The distinguished board of medical specialists behind

The Doctors' Guide to Over-the-Counter Drugs

Stephen W. Bent, M.D.
University of California at San Francisco
School of Medicine

Andrew Buda, M.D.
Tulane University School of Medicine

Nancy C. Chescheir, M.D.
University of North Carolina School of Medicine

Raymond Dingledine, Ph.D.
Emory University School of Medicine

Michael Frank, M.D.
Duke University Medical School

Michael Friedman, M.D.
New York University Medical Center

Ernesto Gonzalez, M.D.
Harvard Medical School

Daniel Robinson, Pharm.D.
University of Southern California School of Pharmacy

Elmer Y. Tu, M.D.
University of Texas School of Medical Science

James Webster, M.D.
Northwestern University School of Medicine

THE DOCTORS' GUIDE TO OVER-THE-COUNTER DRUGS

Created in Association with an Advisory Panel of Specialists from America's Top Medical Schools

Edited and Compiled by
BRENDA D. ADDERLY, M.H.A.

WARNER BOOKS

A Time Warner Company

WARNER BOOKS EDITION

Cover design by Cathy Saksa

Warner Books, Inc.
1271 Avenue of the Americas
New York, NY 10020

Visit our Web site at
www.warnerbooks.com

Visit Brenda Adderly's Web site at
www.BrendaAdderly.com

A Time Warner Company

Printed in the United States of America

ISBN: 0-446-60525-5

First Printing, June, 1998

10 9 8 7 6 5 4 3 2 1

I dedicate this book to my husband
and family for their constant support,
encouragement, and love.

Publisher's Note

The Doctors' Guide to Over-the-Counter Drugs was written to provide a reference tool for consumers who want easy-to-understand information on the many over-the-counter medications on the market. It is meant to help the reader sift through the many medications available, not to be used as a recommendation of treatment or endorsement of any product. The information contained in this book is not meant to take the place of any information provided by the product's maker or your doctor. If you have any questions regarding the safety or efficacy of any over-the-counter medication, or any potential drug interactions, please ask your pharmacist or doctor.

Acknowledgments

I would like to acknowledge the enormous contributions of several individuals. Without them, this wouldn't be a book: Janet Brandt, Skye Van Raalte-Herzog, Sheryl Winter, Larry Underhill, and special thanks to Carl Byron and Amy Inouye for your tireless, meticulous work and great ideas. Both of you made this *Guide* what it is. Finally to Mari Florence, my sincerest appreciation for pulling this major effort together, smoothing out the bumps along the way, and handling everything beautifully. Thanks, Mari.

—Brenda D. Adderly

Contents

Foreword

Americans self-diagnose and self-medicate over 80 percent of the time. And if we do decide to see a doctor, getting an appointment often takes time. In the meanwhile, we want relief for what is ailing us.

With a plethora of over-the-counter medications available, choosing the appropriate one(s) can be a bewildering experience. For any given condition, there are several brands, each with many variations from which to choose. Faced with so many products, it is a tough task to differentiate one brand from the next.

When it comes to determining which active ingredient will alleviate the particular ailment, selecting the best medication becomes even more daunting. Since most of us aren't trained pharmacologists, reading the labels and attempting to discern what these ingredients do is almost impossible. We can barely pronounce many of them!

The Doctors' Guide to Over-the-Counter Drugs is the answer to consumers' anxiety. The *Doctors' Guide* demystifies the process of selecting the most appropriate over-the-counter medication. The *Guide* profiles over 3,000 medications and gives accurate, easy-to-understand information. In each entry, those active ingredients which leave us scratching our head are clearly defined—the reader learns in what brands they are found, as well as the specific symptoms they relieve. For example, readers will learn which brand of analgesic is best for which type of pain.

The *Guide* has been reviewed by a distinguished panel of medical experts from the leading American medical schools and hospitals. This panel endorsed the *Guide* as being a comprehensive, easy-to-use reference. And as a pharmaceutical industry representative who sees the growing impact of managed care, I too endorse the *Guide*. With the advent of managed care, the time patients have with their doctor is shrinking. Therefore, the most knowledgeable patients—those who come with information and prepared with questions—get the best care. The *Doctors' Guide* is an excellent resource.

Brenda Adderly, the *Guide*'s author, should be commended on a job well-done. The *Guide* is a must-have medical reference for all American households.

Fred Tarter
Chairman
The Pharmacy Fund

Introduction

It starts out subtly, a little ache around your temples. Then before you know it, a full-fledged headache has set in. Or perhaps your spouse comes home from work, feeling a bit under the weather. The next thing you know, you're coughing and sneezing and a fever makes you just miserable. You look in the medicine cabinet and there's nothing there, so you bundle up and head to the store where you're faced with a seemingly endless aisle of over-the-counter drugs—all promising to make you good as new. What do you do?

The Doctors' Guide to Over-the-Counter Drugs answers this question by providing the most current and most essential information about the medicines you'll encounter. In our easy-to-use format, you'll be able to quickly access the information necessary to keep you and your family healthy and happy.

What you need to know about over-the-counter drugs

To ensure the best results from over-the-counter medications, consider the following important questions:

1. What symptoms are you looking to relieve?

2. How do you take the medicine? Does the dosage vary? What is the typical adult dose? Child's dose?

3. What side effects could occur? What do the symptoms of overdose look like?

4. What about interactions with other drugs?

5. Can a pregnant or breastfeeding woman safely use the product?

6. Are there special indications for seniors or children?

7. Can you take this drug with alcohol?

The Doctors' Guide to Over-the-Counter Drugs answers all these questions—and more—by providing the most comprehensive, easy-to-find information available on over-the-counter drugs. In fact, it may be the most valuable book you ever buy.

Advisory Panel of Medical Experts

Stephen W. Bent, M.D.
Clinical Research Fellow,
Department of Internal Medicine
University of California at San Francisco
School of Medicine

Andrew Buda, M.D.
Robert Morgan Danes Professor of Medicine,
Section Chief
Cardiology
Tulane University School of Medicine

Nancy C. Chescheir, M.D.
Associate Professor and Acting Chair of
Obstetrics & Gynecology
University of North Carolina School of
Medicine

Raymond Dingledine, Ph.D.
Chair, Department of Pharmacology
Emory University School of Medicine

Michael Frank, M.D.
Chairman, Pediatrics
Duke University Medical School

Michael Friedman, M.D.
The Diane & Arthur Befer Professor of
Geriatric Medicine
New York University Medical Center

Ernesto Gonzalez
Associate Professor of Dermatology
Harvard Medical School

Daniel Robinson, Pharm.D.
Chair, Department of Clinical Pharmacy
Associate Professor of Clinical Pharmacy & Medicine
University of Southern California School of Pharmacy

Elmer Y. Tu, M.D.
Assistant Professor of the Department of Ophthalmology
Head of the Cornea and External Diseases Services
University of Texas School of Medicine

James Webster, M.D.
Director, Bueller Center on Aging,
Professor of Geriatric Medicine
Northwestern University School of Medicine

How to Use This Book

When you don't feel good and you need something that will ease your discomfort, it's easy to be comforted by the wealth of products available to you. Until you look closely. Then, you ask, "What's the difference between an analgesic and an antitussive?" "What if I have a cough, but no aches and pains?" The answer should be simple, and it is if you've come this far.

The Doctors' Guide to Over-the-Counter Drugs is your easy-reference guide to the overwhelming world of over-the-counter medications. By helping you to find the right drug for you—by your most important concern, your symptom(s)—this helpful guide will help you quickly and effectively determine what active ingredient or ingredient combination is most effective for your condition.

Under each symptom category, the appropriate "active ingredient" is listed, along with its known therapeutic properties. Following these brief introductions, a listing of the appropriate medications and all its pertinent information is illustrated by a clever range of user-friendly icons. Our innovative format, which uses exciting visuals and clear, concise language, is intended to help you, the reader, find out what you need—quickly, accurately, and helpfully.

How to Get the Best Results from Over-the-Counter Medications

Here are some tips to help you safely get the most relief from over-the-counter medications.

1. **Choose a medication that is clearly labeled to treat your symptoms.** Do not take a medication simply because someone gives it to you. Make sure you understand what you are taking at all times. If you have questions, ask your pharmacist or doctor.

2. **Follow the instructions on the packaging.** If an instruction is unclear to you, dial the toll-free number on the package (if applicable), or ask your pharmacist to help you.

3. **Check package labels for specific instructions or warnings,** such as "do not take with alcohol," or "do not drive or operate heavy machinery while taking this drug."

4. **If you are taking prescription medications, check with your pharmacist of doctor** to make sure there is no interaction with the over-the-counter substance you want to take.

5. **Understand that because this medication is sold "over-the-counter," this does not guarantee its safety or efficacy.** Be aware that a particular drug may have unpleasant side-effects for you, or you may find that it doesn't relieve your symptoms to your satisfaction—or at all.

6. **Do not continue taking the medication once your symptoms have been relieved.** With some medications, you can build up a resistance to the active ingredient—making it less effective when you really need it.

7. **Never take any medication without looking at the label first.** Make a mental note of the medication's bottle and label so you can easily identify it when necessary. Don't take medicine at night without looking at the label under the light to make sure you're taking the correct medication.

8. **Don't transfer medications from the original container,** even if it seems more convenient for use. The original containers protect the drugs and are also essential for proper identification.

9. **Do not keep over-the-counter medications that have expired or have been compromised in any way** (i.e. the packaging has been damaged or has become wet). Destroy these medications by flushing them down the toilet and by disposing of the containers in a way that children can't find them.

10. **Always keep medicines out of the reach of children.** Although most medications come in child-proof containers, children can often open these bottles and

swallow the contents. Be especially careful of "good-tasting" children's medications. Children can confuse these for candy and may seek them out.

11. **Do not assume that children can take "a half dose" of a medication suitable for adults.** While children can take smaller doses of some adult medications, in some cases, over-the-counter medications are unsuitable for children. Check the dosage before administering any medication to a child.

12. **Keep a list of these medications, and tell your doctor or pharmacist you are taking them before you take any other medications.**

13. **If you have a bad reaction to a drug, or it makes you feel uncomfortable in any way, stop taking it.** If you have an extreme reaction, immediately seek medical attention. When you seek medical attention, take the bottle or box with you so that the doctor can see what you've taken.

How to Find the Information You Need

The Doctors' Guide to Over-the-Counter Drugs has created an easy-use format for finding out what medications are most appropriate for your condition. Each detailed entry contains a host of user-friendly icons that breaks down the essential information into easy-to-read sections.

The over-the-counter drugs described in the book are explained using the following format:

BRAND NAMES
Indicates the names of the drugs under the specific active ingredients or active ingredient combinations.

SYMPTOMS RELIEVED
Tells you the symptoms and conditions that this drug is formulated to treat and what it is most commonly used for.

HOW TO TAKE/HOW TO USE
Tells you precisely how to take the drug.

USUAL ADULT DOSE
Indicates the recommended adult dose.

USUAL CHILD DOSE
Indicates the recommended child dose by age.

CONCERNS

OVERDOSE SYMPTOMS
Tells you what symptoms are signs of an overdose or reaction.

SIDE EFFECTS
Gives you the most common—and less frequently experienced—side effects to the drug.

CHECK WITH YOUR DOCTOR OR PHARMACIST
Helps you understand which drugs could present potential drug interaction problems to discuss with your doctor or pharmacist.

PREGNANCY OR BREASTFEEDING
Helps you understand the safety and/or concerns of a drug on a pregnant or breast-feeding woman.

SPECIAL PRECAUTIONS

PRECAUTIONS FOR CHILDREN
Are issues that the reader should be aware of that pertain specifically to children.

55+

PRECAUTIONS FOR SENIORS
Are issues that the reader should be aware of that pertain specifically to seniors.

WARNINGS

SPECIAL WARNINGS

Are red flags for specific side effects related to health condition or lifestyle, such as heightened drug effects due to alcohol consumption.

ADDITIONAL WARNINGS

Are indicated sporadically in the book for certain drugs in which special issues, such as dependency and abuse, can be an issue.

INFORM YOUR DOCTOR BEFORE TAKING [THIS DRUG] IF YOU HAVE:

Helps you determine what conditions or illnesses you should communicate to your doctor before taking the indicated over-the-counter drug.

ALLERGIES AND SINUS RELIEF

QUICK REVIEW

• ANALGESIC •

The most important considerations in choosing an analgesic are: pain relief; anti-inflammatory activity, and allergic reaction or sensitivity to certain active ingredients.

ANALGESICS (NONNARCOTIC) ARE A CLASS OF DRUGS WHICH:

- inhibit the action of prostaglandins (hormonelike substances) in the central nervous system, thereby temporarily reducing the perception of physical pain with little loss of sensibility to other physical sensation,
- are used to temporarily alleviate symptoms such as: headache, fever, backache, sinus pain, muscle strain, menstrual pain, and similar ailments. Some analgesics, such as aspirin (acetylsalicylic acid) and ibuprofen, also provide temporary anti-inflammatory relief for ailments such as arthritis. Aspirin has also been shown to be effective as a blood thinning antiplatelet agent in reducing heart attack and stroke risk,
- can have adverse effects in some instances. Aspirin intolerance can produce allergic and anaphylactic reactions in hypersensitive and asthmatic individuals. Aspirin can also aggravate aggravate gastrointestinal conditions such as heartburn and ulcer. Long-term acetaminophen use can damage liver (hepatic) and kidney (renal) functions.

Q U I C K F A C T S

ACTIVE INGREDIENT:
IBUPROFEN

BRAND NAMES:
- Advil Cold & Sinus Caplets
- Bayer Select Pain Relief
- Dimetapp
- Dristan Sinus Caplets
- Motrin IB Sinus Caplets
- Sine-Aid IB Caplets (combination with pseudoephedrine hydrochloride)

SYMPTOMS RELIEVED:
Minor aches and pains such as those associated with the common cold, flu, headache, sinusitis, hay fever, and other respiratory allergies.

HOW TO TAKE:
Comes in tablet, caplet, and gelcap forms. Swallow with liquid. Do not crush or chew timed-release tablet. Ibuprofen can cause gastrointestinal (GI) irritation and should be taken with food or following meal.

USUAL ADULT DOSE:
Minor aches and pains: 200 milligrams every 4 to 6 hours as needed, not to exceed 1.2 grams per day.

USUAL CHILD DOSE:
Always consult with a pharmacist or physician. Dosage may vary based on infant or child's age. Fever reduction: Maximum daily dose not to exceed 400 milligrams. Dosage should be adjusted based on initial temperature level. If less or equal to 102.5°F, 5 milligrams per dose is recommended. If temperature is greater than 102.5°F, 10 milligrams per dose is recommended.

QUICK FACTS

OVERDOSE SYMPTOMS:
Nervous agitation, disorientation, confusion, severe headache, convulsions, GI bleeding or hemorrhage. If you suspect an overdose, immediately seek medical attention.

SIDE EFFECTS:
No serious effects in most cases of common use, however normal use of ibuprofen can result in common GI irritations such as heartburn and indigestion. Less common side effects include dizziness, nausea, stomach cramps, and headache.

CHECK WITH YOUR DOCTOR OR PHARMACIST BEFORE COMBINING IBUPROFEN WITH:
Antacids, anticoagulants, aspirin, asthma medication, other nonsteroidal anti-inflammatory drugs (NSAIDs), tetracycline, and any other medication. Combination with acetaminophen increases risk of kidney damage. Ingestion of alcohol while taking ibuprofen can increase risk of GI ulceration. Avoid ibuprofen if you have a history of anemia. Also avoid use of ibuprofen, if possible, one week prior to surgery, as it may increase possibility of postoperative bleeding.

PREGNANCY OR BREASTFEEDING:
No harmful effects have been reported regarding pregnancy or breastfeeding of infants, but ibuprofen use by a nursing mother should be considered a potential risk for a nursing child as the drug will be passed on to the infant in the mother's milk. In all cases, a physician should be consulted.

PRECAUTIONS FOR CHILDREN:
In general, ibuprofen and other NSAIDs are not advised for children under 15. Administer ibuprofen to infants or children only when consulting a physician and follow instructions on medication.

PRECAUTIONS FOR SENIORS:
Seniors generally don't eliminate drugs as efficiently as younger persons, and should avoid high dosages. Seniors (over 65) are at special risk for development of ulcers if taking ibuprofen in high doses. Prolonged use can also lead to kidney and liver damage.

SPECIAL WARNINGS:
Don't take ibuprofen medication if you are aspirin intolerant or allergic to other NSAIDs. If in doubt, always consult a pharmacist or physician. Also avoid if you have GI conditions such as gastritis, peptic ulcer, enteritis, ileitis, colitis; asthma, high blood pressure, or hematologic (bleeding) problems. Avoid alcohol while taking this or any other NSAID.

INFORM YOUR DOCTOR BEFORE TAKING IBUPROFEN IF YOU HAVE:
An allergy or intolerance to aspirin or other NSAIDs, damaged or impaired renal (kidney) or hepatic (liver) functions, epilepsy, Parkinson's disease, or mental illness.

QUICK REVIEW

•ANTI-INFLAMMATORY•

The most important considerations in choosing an anti-inflammatory agent (nonsteroidal anti-inflammatory drug or "NSAID") are: pain relief; anti-inflammatory activity, and the potential for allergic reaction or sensitivity to certain active ingredients.

ANTI-INFLAMMATORY AGENTS (NSAIDS) ARE A CLASS OF DRUGS WHICH:

- inhibit the action of prostaglandins (hormonelike substances) in the central nervous system, thereby temporarily reducing the perception of physical pain with little loss of sensibility to other physical sensation,
- are used both for their anti-inflammatory and analgesic properties, to temporarily alleviate symptoms such as: headache, fever, backache, sinus pain, muscle strain, menstrual pain, and similar ailments. Some NSAIDs also provide temporary anti-inflammatory relief for ailments such as rheumatoid arthritis and osteoarthritis,
- can have adverse effects in some instances such as aggravation of gastrointestinal (GI) conditions such as heartburn and ulcer, and can produce allergic reactions in persons who are aspirin-intolerant or hypersensitive.

See *also:* Analgesics

ACTIVE INGREDIENT:
IBUPROFEN

BRAND NAMES:
- ADVIL
- ADVIL COLD & SINUS CAPLETS
- ARTHRITIS FOUNDATION
- BAYER SELECT PAIN RELIEF
- DIMETAPP
- DRISTAN SINUS CAPLETS
- GENPRIL
- IBUPROHM
- MOTRIN
- MOTRIN IB SINUS CAPLETS
- NUPRON
- OBUPRIN
- SINE-AID IB CAPLETS

SYMPTOMS RELIEVED:
Minor aches and pains such as those associated with the common cold, flu, headache, sinusitis, hay fever and other respiratory allergies. Ibuprofen can also be used for related conditions such as the reduction of fever.

HOW TO TAKE:
Comes in tablet, caplet, and gelcap forms. Swallow with liquid. Do not crush or chew timed-release tablet. Ibuprofen can cause gastrointestinal (GI) irritation and should be taken with food or following meal.

USUAL ADULT DOSE:
Minor aches and pains: 200 milligrams every 4 to 6 hours as needed, not to exceed 1.2 grams per day.

Q U I C K F A C T S

USUAL CHILD DOSE:
Always consult with a pharmacist or physician. Dosage may vary based on infant or child's age.

Fever reduction: Maximum daily dose not to exceed 400 milligrams. Dosage should be adjusted based on initial temperature level. If less or equal to 102.5°F, 5 milligrams per dose is recommended.

Juvenile arthritis: 30 to 70 milligrams per day in 3 or 4 equal doses or as indicated.

OVERDOSE SYMPTOMS:
Nervous agitation, disorientation, confusion, severe headache, convulsions, GI bleeding, or hemorrhage. If you suspect an overdose, immediately seek medical attention.

SIDE EFFECTS:
No serious effects in most cases of common use, however normal use can result in common GI irritations such as heartburn and indigestion. Less common side effects include dizziness, nausea, stomach cramps, and headache. If you experience these side effects, inform your doctor immediately.

CHECK WITH YOUR DOCTOR OR PHARMACIST BEFORE COMBINING IBUPROFEN WITH:
Antacids, anticoagulants, aspirin, asthma medication, other nonsteroidal anti-inflammatory drugs (NSAIDs), tetracycline, and any other medication. Combination with acetaminophen increases risk of kidney damage. Ingestion of alcohol while taking ibuprofen can increase risk of GI ulceration. Avoid ibuprofen if you have a history

of anemia. Also avoid use of ibuprofen, if possible, one week prior to surgery, as it may increase possibility of postoperative bleeding.

PREGNANCY OR BREASTFEEDING:
No harmful effects have been reported regarding pregnancy or breastfeeding of infants, but ibuprofen use by a nursing mother should be considered a potential risk for a nursing child as the drug will be passed on to the infant in the mother's milk. In all cases, a physician should be consulted.

PRECAUTIONS FOR CHILDREN:
In general, ibuprofen and other NSAIDs are not advised for children under 15. Administer ibuprofen to infants or children only when consulting a physician and follow instructions on medication.

55+ **PRECAUTIONS FOR SENIORS:**
Seniors generally don't eliminate drugs as efficiently as younger persons, and should avoid high dosages. Seniors (over 65) are at special risk for development of ulcers if taking ibuprofen in high doses.

SPECIAL WARNINGS:
Don't take ibuprofen medication if you are aspirin intolerant or allergic to other NSAIDs. If in doubt, always consult a pharmacist or physician. Also avoid if you have GI conditions such as gastritis, peptic ulcer, enteritis, ileitis, colitis; asthma, high blood pressure, or hematologic (bleeding) problems. Avoid alcohol while taking this or any other NSAID.

QUICK FACTS

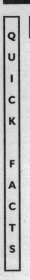

INFORM YOUR DOCTOR BEFORE TAKING IBUPROFEN IF YOU HAVE:
An allergy or intolerance to aspirin or other NSAIDs, damaged or impaired renal (kidney) or hepatic (liver) functions, epilepsy, Parkinson's disease, or mental illness.

• ANTIHISTAMINES •

The most important considerations in choosing an antihistamine are: its effectiveness in blocking or alleviating effects of histamine on the respiratory system, and the nature and extent of side effects which the drug may produce.

QUICK REVIEW

ANTIHISTAMINES ARE A CLASS OF DRUGS WHICH:

- are used in treating allergies and motion sickness,
- block the effects of histamine, a chemical substance released by the body as the result of injury or in reaction to an allergen. Histamine increases capillary permeability, which allows fluids to escape and cause swelling. It also constricts small air passages in the lungs. These properties result in symptoms such as sinus headache, congestion, sneezing, runny nose,wheezing, puffiness, and lowered blood pressure,
- act by blocking or displacing histamine, particularly in the blood vessels, skin, uterus, and bronchioles,
- as a result of the drugs' drying effects, thereby impede drainage and expectoration,
- may produce side effects such as drowsiness, nasal stuffiness, dryness of mouth and sinus passages, dizziness, and common gastrointestinal (GI) irritation or distress,
- are not recommended in treating lower respiratory symptoms including asthma, as the drug's effects may impede expectoration.

QUICK FACTS

ACTIVE INGREDIENT:

BROMPHENIRAMINE MALEATE

BRAND NAMES:

- Dimetane Elixir (also contains alcohol)
- Dimetane Extentabs
- Dimetane Tablets

SYMPTOMS RELIEVED:

Nasal congestion, runny nose, itchy and watery eyes, sneezing, scratchy throat, and irritated sinuses due to common cold, sinusitis, hay fever, and other upper respiratory allergies.

HOW TO TAKE:

Comes in tablet, and liquid forms. Swallow tablet with liquid. Do not crush or chew timed-release tablets. Brompheniramine maleate and other antihistamines can cause gastrointestinal (GI) irritation and should be taken with food or following meal.

USUAL ADULT DOSE:

4 milligrams 4 to 6 times per day, or 8 to 12 milligrams of timed-release medication 2 to 3 times per day, not to exceed 24 milligrams in a 24 hour period.

USUAL CHILD DOSE:

For children 6 to 12: 2 milligrams 4 to 6 times per day, not to exceed 12 milligrams in a 24 hour period. Timed-release medications should only be administered under direction of physician.

Do not administer to children under 6 unless under direction of physician. Dosage may vary based on infant or child's age.

QUICK FACTS

OVERDOSE SYMPTOMS:
Nervous agitation, severe anxiety, insomnia (sleeplessness), hallucinations, tremors, coma. If you suspect an overdose, immediately seek medical attention.

SIDE EFFECTS:
The most frequent side effect of antihistamine use is drowsiness. Other common side effects include: include dryness of mouth, throat, and nasal passages, dizziness, GI distress (including vomiting, diarrhea, and constipation or change in bowel regularity), and diminished muscle coordination. In rare cases, more severe side effects may result, such as painful and frequent urination or urinary retention, vision problems, loss of appetite, and respiratory difficulty. In these cases, discontinue medication and call your doctor immediately.

CHECK WITH YOUR DOCTOR OR PHARMACIST BEFORE COMBINING BROMPHENIRAMINE MALEATE WITH:
Cold, cough, or allergy medication—including other antihistamines; aspirin, stimulants, antidepressants, antihypertensives, digitalis or other heart medication, diuretics, or MAO (monoamine oxidase inhibitors) drugs. Avoid ingestion of alcohol or use of sedatives or tranquilizers while taking brompheniramine maleate-containing medication or most other antihistamine-containing medication as the combination can produce severe drowsiness or sedation.

PREGNANCY OR BREASTFEEDING:
Brompheniramine maleate use by a nursing mother should be considered a potential risk for

QUICK FACTS

a nursing child as the drug will be passed on to the infant in the mother's milk. In all cases, whether pregnant or nursing, a physician should be consulted.

PRECAUTIONS FOR CHILDREN:
In general, brompheniramine maleate is not advised for children under 6. Administer brompheniramine maleate to infants or children only when consulting a physician and follow instructions on medication (see above).

55+ **PRECAUTIONS FOR SENIORS:**
Seniors generally don't eliminate drugs as efficiently as younger persons, and should avoid high dosages. Use of brompheniramine maleate medications by seniors can lead to urinary difficulties. In addition, seniors are more likely to experience sedatory effects of the drug.

SPECIAL WARNINGS:
Because antihistamines often cause drowsiness, you should avoid activities or tasks such as driving, or other operations which require alertness, coordination, dexterity or quick reflexes. Do not use continuously for longer than 3 months.

INFORM YOUR DOCTOR BEFORE TAKING BROMPHENIRAMINE MALEATE IF YOU HAVE:
Urinary difficulty, glaucoma, ulcer, or if you are pregnant. If you anticipate any surgery requiring general or spinal anesthesia within 2 months of taking brompheniramine maleate-containing medication, inform your doctor.

ACTIVE INGREDIENT:
DIPHENHYDRAMINE HYDROCHLORIDE

Q U I C K F A C T S

BRAND NAMES:
- ALLERMAX CAPLETS
- BANOPHEN/BANOPHEN CAPLETS
- BELIX (also contains alcohol)
- BENADRYL 25
- BENILYN COUGH (also contains alcohol, saccharin)
- BYDRAMINE COUGH (also contains alcohol)
- DIPHEN COUGH
- DORMAREX
- GENAHIST (also contains alcohol)
- HYDRAMINE COUGH (also contains alcohol)
- NIDRYL (also contains alcohol)
- NORDRYL COUGH (also contains alcohol)
- PHENDRY/CHILDREN'S ALLERGY MEDICINE (also contains alcohol)

Note: *Diphenhydramine* is also used as a sleep aid, and as active ingredient in combination with other drugs in antitussive products.

SYMPTOMS RELIEVED:
Nasal congestion, runny nose, itchy and watery eyes, sneezing, scratchy throat, and irritate sinuses due to common cold, sinusitis, hay fever, and other upper respiratory allergies.

HOW TO TAKE:
Comes in tablet, capsule, and liquid forms.
Swallow tablet or capsule with liquid.
Do not crush or chew timed-release tablets.
Diphenhydramine and other antihistamines can cause gastrointestinal (GI) irritation and should be taken with food or following meal.

QUICK FACTS

USUAL ADULT DOSE:
25 to 50 milligrams 3 to 4 times per day, not to exceed 150 milligrams in a 24 hour period.

USUAL CHILD DOSE:
For children 6 to 12: 12.5 milligrams 3 to 4 times per day, not to exceed 50 milligrams in a 24 hour period. Timed release medications should only be administered under direction of physician.

Do not administer to children under 6 unless under direction of physician. Dosage may vary based on infant or child's age.

OVERDOSE SYMPTOMS:
Nervous agitation, severe anxiety, insomnia (sleeplessness), hallucinations, tremors, coma. If you suspect an overdose, immediately seek medical attention.

SIDE EFFECTS:
The most frequent side effect of antihistamines use is drowsiness. Other common side effects include: include dryness of mouth, throat, and nasal passages, dizziness, GI distress (including vomiting, diarrhea, and constipation or change in bowel regularity), and diminished muscle coordination. In rare cases, more severe side effects may result, such as painful and frequent urination or urinary retention, vision problems, loss of appetite, and respiratory difficulty. In these cases, discontinue medication and call your doctor immediately.

CHECK WITH YOUR DOCTOR OR PHARMACIST BEFORE COMBINING DIPHENHYDRAMINE WITH:
Cold, cough, or allergy medication—including

other antihistamines; aspirin, stimulants, antidepressants, antihypertensives, digitalis or other heart medication, diuretics, or MAO (monoamine oxidase inhibitors) drugs. Avoid ingestion of alcohol or use of sedatives or tranquilizers while taking diphenhydramine-containing medication or most other antihistamine-containing medication as the combination can produce severe drowsiness or sedation.

PREGNANCY OR BREASTFEEDING:
Diphenhydramine use by a nursing mother should be considered a potential risk for a nursing child as the drug will be passed on to the infant in the mother's milk. In all cases, whether pregnant or breastfeeding, a physician should be consulted.

PRECAUTIONS FOR CHILDREN:
In general, diphenhydramine is not advised for children under 6. Administer diphenhydramine to infants or children only when consulting a physician and follow instructions on medication (see above).

55+ **PRECAUTIONS FOR SENIORS:**
Seniors generally don't eliminate drugs as efficiently as younger persons, and should avoid high dosages. Use of diphenhydramine medications by seniors can lead to urinary difficulties. In addition, seniors are more likely to experience drowsiness effects of the drug.

SPECIAL WARNINGS:
Because antihistamines often cause drowsiness, you should avoid activities or tasks such as driving, or other operations which require

alertness, coordination, dexterity, or quick reflexes. Do not use continuously for longer than 3 months. Do not use diphenhydramine medications containing tartrazine if you are intolerant or hypersensitive to aspirin. Allergic reactions, including bronchial asthma, have occurred in susceptible individuals.

INFORM YOUR DOCTOR BEFORE TAKING DIPHENHYDRAMINE IF YOU HAVE:
Urinary difficulty, glaucoma, ulcer, or if you are pregnant. If you anticipate any surgery requiring general or spinal anesthesia within 2 months of taking diphenhydramine-containing medication, inform your doctor.

ACTIVE INGREDIENT:
TRIPOLIDINE HYDROCHLORIDE

QUICK FACTS

BRAND NAMES:
- ACTIDIL

SYMPTOMS RELIEVED:
Nasal congestion, runny nose, itchy and watery eyes, sneezing, scratchy throat, and irritate sinuses due to common cold, sinusitis, hay fever, and other upper respiratory allergies.

HOW TO TAKE:
Comes in tablet, capsule, and liquid forms. Swallow tablet or capsule with liquid. Do not crush or chew timed-release tablets. Tripolidine and other antihistamines can cause gastrointestinal (GI) irritation and should be taken with food or following meal.

USUAL ADULT DOSE:
2.5 milligrams 3 to 4 times per day, not to exceed 10 milligrams in a 24 hour period.

USUAL CHILD DOSE:
For children 6 to 12: 2 milligrams 4 to 6 times per day, or 8 milligrams of timed release medication at bedtime or during day, not to exceed 12 milligrams in a 24 hour period.

For children 2 to 6: 1.25 milligrams 4 to 6 times per day, not to exceed 5 milligrams in a 24 hour period. Timed release medications are not advised for children 2 to 6 or younger. Do not administer to children in this age group unless under direction of physician. Dosage may vary based on infant or child's age.

QUICK FACTS

OVERDOSE SYMPTOMS:
Nervous agitation, severe anxiety, insomnia (sleeplessness), hallucinations, tremors, coma. If you suspect an overdose, immediately seek medical attention.

SIDE EFFECTS:
The most frequent side effect of antihistamines use is drowsiness. Other common side effects include: include dryness of mouth, throat, and nasal passages, dizziness, GI distress (including vomiting, diarrhea, and constipation or change in bowel regularity), and diminished muscle coordination. In rare cases, more severe side effects may result, such as painful and frequent urination or urinary retention, vision problems, loss of appetite, and respiratory difficulty. In these cases, discontinue medication and call your doctor immediately.

CHECK WITH YOUR DOCTOR OR PHARMACIST BEFORE COMBINING TRIPOLIDINE WITH:
Cold, cough, or allergy medication—including other antihistamines; aspirin, stimulants, antidepressants, antihypertensives, digitalis or other heart medication, diuretics, or MAO (monoamine oxidase inhibitors) drugs. Avoid ingestion of alcohol or use of sedatives or tranquilizers while taking tripolidine-containing medication or most other antihistamine-containing medication as the combination can produce severe drowsiness or sedation.

PREGNANCY OR BREASTFEEDING:
Tripolidine use by a nursing mother should be considered a potential risk for a nursing child as the drug will be passed on to the infant in the

mother's milk. In all cases, a physician should be consulted.

PRECAUTIONS FOR CHILDREN:
In general, tripolidine is not advised for children under 6. Administer tripolidine to infants or children only when consulting a physician and follow instructions on medication (see above).

55+

PRECAUTIONS FOR SENIORS:
Seniors generally don't eliminate drugs as efficiently as younger persons, and should avoid high dosages. Use of tripolidine medications by seniors can lead to urinary difficulties. In addition, seniors are more likely to experience stimulant effects of the drug.

SPECIAL WARNINGS:
Because antihistamines often cause drowsiness, you should avoid activities or tasks such as driving, or other operations which require alertness, coordination, dexterity or quick reflexes. Do not use continuously for longer than 3 months. Do not use tripolidine medications containing tartrazine if you are intolerant or hypersensitive to aspirin. Allergic reactions, including bronchial asthma, have occurred in susceptible individuals.

INFORM YOUR DOCTOR BEFORE TAKING TRIPOLIDINE IF YOU HAVE:
Urinary difficulty, glaucoma, ulcer, or if you are pregnant. If you anticipate any surgery requiring general or spinal anesthesia within 2 months of taking tripolidine-containing medication, inform your doctor.

QUICK REVIEW

• ANTITUSSIVE •

The most important considerations in choosing an antitussive are: cough suppressant and relief action; and potential side effects associated with the drug.

ANTITUSSIVES ARE A CLASS OF DRUGS WHICH:

- help to suppress and relieve the spasmodic cough reflex typical of symptoms of various allergies, colds, bronchitis, flu, and other nonchronic ailments,
- are commonly used to give an allergy, cold, bronchitis, flu, and other nonchronic respiratory ailment-sufferer sufficient relief from coughing spasms, so that the person can rest, thereby increasing the chances of recovering from the illness,
- may produce side effects such as drowsiness, nasal stuffiness, dryness of mouth and sinus passages, dizziness, and common gastrointestinal (GI) irritation or distress,
- are not recommended in treating chronic and lower respiratory symptoms including asthma, and emphysema,
- are often combined with other cough-related active ingredients such as expectorants, as well as analgesics, antihistamines, and decongestants—as well as other ingredients such as alcohol, sweeteners (natural and artificial) and flavorings (natural and artificial),
- do not affect the underlying cause of the symptoms which they are designed to relieve or suppress.

ACTIVE INGREDIENTS:

GUAIFENESIN, DEXTROMETHORPHAN HYDROBROMIDE, AND PHENYLPROPANOLAMINE HYDROCHLORIDE

QUICK FACTS

℞ **BRAND NAMES:**

- GuiaCough CF Liquid (also contains alcohol, parabens, saccharin, sorbitol, sucrose)
- Guiatuss CF Liquid (also contains alcohol)
- Naldecon DX Adult Liquid (also contains saccharin, sorbitol)
- Naldelate DX Adult Liquid (also contains saccharin, sorbitol)
- Robafen CF Liquid (also contains alcohol)
- Robitussin–CF Liquid (also contains alcohol, saccharin, sorbitol)

Note: *Guaifenesin* and *dextromethorphan hydrobromide* are also active ingredients in other multi-symptom antitussive/expectorant medications which are formulated with other active ingredients.

Phenylpropanolamine hydrochloride is used as an active ingredient in decongestant and stimulant products.

SYMPTOMS RELIEVED:
Cough, nasal congestion and runny nose, itchy and watery eyes, sneezing, scratchy throat, and irritated sinuses associated with common cold, minor throat and bronchial irritations, sinusitis, hay fever and other upper respiratory allergies.

HOW TO TAKE:
Comes in liquid forms.

QUICK FACTS

USUAL ADULT DOSE:
Dosage varies per product and active ingredient formulation. Follow product dosage instructions.

USUAL CHILD DOSE:
Do not administer to children under 6 unless under direction of physician. Dosage may vary based on infant or child's age.

OVERDOSE SYMPTOMS:
Nervous agitation, severe anxiety, insomnia (sleeplessness), hallucinations, tremors, convulsions, nausea, vomiting, cardiac arrhythmia (irregular pulse and heartbeat), drowsiness, dizziness, fatigue, rash. If you suspect an overdose, immediately seek medical attention.

SIDE EFFECTS:
No serious effects in most cases of common use. Less common side effects include nasal dryness, dizziness, nausea, and mild insomnia palpitations, insomnia, gastrointestinal (GI) upset including stomach cramps and diarrhea, drowsiness, and fatigue. In rare cases, more severe side effects may result, including: painful and frequent urination, hypertension, and heart palpitations. In these cases, discontinue medication and call your doctor immediately.

CHECK WITH YOUR DOCTOR OR PHARMACIST BEFORE COMBINING THESE COMBINATION PRODUCTS WITH:
Anticoagulant medications, other cold, cough, or allergy medication, stimulants, antidepressants, antihypertensives, digitalis or other heart medication, diuretics, or MAO (monoamine oxidase inhibitors) drugs. Ingestion of caffeinated bever-

ages (coffee, tea, caffeine-containing soft drinks) while taking phenylpropanolamine-containing medication can result in agitation and insomnia.

Q U I C K F A C T S

PREGNANCY OR BREASTFEEDING:
No harmful effects have been reported regarding pregnancy or breastfeeding of infants, however, use of medications containing any of the active ingredients in these products by a nursing mother should be considered a potential risk for a nursing child as the drug(s) will be passed on to the infant in the mother's milk. In all cases, a physician should be consulted.

PRECAUTIONS FOR CHILDREN:
In general, these active ingredients are not advised for children under 2. Administer to infants or children only when consulting a physician and follow instructions on medication (see above).

55+ **PRECAUTIONS FOR SENIORS:**
Seniors generally don't eliminate drugs as efficiently as younger persons, and should avoid high dosages.

SPECIAL WARNINGS:
Do not use for control of chronic cough related to conditions such as emphysema, asthma, or smoking, or if coughs are producing excessive secretions. If cough is accompanied by high fever, rash, nausea or vomiting, or persistent headache, use only if directed by your doctor.

ADDITIONAL WARNING:
Alcohol: Some cough/cold medications contain various amounts of alcohol. Check label of any

QUICK FACTS

cough medication if concerned about ingestion of alcohol.

Sugar/Sweeteners: Some cough/cold medications contain various amounts of sugar, sucrose, glucose, and/or artificial sweeteners such as aspartame, saccharin, sorbitol. Check label of cough medication before selecting, if concerned about diabetes and ingestion of sugar or artificial sweeteners.

Abuse/Dependency: Reports indicate a rising rate of abuse of dextromethorphan-containing medications, particularly among teens. Sufficient data has not yet been collected, however, to determine the abuse and dependency potential of dextromethorphan-containing medications.

INFORM YOUR DOCTOR BEFORE TAKING PRODUCTS CONTAINING THIS COMBINATION OF ACTIVE INGREDIENTS IF YOU HAVE:

Asthma, emphysema or other respiratory condition, liver impairment or liver disease, allergies to aspirin or other salicylates, or if you have diabetes, thyroid condition, or urinary difficulty.

If you anticipate any surgery requiring general or spinal anesthesia within 2 months of taking medication which contains phenylpropanolamine, inform your doctor.

ACTIVE INGREDIENT:

TRIPOLIDINE HYDROCHLORIDE

BRAND NAMES:
- ACTIDIL

SYMPTOMS RELIEVED:
Nasal congestion, runny nose, itchy and watery eyes, sneezing, scratchy throat, and irritate sinuses due to common cold, sinusitis, hay fever, and other upper respiratory allergies.

HOW TO TAKE:
Comes in tablet, capsule, and liquid forms. Swallow tablet or capsule with liquid. Do not crush or chew timed-release tablets. Tripolidine and other antihistamines can cause gastrointestinal (GI) irritation and should be taken with food or following meal.

USUAL ADULT DOSE:
2.5 milligrams 3 to 4 times per day, not to exceed 10 milligrams in a 24 hour period.

USUAL CHILD DOSE:
For children 6 to 12: 2 milligrams 4 to 6 times per day, or 8 milligrams of timed release medication at bedtime or during day, not to exceed 12 milligrams in a 24 hour period.

For children 2 to 6: 1.25 milligrams 4 to 6 times per day, not to exceed 5 milligrams in a 24 hour period. Timed release medications are not advised for children 2 to 6 or younger. Do not administer to children in this age group unless under direction of physician. Dosage may vary based on infant or child's age.

QUICK FACTS

QUICK FACTS

OVERDOSE SYMPTOMS:
Nervous agitation, severe anxiety, insomnia (sleeplessness), hallucinations, tremors, coma. If you suspect an overdose, immediately seek medical attention.

SIDE EFFECTS:
The most frequent side effect of antihistamines use is drowsiness. Other common side effects include: include dryness of mouth, throat, and nasal passages, dizziness, GI distress (including vomiting, diarrhea, and constipation or change in bowel regularity), and diminished muscle coordination. In rare cases, more severe side effects may result, such as painful and frequent urination or urinary retention, vision problems, loss of appetite, and respiratory difficulty. In these cases, discontinue medication and call your doctor immediately.

CHECK WITH YOUR DOCTOR OR PHARMACIST BEFORE COMBINING TRIPOLIDINE WITH:
Cold, cough, or allergy medication—including other antihistamines; aspirin, stimulants, antidepressants, antihypertensives, digitalis or other heart medication, diuretics, or MAO (monoamine oxidase inhibitors) drugs. Avoid ingestion of alcohol or use of sedatives or tranquilizers while taking tripolidine-containing medication or most other antihistamine-containing medication as the combination can produce severe drowsiness or sedation.

PREGNANCY OR BREASTFEEDING:
No harmful effects have been reported regarding pregnancy or breastfeeding of infants. However, tripolidine use by a nursing mother

should be considered a potential risk for a nursing child as the drug will be passed on to the infant in the mother's milk. In all cases, a physician should be consulted.

PRECAUTIONS FOR CHILDREN:
In general, tripolidine is not advised for children under 6. Administer tripolidine to infants or children only when consulting a physician and follow instructions on medication (see above).

55+

PRECAUTIONS FOR SENIORS:
Seniors generally don't eliminate drugs as efficiently as younger persons, and should avoid high dosages. Use of tripolidine medications by seniors can lead to urinary difficulties. In addition, seniors are more likely to experience stimulant effects of the drug.

SPECIAL WARNINGS:
Because antihistamines often cause drowsiness, you should avoid activities or tasks such as driving, or other operations which require alertness, coordination, dexterity or quick reflexes. Do not use continuously for longer than 3 months. Do not use tripolidine medications containing tartrazine if you are intolerant or hypersensitive to aspirin. Allergic reactions, including bronchial asthma, have occurred in susceptible individuals.

INFORM YOUR DOCTOR BEFORE TAKING TRIPOLIDINE IF YOU HAVE:
urinary difficulty, glaucoma, ulcer, or if you are pregnant. If you anticipate any surgery requiring general or spinal anesthesia within 2 months of taking tripolidine-containing medication, inform your doctor.

QUICK REVIEW

• DECONGESTANT •
(NASAL)

The most important considerations in choosing a decongestant are: relief of membrane congestion (usually in sinus areas) in cases of allergy, hay fever, and common cold; and potential side effects associated with these drugs.

DECONGESTANTS ARE A CLASS OF DRUGS WHICH:

- shrink swollen and irritated mucosal membranes. Decongestants function by acting on the sympathetic nervous system to constrict blood vessels. Many of these drugs can be effective in relieving nasal congestion, respiratory allergies, or sinusitis,
- often are often combined with other agents such as antihistamines, antipyretics, analgesics, antitussives, or expectorants to provide multisymptomatic relief for headaches, fever, cough, sleeplessness, and other symptoms of the common cold, flu, hay fever, and similar ailments. However, these drugs do not affect the underlying cause or course of such ailments,
- may produce side effects which can include dryness of mouth and sinuses, nervous agitation, sleeplessness, or drowsiness.

ACTIVE INGREDIENTS:

ACETAMINOPHEN, CHLORPHENIRAMINE MALEATE, DEXTROMETHORPHAN HYDROBROMIDE, AND PSEUDOEPHREDINE HYDROCHLORIDE

℞ **BRAND NAMES:**

- Alka-Seltzer Plus Cold & Cough Liqui-Gels (also contains sorbitol)
- Bayer Select Flu Relief Caplets
- Co-Apap Tablets
- Comtrex Liquid (also contains alcohol, sucrose)
- Comtrex Liqui-Gels (contains sorbitol)
- Comtrex Maximum Liqui-Gels (contains sorbitol)
- Comtrex Max Strength Multi-Symptom Cold & Flu Relief Liqui-Gels
- Comtrex Maximum Strength Multi-Symptom Cold & Flu Relief Caplets & Tablets (contains parabens)
- Contac Severe Cold & Flu Nighttime Liquid (also contains alcohol, saccharin, sorbitol, glucose)
- Genacol Tablets
- Kolephrin/DM Caplets
- Mapap Cold Formula Tablets
- Medi-Flu Liquid (also contains alcohol, saccharin, sorbitol, sugar)
- TheraFlu Flu, Cold & Cough Powder (contains sucrose)
- TheraFlu Nighttime Flu Powder (contains sucrose)
- Tylenol Children's Cold Multi-Symptom Plus Cough Liquid (also contains sorbitol, corn syrup)

QUICK FACTS

- Tylenol Multi-Symptom Cold Caplets & Tablets
- Tylenol Multi-Symptom Hot Medication Powder (combination with phenylalanine, also contains aspartame, sucrose)
- Vicks Children's NyQuil Nighttime Cold/Cough Liquid (also contains sucrose)
- Vicks 44M Cold, Flu & Cough LiquiCaps
- Vicks Pediatric Formula 44M Multi-Symptom Cough & Cold Liquid (also contains sorbitol, sucrose)

Note: *Dextromethorphan hydrobromide* is also an active ingredient in other multi-symptom antitussive/expectorant medications which are formulated with other active ingredients.

Pseudoephredine hydrochloride is a used as an active ingredient in decongestant and stimulant products.

Acetaminophen is a non-aspirin analgesic which is used primarily in pain-relief products.

Chlorpheniramine maleate is an antihistamine which is mostly used in combination with analgesic, antitussive, decongestant and expectorant active ingredients in over-the-counter medications to provide relief of allergy, common cold, cough or flu symptoms.

SYMPTOMS RELIEVED:
Minor aches and pains, nasal congestion, and coughing such as those associated with the common cold, flu, sore throat, sinusitis, hay fever and other respiratory allergies, and reduction of fever.

HOW TO TAKE:
Comes in tablet, caplet, capsule, and liquid forms. Swallow tablet, caplet, or capsule with liquid. Sprinkle powder over liquid, then swallow. Do not crush or chew timed-release tablet.

USUAL ADULT DOSE:
Dosage varies per product and active ingredient formulation. Follow product dosage instructions.

USUAL CHILD DOSE:
Do not administer to children under 6 unless under direction of physician. Dosage may vary based on infant or child's age.

OVERDOSE SYMPTOMS:
Nervous agitation, severe anxiety, insomnia (sleeplessness), hallucinations, tremors, convulsions, nausea, vomiting, cardiac arrhythmia (irregular pulse and heartbeat), drowsiness, dizziness, fatigue, rash. If you suspect an overdose, immediately seek medical attention.

SIDE EFFECTS:
No serious effects in most cases of common use, although antihistamines can cause drowsiness. Less common side effects include nasal dryness, dizziness, nausea, and mild insomnia palpitations, insomnia, gastrointestinal (GI) upset including stomach cramps and diarrhea, drowsiness, and fatigue. In rare cases, more severe side effects may result, including: painful and frequent urination, hypertension, and heart palpitations. In these cases, discontinue medication and call your doctor immediately. Long-term ingestion of high dosages of acetaminophen-containing products may increase risk of liver and kidney damage.

QUICK FACTS

CHECK WITH YOUR DOCTOR OR PHARMACIST BEFORE COMBINING THESE COMBINATION PRODUCTS WITH:

Anticoagulant medications, other cold, cough, or allergy medication, stimulants, antidepressants, antihypertensives, digitalis or other heart medication, diuretics, or MAO (monoamine oxidase inhibitors) drugs. Ingestion of caffeinated beverages (coffee, tea, caffeine-containing soft drinks) while taking pseudoephredine-containing medication can result in agitation and insomnia.

If taking combination products which contain acetaminophen, you should avoid Isoniazid (anti-tuberculosis) medication. Excessive ingestion of alcohol while taking acetaminophen-containing medication can increase the risk of liver damage or disease (hepatic toxicity). Alcohol use may also increase possible drowsiness effect of the antihistamine in these combination products.

PREGNANCY OR BREASTFEEDING:

No harmful effects have been reported regarding pregnancy or breastfeeding of infants, however, use of medications containing any of the active ingredients in these products by a nursing mother should be considered a potential risk for a nursing child as the drug(s) will be passed on to the infant in the mother's milk. In all cases, a physician should be consulted.

PRECAUTIONS FOR CHILDREN:

In general, these active ingredients are not advised for children under 2. Administer to infants or children only when consulting a physician and follow instructions on medication (see above).

55+ **PRECAUTIONS FOR SENIORS:**
Seniors generally don't eliminate drugs as efficiently as younger persons, and should avoid high dosages. Use of antihistamine-containing medications by seniors can lead to urinary difficulties. In addition, seniors are more likely to experience potential drowsiness effects of the antihistamine in this combination.

SPECIAL WARNINGS:
Do not use for control of chronic cough related to conditions such as emphysema, asthma, or smoking, or if coughs are producing excessive secretions. If cough is accompanied by high fever, rash, nausea or vomiting, or persistent headache, use only if directed by your doctor. Because antihistamines may cause drowsiness, you should avoid activities or tasks such as driving, or other operations which require alertness, coordination, dexterity, or quick reflexes. Chronic alcoholics are at risk for hepatic (liver) function impairment if taking high dosages of acetaminophen-containing medication. Do not use medications which combine doxylamine succinate with tartrazine if you are intolerant or hypersensitive to aspirin. Allergic reactions, including bronchial asthma, have occurred in susceptible individuals.

ADDITIONAL WARNING:
Alcohol: Some cough/cold medications contain various amounts of alcohol. Check label of any cough medication if concerned about ingestion of alcohol.

Sugar/Sweeteners: Some cough/cold medications contain various amounts of sugar, sucrose,

Q U I C K F A C T S

glucose, and/or artificial sweeteners such as aspartame, saccharin, sorbitol. Check label of cough medication before selecting, if concerned about diabetes and ingestion of sugar or artificial sweeteners.

Abuse/Dependency: Reports indicate a rising rate of abuse of dextromethorphan-containing medications, particularly among teens. Sufficient data has not yet been collected, however, to determine the abuse and dependency potential of dextromethorphan-containing medications.

INFORM YOUR DOCTOR BEFORE TAKING PRODUCTS CONTAINING THIS COMBINATION OF ACTIVE INGREDIENTS IF YOU HAVE:

Asthma, emphysema or other respiratory condition, liver impairment or liver disease, allergies to aspirin or other salicylates, or if you have diabetes, thyroid condition, or urinary difficulty.

If you anticipate any surgery requiring general or spinal anesthesia within 2 months of taking medication which contains pseudoephredine, inform your doctor.

ACTIVE INGREDIENTS:

ACETAMINOPHEN, DEXTROMETHORPHAN HYDROBROMIDE, AND PSEUDOEPHREDINE HYDROCHLORIDE

QUICK FACTS

℞ **BRAND NAMES:**

- ALKA-SELTZER PLUS FLU & BODY ACHES NON-DROWSY LIQUI-GELS
- BAYER SELECT NIGHTTIME COLD CAPLETS (combination with tripolidine hydrochloride)
- COMTREX MAXIMUM STRENGTH NON-DROWSY CAPLETS
- CONTAC DAY & NIGHT COLD & FLU CAPLETS (combination with diphenhydramine hydrochloride)
- ROBITUSSIN NIGHT RELIEF LIQUID (also contains saccharin, sorbitol)
- SALETO CF TABLETS
- SUDAFED SEVERE COLD CAPLETS & TABLETS
- THERAFLU NON-DROWSY FORMULA MAXIMUM STRENGTH CAPLETS (also contains lactose, methylparaben)
- THERAFLU NON-DROWSY FLU, COLD & COUGH MAXIMUM STRENGTH POWDER (also contains sucrose)
- TRIAMINIC SORE THROAT FORMULA LIQUID (also contains EDTA, sucrose)
- TYLENOL COLD NO DROWSINESS CAPLETS & GELCAPS/MAXIMUM STRENGTH GELCAPS
- TYLENOL MAXIMUM STRENGTH COUGH WITH DECONGESTANT LIQUID (also contains alcohol, saccharin, sorbitol, sucrose)

Note: *Dextromethorphan hydrobromide* is also an active ingredient in other multi-symptom antitussive/expectorant medications which are formulated with other active ingredients.

QUICK FACTS

Pseudoephredine hydrochloride is a used as an active ingredient in decongestant and stimulant products.

Acetaminophen is a non-aspirin analgesic which is used primarily in pain-relief products.

SYMPTOMS RELIEVED:
Minor aches and pains, nasal congestion and coughing such as those associated with the common cold, flu, sore throat, sinusitis, hay fever and other respiratory allergies.

HOW TO TAKE:
Comes in caplet, capsule, and liquid forms. Swallow caplet or capsule with liquid. Sprinkle powder over liquid, then swallow. Do not crush or chew timed-release tablet.

USUAL ADULT DOSE:
Dosage varies per product and active ingredient formulation. Follow product dosage instructions.

USUAL CHILD DOSE:
Do not administer to children under 6 unless under direction of physician. Dosage may vary based on infant or child's age.

OVERDOSE SYMPTOMS:
Nervous agitation, severe anxiety, insomnia (sleeplessness), hallucinations, tremors, convulsions, nausea, vomiting, cardiac arrhythmia (irregular pulse and heartbeat), drowsiness, dizziness, fatigue, rash. If you suspect an overdose, immediately seek medical attention.

SIDE EFFECTS:
No serious effects in most cases of common use. Less common side effects include nasal dry-

ness, dizziness, nausea, and mild insomnia palpitations, insomnia, gastrointestinal (GI) upset including stomach cramps and diarrhea, drowsiness and fatigue. In rare cases, more severe side effects may result, including: painful and frequent urination, hypertension, and heart palpitations. In these cases, discontinue medication and call your doctor immediately. Long-term ingestion of high dosages of acetaminophen-containing products may increase risk of liver and kidney damage.

QUICK FACTS

CHECK WITH YOUR DOCTOR OR PHARMACIST BEFORE COMBINING THESE COMBINATION PRODUCTS WITH:
Anticoagulant medications , other cold, cough, or allergy medication, stimulants, antidepressants, antihypertensives, digitalis or other heart medication, diuretics, or MAO (monoamine oxidase inhibitors) drugs. Ingestion of caffeinated beverages (coffee, tea, caffeine-containing soft drinks) while taking pseudoephredine-containing medication can result in agitation and insomnia. If taking combination products which contain acetaminophen, you should avoid Isoniazid (antituberculosis) medication. Excessive ingestion of alcohol while taking acetaminophen-containing medication can increase the risk of liver damage or disease (hepatic toxicity).

PREGNANCY OR BREASTFEEDING:
No harmful effects have been reported regarding pregnancy or breastfeeding of infants, however, use of medications containing any of the active ingredients in these products by a nursing mother should be considered a potential risk for a nursing child as the drug(s) will be passed on

to the infant in the mother's milk. In all cases, a physician should be consulted.

PRECAUTIONS FOR CHILDREN:
In general, these active ingredients are not advised for children under 2. Administer to infants or children only when consulting a physician and follow instructions on medication (see above).

55+ **PRECAUTIONS FOR SENIORS:**
Seniors generally don't eliminate drugs as efficiently as younger persons, and should avoid high dosages. Use of pseudoephedrine-containing medications by seniors can lead to urinary difficulties. In addition, seniors are more likely to experience stimulant effects of pseudoephedrine.

SPECIAL WARNINGS:
Do not use for control of chronic cough related to conditions such as emphysema, asthma, or smoking, or if coughs are producing excessive secretions. If cough is accompanied by high fever, rash, nausea or vomiting, or persistent headache, use only if directed by your doctor. Chronic alcoholics are at risk for hepatic (liver) function impairment if taking high dosages of acetaminophen-containing medication.

ADDITIONAL WARNING:
Alcohol: Some cough/cold medications contain various amounts of alcohol. Check label of any cough medication if concerned about ingestion of alcohol.

Sugar/Sweeteners: Some cough/cold medications contain various amounts of sugar, sucrose, glucose, and/or artificial sweeteners such as aspartame, saccharin, sorbitol. Check label of cough medication before selecting, if concerned about diabetes and ingestion of sugar or artificial sweeteners.

Abuse/Dependency: Reports indicate a rising rate of abuse of dextromethorphan-containing medications, particularly among teens. Sufficient data has not yet been collected, however, to determine the abuse and dependency potential of dextromethorphan-containing medications.

INFORM YOUR DOCTOR BEFORE TAKING PRODUCTS CONTAINING THIS COMBINATION OF ACTIVE INGREDIENTS IF YOU HAVE:
Asthma, emphysema, or other respiratory condition, liver impairment or liver disease, allergies to any sympathomimetic drug, aspirin or other salicylates, or if you have diabetes, thyroid condition, or urinary difficulty. If you anticipate any surgery requiring general or spinal anesthesia within 2 months of taking medication which contains pseudoephredine, inform your doctor.

QUICK FACTS

ACTIVE INGREDIENT:
PHENYLPROPANOLAMINE HYDROCHLORIDE

BRAND NAMES:
- A.R.M. Caplets
- Chlor-Rest
- Cold-Gest Capsules
- Contac 12-Hour Capsules
- Demazin
- Demazin Syrup
- Gencold Capsules
- Propagest
- Rescon Liquid
- Silaminic Cold Syrup
- Spec-T Sore Throat/Decongestant Lozenges
- Tavist-D Tablets
- Teldrin 12-Hour Allergy Relief
- Temazin Cold Syrup
- Thera-Hist Syrup
- Tri-Nefrin
- Triaminic

SYMPTOMS RELIEVED:
Nasal congestion, runny nose, itchy and watery eyes, sneezing, scratchy throat, and irritated sinuses due to common cold, sinusitis, hay fever, and other upper respiratory allergies.

HOW TO TAKE:
Comes in tablet, capsule, chewable forms. Swallow with liquid. Do not crush or chew timed-release tablets.

USUAL ADULT DOSE:
25 milligrams every 4 hours, not to exceed 150 milligrams in a 24 hour period, or 75 milligrams

in a 24 hour period for timed-release tablets or capsules.

QUICK FACTS

USUAL CHILD DOSE:

For children 6 to 12: 12.5 milligrams 6 times per day, not to exceed 75 milligrams in a 24 hour period.

For children 2 to 6: 6.25 milligrams 6 times per day, not to exceed 37.5 milligrams in a 24 hour period.

Timed-release medications should only be administered under direction of physician. Do not administer to children under 6 unless under direction of physician. Dosage may vary based on infant or child's age.

OVERDOSE SYMPTOMS:

Nervous agitation, severe anxiety, insomnia (sleeplessness), hallucinations, tremors, convulsions, nausea, vomiting, cardiac arrhythmia (irregular pulse and heartbeat). If you suspect an overdose, immediately seek medical attention.

SIDE EFFECTS:

No serious effects in most cases of common use. Less common side effects include nasal dryness, dizziness, nausea, and mild insomnia. In rare cases, more severe side effects may result, including: painful and frequent urination, hypertension, and heart palpitations. In these cases, discontinue medication and call your doctor immediately.

CHECK WITH YOUR DOCTOR OR PHARMACIST BEFORE COMBINING PHENYLPROPANOLAMINE WITH:

Cold, cough, or allergy medication, stimulants,

antidepressants, antihypertensives, digitalis or other heart medication, diuretics, or MAO (monoamine oxidase inhibitors) drugs. Ingestion of caffeinated beverages (coffee, tea, caffeine-containing soft drinks) while taking phenylpropanolamine-containing medication can result in agitation and insomnia.

PREGNANCY OR BREASTFEEDING:
No harmful effects have been reported regarding pregnancy or breastfeeding of infants. Phenylpropanolamine use by a nursing mother should be considered a potential risk for a nursing child as the drug will be passed on to the infant in the mother's milk. In all cases, a physician should be consulted.

PRECAUTIONS FOR CHILDREN:
In general, phenylpropanolamine is not advised for children under 6. Administer phenylpropanolamine to infants or children only when consulting a physician and follow instructions on medication (see above).

55+

PRECAUTIONS FOR SENIORS:
Seniors generally don't eliminate drugs as efficiently as younger persons, and should avoid high dosages. Use of phenylpropanolamine medications by seniors can lead to cardiac arrhythmia (irregular pulse and heartbeat). In addition, seniors are more likely to experience stimulant effects of the drug.

SPECIAL WARNINGS:
Do not use continuously for longer than 3 months. Do not use phenylpropanolamine medications containing tartrazine if you are

intolerant or hypersensitive to aspirin. Allergic reactions, including bronchial asthma, have occurred in susceptible individuals.

INFORM YOUR DOCTOR BEFORE TAKING PHENYLPROPANOLAMINE IF YOU HAVE:
Allergies to: any sympathomimetic drug, aspirin or other salicylates, or if you have diabetes, thyroid condition, or urinary difficulty. If you anticipate any surgery requiring general or spinal anesthesia within 2 months of taking phenylpropanolamine medication, inform your doctor.

QUICK FACTS

ACTIVE INGREDIENT:
PHENYLPROPANOLAMINE AND BROMPHENIRAMINE MALEATE

BRAND NAMES:
- Dimaphen Release Tablets
- Dimetane Decongestant Capsules
- Dimetapp Extentabs Tablets
- Vicks DayQuil Allergy Relief 12-Hour Tablets

HOW TO TAKE:
Comes in tablet and capsule forms. Swallow with liquid. Do not crush or chew timed-release tablets.

USUAL ADULT DOSE:
25 milligrams 3 times per day, (75 milligrams once daily for time release capsules) 1/2 hour before meals, not to exceed 75 milligrams in a 24 hour period.

USUAL CHILD DOSE:
Do not administer to children under 6 unless under direction of physician. Dosage may vary based on infant or child's age.

OVERDOSE SYMPTOMS:
Nervous agitation, severe anxiety, insomnia (sleeplessness), hallucinations, tremors, convulsions, nausea, vomiting, cardiac arrhythmia (irregular pulse and heartbeat). If you suspect an overdose, immediately seek medical attention.

SIDE EFFECTS:
No serious effects in most cases of common use. Less common side effects include nasal dryness, dizziness, nausea, and mild insomnia palpitations, insomnia. In rare cases, more severe

side effects may result, including: painful and frequent urination, hypertension, and heart palpitations. In these cases, discontinue medication and call your doctor immediately.

CHECK WITH YOUR DOCTOR OR PHARMACIST BEFORE COMBINING PHENYLPROPANOLAMINE WITH:

Cold, cough,or allergy medication, stimulants, antidepressants, antihypertensives, digitalis or other heart medication, diuretics, or MAO (monoamine oxidase inhibitors) drugs. Ingestion of caffeinated beverages (coffee, tea, caffeine-containing soft drinks) while taking phenylpropanolamine-containing medication can result in agitation and insomnia.

PREGNANCY OR BREASTFEEDING:

No harmful effects have been reported regarding pregnancy or breastfeeding of infants. Phenylpropanolamine use by a nursing mother should be considered a potential risk for a nursing child as the drug will be passed on to the infant in the mother's milk. In all cases, a physician should be consulted.

PRECAUTIONS FOR CHILDREN:

In general, phenylpropanolamine is not advised for children under 6. Administer phenylpropanolamine to infants or children only when consulting a physician and follow instructions on medication (see above).

55+

PRECAUTIONS FOR SENIORS:

Seniors generally don't eliminate drugs as efficiently as younger persons, and should avoid high dosages. Use of phenylpropanolamine medications by seniors can lead to cardiac arrhythmia (irregular pulse and heartbeat). In addition, seniors are more likely to experience stimulant effects of the drug.

SPECIAL WARNINGS:
Do not use continuously for longer than 3 months. Do not use phenylpropanolamine medications containing tartazine if you are intolerant or hypersensitive to aspirin. Allergic reactions, including bronchial asthma, have occurred in susceptible individuals.

INFORM YOUR DOCTOR BEFORE TAKING PHENYLPROPANOLAMINE IF YOU HAVE:
Allergies to aspirin or other salicylates, or if you have diabetes, thyroid condition, or urinary difficulty. If you anticipate any surgery requiring general or spinal anesthesia within 2 months of taking phenylpropanolamine medication, inform your doctor.

ACTIVE INGREDIENTS:

PHENYLPROPANOLAMINE HYDROCHLORIDE COMBINATION WITH CHLOPHENIRAMINE MALEATE

Q U I C K F A C T S

BRAND NAMES:

- A.R.M. Caplets
- Cold-Gest Capsules
- Contac 12-Hour Capsules
- Tavist-D Tablets
- Teldrin 12-Hour Allergy Relief
- Thera-Hist Syrup
- Tri-Nefrin
- Triaminic Allergy Tablets
- Triaminic AM Decongestant Formula

SYMPTOMS RELIEVED:

Nasal congestion, runny nose, itchy and watery eyes, sneezing, scratchy throat, and irritated sinuses due to common cold, sinusitis, hay fever and other upper respiratory allergies.

HOW TO TAKE:

Comes in tablet, capsule, liquid, lozenge, and chewable forms. Swallow tablets and capsules with liquid. Do not crush or chew timed-release tablets.

USUAL ADULT DOSE:

25 milligrams every 4 hours, not to exceed 150 milligrams in a 24 hour period, or 75 milligrams in a 24 hour period for timed-release tablets or capsules.

USUAL CHILD DOSE:

Do not administer to children under 6 unless under direction of physician.

Q U I C K F A C T S

Children 6 to 12: 12.5 milligrams every 4 hours, not to exceed 75 milligrams in a 24 hour period. (Dosage may vary based on child's age.)

OVERDOSE SYMPTOMS:
Nervous agitation, severe anxiety, insomnia (sleeplessness), hallucinations, tremors, convulsions, nausea, vomiting, cardiac arrhythmia (irregular pulse and heartbeat). If you suspect an overdose, immediately seek medical attention.

SIDE EFFECTS:
No serious effects in most cases of common use. Less common side effects include nasal dryness, dizziness, nausea, and mild insomnia palpitations, insomnia. In rare cases, more severe side effects may result, including: painful and frequent urination, hypertension, and heart palpitations. In these cases, discontinue medication and call your doctor immediately.

CHECK WITH YOUR DOCTOR OR PHARMACIST BEFORE COMBINING PHENYLPROPANOLAMINE WITH:
Cold, cough, or allergy medication, stimulants, antidepressants, antihypertensives, digitalis or other heart medication, diuretics, or MAO (monoamine oxidase inhibitors) drugs. Ingestion of caffeinated beverages (coffee, tea, caffeine-containing soft drinks) while taking phenylpropanolamine-containing medication can result in agitation and insomnia.

PREGNANCY OR BREASTFEEDING:
No harmful effects have been reported regarding pregnancy or breastfeeding of infants, Phenylpropanolamine use by a nursing mother

should be considered a potential risk for a nursing child as the drug will be passed on to the infant in the mother's milk. In all cases, a physician should be consulted.

PRECAUTIONS FOR CHILDREN:
In general, phenylpropanolamine is not advised for children under 6. Administer to infants or children only when consulting a physician.

55+

PRECAUTIONS FOR SENIORS:
Seniors generally don't eliminate drugs as efficiently as younger persons, and should avoid high dosages. Use of phenylpropanolamine medications by seniors can lead to cardiac arrhythmia (irregular pulse and heartbeat). In addition, seniors are more likely to experience stimulant effects of the drug.

SPECIAL WARNINGS:
Do not use continuously for longer than 3 months. Do not use phenylpropanolamine medications containing tartrazine if you are intolerant or hypersensitive to aspirin. Allergic reactions, including bronchial asthma, have occurred in susceptible individuals.

INFORM YOUR DOCTOR BEFORE TAKING PHENYLPROPANOLAMINE IF YOU HAVE:
Allergies to: any sympathomimetic drug, aspirin or other salicylates, or if you have diabetes, thyroid condition, or urinary difficulty. If you anticipate any surgery requiring general or spinal anesthesia within 2 months of taking phenylpropanolamine medication, inform your doctor.

QUICK FACTS

ACTIVE INGREDIENTS:
PHENYLPROPANOLAMINE AND CHLORPHENIRAMINE MALEATE

℞ **BRAND NAMES:**
- A.R.M. Caplets
- Allerest Sinus Pain Formula (combination with acetaminophen)
- Aspirin-Free Bayer Select Allergy Sinus Caplets (combination with acetaminophen)
- BC Cold–Sinus–Allergy Powder (combination with aspirin)
- Children's Allerest (also contains saccharin and sorbitol)
- Chlor-Trimeton Allergy Sinus Caplets (combination with acetaminophen)
- Chlor-Rest
- Cold-Gest Capsules
- Contac 12-Hour Capsules
- Coricidin D Tablets (combination with acetaminophen)
- Dapacin Cold Capsules (combination with acetaminophen)
- Demazin Syrup (also contains 7.5% alcohol, menthol, sugar, parabens)
- Duadacin Capsules (combination with acetaminophen)
- Gelpirin-CCF Tablets (combination with acetaminophen and guaifenesin)
- Gencold Capsules
- Histosal Tablets (combination with acetaminophen and caffeine)
- Maximum Strength Tylenol Allergy Sinus (combination with acetaminophen)
- Naldecon Pediatric Syrup/Drops (also contains sorbitol)

- Naldelate Pediatric Syrup (also contains sorbitol)
- Nalgest Pediatric Syrup/Drops (also contains sorbitol)
- Pyrroxate (combination with acetaminophen)
- Rescon Liquid (also contains 7.5% alcohol, menthol, sugar, parabens)
- Silaminic Cold Syrup (also contains 7.5% alcohol, menthol, sugar, parabens)
- Sinapils Tablets (combination with acetaminophen and caffeine)
- Sinarest Extra Strength Tablets (combination with acetaminophen)
- Sinulin (combination with acetaminophen)
- Teldrin 12-Hour Allergy Relief
- Temazin Cold Syrup (also contains 7.5% alcohol, menthol, sugar, parabens)
- Thera-Hist Syrup (also contains sorbitol and sucrose)
- Tri-Nefrin
- Tri-Phen-Chlor Pediatric Syrup/Drops (also contains sorbitol)
- Tri-Phen-Mine Pediatric Syrup/Drops (also contains sorbitol)
- Triaminic
- Triaminicin Cold, Allergy, Sinus Tablets (combination with acetaminophen)
- Triaminicol Multi-Symptom Cough & Cold Tablets (combination with acetaminophen and caffeine)

HOW TO TAKE:

Comes in tablet, capsule, and chewable forms. Swallow with liquid. Do not crush or chew timed-release tablets. Phenylpropanolamine can cause GI (gastrointestinal) irritation and should be taken with food or following meal.

QUICK FACTS

USUAL ADULT DOSE:
25 milligrams 3 times per day, (75 milligrams once daily for time release capsules) ½ hour before meals, not to exceed 75 milligrams in a 24 hour period.

USUAL CHILD DOSE:
Do not administer to children under 6 unless under direction of physician. Dosage may vary based on infant or child's age.

OVERDOSE SYMPTOMS:
Nervous agitation, severe anxiety, insomnia (sleeplessness), hallucinations, tremors, convulsions, nausea, vomiting, cardiac arrhythmia (irregular pulse and heartbeat). If you suspect an overdose, immediately seek medical attention.

SIDE EFFECTS:
No serious effects in most cases of common use. Less common side effects include nasal dryness, dizziness, nausea, and mild insomnia palpitations, insomnia. In rare cases, more severe side effects may result, including: painful and frequent urination, hypertension, and heart palpitations. In these cases, discontinue medication and call your doctor immediately.

CHECK WITH YOUR DOCTOR OR PHARMACIST BEFORE COMBINING PHENYLPROPANOLAMINE WITH:
Stimulants, antidepressants, antihypertensives, digitalis or other heart medication, diuretics, or MAO (monoamine oxidase inhibitors) drugs. Ingestion of caffeinated beverages (coffee, tea, caffeine-containing soft drinks) while taking phenylpropanolamine-containing medication can result in agitation and insomnia.

PREGNANCY OR BREASTFEEDING:
No harmful effects have been reported regarding pregnancy or breastfeeding of infants. Phenylpropanolamine use by a nursing mother should be considered a potential risk for a nursing child as the drug will be passed on to the infant in the mother's milk. In all cases, a physician should be consulted.

PRECAUTIONS FOR CHILDREN:
In general, phenylpropanolamine is not advised for children under 6. Administer to infants or children only when consulting a physician.

55+

PRECAUTIONS FOR SENIORS:
Seniors generally don't eliminate drugs as efficiently as younger persons, and should avoid high dosages. Use of phenylpropanolamine medications by seniors can lead to cardiac arrhythmia (irregular pulse and heartbeat). In addition, seniors are more likely to experience stimulant effects of the drug.

SPECIAL WARNINGS:
Do not use continuously for longer the 3 months. Do not use phenylpropanolamine medications containing tartazine if you are intolerant or hypersensitive to aspirin. Allergic reactions, including bronchial asthma, have occurred in susceptible individuals.

INFORM YOUR DOCTOR BEFORE TAKING PHENYLPROPANOLAMINE IF YOU HAVE:
Allergies to aspirin or other salicylates, diabetes, thyroid condition, urinary difficulty. If you anticipate any surgery requiring general or spinal anesthesia within 2 months of taking phenylpropanolamine medication, inform your doctor.

QUICK FACTS

ACTIVE INGREDIENTS:

PHENYLPROPANOLAMINE AND CHLORPHENIRAMINE MALEATE COMBINATION WITH ACETAMINOPHEN

BRAND NAMES:

- ALLEREST SINUS PAIN FORMULA
- ASPIRIN-FREE BAYER SELECT ALLERGY SINUS CAPLETS
- CHLOR-TRIMETON ALLERGY SINUS CAPLETS
- CORICIDIN D TABLETS
- HISTOSAL TABLETS (combination with caffeine)
- MAXIMUM STRENGTH TYLENOL ALLERGY SINUS
- PYRROXATE
- SINAPILS TABLETS (combination with caffeine)
- SINAREST EXTRA STRENGTH TABLETS
- SINULIN
- TRIAMINICIN COLD, ALLERGY, SINUS TABLETS

HOW TO TAKE:
Comes in tablet, capsule, and chewable forms. Swallow with liquid. Do not crush or chew timed-release tablets.

USUAL ADULT DOSE:
25 milligrams 3 times per day, (75 milligrams once daily for time release capsules) 1/2 hour before meals, not to exceed 75 milligrams in a 24 hour period.

USUAL CHILD DOSE:
Do not administer to children under 6 unless under direction of physician. Dosage may vary based on infant or child's age.

OVERDOSE SYMPTOMS:
Nervous agitation, severe anxiety, insomnia

(sleeplessness), hallucinations, tremors, convulsions, nausea, vomiting, cardiac arrhythmia (irregular pulse and heartbeat). If you suspect an overdose, immediately seek medical attention.

SIDE EFFECTS:

No serious effects in most cases of common use. Less common side effects include nasal dryness, dizziness, nausea, and mild insomnia palpitations, insomnia. In rare cases, more severe side effects may result, including: painful and frequent urination, hypertension, and heart palpitations. In these cases, discontinue medication and call your doctor immediately.

CHECK WITH YOUR DOCTOR OR PHARMACIST BEFORE COMBINING PHENYLPROPANOLAMINE WITH:

Cold, cough,or allergy medication, stimulants, antidepressants, antihypertensives, digitalis or other heart medication, diuretics, or MAO (monoamine oxidase inhibitors) drugs. Ingestion of caffeinated beverages (coffee, tea, caffeine-containing soft drinks) while taking phenylpropanolamine-containing medication can result in agitation and insomnia.

PREGNANCY OR BREASTFEEDING:

No harmful effects have been reported regarding pregnancy or breastfeeding of infants. Phenylpropanolamine use by a nursing mother should be considered a potential risk for a nursing child as the drug will be passed on to the infant in the mother's milk. In all cases, a physician should be consulted.

QUICK FACTS

PRECAUTIONS FOR CHILDREN:
In general, phenylpropanolamine is not advised for children under 6. Administer phenylpropanolamine to infants or children only when consulting a physician and follow instructions on medication (see above).

PRECAUTIONS FOR SENIORS:
Seniors generally don't eliminate drugs as efficiently as younger persons, and should avoid high dosages. Use of phenylpropanolamine medications by seniors can lead to cardiac arrhythmia (irregular pulse and heartbeat). In addition, seniors are more likely to experience stimulant effects of the drug.

SPECIAL WARNINGS:
Do not use continuously for longer than 3 months. Do not use phenylpropanolamine medications containing tartrazine if you are intolerant or hypersensitive to aspirin. Allergic reactions, including bronchial asthma, have occurred in susceptible individuals.

INFORM YOUR DOCTOR BEFORE TAKING PHENYLPROPANOLAMINE IF YOU HAVE:
Allergies to: any sympathomimetic drug, aspirin or other salicylates, or if you have diabetes, thyroid condition, or urinary difficulty. If you anticipate any surgery requiring general or spinal anesthesia within 2 months of taking phenylpropanolamine medication, inform your doctor.

ACTIVE INGREDIENTS:

PHENYLPROPANOLAMINE AND CHLORPHENIRAMINE MALEATE (DECONGESTANT) COMBINATION WITH ACETAMINOPHEN

QUICK FACTS

BRAND NAMES:
- Allerest Sinus Pain Formula
- Aspirin-Free Bayer Select Allergy Sinus Caplets
- Chlor-Trimeton Allergy Sinus Caplets
- Coricidin D Tablets
- Dapacin Cold Capsules
- Gelpirin-CCF Tablets (combination with guaifenesin)
- Gencold Capsules
- Histosal Tablets (combination with caffeine)
- Maximum Strength Tylenol Allergy Sinus
- Pyrroxate
- Sinapils Tablets (combination with caffeine)
- Sinarest Extra Strength Tablets
- Sinulin
- Triaminicin Cold, Allergy, Sinus Tablets
- Triaminicol Multi-Symptom Cough & Cold Tablets (combination with caffeine)

HOW TO TAKE:
Comes in tablet, capsule, and chewable forms. Swallow with liquid. Do not crush or chew timed-release tablets.

USUAL ADULT DOSE:
25 milligrams 3 times per day, (75 milligrams once daily for time release capsules) 1/2 hour before meals, not to exceed 75 milligrams in a 24 hour period.

QUICK FACTS

55+ **USUAL CHILD DOSE:**
Do not administer to children under 6 unless under direction of physician. Dosage may vary based on infant or child's age.

OVERDOSE SYMPTOMS:
Nervous agitation, severe anxiety, insomnia (sleeplessness), hallucinations, tremors, convulsions, nausea, vomiting, cardiac arrhythmia (irregular pulse and heartbeat). If you suspect an overdose, immediately seek medical attention.

SIDE EFFECTS:
No serious effects in most cases of common use. Less common side effects include nasal dryness, dizziness, nausea, and mild insomnia palpitations, insomnia. In rare cases, more severe side effects may result, including: painful and frequent urination, hypertension, and heart palpitations. In these cases, discontinue medication and call your doctor immediately.

CHECK WITH YOUR DOCTOR OR PHARMACIST BEFORE COMBINING PHENYLPROPANOLAMINE WITH:
Cold, cough,or allergy medication, stimulants, antidepressants, antihypertensives, digitalis or other heart medication, diuretics, or MAO (monoamine oxidase inhibitors) drugs. Ingestion of caffeinated beverages (coffee, tea, caffeine-containing soft drinks) while taking phenylpropanolamine-containing medication can result in agitation and insomnia.

PREGNANCY OR BREASTFEEDING:
No harmful effects have been reported regarding pregnancy or breastfeeding of infants.

Phenylpropanolamine use by a nursing mother should be considered a potential risk for a nursing child as the drug will be passed on to the infant in the mother's milk. In all cases, a physician should be consulted.

PRECAUTIONS FOR CHILDREN:
In general, phenylpropanolamine is not advised for children under 6. Administer phenylpropanolamine to infants or children only when consulting a physician and follow instructions on medication (see above).

55+

PRECAUTIONS FOR SENIORS:
Seniors generally don't eliminate drugs as efficiently as younger persons, and should avoid high dosages. Use of phenylpropanolamine medications by seniors can lead to cardiac arrhythmia (irregular pulse and heartbeat). In addition, seniors are more likely to experience stimulant effects of the drug.

SPECIAL WARNINGS:
Do not use continuously for longer than 3 months. Do not use phenylpropanolamine medications containing tartrazine if you are intolerant or hypersensitive to aspirin. Allergic reactions, including bronchial asthma, have occurred in susceptible individuals.

INFORM YOUR DOCTOR BEFORE TAKING PHENYLPROPANOLAMINE IF YOU HAVE:
Allergies to aspirin or other salicylates, or if you have diabetes,thyroid condition, or urinary difficulty. If you anticipate any surgery requiring general or spinal anesthesia within 2 months of taking phenylpropanolamine medication, inform your doctor.

QUICK FACTS

ACTIVE INGREDIENT:
PSEUDOEPHEDRINE HYDROCHLORIDE

BRAND NAMES:
- ALLERMED
- CENAFED
- CENAPHED SYRUP (also contains methylparaben)
- DEFED-60
- DORCOL CHILDREN'S DECONGESTANT (also contains sucrose, sorbitol)
- GENAPHED
- HALOFED (some formulations are sugar-coated)
- PEDIACARE INFANTS' DECONGESTANT (also contains sucrose, sorbitol)
- PSEUDO-GEST
- SEDOTABS (also contains sucrose)
- SINUSTOP PRO
- SUDAFED (also contains sucrose)
- SUDAFED CHILDREN'S (also contains methylparaben, sodium benzoate, sorbitol, sucrose—some formulations contain raspberry flavor)
- SUDAFED 12-HOUR CAPLETS

SYMPTOMS RELIEVED:
Nasal congestion, runny nose, itchy and watery eyes, sneezing, scratchy throat, and irritated sinuses due to common cold, sinusitis, hay fever, and other upper respiratory allergies.

HOW TO TAKE:
Comes in tablet, capsule, liquid, and drop forms. Swallow with liquid. Do not crush or chew timed-release tablets. Use dropper per instructions on medication.

USUAL ADULT DOSE:
60 milligrams 4 to 6 times per day, (120 milli-

grams twice daily for timed-release capsules), not to exceed 240 milligrams in a 24 hour period.

USUAL CHILD DOSE:

For children 6 to 12: 30 milligrams 4 to 6 times per day, not to exceed 120 milligrams in a 24 hour period.

For children 2 to 6: 15 milligrams 4 to 6 times per day, not to exceed 60 milligrams in a 24 hour period.

For children 1 to 2: 7 drops (0.2 milliliters) per kilogram of child's weight not to exceed 4 doses in a 24 hour period.

Timed-release medications should only be administered to children under direction of physician. Do not administer to children under 6 unless under direction of physician. Dosage may vary based on infant or child's age.

OVERDOSE SYMPTOMS:

Severe nervous agitation, disorientation, anxiety, headache, nausea and vomiting, heavy sweats, cardiac arrhythmia (irregular pulse and heartbeat), muscle tremors and spasms. If you suspect an overdose, immediately seek medical attention.

SIDE EFFECTS:

No serious effects in most cases of common use. Less common side effects include nasal dryness, dizziness, nausea, and mild insomnia palpitations, insomnia. In rare cases, more severe side effects may result, including: nausea or vomiting, painful and frequent urination,

Q U I C K F A C T S

hypertension, and irregular heartbeat. In these cases, discontinue medication and call your doctor immediately.

CHECK WITH YOUR DOCTOR OR PHARMACIST BEFORE COMBINING PSEUDOEPHEDRINE HYDROCHLORIDE WITH:
Cold, cough, or allergy medication, stimulants, antidepressants, antihypertensives, digitalis or other heart medication, diuretics, or MAO (monoamine oxidase inhibitors) drugs. Ingestion of caffeinated beverages (coffee, tea, caffeine-containing soft drinks) while taking pseudoephedrine hydrochloride-containing medication can result in agitation and insomnia.

PREGNANCY OR BREASTFEEDING:
No harmful effects have been reported regarding pregnancy or breastfeeding of infants. Pseudoephedrine hydrochloride use by a nursing mother should be considered a potential risk for a nursing child as the drug will be passed on to the infant in the mother's milk. In all cases, a physician should be consulted.

PRECAUTIONS FOR CHILDREN:
In general, pseudoephedrine hydrochloride is not advised for children under 12. Administer pseudoephedrine hydrochloride to infants or children only when consulting a physician and follow instructions on medication (see above).

55+

PRECAUTIONS FOR SENIORS:
Seniors generally don't eliminate drugs as efficiently as younger persons, and should avoid high dosages. Use of pseudoephedrine hydrochloride medications by seniors can lead to

cardiac arrhythmia (irregular pulse and heartbeat). In addition, seniors are more likely to experience stimulant effects of the drug.

SPECIAL WARNINGS:
Do not combine with any medication which contains caffeine. Do not use continuously for longer than 3 months. Do not use pseudoephedrine hydrochloride medications containing tartazine if you are intolerant or hypersensitive to aspirin. Allergic reactions, including bronchial asthma, have occurred in susceptible individuals.

INFORM YOUR DOCTOR BEFORE TAKING PSEUDOEPHEDRINE HYDROCHLORIDE IF YOU HAVE:
Allergies to: any sympathomimetic drug, aspirin or other salicylates, or if you have diabetes, thyroid condition, or urinary difficulty. If you anticipate any surgery requiring general or spinal anesthesia within 2 months of taking pseudoephedrine hydrochloride medication, inform your doctor.

Q U I C K F A C T S

ACTIVE INGREDIENT:

TRIPOLIDINE HYDROCHLORIDE

BRAND NAMES:

- ACTIDIL

SYMPTOMS RELIEVED:

Nasal congestion, runny nose, itchy and watery eyes, sneezing, scratchy throat, and irritate sinuses due to common cold, sinusitis, hay fever, and other upper respiratory allergies.

HOW TO TAKE:

Comes in tablet, capsule, and liquid forms. Swallow tablet or capsule with liquid. Do not crush or chew timed-release tablets. Tripolidine and other antihistamines can cause gastro-intestinal (GI) irritation and should be taken with food or following meal.

USUAL ADULT DOSE:

2.5 milligrams 3 to 4 times per day, not to exceed 10 milligrams in a 24 hour period.

USUAL CHILD DOSE:

For children 6 to 12: 2 milligrams 4 to 6 times per day, or 8 milligrams of timed release medication at bedtime or during day, not to exceed 12 milligrams in a 24 hour period.

For children 2 to 6: 1.25 milligrams 4 to 6 times per day, not to exceed 5 milligrams in a 24 hour period. Timed-release medications are not advised for children 2 to 6 or younger. Do not administer to children in this age group unless under direction of physician. Dosage may vary based on infant or child's age.

OVERDOSE SYMPTOMS:
Nervous agitation, severe anxiety, insomnia (sleeplessness), hallucinations, tremors, coma. If you suspect an overdose, immediately seek medical attention.

SIDE EFFECTS:
The most frequent side effect of antihistamines use is drowsiness. Other common side effects include: include dryness of mouth, throat, and nasal passages, dizziness, GI distress (including vomiting, diarrhea, and constipation or change in bowel regularity), and diminished muscle coordination. In rare cases, more severe side effects may result, such as painful and frequent urination or urinary retention, vision problems, loss of appetite, and respiratory difficulty. In these cases, discontinue medication and call your doctor immediately.

CHECK WITH YOUR DOCTOR OR PHARMACIST BEFORE COMBINING TRIPOLIDINE WITH:
Cold, cough, or allergy medication—including other antihistamines; aspirin, stimulants, antidepressants, antihypertensives, digitalis or other heart medication, diuretics, or MAO (monoamine oxidase inhibitors) drugs. Avoid ingestion of alcohol or use of sedatives or tranquilizers while taking tripolidine-containing medication or most other antihistamine-containing medication as the combination can produce severe drowsiness or sedation.

PREGNANCY OR BREASTFEEDING:
No harmful effects have been reported regarding pregnancy or breastfeeding of infants. Tripolidine use by a nursing mother should be

Q U I C K F A C T S

considered a potential risk for a nursing child as the drug will be passed on to the infant in the mother's milk. In all cases, a physician should be consulted.

PRECAUTIONS FOR CHILDREN:
In general, tripolidine is not advised for children under 6. Administer tripolidine to infants or children only when consulting a physician and follow instructions on medication (see above).

55+ **PRECAUTIONS FOR SENIORS:**
Seniors generally don't eliminate drugs as efficiently as younger persons, and should avoid high dosages. Use of tripolidine medications by seniors can lead to urinary difficulties. In addition, seniors are more likely to experience stimulant effects of the drug.

SPECIAL WARNINGS:
Because antihistamines often cause drowsiness, you should avoid activities or tasks such as driving, or other operations which require alertness, coordination, dexterity or quick reflexes. Do not use continuously for longer than 3 months. Do not use tripolidine medications containing tartrazine if you are intolerant or hypersensitive to aspirin. Allergic reactions, including bronchial asthma, have occurred in susceptible individuals.

INFORM YOUR DOCTOR BEFORE TAKING TRIPOLIDINE IF YOU HAVE:
Urinary difficulty, glaucoma, ulcer, or if you are pregnant. If you anticipate any surgery requiring general or spinal anesthesia within 2 months of taking tripolidine-containing medication, inform your doctor.

ACTIVE INGREDIENT:
CROMOLYN SODIUM (DISODIUM CROMOGLYCATE)

BRAND NAMES:
• NASALCROM

SYMPTOMS RELIEVED:
Nasal symptoms of hay fever and other nasal allergies.

HOW TO TAKE:
Comes in metered spray form. Spray in each nostril (see below). Do not under any conditions ingest internally or use in eyes.

USUAL ADULT DOSE:
Before administration of spray, clear nasal passages. Spray each nostril once, at regular intervals, 3 to 6 times per day. Inhale through nose. In all cases follow specific product instructions.

USUAL CHILD DOSE:
Ages 6 to 12: Before administration of spray, clear nasal passages. Spray each nostril once, at regular intervals, 3 to 6 times per day. Inhale through nose (same as adult dose).

Only administer to children between under 6 under doctor's supervision or direction. These products are generally not advised for children younger than 2, and never for infants. In all cases follow specific product instructions.

OVERDOSE SYMPTOMS:
None known.

SIDE EFFECTS:
No serious effects in most cases of common

Q U I C K F A C T S

use. Common side effects with this product may include: sneezing, nasal irritation, headache, unpleasant taste in mouth, postnasal drip, and skin rash. In rare cases, hives, intense itching and irritation, burning or stinging sensation in nose, and lightheadedness or fainting have been reported. In any of these cases, discontinue use of the product and call your doctor immediately.

CHECK WITH YOUR DOCTOR OR PHARMACIST BEFORE COMBINING THIS COMBINATION WITH:
Antiasthma medication, any other allergy products, or any other drugs and preparations.

PREGNANCY OR BREASTFEEDING:
Safety of this drug for use during pregnancy or while nursing has not been established. In all cases you should consult your doctor before using any drug during pregnancy or while nursing.

PRECAUTIONS FOR CHILDREN:
These products should only be used with doctor's supervision or direction for children under 6. These products are not recommended for use with children under 2 and should never be used with infants. Consult your doctor and follow instructions on medication (see above).

55+

PRECAUTIONS FOR SENIORS:
Seniors generally don't eliminate drugs as efficiently as younger persons, and should avoid high dosages.

SPECIAL WARNINGS:
Do not use these products if you are allergic to cromolyn sodium, lactose, milk or other dairy

products, or any of the inactive ingredients contained in these products. Although this product may relieve common asthma symptoms, do not use it to treat acute asthma.

INFORM YOUR DOCTOR BEFORE TAKING THIS PRODUCT IF YOU HAVE:
Any form of liver or kidney disease (including kidney stones), or if you are or plan to become pregnant during time that you will be taking this product.

QUICK FACTS

ACTIVE INGREDIENT:
EPHEDRINE HYDROCHLORIDE

BRAND NAMES:
- KONDON'S NASAL (jelly)
- PRETZ-D (spray)
- VICKS VATRONOL (drops)

SYMPTOMS RELIEVED:
Nasal congestion due to common cold, sinusitis, hay fever, and other upper respiratory allergies.

HOW TO TAKE:
Comes in nasal spray, drop, or jelly forms. Use dropper and spray pump per instructions on medication label. Apply jelly with sterile swab. Always wash hands before applying product directly.

USUAL ADULT DOSE:
Dosage varies per product formulation. Follow product dosage instructions.

USUAL CHILD DOSE:
Do not administer to children under 6 unless under direction of physician. Dosage may vary based on infant or child's age.

OVERDOSE SYMPTOMS:
Headache, nausea and vomiting, heart palpitations, raised blood pressure, muscle tremors and spasms. If you suspect an overdose, immediately seek medical attention.

SIDE EFFECTS:
Most common include: nasal dryness and stinging, headache, burning sensation. In rare cases, more severe side effects may result, including:

heavy sweats, nervous agitation, hypertension, and irregular heartbeat. In these cases, discontinue medication and call your doctor immediately.

CHECK WITH YOUR DOCTOR OR PHARMACIST BEFORE COMBINING EPHEDRINE WITH:
Cold, cough, allergy or asthma medication, stimulants, sedatives, sleep aids, antidepressants, antihypertensives, digitalis or other heart medication, diuretics, or MAO (monoamine oxidase inhibitors) drugs. Ingestion of caffeinated beverages (coffee, tea, caffeine-containing soft drinks) while taking ephedrine-containing medication can result in agitation and insomnia.

PREGNANCY OR BREASTFEEDING:
No harmful effects have been reported regarding pregnancy or breastfeeding of infants. Ephedrine use by a nursing mother should be considered a potential risk for a nursing child as the drug will be passed on to the infant in the mother's milk. In all cases, a physician should be consulted.

PRECAUTIONS FOR CHILDREN:
In general, ephedrine is not advised for children under 6. Administer ephedrine to infants or children only when consulting a physician and follow instructions on medication (see above).

55+ **PRECAUTIONS FOR SENIORS:**
Seniors generally don't eliminate drugs as efficiently as younger persons, and should avoid high dosages. Seniors are more likely to experience stimulant effects of the drug.

Q U I C K F A C T S

SPECIAL WARNINGS:
Do not combine with any medication which contains caffeine. Prolonged, continuous use may lead to dependence.

INFORM YOUR DOCTOR BEFORE TAKING EPHEDRINE IF YOU HAVE:
Diabetes, high blood pressure, heart disease, or thyroid condition. If you anticipate any surgery requiring general or spinal anesthesia within 2 months of taking ephedrine medication, inform your doctor.

ACTIVE INGREDIENT:
NAPHAZOLINE HYDROCHLORIDE

QUICK FACTS

BRAND NAMES:
- PRIVINE

SYMPTOMS RELIEVED:
Nasal congestion due to common cold, sinusitis, hay fever and other upper respiratory allergies.

HOW TO TAKE:
Comes in nasal spray or drops forms. Use dropper and spray pump per instructions on medication label. Always wash hands before applying product directly.

USUAL ADULT DOSE:
1 to 2 sprays or drops per nostril as needed, not to exceed 1 dose every 6 hours

USUAL CHILD DOSE:
Do not administer to children under 12 unless under direction of physician. Dosage may vary based on infant or child's age.

OVERDOSE SYMPTOMS:
Headache, nausea, and vomiting, heart palpitations, raised blood pressure, muscle tremors and spasms. If you suspect an overdose, immediately seek medical attention.

SIDE EFFECTS:
Most common include: nasal dryness and stinging, headache, burning sensation. In rare cases, more severe side effects may result, including: heavy sweats, nervous agitation, hypertension, and irregular heartbeat. In these cases, discontinue medication and call your doctor immediately.

QUICK FACTS

CHECK WITH YOUR DOCTOR OR PHARMACIST BEFORE COMBINING NAPHAZOLINE WITH:
Cold, cough, allergy, or asthma medication, stimulants, sedatives, sleep aids, antidepressants, antihypertensives, digitalis or other heart medication, diuretics, or MAO (monoamine oxidase inhibitors) drugs.

PREGNANCY OR BREASTFEEDING:
No harmful effects have been reported regarding pregnancy or breastfeeding of infant. Naphazoline use by a nursing mother should be considered a potential risk for a nursing child as the drug will be passed on to the infant in the mother's milk. In all cases, a physician should be consulted.

PRECAUTIONS FOR CHILDREN:
Administer naphazoline to infants or children only when consulting a physician and follow instructions on medication (see above).

55+ **PRECAUTIONS FOR SENIORS:**
Seniors should avoid high dosages and are more likely to experience stimulant effects of the drug.

SPECIAL WARNINGS:
Do not combine with any medication which contains caffeine. Prolonged, continuous use may lead to dependence.

INFORM YOUR DOCTOR BEFORE TAKING NAPHAZOLINE IF YOU HAVE:
Diabetes, high blood pressure, heart disease, or thyroid condition. If you anticipate any surgery requiring general or spinal anesthesia within 2 months of taking naphazoline medication, inform your doctor.

ACTIVE INGREDIENT:
OXYMETAZOLINE HYDROCHLORIDE

QUICK FACTS

BRAND NAMES:
- AFRIN/AFRIN CHILDREN'S NOSE DROPS
- ALLEREST 12-HOUR NASAL
- CHLORPHED-LA
- DRISTAN LONG LASTING
- DURAMIST PLUS
- DURATION
- GENASAL
- NEO-SYNEPHRINE 12-HOUR
- NOSTRILLA
- SINAREST 12-HOUR
- SINEX LONG-ACTING
- TWICE-A-DAY

SYMPTOMS RELIEVED:
Nasal congestion due to common cold, sinusitis, hay fever and other upper respiratory allergies.

HOW TO TAKE:
Comes in nasal spray or drop forms. Use dropper and spray pump per instructions on medication label. Always wash hands before applying product directly.

USUAL ADULT DOSE:
2 to 3 sprays or drops of 0.05% solution per nostril 2 times per day.

USUAL CHILD DOSE:
For children 6 and older: Same dosage as adults.

For children 2 to 6: 2 to 3 sprays or drops of 0.025% solution per nostril 2 times per day.

Do not administer to children under 2 unless under direction of physician. Dosage may vary based on infant or child's age.

QUICK FACTS

OVERDOSE SYMPTOMS:
Headache, nausea, and vomiting, heart palpitations, raised blood pressure, muscle tremors and spasms. If you suspect an overdose, immediately seek medical attention.

SIDE EFFECTS:
Most common include: nasal dryness and stinging, headache, burning sensation. In rare cases, more severe side effects may result, including: heavy sweats, nervous agitation, hypertension, and irregular heartbeat. In these cases, discontinue medication and call your doctor immediately.

CHECK WITH YOUR DOCTOR OR PHARMACIST BEFORE COMBINING OXYMETAZOLINE WITH:
Cold, cough, allergy, or asthma medication, stimulants, sedatives, sleep aids, antidepressants, antihypertensives, digitalis or other heart medication, diuretics, or MAO (monoamine oxidase inhibitors) drugs. Ingestion of caffeinated beverages (coffee, tea, caffeine-containing soft drinks) while taking oxymetazoline-containing medication can result in agitation and insomnia.

PREGNANCY OR BREASTFEEDING:
No harmful effects have been reported regarding pregnancy or breastfeeding of infants. Oxymetazoline use by a nursing mother should be considered a potential risk for a nursing child as the drug will be passed on to the infant in the mother's milk. In all cases, a physician should be consulted.

PRECAUTIONS FOR CHILDREN:
In general, oxymetazoline is not advised for

children under 6. Administer oxymetazoline to infants or children only when consulting a physician and follow instructions on medication (see above).

55+ **PRECAUTIONS FOR SENIORS:**
Seniors generally don't eliminate drugs as efficiently as younger persons, and should avoid high dosages. Seniors are more likely to experience stimulant effects of the drug.

SPECIAL WARNINGS:
Do not combine with any medication which contains caffeine. Prolonged, continuous use may lead to dependence.

INFORM YOUR DOCTOR BEFORE TAKING OXYMETAZOLINE IF YOU HAVE:
Diabetes, high blood pressure, heart disease, or thyroid condition. If you anticipate any surgery requiring general or spinal anesthesia within 2 months of taking oxymetazoline medication, inform your doctor.

QUICK FACTS

ACTIVE INGREDIENT:

PHENYLEPHRINE HYDROCHLORIDE

BRAND NAMES:

- ALCONEFRIN/ ALCONEFRIN 25
- NEO-SYNEPHRINE
- NOSTRIL/CHILDREN'S NOSTRIL
- RHINALL
- SINEX

SYMPTOMS RELIEVED:
Nasal congestion due to common cold, sinusitis, hay fever, and other upper respiratory allergies.

HOW TO TAKE:
Comes in nasal spray or drop forms. Use dropper and spray pump per instructions on medication label. Always wash hands before applying product directly.

USUAL ADULT DOSE:
0.25% and 0.5% solutions: 2 to 3 sprays or drops per nostril every 3 to 4 hours.

1% solution: 2 to 3 sprays or drops per nostril no more than every 4 hours

USUAL CHILD DOSE:
For children 6 to 12:
0.25% and 0.5% solutions: 2 to 3 sprays or drops per nostril every 3 to 4 hours.

Do not administer to children under 6 unless under direction of physician. Dosage may vary based on infant or child's age.

OVERDOSE SYMPTOMS:
Headache, nausea and vomiting, heart palpitations, raised blood pressure, muscle tremors

and spasms. If you suspect an overdose, immediately seek medical attention.

SIDE EFFECTS:
Most common include: nasal dryness and stinging, headache, burning sensation. In rare cases, more severe side effects may result, including: heavy sweats, nervous agitation, hypertension, and irregular heartbeat. In these cases, discontinue medication and call your doctor immediately.

CHECK WITH YOUR DOCTOR OR PHARMACIST BEFORE COMBINING PHENYLEPHRINE WITH:
Cold, cough, allergy, or asthma medication, stimulants, sedatives, sleep aids, antidepressants, antihypertensives, digitalis or other heart medication, diuretics, or MAO (monoamine oxidase inhibitors) drugs. Ingestion of caffeinated beverages (coffee, tea, caffeine-containing soft drinks) while taking phenylephrine-containing medication can result in agitation and insomnia.

PREGNANCY OR BREASTFEEDING:
No harmful effects have been reported regarding pregnancy or breastfeeding of infants. Phenylephrine use by a nursing mother should be considered a potential risk for a nursing child as the drug will be passed on to the infant in the mother's milk. In all cases, a physician should be consulted.

PRECAUTIONS FOR CHILDREN:
In general, phenylephrine is not advised for children under 6. Administer phenylephrine to infants or children only when consulting a physician and follow instructions on medication (see above).

Q U I C K F A C T S

55+ **PRECAUTIONS FOR SENIORS:**
Seniors generally don't eliminate drugs as efficiently as younger persons, and should avoid high dosages. Seniors are more likely to experience stimulant effects of the drug.

SPECIAL WARNINGS:
Do not combine with any medication which contains caffeine. Prolonged, continuous use may lead to dependence.

INFORM YOUR DOCTOR BEFORE TAKING PHENYLEPHRINE IF YOU HAVE:
Diabetes, high blood pressure, heart disease, or thyroid condition. If you anticipate any surgery requiring general or spinal anesthesia within 2 months of taking phenylephrine medication, inform your doctor.

ACTIVE INGREDIENTS:
PHENYLEPHRINE HYDROCHLORIDE, NAPHAZOLINE HYDROCHLORIDE, AND PYRLAMINE MALEATE

QUICK FACTS

BRAND NAMES:
- 4-WAY FAST ACTING ORIGINAL (regular and menthol)

SYMPTOMS RELIEVED:
Nasal congestion, runny nose, itchy and watery eyes, sneezing, scratchy throat, and irritated sinuses due to common cold, sinusitis, hay fever, and other upper respiratory allergies.

HOW TO TAKE:
Comes in nasal spray or drops forms. Use dropper and spray pump per instructions on medication label. Always wash hands before applying product directly.

USUAL ADULT DOSE:
1 to 2 sprays or drops per nostril as needed, not to exceed 1 dose every 6 hours

USUAL CHILD DOSE:
Do not administer to children under 12 unless under direction of physician. Dosage may vary based on infant or child's age.

OVERDOSE SYMPTOMS:
Headache, nausea and vomiting, heart palpitations, raised blood pressure, muscle tremors and spasms. If you suspect an overdose, immediately seek medical attention.

SIDE EFFECTS:
No harmful effects have been reported regarding pregnancy or breastfeeding of infants.

QUICK FACTS

The most frequent side effect of antihistamine use is drowsiness. Other common side effects include: nasal dryness and stinging, headache, burning sensation. In rare cases, more severe side effects may result, including: heavy sweats, nervous agitation, hypertension, and irregular heartbeat. In these cases, discontinue medication and call your doctor immediately.

CHECK WITH YOUR DOCTOR OR PHARMACIST BEFORE COMBINING THIS COMBINATION PRODUCT WITH:
Cold, cough, allergy, or asthma medication, stimulants, sedatives, sleep aids, antidepressants, antihypertensives, digitalis or other heart medication, diuretics, or MAO (monoamine oxidase inhibitors) drugs. Ingestion of caffeinated beverages (coffee, tea, caffeine-containing soft drinks) while taking naphazoline-containing medication can result in agitation and insomnia.

PREGNANCY OR BREASTFEEDING:
No harmful effects have been reported regarding pregnancy or breastfeeding of infants. Use of this combination product by a nursing mother should be considered a potential risk for a nursing child as the drugs will be passed on to the infant in the mother's milk. In all cases, a physician should be consulted.

PRECAUTIONS FOR CHILDREN:
In general, this combination product is not advised for children under 6. Administer this combination product to infants or children only when consulting a physician and follow instructions on medication (see above).

55+ **PRECAUTIONS FOR SENIORS:**
Seniors generally don't eliminate drugs as efficiently as younger persons, and should avoid high dosages. Seniors are more likely to experience stimulant effects of the drugs in this product.

SPECIAL WARNINGS:
Because antihistamines often cause drowsiness, you should avoid activities or tasks such as driving, or other operations which require alertness, coordination, dexterity or quick reflexes. Do not use continuously for longer than 3 months.

INFORM YOUR DOCTOR BEFORE TAKING THIS COMBINATION PRODUCT IF YOU HAVE:
Diabetes, high blood pressure, heart disease, or thyroid condition. If you anticipate any surgery requiring general or spinal anesthesia within 2 months of taking this medication, inform your doctor.

QUICK FACTS

ACTIVE INGREDIENTS:

PHENYLEPHRINE HYDROCHLORIDE AND PHENIRAMINE MALEATE

BRAND NAMES:

- DRISTAN NASAL (regular and menthol)

SYMPTOMS RELIEVED:

Nasal congestion, runny nose, itchy and watery eyes, sneezing, scratchy throat, and irritated sinuses due to common cold, sinusitis, hay fever, and other upper respiratory allergies.

HOW TO TAKE:

Comes in nasal spray form. Use spray pump per instructions on medication label. Always wash hands before applying product directly.

USUAL ADULT DOSE:

0.25% and 0.5% solutions: 2 to 3 sprays or drops per nostril every 3 to 4 hours.

1% solution: 2 to 3 sprays or drops per nostril no more than every 4 hours

USUAL CHILD DOSE:

For children 6 to 12:

0.25% and 0.5% solutions: 2 to 3 sprays or drops per nostril every 3 to 4 hours.

Do not administer to children under 6 unless under direction of physician. Dosage may vary based on infant or child's age.

OVERDOSE SYMPTOMS:

Headache, nausea, and vomiting, heart palpitations, raised blood pressure, muscle tremors and spasms. If you suspect an overdose, immediately seek medical attention.

SIDE EFFECTS:
The most frequent side effect of antihistamine use is drowsiness. Other common side effects include: nasal dryness and stinging, headache, burning sensation. In rare cases, more severe side effects may result, including: heavy sweats, nervous agitation, hypertension, and irregular heartbeat. In these cases, discontinue medication and call your doctor immediately.

CHECK WITH YOUR DOCTOR OR PHARMACIST BEFORE COMBINING PHENYLEPHRINE AND PHENIRAMINE MALEATE WITH:
Cold, cough, allergy, or asthma medication, stimulants, sedatives, sleep aids, antidepressants, antihypertensives, digitalis or other heart medication, diuretics, or MAO (monoamine oxidase inhibitors) drugs. Ingestion of caffeinated beverages (coffee, tea, caffeine-containing soft drinks) while taking phenylephrine and pheniramine maleate-containing medication can result in agitation and insomnia. Avoid ingestion of alcohol or use of sedatives or tranquilizers while taking chlorpheniramine maleate-containing medication or most other antihistamine-containing medication as the combination can produce severe drowsiness or sedation.

PREGNANCY OR BREASTFEEDING:
No harmful effects have been reported regarding pregnancy or breastfeeding of infants. Phenylephrine and pheniramine maleate use by a nursing mother should be considered a potential risk for a nursing child as the drug will be passed on to the infant in the mother's milk. In all cases, a physician should be consulted.

QUICK FACTS

PRECAUTIONS FOR CHILDREN:
In general, phenylephrine and pheniramine maleate use is not advised for children under 6. Administer phenylephrine and pheniramine maleate to infants or children only when consulting a physician and follow instructions on medication (see above).

PRECAUTIONS FOR SENIORS:
Seniors generally don't eliminate drugs as efficiently as younger persons, and should avoid high dosages. Seniors are more likely to experience stimulant effects of the drug.

SPECIAL WARNINGS:
Because antihistamines often cause drowsiness, you should avoid activities or tasks such as driving, or other operations which require alertness, coordination, dexterity or quick reflexes. Do not use continuously for longer than 3 months.

INFORM YOUR DOCTOR BEFORE TAKING PHENYLEPHRINE AND PHENIRAMINE MALEATE IF YOU HAVE:
Diabetes, high blood pressure, heart disease, or thyroid condition.

ACTIVE INGREDIENTS:

PHENYLEPHRINE HYDROCHLORIDE AND PYRLAMINE MALEATE

BRAND NAMES:
- MYCI-SPRAY

SYMPTOMS RELIEVED:
Nasal congestion, runny nose, itchy and watery eyes, sneezing, scratchy throat, and irritated sinuses due to common cold, sinusitis, hay fever, and other upper respiratory allergies.

HOW TO USE:
Comes in nasal spray form. Use spray pump per instructions on medication label. Always wash hands before applying product directly.

USUAL ADULT DOSE:
0.25% and 0.5% solutions: 2 to 3 sprays or drops per nostril every 3 to 4 hours.

1% solution: 2 to 3 sprays or drops per nostril no more than every 4 hours

USUAL CHILD DOSE:
For children 6 to 12:
0.25% and 0.5% solutions: 2 to 3 sprays or drops per nostril every 3 to 4 hours.

Do not administer to children under 6 unless under direction of physician. Dosage may vary based on infant or child's age.

OVERDOSE SYMPTOMS:
Headache, nausea and vomiting, heart palpitations, raised blood pressure, muscle tremors and spasms. If you suspect an overdose, immediately seek medical attention.

Q U I C K F A C T S

Q U I C K F A C T S

SIDE EFFECTS:
The most frequent side effect of antihistamine use is drowsiness. Other common side effects include: nasal dryness and stinging, headache, burning sensation. In rare cases, more severe side effects may result, including: heavy sweats, nervous agitation, hypertension, and irregular heartbeat. In these cases, discontinue medication and call your doctor immediately.

CHECK WITH YOUR DOCTOR OR PHARMACIST BEFORE COMBINING PHENYLEPHRINE AND PYRILAMINE MALEATE WITH:
Cold, cough, allergy, or asthma medication, stimulants, sedatives, sleep aids, antidepressants, antihypertensives, digitalis or other heart medication, diuretics, or MAO (monoamine oxidase inhibitors) drugs. Ingestion of caffeinated beverages (coffee, tea, caffeine-containing soft drinks) while taking phenylephrine and pyrilamine maleate-containing medication can result in agitation and insomnia. Avoid ingestion of alcohol or use of sedatives or tranquilizers while taking chlorpheniramine maleate-containing medication or most other antihistamine-containing medication as the combination can produce severe drowsiness or sedation.

PREGNANCY OR BREASTFEEDING:
No harmful effects have been reported regarding pregnancy or breastfeeding of infants. Phenylephrine and pyrilamine maleate use by a nursing mother should be considered a potential risk for a nursing child as the drug will be passed on to the infant in the mother's milk. In all cases, a physician should be consulted.

PRECAUTIONS FOR CHILDREN:
In general, phenylephrine and pyrilamine maleate use is not advised for children under 6. Administer phenylephrine and pyrilamine maleate to infants or children only when consulting a physician and follow instructions on medication (see above).

55+ **PRECAUTIONS FOR SENIORS:**
Seniors generally don't eliminate drugs as efficiently as younger persons, and should avoid high dosages. Seniors are more likely to experience stimulant effects of the drug.

SPECIAL WARNINGS:
Because antihistamines often cause drowsiness, you should avoid activities or tasks such as driving, or other operations which require alertness, coordination, dexterity or quick reflexes. Do not use continuously for longer than 3 months.

INFORM YOUR DOCTOR BEFORE TAKING PHENYLEPHRINE AND PYRILAMINE MALEATE IF YOU HAVE:
Diabetes, high blood pressure, heart disease, or thyroid condition.

QUICK FACTS

ACTIVE INGREDIENT:
SODIUM CHLORIDE

BRAND NAMES:
- Afrin Saline Mist
- Ayr Saline
- Breathe Free
- Dristan Saline Spray
- HuMist Nasal Mist
- Nasal
- Nasal Moist
- Ocean
- Pretz/Pretz Irrigating/Pretz Moisturizing
- SalineX
- SeaMist

SYMPTOMS RELIEVED:
Nasal congestion, runny nose, itchy and watery eyes, sneezing, scratchy throat, and irritated sinuses due to common cold, sinusitis, hay fever, and other upper respiratory allergies.

HOW TO TAKE:
Comes in nasal spray, mist, or drop forms. Use dropper and spray pump per instructions on medication label. Always wash hands before applying product directly.

USUAL ADULT DOSE:
2 to 6 sprays or drops per nostril as needed or as directed by your doctor.

USUAL CHILD DOSE:
2 to 6 sprays or drops per nostril as needed or as directed by your doctor.

OVERDOSE SYMPTOMS:
Headache, nausea and vomiting, heart palpitations, raised blood pressure, muscle tremors

and spasms. If you suspect an overdose, immediately seek medical attention.

SIDE EFFECTS:
Most common include: nasal burning and itching of membrane on application, and dryness and stinging during use. In rare cases, more severe side effects may result, including: heavy sweats, nervous agitation, hypertension, and irregular heartbeat. In these cases, discontinue medication and call your doctor immediately.

CHECK WITH YOUR DOCTOR OR PHARMACIST BEFORE COMBINING SODIUM CHLORIDE WITH:
Safe to use with other medications.

PREGNANCY OR BREASTFEEDING:
Adequate studies in pregnant women have failed to show a risk to the fetus in the first trimester of pregnancy, and no evidence of risk has been shown in later trimesters.

PRECAUTIONS FOR CHILDREN:
Carefully administer or supervise the use of these products with children and infants. To avoid contamination, always wipe nozzle clean after each use. Always follow instructions on medication (see above).

55+ **PRECAUTIONS FOR SENIORS:**
No known precautions.

SPECIAL WARNINGS:
Prolonged, continuous use may lead to dependence.

INFORM YOUR DOCTOR BEFORE TAKING SODIUM CHLORIDE IF YOU HAVE:
No known contraindications.

QUICK FACTS

ACTIVE INGREDIENT:
XYLOMETAZOLINE HYDROCHLORIDE

BRAND NAMES:
- OTRIVIN/OTRIVIN PEDIATRIC NASAL DROPS

SYMPTOMS RELIEVED:
Nasal congestion, runny nose, itchy and watery eyes, sneezing, scratchy throat, and irritated sinuses due to common cold, sinusitis, hay fever, and other upper respiratory allergies.

HOW TO TAKE:
Comes in nasal spray or drop forms. Use dropper and spray pump per instructions on medication label. Always wash hands before applying product directly.

USUAL ADULT DOSE:
2 to 3 sprays or drops of 0.1% solution per nostril 2 to 3 times per day.

USUAL CHILD DOSE:
For children 2 to 12: 2 to 3 sprays or drops of 0.05% solution per nostril 2 to 3 times per day.

Do not administer to children under 2 unless under direction of physician. Dosage may vary based on infant or child's age.

OVERDOSE SYMPTOMS:
Headache, nausea and vomiting, heart palpitations, raised blood pressure, muscle tremors and spasms. If you suspect an overdose, immediately seek medical attention.

SIDE EFFECTS:
Most common include: nasal dryness and stinging, headache, burning sensation. In rare cases,

more severe side effects may result, including: heavy sweats, nervous agitation, hypertension, and irregular heartbeat. In these cases, discontinue medication and call your doctor immediately.

CHECK WITH YOUR DOCTOR OR PHARMACIST BEFORE COMBINING XYLOMETAZOLINE WITH:
Cold, cough, allergy, or asthma medication, stimulants, sedatives, sleep aids, antidepressants, antihypertensives, digitalis or other heart medication, diuretics, or MAO (monoamine oxidase inhibitors) drugs. Ingestion of caffeinated beverages (coffee, tea, caffeine-containing soft drinks) while taking xylometazoline-containing medication can result in agitation and insomnia.

PREGNANCY OR BREASTFEEDING:
No harmful effects have been reported regarding pregnancy or breastfeeding of infants. Xylometazoline use by a nursing mother should be considered a potential risk for a nursing child as the drug will be passed on to the infant in the mother's milk. In all cases, a physician should be consulted.

PRECAUTIONS FOR CHILDREN:
In general, xylometazoline is not advised for children under 6. Administer xylometazoline to infants or children only when consulting a physician and follow instructions on medication (see above).

55+ **PRECAUTIONS FOR SENIORS:**
Seniors generally don't eliminate drugs as efficiently as younger persons, and should avoid high dosages. Seniors are more likely to experience stimulant effects of the drug.

Q U I C K F A C T S

SPECIAL WARNINGS:
Do not combine with any medication which contains caffeine. Prolonged, continuous use may lead to dependence.

INFORM YOUR DOCTOR BEFORE TAKING XYLOMETAZOLINE IF YOU HAVE:
Diabetes, high blood pressure, heart disease, or thyroid condition. If you anticipate any surgery requiring general or spinal anesthesia within 2 months of taking xylometazoline medication, inform your doctor.

• EXPECTORANT •

The most important considerations in choosing an expectorant are: its action in increasing productivity of coughs and potential side effects associated with the drug.

EXPECTORANTS ARE A CLASS OF DRUGS WHICH:

- help to relieve the typical coughing symptoms of various allergies, colds, bronchitis, flu and other nonchronic respiratory ailments, by reducing adhesiveness of respiratory tract and increasing the productivity of coughs, thereby lessening their occurrence,
- are commonly used to give an allergy, cold, bronchitis, flu, and other nonchronic respiratory ailment-sufferer sufficient relief from coughing spasms, so that the person can rest,
- may produce side effects such as drowsiness, nasal stuffiness, dryness of mouth and sinus passages, dizziness, and common gastrointestinal (GI) irritation or distress,
- are not recommended in treating chronic and lower respiratory symptoms including asthma, and emphysema,
- are often combined with other cough-related active ingredients such as antitussives, as well as analgesics, antihistamines, and decongestants—as well as other ingredients such as alcohol, sweeteners (natural and artificial) and flavorings (natural and artificial),
- do not affect the underlying cause of the symptoms which they are designed to relieve or suppress.

QUICK REVIEW

Q U I C K F A C T S

ACTIVE INGREDIENT:
GUAIFENESIN

℞ **BRAND NAMES:**

Capsules:
- AMONIDRIN
- BREONESIN
- GG-CEN
- GEE-GEE
- GLYCOTUSS
- GLYTUSS
- HYTUSS/HYTUSS 2X

Liquid:
- NALDECON SENIOR EX (also contains saccharin, sorbitol)

Syrup:
- ANTI-TUSS (also contains alcohol)
- GENATUSS (also contains alcohol)
- GLYATE (also contains alcohol)
- GUIATUSS
- HALOTUSSIN (also contains alcohol)
- MALOTUSS (also contains alcohol)
- MYTUSSIN (also contains alcohol, sugar, menthol, raspberry flavor)
- RESCON–GGLIQUID (combination with phenylephrine hydrochloride—a decongestant)
- ROBITUSSIN (also contains alcohol, glucose, corn syrup, saccharin)
- SCOT-TUSSIN EXPECTORANT (also contains alcohol, saccharin, menthol, sorbitol)
- UNI-TUSSIN (also contains alcohol)

Note: *Guaifenesin* is an active ingredient in many multi-symptom antitussive/expectorant medications which are formulated with other active ingredients.

SYMPTOMS RELIEVED:
Coughs associated with common cold, flu, hay fever, and other respiratory allergies by loosening bronchial congestion and phlegm, resulting in more productive coughs.

HOW TO TAKE:
Comes in capsule, liquid, or syrup forms. Swallow capsule with liquid. Do not crush or chew timed-release capsules.

USUAL ADULT DOSE:
Dosage varies per product and active ingredient formulation. Follow product dosage instructions.

USUAL CHILD DOSE:
Dosage varies per product and active ingredient formulation. Follow product dosage instructions.

Do not administer to children under 2 unless under direction of physician. Dosage may vary based on infant or child's age.

OVERDOSE SYMPTOMS:
Nausea and vomiting, drowsiness, dizziness, fatigue, rash. If you suspect an overdose, immediately seek medical attention.

SIDE EFFECTS:
No serious effects in most cases of common use. Less common side effects include dizziness, gastrointestinal (GI) upset including stomach cramps and diarrhea, drowsiness, fatigue.

CHECK WITH YOUR DOCTOR OR PHARMACIST BEFORE COMBINING GUAIFENESIN WITH:
Any anticoagulant medication.

QUICK FACTS

PREGNANCY OR BREASTFEEDING:
No harmful effects have been reported regarding pregnancy or breastfeeding of infants. Guaifenesin use by a nursing mother should be considered a potential risk for a nursing child as the drug will be passed on to the infant in the mother's milk. In all cases, a physician should be consulted.

PRECAUTIONS FOR CHILDREN:
In general, guaifenesin is not advised for children under 2. Administer guaifenesin to infants or children only when consulting a physician and follow instructions on medication (see above).

55+

PRECAUTIONS FOR SENIORS:
Seniors generally don't eliminate drugs as efficiently as younger persons, and should avoid high dosages.

SPECIAL WARNINGS:
Do not use for control of chronic cough related to conditions such as emphysema, asthma, or smoking, or if coughs are producing excessive secretions. If cough is accompanied by high fever, rash, nausea or vomiting, or persistent headache, use only if directed by your doctor.

ADDITIONAL WARNING:
Alcohol: Some guaifenesin-containing medications contain various amounts of alcohol. Check label of any cough medication if concerned about ingestion of alcohol.

Sugar/Sweeteners: Some dextromethorphan-containing medications contain various amounts of sugar, sucrose, glucose, and/or artificial sweeteners such as aspartame, saccharin, sorbitol. Check label of cough medication before selecting, if concerned about diabetes and ingestion of sugar or artificial sweeteners.

INFORM YOUR DOCTOR BEFORE TAKING GUAIFENESIN IF YOU HAVE:
Asthma, emphysema, or other respiratory condition.

QUICK FACTS

ACTIVE INGREDIENTS:
GUAIFENESIN AND DEXTROMETHORPHAN HYDROBROMIDE

℞ **BRAND NAMES:**

Liquid:
- Benylin Expectorant Liquid (also contains alcohol, saccharin, menthol, sucrose)
- Cheracol D Cough Liquid (also contains alcohol, fructose, sucrose)
- Diabetic Tussin DM (also contains saccharin, methylparaben, menthol)
- Guiatussin with Dextromethorphan Liquid (also contains alcohol)
- Halotussin-DM Liquid (also contains corn syrup, menthol, saccharin, sucrose, parabens)
- Halotussin-DM Sugar-Free Liquid (also contains saccharin, sorbitol, parabens)
- Kolephrin GG/DM Liquid (also contains glucose, saccharin, sucrose)
- Mytussin DM Liquid (also contains alcohol)
- Naldecon Senior DX Liquid (also contains saccharin, sorbitol)
- Robitussin–DM Liquid (also contains saccharin, glucose, high fructose corn syrup)
- Safe Tussin 30 Liquid
- Vicks Pediatric Formula 44E Liquid (also contains sorbitol, sucrose)

Syrup:
- Extra Action Cough Syrup (also contains alcohol, corn syrup, saccharin, sucrose)
- Genatuss DM Syrup (also contains sucrose)
- Rhinosyn–DMX Syrup
- Robafen DM Syrup (also contains alcohol, sugar, menthol, sorbitol, parabens)

- Tolu-Sed DM Syrup (also contains alcohol)
- Uni-Tussin DM Syrup (also contains saccharin, sucrose, methylparaben)

Tablets:

- Glycotuss-DM Tablets
- Tuss–DM Tablets

Note: *Guaifenesin* and *dextromethorphan hydrobromide* are also active ingredient in other multi-symptom antitussive/expectorant medications which are formulated with other active ingredients.

SYMPTOMS RELIEVED:
Coughs associated with common cold, flu, hay fever, and other respiratory allergies by suppressing or moderating extreme cough activity, and by loosening bronchial congestion and phlegm, resulting in more productive coughs.

HOW TO TAKE:
Comes in tablet, liquid, or syrup forms. Swallow tablet with liquid. Do not crush or chew timed-release capsules.

USUAL ADULT DOSE:
Dosage varies per product and active ingredient formulation. Follow product dosage instructions.

USUAL CHILD DOSE:
Do not administer to children under 6 unless under direction of physician. Dosage may vary based on infant or child's age.

OVERDOSE SYMPTOMS:
Nervous agitation, severe anxiety, insomnia (sleeplessness), hallucinations, tremors,

QUICK FACTS

convulsions, nausea, vomiting, cardiac arrhythmia (irregular pulse and heartbeat), drowsiness, dizziness, fatigue, rash. If you suspect an overdose, immediately seek medical attention.

SIDE EFFECTS:
No serious effects in most cases of common use. Less common side effects include nasal dryness, dizziness, nausea, and mild insomnia palpitations, insomnia, gastrointestinal (GI) upset including stomach cramps and diarrhea, drowsiness and fatigue. In rare cases, more severe side effects may result, including: painful and frequent urination, hypertension, and heart palpitations. In these cases, discontinue medication and call your doctor immediately.

CHECK WITH YOUR DOCTOR OR PHARMACIST BEFORE COMBINING GUAIFENESIN AND DEXTROMETHORPHAN WITH:
Anticoagulant medications and MAO (monoamine oxidase inhibitors) drugs.

PREGNANCY OR BREASTFEEDING:
Guaifenesin and dextromethorphan use by a nursing mother should be considered a potential risk for a nursing child as the drug will be passed on to the infant in the mother's milk. In all cases, a physician should be consulted.

PRECAUTIONS FOR CHILDREN:
In general, guaifenesin and dextromethorphan are not advised for children under 2. Administer guaifenesin and dextromethorphan to infants or children only when consulting a physician and follow instructions on medication (see above).

55+ **PRECAUTIONS FOR SENIORS:**
Seniors generally don't eliminate drugs as efficiently as younger persons, and should avoid high dosages.

SPECIAL WARNINGS:
Do not use for control of chronic cough related to conditions such as emphysema, asthma, or smoking, or if coughs are producing excessive secretions. If cough is accompanied by high fever, rash, nausea or vomiting, or persistent headache, use only if directed by your doctor.

ADDITIONAL WARNING:
Alcohol: Some cough/cold medications contain various amounts of alcohol. Check label of any cough medication if concerned about ingestion of alcohol.

Sugar/Sweeteners: Some cough/cold medications contain various amounts of sugar, sucrose, glucose, and/or artificial sweeteners such as aspartame, saccharin, sorbitol. Check label of cough medication before selecting, if concerned about diabetes and ingestion of sugar or artificial sweeteners.

Abuse/Dependency: Reports indicate a rising rate of abuse of dextromethorphan-containing medications, particularly among teens. Sufficient data has not yet been collected, however, to determine the abuse and dependency potential of dextromethorphan-containing medications.

℞ **INFORM YOUR DOCTOR BEFORE TAKING GUAIFENESIN AND DEXTROMETHORPHAN IF YOU HAVE:**
Asthma, emphysema, or other respiratory condition, or liver impairment or liver disease.

APPETITE SUPPRESSANT

QUICK REVIEW

•APPETITE SUPPRESSANT•

The most important considerations in choosing an appetite suppressant are: its effectiveness in helping to suppress appetite, and potential side effects associated with the drug.

DIET AIDS ARE A CLASS OF DRUGS WHICH:

- are only intended to help a person lose excessive weight in cases such as obesity,
- should only be used as part of an overall reduced calorie diet, and not as a substitute for sensible diet,
- act by stimulating the central nervous system (CNS) and suppressing appetite,
- in over-the-counter (OTC) products, mostly contain either phenylpropanolamine hydrochloride, benzocaine, or caffeine as the active ingredient,
- can produce serious adverse side effects, such as stroke, seizure, heart attack, psychosis, and death in cases of abuse or overdose.

ACTIVE INGREDIENT:
BENZOCAINE

BRAND NAMES:
- Diet Ayds
- Slim-Mint
(combination with lecithin and tartrazine)

SYMPTOMS RELIEVED:
Sweet tooth—anesthetic appears to decreases ability to discern degrees of sweetness, resulting in less caloric intake.

HOW TO TAKE:
Comes in chewable forms (candy and gum).

USUAL ADULT DOSE:
6 to 15 milligrams just before eating, not to exceed 45 milligrams in a 24 hour period.

USUAL CHILD DOSE:
Do not administer to children under 6 unless under direction of physician. Dosage may vary based on infant or child's age.

OVERDOSE SYMPTOMS:
Nervous agitation, severe anxiety, insomnia (sleeplessness), hallucinations, tremors, convulsions, nausea, vomiting, cardiac arrhythmia (irregular pulse and heartbeat). If you suspect an overdose, immediately seek medical attention.

SIDE EFFECTS:
No serious effects in most cases of common use. Less common side effects include nasal dryness, dizziness, nausea, and mild insomnia palpitations, insomnia. In rare cases, more severe side effects may result, including: painful and

frequent urination, hypertension, and heart palpitations. In these cases, discontinue medication and call your doctor immediately.

CHECK WITH YOUR DOCTOR OR PHARMACIST BEFORE COMBINING BENZOCAINE WITH:
Cold, cough, or allergy medication, stimulants, antidepressants, antihypertensives, digitalis or other heart medication, diuretics, or MAO (monoamine oxidase inhibitors) drugs. Ingestion of caffeinated beverages (coffee, tea, caffeine-containing soft drinks) while taking benzocaine-containing medication can result in agitation and insomnia.

PREGNANCY OR BREASTFEEDING:
No harmful effects have been reported for pregnant women or nursing mothers. Benzocaine use by a nursing mother should be considered a potential risk for a nursing child as the drug will be passed on to the infant in the mother's milk. In all cases, a physician should be consulted.

PRECAUTIONS FOR CHILDREN:
In general, benzocaine is not advised for children under 6. Administer benzocaine to infants or children only when consulting a physician and follow instructions on medication (see above).

55+

PRECAUTIONS FOR SENIORS:
Seniors generally don't eliminate drugs as efficiently as younger persons, and should avoid high dosages. Use of benzocaine medications by seniors can lead to cardiac arrhythmia (irregular pulse and heartbeat). In addition, seniors are more likely to experience stimulant effects of the drug.

SPECIAL WARNINGS:
Do not use continuously for longer than 3 months. Do not use benzocaine medications containing tartrazine if you are intolerant or hypersensitive to aspirin. Allergic reactions, including bronchial asthma, have occurred in susceptible individuals.

INFORM YOUR DOCTOR BEFORE TAKING BENZOCAINE IF YOU HAVE:
Allergies to: any sympathomimetic drug, aspirin or other salicylates, or if you have diabetes, thyroid condition, or urinary difficulty. If you anticipate any surgery requiring general or spinal anesthesia within 2 months of taking benzocaine medication, inform your doctor.

QUICK FACTS

ACTIVE INGREDIENTS:

PHENYLPROPANOLAMINE HYDROCHLORIDE AND COMBINATIONS

BRAND NAMES:

- ACUTRIM
- APPEDRINE (combination with multivitamin)
- CONTROL
- DEX-A-DIET
- DEX-A-DIET PLUS VITAMIN C (combination with vitamin C)
- DEXATRIM
- DEXATRIM PLUS VITAMIN C (combination with vitamin C)
- GRAPEFRUIT DIET PLAN WITH DIADAX (combination with grapefruit extract)
- PHENOXINE
- PHENYLDRINE
- PROLAMINE
- UNITROL

SYMPTOMS RELIEVED:
Decreases or suppresses appetite.

HOW TO TAKE:
Comes in tablet, capsule, chewable forms. Swallow with liquid. Do not crush or chew timed-release tablets.

USUAL ADULT DOSE:
25 milligrams 3 times per day, (75 milligrams once daily for time release capsules) 1/2 hour before meals, not to exceed 75 milligrams in a 24 hour period.

USUAL CHILD DOSE:
Do not administer to children under 6 unless

under direction of physician. Dosage may vary based on infant or child's age.

OVERDOSE SYMPTOMS:
Nervous agitation, severe anxiety, insomnia (sleeplessness), hallucinations, tremors, convulsions, nausea, vomiting, cardiac arrhythmia (irregular pulse and heartbeat). If you suspect an overdose, immediately seek medical attention.

SIDE EFFECTS:
No serious effects in most cases of common use. Less common side effects include nasal dryness, dizziness, nausea, and mild insomnia palpitations, insomnia. In rare cases, more severe side effects may result, including: painful and frequent urination, hypertension, and heart palpitations. In these cases, discontinue medication and call your doctor immediately.

CHECK WITH YOUR DOCTOR OR PHARMACIST BEFORE COMBINING PHENYLPROPANOLAMINE WITH:
Cold, cough, or allergy medication, stimulants, antidepressants, antihypertensives, digitalis or other heart medication, diuretics, or MAO (monoamine oxidase inhibitors) drugs. Ingestion of caffeinated beverages (coffee, tea, caffeine-containing soft drinks) while taking phenylpropanolamine-containing medication can result in agitation and insomnia.

PREGNANCY OR BREASTFEEDING:
No harmful effects have been reported for pregnant women or nursing mothers. Phenylpropanolamine use by a nursing mother should be

considered a potential risk for a nursing child as the drug will be passed on to the infant in the mother's milk. In all cases, a physician should be consulted.

PRECAUTIONS FOR CHILDREN:
In general, phenylpropanolamine is not advised for children under 6. Administer phenylpropanolamine to infants or children only when consulting a physician and follow instructions on medication (see above).

PRECAUTIONS FOR SENIORS:
Seniors generally don't eliminate drugs as efficiently as younger persons, and should avoid high dosages. Use of phenylpropanolamine medications by seniors can lead to cardiac arrhythmia (irregular pulse and heartbeat). In addition, seniors are more likely to experience stimulant effects of the drug.

SPECIAL WARNINGS:
Do not use continuously for longer than 3 months. Do not use phenylpropanolamine medications containing tartrazine if you are intolerant or hypersensitive to aspirin. Allergic reactions, including bronchial asthma, have occurred in susceptible individuals.

INFORM YOUR DOCTOR BEFORE TAKING PHENYLPROPANOLAMINE IF YOU HAVE:
Allergies to aspirin or other salicylates, or if you have diabetes, thyroid condition, or urinary difficulty. If you anticipate any surgery requiring general or spinal anesthesia within 2 months of taking phenylpropanolamine medication, inform your doctor.

ARTHRITIS

QUICK REVIEW

• ANALGESIC •

The most important considerations in choosing an analgesic are: pain relief; anti-inflammatory activity, and allergic reaction or sensitivity to certain active ingredients.

ANALGESICS (NONNARCOTIC) ARE A CLASS OF DRUGS WHICH:

- inhibit the action of prostaglandins (hormonelike substances) in the central nervous system, thereby temporarily reducing the perception of physical pain with little loss of sensibility to other physical sensation,
- are used to temporarily alleviate symptoms such as: headache, fever, backache, sinus pain, muscle strain, menstrual pain, and similar ailments. Some analgesics, such as aspirin (acetylsalicylic acid) and ibuprofen, also provide temporary anti-inflammatory relief for ailments such as arthritis. Aspirin has also been shown to be effective as a blood thinning antiplatelet agent in reducing heart attack and stroke risk,
- can have adverse effects in some instances. Aspirin intolerance can produce allergic and anaphylactic reactions in hypersensitive and asthmatic individuals. Aspirin can also aggravate aggravate gastrointestinal conditions such as heartburn and ulcer. Long-term acetaminophen use can damage liver (hepatic) and kidney (renal) functions.

ACTIVE INGREDIENTS:

ACETAMINOPHEN, ASPIRIN, AND CAFFEINE COMBINATION

QUICK FACTS

BRAND NAMES:

- Buffets II Tablets
- Excedrin Extra-Strength
- Gelpirin
- Goody's Extra Strength Headache Powders
- Pain Reliever Tabs
- Supac
- Vanquish

SYMPTOMS RELIEVED:

Minor aches and pains such as those associated with arthritis.

HOW TO TAKE:

Comes in tablet, caplet, capsule, and powder forms. Swallow with liquid. Sprinkle powder over liquid, then swallow. Do not crush or chew timed-release tablets. Aspirin and caffeine both can cause gastrointestinal (GI) irritation and should be taken with food or following meal.

USUAL ADULT DOSE:

1 or 2 capsules, tablets, caplets or 1 powder packet every 2 to 6 hours.

Q U I C K F A C T S

ACTIVE INGREDIENTS:

ACETAMINOPHEN AND CAFFEINE COMBINATION

BRAND NAMES:

- Bayer Select Maximum Strength
- Excedrin Aspirin-Free
- Fendol

SYMPTOMS RELIEVED:

Minor aches and pains such as those associated with the common cold, flu, headache, toothache, sinusitis, hay fever, and other respiratory allergies, muscular aches, backache, minor arthritis pain, menstrual discomfort, and reduction of fever.

HOW TO TAKE:

Comes in tablet, caplet, capsule, and powder forms. Swallow with liquid. Sprinkle powder over liquid, then swallow. Do not crush or chew timed-release tablets. Caffeine can cause gastrointestinal (GI) irritation and should be taken with food or following a meal.

USUAL ADULT DOSE:

12.5 milligrams every 4 to 6 hours, not to exceed 25 milligrams in a 4 to 6 hour period or 75 milligrams in a 24 hour period.

USUAL CHILD DOSE:

Do not administer to children under 16 unless under direction of physician. Dosage may vary based on infant or child's age.

OVERDOSE SYMPTOMS:

Nervous agitation, disorientation, confusion, severe headache, convulsions, GI bleeding, or

hemorrhage. If you suspect an overdose, seek medical attention immediately.

SIDE EFFECTS:
No serious effects in most cases of common use, however normal use of caffeine can result in common GI irritations such as heartburn and indigestion. Less common side effects include dizziness, nausea, stomach cramps, and headache.

CHECK WITH YOUR DOCTOR OR PHARMACIST BEFORE COMBINING ACETAMINOPHEN OR CAFFEINE WITH:
Antacids, anticoagulants, aspirin, asthma medication, other nonsteroidal anti-inflammatory drugs (NSAIDs), tetracycline, and any other medication.

PREGNANCY OR BREASTFEEDING:
Animal studies have indicated an adverse effect on fetus, but no adequate studies have been performed on humans. No harmful effects have been reported regarding nursing infants, but caffeine use by a nursing mother should be considered a potential risk for a nursing child as the drug will be passed on to the infant in the mother's milk. In all cases, a physician should be consulted.

PRECAUTIONS FOR CHILDREN:
In general, caffeine and other NSAIDs are not advised for children under 15. Administer caffeine to infants or children only when consulting a physician and follow instructions on medication (see above).

Q U I C K F A C T S

55+ **PRECAUTIONS FOR SENIORS:**

Seniors generally don't eliminate drugs as efficiently as younger persons, and should avoid high dosages. Seniors (over 65) are at special risk for development of ulcers if taking caffeine in high doses. Prolonged use can also lead to kidney and liver damage.

SPECIAL WARNINGS:

Don't take caffeine medication if you are aspirin intolerant or allergic to other NSAIDs. If in doubt, always consult a pharmacist or physician. Also avoid if you have GI conditions such as gastritis, peptic ulcer, enteritis, ileitis, colitis; asthma, high blood pressure, or hematologic (bleeding) problems. Avoid alcohol while taking this or any other NSAID.

INFORM YOUR DOCTOR BEFORE TAKING CAFFEINE IF YOU HAVE:

An allergy or intolerance to aspirin or other NSAIDs, damaged or impaired renal (kidney) or hepatic (liver) functions, epilepsy, Parkinson's disease, or mental illness.

ACTIVE INGREDIENT:
ASPIRIN

BRAND NAMES:
- ASCRIPTIN
- CAMA ARTHRITIS PAIN RELIEVER
- EMPIRIN
- GOODY'S
- MAGNAPRIN

SYMPTOMS RELIEVED:
Minor aches and pains such as those associated with arthritis.

HOW TO TAKE:
Comes in tablet, caplet, capsule, and powder forms. Swallow tablet, capsule, or caplet with liquid. Sprinkle powder over liquid, then swallow. Do not crush or chew timed-release tablet. Aspirin can cause gastrointestinal (GI) irritation and should be taken with food or following meal.

USUAL ADULT DOSE:
Minor aches and pains: 325 to 650 milligrams every 4 hours or as needed, not to exceed 4 grams a day. For extra strength products, dosage may range to 500 milligrams every 3 hours to 1,000 milligrams every 6 hours.

For arthritis and related conditions: 3.2 to 6 grams divided into equal doses over 24 hours.

USUAL CHILD DOSE:
4 to 5 doses per day, not to exceed 5 doses in 24 hours. Dosage varies based on infant or child's age.

OVERDOSE SYMPTOMS:
Respiratory difficulty, hyperventilation, hyper-

thermia, nausea and vomiting, severe diarrhea, impaired vision, bloody urine, abnormal thirst, nervous agitation, disorientation and dizziness. In some cases, capillary and other hematological abnormalities may result. If you suspect an overdose, immediately seek medical attention.

SIDE EFFECTS:
No serious effects in most cases of common use, however normal aspirin use can result in common gastrointestinal (GI) irritations such as heartburn and indigestion. Aspirin affects hypothalamus, resulting in dilation of small blood vessels in skin. Low dosages may reduce risk of blood clotting as aspirin inhibits blood clotting. Aspirin use may however contribute to anemia in anemic individuals.

CHECK WITH YOUR DOCTOR OR PHARMACIST BEFORE COMBINING ASPIRIN WITH:
Anticoagulants, asthma medication, other salicylates, tetracycline, and any other medication. Ingestion of alcohol while taking aspirin can increase risk of GI ulceration. Avoid aspirin use if you have aspirin intolerance, asthma, rhinitis, or a history of anemia (iron poor blood). Also avoid use of aspirin, if possible, one week prior to surgery, as it may increase possibility of postoperative bleeding.

PREGNANCY OR BREASTFEEDING:
In third trimester, aspirin use should be discouraged. No harmful effects have been reported regarding nursing infants, but aspirin use by a nursing mother should be considered a potential risk for a nursing child as the drug will be passed on to the infant in milk. In all cases, a physician should be consulted.

PRECAUTIONS FOR CHILDREN:
In general, administer to infants or children only when consulting a physician and follow instructions on medication.

SPECIAL WARNING:
Aspirin use in children and teenagers with influenza (flu), chickenpox, and other viral infections may be associated with development of Reyes syndrome. This rare but acute and often life-threatening condition has caused permanent brain damage in survivors. Symptoms include: vomiting, lethargy, bellicosity, leading possibly to delirium and coma.

55+

PRECAUTIONS FOR SENIORS:
Seniors generally don't eliminate drugs as efficiently as younger persons, and should avoid high dosages. Buffered effervescent aspirin products contain high sodium content and should be avoided if on a restricted sodium diet. Aspirin use can cause GI irritation and possibly stomach or intestinal bleeding in seniors, manifested usually by dark stools.

SPECIAL WARNINGS:
Always check expiration date on label of medication. Do not take aspirin which emits a vinegar-like odor. This indicates that it is decomposing and is unsafe for use.

INFORM YOUR DOCTOR BEFORE TAKING ASPIRIN IF YOU HAVE:
An allergy to aspirin, are asthmatic, anemic, or have GI sensitivity.

Q U I C K F A C T S

ACTIVE INGREDIENT:

IBUPROFEN

BRAND NAMES:

- ADVIL
- ARTHRITIS FOUNDATION
- BAYER SELECT PAIN RELIEF
- GENPRIL
- IBUPROHM
- MOTRIN
- NUPRON
- OBUPRIN

SYMPTOMS RELIEVED:
Minor aches and pains such as those associated with arthritis.

HOW TO TAKE:
Comes in tablet, caplet, and gelcap forms. Swallow with liquid. Do not crush or chew timed-release tablet. Ibuprófen can cause gastrointestinal (GI) irritation and should be taken with food or following meal.

USUAL ADULT DOSE:
Minor aches and pains: 200 milligrams every 4 to 6 hours as needed, not to exceed 1.2 grams per day.

Arthritis and related conditions: 1.2 grams to 3.2 grams per day divided into equal doses over 24 hours.

USUAL CHILD DOSE:
Always consult with a pharmacist or physician. Dosage may vary based on infant or child's age. Juvenile arthritis: 30 to 70 milligrams per day in 3 or 4 equal doses or as indicated.

Fever reduction: Maximum daily dose not to exceed 40 milligrams. Dosage should be adjusted based on initial temperature level. If less or equal to 102.5°F, 5 milligrams per dose is recommended. If temperature is greater than 102.5°F, 10 milligrams per dose is recommended.

OVERDOSE SYMPTOMS:
Nervous agitation, disorientation, confusion, severe headache, convulsions, GI bleeding or hemorrhage. If you suspect an overdose, immediately seek medical attention.

SIDE EFFECTS:
No serious effects in most cases of common use, however normal use of ibuprofen can result in common GI irritations such as heartburn and indigestion. Less common side effects include dizziness, nausea, stomach cramps, and headache.

CHECK WITH YOUR DOCTOR OR PHARMACIST BEFORE COMBINING IBUPROFEN WITH:
Antacids, anticoagulants, aspirin, asthma medication, other nonsteroidal anti-inflammatory drugs (NSAIDs), tetracycline, and any other medication. Combination with acetaminophen increases risk of kidney damage. Ingestion of alcohol while taking ibuprofen can increase risk of GI ulceration. Avoid ibuprofen if you have a history of anemia. Also avoid use of ibuprofen, if possible, one week prior to surgery, as it may increase possibility of postoperative bleeding.

PREGNANCY OR BREASTFEEDING:
No harmful effects have been reported regarding pregnancy or breastfeeding of infants, but ibuprofen use by a nursing mother should be

considered a potential risk for a nursing child as the drug will be passed on to the infant in the mother's milk. In all cases, a physician should be consulted.

PRECAUTIONS FOR CHILDREN:

In general, ibuprofen and other NSAIDs are not advised for children under 15. Administer ibuprofen to infants or children only when consulting a physician and follow instructions on medication.

PRECAUTIONS FOR SENIORS:

55+

Seniors generally don't eliminate drugs as efficiently as younger persons, and should avoid high dosages. Seniors (over 65) are at special risk for development of ulcers if taking ibuprofen in high doses. Prolonged use can also lead to kidney and liver damage.

SPECIAL WARNINGS:

Don't take ibuprofen medication if you are aspirin intolerant or allergic to other NSAIDs drugs. If in doubt, always consult a pharmacist or physician. Avoid alcohol while taking this or any other NSAID.

INFORM YOUR DOCTOR BEFORE TAKING IBUPROFEN IF YOU HAVE:

An allergy or intolerance to aspirin or other NSAIDs, damaged or impaired renal (kidney) or hepatic (liver) functions, epilepsy, Parkinson's disease, or mental illness.

ACTIVE INGREDIENT:

CAPSAICIN (CAPSICUM OLEORESIN)

BRAND NAMES:

- ArthriCare Odor-Free
  (combination with menthol, methyl nicotinate —also contains aloe vera gel, carbomer 940, cetyl alcohol, glyceryl stereate SE, isocetyl alcohol, propylparaben, stearyl alcohol, triethanolamine)
- ArthriCare Ultra
  (combination with menthol USP—also contains aloe vera gel, carbomer, cetyl alcohol, glyceryl stereate SE, isocetyl alcohol, propylparaben, stearyl alcohol)
- Menthacin
  (combination with menthol, methyl nicotinate —also contains capric triglyceride, carbomer 1342, carbomer 940, cetyl alcohol, diazolidinyl urea, glyceryl stereate, sodium lauryl sulfate, maleated soybean oil, methylparaben, polysorbate 60, propylene glycol, propylparaben, sorbitan stearate trolamine)

SYMPTOMS RELIEVED:

Minor aches and pains of muscles and joints associated with arthritis, common back pain, and sprains and strains.

HOW TO USE:

Comes in ointment and cream forms. Apply to affected areas. These products are for external use only. Do not swallow. Avoid contact with eyes while applying.

USUAL ADULT DOSE:

Apply to affected area(s), not more than 3 to

QUICK FACTS

Q U I C K F A C T S

4 times per day, or as directed by your doctor. In all cases follow specific product instructions.

USUAL CHILD DOSE:
For ages 2 to 12: Applications is same as adult, or as directed by your doctor. In all cases follow specific product instructions.

Only apply to children under 2 under doctor's supervision or direction. In all cases follow specific product instructions.

OVERDOSE SYMPTOMS:
None known.

SIDE EFFECTS:
No serious effects in most cases of common use. In some cases, stinging or burning sensation may be felt where rub has been applied. Because these products warm the affected area, temporary redness may also occur.

CHECK WITH YOUR DOCTOR OR PHARMACIST BEFORE COMBINING THESE PRODUCTS WITH:
Any other drugs and preparations.

PREGNANCY OR BREASTFEEDING:
Safety of this drug for use during pregnancy or while nursing has not been established. In all cases you should consult your doctor before using any drug during pregnancy or while nursing.

PRECAUTIONS FOR CHILDREN:
These products should only be used with doctor's supervision or direction for children under 2. Consult your doctor and follow instructions on medication (see above).

55+ **PRECAUTIONS FOR SENIORS:**
None known.

SPECIAL WARNINGS:
Do not use these products if you are allergic to capsaicin, fruits of Capsicum plants, (e.g. cayenne peppers), or any of the inactive ingredients contained in these products. Do not apply these products to wounds, lesions, broken, damaged, or sensitive skin. Avoid contact with eyes and mucous membranes. Do not use a heating pad or other forms of topical heating while using these products. Do not apply these products immediately before or after a bath or shower.

INFORM YOUR DOCTOR BEFORE USING THESE PRODUCTS IF YOU HAVE:
Any allergies, or if you are or plan to become pregnant during time that you will be taking this product.

QUICK FACTS

ACTIVE INGREDIENT:
METHYL SALICYLATE

BRAND NAMES:
- ARTHRICARE TRIPLE MEDICATED (combination with menthol, methyl nicotinate—also contains carbomer 940, dioctyl sodium sulfosuccinate, glycerin, isopropyl alcohol, polysorbate 60, propylene glycol)
- MENTHOLATUM DEEP HEATING (combination with menthol—also contains glyceryl stearate, sodium lauryl sulfate, isoceteth-20, poloxamer 407, quaternium-15, sorbitan stearate)

SYMPTOMS RELIEVED:
Minor aches and pains of muscles and joints associated with arthritis, common back pain, and sprains and strains.

HOW TO USE:
Comes in ointment form. Apply to affected areas. These products are for external use only. Do not swallow. Avoid contact with eyes while applying.

USUAL ADULT DOSE:
Apply to affected area(s), not more than 3 to 4 times per day, or as directed by your doctor. In all cases follow specific product instructions.

USUAL CHILD DOSE:
For ages 2 to 12: Apply same as adult, or as directed by your doctor. In all cases follow specific product instructions.

Only apply to children under 2 under doctor's supervision or direction. In all cases follow specific product instructions.

OVERDOSE SYMPTOMS:
None known.

SIDE EFFECTS:
No serious effects in most cases of common use. In some cases, stinging or burning sensation may be felt where rub has been applied. Because these products warm the affected area, temporary redness may also occur.

CHECK WITH YOUR DOCTOR OR PHARMACIST BEFORE COMBINING THIS PRODUCT WITH:
Any other drugs and preparations.

PREGNANCY OR BREASTFEEDING:
Safety of this drug for use during pregnancy or while nursing has not been established. In all cases you should consult your doctor before using any drug during pregnancy or while nursing.

PRECAUTIONS FOR CHILDREN:
These products should only be used with doctor's supervision or direction for children under 2. Consult your doctor and follow instructions on medication (see above).

55+ **PRECAUTIONS FOR SENIORS:**
None known.

SPECIAL WARNINGS:
Do not use these products if you are allergic to methyl salicylate, menthol, methyl nicotinate, or any of the inactive ingredients contained in these products. Do not apply these products to wounds, lesions, broken, damaged, or sensitive skin. Avoid contact with eyes and mucous membranes. Do not use a heating pad or other forms

Q U I C K F A C T S

of topical heating while using these products. Do not apply these products immediately before or after a bath or shower.

INFORM YOUR DOCTOR BEFORE USING THESE PRODUCTS IF YOU HAVE:
Any allergies, or if you are or plan to become pregnant during time that you will be taking this product.

• ANTI-INFLAMMATORY •

The most important considerations in choosing an anti-inflammatory agent (nonsteroidal anti-inflammatory drug or "NSAID") are: pain relief; anti-inflammatory activity, and the potential for allergic reaction or sensitivity to certain active ingredients.

ANTI-INFLAMMATORY AGENTS (NSAIDS) ARE A CLASS OF DRUGS WHICH:

- inhibit the action of prostaglandins (hormonelike substances) in the central nervous system, thereby temporarily reducing the perception of physical pain with little loss of sensibility to other physical sensation,
- are used both for their anti-inflammatory and analgesic properties, to temporarily alleviate symptoms such as: headache, fever, backache, sinus pain, muscle strain, menstrual pain, and similar ailments. Some NSAIDs also provide temporary anti-inflammatory relief for ailments such as rheumatoid arthritis and osteoarthritis,
- can have adverse effects in some instances such as aggravation of gastrointestinal (GI) conditions such as heartburn and ulcer, and can produce allergic reactions in persons who are aspirin-intolerant or hypersensitive.

See *also:* Analgesics

QUICK FACTS

ACTIVE INGREDIENT:
ACETAMINOPHEN

BRAND NAMES:
- BANESIN
- DOLANEX
- EXCEDRIN ASPIRIN-FREE
- PANADOL
- PERCOGESIC ANALGESIC TABLETS (combination with phenyltoloxamine citrate, also contains sucrose)
- PHENAPHEN
- TAPAÑOL
- TYLENOL (various formulations)
- UNISOM WITH PAIN RELIEF (combination with diphenhydramine hydrochloride)
- VANQUISH (combination with aspirin and caffeine)

SYMPTOMS RELIEVED:
Minor aches and pains such as those associated with arthritis.

HOW TO TAKE:
Comes in tablet, chewable tablet, caplet, capsule, elixir, liquid, powder, solution, and suppository forms. Swallow tablet, capsule, or elixir with liquid. Sprinkle powder over liquid, then swallow. Follow medication instructions carefully for proper insertion of suppositories. Do not crush or chew timed-release tablet. In proper dosages in most cases, acetaminophen does not cause gastrointestinal (GI) irritation and can be taken with or without food.

USUAL ADULT DOSE:
325 to 650 milligrams every 4 to 6 hours,

or 1 gram 3 to 4 times per day, not to exceed 4 grams a day.

USUAL CHILD DOSE:
4 to 5 doses per day, not to exceed 5 doses in 24 hours. Dosage varies based on infant or child's age.

OVERDOSE SYMPTOMS:
Nausea, vomiting, diaphoresis, discomfort, and malaise. In some cases, hepatic toxicity (liver poisoning) may result. If you suspect an overdose, immediately seek medical attention.

SIDE EFFECTS:
None in most cases of common use. Long-term ingestion of high dosages may increase risk of liver and kidney damage. In rare cases, extreme fatigue and drowsiness, allergic skin eruptions (rash, hives, itch), sore throat and fever, bleeding or bruising, urinary discomfort or blood in urine, jaundiced skin or eyes may result.

CHECK WITH YOUR DOCTOR OR PHARMACIST BEFORE COMBINING ACETAMINOPHEN WITH:
Anticoagulants, aspirin and other salicylates, Isoniazid (anti-tuberculosis) medication. Excessive ingestion of alcohol while taking acetaminophen can increase the risk of liver damage or disease (hepatic toxicity).

PREGNANCY OR BREASTFEEDING:
No conclusive evidence of effects on fetus—benign or adverse—has been established. High dosage has in isolated cases caused anemia in mother and kidney failure in fetus. Nursing infants have shown no harmful effects.

Q U I C K F A C T S

PRECAUTIONS FOR CHILDREN:
In general, administer to infants or children only when consulting a physician and follow instructions on medication.

PRECAUTIONS FOR SENIORS:
Seniors generally don't eliminate drugs as efficiently as younger persons, and should avoid high dosages.

SPECIAL WARNINGS:
Chronic alcoholics are at risk for hepatic (liver) function impairment if taking high dosages of acetaminophen.

INFORM YOUR DOCTOR BEFORE TAKING ACETAMINOPHEN IF YOU HAVE:
Liver or kidney disease or damage, an allergy to acetaminophen, or hypoglycemia.

ACTIVE INGREDIENT:
ASPIRIN

Q U I C K F A C T S

BRAND NAMES:
- ASCRIPTIN
- CAMA ARTHRITIS PAIN RELIEVER
- EMPIRIN
- GOODY'S
- MAGNAPRIN

SYMPTOMS RELIEVED:
Minor aches and pains such as those associated with arthritis.

HOW TO TAKE:
Comes in tablet, caplet, capsule, and powder forms. Swallow tablet, capsule, or caplet with liquid. Sprinkle powder over liquid, then swallow. Do not crush or chew timed-release tablet. Aspirin can cause gastrointestinal (GI) irritation and should be taken with food or following meal.

USUAL ADULT DOSE:
Minor aches and pains: 325 to 650 milligrams every 4 hours or as needed, not to exceed 4 grams a day. For extra strength products, dosage may range to 500 milligrams every 3 hours to 1,000 milligrams every 6 hours. For arthritis and related conditions: 3.2 to 6 grams divided into equal doses over 24 hours.

USUAL CHILD DOSE:
4 to 5 doses per day, not to exceed 5 doses in 24 hours. Dosage varies based on infant or child's age.

OVERDOSE SYMPTOMS:
Respiratory difficulty, hyperventilation, hyper-

QUICK FACTS

thermia, nausea and vomiting, severe diarrhea, impaired vision, bloody urine, abnormal thirst, nervous agitation, disorientation and dizziness. In some cases, capillary and other hematological abnormalities may result. If you suspect an overdose, immediately seek medical attention.

SIDE EFFECTS:
No serious effects in most cases of common use, however normal aspirin use can result in common gastrointestinal (GI) irritations such as heartburn and indigestion. Aspirin affects hypothalamus, resulting in dilation of small blood vessels in skin. Low dosages may reduce risk of blood clotting as aspirin inhibits blood clotting. Aspirin use may however contribute to anemia in anemic individuals.

CHECK WITH YOUR DOCTOR OR PHARMACIST BEFORE COMBINING ASPIRIN WITH:
Anticoagulants, asthma medication, other salicylates, tetracycline, and any other medication. Ingestion of alcohol while taking aspirin can increase risk of GI ulceration. Avoid aspirin use if you have aspirin intolerance, asthma, rhinitis, or a history of anemia (iron poor blood). Also avoid use of aspirin, if possible, one week prior to surgery, as it may increase possibility of postoperative bleeding.

PREGNANCY OR BREASTFEEDING:
In third trimester, aspirin use should be discouraged. No harmful effects have been reported regarding nursing infants, but aspirin use by a nursing mother should be considered a potential risk for a nursing child as the drug will be passed on to the infant in milk. In all cases, a physician should be consulted.

PRECAUTIONS FOR CHILDREN:
In general, administer to infants or children only when consulting a physician and follow instructions on medication.

SPECIAL WARNING:
Aspirin use in children and teenagers with influenza (flu), chicken pox, and other viral infections may be associated with development of Reye's syndrome. This rare but acute and often life-threatening condition has caused permanent brain damage in survivors. Symptoms include: vomiting, lethargy, bellicosity, leading possibly to delirium and coma.

55+

PRECAUTIONS FOR SENIORS:
Seniors generally don't eliminate drugs as efficiently as younger persons, and should avoid high dosages. Buffered effervescent aspirin products contain high sodium content and should be avoided if on a restricted sodium diet. Aspirin use can cause GI irritation and possibly stomach or intestinal bleeding in seniors, manifested usually by dark stools.

SPECIAL WARNINGS:
Always check expiration date on label of medication. Do not take aspirin which emits a vinegar-like odor. This indicates that it is decomposing and is unsafe for use.

INFORM YOUR DOCTOR BEFORE TAKING ASPIRIN IF YOU HAVE:
An allergy to aspirin, are asthmatic, anemic, or have GI sensitivity.

Q U I C K F A C T S

ACTIVE INGREDIENT:
IBUPROFEN

BRAND NAMES:
- Advil
- Arthritis Foundation (backache and muscle pain)
- Bayer Select Pain Relief
- Genpril
- Ibuprohm
- Motrin
- Nupron
- Obuprin

SYMPTOMS RELIEVED:
Minor aches and pains such as those associated with arthritis.

HOW TO TAKE:
Comes in tablet, caplet, and gelcap forms. Swallow with liquid. Do not crush or chew timed-release tablet. Ibuprofen can cause gastrointestinal (GI) irritation and should be taken with food or following meal.

USUAL ADULT DOSE:
Minor aches and pains: 200 milligrams every 4 to 6 hours as needed, not to exceed 1.2 grams per day.

USUAL CHILD DOSE:
Always consult with a pharmacist or physician. Dosage may vary based on infant or child's age. Juvenile arthritis: 30 to 70 milligrams per day in 3 or 4 equal doses or as indicated.

OVERDOSE SYMPTOMS:
Nervous agitation, disorientation, confusion, severe headache, convulsions, GI bleeding or hemorrhage. If you suspect an overdose, immediately seek medical attention.

SIDE EFFECTS:
No serious effects in most cases of common use, however normal use of ibuprofen can result in common GI irritations such as heartburn and indigestion. Less common side effects include dizziness, nausea, stomach cramps, and headache.

CHECK WITH YOUR DOCTOR OR PHARMACIST BEFORE COMBINING IBUPROFEN WITH:
Antacids, anticoagulants, aspirin, asthma medication, other nonsteroidal anti-inflammatory drugs (NSAIDs), tetracycline, and any other medication. Combination with acetaminophen increases risk of kidney damage. Ingestion of alcohol while taking ibuprofen can increase risk of GI ulceration. Avoid ibuprofen if you have a history of anemia. Also avoid use of ibuprofen, if possible, one week prior to surgery, as it may increase possibility of postoperative bleeding.

PREGNANCY OR BREASTFEEDING:
No harmful effects have been reported regarding nursing infants, but ibuprofen use by a nursing mother should be considered a potential risk for a nursing child as the drug will be passed on to the infant in the mother's milk. In all cases, a physician should be consulted.

PRECAUTIONS FOR CHILDREN:
In general, ibuprofen and other NSAIDs are not advised for children under 15. Administer ibuprofen to infants or children only when consulting a physician and follow instructions on medication.

PRECAUTIONS FOR SENIORS:
Seniors generally don't eliminate drugs as efficiently as younger persons, and should avoid high dosages. Seniors (over 65) are at special risk for development of ulcers if taking ibuprofen in high doses. Prolonged use can also lead to kidney and liver damage.

SPECIAL WARNINGS:
Don't take ibuprofen medication if you are aspirin intolerant or allergic to other NSAIDs. If in doubt, always consult a pharmacist or physician. Also avoid if you have GI conditions such as gastritis, peptic ulcer, enteritis, ileitis, colitis; asthma, high blood pressure, or hematologic (bleeding) problems. Avoid alcohol while taking this or any other NSAID.

INFORM YOUR DOCTOR BEFORE TAKING IBUPROFEN IF YOU HAVE:
An allergy or intolerance to aspirin or other NSAIDs, damaged or impaired renal (kidney) or hepatic (liver) functions, epilepsy, Parkinson's disease, or mental illness.

BACKACHE AND PAIN RELIEF

QUICK REVIEW

• ANALGESIC •

The most important considerations in choosing an analgesic are: pain relief; anti-inflammatory activity, and allergic reaction or sensitivity to certain active ingredients.

ANALGESICS (NONNARCOTIC) ARE A CLASS OF DRUGS WHICH:

- inhibit the action of prostaglandins (hormonelike substances) in the central nervous system, thereby temporarily reducing the perception of physical pain with little loss of sensibility to other physical sensation,
- are used to temporarily alleviate symptoms such as: headache, fever, backache, sinus pain, muscle strain, menstrual pain, and similar ailments. Some analgesics, such as aspirin (acetylsalicylic acid) and ibuprofen, also provide temporary anti-inflammatory relief for ailments such as arthritis. Aspirin has also been shown to be effective as a blood thinning antiplatelet agent in reducing heart attack and stroke risk,
- can have adverse effects in some instances. Aspirin intolerance can produce allergic and anaphylactic reactions in hypersensitive and asthmatic individuals. Aspirin can also aggravate aggravate gastrointestinal conditions such as heartburn and ulcer. Long-term acetaminophen use can damage liver (hepatic) and kidney (renal) functions.

ACTIVE INGREDIENT:
ACETAMINOPHEN

Q U I C K F A C T S

BRAND NAMES:
- BANESIN
- DOLANEX
- EXCEDRIN ASPIRIN-FREE
- PANADOL
- PERCOGESIC ANALGESIC TABLETS (combination with phenyltoloxamine citrate, also contains sucrose)
- PHENAPHEN
- TAPANOL
- TYLENOL (various formulations)
- VANQUISH (combination with aspirin and caffeine)

SYMPTOMS RELIEVED:
Minor aches and pains such as those associated with the common cold, flu, headache, toothache, sinusitis, hay fever, and other respiratory allergies, muscular aches, backache, minor arthritis pain, menstrual discomfort, and reduction of fever.

HOW TO TAKE:
Comes in tablet, chewable tablet, caplet, capsule, elixir, liquid, powder, solution, and suppository forms. Swallow tablet, capsule, or elixir with liquid. Sprinkle powder over liquid, then swallow. Follow medication instructions carefully for proper insertion of suppositories. Do not crush or chew timed-release tablet. In proper dosages in most cases, acetaminophen does not cause gastrointestinal (GI) irritation and can be taken with or without food.

Q U I C K F A C T S

USUAL ADULT DOSE:
325 to 650 milligrams every 4 to 6 hours, or 1 gram 3 to 4 times per day, not to exceed 4 grams a day.

USUAL CHILD DOSE:
4 to 5 doses per day, not to exceed 5 doses in 24 hours. Dosage varies based on infant or child's age.

OVERDOSE SYMPTOMS:
Nausea, vomiting, diaphoresis, discomfort, and malaise. In some cases, hepatic toxicity (liver poisoning) may result. If you suspect an overdose, immediately seek medical attention.

SIDE EFFECTS:
None in most cases of common use. Long-term ingestion of high dosages may increase risk of liver and kidney damage. In rare cases, extreme fatigue and drowsiness, allergic skin eruptions (rash, hives, itch), sore throat and fever, bleeding or bruising, urinary discomfort or blood in urine, jaundiced skin or eyes may result.

CHECK WITH YOUR DOCTOR OR PHARMACIST BEFORE COMBINING ACETAMINOPHEN WITH:
Anticoagulants, aspirin and other salicylates, Isoniazid (anti-tuberculosis) medication. Excessive ingestion of alcohol while taking acetaminophen can increase the risk of liver damage or disease (hepatic toxicity).

PREGNANCY OR BREASTFEEDING:
No conclusive evidence of effects on fetus—benign or adverse—has been established. High dosage has in isolated cases caused anemia in

mother and kidney failure in fetus. Nursing infants have shown no harmful effects.

PRECAUTIONS FOR CHILDREN:
In general, administer to infants or children only when consulting a physician and follow instructions on medication.

PRECAUTIONS FOR SENIORS:
Seniors generally don't eliminate drugs as efficiently as younger persons, and should avoid high dosages.

SPECIAL WARNINGS:
Chronic alcoholics are at risk for hepatic (liver) function impairment if taking high dosages of acetaminophen.

INFORM YOUR DOCTOR BEFORE TAKING ACETAMINOPHEN IF YOU HAVE:
Liver or kidney disease or damage, an allergy to acetaminophen, or hypoglycemia.

QUICK FACTS

ACTIVE INGREDIENTS:

ACETAMINOPHEN, ASPIRIN, AND CAFFEINE COMBINATION

BRAND NAMES:

- Buffets II Tablets
- Excedrin Extra-Strength
- Gelpirin
- Goody's Extra Strength Headache Powders
- Pain Reliever Tabs
- Supac
- Vanquish

SYMPTOMS RELIEVED:
Minor aches and pains such as those associated with the common cold, flu, headache, toothache, sinusitis, hay fever, and other respiratory allergies, muscular aches, backache, minor arthritis pain, menstrual discomfort, and reduction of fever.

HOW TO TAKE:
Comes in tablet, caplet, capsule, and powder forms. Swallow with liquid. Sprinkle powder over liquid, then swallow. Do not crush or chew timed-release tablets. Aspirin and caffeine both can cause gastrointestinal (GI) irritation and should be taken with food or following meal.

USUAL ADULT DOSE:
1 or 2 capsules, tablets, caplets or 1 powder packet every 2 to 6 hours.

For important information regarding each active ingredient, also see: Acetaminophen, Aspirin, Caffeine Quick Facts

ACTIVE INGREDIENTS:
ACETAMINOPHEN AND CAFFEINE COMBINATION

BRAND NAMES:
- BAYER SELECT MAXIMUM STRENGTH
- EXCEDRIN ASPIRIN-FREE
- FENDOL

SYMPTOMS RELIEVED:
Minor aches and pains such as those associated with the common cold, flu, headache, toothache, sinusitis, hay fever, and other respiratory allergies, muscular aches, backache, minor arthritis pain, menstrual discomfort, and reduction of fever.

HOW TO TAKE:
Comes in tablet, caplet, capsule, and powder forms. Swallow with liquid. Sprinkle powder over liquid, then swallow. Do not crush or chew timed-release tablets. Caffeine can cause gastrointestinal (GI) irritation and should be taken with food or following a meal.

USUAL ADULT DOSE:
12.5 milligrams every 4 to 6 hours, not to exceed 25 milligrams in a 4 to 6 hour period or 75 milligrams in a 24 hour period.

USUAL CHILD DOSE:
Do not administer to children under 16 unless under direction of physician. Dosage may vary based on infant or child's age.

OVERDOSE SYMPTOMS:
Nervous agitation, disorientation, confusion, severe headache, convulsions, GI bleeding, or

QUICK FACTS

hemorrhage. If you suspect an overdose, seek medical attention immediately.

SIDE EFFECTS:
No serious effects in most cases of common use, however normal use of caffeine can result in common GI irritations such as heartburn and indigestion. Less common side effects include dizziness, nausea, stomach cramps, and headache.

CHECK WITH YOUR DOCTOR OR PHARMACIST BEFORE COMBINING ACETAMINOPHEN OR CAFFEINE WITH:
Antacids, anticoagulants, aspirin, asthma medication, other nonsteroidal anti-inflammatory drugs (NSAIDs), tetracycline, and any other medication.

PREGNANCY OR BREASTFEEDING:
Animal studies have indicated an adverse effect on fetus, but no adequate studies have been performed on humans. No harmful effects have been reported regarding nursing infants, but caffeine use by a nursing mother should be considered a potential risk for a nursing child as the drug will be passed on to the infant in the mother's milk. In all cases, a physician should be consulted.

PRECAUTIONS FOR CHILDREN:
In general, caffeine and other NSAIDs are not advised for children under 15. Administer caffeine to infants or children only when consulting a physician and follow instructions on medication (see above).

55+

PRECAUTIONS FOR SENIORS:

Seniors generally don't eliminate drugs as efficiently as younger persons, and should avoid high dosages. Seniors (over 65) are at special risk for development of ulcers if taking caffeine in high doses. Prolonged use can also lead to kidney and liver damage.

SPECIAL WARNINGS:

Don't take caffeine medication if you are aspirin intolerant or allergic to other NSAIDs. If in doubt, always consult a pharmacist or physician. Also avoid if you have GI conditions such as gastritis, peptic ulcer, enteritis, ileitis, colitis; asthma, high blood pressure, or hematologic (bleeding) problems. Avoid alcohol while taking this or any other NSAID.

INFORM YOUR DOCTOR BEFORE TAKING CAFFEINE IF YOU HAVE:

An allergy or intolerance to aspirin or other NSAIDs, damaged or impaired renal (kidney) or hepatic (liver) functions, epilepsy, Parkinson's disease or mental illness.

QUICK FACTS

ACTIVE INGREDIENT:
ASPIRIN

BRAND NAMES:
- Ascriptin
- Cama Arthritis Pain Reliever
- Empirin
- Goody's
- Magnaprin

SYMPTOMS RELIEVED:
Minor aches and pains such as those associated with the common cold, flu, headache, toothache, sinusitis, hay fever, and other respiratory allergies, muscular aches, backache, minor arthritis pain, menstrual discomfort, and reduction of fever.

HOW TO TAKE:
Comes in tablet, caplet, capsule, and powder forms. Swallow tablet, capsule, or caplet with liquid. Sprinkle powder over liquid, then swallow. Do not crush or chew timed-release tablet. Aspirin can cause gastrointestinal (GI) irritation and should be taken with food or following meal.

USUAL ADULT DOSE:
325 to 650 milligrams every 4 hours or as needed, not to exceed 4 grams a day. For extra strength products, dosage may range to 500 milligrams every 3 hours to 1,000 milligrams every 6 hours.

USUAL CHILD DOSE:
4 to 5 doses per day, not to exceed 5 doses in 24 hours. Dosage varies based on infant or child's age.

OVERDOSE SYMPTOMS:
Respiratory difficulty, hyperventilation, hyperthermia, nausea and vomiting, severe diarrhea, impaired vision, bloody urine, abnormal thirst, nervous agitation, disorientation and dizziness. In some cases, capillary and other hematological abnormalities may result. If you suspect an overdose, immediately seek medical attention.

SIDE EFFECTS:
No serious effects in most cases of common use, however normal aspirin use can result in common GI irritations such as heartburn and indigestion. Aspirin affects hypothalamus, resulting in dilation of small blood vessels in skin. Low dosages may reduce risk of blood clotting as aspirin inhibits blood clotting. Aspirin use may however contribute to anemia in anemic individuals.

CHECK WITH YOUR DOCTOR OR PHARMACIST BEFORE COMBINING ASPIRIN WITH:
Anticoagulants, asthma medication, other salicylates, tetracycline, and any other medication. Ingestion of alcohol while taking aspirin can increase risk of GI ulceration. Avoid aspirin use if you have aspirin intolerance, asthma, rhinitis, or a history of anemia (iron poor blood). Also avoid use of aspirin, if possible, one week prior to surgery, as it may increase possibility of postoperative bleeding.

PREGNANCY OR BREASTFEEDING:
In third trimester, aspirin use should be discouraged. No harmful effects have been reported regarding nursing infants, but aspirin use by a nursing mother should be considered a potential risk for a nursing child as the drug will be passed

on to the infant in milk. In all cases, a physician should be consulted.

PRECAUTIONS FOR CHILDREN:
In general, administer to infants or children only when consulting a physician and follow instructions on medication.

SPECIAL WARNING:
Aspirin use in children and teenagers with influenza (flu), chicken pox, and other viral infections may be associated with development of Reye's syndrome. This rare but acute and often life-threatening condition has caused permanent brain damage in survivors. Symptoms include: vomiting, lethargy, bellicosity, leading possibly to delirium and coma.

55+ **PRECAUTIONS FOR SENIORS:**
Seniors generally don't eliminate drugs as efficiently as younger persons, and should avoid high dosages. Buffered effervescent aspirin products contain high sodium content and should be avoided if on a restricted sodium diet. Aspirin use can cause GI irritation and possibly stomach or intestinal bleeding in seniors, manifested usually by dark stools.

SPECIAL WARNINGS:
Always check expiration date on label of medication. Do not take aspirin which emits a vinegar-like odor. This indicates that it is decomposing and is unsafe for use.

INFORM YOUR DOCTOR BEFORE TAKING ASPIRIN IF YOU HAVE:
An allergy to aspirin, are asthmatic, anemic, or have GI sensitivity.

QUICK FACTS

ACTIVE INGREDIENTS:

ASPIRIN AND CAFFEINE COMBINATION

QUICK FACTS

BRAND NAMES:
- ANACIN
- BC POWDER
- COPE
- DRISTAN
- EXCEDRIN
- FENDOL
- GENSAN

SYMPTOMS RELIEVED:
Minor aches and pains such as those associated with the common cold, flu, headache, toothache, sinusitis, hay fever, and other respiratory allergies, muscular aches, backache, minor arthritis pain, menstrual discomfort, and reduction of fever.

HOW TO TAKE:
Comes in tablet, caplet, capsule, and powder forms. Swallow with liquid. Sprinkle powder over liquid, then swallow. Do not crush or chew timed-release tablets. Caffeine can cause gastrointestinal (GI) irritation and should be taken with food or following meal.

USUAL ADULT DOSE:
12.5 milligrams every 4 to 6 hours, not to exceed 25 milligrams in a 4 to 6 hour period or 75 milligrams in a 24 hour period.

USUAL CHILD DOSE:
Do not administer to children under 16 unless under direction of physician. Dosage may vary based on infant or child's age.

QUICK FACTS

OVERDOSE SYMPTOMS:
Nervous agitation, disorientation, confusion, severe headache, convulsions, GI bleeding or hemorrhage. If you suspect an overdose, immediately seek medical attention.

SIDE EFFECTS:
No serious effects in most cases of common use, however normal use of caffeine can result in common GI irritations such as heartburn and indigestion. Less common side effects include dizziness, nausea, stomach cramps, and headache.

CHECK WITH YOUR DOCTOR OR PHARMACIST BEFORE COMBINING CAFFEINE WITH:
Antacids, anticoagulants, aspirin, asthma medication, other nonsteroidal anti-inflammatory drugs (NSAIDs), tetracycline, and any other medication. Combination with acetaminophen increases risk of kidney damage. Ingestion of alcohol while taking salicylates can increase risk of GI ulceration. Avoid caffeine if you have a history of anemia. Also avoid use of caffeine, if possible, one week prior to surgery, as it may increase possibility of postoperative bleeding.

PREGNANCY OR BREASTFEEDING:
Animal studies have indicated an adverse effect on fetus, but no adequate studies have been performed on humans. No harmful effects have been reported regarding nursing infants, but caffeine use by a nursing mother should be considered a potential risk for a nursing child as the drug will be passed on to the infant in the mother's milk. In all cases, a physician should be consulted.

PRECAUTIONS FOR CHILDREN:
In general, caffeine and other NSAIDs are not advised for children under 15. Administer caffeine to infants or children only when consulting a physician and follow instructions on medication (see above).

PRECAUTIONS FOR SENIORS:
Seniors generally don't eliminate drugs as efficiently as younger persons, and should avoid high dosages. Seniors (over 65) are at special risk for development of ulcers if taking caffeine in high doses. Prolonged use can also lead to kidney and liver damage.

SPECIAL WARNINGS:
Don't take caffeine medication if you are aspirin intolerant or allergic to other NSAIDs. If in doubt, always consult a pharmacist or physician. Also avoid if you have GI conditions such as gastritis, peptic ulcer, enteritis, ileitis, colitis; asthma, high blood pressure, or hematologic (bleeding) problems. Avoid alcohol while taking this or any other NSAID.

INFORM YOUR DOCTOR BEFORE TAKING CAFFEINE IF YOU HAVE:
An allergy or intolerance to aspirin or other NSAIDs, damaged or impaired renal (kidney) or hepatic (liver) functions, epilepsy, Parkinson's disease or mental illness.

QUICK FACTS

ACTIVE INGREDIENT:

IBUPROFEN

BRAND NAMES:

- ADVIL
- ARTHRITIS FOUNDATION (backache and muscle pain)
- BAYER SELECT PAIN RELIEF
- GENPRIL
- IBUPROHM
- MOTRIN
- NUPRON
- OBUPRIN

SYMPTOMS RELIEVED:

Minor aches and pains such as those associated with the common cold, flu, headache, toothache, sinusitis, hay fever, and other respiratory allergies, muscular aches, backache, minor arthritis pain, menstrual discomfort, and reduction of fever.

HOW TO TAKE:

Comes in tablet, caplet, and gelcap forms. Swallow with liquid. Do not crush or chew timed-release tablet. Ibuprofen can cause gastrointestinal (GI) irritation and should be taken with food or following meal.

USUAL ADULT DOSE:

Minor aches and pains: 200 milligrams every 4 to 6 hours as needed, not to exceed 1.2 grams per day.

Arthritis and related conditions: 1.2 grams to 3.2 grams per day divided into equal doses over 24 hours.

USUAL CHILD DOSE:
Always consult with a pharmacist or physician. Dosage may vary based on infant or child's age. Juvenile arthritis: 30 to 70 milligrams per day in 3 or 4 equal doses or as indicated.

Fever reduction: Maximum daily dose not to exceed 40 milligrams. Dosage should be adjusted based on initial temperature level. If less or equal to 102.5°F, 5 milligrams per dose is recommended. If temperature is greater than 102.5°F, 10 milligrams per dose is recommended.

OVERDOSE SYMPTOMS:
Nervous agitation, disorientation, confusion, severe headache, convulsions, GI bleeding or hemorrhage. If you suspect an overdose, immediately seek medical attention.

SIDE EFFECTS:
No serious effects in most cases of common use, however normal use of ibuprofen can result in common GI irritations such as heartburn and indigestion. Less common side effects include dizziness, nausea, stomach cramps, and headache.

CHECK WITH YOUR DOCTOR OR PHARMACIST BEFORE COMBINING IBUPROFEN WITH:
Antacids, anticoagulants, aspirin, asthma medication, other nonsteroidal anti-inflammatory drugs (NSAIDs), tetracycline, and any other medication. Combination with acetaminophen increases risk of kidney damage. Ingestion of alcohol while taking ibuprofen can increase risk of GI ulceration. Avoid ibuprofen if you have a history of anemia. Also avoid use of ibuprofen, if possible, one week prior to surgery, as it may increase possibility of postoperative bleeding.

QUICK FACTS

PREGNANCY OR BREASTFEEDING:
No harmful effects have been reported regarding nursing infants, but ibuprofen use by a nursing mother should be considered a potential risk for a nursing child as the drug will be passed on to the infant in the mother's milk. In all cases, a physician should be consulted.

PRECAUTIONS FOR CHILDREN:
In general, ibuprofen and other NSAIDs are not advised for children under 15. Administer ibuprofen to infants or children only when consulting a physician and follow instructions on medication.

PRECAUTIONS FOR SENIORS:
Seniors generally don't eliminate drugs as efficiently as younger persons, and should avoid high dosages. Seniors (over 65) are at special risk for development of ulcers if taking ibuprofen in high doses. Prolonged use can also lead to kidney and liver damage.

SPECIAL WARNINGS:
Don't take ibuprofen medication if you are aspirin intolerant or allergic to other NSAIDs (anti-inflammatory nonsteroidal) drugs. If in doubt, always consult a pharmacist or physician. Avoid alcohol while taking this or any other NSAID.

INFORM YOUR DOCTOR BEFORE TAKING IBUPROFEN IF YOU HAVE:
An allergy or intolerance to aspirin or other NSAIDs, damaged or impaired renal (kidney) or hepatic (liver) functions, epilepsy, Parkinson's disease, or mental illness.

ACTIVE INGREDIENT:
KETOPROFEN

QUICK FACTS

BRAND NAMES:
- ACTRON
- ORUDIS

SYMPTOMS RELIEVED:
Minor aches and pains such as those associated with the common cold, flu, headache, toothache, sinusitis, hay fever, and other respiratory allergies, muscular aches, backache, minor arthritis pain, menstrual discomfort, and reduction of fever.

HOW TO TAKE:
Comes in tablet forms. Swallow with liquid. Do not crush or chew timed-release tablets. Ketoprofen can cause gastrointestinal (GI) irritation and should be taken with food or following meal.

USUAL ADULT DOSE:
12.5 milligrams every 4 to 6 hours, not to exceed 25 milligrams in a 4 to 6 hour period or 75 milligrams in a 24 hour period.

USUAL CHILD DOSE:
Do not administer to children under 16 unless under direction of physician. Dosage may vary based on infant or child's age.

OVERDOSE SYMPTOMS:
Nervous agitation, disorientation, confusion, severe headache, convulsions, GI bleeding or hemorrhage. If you suspect an overdose, immediately seek medical attention.

Q U I C K F A C T S

SIDE EFFECTS:
No serious effects in most cases of common use, however normal use of ketoprofen can result in common GI irritations such as heartburn and indigestion. Less common side effects include dizziness, nausea, stomach cramps, and headache.

CHECK WITH YOUR DOCTOR OR PHARMACIST BEFORE COMBINING KETOPROFEN WITH:
Antacids, anticoagulants, aspirin, asthma medication, other nonsteroidal anti-inflammatory drugs (NSAIDs), tetracycline, and any other medication. Combination with acetaminophen increases risk of kidney damage. Ingestion of alcohol while taking ketoprofen can increase risk of GI ulceration. Avoid ketoprofen if you have a history of anemia. Also avoid use of ketoprofen, if possible, one week prior to surgery, as it may increase possibility of postoperative bleeding.

PREGNANCY OR BREASTFEEDING:
Animal studies have indicated an adverse effect on fetus, but no adequate studies have been performed on humans. No harmful effects have been reported regarding nursing infants, but ketoprofen use by a nursing mother should be considered a potential risk for a nursing child as the drug will be passed on to the infant in the mother's milk. In all cases, a physician should be consulted.

PRECAUTIONS FOR CHILDREN:
In general, ketoprofen and other NSAIDs are not advised for children under 15. Administer ketoprofen to infants or children only when

consulting a physician and follow instructions on medication (see above).

55+ **PRECAUTIONS FOR SENIORS:**
Seniors generally don't eliminate drugs as efficiently as younger persons, and should avoid high dosages. Seniors (over 65) are at special risk for development of ulcers if taking ketoprofen in high doses. Prolonged use can also lead to kidney and liver damage.

SPECIAL WARNINGS:
Don't take ketoprofen medication if you are aspirin intolerant or allergic to other NSAIDs. If in doubt, always consult a pharmacist or physician. Also avoid if you have GI conditions such as gastritis, peptic ulcer, enteritis, ileitis, colitis; asthma, high blood pressure, or hematologic (bleeding) problems. Avoid alcohol while taking this or any other NSAID.

INFORM YOUR DOCTOR BEFORE TAKING KETOPROFEN IF YOU HAVE:
An allergy or intolerance to aspirin or other NSAIDs, damaged or impaired renal (kidney) or hepatic (liver) functions, epilepsy, Parkinson's disease, or mental illness.

QUICK FACTS

ACTIVE INGREDIENT:
NAPROXEN

BRAND NAMES:
• ALEVE

SYMPTOMS RELIEVED:
Minor aches and pains such as those associated with the common cold, flu, headache, toothache, sinusitis, hay fever, and other respiratory allergies, muscular aches, backache, minor arthritis pain, menstrual discomfort, and reduction of fever.

HOW TO TAKE:
Comes in tablet forms. Swallow with liquid. Do not crush or chew timed-release tablets. Naproxen can cause gastrointestinal (GI) irritation and should be taken with food or following meal.

USUAL ADULT DOSE:
200 milligrams every 8 to 12 hours with full glass of liquid, not to exceed 600 milligrams in a 24 hour period. Seniors (over 65) should not exceed 200 milligrams in a 12 hour period.

USUAL CHILD DOSE:
Do not administer to children under 12 unless under direction of physician. Dosage may vary based on infant or child's age.

OVERDOSE SYMPTOMS:
Nervous agitation, disorientation, confusion, severe headache, convulsions, GI bleeding, or hemorrhage. If you suspect an overdose, immediately seek medical attention.

SIDE EFFECTS:
No serious effects in most cases of common use, however normal use of naproxen can result in common GI irritations such as heartburn and indigestion. Less common side effects include dizziness, nausea, stomach cramps, and headache.

CHECK WITH YOUR DOCTOR OR PHARMACIST BEFORE COMBINING NAPROXEN WITH:
Antacids, anticoagulants, aspirin, asthma medication, other nonsteroidal anti-inflammatory drugs (NSAIDs), tetracycline, and any other medication. Combination with acetaminophen increases risk of kidney damage. Ingestion of alcohol while taking naproxen can increase risk of GI ulceration. Avoid naproxen if you have a history of anemia. Also avoid use of naproxen, if possible, one week prior to surgery, as it may increase possibility of postoperative bleeding.

PREGNANCY OR BREASTFEEDING:
Animal studies have indicated an adverse effect on fetus, but no adequate studies have been performed on humans. No harmful effects have been reported regarding nursing infants, but naproxen use by a nursing mother should be considered a potential risk for a nursing child as the drug will be passed on to the infant in the mother's milk. In all cases, a physician should be consulted.

PRECAUTIONS FOR CHILDREN:
In general, naproxen and other NSAIDs are not advised for children under 15. Administer naproxen to infants or children only when consulting a physician and follow instructions on medication (see above).

Q U I C K F A C T S

55+ **PRECAUTIONS FOR SENIORS:**
Seniors generally don't eliminate drugs as efficiently as younger persons, and should avoid high dosages. Seniors (over 65) are at special risk for development of ulcers if taking naproxen in high doses. Prolonged use can also lead to kidney and liver damage.

SPECIAL WARNINGS:
Don't take naproxen medication if you are aspirin intolerant or allergic to other NSAIDs. If in doubt, always consult a pharmacist or physician. Also avoid if you have GI conditions such as gastritis, peptic ulcer, enteritis, ileitis, colitis; asthma, high blood pressure, or hematologic (bleeding) problems. Avoid alcohol while taking this or any other NSAID.

INFORM YOUR DOCTOR BEFORE TAKING NAPROXEN IF YOU HAVE:
An allergy or intolerance to aspirin or other NSAIDs, damaged or impaired renal (kidney) or hepatic (liver) functions, epilepsy, Parkinson's disease, or mental illness.

ACTIVE INGREDIENT:

SALICYLATES

BRAND NAMES:
- BACKACHE CAPLETS
- DOAN'S ANALGESIC
- MOBIGESIC

SYMPTOMS RELIEVED:
Minor aches and pains such as those associated with the common cold, flu, headache, toothache, sinusitis, hay fever, and other respiratory allergies, muscular aches, backache, minor arthritis pain, menstrual discomfort, and reduction of fever.

HOW TO TAKE:
Comes in tablet, chewable tablet, caplet, capsule, powder, and solution forms. Swallow tablet, capsule, or caplet with liquid. Sprinkle powder over liquid, then swallow. Do not crush or chew timed-release tablet. Salicylates can cause gastrointestinal (GI) irritation and should be taken with food or following meal.

USUAL ADULT DOSE:
SODIUM SALICYLATE:
Minor aches and pains: 325 to 650 milligrams every 4 hours or as needed, not to exceed 4 grams a day. For extra strength products, dosage may range to 500 milligrams every 3 hours to 1,000 milligrams every 6 hours.

Arthritis and related conditions: 3.2 to 6 grams divided into equal doses over 24 hours.

MAGNESIUM SALICYLATE:
650 milligrams every 4 hours, as needed.

Q U I C K F A C T S

QUICK FACTS

USUAL CHILD DOSE:
Dosage varies based on infant or child's age. Consult with a pharmacist or physician.

OVERDOSE SYMPTOMS:
Respiratory difficulty, hyperventilation, hyperthermia, nausea and vomiting, severe diarrhea, impaired vision, bloody urine, abnormal thirst, nervous agitation, disorientation and dizziness. In some cases, capillary and other hematological abnormalities may result. If you suspect an overdose, immediately seek medical attention.

SIDE EFFECTS:
No serious effects in most cases of common use, however normal use of sodium salicylate can result in common GI irritations such as heartburn and indigestion. Sodium salicylate is not advised for individuals on low sodium diet. Magnesium salicylate, which is a sodium free salicylate may result in lower incidence of GI upset. Salicylates affect hypothalamus, resulting in dilation of small blood vessels in skin. Low dosages may reduce risk of blood clotting as salicylates inhibit blood clotting. Salicylate use may however contribute to anemia in anemic individuals.

CHECK WITH YOUR DOCTOR OR PHARMACIST BEFORE COMBINING SALICYLATES WITH:
Acetaminophen, anticoagulants, asthma medication, other salicylates, tetracycline, and any other medication. Combination with acetaminophen increases risk of kidney damage. Ingestion of alcohol while taking salicylates can increase risk of GI ulceration. Avoid salicylates if you have a history of anemia. Also avoid use of salicylates, if possible, one week prior to

surgery, as it may increase possibility of post-operative bleeding.

PREGNANCY OR BREASTFEEDING:
Animal studies have indicated an adverse effect on fetus, but no adequate studies have been performed on humans. In third trimester, salicylate use should be discouraged. No harmful effects have been reported regarding nursing infants, but salicylate use by a nursing mother should be considered a potential risk for a nursing child as the drug will be passed on to the infant in milk. In all cases, a physician should be consulted.

PRECAUTIONS FOR CHILDREN:
In general, administer salicylates to infants or children only when consulting a physician and follow instructions on medication.

SPECIAL WARNING:
Use of salicylates in children and teenagers with influenza (flu), chicken pox, and other viral infections may be associated with development of Reye's syndrome. This rare but acute and often life-threatening condition has caused permanent brain damage in survivors. Symptoms include: vomiting, lethargy, bellicosity, leading possibly to delirium and coma.

55+

PRECAUTIONS FOR SENIORS:
Seniors generally don't eliminate drugs as efficiently as younger persons, and should avoid high dosages. Sodium salicylate and buffered effervescent salicylate medications contain high sodium content and should be avoided if on a restricted sodium diet. Salicylate use can cause

Q U I C K F A C T S

GI irritation and possibly stomach or intestinal bleeding in seniors, manifested usually by dark stools. Prolonged use can lead to kidney damage.

SPECIAL WARNINGS:

Always check expiration date on label of medication. Do not take if medication has expired. Do not take salicylate medication which emits a vinegar-like odor. This indicates that it is decomposing and is unsafe for use.

INFORM YOUR DOCTOR BEFORE TAKING SALICYLATES IF YOU HAVE:

An allergy to salicylates (including aspirin), are asthmatic, are anemic or have other hematological conditions, or susceptible to GI irritation.

ACTIVE INGREDIENT:

CAPSAICIN (CAPSICUM OLEORESIN)

QUICK FACTS

BRAND NAMES:

- ArthriCare Odor Free (combination with menthol, methyl nicotinate—also contains aloe vera gel, carbomer 940, cetyl alcohol, glyceryl stereate SE, isocetyl alcohol, propylparaben, stearyl alcohol, triethanolamine)
- ArthriCare Ultra (combination with menthol USP—also contains aloe vera gel, carbomer, cetyl alcohol, glyceryl stereate SE, isocetyl alcohol, propylparaben, stearyl alcohol)
- Menthacin (combination with menthol, methyl nicotinate—also contains capric triglyceride, carbomer 1342, carbomer 940, cetyl alcohol, diazolidinyl urea, glyceryl stereate, sodium lauryl sulfate, maleated soybean oil, methylparaben, polysorbate 60, propylene glycol, propylparaben, sorbitan stearate trolamine)

SYMPTOMS RELIEVED:
Minor aches and pains of muscles and joints associated with arthritis, common back pain, and sprains and strains.

HOW TO USE:
Comes in ointment and cream forms. Apply to affected areas. These products are for external use only. Do not swallow. Avoid contact with eyes while applying.

USUAL ADULT DOSE:
Apply to affected area(s), not more than 3 to

QUICK FACTS

4 times per day, or as directed by your doctor. In all cases follow specific product instructions.

USUAL CHILD DOSE:
For ages 2 to 12: Application is same as adult, or as directed by your doctor. In all cases follow specific product instructions.

Only apply to children under 2 under doctor's supervision or direction. In all cases follow specific product instructions.

OVERDOSE SYMPTOMS:
None known.

SIDE EFFECTS:
No serious effects in most cases of common use. In some cases, stinging or burning sensation may be felt where rub has been applied. Because these products warm the affected area, temporary redness may also occur.

CHECK WITH YOUR DOCTOR OR PHARMACIST BEFORE COMBINING THESE PRODUCTS WITH:
Any other drugs and preparations.

PREGNANCY OR BREASTFEEDING:
Safety of this drug for use during pregnancy or while nursing has not been established. In all cases you should consult your doctor before using any drug during pregnancy or while nursing.

PRECAUTIONS FOR CHILDREN:
These products should only be used with doctor's supervision or direction for children under 2. Consult your doctor and follow instructions on medication (see above).

55+ **PRECAUTIONS FOR SENIORS:**
None known.

SPECIAL WARNINGS:
Do not use these products if you are allergic to capsaicin, fruits of Capsicum plants, (e.g. cayenne peppers), or any of the inactive ingredients contained in these products. Do not apply these products to wounds, lesions, broken, damaged, or sensitive skin. Avoid contact with eyes and mucous membranes. Do not use a heating pad or other forms of topical heating while using these products. Do not apply these products immediately before or after a bath or shower.

INFORM YOUR DOCTOR BEFORE USING THESE PRODUCTS IF YOU HAVE:
Any allergies, or if you are or plan to become pregnant during time that you will be taking this product.

QUICK FACTS

ACTIVE INGREDIENT:

METHYL SALICYLATE

BRAND NAMES:

- ArthriCare Triple Medicated (combination with menthol, methyl nicotinate —also contains carbomer 940, dioctyl sodium sulfosuccinate, glycerin, isopropyl alcohol, polysorbate 60, propylene glycol)
- Mentholatum Deep Heating (combination with menthol—also contains glyceryl stearate, sodium lauryl sulfate, isoceteth-20, poloxamer 407, quaternium-15, sorbitan stearate)

SYMPTOMS RELIEVED:

Minor aches and pains of muscles and joints associated with arthritis, common back pain, and sprains and strains.

HOW TO USE:

Comes in ointment form. Apply to affected areas. These products are for external use only. Do not swallow. Avoid contact with eyes while applying.

USUAL ADULT DOSE:

Apply to affected area(s), not more than 3 to 4 times per day, or as directed by your doctor. In all cases follow specific product instructions.

USUAL CHILD DOSE:

For ages 2 to 12: Apply same as adult, or as directed by your doctor. In all cases follow specific product instructions.

Only apply to children under 2 under doctor's supervision or direction. In all cases follow specific product instructions.

OVERDOSE SYMPTOMS:
None known.

SIDE EFFECTS:
No serious effects in most cases of common use. In some cases, stinging or burning sensation may be felt where rub has been applied. Because these products warm the affected area, temporary redness may also occur.

CHECK WITH YOUR DOCTOR OR PHARMACIST BEFORE COMBINING THIS PRODUCT WITH:
Any other drugs and preparations.

PREGNANCY OR BREASTFEEDING:
Safety of this drug for use during pregnancy or while nursing has not been established. In all cases you should consult your doctor before using any drug during pregnancy or while nursing.

PRECAUTIONS FOR CHILDREN:
These products should only be used with doctor's supervision or direction for children under 2. Consult your doctor and follow instructions on medication (see above).

PRECAUTIONS FOR SENIORS:
None known.

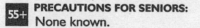

SPECIAL WARNINGS:
Do not use these products if you are allergic to methyl salicylate, menthol, methyl nicotinate, or any of the inactive ingredients contained in these products. Do not apply these products to wounds, lesions, broken, damaged, or sensitive skin. Avoid contact with eyes and mucous

membranes. Do not use a heating pad or other forms of topical heating while using these products. Do not apply these products immediately before or after a bath or shower.

INFORM YOUR DOCTOR BEFORE USING THESE PRODUCTS IF YOU HAVE:

Any allergies, or if you are or plan to become pregnant during time that you will be taking this product.

• ANTI-INFLAMMATORY •

The most important considerations in choosing an anti-inflammatory agent (nonsteroidal anti-inflammatory or "NSAID") are: pain relief; anti-inflammatory activity, and the potential for allergic reaction or sensitivity to certain active ingredients.

QUICK REVIEW

ANTI-INFLAMMATORY AGENTS (NSAIDS) ARE A CLASS OF DRUGS WHICH:

- inhibit the action of prostaglandins (hormonelike substances) in the central nervous system, thereby temporarily reducing the perception of physical pain with little loss of sensibility to other physical sensation,
- are used both for their anti-inflammatory and analgesic properties, to temporarily alleviate symptoms such as: headache, fever, backache, sinus pain, muscle strain, menstrual pain, and similar ailments. Some NSAIDs also provide temporary anti-inflammatory relief for ailments such as rheumatoid arthritis and osteoarthritis,
- can have adverse effects in some instances such as aggravation of gastrointestinal (GI) conditions such as heartburn and ulcer, and can produce allergic reactions in persons who are aspirin-intolerant or hypersensitive.

See also: Analgesics

QUICK FACTS

ACTIVE INGREDIENT:
ACETAMINOPHEN

BRAND NAMES:
- BANESIN
- DOLANEX
- EXCEDRIN ASPIRIN-FREE
- PANADOL
- PERCOGESIC ANALGESIC TABLETS (combination with phenyltoloxamine citrate, also contains sucrose)
- PHENAPHEN
- TAPANOL
- TYLENOL (various formulations)
- VANQUISH (combination with aspirin and caffeine)

SYMPTOMS RELIEVED:
Minor aches and pains such as those associated with the common cold, flu, headache, toothache, sinusitis, hay fever and other respiratory allergies, muscular aches, backache, minor arthritis pain, menstrual discomfort, and reduction of fever.

HOW TO TAKE:
Comes in tablet, chewable tablet, caplet, capsule, elixir, liquid, powder, solution, and suppository forms. Swallow tablet, capsule, or elixir with liquid. Sprinkle powder over liquid, then swallow. Follow medication instructions carefully for proper insertion of suppositories. Do not crush or chew timed-release tablet. In proper dosages in most cases, acetaminophen does not cause gastrointestinal (GI) irritation and can be taken with or without food.

USUAL ADULT DOSE:
325 to 650 milligrams every 4 to 6 hours, or 1 gram 3 to 4 times per day, not to exceed 4 grams a day.

USUAL CHILD DOSE:
4 to 5 doses per day, not to exceed 5 doses in 24 hours. Dosage varies based on infant or child's age.

OVERDOSE SYMPTOMS:
Nausea, vomiting, diaphoresis, discomfort, and malaise. In some cases, hepatic toxicity (liver poisoning) may result. If you suspect an overdose, immediately seek medical attention.

SIDE EFFECTS:
None in most cases of common use. Long-term ingestion of high dosages may increase risk of liver and kidney damage. In rare cases, extreme fatigue and drowsiness, allergic skin eruptions (rash, hives, itch), sore throat and fever, bleeding or bruising, urinary discomfort or blood in urine, jaundiced skin or eyes may result.

CHECK WITH YOUR DOCTOR OR PHARMACIST BEFORE COMBINING ACETAMINOPHEN WITH:
Anticoagulants, aspirin and other salicylates, Isoniazid (anti-tuberculosis) medication. Excessive ingestion of alcohol while taking acetaminophen can increase the risk of liver damage or disease (hepatic toxicity).

PREGNANCY OR BREASTFEEDING:
No conclusive evidence of effects on fetus—benign or adverse—has been established. High dosage has in isolated cases caused anemia in

Q U I C K F A C T S

mother and kidney failure in fetus. Nursing infants have shown no harmful effects.

PRECAUTIONS FOR CHILDREN:
In general, administer to infants or children only when consulting a physician and follow instructions on medication.

55+ **PRECAUTIONS FOR SENIORS:**
Seniors generally don't eliminate drugs as efficiently as younger persons, and should avoid high dosages.

SPECIAL WARNINGS:
Chronic alcoholics are at risk for hepatic (liver) function impairment if taking high dosages of acetaminophen.

INFORM YOUR DOCTOR BEFORE TAKING ACETAMINOPHEN IF YOU HAVE:
Liver or kidney disease or damage, an allergy to acetaminophen, or hypoglycemia.

ACTIVE INGREDIENTS:
ACETAMINOPHEN AND ASPIRIN

QUICK FACTS

BRAND NAMES:
- EXTRA STRENGTH EXCEDRIN
- GOODY'S EXTRA STRENGTH HEADACHE POWDERS

SYMPTOMS RELIEVED:
Minor aches and pains such as those associated with the common cold, flu, headache, toothache, sinusitis, hay fever and other respiratory allergies, muscular aches, backache, minor arthritis pain, menstrual discomfort, and reduction of fever.

HOW TO TAKE:
Comes in tablet, chewable tablet, caplet, capsule, and powder forms. Swallow tablet or capsule with liquid. Sprinkle powder over liquid, then swallow. Do not crush or chew timed-release tablet. Although acetaminophen does not normally cause GI irritation, aspirin can—as a result these medications should be taken with food.

USUAL ADULT DOSE:
Minor aches and pains: 325 to 650 milligrams every 4 hours or as needed, not to exceed 4 grams a day. For extra strength products, dosage may range to 500 milligrams every 3 hours to 1,000 milligrams every 6 hours.

USUAL CHILD DOSE:
4 to 5 doses per day, not to exceed 5 doses in 24 hours. Dosage varies based on infant or child's age.

QUICK FACTS

OVERDOSE SYMPTOMS:
Nausea, vomiting, diaphoresis, diarrhea, discomfort, fever, impaired vision, sweats, bloody urine, abnormal thirst, nervous agitation, and malaise. In some cases, hepatic toxicity (liver poisoning), or capillary and other hematological abnormalities may result. If you suspect an overdose, immediately seek medical attention.

SIDE EFFECTS:
Aspirin: None in most cases of common use, however normal aspirin use can result in common gastrointestinal (GI) irritations such as heartburn and indigestion. Aspirin affects the hypothalamus, resulting in dilation of small blood vessels in skin. Low dosages may reduce risk of blood clotting as aspirin inhibits clotting of small blood cells. Aspirin use may however contribute to anemia in anemic individuals.

Acetaminophen: Long-term ingestion of high dosages of acetaminophen may increase risk of liver and kidney damage. In rare cases, extreme fatigue and drowsiness, allergic skin eruptions (rash, hives, itch), sore throat and fever, bleeding or bruising, urinary discomfort or blood in urine, jaundiced skin or eyes may result.

CHECK WITH YOUR DOCTOR OR PHARMACIST BEFORE COMBINING ACETAMINOPHEN/ASPIRIN COMBINATION WITH:
Anticoagulants, aspirin, and other salicylates, tetracycline, cellulose-based laxatives, Isoniazid (anti-tuberculosis) medication. Excessive ingestion of alcohol while taking acetaminophen can increase the risk of liver damage or disease (hepatic toxicity). Ingestion of alcohol while

taking aspirin can increase risk of GI ulceration. Avoid use of medication containing aspirin if you have a history of anemia. Also avoid use of medication containing aspirin, if possible, one week prior to surgery, as aspirin may increase possibility of postoperative bleeding.

PREGNANCY OR BREASTFEEDING:
High dosage of acetaminophen has in isolated cases caused anemia in mother and kidney failure in fetus. In third trimester, use of medication containing aspirin should be discouraged. No harmful effects have been reported regarding nursing infants, but aspirin use by a nursing mother should be considered a potential risk for a nursing child as the drug will be passed on to the infant in milk. In all cases, a physician should be consulted.

PRECAUTIONS FOR CHILDREN:
In general, administer to infants or children only when consulting a physician and follow instructions on medication.

SPECIAL WARNING:
Aspirin use in children and teenagers with influenza (flu), chickenpox, and other viral infections may be associated with development of Reyes syndrome. This rare but acute and often life-threatening condition has caused permanent brain damage in survivors. Symptoms include: vomiting, lethargy, bellicosity, leading possibly to delirium and coma.

55+ **PRECAUTIONS FOR SENIORS:**
Seniors generally don't eliminate drugs as efficiently as younger persons, and should avoid

QUICK FACTS

high dosages. Aspirin use can cause GI irritation and possibly stomach or intestinal bleeding in seniors, manifested usually by dark stools.

SPECIAL WARNINGS:
Chronic alcoholics are at risk for hepatic (liver) function impairment if taking high dosages of acetaminophen. Always check expiration date on label of medication. Do not take if medication has expired. Do not take medication containing aspirin which emits a vinegar-like odor. This indicates that it is decomposing and is unsafe for use.

INFORM YOUR DOCTOR BEFORE TAKING ACETAMINOPHEN/ASPIRIN COMBINATION IF YOU HAVE:
Liver or kidney disease or damage, an allergy to acetaminophen or aspirin, asthma, anemia, or other hematological condition, GI sensitivity, viral infection, hypoglycemia.

ACTIVE INGREDIENTS:

ACETAMINOPHEN AND CAFFEINE COMBINATION

BRAND NAMES:

- BAYER SELECT MAXIMUM STRENGTH
- EXCEDRIN ASPIRIN-FREE
- FENDOL

SYMPTOMS RELIEVED:

Minor aches and pains such as those associated with the common cold, flu, headache, toothache, sinusitis, hay fever and other respiratory allergies, muscular aches, backache, minor arthritis pain, menstrual discomfort, and reduction of fever.

HOW TO TAKE:

Comes in tablet, caplet, capsule, and powder forms. Swallow with liquid. Sprinkle powder over liquid, then swallow. Do not crush or chew timed-release tablets. Caffeine can cause gastrointestinal (GI) irritation and should be taken with food or following a meal.

USUAL ADULT DOSE:

12.5 milligrams every 4 to 6 hours, not to exceed 25 milligrams in a 4 to 6 hour period or 75 milligrams in a 24 hour period.

USUAL CHILD DOSE:

Do not administer to children under 16 unless under direction of physician. Dosage may vary based on infant or child's age.

OVERDOSE SYMPTOMS:

Nervous agitation, disorientation, confusion, severe headache, convulsions, GI bleeding, or

hemorrhage. If you suspect an overdose, seek medical attention immediately.

SIDE EFFECTS:
No serious effects in most cases of common use, however normal use of caffeine can result in common GI irritations such as heartburn and indigestion. Less common side effects include dizziness, nausea, stomach cramps, and headache.

CHECK WITH YOUR DOCTOR OR PHARMACIST BEFORE COMBINING ACETAMINOPHEN OR CAFFEINE WITH:
Antacids, anticoagulants, aspirin, asthma medication, other nonsteroidal anti-inflammatory drugs (NSAIDs), tetracycline, and any other medication.

PREGNANCY OR BREASTFEEDING:
Animal studies have indicated an adverse effect on fetus, but no adequate studies have been performed on humans. No harmful effects have been reported regarding nursing infants, but caffeine use by a nursing mother should be considered a potential risk for a nursing child as the drug will be passed on to the infant in the mother's milk. In all cases, a physician should be consulted.

PRECAUTIONS FOR CHILDREN:
In general, caffeine and other NSAIDs are not advised for children under 15. Administer caffeine to infants or children only when consulting a physician and follow instructions on medication (see above).

55+ **PRECAUTIONS FOR SENIORS:**
Seniors generally don't eliminate drugs as efficiently as younger persons, and should avoid high dosages. Seniors (over 65) are at special risk for development of ulcers if taking caffeine in high doses. Prolonged use can also lead to kidney and liver damage.

SPECIAL WARNINGS:
Don't take caffeine medication if you are aspirin intolerant or allergic to other NSAIDs. If in doubt, always consult a pharmacist or physician. Also avoid if you have GI conditions such as gastritis, peptic ulcer, enteritis, ileitis, colitis; asthma, high blood pressure, or hematologic (bleeding) problems. Avoid alcohol while taking this or any other NSAID.

INFORM YOUR DOCTOR BEFORE TAKING CAFFEINE IF YOU HAVE:
An allergy or intolerance to aspirin or other NSAIDs, damaged or impaired renal (kidney) or hepatic (liver) functions, epilepsy, Parkinson's disease or mental illness.

QUICK FACTS

ACTIVE INGREDIENT:
ASPIRIN

BRAND NAMES:
- Ascriptin
- Cama Arthritis Pain Reliever
- Empirin
- Goody's
- Magnaprin

SYMPTOMS RELIEVED:
Minor aches and pains such as those associated with the common cold, flu, headache, toothache, sinusitis, hay fever and other respiratory allergies, muscular aches, backache, minor arthritis pain, menstrual discomfort, and reduction of fever.

HOW TO TAKE:
Comes in tablet, caplet, capsule, and powder forms. Swallow tablet, capsule, or caplet with liquid. Sprinkle powder over liquid, then swallow. Do not crush or chew timed-release tablet. Aspirin can cause gastrointestinal (GI) irritation and should be taken with food or following meal.

USUAL ADULT DOSE:
Minor aches and pains: 325 to 650 milligrams every 4 hours or as needed, not to exceed 4 grams a day. For extra strength products, dosage may range to 500 milligrams every 3 hours to 1,000 milligrams every 6 hours. For arthritis and related conditions: 3.2 to 6 grams divided into equal doses over 24 hours.

USUAL CHILD DOSE:
4 to 5 doses per day, not to exceed 5 doses

in 24 hours. Dosage varies based on infant or child's age.

OVERDOSE SYMPTOMS:
Respiratory difficulty, hyperventilation, hyperthermia, nausea and vomiting, severe diarrhea, impaired vision, bloody urine, abnormal thirst, nervous agitation, disorientation and dizziness. In some cases, capillary and other hematological abnormalities may result. If you suspect an overdose, immediately seek medical attention.

SIDE EFFECTS:
No serious effects in most cases of common use, however normal aspirin use can result in common gastrointestinal (GI) irritations such as heartburn and indigestion. Aspirin affects hypothalamus, resulting in dilation of small blood vessels in skin. Low dosages may reduce risk of blood clotting as aspirin inhibits blood clotting. Aspirin use may however contribute to anemia in anemic individuals.

CHECK WITH YOUR DOCTOR OR PHARMACIST BEFORE COMBINING ASPIRIN WITH:
Anticoagulants, asthma medication, other salicylates, tetracycline, and any other medication. Ingestion of alcohol while taking aspirin can increase risk of GI ulceration. Avoid aspirin use if you have aspirin intolerance, asthma, rhinitis, or a history of anemia (iron poor blood). Also avoid use of aspirin, if possible, one week prior to surgery, as it may increase possibility of post-operative bleeding.

PREGNANCY OR BREASTFEEDING:
Animal studies have indicated an adverse effect

on fetus, but no adequate studies have been performed on humans. In third trimester, aspirin use should be discouraged. No harmful effects have been reported regarding nursing infants, but aspirin use by a nursing mother should be considered a potential risk for a nursing child as the drug will be passed on to the infant in milk. In all cases, a physician should be consulted.

PRECAUTIONS FOR CHILDREN:
In general, administer to infants or children only when consulting a physician and follow instructions on medication.

SPECIAL WARNING:
Aspirin use in children and teenagers with influenza (flu), chicken pox, and other viral infections may be associated with development of Reye's syndrome. This rare but acute and often life-threatening condition has caused permanent brain damage in survivors. Symptoms include: vomiting, lethargy, bellicosity, leading possibly to delirium and coma.

55+

PRECAUTIONS FOR SENIORS:
Seniors generally don't eliminate drugs as efficiently as younger persons, and should avoid high dosages. Buffered effervescent aspirin products contain high sodium content and should be avoided if on a restricted sodium diet. Aspirin use can cause GI irritation and possibly stomach or intestinal bleeding in seniors, manifested usually by dark stools.

SPECIAL WARNINGS:
Always check expiration date on label of medication. Do not take if medication has expired.

Do not take aspirin which emits a vinegar-like odor. This indicates that it is decomposing and is unsafe for use.

INFORM YOUR DOCTOR BEFORE TAKING ASPIRIN IF YOU HAVE:

An allergy to aspirin, are asthmatic, anemic or have other hematological conditions, or have GI sensitivity.

QUICK FACTS

ACTIVE INGREDIENTS:

ASPIRIN AND CAFFEINE COMBINATION

BRAND NAMES:

- ANACIN
- BC POWDER
- COPE
- DRISTAN
- EXCEDRIN
- FENDOL
- GENSAN

SYMPTOMS RELIEVED:

Minor aches and pains such as those associated with the common cold, flu, headache, toothache, sinusitis, hay fever and other respiratory allergies, muscular aches, backache, minor arthritis pain, menstrual discomfort, and reduction of fever.

HOW TO TAKE:

Comes in tablet, caplet, capsule, and powder forms. Swallow with liquid. Sprinkle powder over liquid, then swallow. Do not crush or chew timed-release tablets. Caffeine can cause gastrointestinal (GI) irritation and should be taken with food or following meal.

USUAL ADULT DOSE:

12.5 milligrams every 4 to 6 hours, not to exceed 25 milligrams in a 4 to 6 hour period or 75 milligrams in a 24 hour period.

USUAL CHILD DOSE:

Do not administer to children under 16 unless under direction of physician. Dosage may vary based on infant or child's age.

OVERDOSE SYMPTOMS:
Nervous agitation, disorientation, confusion, severe headache, convulsions, GI bleeding or hemorrhage. If you suspect an overdose, immediately seek medical attention.

SIDE EFFECTS:
No serious effects in most cases of common use, however normal use of caffeine can result in common GI irritations such as heartburn and indigestion. Less common side effects include dizziness, nausea, stomach cramps, and headache.

CHECK WITH YOUR DOCTOR OR PHARMACIST BEFORE COMBINING CAFFEINE WITH:
Antacids, anticoagulants, aspirin, asthma medication, other nonsteroidal anti-inflammatory drugs (NSAIDs), tetracycline, and any other medication. Combination with acetaminophen increases risk of kidney damage. Ingestion of alcohol while taking salicylates can increase risk of GI ulceration. Avoid caffeine if you have a history of anemia. Also avoid use of caffeine, if possible, one week prior to surgery, as it may increase possibility of postoperative bleeding.

PREGNANCY OR BREASTFEEDING:
Animal studies have indicated an adverse effect on fetus, but no adequate studies have been performed on humans. No harmful effects have been reported regarding nursing infants, but caffeine use by a nursing mother should be considered a potential risk for a nursing child as the drug will be passed on to the infant in the mother's milk. In all cases, a physician should be consulted.

QUICK FACTS

PRECAUTIONS FOR CHILDREN:
In general, caffeine and other NSAIDs are not advised for children under 15. Administer caffeine to infants or children only when consulting a physician and follow instructions on medication (see above).

PRECAUTIONS FOR SENIORS:
Seniors generally don't eliminate drugs as efficiently as younger persons, and should avoid high dosages. Seniors (over 65) are at special risk for development of ulcers if taking caffeine in high doses. Prolonged use can also lead to kidney and liver damage.

SPECIAL WARNINGS:
Don't take caffeine medication if you are aspirin intolerant or allergic to other NSAIDs. If in doubt, always consult a pharmacist or physician. Also avoid if you have GI conditions such as gastritis, peptic ulcer, enteritis, ileitis, colitis; asthma, high blood pressure, or hematologic (bleeding) problems. Avoid alcohol while taking this or any other NSAID.

INFORM YOUR DOCTOR BEFORE TAKING CAFFEINE IF YOU HAVE:
An allergy or intolerance to aspirin or other NSAIDs, damaged or impaired renal (kidney) or hepatic (liver) functions, epilepsy, Parkinson's disease or mental illness.

QUICK FACTS

ACTIVE INGREDIENT:
IBUPROFEN

BRAND NAMES:
- Advil
- Advil Cold & Sinus Caplets
- Arthritis Foundation (backache and muscle pain)
- Bayer Select Pain Relief
- Dimetapp
- Dristan Sinus Caplets
- Genpril
- Ibuprohm
- Motrin
- Motrin IB Sinus Caplets
- Nupron
- Obuprin
- Sine-Aid IB Caplets (combination with pseudoephedrine hydrochloride)

SYMPTOMS RELIEVED:
Minor aches and pains such as those associated with the common cold, flu, headache, toothache, sinusitis, hay fever and other respiratory allergies, muscular aches, backache, minor arthritis pain, menstrual discomfort, and reduction of fever.

HOW TO TAKE:
Comes in tablet, caplet, and gelcap forms. Swallow with liquid. Do not crush or chew timed-release tablet. Ibuprofen can cause gastrointestinal (GI) irritation and should be taken with food or following meal.

USUAL ADULT DOSE:
Minor aches and pains: 200 milligrams every

QUICK FACTS

4 to 6 hours as needed, not to exceed 1.2 grams per day.

USUAL CHILD DOSE:
Always consult with a pharmacist or physician. Dosage may vary based on infant or child's age.

Juvenile arthritis: 30 to 70 milligrams per day in 3 or 4 equal doses or as indicated.

Fever reduction: Maximum daily dose not to exceed 40 milligrams. Dosage should be adjusted based on initial temperature level. If less or equal to 102.5°F, 5 milligrams per dose is recommended.

OVERDOSE SYMPTOMS:
Nervous agitation, disorientation, confusion, severe headache, convulsions, GI bleeding or hemorrhage. If you suspect an overdose, immediately seek medical attention.

SIDE EFFECTS:
No serious effects in most cases of common use, however normal use of ibuprofen can result in common GI irritations such as heartburn and indigestion. Less common side effects include dizziness, nausea, stomach cramps, and headache.

CHECK WITH YOUR DOCTOR OR PHARMACIST BEFORE COMBINING IBUPROFEN WITH:
Antacids, anticoagulants, aspirin, asthma medication, other nonsteroidal anti-inflammatory drugs (NSAIDs), tetracycline, and any other medication. Combination with acetaminophen increases risk of kidney damage. Ingestion of alcohol while taking ibuprofen can increase risk of GI ulcera-

tion. Avoid ibuprofen if you have a history of anemia. Also avoid use of ibuprofen, if possible, one week prior to surgery, as it may increase possibility of postoperative bleeding.

PREGNANCY OR BREASTFEEDING:
No harmful effects have been reported regarding nursing infants, but ibuprofen use by a nursing mother should be considered a potential risk for a nursing child as the drug will be passed on to the infant in the mother's milk. In all cases, a physician should be consulted.

PRECAUTIONS FOR CHILDREN:
In general, ibuprofen and other NSAIDs are not advised for children under 15. Administer ibuprofen to infants or children only when consulting a physician and follow instructions on medication.

55+ **PRECAUTIONS FOR SENIORS:**
Seniors generally don't eliminate drugs as efficiently as younger persons, and should avoid high dosages. Seniors (over 65) are at special risk for development of ulcers if taking ibuprofen in high doses. Prolonged use can also lead to kidney and liver damage.

SPECIAL WARNINGS:
Don't take ibuprofen medication if you are aspirin intolerant or allergic to other NSAIDs. If in doubt, always consult a pharmacist or physician. Also avoid if you have GI conditions such as gastritis, peptic ulcer, enteritis, ileitis, colitis; asthma, high blood pressure, or hematologic (bleeding) problems. Avoid alcohol while taking this or any other NSAID.

QUICK FACTS

INFORM YOUR DOCTOR BEFORE TAKING IBUPROFEN IF YOU HAVE:
An allergy or intolerance to aspirin or other NSAIDs, damaged or impaired renal (kidney) or hepatic (liver) functions, epilepsy, Parkinson's disease, or mental illness.

ACTIVE INGREDIENT:
KETOPROFEN

Q U I C K F A C T S

BRAND NAMES:
- ACTRON
- ORUDIS

SYMPTOMS RELIEVED:
Minor aches and pains such as those associated with the common cold, flu, headache, toothache, sinusitis, hay fever and other respiratory allergies, muscular aches, backache, minor arthritis pain, menstrual discomfort, and reduction of fever.

HOW TO TAKE:
Comes in tablet forms. Swallow with liquid. Do not crush or chew timed-release tablets. Ketoprofen can cause gastrointestinal (GI) irritation and should be taken with food or following meal.

USUAL ADULT DOSE:
12.5 milligrams every 4 to 6 hours, not to exceed 25 milligrams in a 4 to 6 hour period or 75 milligrams in a 24 hour period.

USUAL CHILD DOSE:
Do not administer to children under 16 unless under direction of physician. Dosage may vary based on infant or child's age.

OVERDOSE SYMPTOMS:
Nervous agitation, disorientation, confusion, severe headache, convulsions, GI bleeding or hemorrhage. If you suspect an overdose, immediately seek medical attention.

QUICK FACTS

SIDE EFFECTS:
No serious effects in most cases of common use, however normal use of ketoprofen can result in common GI irritations such as heartburn and indigestion. Less common side effects include dizziness, nausea, stomach cramps, and headache.

CHECK WITH YOUR DOCTOR OR PHARMACIST BEFORE COMBINING KETOPROFEN WITH:
Antacids, anticoagulants, aspirin, asthma medication, other nonsteroidal anti-inflammatory drugs (NSAIDs), tetracycline, and any other medication. Combination with acetaminophen increases risk of kidney damage. Ingestion of alcohol while taking ketoprofen can increase risk of GI ulceration. Avoid ketoprofen if you have a history of anemia. Also avoid use of ketoprofen, if possible, one week prior to surgery, as it may increase possibility of postoperative bleeding.

PREGNANCY OR BREASTFEEDING:
Animal studies have indicated an adverse effect on fetus, but no adequate studies have been performed on humans. No harmful effects have been reported regarding nursing infants, but ketoprofen use by a nursing mother should be considered a potential risk for a nursing child as the drug will be passed on to the infant in the mother's milk. In all cases, a physician should be consulted.

PRECAUTIONS FOR CHILDREN:
In general, ketoprofen and other NSAIDs are not advised for children under 15. Administer ketoprofen to infants or children only when

consulting a physician and follow instructions on medication (see above).

PRECAUTIONS FOR SENIORS:
Seniors generally don't eliminate drugs as efficiently as younger persons, and should avoid high dosages. Seniors (over 65) are at special risk for development of ulcers if taking ketoprofen in high doses. Prolonged use can also lead to kidney and liver damage.

SPECIAL WARNINGS:
Don't take ketoprofen medication if you are aspirin intolerant or allergic to other NSAIDs. If in doubt, always consult a pharmacist or physician. Also avoid if you have GI conditions such as gastritis, peptic ulcer, enteritis, ileitis, colitis; asthma, high blood pressure, or hematologic (bleeding) problems. Avoid alcohol while taking this or any other NSAID.

INFORM YOUR DOCTOR BEFORE TAKING KETOPROFEN IF YOU HAVE:
An allergy or intolerance to aspirin or other NSAIDs, damaged or impaired renal (kidney) or hepatic (liver) functions, epilepsy, Parkinson's disease, or mental illness.

QUICK REVIEW

• ANTIHISTAMINES •

The most important considerations in choosing an antihistamine are: its effectiveness in blocking or alleviating effects of histamine on the respiratory system, and the nature and extent of side effects which the drug may produce.

ANTIHISTAMINES ARE A CLASS OF DRUGS WHICH:

- are used in treating allergies and motion sickness,
- block the effects of histamine, a chemical substance released by the body as the result of injury or in reaction to an allergen. Histamine increases capillary permeability, which allows fluids to escape and cause swelling. It also constricts small air passages in the lungs. These properties result in symptoms such as sinus headache, congestion, sneezing, runny nose,wheezing, puffiness, and lowered blood pressure,
- act by blocking or displacing histamine, particularly in the blood vessels, skin, uterus, and bronchioles,
- as a result of the drugs' drying effects, thereby impede drainage and expectoration,
- may produce side effects such as drowsiness, nasal stuffiness, dryness of mouth and sinus passages, dizziness, and common gastrointestinal (GI) irritation or distress,
- are not recommended in treating lower respiratory symptoms including asthma, as the drug's effects may impede expectoration.

Q U I C K F A C T S

ACTIVE INGREDIENT:
ACETAMINOPHEN

BRAND NAMES:
- Unisom with Pain Relief (combination with diphenhydramine hydrochloride)

SYMPTOMS RELIEVED:
Minor aches and pains such as those associated with the common cold, flu, headache, toothache, sinusitis, hay fever and other respiratory allergies, muscular aches, backache, minor arthritis pain, menstrual discomfort, and reduction of fever.

HOW TO TAKE:
Comes in tablet forms. Swallow tablet with liquid. Do not crush or chew timed-release tablet. In proper dosages in most cases, acetaminophen does not cause gastrointestinal (GI) irritation and can be taken with or without food.

USUAL ADULT DOSE:
650 milligrams at bedtime or as directed by your doctor.

USUAL CHILD DOSE:
Unisom is intended for adults only and should not be given to children under 12.

OVERDOSE SYMPTOMS:
Nausea, vomiting, diaphoresis, discomfort, and malaise. In some cases, hepatic toxicity (liver poisoning) may result. If you suspect an overdose, immediately seek medical attention.

SIDE EFFECTS:
Drowsiness. In rare cases: allergic skin eruptions (rash, hives, itch), sore throat and fever,

Q U I C K F A C T S

bleeding or bruising, urinary discomfort or blood in urine, jaundiced skin or eyes may result.

CHECK WITH YOUR DOCTOR OR PHARMACIST BEFORE COMBINING ACETAMINOPHEN AND ANTIHISTAMINE WITH:
Sedatives, tranquilizers, anticoagulants, aspirin and other salicylates, Isoniazid (anti-tuberculosis) medication. Ingestion of alcohol while taking acetaminophen can increase the risk of liver damage or disease (hepatic toxicity).

PREGNANCY OR BREASTFEEDING:
No harmful effects have been reported regarding nursing infants, but ibuprofen use by a nursing mother should be considered a potential risk for a nursing child as the drug will be passed on to the infant in the mother's milk. In all cases, a physician should be consulted.

PRECAUTIONS FOR CHILDREN:
See above.

55+

PRECAUTIONS FOR SENIORS:
Seniors generally don't eliminate drugs as efficiently as younger persons, and should avoid high dosages or chronic use as hepatic (liver) function impairment may result.

SPECIAL WARNINGS:
Avoid alcohol when taking this combination. Chronic alcoholics are also at risk for hepatic (liver) function impairment if taking high dosages.

INFORM YOUR DOCTOR BEFORE TAKING ACETAMINOPHEN IF YOU HAVE:
Liver or kidney disease or damage, an allergy to acetaminophen, or hypoglycemia.

COLDS AND FLU

Q U I C K   R E V I E W

• ANALGESIC •

The most important considerations in choosing an analgesic are: pain relief; anti-inflammatory activity, and allergic reaction or sensitivity to certain active ingredients.

ANALGESICS (NONNARCOTIC) ARE A CLASS OF DRUGS WHICH:

- inhibit the action of prostaglandins (hormonelike substances) in the central nervous system, thereby temporarily reducing the perception of physical pain with little loss of sensibility to other physical sensation,
- are used to temporarily alleviate symptoms such as: headache, fever, backache, sinus pain, muscle strain, menstrual pain, and similar ailments. Some analgesics, such as aspirin (acetylsalicylic acid) and ibuprofen, also provide temporary anti-inflammatory relief for ailments such as arthritis. Aspirin has also been shown to be effective as a blood thinning antiplatelet agent in reducing heart attack and stroke risk,
- can have adverse effects in some instances. Aspirin intolerance can produce allergic and anaphylactic reactions in hypersensitive and asthmatic individuals. Aspirin can also aggravate aggravate gastrointestinal conditions such as heartburn and ulcer. Long-term acetaminophen use can damage liver (hepatic) and kidney (renal) functions.

QUICK FACTS

ACTIVE INGREDIENT:
ACETAMINOPHEN

BRAND NAMES:
Combination with pseudoephedrine hydrochloride:
- Bayer Select Head Cold Caplets/ Maximum Strength Sinus Pain Relief Caplets
- Coldrine Tablets
- Dristan AF (combination with caffeine)
- Dristan Cold Caplets
- Dynafed
- Excedrin Sinus Extra Strength Tablets & Caplets
- Ornex
- Tylenol (various formulations)

SYMPTOMS RELIEVED:
Minor aches and pains such as those associated with the common cold and flu; reduction of fever.

HOW TO TAKE:
Comes in tablet, chewable tablet, caplet, capsule, elixir, liquid, powder, solution. Swallow tablet, capsule, or elixir with liquid. Sprinkle powder over liquid, then swallow. Do not crush or chew timed-release tablet. In proper dosages in most cases, acetaminophen does not cause gastrointestinal (GI) irritation and can be taken with or without food.

USUAL ADULT DOSE:
325 to 650 milligrams every 4 to 6 hours, or 1 gram 3 to 4 times per day, not to exceed 4 grams a day.

Q U I C K F A C T S

USUAL CHILD DOSE:
4 to 5 doses per day, not to exceed 5 doses in 24 hours. Dosage varies based on infant or child's age.

OVERDOSE SYMPTOMS:
Nausea, vomiting, diaphoresis, discomfort, and malaise. In some cases, hepatic toxicity (liver poisoning) may result. If you suspect an overdose, immediately seek medical attention.

SIDE EFFECTS:
None in most cases of common use. Long-term ingestion of high dosages may increase risk of liver and kidney damage. In rare cases, extreme fatigue and drowsiness, allergic skin eruptions (rash, hives, itch), sore throat and fever, bleeding or bruising, urinary discomfort or blood in urine, jaundiced skin or eyes may result.

CHECK WITH YOUR DOCTOR OR PHARMACIST BEFORE COMBINING ACETAMINOPHEN WITH:
Anticoagulants, aspirin and other salicylates, Isoniazid (anti-tuberculosis) medication. Excessive ingestion of alcohol while taking acetaminophen can increase the risk of liver damage or disease (hepatic toxicity).

PREGNANCY OR BREASTFEEDING:
No conclusive evidence of effects on fetus—benign or adverse—has been established. High dosage has in isolated cases caused anemia in mother and kidney failure in fetus. Nursing infants have shown no harmful effects.

PRECAUTIONS FOR CHILDREN:
In general, administer to infants or children

only when consulting a physician and follow instructions on medication.

55+ **PRECAUTIONS FOR SENIORS:**
Seniors generally don't eliminate drugs as efficiently as younger persons, and should avoid high dosages.

SPECIAL WARNINGS:
Chronic alcoholics are at risk for hepatic (liver) function impairment if taking high dosages of acetaminophen.

INFORM YOUR DOCTOR BEFORE TAKING ACETAMINOPHEN IF YOU HAVE:
Liver or kidney disease or damage, an allergy to acetaminophen, or hypoglycemia.

QUICK FACTS

QUICK FACTS

ACTIVE INGREDIENTS:

ACETAMINOPHEN, ASPIRIN, AND CAFFEINE COMBINATION

BRAND NAMES:

- Buffets II Tablets
- Excedrin Extra-Strength
- Gelpirin
- Goody's Extra Strength Headache Powders
- Pain Reliever Tabs
- Supac
- Vanquish

SYMPTOMS RELIEVED:
Minor aches and pains such as those associated with the common cold and flu; reduction of fever.

HOW TO TAKE:
Comes in tablet, caplet, capsule, and powder forms. Swallow with liquid. Sprinkle powder over liquid, then swallow. Do not crush or chew timed-release tablets. Aspirin and caffeine both can cause gastrointestinal (GI) irritation and should be taken with food or following meal.

USUAL ADULT DOSE:
1 or 2 capsules, tablets, caplets or 1 powder packet every 2 to 6 hours.

ACTIVE INGREDIENTS:

ACETAMINOPHEN AND CAFFEINE COMBINATION

BRAND NAMES:
- Bayer Select Maximum Strength
- Excedrin Aspirin-Free
- Fendol

SYMPTOMS RELIEVED:
Minor aches and pains such as those associated with the common cold and flu; reduction of fever.

HOW TO TAKE:
Comes in tablet, caplet, capsule, and powder forms. Swallow with liquid. Sprinkle powder over liquid, then swallow. Do not crush or chew timed-release tablets. Caffeine can cause gastrointestinal (GI) irritation and should be taken with food or following a meal.

USUAL ADULT DOSE:
12.5 milligrams every 4 to 6 hours, not to exceed 25 milligrams in a 4 to 6 hour period or 75 milligrams in a 24 hour period.

USUAL CHILD DOSE:
Do not administer to children under 16 unless under direction of physician. Dosage may vary based on infant or child's age.

OVERDOSE SYMPTOMS:
Nervous agitation, disorientation, confusion, severe headache, convulsions, GI bleeding, or hemorrhage. If you suspect an overdose, seek medical attention immediately.

Q U I C K F A C T S

SIDE EFFECTS:
No serious effects in most cases of common use, however normal use of caffeine can result in common GI irritations such as heartburn and indigestion. Less common side effects include dizziness, nausea, stomach cramps, and headache.

CHECK WITH YOUR DOCTOR OR PHARMACIST BEFORE COMBINING ACETAMINOPHEN OR CAFFEINE WITH:
Antacids, anticoagulants, aspirin, asthma medication, other nonsteroidal anti-inflammatory drugs (NSAIDs), tetracycline, and any other medication.

PREGNANCY OR BREASTFEEDING:
Animal studies have indicated an adverse effect on fetus, but no adequate studies have been performed on humans. No harmful effects have been reported regarding nursing infants, but caffeine use by a nursing mother should be considered a potential risk for a nursing child as the drug will be passed on to the infant in the mother's milk. In all cases, a physician should be consulted.

PRECAUTIONS FOR CHILDREN:
In general, caffeine and other NSAIDs are not advised for children under 15. Administer caffeine to infants or children only when consulting a physician and follow instructions on medication (see above).

PRECAUTIONS FOR SENIORS:
Seniors generally don't eliminate drugs as efficiently as younger persons, and should avoid

high dosages. Seniors (over 65) are at special risk for development of ulcers if taking caffeine in high doses. Prolonged use can also lead to kidney and liver damage.

SPECIAL WARNINGS:
Don't take caffeine medication if you are aspirin intolerant or allergic to other NSAIDs. If in doubt, always consult a pharmacist or physician. Also avoid if you have GI conditions such as gastritis, peptic ulcer, enteritis, ileitis, colitis; asthma, high blood pressure, or hematologic (bleeding) problems. Avoid alcohol while taking this or any other NSAID.

INFORM YOUR DOCTOR BEFORE TAKING CAFFEINE IF YOU HAVE:
An allergy or intolerance to aspirin or other NSAIDs, damaged or impaired renal (kidney) or hepatic (liver) functions, epilepsy, Parkinson's disease or mental illness.

QUICK FACTS

ACTIVE INGREDIENTS:

ACETAMINOPHEN, CHLORPHENIRAMINE MALEATE, DEXTROMETHORPHAN HYDROBROMIDE, AND PSEUDOEPHREDINE HYDROCHLORIDE

℞ **BRAND NAMES:**

- Alka-Seltzer Plus Cold & Cough Liqui-Gels (also contains sorbitol)
- Bayer Select Flu Relief Caplets
- Co-Apap Tablets
- Comtrex Liquid (also contains alcohol, sucrose)
- Comtrex Liqui-Gels (contains sorbitol)
- Comtrex Maximum Liqui-Gels (contains sorbitol)
- Comtrex Max Strength Multi-Symptom Cold & Flu Relief Liqui-Gels
- Comtrex Maximum Strength Multi-Symptom Cold & Flu Relief Caplets & Tablets (contains parabens)
- Contac Severe Cold & Flu Nighttime Liquid (also contains alcohol, saccharin, sorbitol, glucose)
- Genacol Tablets
- Kolephrin/DM Caplets
- Mapap Cold Formula Tablets
- Medi-Flu Liquid (also contains alcohol, saccharin, sorbitol, sugar)
- TheraFlu Flu Cold & Cough Powder (contains sucrose)
- TheraFlu Nighttime Flu Powder (contains sucrose)
- Tylenol Children's Cold Multi-Symptom Plus Cough Liquid (also contains sorbitol, corn syrup)

- Tylenol Multi-Symptom Cold Caplets & Tablets
- Tylenol Multi-Symptom Hot Medication Powder (combination with phenylalanine, also contains aspartame, sucrose)
- Vicks Children's NyQuil Nighttime Cold/Cough Liquid (also contains sucrose)
- Vicks 44M Cold, Flu & Cough LiquiCaps
- Vicks Pediatric Formula 44M Multi-Symptom Cough & Cold Liquid (also contains sorbitol, sucrose)

Note: *Dextromethorphan hydrobromide* is also an active ingredient in other multi-symptom antitussive/expectorant medications which are formulated with other active ingredients.

Pseudoephredine hydrochloride is a used as an active ingredient in decongestant and stimulant products.

Acetaminophen is a non-aspirin analgesic which is used primarily in pain-relief products.

Chlorpheniramine maleate is an antihistamine which is mostly used in combination with analgesic, antitussive, decongestant, and expectorant active ingredients in OTC medications to provide relief of allergy, common cold, cough, or flu symptoms.

SYMPTOMS RELIEVED:

Minor aches and pains such as those associated with the common cold and flu; reduction of fever.

HOW TO TAKE:

Comes in tablet, caplet, capsule, and liquid forms. Swallow tablet, caplet, or capsule with liquid. Sprinkle powder over liquid, then swallow. Do not crush or chew timed-release tablet.

USUAL ADULT DOSE:
Dosage varies per product and active ingredient formulation. Follow product dosage instructions.

USUAL CHILD DOSE:
Do not administer to children under 6 unless under direction of physician. Dosage may vary based on infant or child's age.

OVERDOSE SYMPTOMS:
Nervous agitation, severe anxiety, insomnia (sleeplessness), hallucinations, tremors, convulsions, nausea, vomiting, cardiac arrhythmia (irregular pulse and heartbeat), drowsiness, dizziness, fatigue, rash. If you suspect an overdose, immediately seek medical attention.

SIDE EFFECTS:
No serious effects in most cases of common use, although antihistamines can cause drowsiness. Less common side effects include nasal dryness, dizziness, nausea, and mild insomnia palpitations, insomnia, gastrointestinal (GI) upset including stomach cramps and diarrhea, drowsiness, and fatigue. In rare cases, more severe side effects may result, including: painful and frequent urination, hypertension, and heart palpitations. In these cases, discontinue medication and call your doctor immediately. Long-term ingestion of high dosages of acetaminophen-containing products may increase risk of liver and kidney damage.

CHECK WITH YOUR DOCTOR OR PHARMACIST BEFORE COMBINING THESE COMBINATION PRODUCTS WITH:
Anticoagulant medications, other cold, cough, or allergy medication, stimulants, antidepressants, antihypertensives, digitalis or other heart medication, diuretics, or MAO (monoamine oxidase inhibitors) drugs. Ingestion of caffeinated beverages (coffee, tea, caffeine-containing soft drinks) while taking pseudoephredine-containing medication can result in agitation and insomnia.
If taking combination products which contain acetaminophen, you should avoid Isoniazid (anti-tuberculosis) medication. Excessive ingestion of alcohol while taking acetaminophen-containing medication can increase the risk of liver damage or disease (hepatic toxicity). Alcohol use may also increase possible drowsiness effect of the antihistamine in these combination products.

PREGNANCY OR BREASTFEEDING:
Use of medications containing any of the active ingredients in these products by a nursing mother should be considered a potential risk for a nursing child as the drug(s) will be passed on to the infant in the mother's milk. In all cases, a physician should be consulted.

PRECAUTIONS FOR CHILDREN:
In general, these active ingredients are not advised for children under 2. Administer to infants or children only when consulting a physician and follow instructions on medication (see above).

55+ **PRECAUTIONS FOR SENIORS:**
Seniors generally don't eliminate drugs as

efficiently as younger persons, and should avoid high dosages. Use of antihistamine-containing medications by seniors can lead to urinary difficulties. In addition, seniors are more likely to experience potential drowsiness effects of the antihistamine in this combination.

SPECIAL WARNINGS:
Do not use for control of chronic cough related to conditions such as emphysema, asthma, or smoking, or if coughs are producing excessive secretions. If cough is accompanied by high fever, rash, nausea or vomiting, or persistent headache, use only if directed by your doctor. Because antihistamines may cause drowsiness, you should avoid activities or tasks such as driving, or other operations which require alertness, coordination, dexterity, or quick reflexes. Chronic alcoholics are at risk for hepatic (liver) function impairment if taking high dosages of acetaminophen-containing medication. Do not use medications which combine doxylamine succinate with tartrazine if you are intolerant or hypersensitive to aspirin. Allergic reactions, including bronchial asthma, have occurred in susceptible individuals.

ADDITIONAL WARNING:
Alcohol: Some cough/cold medications contain various amounts of alcohol. Check label of any cough medication if concerned about ingestion of alcohol.

Sugar/Sweeteners: Some cough/cold medications contain various amounts of sugar, sucrose, glucose, and/or artificial sweeteners such as aspartame, saccharin, sorbitol. Check label of cough medication before selecting, if concerned about diabetes and ingestion of sugar or artificial sweeteners.

Abuse/Dependency: Reports indicate a rising rate of abuse of dextromethorphan-containing medications, particularly among teens. Sufficient data has not yet been collected, however, to determine the abuse and dependency potential of dextromethorphan-containing medications.

INFORM YOUR DOCTOR BEFORE TAKING PRODUCTS CONTAINING THIS COMBINATION OF ACTIVE INGREDIENTS IF YOU HAVE:
Asthma, emphysema or other respiratory condition, liver impairment or liver disease, allergies to any sympathomimetic drug, aspirin or other salicylates, or if you have diabetes, thyroid condition, or urinary difficulty. If you anticipate any surgery requiring general or spinal anesthesia within 2 months of taking medication which contains pseudoephredine, inform your doctor.

QUICK FACTS

ACTIVE INGREDIENTS:
ACETAMINOPHEN, DEXTROMETHORPHAN HYDROBROMIDE, DOXYLAMINE SUCCINATE, AND PSEUDOEPHREDINE HYDROCHLORIDE

Rx **BRAND NAMES:**

- Alka-Seltzer Plus Nighttime Cold Liqui-Gels
  (also contains sorbitol)
- Genite Liquid
  (also contains alcohol, tartrazine)
- NyQuil Hot Therapy Powder
  (also contains sucrose)
- NyQuil Nighttime Cold/Flu Medicine Liquid
  (also contains alcohol, sucrose, saccharin [cherry flavor], tartrazine [original flavor])
- Vicks NyQuil LiquiCaps

Note: *Dextromethorphan hydrobromide* is also an active ingredient in other multi-symptom antitussive/expectorant medications which are formulated with other active ingredients.

Pseudoephredine hydrochloride is a used as an active ingredient in decongestant and stimulant products.

Acetaminophen is a non-aspirin analgesic which is used primarily in pain-relief products.

Doxylamine succinate is a drowsiness-producing antihistamine which is mostly used in combination with analgesic, antitussive, decongestant, and expectorant active ingredients in OTC medications to provide nighttime relief of allergy, common cold, cough or flu symptoms. It is also used as a sleep aid.

SYMPTOMS RELIEVED:
Minor aches and pains such as those associated with the common cold and flu; reduction of fever.

HOW TO TAKE:
Comes in capsule, liquid, and powder forms. Swallow capsule with liquid. Sprinkle powder over liquid, then swallow. Do not crush or chew timed-release capsule.

USUAL ADULT DOSE:
Dosage varies per product and active ingredient formulation. Follow product dosage instructions.

USUAL CHILD DOSE:
Do not administer to children under 6 unless under direction of physician. Dosage may vary based on infant or child's age.

OVERDOSE SYMPTOMS:
Nervous agitation, severe anxiety, insomnia (sleeplessness), hallucinations, tremors, convulsions, nausea, vomiting, cardiac arrhythmia (irregular pulse and heartbeat), drowsiness, dizziness, fatigue, rash. If you suspect an overdose, immediately seek medical attention.

SIDE EFFECTS:
No serious effects in most cases of common use, although antihistamines often cause drowsiness. Less common side effects include nasal dryness, dizziness, nausea, and mild insomnia palpitations, insomnia, gastrointestinal (GI) upset including stomach cramps and diarrhea, drowsiness, and fatigue. In rare cases, more severe side effects may result, including: painful and

QUICK FACTS

QUICK FACTS

frequent urination, hypertension, and heart palpitations. In these cases, discontinue medication and call your doctor immediately. Long-term ingestion of high dosages of acetaminophen-containing products may increase risk of liver and kidney damage.

CHECK WITH YOUR DOCTOR OR PHARMACIST BEFORE COMBINING THESE COMBINATION PRODUCTS WITH:

Anticoagulant medications, other cold, cough, or allergy medication, stimulants, antidepressants, antihypertensives, digitalis or other heart medication, diuretics, or MAO (monoamine oxidase inhibitors) drugs. Ingestion of caffeinated beverages (coffee, tea, caffeine-containing soft drinks) while taking pseudoephredine-containing medication can result in agitation and insomnia.

If taking combination products which contain acetaminophen, you should avoid Isoniazid (anti-tuberculosis) medication. Excessive ingestion of alcohol while taking acetaminophen-containing medication can increase the risk of liver damage or disease (hepatic toxicity). Alcohol use may also increase drowsiness effect of the antihistamine doxylamine succinate in these combination products.

PREGNANCY OR BREASTFEEDING:

Use of medications containing any of the active ingredients in these products by a nursing mother should be considered a potential risk for a nursing child as the drug(s) will be passed on to the infant in the mother's milk. In all cases, a physician should be consulted.

PRECAUTIONS FOR CHILDREN:
In general, these active ingredients are not advised for children under 2. Administer to infants or children only when consulting a physician and follow instructions on medication (see above).

PRECAUTIONS FOR SENIORS:
Seniors generally don't eliminate drugs as efficiently as younger persons, and should avoid high dosages. Use of doxylamine succinate-containing medications by seniors can lead to urinary difficulties. In addition, seniors are more likely to experience drowsiness effects of doxylamine succinate.

SPECIAL WARNINGS:
Do not use for control of chronic cough related to conditions such as emphysema, asthma, or smoking, or if coughs are producing excessive secretions. If cough is accompanied by high fever, rash, nausea or vomiting, or persistent headache, use only if directed by your doctor. Because antihistamines such as doxylamine succinate often cause drowsiness, you should avoid activities or tasks such as driving, or other operations which require alertness, coordination, dexterity, or quick reflexes. Chronic alcoholics are at risk for hepatic (liver) function impairment if taking high dosages of acetaminophen-containing medication. Do not use medications which combine doxylamine succinate with tartrazine if you are intolerant or hypersensitive to aspirin. Allergic reactions, including bronchial asthma, have occurred in susceptible individuals.

Q U I C K F A C T S

ADDITIONAL WARNING:
Alcohol: Some cough/cold medications contain various amounts of alcohol. Check label of any cough medication if concerned about ingestion of alcohol.

Sugar/Sweeteners: Some cough/cold medications contain various amounts of sugar, sucrose, glucose, and/or artificial sweeteners such as aspartame, saccharin, sorbitol. Check label of cough medication before selecting, if concerned about diabetes and ingestion of sugar or artificial sweeteners.

Abuse/Dependency: Reports indicate a rising rate of abuse of dextromethorphan-containing medications, particularly among teens. Sufficient data has not yet been collected, however, to determine the abuse and dependency potential of dextromethorphan-containing medications.

INFORM YOUR DOCTOR BEFORE TAKING PRODUCTS CONTAINING THIS COMBINATION OF ACTIVE INGREDIENTS IF YOU HAVE:
Asthma, emphysema or other respiratory condition, liver impairment or liver disease, allergies to any sympathomimetic drug, aspirin or other salicylates, or if you have diabetes, thyroid condition, or urinary difficulty. If you anticipate any surgery requiring general or spinal anesthesia within 2 months of taking medication which contains pseudoephredine, inform your doctor.

ACTIVE INGREDIENTS:

ACETAMINOPHEN, DEXTROMETHORPHAN HYDROBROMIDE, AND PSEUDOEPHREDINE HYDROCHLORIDE

QUICK FACTS

℞ **BRAND NAMES:**

- ALKA-SELTZER PLUS FLU & BODY ACHES NON-DROWSY LIQUI-GELS
- BAYER SELECT NIGHTTIME COLD CAPLETS (combination with tripolidine hydrochloride)
- COMTREX MAXIMUM STRENGTH NON-DROWSY CAPLETS
- CONTAC DAY & NIGHT COLD & FLU CAPLETS (combination with diphenhydramine hydrochloride)
- ROBITUSSIN NIGHT RELIEF LIQUID (also contains saccharin, sorbitol)
- SALETO CF TABLETS
- SUDAFED SEVERE COLD CAPLETS & TABLETS
- THERAFLU NON-DROWSY FORMULA MAXIMUM STRENGTH CAPLETS (also contains lactose, methylparaben)
- THERAFLU NON-DROWSY FLU, COLD & COUGH MAXIMUM STRENGTH POWDER (also contains sucrose)
- TRIAMINIC SORE THROAT FORMULA LIQUID (also contains EDTA, sucrose)
- TYLENOL COLD NO DROWSINESS CAPLETS & GELCAPS/MAXIMUM STRENGTH GELCAPS
- TYLENOL MAXIMUM STRENGTH COUGH WITH DECONGESTANT LIQUID (also contains alcohol, saccharin, sorbitol, sucrose)

Note: *Dextromethorphan hydrobromide* is also an active ingredient in other multi-symptom

QUICK FACTS

antitussive/expectorant medications which are formulated with other active ingredients.

Pseudoephredine hydrochloride is a used as an active ingredient in decongestant and stimulant products.

Acetaminophen is a non-aspirin analgesic which is used primarily in pain-relief products.

SYMPTOMS RELIEVED:
Minor aches and pains such as those associated with the common cold and flu; reduction of fever.

HOW TO TAKE:
Comes in caplet, capsule, and liquid forms. Swallow caplet or capsule with liquid. Sprinkle powder over liquid, then swallow. Do not crush or chew timed-release tablet.

USUAL ADULT DOSE:
Dosage varies per product and active ingredient formulation. Follow product dosage instructions.

USUAL CHILD DOSE:
Do not administer to children under 6 unless under direction of physician. Dosage may vary based on infant or child's age.

OVERDOSE SYMPTOMS:
Nervous agitation, severe anxiety, insomnia (sleeplessness), hallucinations, tremors, convulsions, nausea, vomiting, cardiac arrhythmia (irregular pulse and heartbeat), drowsiness, dizziness, fatigue, rash. If you suspect an overdose, immediately seek medical attention.

SIDE EFFECTS:
No serious effects in most cases of common use. Less common side effects include nasal dryness, dizziness, nausea, and mild insomnia palpitations, insomnia, gastrointestinal (GI) upset including stomach cramps and diarrhea, drowsiness and fatigue. In rare cases, more severe side effects may result, including: painful and frequent urination, hypertension, and heart palpitations. In these cases, discontinue medication and call your doctor immediately. Long-term ingestion of high dosages of acetaminophen-containing products may increase risk of liver and kidney damage.

CHECK WITH YOUR DOCTOR OR PHARMACIST BEFORE COMBINING THESE COMBINATION PRODUCTS WITH:
Anticoagulant medications, other cold, cough, or allergy medication, stimulants, antidepressants, antihypertensives, digitalis or other heart medication, diuretics, or MAO (monoamine oxidase inhibitors) drugs. Ingestion of caffeinated beverages (coffee, tea, caffeine-containing soft drinks) while taking pseudoephredine-containing medication can result in agitation and insomnia.
If taking combination products which contain acetaminophen, you should avoid Isoniazid (anti-tuberculosis) medication. Excessive ingestion of alcohol while taking acetaminophen-containing medication can increase the risk of liver damage or disease (hepatic toxicity).

PREGNANCY OR BREASTFEEDING:
Use of medications containing any of the active ingredients in these products by a nursing

Q U I C K F A C T S

mother should be considered a potential risk for a nursing child as the drug(s) will be passed on to the infant in the mother's milk. In all cases, a physician should be consulted.

PRECAUTIONS FOR CHILDREN:
In general, these active ingredients are not advised for children under 2.

55+ **PRECAUTIONS FOR SENIORS:**
Seniors generally don't eliminate drugs as efficiently as younger persons, and should avoid high dosages. Use of pseudoephedrine-containing medications by seniors can lead to urinary difficulties. In addition, seniors are more likely to experience stimulant effects of pseudoephedrine.

SPECIAL WARNINGS:
Do not use for control of chronic cough related to conditions such as emphysema, asthma, or smoking, or if coughs are producing excessive secretions. If cough is accompanied by high fever, rash, nausea or vomiting, or persistent headache, use only if directed by your doctor. Chronic alcoholics are at risk for hepatic (liver) function impairment if taking high dosages of acetaminophen-containing medication.

ADDITIONAL WARNING:
Alcohol: Some cough/cold medications contain various amounts of alcohol. Check label of any cough medication if concerned about ingestion of alcohol.

Sugar/Sweeteners: Some cough/cold medications contain various amounts of sugar, sucrose, glucose, and/or artificial sweeteners such as aspartame, saccharin, sorbitol. Check label of cough medication before selecting, if concerned about diabetes and ingestion of sugar or artificial sweeteners.

Abuse/Dependency: Reports indicate a rising rate of abuse of dextromethorphan-containing medications, particularly among teens. Sufficient data has not yet been collected, however, to determine the abuse and dependency potential of dextromethorphan-containing medications.

INFORM YOUR DOCTOR BEFORE TAKING PRODUCTS CONTAINING THIS COMBINATION OF ACTIVE INGREDIENTS IF YOU HAVE:
Asthma, emphysema or other respiratory condition, liver impairment or liver disease, allergies to any sympathomimetic drug, aspirin or other salicylates, or if you have diabetes, thyroid condition, or urinary difficulty. If you anticipate any surgery requiring general or spinal anesthesia within 2 months of taking medication which contains pseudoephredine, inform your doctor.

QUICK FACTS

ACTIVE INGREDIENT:
IBUPROFEN

BRAND NAMES:
- ADVIL COLD & SINUS CAPLETS
- DIMETAPP
- DRISTAN SINUS CAPLETS
- MOTRIN IB SINUS CAPLETS
- NUPRON
- SINE-AID IB CAPLETS (combination with pseudoephedrine hydrochloride)

SYMPTOMS RELIEVED:
Minor aches and pains such as those associated with the common cold and flu; reduction of fever.

HOW TO TAKE:
Comes in tablet, caplet, and gelcap forms. Swallow with liquid. Do not crush or chew timed-release tablet. Ibuprofen can cause gastrointestinal (GI) irritation and should be taken with food or following meal.

USUAL ADULT DOSE:
Minor aches and pains: 200 milligrams every 4 to 6 hours as needed, not to exceed 1.2 grams per day.

USUAL CHILD DOSE:
Always consult with a pharmacist or physician. Dosage may vary based on infant or child's age.

Fever reduction: Maximum daily dose not to exceed 40 milligrams. Dosage should be adjusted based on initial temperature level. If less or equal to 102.5°F, 5 milligrams per dose is recommended. If temperature is greater than 102.5°F, 10 milligrams per dose is recommended.

OVERDOSE SYMPTOMS:
Nervous agitation, disorientation, confusion, severe headache, convulsions, GI bleeding or hemorrhage. If you suspect an overdose, immediately seek medical attention.

SIDE EFFECTS:
No serious effects in most cases of common use, however normal use of ibuprofen can result in common GI irritations such as heartburn and indigestion. Less common side effects include dizziness, nausea, stomach cramps, and headache.

CHECK WITH YOUR DOCTOR OR PHARMACIST BEFORE COMBINING IBUPROFEN WITH:
Antacids, anticoagulants, aspirin, asthma medication, other nonsteroidal anti-inflammatory drugs (NSAIDs), tetracycline, and any other medication. Combination with acetaminophen increases risk of kidney damage. Ingestion of alcohol while taking ibuprofen can increase risk of GI ulceration. Avoid ibuprofen if you have a history of anemia. Also avoid use of ibuprofen, if possible, one week prior to surgery, as it may increase possibility of postoperative bleeding.

PREGNANCY OR BREASTFEEDING:
Animal studies have indicated an adverse effect on fetus, but no adequate studies have been performed on humans. No harmful effects have been reported regarding nursing infants, but ibuprofen use by a nursing mother should be considered a potential risk for a nursing child as the drug will be passed on to the infant in the mother's milk. In all cases, a physician should be consulted.

Q U I C K F A C T S

PRECAUTIONS FOR CHILDREN:
In general, ibuprofen and other NSAIDs are not advised for children under 15.

PRECAUTIONS FOR SENIORS:
Seniors generally don't eliminate drugs as efficiently as younger persons, and should avoid high dosages. Seniors (over 65) are at special risk for development of ulcers if taking ibuprofen in high doses. Prolonged use can also lead to kidney and liver damage.

SPECIAL WARNINGS:
Don't take ibuprofen medication if you are aspirin intolerant or allergic to other NSAIDs. If in doubt, always consult a pharmacist or physician. Also avoid if you have GI conditions such as gastritis, peptic ulcer, enteritis, ileitis, colitis; asthma, high blood pressure, or hematologic (bleeding) problems. Avoid alcohol while taking this or any other NSAID.

INFORM YOUR DOCTOR BEFORE TAKING IBUPROFEN IF YOU HAVE:
An allergy or intolerance to aspirin or other NSAIDs, damaged or impaired renal (kidney) or hepatic (liver) functions, epilepsy, Parkinson's disease, or mental illness.

ACTIVE INGREDIENT:

CAMPHOR

Q U I C K F A C T S

BRAND NAMES:

- MENTHOLATUM CHERRY CHEST RUB FOR KIDS (combination with menthol, eucalyptus oil—also contains fragrance, petrolatum, steareth-2, titanium dioxide)
- MENTHOLATUM OINTMENT (combination with menthol, eucalyptus oil—also contains fragrance, petrolatum, titanium dioxide)
- VICKS VAPORUB–CREAM (combination with menthol, eucalyptus oil—also contains cedarleaf oil, nutmeg oil, special petrolatum, spirits of turpentine, thymol)
- VICKS VAPORUB–OINTMENT (combination with menthol, eucalyptus oil—also contains carbomer 954, cedarleaf oil, cetyl alcohol, cetyl palminate, dimethicone, glycerin, imidazoliyl urea, isopropyl palminate, methylparaben, nutmeg oil, stearate, propylparaben, sodium hydroxide, spirits of turpentine, stearic acid, stearyl alcohol, thymol, titanium dioxide)

SYMPTOMS RELIEVED:

Nasal, sinus, and chest congestion, cough, and minor aches and pains of muscles associated with common cold, head cold, and flu.

HOW TO USE:

Comes in ointment and cream forms. Apply to affected areas. These products are for external use only. Do not swallow. Avoid contact with eyes while applying.

USUAL ADULT DOSE:

See specific product instructions. Generally,

QUICK FACTS

apply externally to chest, throat, or below nostrils not more than 3 to 4 times per day, or as directed by your doctor. In all cases follow specific product instructions.

USUAL CHILD DOSE:
For ages 2 to 12: Apply same as adult, or as directed by your doctor. In all cases follow specific product instructions.

Only apply to children under 2 under doctor's supervision or direction. In all cases follow specific product instructions.

OVERDOSE SYMPTOMS:
None known.

SIDE EFFECTS:
No serious effects in most cases of common use.

CHECK WITH YOUR DOCTOR OR PHARMACIST BEFORE COMBINING THIS PRODUCT WITH:
Any other drugs and preparations.

PREGNANCY OR BREASTFEEDING:
Safety of this drug for use during pregnancy or while nursing has not been established. In all cases you should consult your doctor before using any drug during pregnancy or while nursing.

PRECAUTIONS FOR CHILDREN:
These products should only be used with doctor's supervision or direction for children under 2. Consult your doctor and follow instructions on medication (see above).

55+ **PRECAUTIONS FOR SENIORS:**
None known.

SPECIAL WARNINGS:
Do not use these products if you are allergic to camphor, menthol, or any of the inactive ingredients contained in these products. Do not apply these products to wounds, lesions, broken, damaged, or sensitive skin. Avoid contact with eyes and mucous membranes. Do not use in mouth or nose. Unless directed by your doctor, do not use these products to treat symptoms of persistent or chronic cough, such as those associated with smoking, asthma, emphysema, or coughs with excessive phlegm.

INFORM YOUR DOCTOR BEFORE USING THESE PRODUCTS IF YOU HAVE:
Any allergies, or if you are or plan to become pregnant during time that you will be taking this product.

QUICK REVIEW

• ANESTHETIC •
(TOPICAL)

The most important considerations in choosing a topical or local anesthetic are: its action in partially or completely eliminating the sensation of physical pain in one part of the body, and potential side effects associated with the drug.

TOPICAL ANESTHETICS ARE A CLASS OF DRUGS WHICH:

- act in some combination of the following ways: by limiting the production of energy in nerve cells—thereby reducing nerve impulses and related sensation of pain, by increasing the body's production of organic compounds which limit the transmission of pain messages through synapses, or by reducing nerve cell energy production, thereby limiting the cell's production of nerve impulses. These actions are not completely understood due to varying effects of topical anesthetics and the complex nature of the body's central nervous system (CNS),
- especially when used in high dosages or for long treatment periods, may be absorbed into the blood stream through the skin or mucous membranes, increasing the anesthetic's effectiveness but also the incidence and probability of adverse side effects,
- do not affect the underlying cause of the symptoms which they are designed to relieve or suppress.

ACTIVE INGREDIENT:
DYCLONINE HYDROCHLORIDE

BRAND NAMES:
- CEPACOL MAXIMUM STRENGTH SORE THROAT SPRAY/CHERRY AND COOL MENTHOL (also contains cetylpyridinium chloride, dibasic sodium phosphate, flavors, glycerin, phosphoric acid, poloxamer, potassium sorbate, sorbitol—may also contain saccharin)

SYMPTOMS RELIEVED:
Minor sore throat and sore mouth pain, including pain associated with common cold, canker sores, and minor oral irritation or pain caused by dental or orthodontic procedures.

HOW TO TAKE:
Comes in spray form. Spray into throat or affected area of mouth or gums, and swallow.

USUAL ADULT DOSE:
Spray 4 times, not to exceed 4 doses per day, or as directed by your doctor or dentist. In all cases follow specific product instructions.

USUAL CHILD DOSE:
For ages 2 to 12: Spray 2 to 3 times, not to exceed 4 doses per day, or as directed by your doctor or dentist. Children should be supervised when administering this product. In all cases follow specific product instructions.

Only administer to children under 2 under doctor or dentist's supervision or direction. In all cases follow specific product instructions.

OVERDOSE SYMPTOMS:
None known.

QUICK FACTS

SIDE EFFECTS:
No serious effects in most cases of common use.

CHECK WITH YOUR DOCTOR OR PHARMACIST BEFORE COMBINING THIS COMBINATION WITH:
Any other drugs and preparations.

PREGNANCY OR BREASTFEEDING:
Safety of this drug for use during pregnancy or while nursing has not been established. In all cases you should consult your doctor before using any drug during pregnancy or while nursing.

PRECAUTIONS FOR CHILDREN:
This product should only be used with doctor or dentist's supervision or direction for children under 2. Consult your doctor or dentist and follow instructions on medication (see above).

PRECAUTIONS FOR SENIORS:
Seniors generally don't eliminate drugs as efficiently as younger persons, and should avoid high dosages.

SPECIAL WARNINGS:
Do not use this product if you are allergic to dyclonine hydrochloride or any of the inactive ingredients contained in this product. Call your doctor if sore throat persists longer than two days, or is severe, and is accompanied by other symptoms such as fever, headache, rash, nausea or vomiting, or other severe symptoms.

INFORM YOUR DOCTOR BEFORE TAKING THIS PRODUCT IF YOU HAVE:
Any allergies, any of the symptoms listed above, or if you are or plan to become pregnant during time that you will be taking this product.

• ANTI-INFLAMMATORY •

The most important considerations in choosing an anti-inflammatory agent (nonsteroidal anti-inflammatory drug or "NSAID") are: pain relief; anti-inflammatory activity, and the potential for allergic reaction or sensitivity to certain active ingredients.

ANTI-INFLAMMATORY AGENTS (NSAIDS) ARE A CLASS OF DRUGS WHICH:

- inhibit the action of prostaglandins (hormonelike substances) in the central nervous system, thereby temporarily reducing the perception of physical pain with little loss of sensibility to other physical sensation,
- are used both for their anti-inflammatory and analgesic properties, to temporarily alleviate symptoms such as: headache, fever, backache, sinus pain, muscle strain, menstrual pain, and similar ailments. Some NSAIDs also provide temporary anti-inflammatory relief for ailments such as rheumatoid arthritis and osteoarthritis,
- can have adverse effects in some instances such as aggravation of gastrointestinal (GI) conditions such as heartburn and ulcer, and can produce allergic reactions in persons who are aspirin-intolerant or hypersensitive.

See also: Analgesics

QUICK FACTS

ACTIVE INGREDIENT:
IBUPROFEN

BRAND NAMES:
- ADVIL COLD & SINUS CAPLETS
- DIMETAPP
- DRISTAN SINUS CAPLETS
- MOTRIN IB SINUS CAPLETS
- NUPRON
- SINE-AID IB CAPLETS
(combination with pseudoephedrine hydrochloride)

SYMPTOMS RELIEVED:
Minor aches and pains such as those associated with the common cold and flu; reduction of fever.

HOW TO TAKE:
Comes in tablet, caplet, and gelcap forms. Swallow with liquid. Do not crush or chew timed-release tablet. Ibuprofen can cause gastrointestinal (GI) irritation and should be taken with food or following meal.

USUAL ADULT DOSE:
Minor aches and pains: 200 milligrams every 4 to 6 hours as needed, not to exceed 1.2 grams per day.

USUAL CHILD DOSE:
Always consult with a pharmacist or physician. Dosage may vary based on infant or child's age. *Fever reduction:* Maximum daily dose not to exceed 40 milligrams. Dosage should be adjusted based on initial temperature level. If less or equal to 102.5°F, 5 milligrams per dose is recommended. If temperature is greater than 102.5°F, 10 milligrams per dose is recommended.

OVERDOSE SYMPTOMS:
Nervous agitation, disorientation, confusion, severe headache, convulsions, GI bleeding or hemorrhage. If you suspect an overdose, immediately seek medical attention.

SIDE EFFECTS:
No serious effects in most cases of common use, however normal use of ibuprofen can result in common GI irritations such as heartburn and indigestion. Less common side effects include dizziness, nausea, stomach cramps, and headache.

CHECK WITH YOUR DOCTOR OR PHARMACIST BEFORE COMBINING IBUPROFEN WITH:
Antacids, anticoagulants, aspirin, asthma medication, other nonsteroidal anti-inflammatory drugs (NSAIDs), tetracycline, and any other medication. Combination with acetaminophen increases risk of kidney damage. Ingestion of alcohol while taking ibuprofen can increase risk of GI ulceration. Avoid ibuprofen if you have a history of anemia. Also avoid use of ibuprofen, if possible, one week prior to surgery, as it may increase possibility of postoperative bleeding.

PREGNANCY OR BREASTFEEDING:
Animal studies have indicated an adverse effect on fetus, but no adequate studies have been performed on humans. No harmful effects have been reported regarding nursing infants, but ibuprofen use by a nursing mother should be considered a potential risk for a nursing child as the drug will be passed on to the infant in the mother's milk. In all cases, a physician should be consulted.

Q U I C K F A C T S

PRECAUTIONS FOR CHILDREN:
In general, ibuprofen and other NSAIDs are not advised for children under 15.

PRECAUTIONS FOR SENIORS:
Seniors generally don't eliminate drugs as efficiently as younger persons, and should avoid high dosages. Seniors (over 65) are at special risk for development of ulcers if taking ibuprofen in high doses. Prolonged use can also lead to kidney and liver damage.

SPECIAL WARNINGS:
Don't take ibuprofen medication if you are aspirin intolerant or allergic to other NSAIDs. If in doubt, always consult a pharmacist or physician. Also avoid if you have GI conditions such as gastritis, peptic ulcer, enteritis, ileitis, colitis; asthma, high blood pressure, or hematologic (bleeding) problems. Avoid alcohol while taking this or any other NSAID.

INFORM YOUR DOCTOR BEFORE TAKING IBUPROFEN IF YOU HAVE:
An allergy or intolerance to aspirin or other NSAIDs, damaged or impaired renal (kidney) or hepatic (liver) functions, epilepsy, Parkinson's disease, or mental illness.

• ANTIHISTAMINES •

The most important considerations in choosing an antihistamine are: its effectiveness in blocking or alleviating effects of histamine on the respiratory system, and the nature and extent of side effects which the drug may produce.

ANTIHISTAMINES ARE A CLASS OF DRUGS WHICH:

- are used in treating allergies and motion sickness,
- block the effects of histamine, a chemical substance released by the body as the result of injury or in reaction to an allergen. Histamine increases capillary permeability, which allows fluids to escape and cause swelling. It also constricts small air passages in the lungs. These properties result in symptoms such as sinus headache, congestion, sneezing, runny nose,wheezing, puffiness, and lowered blood pressure,
- act by blocking or displacing histamine, particularly in the blood vessels, skin, uterus, and bronchioles,
- as a result of the drugs' drying effects, thereby impede drainage and expectoration,
- may produce side effects such as drowsiness, nasal stuffiness, dryness of mouth and sinus passages, dizziness, and common gastrointestinal (GI) irritation or distress,
- are not recommended in treating lower respiratory symptoms including asthma, as the drug's effects may impede expectoration.

QUICK FACTS

ACTIVE INGREDIENTS:
ACETAMINOPHEN, DEXTROMETHORPHAN HYDROBROMIDE, DOXYLAMINE SUCCINATE, AND PSEUDOEPHREDINE HYDROCHLORIDE

℞ **BRAND NAMES:**

- Alka-Seltzer Plus Nighttime Cold Liqui-Gels (also contains sorbitol)
- Genite Liquid (also contains alcohol, tartrazine)
- NyQuil Hot Therapy Powder (also contains sucrose)
- NyQuil Nighttime Cold/Flu Medicine Liquid (also contains alcohol, sucrose, saccharin [cherry flavor], tartrazine [original flavor])
- Vicks NyQuil LiquiCaps

Note: *Dextromethorphan hydrobromide* is also an active ingredient in other multi-symptom antitussive/expectorant medications which are formulated with other active ingredients.

Pseudoephredine hydrochloride is a used as an active ingredient in decongestant and stimulant products.

Acetaminophen is a non-aspirin analgesic which is used primarily in pain-relief products.

Doxylamine succinate is a drowsiness-producing antihistamine which is mostly used in combination with analgesic, antitussive, decongestant, and expectorant active ingredients in OTC medications to provide nighttime relief of allergy, common cold, cough or flu symptoms. It is also used as a sleep aid.

SYMPTOMS RELIEVED:
Minor aches and pains, nasal congestion and coughing such as those associated with the common cold, flu, sore throat, sinusitis, hay fever and other respiratory allergies, and reduction of fever.

HOW TO TAKE:
Comes in capsule, liquid, and powder forms. Swallow capsule with liquid. Sprinkle powder over liquid, then swallow. Do not crush or chew timed-release capsule.

USUAL ADULT DOSE:
Dosage varies per product and active ingredient formulation. Follow product dosage instructions.

USUAL CHILD DOSE:
Do not administer to children under 6 unless under direction of physician. Dosage may vary based on infant or child's age.

OVERDOSE SYMPTOMS:
Nervous agitation, severe anxiety, insomnia (sleeplessness), hallucinations, tremors, convulsions, nausea, vomiting, cardiac arrhythmia (irregular pulse and heartbeat), drowsiness, dizziness, fatigue, rash. If you suspect an overdose, immediately seek medical attention.

SIDE EFFECTS:
No serious effects in most cases of common use, although antihistamines often cause drowsiness. Less common side effects include nasal dryness, dizziness, nausea, and mild insomnia palpitations, insomnia, gastrointestinal (GI) upset including stomach cramps and diarrhea, drowsiness, and fatigue. In rare cases, more severe

QUICK FACTS

side effects may result, including: painful and frequent urination, hypertension, and heart palpitations. In these cases, discontinue medication and call your doctor immediately. Long-term ingestion of high dosages of acetaminophen-containing products may increase risk of liver and kidney damage.

CHECK WITH YOUR DOCTOR OR PHARMACIST BEFORE COMBINING THESE COMBINATION PRODUCTS WITH:

Anticoagulant medications, other cold, cough, or allergy medication, stimulants, antidepressants, antihypertensives, digitalis or other heart medication, diuretics, or MAO (monoamine oxidase inhibitors) drugs. Ingestion of caffeinated beverages (coffee, tea, caffeine-containing soft drinks) while taking pseudoephredine-containing medication can result in agitation and insomnia.

If taking combination products which contain acetaminophen, you should avoid Isoniazid (antituberculosis) medication. Excessive ingestion of alcohol while taking acetaminophen-containing medication can increase the risk of liver damage or disease (hepatic toxicity). Alcohol use may also increase drowsiness effect of the antihistamine doxylamine succinate in these combination products.

PREGNANCY OR BREASTFEEDING:

Use of medications containing any of the active ingredients in these products by a nursing mother should be considered a potential risk for a nursing child as the drug(s) will be passed on to the infant in the mother's milk. In all cases, a physician should be consulted.

PRECAUTIONS FOR CHILDREN:
In general, these active ingredients are not advised for children under 2. Administer to infants or children only when consulting a physician and follow instructions on medication (see above).

55+ **PRECAUTIONS FOR SENIORS:**
Seniors generally don't eliminate drugs as efficiently as younger persons, and should avoid high dosages. Use of doxylamine succinate-containing medications by seniors can lead to urinary difficulties. In addition, seniors are more likely to experience drowsiness effects of doxylamine succinate.

SPECIAL WARNINGS:
Do not use for control of chronic cough related to conditions such as emphysema, asthma, or smoking, or if coughs are producing excessive secretions. If cough is accompanied by high fever, rash, nausea or vomiting, or persistent headache, use only if directed by your doctor. Because antihistamines such as doxylamine succinate often cause drowsiness, you should avoid activities or tasks such as driving, or other operations which require alertness, coordination, dexterity, or quick reflexes. Chronic alcoholics are at risk for hepatic (liver) function impairment if taking high dosages of acetaminophen-containing medication. Do not use medications which combine doxylamine succinate with tartrazine if you are intolerant or hypersensitive to aspirin. Allergic reactions, including bronchial asthma, have occurred in susceptible individuals.

Q U I C K F A C T S

ADDITIONAL WARNING:

Alcohol: Some cough/cold medications contain various amounts of alcohol. Check label of any cough medication if concerned about ingestion of alcohol.

Sugar/Sweeteners: Some cough/cold medications contain various amounts of sugar, sucrose, glucose, and/or artificial sweeteners such as aspartame, saccharin, sorbitol. Check label of cough medication before selecting, if concerned about diabetes and ingestion of sugar or artificial sweeteners.

Abuse/Dependency: Reports indicate a rising rate of abuse of dextromethorphan-containing medications, particularly among teens. Sufficient data has not yet been collected, however, to determine the abuse and dependency potential of dextromethorphan-containing medications.

INFORM YOUR DOCTOR BEFORE TAKING PRODUCTS CONTAINING THIS COMBINATION OF ACTIVE INGREDIENTS IF YOU HAVE:

Asthma, emphysema or other respiratory condition, liver impairment or liver disease, allergies to any sympathomimetic drug, aspirin or other salicylates, or if you have diabetes, thyroid condition, or urinary difficulty. If you anticipate any surgery requiring general or spinal anesthesia within 2 months of taking medication which contains pseudoephredine, inform your doctor.

ACTIVE INGREDIENT:

BROMPHENIRAMINE MALEATE

Q U I C K F A C T S

BRAND NAMES:

- Dimetane Elixir (also contains alcohol)
- Dimetane Extentabs
- Dimetane Tablets

SYMPTOMS RELIEVED:

Nasal congestion, runny nose, itchy and watery eyes, sneezing, scratchy throat, and irritated sinuses due to common cold, sinusitis, hay fever, and other upper respiratory allergies.

HOW TO TAKE:

Comes in tablet, and liquid forms. Swallow tablet with liquid. Do not crush or chew timed-release tablets. Brompheniramine maleate and other antihistamines can cause gastrointestinal (GI) irritation and should be taken with food or following meal.

USUAL ADULT DOSE:

4 milligrams 4 to 6 times per day, or 8 to 12 milligrams of timed-release medication 2 to 3 times per day, not to exceed 24 milligrams in a 24 hour period.

USUAL CHILD DOSE:

For children 6 to 12: 2 milligrams 4 to 6 times per day, not to exceed 12 milligrams in a 24 hour period. Timed-release medications should only be administered under direction of physician.

Do not administer to children under 6 unless under direction of physician. Dosage may vary based on infant or child's age.

QUICK FACTS

OVERDOSE SYMPTOMS:
Nervous agitation, severe anxiety, insomnia (sleeplessness), hallucinations, tremors, coma. If you suspect an overdose, immediately seek medical attention.

SIDE EFFECTS:
The most frequent side effect of antihistamines use is drowsiness. Other common side effects include: include dryness of mouth, throat, and nasal passages, dizziness, GI distress (including vomiting, diarrhea and constipation or change in bowel regularity), and diminished muscle coordination. In rare cases, more severe side effects may result, such as painful and frequent urination or urinary retention, vision problems, loss of appetite, and respiratory difficulty. In these cases, discontinue medication and call your doctor immediately.

CHECK WITH YOUR DOCTOR OR PHARMACIST BEFORE COMBINING BROMPHENIRAMINE MALEATE WITH:
Cold, cough, or allergy medication—including other antihistamines; aspirin, stimulants, antidepressants, antihypertensives, digitalis or other heart medication, diuretics, or MAO (monoamine oxidase inhibitors) drugs. Avoid ingestion of alcohol or use of sedatives or tranquilizers while taking brompheniramine maleate-containing medication or most other antihistamine-containing medication as the combination can produce severe drowsiness or sedation.

PREGNANCY OR BREASTFEEDING:
Brompheniramine maleate use by a nursing mother should be considered a potential risk for

a nursing child as the drug will be passed on to the infant in the mother's milk. In all cases, a physician should be consulted.

PRECAUTIONS FOR CHILDREN:
In general, brompheniramine maleate is not advised for children under 6. Administer brompheniramine maleate to infants or children only when consulting a physician and follow instructions on medication (see above).

55+ **PRECAUTIONS FOR SENIORS:**
Seniors generally don't eliminate drugs as efficiently as younger persons, and should avoid high dosages. Use of brompheniramine maleate medications by seniors can lead to urinary difficulties. In addition, seniors are more likely to experience sedatory effects of the drug.

SPECIAL WARNINGS:
Because antihistamines often cause drowsiness, you should avoid activities or tasks such as, driving, or other operations which require alertness, coordination, dexterity or quick reflexes. Do not use continuously for longer than 3 months.

INFORM YOUR DOCTOR BEFORE TAKING BROMPHENIRAMINE MALEATE IF YOU HAVE:
Urinary difficulty, glaucoma, ulcer, or if you are pregnant. If you anticipate any surgery requiring general or spinal anesthesia within 2 months of taking brompheniramine maleate-containing medication, inform your doctor.

QUICK FACTS

QUICK FACTS

ACTIVE INGREDIENT:

TRIPOLIDINE HYDROCHLORIDE

BRAND NAMES:

- ACTIDIL

SYMPTOMS RELIEVED:

Nasal congestion, runny nose, itchy and watery eyes, sneezing, scratchy throat, and irritated sinuses due to common cold, sinusitis, hay fever, and other upper respiratory allergies.

HOW TO TAKE:

Comes in tablet, capsule, and liquid forms. Swallow tablet or capsule with liquid. Do not crush or chew timed-release tablets. Tripolidine and other antihistamines can cause gastrointestinal (GI) irritation and should be taken with food or following meal.

USUAL ADULT DOSE:

2.5 milligrams 3 to 4 times per day, not to exceed 10 grams in a 24 hour period.

USUAL CHILD DOSE:

For children 6 to 12: 2 milligrams 4 to 6 times per day, or 8 milligrams of timed-release medication at bedtime or during day, not to exceed 12 milligrams in a 24 hour period.

For children 2 to 6: 1.25 milligrams 4 to 6 times per day, not to exceed 5 milligrams in a 24 hour period. Timed-release medications are not advised for children 2 to 6 or younger. Do not administer to children in this age group unless under direction of physician. Dosage may vary based on infant or child's age.

OVERDOSE SYMPTOMS:
Nervous agitation, severe anxiety, insomnia (sleeplessness), hallucinations, tremors, coma. If you suspect an overdose, immediately seek medical attention.

SIDE EFFECTS:
The most frequent side effect of antihistamines use is drowsiness. Other common side effects include: include dryness of mouth, throat, and nasal passages, dizziness, GI distress (including vomiting, diarrhea, and constipation or change in bowel regularity), and diminished muscle coordination. In rare cases, more severe side effects may result, such as painful and frequent urination or urinary retention, vision problems, loss of appetite, and respiratory difficulty. In these cases, discontinue medication and call your doctor immediately.

CHECK WITH YOUR DOCTOR OR PHARMACIST BEFORE COMBINING TRIPOLIDINE WITH:
Cold, cough, or allergy medication—including other antihistamines; aspirin, stimulants, antidepressants, antihypertensives, digitalis or other heart medication, diuretics, or MAO (monoamine oxidase inhibitors) drugs. Avoid ingestion of alcohol or use of sedatives or tranquilizers while taking tripolidine-containing medication or most other antihistamine-containing medication as the combination can produce severe drowsiness or sedation.

PREGNANCY OR BREASTFEEDING:
Tripolidine use by a nursing mother should be considered a potential risk for a nursing child as

QUICK FACTS

the drug will be passed on to the infant in the mother's milk. In all cases, a physician should be consulted.

PRECAUTIONS FOR CHILDREN:
In general, tripolidine is not advised for children under 6. Administer tripolidine to infants or children only when consulting a physician and follow instructions on medication (see above).

PRECAUTIONS FOR SENIORS:
Seniors generally don't eliminate drugs as efficiently as younger persons, and should avoid high dosages. Use of tripolidine medications by seniors can lead to urinary difficulties. In addition, seniors are more likely to experience stimulant effects of the drug.

SPECIAL WARNINGS:
Because antihistamines often cause drowsiness, you should avoid activities or tasks such as driving, or other operations which require alertness, coordination, dexterity or quick reflexes. Do not use continuously for longer than 3 months. Do not use tripolidine medications containing tartrazine if you are intolerant or hypersensitive to aspirin. Allergic reactions, including bronchial asthma, have occurred in susceptible individuals.

INFORM YOUR DOCTOR BEFORE TAKING TRIPOLIDINE IF YOU HAVE:
Urinary difficulty, glaucoma, ulcer, or if you are pregnant. If you anticipate any surgery requiring general or spinal anesthesia within 2 months of taking tripolidine-containing medication, inform your doctor.

• ANTITUSSIVE •

The most important considerations in choosing an antitussive are: cough suppressant and relief action; and potential side effects associated with the drug.

QUICK REVIEW

ANTITUSSIVES ARE A CLASS OF DRUGS WHICH:

- help to suppress and relieve the spasmodic cough reflex typical of symptoms of various allergies, colds, bronchitis, flu, and other nonchronic respiratory ailments,
- are commonly used to give an allergy, cold, bronchitis, flu, and other nonchronic respiratory ailment-sufferer sufficient relief from coughing spasms, so that the person can rest, thereby increasing the chances of recovering from the illness,
- may produce side effects such as drowsiness, nasal stuffiness, dryness of mouth and sinus passages, dizziness, and common gastrointestinal (GI) irritation or distress,
- are not recommended in treating chronic and lower respiratory symptoms including asthma, and emphysema, as the drug's effects may impede expectoration,
- are often combined with other cough-related active ingredients such as expectorants, as well as analgesics, antihistamines, and decongestants—as well as other ingredients such as alcohol, sweeteners (natural and artificial) and flavorings (natural and artificial),
- do not affect the underlying cause of the symptoms which they are designed to relieve or suppress.

QUICK FACTS

ACTIVE INGREDIENTS:

ACETAMINOPHEN, CHLORPHENIRAMINE MALEATE, DEXTROMETHORPHAN HYDROBROMIDE, AND PSEUDOEPHREDINE HYDROCHLORIDE

℞ **BRAND NAMES:**

- ALKA-SELTZER PLUS COLD & COUGH LIQUI-GELS (also contains sorbitol)
- BAYER SELECT FLU RELIEF CAPLETS
- CO-APAP TABLETS
- COMTREX LIQUID (also contains alcohol, sucrose)
- COMTREX LIQUI-GELS (contains sorbitol)
- COMTREX MAXIMUM LIQUI-GELS (contains sorbitol)
- COMTREX MAX STRENGTH MULTI-SYMPTOM COLD & FLU RELIEF LIQUI-GELS
- COMTREX MAXIMUM STRENGTH MULTI-SYMPTOM COLD & FLU RELIEF CAPLETS & TABLETS (contains parabens)
- CONTAC SEVERE COLD & FLU NIGHTTIME LIQUID (also contains alcohol, saccharin, sorbitol, glucose)
- GENACOL TABLETS
- KOLEPHRIN/DM CAPLETS
- MAPAP COLD FORMULA TABLETS
- MEDI-FLU LIQUID (also contains alcohol, saccharin, sorbitol, sugar)
- THERAFLU FLU, COLD & COUGH POWDER (contains sucrose)
- THERAFLU NIGHTTIME FLU POWDER (contains sucrose)
- TYLENOL CHILDREN'S COLD MULTI-SYMPTOM PLUS COUGH LIQUID (also contains sorbitol, corn syrup)

- Tylenol Multi-Symptom Cold Caplets & Tablets
- Tylenol Multi-Symptom Hot Medication Powder (combination with phenylalanine, also contains aspartame, sucrose)
- Vicks Children's NyQuil Nighttime Cold/Cough Liquid (also contains sucrose)
- Vicks 44M Cold, Flu & Cough LiquiCaps
- Vicks Pediatric Formula 44M Multi-Symptom Cough & Cold Liquid
  (also contains sorbitol, sucrose)

Note: *Dextromethorphan hydrobromide* is also an active ingredient in other multi-symptom antitussive/expectorant medications which are formulated with other active ingredients.

Pseudoephredine hydrochloride is a used as an active ingredient in decongestant and stimulant products.

Acetaminophen is a non-aspirin analgesic which is used primarily in pain-relief products.

Chlorpheniramine maleate is an antihistamine which is mostly used in combination with analgesic, antitussive, decongestant and expectorant active ingredients in OTC medications to provide relief of allergy, common cold, cough or flu symptoms.

SYMPTOMS RELIEVED:
Minor aches and pains, nasal congestion, and coughing such as those associated with the common cold, flu, sore throat, sinusitis, hay fever and other respiratory allergies, and reduction of fever.

QUICK FACTS

HOW TO TAKE:
Comes in tablet, caplet, capsule, and liquid forms. Swallow tablet, caplet, or capsule with liquid. Sprinkle powder over liquid, then swallow. Do not crush or chew timed-release tablet.

USUAL ADULT DOSE:
Dosage varies per product and active ingredient formulation. Follow product dosage instructions.

USUAL CHILD DOSE:
Do not administer to children under 6 unless under direction of physician. Dosage may vary based on infant or child's age.

OVERDOSE SYMPTOMS:
Nervous agitation, severe anxiety, insomnia (sleeplessness), hallucinations, tremors, convulsions, nausea, vomiting, cardiac arrhythmia (irregular pulse and heartbeat), drowsiness, dizziness, fatigue, rash. If you suspect an overdose, immediately seek medical attention.

SIDE EFFECTS:
No serious effects in most cases of common use, although antihistamines can cause drowsiness. Less common side effects include nasal dryness, dizziness, nausea, and mild insomnia palpitations, insomnia, gastrointestinal (GI) upset including stomach cramps and diarrhea, drowsiness, and fatigue. In rare cases, more severe side effects may result, including: painful and frequent urination, hypertension, and heart palpitations. In these cases, discontinue medication and call your doctor immediately. Long-term ingestion of high dosages of acetaminophen-containing products may increase risk of liver and kidney damage.

CHECK WITH YOUR DOCTOR OR PHARMACIST BEFORE COMBINING THESE COMBINATION PRODUCTS WITH:

Anticoagulant medications, other cold, cough, or allergy medication, stimulants, antidepressants, antihypertensives, digitalis or other heart medication, diuretics, or MAO (monoamine oxidase inhibitors) drugs. Ingestion of caffeinated beverages (coffee, tea, caffeine-containing soft drinks) while taking pseudoephredine-containing medication can result in agitation and insomnia.

If taking combination products which contain acetaminophen, you should avoid Isoniazid (anti-tuberculosis) medication. Excessive ingestion of alcohol while taking acetaminophen-containing medication can increase the risk of liver damage or disease (hepatic toxicity). Alcohol use may also increase possible drowsiness effect of the antihistamine in these combination products.

PREGNANCY OR BREASTFEEDING:

Use of medications containing any of the active ingredients in these products by a nursing mother should be considered a potential risk for a nursing child as the drug(s) will be passed on to the infant in the mother's milk. In all cases, a physician should be consulted.

PRECAUTIONS FOR CHILDREN:

In general, these active ingredients are not advised for children under 2. Administer to infants or children only when consulting a physician and follow instructions on medication (see above).

55+ PRECAUTIONS FOR SENIORS:

Seniors generally don't eliminate drugs as

efficiently as younger persons, and should avoid high dosages. Use of antihistamine-containing medications by seniors can lead to urinary difficulties. In addition, seniors are more likely to experience potential drowsiness effects of the antihistamine in this combination.

SPECIAL WARNINGS:
Do not use for control of chronic cough related to conditions such as emphysema, asthma, or smoking, or if coughs are producing excessive secretions. If cough is accompanied by high fever, rash, nausea or vomiting, or persistent headache, use only if directed by your doctor. Because antihistamines may cause drowsiness, you should avoid activities or tasks such as driving, or other operations which require alertness, coordination, dexterity, or quick reflexes. Chronic alcoholics are at risk for hepatic (liver) function impairment if taking high dosages of acetaminophen-containing medication. Do not use medications which combine doxylamine succinate with tartrazine if you are intolerant or hypersensitive to aspirin. Allergic reactions, including bronchial asthma, have occurred in susceptible individuals.

ADDITIONAL WARNING:
Alcohol: Some cough/cold medications contain various amounts of alcohol. Check label of any cough medication if concerned about ingestion of alcohol.

Sugar/Sweeteners: Some cough/cold medications contain various amounts of sugar, sucrose, glucose, and/or artificial sweeteners such as aspartame, saccharin, sorbitol. Check label of cough medication before selecting, if concerned about diabetes and ingestion of sugar or artificial sweeteners.

Abuse/Dependency: Reports indicate a rising rate of abuse of dextromethorphan-containing medications, particularly among teens. Sufficient data has not yet been collected, however, to determine the abuse and dependency potential of dextromethorphan-containing medications.

INFORM YOUR DOCTOR BEFORE TAKING PRODUCTS CONTAINING THIS COMBINATION OF ACTIVE INGREDIENTS IF YOU HAVE:
Asthma, emphysema or other respiratory condition, liver impairment or liver disease, allergies to any sympathomimetic drug, aspirin or other salicylates, or if you have diabetes, thyroid condition, or urinary difficulty. If you anticipate any surgery requiring general or spinal anesthesia within 2 months of taking medication which contains pseudoephredine, inform your doctor.

QUICK FACTS

ACTIVE INGREDIENTS:

ACETAMINOPHEN AND DEXTROMETHORPHAN HYDROBROMIDE

BRAND NAMES:
- BAYER SELECT CHEST COLD CAPLETS
- CONTAC COUGH & SORE THROAT LIQUID (also contains alcohol, saccharin, sorbitol)
- DRIXORAL COUGH & SORE THROAT LIQUID CAPS (contains sorbitol)
- TYLENOL MAXIMUM STRENGTH COUGH LIQUID (also contains alcohol, saccharin, sorbitol, sucrose)

Note: *Dextromethorphan hydrobromide* is also an active ingredient in other multisymptom antitussive/expectorant medications which are formulated with other active ingredients.

Acetaminophen is a non-aspirin analgesic which is used primarily in pain-relief products.

SYMPTOMS RELIEVED:
Minor aches and pains, nasal congestion and coughing such as those associated with the common cold, flu, sinusitis, hay fever and other respiratory allergies, as well as relief of headache, toothache, muscular aches, backache, minor arthritis pain, menstrual discomfort, and reduction of fever.

HOW TO TAKE:
Comes in caplet, capsule, and liquid forms. Swallow caplet or capsule with liquid. Do not crush or chew timed-release tablet.

USUAL ADULT DOSE:
Dosage varies per product and active ingredient formulation. Follow product dosage instructions.

USUAL CHILD DOSE:
Do not administer to children under 6 unless under direction of physician. Dosage may vary based on infant or child's age.

OVERDOSE SYMPTOMS:
Nervous agitation, severe anxiety, insomnia (sleeplessness), hallucinations, tremors, convulsions, nausea, vomiting, cardiac arrhythmia (irregular pulse and heartbeat), drowsiness, dizziness, fatigue, rash. If you suspect an overdose, immediately seek medical attention.

SIDE EFFECTS:
No serious effects in most cases of common use. Less common side effects include nasal dryness, dizziness, nausea, and mild insomnia palpitations, insomnia, gastrointestinal (GI) upset including stomach cramps and diarrhea, drowsiness and fatigue. In rare cases, more severe side effects may result, including: painful and frequent urination, hypertension, and heart palpitations. In these cases, discontinue medication and call your doctor immediately. Long-term ingestion of high dosages of acetaminophen-containing products may increase risk of liver and kidney damage.

CHECK WITH YOUR DOCTOR OR PHARMACIST BEFORE COMBINING THESE COMBINATION PRODUCTS WITH:
Anticoagulant medications, other cold, cough, or allergy medication, stimulants, antidepres-

Q U I C K F A C T S

sants, antihypertensives, digitalis or other heart medication, diuretics, or MAO (monoamine oxidase inhibitors) drugs. If taking combination products which contain acetaminophen, you should avoid Isoniazid (anti-tuberculosis) medication. Excessive ingestion of alcohol while taking acetaminophen-containing medication can increase the risk of liver damage or disease (hepatic toxicity).

PREGNANCY OR BREASTFEEDING:
Use of medications containing any of the active ingredients in these products by a nursing mother should be considered a potential risk for a nursing child as the drug(s) will be passed on to the infant in the mother's milk. In all cases, a physician should be consulted.

PRECAUTIONS FOR CHILDREN:
In general, these active ingredients are not advised for children under 2. Administer to infants or children only when consulting a physician and follow instructions on medication (see above).

55+

PRECAUTIONS FOR SENIORS:
Seniors generally don't eliminate drugs as efficiently as younger persons, and should avoid high dosages.

SPECIAL WARNINGS:
Do not use for control of chronic cough related to conditions such as emphysema, asthma, or smoking, or if coughs are producing excessive secretions. If cough is accompanied by high fever, rash, nausea or vomiting, or persistent headache, use only if directed by your doctor.

Chronic alcoholics are at risk for hepatic (liver) function impairment if taking high dosages of acetaminophen-containing medication.

ADDITIONAL WARNING:
Alcohol: Some cough/cold medications contain various amounts of alcohol. Check label of any cough medication if concerned about ingestion of alcohol.

Sugar/Sweeteners: Some cough/cold medications contain various amounts of sugar, sucrose, glucose, and/or artificial sweeteners such as aspertame, saccharin, sorbitol. Check label of cough medication before selecting, if concerned about diabetes and ingestion of sugar or artificial sweeteners.

Abuse/Dependency: Reports indicate a rising rate of abuse of dextromethorphan-containing medications, particularly among teens. Sufficient data has not yet been collected, however, to determine the abuse and dependency potential of dextromethorphan-containing medications.

INFORM YOUR DOCTOR BEFORE TAKING PRODUCTS CONTAINING THIS COMBINATION OF ACTIVE INGREDIENTS IF YOU HAVE:
Asthma, emphysema, or other respiratory condition, liver impairment or liver disease, allergies to any sympathomimetic drug, aspirin or other salicylates, or if you have diabetes, thyroid condition, or urinary difficulty. If you anticipate any surgery requiring general or spinal anesthesia within 2 months of taking medication which contains pseudoephredine, inform your doctor.

QUICK FACTS

ACTIVE INGREDIENTS:

ACETAMINOPHEN, DEXTROMETHORPHAN HYDROBROMIDE, DOXYLAMINE SUCCINATE, AND PSEUDOEPHREDINE HYDROCHLORIDE

BRAND NAMES:

- ALKA-SELTZER PLUS NIGHTTIME COLD LIQUI-GELS (also contains sorbitol)
- GENITE LIQUID (also contains alcohol, tartrazine)
- NYQUIL HOT THERAPY POWDER (also contains sucrose)
- NYQUIL NIGHTTIME COLD/FLU MEDICINE LIQUID (also contains alcohol, sucrose, saccharin [cherry flavor], tartrazine [original flavor])
- VICKS NYQUIL LIQUICAPS

SYMPTOMS RELIEVED:

Minor aches and pains, nasal congestion and coughing such as those associated with the common cold, flu, sore throat, sinusitis, hay fever and other respiratory allergies, and reduction of fever.

HOW TO TAKE:

Comes in capsule, liquid, and powder forms. Swallow capsule with liquid. Sprinkle powder over liquid, then swallow. Do not crush or chew timed-release capsule.

USUAL ADULT DOSE:

Dosage varies per product and active ingredient formulation. Follow product dosage instructions.

USUAL CHILD DOSE:
Do not administer to children under 6 unless under direction of physician. Dosage may vary based on infant or child's age.

OVERDOSE SYMPTOMS:
Nervous agitation, severe anxiety, insomnia (sleeplessness), hallucinations, tremors, convulsions, nausea, vomiting, cardiac arrhythmia (irregular pulse and heartbeat), drowsiness, dizziness, fatigue, rash. If you suspect an overdose, immediately seek medical attention.

SIDE EFFECTS:
No serious effects in most cases of common use, although antihistamines often cause drowsiness. Less common side effects include nasal dryness, dizziness, nausea, and mild insomnia palpitations, insomnia, gastrointestinal (GI) upset including stomach cramps and diarrhea, drowsiness, and fatigue. In rare cases, more severe side effects may result, including: painful and frequent urination, hypertension, and heart palpitations. In these cases, discontinue medication and call your doctor immediately. Long-term ingestion of high dosages of acetaminophen-containing products may increase risk of liver and kidney damage.

CHECK WITH YOUR DOCTOR OR PHARMACIST BEFORE COMBINING THESE COMBINATION PRODUCTS WITH:
Anticoagulant medications, other cold, cough, or allergy medication, stimulants, antidepressants, antihypertensives, digitalis or other heart medication, diuretics, or MAO (monoamine oxidase

QUICK FACTS

inhibitors) drugs. Ingestion of caffeinated beverages (coffee, tea, caffeine-containing soft drinks) while taking pseudoephredine-containing medication can result in agitation and insomnia. If taking combination products which contain acetaminophen, you should avoid Isoniazid (anti-tuberculosis) medication. Excessive ingestion of alcohol while taking acetaminophen-containing medication can increase the risk of liver damage or disease (hepatic toxicity). Alcohol use may also increase drowsiness effect of the antihistamine doxylamine succinate in these combination products.

PREGNANCY OR BREASTFEEDING:
Use of medications containing any of the active ingredients in these products by a nursing mother should be considered a potential risk for a nursing child as the drug(s) will be passed on to the infant in the mother's milk. In all cases, a physician should be consulted.

PRECAUTIONS FOR CHILDREN:
In general, these active ingredients are not advised for children under 2. Administer to infants or children only when consulting a physician and follow instructions on medication (see above).

55+ **PRECAUTIONS FOR SENIORS:**
Seniors generally don't eliminate drugs as efficiently as younger persons, and should avoid high dosages. Use of doxylamine succinate-containing medications by seniors can lead to urinary difficulties. In addition, seniors are more likely to experience drowsiness effects of doxylamine succinate.

SPECIAL WARNINGS:
Do not use for control of chronic cough related to conditions such as emphysema, asthma, or smoking, or if coughs are producing excessive secretions. If cough is accompanied by high fever, rash, nausea or vomiting, or persistent headache, use only if directed by your doctor. Because antihistamines such as doxylamine succinate often cause drowsiness, you should avoid activities or tasks such as driving, or other operations which require alertness, coordination, dexterity, or quick reflexes. Chronic alcoholics are at risk for hepatic (liver) function impairment if taking high dosages of acetaminophen-containing medication. Do not use medications which combine doxylamine succinate with tartrazine if you are intolerant or hypersensitive to aspirin. Allergic reactions, including bronchial asthma, have occurred in susceptible individuals.

ADDITIONAL WARNING:
Alcohol: Some cough/cold medications contain various amounts of alcohol. Check label of any cough medication if concerned about ingestion of alcohol.

Sugar/Sweeteners: Some cough/cold medications contain various amounts of sugar, sucrose, glucose, and/or artificial sweeteners such as aspartame, saccharin, sorbitol. Check label of cough medication before selecting, if concerned about diabetes and ingestion of sugar or artificial sweeteners.

Abuse/Dependency: Reports indicate a rising rate of abuse of dextromethorphan-containing medications, particularly among teens. Sufficient

data has not yet been collected, however, to determine the abuse and dependency potential of dextromethorphan-containing medications.

INFORM YOUR DOCTOR BEFORE TAKING PRODUCTS CONTAINING THIS COMBINATION OF ACTIVE INGREDIENTS IF YOU HAVE:
Asthma, emphysema or other respiratory condition, liver impairment or liver disease, allergies to any sympathomimetic drug, aspirin or other salicylates, or if you have diabetes, thyroid condition, or urinary difficulty. If you anticipate any surgery requiring general or spinal anesthesia within 2 months of taking medication which contains pseudoephredine, inform your doctor.

ACTIVE INGREDIENTS:

ACETAMINOPHEN, DEXTROMETHORPHAN HYDROBROMIDE, AND PSEUDOEPHREDINE HYDROCHLORIDE

Rx **BRAND NAMES:**

- Alka-Seltzer Plus Flu & Body Aches Non-Drowsy Liqui-Gels
- Bayer Select Nighttime Cold Caplets
- Comtrex Maximum Strength Non-Drowsy Caplets
- Contac Day & Night Cold & Flu Caplets
- Robitussin Night Relief Liquid (also contains saccharin, sorbitol)
- Saleto CF Tablets
- Sudafed Severe Cold Caplets & Tablets
- TheraFlu Non-Drowsy Formula Maximum Strength Caplets (also contains lactose, methylparaben)
- TheraFlu Non-Drowsy Flu, Cold & Cough Maximum Strength Powder (also contains sucrose)
- Triaminic Sore Throat Formula Liquid (also contains EDTA, sucrose)
- Tylenol Cold No Drowsiness Caplets & Gelcaps/Maximum Strength Gelcaps
- Tylenol Maximum Strength Cough with Decongestant Liquid (also contains alcohol, saccharin, sorbitol, sucrose)

Note: *Dextromethorphan hydrobromide* is also an active ingredient in other multi-symptom antitussive/expectorant medications which are formulated with other active ingredients.

QUICK FACTS

Pseudoephredine hydrochloride is a used as an active ingredient in decongestant and stimulant products.

Acetaminophen is a non-aspirin analgesic which is used primarily in pain-relief products.

SYMPTOMS RELIEVED:
Minor aches and pains, nasal congestion and coughing such as those associated with the common cold, flu, sore throat, sinusitis, hay fever and other respiratory allergies, and reduction of fever.

HOW TO TAKE:
Comes in caplet, capsule, and liquid forms. Swallow caplet or capsule with liquid. Sprinkle powder over liquid, then swallow. Do not crush or chew timed-release tablet.

USUAL ADULT DOSE:
Dosage varies per product and active ingredient formulation. Follow product dosage instructions.

USUAL CHILD DOSE:
Do not administer to children under 6 unless under direction of physician. Dosage may vary based on infant or child's age.

OVERDOSE SYMPTOMS:
Nervous agitation, severe anxiety, insomnia (sleeplessness), hallucinations, tremors, convulsions, nausea, vomiting, cardiac arrhythmia (irregular pulse and heartbeat), drowsiness, dizziness, fatigue, rash. If you suspect an overdose, immediately seek medical attention.

SIDE EFFECTS:
No serious effects in most cases of common

use. Less common side effects include nasal dryness, dizziness, nausea, and mild insomnia palpitations, insomnia, gastrointestinal (GI) upset including stomach cramps and diarrhea, drowsiness and fatigue. In rare cases, more severe side effects may result, including: painful and frequent urination, hypertension, and heart palpitations. In these cases, discontinue medication and call your doctor immediately. Long-term ingestion of high dosages of acetaminophen-containing products may increase risk of liver and kidney damage.

CHECK WITH YOUR DOCTOR OR PHARMACIST BEFORE COMBINING THESE COMBINATION PRODUCTS WITH:

Anticoagulant medications, other cold, cough, or allergy medication, stimulants, antidepressants, antihypertensives, digitalis or other heart medication, diuretics, or MAO (monoamine oxidase inhibitors) drugs. Ingestion of caffeinated beverages (coffee, tea, caffeine-containing soft drinks) while taking pseudoephredine-containing medication can result in agitation and insomnia.
If taking combination products which contain acetaminophen, you should avoid Isoniazid (anti-tuberculosis) medication. Excessive ingestion of alcohol while taking acetaminophen-containing medication can increase the risk of liver damage or disease (hepatic toxicity).

PREGNANCY OR BREASTFEEDING:

Use of medications containing any of the active ingredients in these products by a nursing mother should be considered a potential risk for a nursing child as the drug(s) will be passed on to the infant in the mother's milk. In all cases, a physician should be consulted.

PRECAUTIONS FOR CHILDREN:
In general, these active ingredients are not advised for children under 2. Administer to infants or children only when consulting a physician and follow instructions on medication (see above).

PRECAUTIONS FOR SENIORS:
Seniors generally don't eliminate drugs as efficiently as younger persons, and should avoid high dosages. Use of pseudoephedrine-containing medications by seniors can lead to urinary difficulties. In addition, seniors are more likely to experience stimulant effects of pseudoephedrine.

SPECIAL WARNINGS:
Do not use for control of chronic cough related to conditions such as emphysema, asthma, or smoking, or if coughs are producing excessive secretions. If cough is accompanied by high fever, rash, nausea or vomiting, or persistent headache, use only if directed by your doctor. Chronic alcoholics are at risk for hepatic (liver) function impairment if taking high dosages of acetaminophen-containing medication.

ADDITIONAL WARNING:
Alcohol: Some cough/cold medications contain various amounts of alcohol. Check label of any cough medication if concerned about ingestion of alcohol.

Sugar/Sweeteners: Some cough/cold medications contain various amounts of sugar, sucrose, glucose, and/or artificial sweeteners such as aspartame, saccharin, sorbitol. Check label of cough medication before selecting, if concerned about diabetes and ingestion of sugar or artificial sweeteners.

Abuse/Dependency: Reports indicate a rising rate of abuse of dextromethorphan-containing medications, particularly among teens. Sufficient data has not yet been collected, however, to determine the abuse and dependency potential of dextromethorphan-containing medications.

INFORM YOUR DOCTOR BEFORE TAKING PRODUCTS CONTAINING THIS COMBINATION OF ACTIVE INGREDIENTS IF YOU HAVE:
Asthma, emphysema or other respiratory condition, liver impairment or liver disease, allergies to any sympathomimetic drug, aspirin or other salicylates, or if you have diabetes, thyroid condition, or urinary difficulty. If you anticipate any surgery requiring general or spinal anesthesia within 2 months of taking medication which contains pseudoephredine, inform your doctor.

QUICK FACTS

ACTIVE INGREDIENT:

DEXTROMETHORPHAN HYDROBROMIDE

℞ **BRAND NAMES:**

Lozenges:

- Hold DM/Children's Hold (also contains sucrose, corn syrup)
- Robitussin Cough Calmers (also contains sorbitol, sucrose, cherry flavor)
- Scot-Tussin DM Cough Chasers (also contains sorbitol)
- Sucrets Cough Control (also contains corn syrup, sucrose)
- Suppress
- Trocal

Liquid:

- Pertussin CS (also contains sorbitol, sucrose, wild berry flavor)
- Robitussin Pediatric (also contains saccharin, sorbitol, cherry flavor)
- St. Joseph Cough Suppressant (also contains sucrose, cherry flavor)

Syrup:

- Benylin DM (also contains alcohol, glucose, menthol, sucrose)
- Pertussin ES (also contains alcohol, sugar, sorbitol)
- Vicks Formula 44 (also contains alcohol, sugar)
- Vicks Formula 44 Pediatric Formula (also contains sorbitol, sucrose, cherry flavor)

Note: *Dextromethorphan hydrobromide* is an active ingredient in many multi-symptom antitussive medications which are formulated with other active ingredients.

SYMPTOMS RELIEVED:
Cough associated with common cold and minor throat and bronchial irritations.

HOW TO TAKE:
Comes in lozenge, liquid, or syrup forms.

USUAL ADULT DOSE:
10 to 30 milligrams 3 to 4 times per day, not to exceed 120 milligrams in a 24 hour period.

USUAL CHILD DOSE:
For children 6 to 12: 5 to10 milligrams 3 to 4 times per day, not to exceed 60 milligrams in a 24 hour period.

For children 2 to 6 (syrup): 2.5 to 7.5 milligrams 3 to 4 times per day, not to exceed 30 milligrams in a 24 hour period.

Do not administer to children under 2 unless under direction of physician. Dosage may vary based on infant or child's age.

OVERDOSE SYMPTOMS:
Intoxication, nervous agitation, and overactivity, hallucinations, respiratory difficulty, convulsions. If you suspect an overdose, immediately seek medical attention.

SIDE EFFECTS:
No serious effects in most cases of common use. Less common side effects include dizziness, stomach cramps, drowsiness, fatigue.

CHECK WITH YOUR DOCTOR OR PHARMACIST BEFORE COMBINING DEXTROMETHORPHAN WITH:
MAO (monoamine oxidase inhibitors) drugs or sedatives.

QUICK FACTS

PREGNANCY OR BREASTFEEDING:
Dextromethorphan use by a nursing mother should be considered a potential risk for a nursing child as the drug will be passed on to the infant in the mother's milk. In all cases, a physician should be consulted.

PRECAUTIONS FOR CHILDREN:
In general, dextromethorphan is not advised for children under 2. Administer dextromethorphan to infants or children only when consulting a physician and follow instructions on medication (see above).

55+

PRECAUTIONS FOR SENIORS:
Seniors generally don't eliminate drugs as efficiently as younger persons, and should avoid high dosages.

SPECIAL WARNINGS:
Do not use for control of chronic cough related to conditions such as emphysema, asthma, or smoking, or if coughs are producing excessive secretions. If cough is accompanied by high fever, rash, nausea or vomiting, or persistent headache, use only if directed by your doctor.

ADDITIONAL WARNING:
Reports indicate a rising rate of abuse of dextromethorphan-containing medications, particularly among teens. Sufficient data has not yet been collected, however, to determine the abuse and dependency potential of dextromethorphan-containing medications.

INFORM YOUR DOCTOR BEFORE TAKING DEXTROMETHORPHAN IF YOU HAVE:
Asthma or liver impairment or liver disease.

ACTIVE INGREDIENTS:

DEXTROMETHORPHAN HYDROBROMIDE AND PSEUDOEPHEDRINE HYDROCHLORIDE

Q U I C K F A C T S

BRAND NAMES:

- DRIXORAL COUGH & CONGESTION LIQUID CAPS
- PEDIA CARE NIGHTREST COUGH–COLD LIQUID (combination with chlorphreniramine maleate—also contains sorbitol, corn syrup)
- ROBITUSSIN MAXIMUM STRENGTH COUGH & COLD LIQUID (also contains alcohol, high fructose corn syrup, saccharin, glucose)
- TRIAMINIC NITE LIGHT LIQUID (combination with chlorphreniramine maleate—also contains sorbitol, sucrose)
- VICKS 44 NON-DROWSY COLD & COUGH LIQUICAPS (also contains sorbitol)
- VICKS PEDIATRIC FORMULA 44D COUGH & DECONGESTANT LIQUID (also contains sorbitol, sucrose)

See also: Pseudoephedrine hydrochloride

SYMPTOMS RELIEVED:
Cough and nasal congestion associated with common cold and minor throat and bronchial irritations.

HOW TO TAKE:
Comes in tablet, capsule, chewable forms. Swallow with liquid. Do not crush or chew timed-release tablets.

USUAL ADULT DOSE:
Dosage varies per product and active ingredient formulation. Follow product dosage instructions.

Q U I C K F A C T S

USUAL CHILD DOSE:
Do not administer to children under 6 unless under direction of physician. Dosage may vary based on infant or child's age.

OVERDOSE SYMPTOMS:
Nervous agitation, severe anxiety, insomnia (sleeplessness), hallucinations, tremors, convulsions, nausea, vomiting, cardiac arrhythmia (irregular pulse and heartbeat). If you suspect an overdose, immediately seek medical attention.

SIDE EFFECTS:
No serious effects in most cases of common use. Less common side effects include nasal dryness, dizziness, nausea, and mild insomnia palpitations, insomnia. In rare cases, more severe side effects may result, including: painful and frequent urination, hypertension, and heart palpitations. In these cases, discontinue medication and call your doctor immediately.

CHECK WITH YOUR DOCTOR OR PHARMACIST BEFORE COMBINING DEXTROMETHORPHAN AND RELATED COMBINATION PRODUCTS WITH:
Cold, cough, or allergy medication, stimulants, antidepressants, antihypertensives, digitalis or other heart medication, diuretics, or MAO (monoamine oxidase inhibitors) drugs. Ingestion of caffeinated beverages (coffee, tea, caffeine-containing soft drinks) while taking dextromethorphan-containing medication can result in agitation and insomnia.

PREGNANCY OR BREASTFEEDING:
Dextromethorphan use by a nursing mother should be considered a potential risk for a

nursing child as the drug will be passed on to the infant in the mother's milk. In all cases, a physician should be consulted.

PRECAUTIONS FOR CHILDREN:
In general, dextromethorphan is not advised for children under 6. Administer dextromethorphan to infants or children only when consulting a physician and follow instructions on medication (see above).

55+

PRECAUTIONS FOR SENIORS:
Seniors generally don't eliminate drugs as efficiently as younger persons, and should avoid high dosages. Use of dextromethorphan medications by seniors can lead to cardiac arrhythmia (irregular pulse and heartbeat). In addition, seniors are more likely to experience stimulant effects of the drug.

SPECIAL WARNINGS:
Do not use continuously for longer than 3 months. Do not use dextromethorphan medications containing tartrazine if you are intolerant or hypersensitive to aspirin. Allergic reactions, including bronchial asthma, have occurred in susceptible individuals.

ADDITIONAL WARNING:
Alcohol: Many dextromethorphan-containing medications contain various amounts of alcohol. Check label of any cough medication if concerned about ingestion of alcohol.

Abuse/Dependency: Reports indicate a rising rate of abuse of dextromethorphan-containing medications, particularly among teens. Sufficient

QUICK FACTS

data has not yet been collected, however, to determine the abuse and dependency potential of dextromethorphan-containing medications.

INFORM YOUR DOCTOR BEFORE TAKING DEXTROMETHORPHAN IF YOU HAVE:
Allergies to: any sympathomimetic drug, aspirin or other salicylates, or if you have diabetes, thyroid condition, or urinary difficulty. If you anticipate any surgery requiring general or spinal anesthesia within 2 months of taking dextromethorphan medication, inform your doctor.

QUICK FACTS

ACTIVE INGREDIENTS:

DEXTROMETHORPHAN HYDROBROMIDE, PHENYLPROPANOLAMINE, AND CHLORPHENIRAMINE MALEATE

Rx

BRAND NAMES:

- ALKA-SELTZER PLUS COLD & COUGH TABLETS (combination with aspirin, phenylalanine, also contains aspartame)
- ALKA-SELTZER PLUS NIGHTTIME COLD & COUGH TABLETS (combination with aspirin, phenylalanine, also contains aspartame, sucrose)
- CEROSE DM LIQUID
- CHERACOL PLUS LIQUID
- KOPHANE COUGH & COLD FORMULA LIQUID
- MYMINICOL LIQUID
- ORTHOXICOL COUGH SYRUP
- RESCON-DM LIQUID
- RHINOSYN–DM LIQUID
- THREAMINE DM SYRUP
- TRIAMINIC–DM SYRUP
- TRIAMINICOL MULTI-SYMPTOM COUGH & COLD TABLETS
- TRIAMINICOL MULTI-SYMPTOM RELIEF LIQUID
- TRICODENE FORTE LIQUID/NN LIQUID
- TRIMINOL COUGH SYRUP
- TUSSAR DM SYRUP
- VICKS 44M COLD, FLU & COUGH LIQUICAPS

SYMPTOMS RELIEVED:

Cough, nasal congestion and runny nose, itchy and watery eyes, sneezing, scratchy throat, and irritated sinuses associated with common cold, minor throat and bronchial irritations, sinusitis, hay fever, and other upper respiratory allergies.

QUICK FACTS

HOW TO TAKE:
Comes in tablet, capsule, liquid, and syrup forms. Swallow tablet or capsule with liquid. Do not crush or chew timed-release tablets.

USUAL ADULT DOSE:
Dosage varies per product and active ingredient formulation. Follow product dosage instructions.

USUAL CHILD DOSE:
Do not administer to children under 6 unless under direction of physician. Dosage may vary based on infant or child's age.

OVERDOSE SYMPTOMS:
Nervous agitation, severe anxiety, insomnia (sleeplessness), hallucinations, tremors, convulsions, nausea, vomiting, cardiac arrhythmia (irregular pulse and heartbeat). If you suspect an overdose, immediately seek medical attention.

SIDE EFFECTS:
No serious effects in most cases of common use, however, drowsiness is a common side effect produced by antihistamines. Less common side effects include nasal dryness, dizziness, nausea, and mild insomnia palpitations, insomnia. In rare cases, more severe side effects may result, including: painful and frequent urination, hypertension, and heart palpitations. In these cases, discontinue medication and call your doctor immediately.

CHECK WITH YOUR DOCTOR OR PHARMACIST BEFORE COMBINING DEXTROMETHORPHAN AND RELATED COMBINATION PRODUCTS WITH:
Cold, cough, or allergy medication, stimulants, antidepressants, antihypertensives, digitalis or

other heart medication, diuretics, or MAO (monoamine oxidase inhibitors) drugs. Ingestion of caffeinated beverages (coffee, tea, caffeine-containing soft drinks) while taking dextromethorphan-containing medication can result in agitation and insomnia.

PREGNANCY OR BREASTFEEDING:
Dextromethorphan use by a nursing mother should be considered a potential risk for a nursing child as the drug will be passed on to the infant in the mother's milk. In all cases, a physician should be consulted.

PRECAUTIONS FOR CHILDREN:
In general, dextromethorphan is not advised for children under 6. Administer dextromethorphan to infants or children only when consulting a physician and follow instructions on medication (see above).

55+

PRECAUTIONS FOR SENIORS:
Seniors generally don't eliminate drugs as efficiently as younger persons, and should avoid high dosages. Use of dextromethorphan medications by seniors can lead to cardiac arrhythmia (irregular pulse and heartbeat). In addition, seniors are more likely to experience stimulant effects of the drug.

SPECIAL WARNINGS:
Do not use for control of chronic cough related to conditions such as emphysema, asthma, or smoking, or if coughs are producing excessive secretions. If cough is accompanied by high fever, rash, nausea or vomiting, or persistent headache, use only if directed by your doctor.

QUICK FACTS

Antihistamines: Because antihistamines often cause drowsiness, you should avoid activities or tasks such as driving, or other operations which require alertness, coordination, dexterity or quick reflexes while taking medications which include antihistamines—such as chlorpheniramine maleate as active ingredients.

Alcohol: Some dextromethorphan-containing medications contain various amounts of alcohol. Check label of any cough medication if concerned about ingestion of alcohol.

Sugar/Sweeteners: Some dextromethorphan-containing medications contain various amounts of sugar, sucrose, glucose, and/or artificial sweeteners such as aspartame, saccharin, sorbitol. Check label of cough medication before selecting, if concerned about diabetes and ingestion of sugar or artificial sweeteners.

ADDITIONAL WARNING:
Abuse/Dependency: Reports indicate a rising rate of abuse of dextromethorphan-containing medications, particularly among teens. Sufficient data has not yet been collected, however, to determine the abuse and dependency potential of dextromethorphan-containing medications.

INFORM YOUR DOCTOR BEFORE TAKING DEXTROMETHORPHAN AND RELATED COMBINATION PRODUCTS IF YOU HAVE:
Allergies to: any sympathomimetic drug, aspirin or other salicylates, or if you have diabetes, thyroid condition, or urinary difficulty. If you anticipate any surgery requiring general or spinal anesthesia within 2 months of taking dextromethorphan medication, inform your doctor.

ACTIVE INGREDIENTS:
DEXTROMETHORPHAN HYDROBROMIDE AND VARIOUS ANTIHISTAMINE COMBINATIONS

Q U I C K F A C T S

BRAND NAMES:
- DIMETAPP DM ELIXIR (combination with phenylpropanolamine hydrochloride and brompheniramine maleate—also contains saccharin, sorbitol)
- PRIMATUSS COUGH MIXTURE 4 LIQUID (combination with chlorpheniramine maleate—contains alcohol, sorbitol, sucrose)
- SCOT-TUSSIN DM LIQUID (combination with chlorpheniramine maleate)
- TRICODENE SUGAR-FREE (combination with chlorpheniramine maleate—also contains sorbitol)

SYMPTOMS RELIEVED:
Cough and nasal congestion associated with common cold, and minor throat and bronchial irritations.

HOW TO TAKE:
Comes in tablet, capsule, and liquid forms. Swallow tablet or capsule with liquid. Do not crush or chew timed-release tablets. Antihistamines can cause gastrointestinal (GI) irritation and should be taken with food or following meal.

USUAL ADULT DOSE:
Dosage varies per product and active ingredient formulation. Follow product dosage instructions.

USUAL CHILD DOSE:
Do not administer to children under 6 unless

QUICK FACTS

under direction of physician. Dosage may vary based on infant or child's age.

OVERDOSE SYMPTOMS:
Nervous agitation, severe anxiety, insomnia (sleeplessness), hallucinations, tremors, convulsions, nausea, vomiting, cardiac arrhythmia (irregular pulse and heartbeat). If you suspect an overdose, immediately seek medical attention.

SIDE EFFECTS:
No serious effects in most cases of common use, however, drowsiness is a common side effect produced by antihistamines. Less common side effects include nasal dryness, dizziness, nausea, and mild insomnia palpitations, insomnia. In rare cases, more severe side effects may result, including: painful and frequent urination, hypertension, and heart palpitations. In these cases, discontinue medication and call your doctor immediately.

CHECK WITH YOUR DOCTOR OR PHARMACIST BEFORE COMBINING DEXTROMETHORPHAN AND RELATED COMBINATION PRODUCTS WITH:
Cold, cough, or allergy medication, stimulants, antidepressants, antihypertensives, digitalis or other heart medication, diuretics, or MAO (monoamine oxidase inhibitors) drugs. Ingestion of caffeinated beverages (coffee, tea, caffeine-containing soft drinks) while taking dextromethorphan-containing medication can result in agitation and insomnia.

PREGNANCY OR BREASTFEEDING:
Dextromethorphan use by a nursing mother should be considered a potential risk for a nurs-

ing child as the drug will be passed on to the infant in the mother's milk. In all cases, a physician should be consulted.

PRECAUTIONS FOR CHILDREN:
In general, dextromethorphan is not advised for children under 6. Administer dextromethorphan to infants or children only when consulting a physician and follow instructions on medication (see above).

55+ **PRECAUTIONS FOR SENIORS:**
Seniors generally don't eliminate drugs as efficiently as younger persons, and should avoid high dosages. Use of dextromethorphan medications by seniors can lead to cardiac arrhythmia (irregular pulse and heartbeat). In addition, seniors are more likely to experience stimulant effects of the drug.

SPECIAL WARNINGS:
Do not use continuously for longer than 3 months. Do not use dextromethorphan medications containing tartrazine if you are intolerant or hypersensitive to aspirin. Allergic reactions, including bronchial asthma, have occurred in susceptible individuals.

Antihistamines: Because antihistamines often cause drowsiness, you should avoid activities or tasks such as driving, or other operations which require alertness, coordination, dexterity or quick reflexes while taking medications which include antihistamines as active ingredients.

ADDITIONAL WARNING:
Abuse/Dependency: Reports indicate a rising rate of abuse of dextromethorphan-containing

medications, particularly among teens. Sufficient data has not yet been collected, however, to determine the abuse and dependency potential of dextromethorphan-containing medications.

INFORM YOUR DOCTOR BEFORE TAKING DEXTROMETHORPHAN IF YOU HAVE:
Allergies to: any sympathomimetic drug, aspirin or other salicylates, or if you have diabetes, thyroid condition, or urinary difficulty. If you anticipate any surgery requiring general or spinal anesthesia within 2 months of taking dextromethorphan medication, inform your doctor.

QUICK FACTS

ACTIVE INGREDIENTS:

DEXTROMETHORPHAN HYDROBROMIDE AND VARIOUS DECONGESTANT COMBINATIONS

BRAND NAMES:

- CODIMAL DM SYRUP (combination with phenylephrine hydrochloride, pyrilamine, also contains menthol, saccharin, sorbitol)
- DIMETAPP DM ELIXIR (combination with phenylpropanolamine hydrochloride and brompheniramine maleate—also contains saccharin, sorbitol)
- ROBITUSSIN PEDIATRIC COUGH & COLD LIQUID (combination with phenylephrine hydrochloride—also contains saccharin, sorbitol)
- SNAPLETS–DM GRANULES (combination with phenylephrine hydrochloride)
- TRICODENE PEDIATRIC COUGH & COLD LIQUID (combination with phenylephrine hydrochloride)

SYMPTOMS RELIEVED:

Cough and nasal congestion associated with common cold, and minor throat and bronchial irritations.

HOW TO TAKE:

Comes in tablet, capsule, liquid, and chewable forms. Swallow with liquid. Do not crush or chew timed-release tablets.

USUAL ADULT DOSE:

Dosage varies per product and active ingredient formulation. Follow product dosage instructions.

USUAL CHILD DOSE:
Do not administer to children under 6 unless under direction of physician. Dosage may vary based on infant or child's age.

OVERDOSE SYMPTOMS:
Nervous agitation, severe anxiety, insomnia (sleeplessness), hallucinations, tremors, convulsions, nausea, vomiting, cardiac arrhythmia (irregular pulse and heartbeat). If you suspect an overdose, immediately seek medical attention.

SIDE EFFECTS:
No serious effects in most cases of common use. Less common side effects include nasal dryness, dizziness, nausea, and mild insomnia palpitations, insomnia. In rare cases, more severe side effects may result, including: painful and frequent urination, hypertension, and heart palpitations. In these cases, discontinue medication and call your doctor immediately.

CHECK WITH YOUR DOCTOR OR PHARMACIST BEFORE COMBINING DEXTROMETHORPHAN AND RELATED COMBINATION PRODUCTS WITH:
Cold, cough, or allergy medication, stimulants, antidepressants, antihypertensives, digitalis or other heart medication, diuretics, or MAO (monoamine oxidase inhibitors) drugs. Ingestion of caffeinated beverages (coffee, tea, caffeine-containing soft drinks) while taking dextromethorphan-containing medication can result in agitation and insomnia.

PREGNANCY OR BREASTFEEDING:
Dextromethorphan use by a nursing mother should be considered a potential risk for a

nursing child as the drug will be passed on to the infant in the mother's milk. In all cases, a physician should be consulted.

PRECAUTIONS FOR CHILDREN:
In general, dextromethorphan is not advised for children under 6. Administer dextromethorphan to infants or children only when consulting a physician and follow instructions on medication (see above).

55+ **PRECAUTIONS FOR SENIORS:**
Seniors generally don't eliminate drugs as efficiently as younger persons, and should avoid high dosages. Use of dextromethorphan medications by seniors can lead to cardiac arrhythmia (irregular pulse and heartbeat). In addition, seniors are more likely to experience stimulant effects of the drug.

SPECIAL WARNINGS:
Do not use continuously for longer than 3 months. Do not use dextromethorphan medications containing tartrazine if you are intolerant or hypersensitive to aspirin. Allergic reactions, including bronchial asthma, have occurred in susceptible individuals.

ADDITIONAL WARNING:
Abuse/Dependency: Reports indicate a rising rate of abuse of dextromethorphan-containing medications, particularly among teens. Sufficient data has not yet been collected, however, to determine the abuse and dependency potential of dextromethorphan-containing medications.

QUICK FACTS

INFORM YOUR DOCTOR BEFORE TAKING DEXTROMETHORPHAN IF YOU HAVE:
Allergies to: any sympathomimetic drug, aspirin or other salicylates, or if you have diabetes, thyroid condition, or urinary difficulty. If you anticipate any surgery requiring general or spinal anesthesia within 2 months of taking dextromethorphan medication, inform your doctor.

ACTIVE INGREDIENT:

DIPHENHYDRAMINE HYDROCHLORIDE

BRAND NAMES:

- BENYLIN COUGH (also contains ammonium chloride, sodium citrate, alcohol, menthol, glucose, sucrose, saccharin)
- BYDRAMINE (also contains alcohol)
- DIPHEN COUGH (also contains ammonium chloride, sodium citrate, alcohol, sugar, menthol, sorbitol, sucrose, raspberry flavor)
- UNI-BENT COUGH (also contains alcohol)

Note: *Diphenhydramine* is an antihistamine which is also used as a sleep aid.

SYMPTOMS RELIEVED:
Nasal congestion, runny nose, itchy and watery eyes, sneezing, scratchy throat, and irritated sinuses due to common cold, sinusitis, hay fever and other upper respiratory allergies.

HOW TO TAKE:
Comes in syrup form. Diphenhydramine and other antihistamines can cause gastrointestinal (GI) irritation and should be taken with food or following meal.

USUAL ADULT DOSE:
25 milligrams 6 times per day, not to exceed 150 milligrams in a 24 hour period.

USUAL CHILD DOSE:
For children 6 to 12: 12.5 milligrams 6 times per day, not to exceed 75 milligrams in a 24 hour period.

For children 2 to 6: 6.25 milligrams 6 times per day, not to exceed 25 milligrams in a 24 hour period.

QUICK FACTS

Do not administer to children under 2 unless under direction of physician. Dosage may vary based on infant or child's age.

OVERDOSE SYMPTOMS:
Nervous agitation, severe anxiety, insomnia (sleeplessness), hallucinations, tremors, convulsions, nausea, vomiting, cardiac arrhythmia (irregular pulse and heartbeat). If you suspect an overdose, immediately seek medical attention.

SIDE EFFECTS:
No serious effects in most cases of common use. Less common side effects include nasal dryness, dizziness, nausea, and mild insomnia palpitations, insomnia. In rare cases, more severe side effects may result, including: painful and frequent urination, hypertension, and heart palpitations. In these cases, discontinue medication and call your doctor immediately.

CHECK WITH YOUR DOCTOR OR PHARMACIST BEFORE COMBINING DIPHENHYDRAMINE WITH:
Cold, cough, or allergy medication, stimulants, antidepressants, antihypertensives, digitalis or other heart medication, diuretics, or MAO (monoamine oxidase inhibitors) drugs. Ingestion of caffeinated beverages (coffee, tea, caffeine-containing soft drinks) while taking diphenhydramine-containing medication can result in agitation and insomnia.

PREGNANCY OR BREASTFEEDING:
Diphenhydramine use by a nursing mother should be considered a potential risk for a nursing child as the drug will be passed on to the infant in the mother's milk. In all cases, a physician should be consulted.

PRECAUTIONS FOR CHILDREN:
In general, diphenhydramine is not advised for children under 6. Administer diphenhydramine to infants or children only when consulting a physician and follow instructions on medication (see above).

PRECAUTIONS FOR SENIORS:
Seniors generally don't eliminate drugs as efficiently as younger persons, and should avoid high dosages. Use of diphenhydramine medications by seniors can lead to urinary difficulties. In addition, seniors are more likely to experience drowsiness effects of the drug.

SPECIAL WARNINGS:
Because antihistamines often cause drowsiness, you should avoid activities or tasks such as driving, or other operations which require alertness, coordination, dexterity or quick reflexes.

INFORM YOUR DOCTOR BEFORE TAKING DIPHENHYDRAMINE IF YOU HAVE:
Allergies to: any sympathomimetic drug, aspirin or other salicylates, or if you have diabetes, thyroid condition, or urinary difficulty. If you anticipate any surgery requiring general or spinal anesthesia within 2 months of taking diphenhydramine medication, inform your doctor.

Q U I C K F A C T S

ACTIVE INGREDIENTS:

GUAIFENESIN, DEXTROMETHORPHAN HYDROBROMIDE, AND PHENYLPROPANOLAMINE HYDROCHLORIDE

℞ **BRAND NAMES:**

- GuiaCough CF Liquid (also contains alcohol, parabens, saccharin, sorbitol, sucrose)
- Guiatuss CF Liquid (also contains alcohol)
- Naldecon DX Adult Liquid (also contains saccharin, sorbitol)
- Naldelate DX Adult Liquid (also contains saccharin, sorbitol)
- Robafen CF Liquid (also contains alcohol)
- Robitussin–CF Liquid (also contains alcohol, saccharin, sorbitol)

Note: *Guaifenesin* and *dextromethorphan hydrobromide* are also active ingredient in other multi-symptom antitussive/expectorant medications which are formulated with other active ingredients.

Phenylpropanolamine hydrochloride is used as an active ingredient in decongestant and stimulant products.

SYMPTOMS RELIEVED:

Cough, nasal congestion and runny nose, itchy and watery eyes, sneezing, scratchy throat, and irritated sinuses associated with common cold, minor throat and bronchial irritations, sinusitis, hay fever and other upper respiratory allergies, by suppressing or moderating extreme cough activity, loosening bronchial congestion and phlegm—resulting in more productive coughs—and by clearing congested sinuses.

HOW TO TAKE:
Comes in liquid forms.

USUAL ADULT DOSE:
Dosage varies per product and active ingredient formulation. Follow product dosage instructions.

USUAL CHILD DOSE:
Do not administer to children under 6 unless under direction of physician. Dosage may vary based on infant or child's age.

OVERDOSE SYMPTOMS:
Nervous agitation, severe anxiety, insomnia (sleeplessness), hallucinations, tremors, convulsions, nausea, vomiting, cardiac arrhythmia (irregular pulse and heartbeat), drowsiness, dizziness, fatigue, rash. If you suspect an overdose, immediately seek medical attention.

SIDE EFFECTS:
No serious effects in most cases of common use. Less common side effects include nasal dryness, dizziness, nausea, and mild insomnia palpitations, insomnia, gastrointestinal (GI) upset including stomach cramps and diarrhea, drowsiness, and fatigue. In rare cases, more severe side effects may result, including: painful and frequent urination, hypertension, and heart palpitations. In these cases, discontinue medication and call your doctor immediately.

CHECK WITH YOUR DOCTOR OR PHARMACIST BEFORE COMBINING THESE COMBINATION PRODUCTS WITH:
Anticoagulant medications, other cold, cough, or allergy medication, stimulants, antidepressants, antihypertensives, digitalis or other heart med-

QUICK FACTS

ication, diuretics, or MAO (monoamine oxidase inhibitors) drugs. Ingestion of caffeinated beverages (coffee, tea, caffeine-containing soft drinks) while taking phenylpropanolamine-containing medication can result in agitation and insomnia.

PREGNANCY OR BREASTFEEDING:
Use of medications containing any of the active ingredients in these products by a nursing mother should be considered a potential risk for a nursing child as the drug(s) will be passed on to the infant in the mother's milk. In all cases, a physician should be consulted.

PRECAUTIONS FOR CHILDREN:
In general, these active ingredients are not advised for children under 2. Administer to infants or children only when consulting a physician and follow instructions on medication (see above).

55+

PRECAUTIONS FOR SENIORS:
Seniors generally don't eliminate drugs as efficiently as younger persons, and should avoid high dosages.

SPECIAL WARNINGS:
Do not use for control of chronic cough related to conditions such as emphysema, asthma, or smoking, or if coughs are producing excessive secretions. If cough is accompanied by high fever, rash, nausea or vomiting, or persistent headache, use only if directed by your doctor.

ADDITIONAL WARNING:
Alcohol: Some cough/cold medications contain various amounts of alcohol. Check label of any

cough medication if concerned about ingestion of alcohol.

Sugar/Sweeteners: Some cough/cold medications contain various amounts of sugar, sucrose, glucose, and/or artificial sweeteners such as aspartame, saccharin, sorbitol. Check label of cough medication before selecting, if concerned about diabetes and ingestion of sugar or artificial sweeteners.

Abuse/Dependency: Reports indicate a rising rate of abuse of dextromethorphan-containing medications, particularly among teens. Sufficient data has not yet been collected, however, to determine the abuse and dependency potential of dextromethorphan-containing medications.

INFORM YOUR DOCTOR BEFORE TAKING PRODUCTS CONTAINING THIS COMBINATION OF ACTIVE INGREDIENTS IF YOU HAVE:

Asthma, emphysema or other respiratory condition, liver impairment or liver disease, allergies to any sympathomimetic drug, aspirin or other salicylates, or if you have diabetes, thyroid condition, or urinary difficulty. If you anticipate any surgery requiring general or spinal anesthesia within 2 months of taking medication which contains phenylpropanolamine, inform your doctor.

Q U I C K F A C T S

ACTIVE INGREDIENTS:

PHENYLPROPANOLAMINE AND CHLORPHENIRAMINE MALEATE COMBINATION WITH ACETAMINOPHEN

BRAND NAMES:

- TRIAMINICOL MULTI-SYMPTOM COUGH & COLD TABLETS (combination with caffeine)

SYMPTOMS RELIEVED:

Cough, nasal congestion and runny nose, itchy and watery eyes, sneezing, scratchy throat, and irritated sinuses associated with common cold, minor throat and bronchial irritations, sinusitis, hay fever and other upper respiratory allergies, by suppressing or moderating extreme cough activity, loosening bronchial congestion and phlegm—resulting in more productive coughs—and by clearing congested sinuses.

HOW TO TAKE:

Comes in tablet, capsule, chewable forms. Swallow with liquid. Do not crush or chew timed-release tablets.

USUAL ADULT DOSE:

25 milligrams 3 times per day, (75 milligrams once daily for timed-release capsules) 1/2 hour before meals, not to exceed 75 milligrams in a 24 hour period.

USUAL CHILD DOSE:

Do not administer to children under 6 unless under direction of physician. Dosage may vary based on infant or child's age.

OVERDOSE SYMPTOMS:

Nervous agitation, severe anxiety, insomnia

(sleeplessness), hallucinations, tremors, convulsions, nausea, vomiting, cardiac arrhythmia (irregular pulse and heartbeat). If you suspect an overdose, immediately seek medical attention.

SIDE EFFECTS:
No serious effects in most cases of common use. Less common side effects include nasal dryness, dizziness, nausea, and mild insomnia palpitations, insomnia. In rare cases, more severe side effects may result, including: painful and frequent urination, hypertension, and heart palpitations. In these cases, discontinue medication and call your doctor immediately.

CHECK WITH YOUR DOCTOR OR PHARMACIST BEFORE COMBINING PHENYLPROPANOLAMINE WITH:
Cold, cough,or allergy medication, stimulants, antidepressants, antihypertensives, digitalis or other heart medication, diuretics, or MAO (monoamine oxidase inhibitors) drugs. Ingestion of caffeinated beverages (coffee, tea, caffeine-containing soft drinks) while taking phenylpropanolamine-containing medication can result in agitation and insomnia.

PREGNANCY OR BREASTFEEDING:
Phenylpropanolamine use by a nursing mother should be considered a potential risk for a nursing child as the drug will be passed on to the infant in the mother's milk. In all cases, a physician should be consulted.

PRECAUTIONS FOR CHILDREN:
In general, phenylpropanolamine is not advised for children under 6. Administer phenylpropa-

QUICK FACTS

nolamine to infants or children only when consulting a physician and follow instructions on medication (see above).

55+ **PRECAUTIONS FOR SENIORS:**
Seniors generally don't eliminate drugs as efficiently as younger persons, and should avoid high dosages. Use of phenylpropanolamine medications by seniors can lead to cardiac arrhythmia (irregular pulse and heartbeat). In addition, seniors are more likely to experience stimulant effects of the drug.

SPECIAL WARNINGS:
Do not use continuously for longer than 3 months. Do not use phenylpropanolamine medications containing tartrazine if you are intolerant or hypersensitive to aspirin. Allergic reactions, including bronchial asthma, have occurred in susceptible individuals.

INFORM YOUR DOCTOR BEFORE TAKING PHENYLPROPANOLAMINE IF YOU HAVE:
Allergies to: any sympathomimetic drug, aspirin or other salicylates, or if you have diabetes, thyroid condition, or urinary difficulty. If you anticipate any surgery requiring general or spinal anesthesia within 2 months of taking phenylpropanolamine medication, inform your doctor.

ACTIVE INGREDIENT:

TRIPOLIDINE HYDROCHLORIDE

BRAND NAMES:

- ACTIDIL

SYMPTOMS RELIEVED:

Nasal congestion, runny nose, itchy and watery eyes, sneezing, scratchy throat, and irritated sinuses due to common cold, sinusitis, hay fever, and other upper respiratory allergies.

HOW TO TAKE:

Comes in tablet, capsule, and liquid forms. Swallow tablet or capsule with liquid. Do not crush or chew timed-release tablets. Tripolidine and other antihistamines can cause gastrointestinal (GI) irritation and should be taken with food or following meal.

USUAL ADULT DOSE:

2.5 milligrams 3 to 4 times per day, not to exceed 10 grams in a 24 hour period.

USUAL CHILD DOSE:

For children 6 to 12: 2 milligrams 4 to 6 times per day, or 8 milligrams of timed-release medication at bedtime or during day, not to exceed 12 milligrams in a 24 hour period.

For children 2 to 6: 1.25 milligrams 4 to 6 times per day, not to exceed 5 milligrams in a 24 hour period. Timed-release medications are not advised for children 2 to 6 or younger. Do not administer to children in this age group unless under direction of physician. Dosage may vary based on infant or child's age.

QUICK FACTS

OVERDOSE SYMPTOMS:
Nervous agitation, severe anxiety, insomnia (sleeplessness), hallucinations, tremors, coma. If you suspect an overdose, immediately seek medical attention.

SIDE EFFECTS:
The most frequent side effect of antihistamines use is drowsiness. Other common side effects include: include dryness of mouth, throat, and nasal passages, dizziness, GI distress (including vomiting, diarrhea, and constipation or change in bowel regularity), and diminished muscle coordination. In rare cases, more severe side effects may result, such as painful and frequent urination or urinary retention, vision problems, loss of appetite, and respiratory difficulty. In these cases, discontinue medication and call your doctor immediately.

CHECK WITH YOUR DOCTOR OR PHARMACIST BEFORE COMBINING TRIPOLIDINE WITH:
Cold, cough, or allergy medication—including other antihistamines; aspirin, stimulants, antidepressants, antihypertensives, digitalis or other heart medication, diuretics, or MAO (monoamine oxidase inhibitors) drugs. Avoid ingestion of alcohol or use of sedatives or tranquilizers while taking tripolidine-containing medication or most other antihistamine-containing medication as the combination can produce severe drowsiness or sedation.

PREGNANCY OR BREASTFEEDING:
Tripolidine use by a nursing mother should be considered a potential risk for a nursing child as the drug will be passed on to the infant in the

mother's milk. In all cases, a physician should be consulted.

PRECAUTIONS FOR CHILDREN:
In general, tripolidine is not advised for children under 6. Administer tripolidine to infants or children only when consulting a physician and follow instructions on medication (see above).

55+
PRECAUTIONS FOR SENIORS:
Seniors generally don't eliminate drugs as efficiently as younger persons, and should avoid high dosages. Use of tripolidine medications by seniors can lead to urinary difficulties. In addition, seniors are more likely to experience stimulant effects of the drug.

SPECIAL WARNINGS:
Because antihistamines often cause drowsiness, you should avoid activities or tasks such as driving, or other operations which require alertness, coordination, dexterity or quick reflexes. Do not use continuously for longer than 3 months. Do not use tripolidine medications containing tartrazine if you are intolerant or hypersensitive to aspirin. Allergic reactions, including bronchial asthma, have occurred in susceptible individuals.

INFORM YOUR DOCTOR BEFORE TAKING TRIPOLIDINE IF YOU HAVE:
urinary difficulty, glaucoma, ulcer, or if you are pregnant. If you anticipate any surgery requiring general or spinal anesthesia within 2 months of taking tripolidine-containing medication, inform your doctor.

QUICK REVIEW

• DECONGESTANT •
(NASAL)

The most important considerations in choosing a decongestant are: relief of membrane congestion (usually in sinus areas) in cases of allergy, hay fever, and common cold; and potential side effects associated with these drugs.

DECONGESTANTS ARE A CLASS OF DRUGS WHICH:

- shrink swollen and irritated mucosal membranes. Decongestants function by acting on the sympathetic nervous system to constrict blood vessels. Many of these drugs can be effective in relieving nasal congestion, respiratory allergies, or sinusitis,
- often are often combined with other agents such as antihistamines, antipyretics, analgesics, antitussives, or expectorants to provide multisymptomatic relief for headaches, fever, cough, sleeplessness, and other symptoms of the common cold, flu, hay fever, and similar ailments. However, these drugs do not affect the underlying cause or course of such ailments,
- may produce side effects which can include dryness of mouth and sinuses, nervous agitation, sleeplessness, or drowsiness.

ACTIVE INGREDIENTS:

ACETAMINOPHEN, CHLORPHENIRAMINE MALEATE, DEXTROMETHORPHAN HYDROBROMIDE, AND PSEUDOEPHREDINE HYDROCHLORIDE

℞ **BRAND NAMES:**

- ALKA-SELTZER PLUS COLD & COUGH LIQUI-GELS (also contains sorbitol)
- BAYER SELECT FLU RELIEF CAPLETS
- CO-APAP TABLETS
- COMTREX LIQUID (also contains alcohol, sucrose)
- COMTREX LIQUI-GELS (contains sorbitol)
- COMTREX MAXIMUM LIQUI-GELS (contains sorbitol)
- COMTREX MAX STRENGTH MULTI-SYMPTOM COLD & FLU RELIEF LIQUI-GELS
- COMTREX MAXIMUM STRENGTH MULTI-SYMPTOM COLD & FLU RELIEF CAPLETS & TABLETS (contains parabens)
- CONTAC SEVERE COLD & FLU NIGHTTIME LIQUID (also contains alcohol, saccharin, sorbitol, glucose)
- GENACOL TABLETS
- KOLEPHRIN/DM CAPLETS
- MAPAP COLD FORMULA TABLETS
- MEDI-FLU LIQUID (also contains alcohol, saccharin, sorbitol, sugar)
- THERAFLU FLU, COLD & COUGH POWDER (contains sucrose)
- THERAFLU NIGHTTIME FLU POWDER (contains sucrose)
- TYLENOL CHILDREN'S COLD MULTI-SYMPTOM PLUS COUGH LIQUID (also contains sorbitol, corn syrup)

QUICK FACTS

- Tylenol Multi-Symptom Cold Caplets & Tablets
- Tylenol Multi-Symptom Hot Medication Powder (combination with phenylalanine, also contains aspartame, sucrose)
- Vicks Children's NyQuil Nighttime Cold/Cough Liquid (also contains sucrose)
- Vicks 44M Cold, Flu & Cough LiquiCaps
- Vicks Pediatric Formula 44M Multi-Symptom Cough & Cold Liquid (also contains sorbitol, sucrose)

Note: *Dextromethorphan hydrobromide* is also an active ingredient in other multi-symptom antitussive/expectorant medications which are formulated with other active ingredients.

Pseudoephredine hydrochloride is a used as an active ingredient in decongestant and stimulant products.

Acetaminophen is a non-aspirin analgesic which is used primarily in pain-relief products.

Chlorpheniramine maleate is an antihistamine which is mostly used in combination with analgesic, antitussive, decongestant and expectorant active ingredients in OTC medications to provide relief of allergy, common cold, cough or flu symptoms.

SYMPTOMS RELIEVED:
Minor aches and pains, nasal congestion, and coughing such as those associated with the common cold, flu, sore throat, sinusitis, hay fever and other respiratory allergies, and reduction of fever.

HOW TO TAKE:
Comes in tablet, caplet, capsule, and liquid forms. Swallow tablet, caplet, or capsule with liquid. Sprinkle powder over liquid, then swallow. Do not crush or chew timed-release tablet.

USUAL ADULT DOSE:
Dosage varies per product and active ingredient formulation. Follow product dosage instructions.

USUAL CHILD DOSE:
Do not administer to children under 6 unless under direction of physician. Dosage may vary based on infant or child's age.

OVERDOSE SYMPTOMS:
Nervous agitation, severe anxiety, insomnia (sleeplessness), hallucinations, tremors, convulsions, nausea, vomiting, cardiac arrhythmia (irregular pulse and heartbeat), drowsiness, dizziness, fatigue, rash. If you suspect an overdose, immediately seek medical attention.

SIDE EFFECTS:
No serious effects in most cases of common use, although antihistamines can cause drowsiness. Less common side effects include nasal dryness, dizziness, nausea, and mild insomnia palpitations, insomnia, gastrointestinal (GI) upset including stomach cramps and diarrhea, drowsiness, and fatigue. In rare cases, more severe side effects may result, including: painful and frequent urination, hypertension, and heart palpitations. In these cases, discontinue medication and call your doctor immediately. Long-term ingestion of high dosages of acetaminophen-containing products may increase risk of liver and kidney damage.

Q U I C K F A C T S

CHECK WITH YOUR DOCTOR OR PHARMACIST BEFORE COMBINING THESE COMBINATION PRODUCTS WITH:

Anticoagulant medications, other cold, cough, or allergy medication, stimulants, antidepressants, antihypertensives, digitalis or other heart medication, diuretics, or MAO (monoamine oxidase inhibitors) drugs. Ingestion of caffeinated beverages (coffee, tea, caffeine-containing soft drinks) while taking pseudoephredine-containing medication can result in agitation and insomnia.

If taking combination products which contain acetaminophen, you should avoid Isoniazid (antituberculosis) medication. Excessive ingestion of alcohol while taking acetaminophen-containing medication can increase the risk of liver damage or disease (hepatic toxicity). Alcohol use may also increase possible drowsiness effect of the antihistamine in these combination products.

PREGNANCY OR BREASTFEEDING:

Use of medications containing any of the active ingredients in these products by a nursing mother should be considered a potential risk for a nursing child as the drug(s) will be passed on to the infant in the mother's milk. In all cases, a physician should be consulted.

PRECAUTIONS FOR CHILDREN:

In general, these active ingredients are not advised for children under 2. Administer to infants or children only when consulting a physician and follow instructions on medication (see above).

55+ **PRECAUTIONS FOR SENIORS:**
Seniors generally don't eliminate drugs as efficiently as younger persons, and should avoid high dosages. Use of antihistamine-containing medications by seniors can lead to urinary difficulties. In addition, seniors are more likely to experience potential drowsiness effects of the antihistamine in this combination.

SPECIAL WARNINGS:
Do not use for control of chronic cough related to conditions such as emphysema, asthma, or smoking, or if coughs are producing excessive secretions. If cough is accompanied by high fever, rash, nausea or vomiting, or persistent headache, use only if directed by your doctor. Because antihistamines may cause drowsiness, you should avoid activities or tasks such as driving, or other operations which require alertness, coordination, dexterity, or quick reflexes. Chronic alcoholics are at risk for hepatic (liver) function impairment if taking high dosages of acetaminophen-containing medication. Do not use medications which combine doxylamine succinate with tartrazine if you are intolerant or hypersensitive to aspirin. Allergic reactions, including bronchial asthma, have occurred in susceptible individuals.

ADDITIONAL WARNING:
Alcohol: Some cough/cold medications contain various amounts of alcohol. Check label of any cough medication if concerned about ingestion of alcohol.

Q U I C K F A C T S

Sugar/Sweeteners: Some cough/cold medications contain various amounts of sugar, sucrose, glucose, and/or artificial sweeteners such as aspartame, saccharin, sorbitol. Check label of cough medication before selecting, if concerned about diabetes and ingestion of sugar or artificial sweeteners.

Abuse/Dependency: Reports indicate a rising rate of abuse of dextromethorphan-containing medications, particularly among teens. Sufficient data has not yet been collected, however, to determine the abuse and dependency potential of dextromethorphan-containing medications.

INFORM YOUR DOCTOR BEFORE TAKING PRODUCTS CONTAINING THIS COMBINATION OF ACTIVE INGREDIENTS IF YOU HAVE:
Asthma, emphysema or other respiratory condition, liver impairment or liver disease, allergies to any sympathomimetic drug, aspirin or other salicylates, or if you have diabetes, thyroid condition, or urinary difficulty. If you anticipate any surgery requiring general or spinal anesthesia within 2 months of taking medication which contains pseudoephredine, inform your doctor.

Q U I C K F A C T S

ACTIVE INGREDIENTS:

ACETAMINOPHEN, DEXTROMETHORPHAN HYDROBROMIDE, AND PSEUDOEPHREDINE HYDROCHLORIDE

℞ **BRAND NAMES:**

- ALKA-SELTZER PLUS FLU & BODY ACHES NON-DROWSY LIQUI-GELS
- BAYER SELECT NIGHTTIME COLD CAPLETS (combination with tripolidine hydrochloride)
- COMTREX MAXIMUM STRENGTH NON-DROWSY CAPLETS
- CONTAC DAY & NIGHT COLD & FLU CAPLETS (combination with diphenhydramine hydrochloride)
- ROBITUSSIN NIGHT RELIEF LIQUID (also contains saccharin, sorbitol)
- SALETO CF TABLETS
- SUDAFED SEVERE COLD CAPLETS & TABLETS
- THERAFLU NON-DROWSY FORMULA MAXIMUM STRENGTH CAPLETS (also contains lactose, methylparaben)
- THERAFLU NON-DROWSY FLU, COLD & COUGH MAXIMUM STRENGTH POWDER (also contains sucrose)
- TRIAMINIC SORE THROAT FORMULA LIQUID (also contains EDTA, sucrose)
- TYLENOL COLD NO DROWSINESS CAPLETS & GELCAPS/MAXIMUM STRENGTH GELCAPS
- TYLENOL MAXIMUM STRENGTH COUGH WITH DECONGESTANT LIQUID (also contains alcohol, saccharin, sorbitol, sucrose)

Note: *Dextromethorphan hydrobromide* is also an active ingredient in other multi-symptom

antitussive/expectorant medications which are formulated with other active ingredients.

Pseudoephredine hydrochloride is a used as an active ingredient in decongestant and stimulant products.

Acetaminophen is a non-aspirin analgesic which is used primarily in pain-relief products.

SYMPTOMS RELIEVED:
Minor aches and pains, nasal congestion and coughing such as those associated with the common cold, flu, sore throat, sinusitis, hay fever and other respiratory allergies, and reduction of fever.

HOW TO TAKE:
Comes in caplet, capsule, and liquid forms. Swallow caplet or capsule with liquid. Sprinkle powder over liquid, then swallow. Do not crush or chew timed-release tablet.

USUAL ADULT DOSE:
Dosage varies per product and active ingredient formulation. Follow product dosage instructions.

USUAL CHILD DOSE:
Do not administer to children under 6 unless under direction of physician. Dosage may vary based on infant or child's age.

OVERDOSE SYMPTOMS:
Nervous agitation, severe anxiety, insomnia (sleeplessness), hallucinations, tremors, convulsions, nausea, vomiting, cardiac arrhythmia (irregular pulse and heartbeat), drowsiness, dizziness, fatigue, rash. If you suspect an overdose, immediately seek medical attention.

SIDE EFFECTS:
No serious effects in most cases of common use. Less common side effects include nasal dryness, dizziness, nausea, and mild insomnia palpitations, insomnia, gastrointestinal (GI) upset including stomach cramps and diarrhea, drowsiness and fatigue. In rare cases, more severe side effects may result, including: painful and frequent urination, hypertension, and heart palpitations. In these cases, discontinue medication and call your doctor immediately. Long-term ingestion of high dosages of acetaminophen-containing products may increase risk of liver and kidney damage.

CHECK WITH YOUR DOCTOR OR PHARMACIST BEFORE COMBINING THESE COMBINATION PRODUCTS WITH:
Anticoagulant medications , other cold, cough, or allergy medication, stimulants, antidepressants, antihypertensives, digitalis or other heart medication, diuretics, or MAO (monoamine oxidase inhibitors) drugs. Ingestion of caffeinated beverages (coffee, tea, caffeine-containing soft drinks) while taking pseudoephredine-containing medication can result in agitation and insomnia. If taking combination products which contain acetaminophen, you should avoid Isoniazid (anti-tuberculosis) medication. Excessive ingestion of alcohol while taking acetaminophen-containing medication can increase the risk of liver damage or disease (hepatic toxicity).

PREGNANCY OR BREASTFEEDING:
Use of medications containing any of the active ingredients in these products by a nursing

mother should be considered a potential risk for a nursing child as the drug(s) will be passed on to the infant in the mother's milk. In all cases, a physician should be consulted.

PRECAUTIONS FOR CHILDREN:
In general, these active ingredients are not advised for children under 2. Administer to infants or children only when consulting a physician and follow instructions on medication (see above).

55+

PRECAUTIONS FOR SENIORS:
Seniors generally don't eliminate drugs as efficiently as younger persons, and should avoid high dosages. Use of pseudoephedrine-containing medications by seniors can lead to urinary difficulties. In addition, seniors are more likely to experience stimulant effects of pseudoephedrine.

SPECIAL WARNINGS:
Do not use for control of chronic cough related to conditions such as emphysema, asthma, or smoking, or if coughs are producing excessive secretions. If cough is accompanied by high fever, rash, nausea or vomiting, or persistent headache, use only if directed by your doctor. Chronic alcoholics are at risk for hepatic (liver) function impairment if taking high dosages of acetaminophen-containing medication.

ADDITIONAL WARNING:
Alcohol: Some cough/cold medications contain various amounts of alcohol. Check label of any cough medication if concerned about ingestion of alcohol.

Sugar/Sweeteners: Some cough/cold medications contain various amounts of sugar, sucrose, glucose, and/or artificial sweeteners such as aspartame, saccharin, sorbitol. Check label of cough medication before selecting, if concerned about diabetes and ingestion of sugar or artificial sweeteners.

Abuse/Dependency: Reports indicate a rising rate of abuse of dextromethorphan-containing medications, particularly among teens. Sufficient data has not yet been collected, however, to determine the abuse and dependency potential of dextromethorphan-containing medications.

INFORM YOUR DOCTOR BEFORE TAKING PRODUCTS CONTAINING THIS COMBINATION OF ACTIVE INGREDIENTS IF YOU HAVE:

Asthma, emphysema or other respiratory condition, liver impairment or liver disease, allergies to any sympathomimetic drug, aspirin or other salicylates, or if you have diabetes, thyroid condition, or urinary difficulty. If you anticipate any surgery requiring general or spinal anesthesia within 2 months of taking medication which contains pseudoephredine, inform your doctor.

QUICK FACTS

ACTIVE INGREDIENT:
PHENYLPROPANOLAMINE HYDROCHLORIDE

BRAND NAMES:
- A.R.M. Caplets
- Chlor-Rest
- Cold-Gest Capsules
- Contac 12-Hour Capsules
- Demazin
- Demazin Syrup
- Gencold Capsules
- Propagest
- Rescon Liquid
- Silaminic Cold Syrup
- Spec-T Sore Throat/Decongestant Lozenges
- Tavist-D Tablets
- Teldrin 12-Hour Allergy Relief
- Temazin Cold Syrup
- Thera-Hist Syrup
- Tri-Nefrin
- Triaminic

SYMPTOMS RELIEVED:
Nasal congestion, runny nose, itchy and watery eyes, sneezing, scratchy throat, and irritated sinuses due to common cold, sinusitis, hay fever, and other upper respiratory allergies.

HOW TO TAKE:
Comes in tablet, capsule, chewable forms. Swallow with liquid. Do not crush or chew timed-release tablets.

USUAL ADULT DOSE:
25 milligrams every 4 hours, not to exceed 150 milligrams in a 24 hour period, or 75 milli-

grams in a 24 hour period for timed-release tablets or capsules.

USUAL CHILD DOSE:

For children 6 to 12: 12.5 milligrams 6 times per day, not to exceed 75 milligrams in a 24 hour period.

For children 2 to 6: 6.25 milligrams 6 times per day, not to exceed 37.5 milligrams in a 24 hour period.

Timed-release medications should only be administered under direction of physician. Do not administer to children under 6 unless under direction of physician. Dosage may vary based on infant or child's age.

OVERDOSE SYMPTOMS:

Nervous agitation, severe anxiety, insomnia (sleeplessness), hallucinations, tremors, convulsions, nausea, vomiting, cardiac arrhythmia (irregular pulse and heartbeat). If you suspect an overdose, immediately seek medical attention.

SIDE EFFECTS:

No serious effects in most cases of common use. Less common side effects include nasal dryness, dizziness, nausea, and mild insomnia. In rare cases, more severe side effects may result, including: painful and frequent urination, hypertension, and heart palpitations. In these cases, discontinue medication and call your doctor immediately.

CHECK WITH YOUR DOCTOR OR PHARMACIST BEFORE COMBINING PHENYLPROPANOLAMINE WITH:

Cold, cough, or allergy medication, stimulants,

Q U I C K F A C T S

antidepressants, antihypertensives, digitalis or other heart medication, diuretics, or MAO (monoamine oxidase inhibitors) drugs. Ingestion of caffeinated beverages (coffee, tea, caffeine-containing soft drinks) while taking phenylpropanolamine-containing medication can result in agitation and insomnia.

PREGNANCY OR BREASTFEEDING:
Phenylpropanolamine use by a nursing mother should be considered a potential risk for a nursing child as the drug will be passed on to the infant in the mother's milk. In all cases, a physician should be consulted.

PRECAUTIONS FOR CHILDREN:
In general, phenylpropanolamine is not advised for children under 6. Administer phenylpropanolamine to infants or children only when consulting a physician and follow instructions on medication (see above).

55+ **PRECAUTIONS FOR SENIORS:**
Seniors generally don't eliminate drugs as efficiently as younger persons, and should avoid high dosages. Use of phenylpropanolamine medications by seniors can lead to cardiac arrhythmia (irregular pulse and heartbeat). In addition, seniors are more likely to experience stimulant effects of the drug.

SPECIAL WARNINGS:
Do not use continuously for longer than 3 months. Do not use phenylpropanolamine medications containing tartrazine if you are intolerant or hypersensitive to aspirin. Allergic reactions, including bronchial asthma, have occurred in susceptible individuals.

INFORM YOUR DOCTOR BEFORE TAKING PHENYLPROPANOLAMINE IF YOU HAVE:

Allergies to: any sympathomimetic drug, aspirin or other salicylates, or if you have diabetes, thyroid condition, or urinary difficulty. If you anticipate any surgery requiring general or spinal anesthesia within 2 months of taking phenylpropanolamine medication, inform your doctor.

Q U I C K F A C T S

ACTIVE INGREDIENTS:

PHENYLPROPANOLAMINE AND BROMPHENIRAMINE MALEATE

BRAND NAMES:

- Bromaline Elixir (contains alcohol, saccharin, sorbitol)
- Bromanate Elixir (contains saccharin, sorbitol)
- Bromtapp Tablets
- Dimaphen Elixir (contains alcohol, saccharin, sorbitol)
- Dimaphen Release Tablets
- Dimetane Decongestant Capsules
- Dimetapp Elixir (contains alcohol, saccharin, sorbitol)
- Dimetapp Exentabs Tablets
- Genatpp Elixir (contains saccharin, sorbitol)

HOW TO TAKE:

Comes in tablet, capsule, chewable forms. Swallow with liquid. Do not crush or chew timed-release tablets.

USUAL ADULT DOSE:

25 milligrams 3 times per day, (75 milligrams once daily for timed-release capsules) 1/2 hour before meals, not to exceed 75 milligrams in a 24 hour period.

USUAL CHILD DOSE:

Do not administer to children under 6 unless under direction of physician. Dosage may vary based on infant or child's age.

OVERDOSE SYMPTOMS:

Nervous agitation, severe anxiety, insomnia (sleeplessness), hallucinations, tremors, convulsions, nausea, vomiting, cardiac arrhythmia (irregular pulse and heartbeat). If you suspect an overdose, immediately seek medical attention.

SIDE EFFECTS:
No serious effects in most cases of common use. Less common side effects include nasal dryness, dizziness, nausea, and mild insomnia palpitations, insomnia. In rare cases, more severe side effects may result, including: painful and frequent urination, hypertension, and heart palpitations. In these cases, discontinue medication and call your doctor immediately.

CHECK WITH YOUR DOCTOR OR PHARMACIST BEFORE COMBINING PHENYLPROPANOLAMINE WITH:
Cold, cough,or allergy medication, stimulants, antidepressants, antihypertensives, digitalis or other heart medication, diuretics, or MAO (monoamine oxidase inhibitors) drugs. Ingestion of caffeinated beverages (coffee, tea, caffeine-containing soft drinks) while taking phenylpropanolamine-containing medication can result in agitation and insomnia.

PREGNANCY OR BREASTFEEDING:
Phenylpropanolamine use by a nursing mother should be considered a potential risk for a nursing child as the drug will be passed on to the infant in the mother's milk. In all cases, a physician should be consulted.

PRECAUTIONS FOR CHILDREN:
In general, phenylpropanolamine is not advised for children under 6. Administer phenylpropanolamine to infants or children only when consulting a physician and follow instructions on medication (see above).

QUICK FACTS

55+ **PRECAUTIONS FOR SENIORS:**
Seniors generally don't eliminate drugs as efficiently as younger persons, and should avoid high dosages. Use of phenylpropanolamine medications by seniors can lead to cardiac arrhythmia (irregular pulse and heartbeat). In addition, seniors are more likely to experience stimulant effects of the drug.

SPECIAL WARNINGS:
Do not use continuously for longer than 3 months. Do not use phenylpropanolamine medications containing tartazine if you are intolerant or hypersensitive to aspirin. Allergic reactions, including bronchial asthma, have occurred in susceptible individuals.

INFORM YOUR DOCTOR BEFORE TAKING PHENYLPROPANOLAMINE IF YOU HAVE:
Allergies to: any sympathomimetic drug, aspirin or other salicylates, or if you have diabetes, thyroid condition, or urinary difficulty. If you anticipate any surgery requiring general or spinal anesthesia within 2 months of taking phenylpropanolamine medication, inform your doctor.

ACTIVE INGREDIENTS:

PHENYLPROPANOLAMINE HYDROCHLORIDE COMBINATION WITH CHLORPHENIRAMINE MALEATE

QUICK FACTS

BRAND NAMES:

- COLD-GEST CAPSULES
- DEMAZIN
- DEMAZIN SYRUP (also contains 7.5% alcohol, menthol, sugar, parabens)
- GENCOLD CAPSULES
- RESCON LIQUID (also contains 7.5% alcohol, menthol, sugar, parabens)
- SILAMINIC COLD SYRUP (also contains 7.5% alcohol, menthol, sugar, parabens)
- SPEC-T SORE THROAT/DECONGESTANT LOZENGES (combination with phenylephrine hydrochloride, benzocaine, tartrazine—also contains dextrose, glucose, sucrose)
- TAVIST-D TABLETS (combination with clemastine fumarate)
- TELDRIN 12-HOUR ALLERGY RELIEF
- TEMAZIN COLD SYRUP (also contains 7.5% alcohol, menthol, sugar, parabens)
- THERA-HIST SYRUP (also contains sorbitol and sucrose)
- TRI-NEFRIN

SYMPTOMS RELIEVED:

Nasal congestion, runny nose, itchy and watery eyes, sneezing, scratchy throat, and irritated sinuses due to common cold, sinusitis, hay fever, and other upper respiratory allergies.

HOW TO TAKE:

Comes in tablet, capsule, liquid, lozenges, and

chewable forms. Swallow tablets and capsules with liquid. Do not crush or chew timed-release tablets.

USUAL ADULT DOSE:
25 milligrams every 4 hours, not to exceed 150 milligrams in a 24 hour period, or 75 milligrams in a 24 hour period for timed-release tablets or capsules.

USUAL CHILD DOSE:
Do not administer to children under 6 unless under direction of physician.

Children 6 to 12: 12.5 milligrams every 4 hours, not to exceed 75 milligrams in a 24 hour period. (Dosage may vary based on child's age.)

OVERDOSE SYMPTOMS:
Nervous agitation, severe anxiety, insomnia (sleeplessness), hallucinations, tremors, convulsions, nausea, vomiting, cardiac arrhythmia (irregular pulse and heartbeat). If you suspect an overdose, immediately seek medical attention.

SIDE EFFECTS:
No serious effects in most cases of common use. Less common side effects include nasal dryness, dizziness, nausea, and mild insomnia. In rare cases, more severe side effects may result, including: painful and frequent urination, hypertension, and heart palpitations. In these cases, discontinue medication and call your doctor immediately.

CHECK WITH YOUR DOCTOR OR PHARMACIST BEFORE COMBINING PHENYLPROPANOLAMINE WITH:
Cold, cough, or allergy medication, stimulants,

antidepressants, antihypertensives, digitalis or other heart medication, diuretics, or MAO (monoamine oxidase inhibitors) drugs. Ingestion of caffeinated beverages (coffee, tea, caffeine-containing soft drinks) while taking phenylpropanolamine-containing medication can result in agitation and insomnia.

PREGNANCY OR BREASTFEEDING:
Phenylpropanolamine use by a nursing mother should be considered a potential risk for a nursing child as the drug will be passed on to the infant in the mother's milk. In all cases, a physician should be consulted.

PRECAUTIONS FOR CHILDREN:
In general, phenylpropanolamine is not advised for children under 6. Administer phenylpropanolamine to infants or children only when consulting a physician and follow instructions on medication (see above).

55+

PRECAUTIONS FOR SENIORS:
Seniors generally don't eliminate drugs as efficiently as younger persons, and should avoid high dosages. Use of phenylpropanolamine medications by seniors can lead to cardiac arrhythmia (irregular pulse and heartbeat). In addition, seniors are more likely to experience stimulant effects of the drug.

SPECIAL WARNINGS:
Do not use continuously for longer than 3 months. Do not use phenylpropanolamine medications containing tartrazine if you are intolerant or hypersensitive to aspirin. Allergic reactions, including bronchial asthma, have occurred in susceptible individuals.

Q U I C K F A C T S

INFORM YOUR DOCTOR BEFORE TAKING PHENYLPROPANOLAMINE IF YOU HAVE:
Allergies to: any sympathomimetic drug, aspirin or other salicylates, or if you have diabetes, thyroid condition, or urinary difficulty. If you anticipate any surgery requiring general or spinal anesthesia within 2 months of taking phenylpropanolamine medication, inform your doctor.

ACTIVE INGREDIENTS:

PHENYLPROPANOLAMINE AND CHLORPHENIRAMINE MALEATE

℞ **BRAND NAMES:**

- A.R.M. Caplets
- Allerest Sinus Pain Formula (combination with acetaminophen)
- Aspirin-Free Bayer Select Allergy Sinus Caplets (combination with acetaminophen)
- BC Cold-Sinus–Allergy Powder (combination with aspirin)
- Children's Allerest (also contains saccharin and sorbitol)
- Chlor-Trimeton Allergy Sinus Caplets (combination with acetaminophen)
- Chlor-Rest
- Cold-Gest Capsules
- Contac 12-Hour Capsules
- Coricidin D Tablets (combination with acetaminophen)
- Dapacin Cold Capsules (combination with acetaminophen)
- Demazin Syrup (also contains 7.5% alcohol, menthol, sugar, parabens)
- Duadacin Capsules (combination with acetaminophen)
- Gelpirin-CCF Tablets (combination with acetaminophen and guaifenesin)
- Gencold Capsules
- Histosal Tablets (combination with acetaminophen and caffeine)
- Maximum Strength Tylenol Allergy Sinus (combination with acetaminophen)
- Naldecon Pediatric Syrup/Drops (also contains sorbitol)

QUICK FACTS

QUICK FACTS

- Naldelate Pediatric Syrup (also contains sorbitol)
- Nalgest Pediatric Syrup/Drops (also contains sorbitol)
- Pyrroxate (combination with acetaminophen)
- Rescon Liquid (also contains 7.5% alcohol, menthol, sugar, parabens)
- Silaminic Cold Syrup (also contains 7.5% alcohol, menthol, sugar, parabens)
- Sinapils Tablets (combination with acetaminophen and caffeine)
- Sinarest Extra Strength Tablets (combination with acetaminophen)
- Sinulin (combination with acetaminophen)
- Teldrin 12-Hour Allergy Relief
- Temazin Cold Syrup (also contains 7.5% alcohol, menthol, sugar, parabens)
- Thera-Hist Syrup (also contains sorbitol and sucrose)
- Tri-Nefrin
- Tri-Phen-Chlor Pediatric Syrup/Drops (also contains sorbitol)
- Tri-Phen-Mine Pediatric Syrup/Drops (also contains sorbitol)
- Triaminic
- Triaminicin Cold, Allergy, Sinus Tablets (combination with acetaminophen)
- Triaminicol Multi-Symptom Cough & Cold Tablets (combination with acetaminophen and caffeine)

HOW TO TAKE:
Comes in tablet, capsule, chewable forms. Swallow with liquid. Do not crush or chew timed-release tablets. Phenylpropanolamine can cause GI irritation and should be taken with food or following meal.

USUAL ADULT DOSE:
25 milligrams 3 times per day, (75 milligrams once daily for time release capsules) 1/2 hour before meals, not to exceed 75 milligrams in a 24 hour period.

USUAL CHILD DOSE:
Do not administer to children under 6 unless under direction of physician. Dosage may vary based on infant or child's age.

OVERDOSE SYMPTOMS:
Nervous agitation, severe anxiety, insomnia (sleeplessness), hallucinations, tremors, convulsions, nausea, vomiting, cardiac arrhythmia (irregular pulse and heartbeat). If you suspect an overdose, immediately seek medical attention.

SIDE EFFECTS:
No serious effects in most cases of common use. Less common side effects include nasal dryness, dizziness, nausea, and mild insomnia palpitations, insomnia. In rare cases, more severe side effects may result, including: painful and frequent urination, hypertension, and heart palpitations. In these cases, discontinue medication and call your doctor immediately.

CHECK WITH YOUR DOCTOR OR PHARMACIST BEFORE COMBINING PHENYLPROPANOLAMINE WITH:
Stimulants, antidepressants, antihypertensives, digitalis or other heart medication, diuretics, or MAO (monoamine oxidase inhibitors) drugs. Ingestion of caffeinated beverages (coffee, tea, caffeine-containing soft drinks) while taking phenylpropanolamine-containing medication can result in agitation and insomnia.

Q U I C K F A C T S

PREGNANCY OR BREASTFEEDING:
Phenylpropanolamine use by a nursing mother should be considered a potential risk for a nursing child as the drug will be passed on to the infant in the mother's milk. In all cases, a physician should be consulted.

PRECAUTIONS FOR CHILDREN:
In general, phenylpropanolamine is not advised for children under 6. Administer to infants or children only when consulting a physician.

PRECAUTIONS FOR SENIORS:
Seniors generally don't eliminate drugs as efficiently as younger persons, and should avoid high dosages. Use of phenylpropanolamine medications by seniors can lead to cardiac arrhythmia (irregular pulse and heartbeat). In addition, seniors are more likely to experience stimulant effects of the drug.

SPECIAL WARNINGS:
Do not use continuously for longer the 3 months. Do not use phenylpropanolamine medications containing tartazine if you are intolerant or hypersensitive to aspirin. Allergic reactions, including bronchial asthma, have occurred in susceptible individuals.

INFORM YOUR DOCTOR BEFORE TAKING PHENYLPROPANOLAMINE IF YOU HAVE:
Allergies to: any sympathomimetic drug, aspirin or other salicylates, diabetes, thyroid condition, urinary difficulty. If you anticipate any surgery requiring general or spinal anesthesia within 2 months of taking phenylpropanolamine medication, inform your doctor.

ACTIVE INGREDIENTS:

PHENYLPROPANOLAMINE AND CHLORPHENIRAMINE MALEATE (DECONGESTANT) COMBINATION WITH ACETAMINOPHEN

QUICK FACTS

BRAND NAMES:

- Allerest Sinus Pain Formula
- Aspirin-Free Bayer Select Allergy Sinus Caplets
- Chlor-Trimeton Allergy Sinus Caplets
- Coricidin D Tablets
- Dapacin Cold Capsules
- Gelpirin-CCF Tablets (combination with guaifenesin)
- Gencold Capsules
- Histosal Tablets (combination with caffeine)
- Maximum Strength Tylenol Allergy Sinus
- Pyrroxate
- Sinapils Tablets (combination with caffeine)
- Sinarest Extra Strength Tablets
- Sinulin
- Triaminicin Cold, Allergy, Sinus Tablets
- Triaminicol Multi-Symptom Cough & Cold Tablets (combination with caffeine)

HOW TO TAKE:
Comes in tablet, capsule, chewable forms. Swallow with liquid. Do not crush or chew timed-release tablets.

USUAL ADULT DOSE:
25 milligrams 3 times per day, (75 milligrams once daily for time release capsules) 1/2 hour before meals, not to exceed 75 milligrams in a 24 hour period.

Q U I C K F A C T S

USUAL CHILD DOSE:
Do not administer to children under 6 unless under direction of physician. Dosage may vary based on infant or child's age.

OVERDOSE SYMPTOMS:
Nervous agitation, severe anxiety, insomnia (sleeplessness), hallucinations, tremors, convulsions, nausea, vomiting, cardiac arrhythmia (irregular pulse and heartbeat). If you suspect an overdose, immediately seek medical attention.

SIDE EFFECTS:
No serious effects in most cases of common use. Less common side effects include nasal dryness, dizziness, nausea, and mild insomnia palpitations, insomnia. In rare cases, more severe side effects may result, including: painful and frequent urination, hypertension, and heart palpitations. In these cases, discontinue medication and call your doctor immediately.

CHECK WITH YOUR DOCTOR OR PHARMACIST BEFORE COMBINING PHENYLPROPANOLAMINE WITH:
Cold, cough, or allergy medication, stimulants, antidepressants, antihypertensives, digitalis or other heart medication, diuretics, or MAO (monoamine oxidase inhibitors) drugs. Ingestion of caffeinated beverages (coffee, tea, caffeine-containing soft drinks) while taking phenylpropanolamine-containing medication can result in agitation and insomnia.

PREGNANCY OR BREASTFEEDING:
Phenylpropanolamine use by a nursing mother should be considered a potential risk for a nurs-

ing child as the drug will be passed on to the infant in the mother's milk. In all cases, a physician should be consulted.

PRECAUTIONS FOR CHILDREN:
In general, phenylpropanolamine is not advised for children under 6. Administer phenylpropanolamine to infants or children only when consulting a physician and follow instructions on medication (see above).

55+ **PRECAUTIONS FOR SENIORS:**
Seniors generally don't eliminate drugs as efficiently as younger persons, and should avoid high dosages. Use of phenylpropanolamine medications by seniors can lead to cardiac arrhythmia (irregular pulse and heartbeat). In addition, seniors are more likely to experience stimulant effects of the drug.

SPECIAL WARNINGS:
Do not use continuously for longer than 3 months. Do not use phenylpropanolamine medications containing tartrazine if you are intolerant or hypersensitive to aspirin. Allergic reactions, including bronchial asthma, have occurred in susceptible individuals.

INFORM YOUR DOCTOR BEFORE TAKING PHENYLPROPANOLAMINE IF YOU HAVE:
Allergies to: any sympathomimetic drug, aspirin or other salicylates, or if you have diabetes, thyroid condition, or urinary difficulty. If you anticipate any surgery requiring general or spinal anesthesia within 2 months of taking phenylpropanolamine medication, inform your doctor.

QUICK FACTS

Q U I C K F A C T S

ACTIVE INGREDIENTS:

PHENYLPROPANOLAMINE AND CHLORPHENIRAMINE MALEATE COMBINATION WITH ACETAMINOPHEN

BRAND NAMES:

- Coricidin D Tablets
- Dapacin Cold Capsules
- Gelpirin–CCF Tablets (combination with guaifenesin)
- Gencold Capsules
- Pyrroxate
- Triaminicin Cold, Allergy, Sinus Tablets
- Triaminicol Multi-Symptom Cough & Cold Tablets (combination with caffeine)

HOW TO TAKE:

Comes in tablet, capsule, chewable forms. Swallow with liquid. Do not crush or chew timed-release tablets.

USUAL ADULT DOSE:

25 milligrams 3 times per day, (75 milligrams once daily for timed-release capsules) ½ hour before meals, not to exceed 75 milligrams in a 24 hour period.

USUAL CHILD DOSE:

Do not administer to children under 6 unless under direction of physician. Dosage may vary based on infant or child's age.

OVERDOSE SYMPTOMS:

Nervous agitation, severe anxiety, insomnia (sleeplessness), hallucinations, tremors, convulsions, nausea, vomiting, cardiac arrhythmia (irregular pulse and heartbeat). If you suspect an overdose, immediately seek medical attention.

SIDE EFFECTS:
No serious effects in most cases of common use. Less common side effects include nasal dryness, dizziness, nausea, and mild insomnia palpitations, insomnia. In rare cases, more severe side effects may result, including: painful and frequent urination, hypertension, and heart palpitations. In these cases, discontinue medication and call your doctor immediately.

CHECK WITH YOUR DOCTOR OR PHARMACIST BEFORE COMBINING PHENYLPROPANOLAMINE WITH:
Cold, cough,or allergy medication, stimulants, antidepressants, antihypertensives, digitalis or other heart medication, diuretics, or MAO (monoamine oxidase inhibitors) drugs. Ingestion of caffeinated beverages (coffee, tea, caffeine-containing soft drinks) while taking phenylpropanolamine-containing medication can result in agitation and insomnia.

PREGNANCY OR BREASTFEEDING:
FDA category C. Animal studies have indicated an adverse effect on fetus, but no adequate studies have been performed on humans. Phenylpropanolamine use by a nursing mother should be considered a potential risk for a nursing child as the drug will be passed on to the infant in the mother's milk. In all cases, a physician should be consulted.

PRECAUTIONS FOR CHILDREN:
In general, phenylpropanolamine is not advised for children under 6. Administer phenylpropanolamine to infants or children only when consulting a physician and follow instructions on medication (see above).

QUICK FACTS

55+ **PRECAUTIONS FOR SENIORS:**
Seniors generally don't eliminate drugs as efficiently as younger persons, and should avoid high dosages. Use of phenylpropanolamine medications by seniors can lead to cardiac arrhythmia (irregular pulse and heartbeat). In addition, seniors are more likely to experience stimulant effects of the drug.

SPECIAL WARNINGS:
Do not use continuously for longer than 3 months. Do not use phenylpropanolamine medications containing tartrazine if you are intolerant or hypersensitive to aspirin. Allergic reactions, including bronchial asthma, have occurred in susceptible individuals.

INFORM YOUR DOCTOR BEFORE TAKING PHENYLPROPANOLAMINE IF YOU HAVE:
Allergies to: any sympathomimetic drug, aspirin or other salicylates, or if you have diabetes, thyroid condition, or urinary difficulty. If you anticipate any surgery requiring general or spinal anesthesia within 2 months of taking phenylpropanolamine medication, inform your doctor.

QUICK FACTS

ACTIVE INGREDIENT:
PSEUDOEPHEDRINE HYDROCHLORIDE

BRAND NAMES:
- ALLERMED
- CENAFED
- CENAPHED SYRUP (also contains methylparaben)
- DEFED-60
- DORCOL CHILDREN'S DECONGESTANT (also contains sucrose, sorbitol)
- GENAPHED
- HALOFED (some formulations are sugar-coated)
- PEDIACARE INFANTS' DECONGESTANT (also contains sucrose, sorbitol)
- PSEUDO-GEST
- SEDOTABS (also contains sucrose)
- SINUSTOP PRO
- SUDAFED (also contains sucrose)
- SUDAFED CHILDREN'S (also contains methylparaben, sodium benzoate, sorbitol, sucrose—some formulations contain raspberry flavor)
- SUDAFED 12-HOUR CAPLETS

SYMPTOMS RELIEVED:
Nasal congestion, runny nose, itchy and watery eyes, sneezing, scratchy throat, and irritated sinuses due to common cold, sinusitis, hay fever, and other upper respiratory allergies.

HOW TO TAKE:
Comes in tablet, capsule, liquid, and drop forms. Swallow with liquid. Do not crush or chew timed-release tablets. Use dropper per instructions on medication.

USUAL ADULT DOSE:
60 milligrams 4 to 6 times per day, (120 milligrams twice daily for time release capsules),

not to exceed 240 milligrams in a 24 hour period.

USUAL CHILD DOSE:

For children 6 to 12: 30 milligrams 4 to 6 times per day, not to exceed 120 milligrams in a 24 hour period.

For children 2 to 6: 15 milligrams 4 to 6 times per day, not to exceed 60 milligrams in a 24 hour period.

For children 1 to 2: 7 drops (0.2 milliliters) per kilograms of child's weight not to exceed 4 doses in a 24 hour period.

Timed-release medications should only be administered to children under direction of physician. Do not administer to children under 6 unless under direction of physician. Dosage may vary based on infant or child's age.

OVERDOSE SYMPTOMS:

Severe nervous agitation, disorientation, anxiety, headache, nausea and vomiting, heavy sweats, cardiac arrhythmia (irregular pulse and heartbeat), muscle tremors and spasms. If you suspect an overdose, immediately seek medical attention.

SIDE EFFECTS:

No serious effects in most cases of common use. Less common side effects include nasal dryness, dizziness, nausea, and mild insomnia palpitations, insomnia. In rare cases, more severe side effects may result, including: nausea or vomiting, painful and frequent urination, hypertension, and irregular heartbeat. In these cases, discontinue medication and call your doctor immediately.

CHECK WITH YOUR DOCTOR OR PHARMACIST BEFORE COMBINING PSEUDOEPHEDRINE HYDROCHLORIDE WITH:
Cold, cough, or allergy medication, stimulants, antidepressants, antihypertensives, digitalis or other heart medication, diuretics, or MAO (monoamine oxidase inhibitors) drugs. Ingestion of caffeinated beverages (coffee, tea, caffeine-containing soft drinks) while taking pseudoephedrine hydrochloride-containing medication can result in agitation and insomnia.

PREGNANCY OR BREASTFEEDING:
Pseudoephedrine hydrochloride use by a nursing mother should be considered a potential risk for a nursing child as the drug will be passed on to the infant in the mother's milk. In all cases, a physician should be consulted.

PRECAUTIONS FOR CHILDREN:
In general, pseudoephedrine hydrochloride is not advised for children under 12. Administer pseudoephedrine hydrochloride to infants or children only when consulting a physician and follow instructions on medication (see above).

55+ **PRECAUTIONS FOR SENIORS:**
Seniors generally don't eliminate drugs as efficiently as younger persons, and should avoid high dosages. Use of pseudoephedrine hydrochloride medications by seniors can lead to cardiac arrhythmia (irregular pulse and heartbeat). In addition, seniors are more likely to experience stimulant effects of the drug.

Q U I C K   F A C T S

SPECIAL WARNINGS:
Do not combine with any medication which contains caffeine. Do not use continuously for longer than 3 months. Do not use pseudo-ephedrine hydrochloride medications containing tartazine if you are intolerant or hypersensitive to aspirin. Allergic reactions, including bronchial asthma, have occurred in susceptible individuals.

INFORM YOUR DOCTOR BEFORE TAKING PSEUDOEPHEDRINE HYDROCHLORIDE IF YOU HAVE:
Allergies to: any sympathomimetic drug, aspirin or other salicylates, or if you have diabetes, thyroid condition, or urinary difficulty. If you anticipate any surgery requiring general or spinal anesthesia within 2 months of taking pseudo-ephedrine hydrochloride medication, inform your doctor.

ACTIVE INGREDIENT:

TRIPOLIDINE HYDROCHLORIDE

BRAND NAMES:
- Actidil

SYMPTOMS RELIEVED:
Nasal congestion, runny nose, itchy and watery eyes, sneezing, scratchy throat, and irritated sinuses due to common cold, sinusitis, hay fever, and other upper respiratory allergies.

HOW TO TAKE:
Comes in tablet, capsule, and liquid forms. Swallow tablet or capsule with liquid. Do not crush or chew timed-release tablets. Tripolidine and other antihistamines can cause gastro-intestinal (GI) irritation and should be taken with food or following meal.

USUAL ADULT DOSE:
2.5 milligrams 3 to 4 times per day, not to exceed 10 milligrams in a 24 hour period.

USUAL CHILD DOSE:
For children 6 to 12: 2 milligrams 4 to 6 times per day, or 8 milligrams of timed-release medication at bedtime or during day, not to exceed 12 milligrams in a 24 hour period.

For children 2 to 6: 1.25 milligrams 4 to 6 times per day, not to exceed 5 milligrams in a 24 hour period. Timed-release medications are not advised for children 2 to 6 or younger. Do not administer to children in this age group unless under direction of physician. Dosage may vary based on infant or child's age.

Q U I C K F A C T S

Q U I C K F A C T S

OVERDOSE SYMPTOMS:
Nervous agitation, severe anxiety, insomnia (sleeplessness), hallucinations, tremors, coma. If you suspect an overdose, immediately seek medical attention.

SIDE EFFECTS:
The most frequent side effect of antihistamines use is drowsiness. Other common side effects include: include dryness of mouth, throat, and nasal passages, dizziness, GI distress (including vomiting, diarrhea, and constipation or change in bowel regularity), and diminished muscle coordination. In rare cases, more severe side effects may result, such as painful and frequent urination or urinary retention, vision problems, loss of appetite, and respiratory difficulty. In these cases, discontinue medication and call your doctor immediately.

CHECK WITH YOUR DOCTOR OR PHARMACIST BEFORE COMBINING TRIPOLIDINE WITH:
Cold, cough, or allergy medication—including other antihistamines; aspirin, stimulants, antidepressants, antihypertensives, digitalis or other heart medication, diuretics, or MAO (monoamine oxidase inhibitors) drugs. Avoid ingestion of alcohol or use of sedatives or tranquilizers while taking tripolidine-containing medication or most other antihistamine-containing medication as the combination can produce severe drowsiness or sedation.

PREGNANCY OR BREASTFEEDING:
Tripolidine use by a nursing mother should be considered a potential risk for a nursing child as the drug will be passed on to the infant in the

mother's milk. In all cases, a physician should be consulted.

PRECAUTIONS FOR CHILDREN:
In general, tripolidine is not advised for children under 6. Administer tripolidine to infants or children only when consulting a physician and follow instructions on medication (see above).

55+ **PRECAUTIONS FOR SENIORS:**
Seniors generally don't eliminate drugs as efficiently as younger persons, and should avoid high dosages. Use of tripolidine medications by seniors can lead to urinary difficulties. In addition, seniors are more likely to experience stimulant effects of the drug.

SPECIAL WARNINGS:
Because antihistamines often cause drowsiness, you should avoid activities or tasks such as driving, or other operations which require alertness, coordination, dexterity or quick reflexes. Do not use continuously for longer than 3 months. Do not use tripolidine medications containing tartrazine if you are intolerant or hypersensitive to aspirin. Allergic reactions, including bronchial asthma, have occurred in susceptible individuals.

INFORM YOUR DOCTOR BEFORE TAKING TRIPOLIDINE IF YOU HAVE:
Urinary difficulty, glaucoma, ulcer, or if you are pregnant. If you anticipate any surgery requiring general or spinal anesthesia within 2 months of taking tripolidine-containing medication, inform your doctor.

Q U I C K F A C T S

ACTIVE INGREDIENT:
CAMPHOR

BRAND NAMES:
- MENTHOLATUM CHERRY CHEST RUB FOR KIDS (combination with menthol, eucalyptus oil—also contains fragrance, petrolatum, steareth-2, titanium dioxide)
- MENTHOLATUM OINTMENT (combination with menthol, eucalyptus oil—also contains fragrance, petrolatum, titanium dioxide)
- VICKS VAPORUB–CREAM (combination with menthol, eucalyptus oil—also contains cedarleaf oil, nutmeg oil, special petrolatum, spirits of turpentine, thymol)
- VICKS VAPORUB–OINTMENT (combination with menthol, eucalyptus oil—also contains carbomer 954, cedarleaf oil, cetyl alcohol, cetyl palminate, dimethicone, glycerin, imidazoliyl urea, isopropyl palminate, methylparaben, nutmeg oil, stearate, propylparaben, sodium hydroxide, spirits of turpentine, stearic acid, stearyl alcohol, thymol, titanium dioxide)

SYMPTOMS RELIEVED:
Nasal, sinus, and chest congestion, cough, and minor aches and pains of muscles associated with common cold, head cold, and flu.

HOW TO USE:
Comes in ointment and cream forms. Apply to affected areas. These products are for external use only. Do not swallow. Avoid contact with eyes while applying.

USUAL ADULT DOSE:
See specific product instructions. Generally,

apply externally to chest, throat, or below nostrils not more than 3 to 4 times per day, or as directed by your doctor. In all cases follow specific product instructions.

USUAL CHILD DOSE:
For ages 2 to 12: Apply same as adult, or as directed by your doctor. In all cases follow specific product instructions.

Only apply to children under 2 under doctor's supervision or direction. In all cases follow specific product instructions.

OVERDOSE SYMPTOMS:
None known.

SIDE EFFECTS:
No serious effects in most cases of common use.

CHECK WITH YOUR DOCTOR OR PHARMACIST BEFORE COMBINING THIS PRODUCT WITH:
Any other drugs and preparations.

PREGNANCY OR BREASTFEEDING:
Safety of this drug for use during pregnancy or while nursing has not been established. In all cases you should consult your doctor before using any drug during pregnancy or while nursing.

PRECAUTIONS FOR CHILDREN:
These products should only be used with doctor's supervision or direction for children under 2. Consult your doctor and follow instructions on medication (see above).

QUICK FACTS

55+ **PRECAUTIONS FOR SENIORS:**
None known.

SPECIAL WARNINGS:
Do not use these products if you are allergic to camphor, menthol, or any of the inactive ingredients contained in these products. Do not apply these products to wounds, lesions, broken, damaged, or sensitive skin. Avoid contact with eyes and mucous membranes. Do not use in mouth or nose. Unless directed by your doctor, do not use these products to treat symptoms of persistent or chronic cough, such as those associated with smoking, asthma, emphysema, or coughs with excessive phlegm.

INFORM YOUR DOCTOR BEFORE USING THESE PRODUCTS IF YOU HAVE:
Any allergies, or if you are or plan to become pregnant during time that you will be taking this product.

ACTIVE INGREDIENT:
EPHEDRINE HYDROCHLORIDE

BRAND NAMES:
- KONDON'S NASAL (jelly)
- PRETZ-D (spray)
- VICKS VATRONOL (drops)

SYMPTOMS RELIEVED:
Nasal congestion due to common cold, sinusitis, hay fever, and other upper respiratory allergies.

HOW TO TAKE:
Comes in nasal spray, drop, or jelly forms. Use dropper and spray pump per instructions on medication label. Apply jelly with sterile swab. Always wash hands before applying product directly.

USUAL ADULT DOSE:
Dosage varies per product formulation. Follow product dosage instructions.

USUAL CHILD DOSE:
Do not administer to children under 6 unless under direction of physician. Dosage may vary based on infant or child's age.

OVERDOSE SYMPTOMS:
Headache, nausea and vomiting, heart palpitations, raised blood pressure, muscle tremors and spasms. If you suspect an overdose, immediately seek medical attention.

SIDE EFFECTS:
Most common include: nasal dryness and stinging, headache, burning sensation. In rare cases, more severe side effects may result, including:

heavy sweats, nervous agitation, hypertension, and irregular heartbeat. In these cases, discontinue medication and call your doctor immediately.

CHECK WITH YOUR DOCTOR OR PHARMACIST BEFORE COMBINING EPHEDRINE WITH:

Cold, cough, allergy or asthma medication, stimulants, sedatives, sleep aids, antidepressants, antihypertensives, digitalis or other heart medication, diuretics, or MAO (monoamine oxidase inhibitors) drugs. Ingestion of caffeinated beverages (coffee, tea, caffeine-containing soft drinks) while taking ephedrine-containing medication can result in agitation and insomnia.

PREGNANCY OR BREASTFEEDING:

Ephedrine use by a nursing mother should be considered a potential risk for a nursing child as the drug will be passed on to the infant in the mother's milk. In all cases, a physician should be consulted.

PRECAUTIONS FOR CHILDREN:

In general, ephedrine is not advised for children under 6. Administer ephedrine to infants or children only when consulting a physician and follow instructions on medication (see above).

55+

PRECAUTIONS FOR SENIORS:

Seniors generally don't eliminate drugs as efficiently as younger persons, and should avoid high dosages. Seniors are more likely to experience stimulant effects of the drug.

SPECIAL WARNINGS:

Do not combine with any medication which

contains caffeine. Prolonged, continuous use may lead to dependence.

INFORM YOUR DOCTOR BEFORE TAKING EPHEDRINE IF YOU HAVE:

Diabetes, high blood pressure, heart disease, or thyroid condition. If you anticipate any surgery requiring general or spinal anesthesia within 2 months of taking ephedrine medication, inform your doctor.

QUICK FACTS

ACTIVE INGREDIENT:

NAPHAZOLINE HYDROCHLORIDE

BRAND NAMES:

- PRIVINE

SYMPTOMS RELIEVED:

Nasal congestion due to common cold, sinusitis, hay fever and other upper respiratory allergies.

HOW TO TAKE:

Comes in nasal spray or drops forms. Use dropper and spray pump per instructions on medication label. Always wash hands before applying product directly.

USUAL ADULT DOSE:

1 to 2 sprays or drops per nostril as needed, not to exceed 1 dose every 6 hours

USUAL CHILD DOSE:

Do not administer to children under 12 unless under direction of physician. Dosage may vary based on infant or child's age.

OVERDOSE SYMPTOMS:

Headache, nausea, and vomiting, heart palpitations, raised blood pressure, muscle tremors and spasms. If you suspect an overdose, immediately seek medical attention.

SIDE EFFECTS:

Most common include: nasal dryness and stinging, headache, burning sensation. In rare cases, more severe side effects may result, including: heavy sweats, nervous agitation, hypertension, and irregular heartbeat. In these cases, discontinue medication and call your doctor immediately.

CHECK WITH YOUR DOCTOR OR PHARMACIST BEFORE COMBINING NAPHAZOLINE WITH:
Cold, cough, allergy, or asthma medication, stimulants, sedatives, sleep aids, antidepressants, antihypertensives, digitalis or other heart medication, diuretics, or MAO (monoamine oxidase inhibitors) drugs.

PREGNANCY OR BREASTFEEDING:
Naphazoline use by a nursing mother should be considered a potential risk for a nursing child as the drug will be passed on to the infant in the mother's milk. In all cases, a physician should be consulted.

PRECAUTIONS FOR CHILDREN:
In general, naphazoline is not advised for children under 6. Administer naphazoline to infants or children only when consulting a physician and follow instructions on medication (see above).

55+

PRECAUTIONS FOR SENIORS:
Seniors generally don't eliminate drugs as efficiently as younger persons, and should avoid high dosages. Seniors are more likely to experience stimulant effects of the drug.

SPECIAL WARNINGS:
Do not combine with any medication which contains caffeine. Prolonged, continuous use may lead to dependence.

INFORM YOUR DOCTOR BEFORE TAKING NAPHAZOLINE IF YOU HAVE:
Diabetes, high blood pressure, heart disease, or thyroid condition. If you anticipate any surgery requiring general or spinal anesthesia within 2 months of taking naphazoline medication, inform your doctor.

Q U I C K F A C T S

ACTIVE INGREDIENT:

OXYMETAZOLINE HYDROCHLORIDE

BRAND NAMES:

- Afrin/Afrin Children's Nose Drops
- Allerest 12-Hour Nasal
- Chlorphed-LA
- Dristan Long Lasting
- Duramist Plus
- Duration
- Genasal
- Neo-Synephrine 12-Hour
- Nostrilla
- Sinarest 12-Hour
- Sinex Long-Acting
- Twice-A-Day

SYMPTOMS RELIEVED:
Nasal congestion due to common cold, sinusitis, hay fever and other upper respiratory allergies.

HOW TO TAKE:
Comes in nasal spray or drop forms. Use dropper and spray pump per instructions on medication label. Always wash hands before applying product directly.

USUAL ADULT DOSE:
2 to 3 sprays or drops of 0.05% solution per nostril 2 times per day.

USUAL CHILD DOSE:
For children 6 and older: Same dosage as adults.

For children 2 to 6: 2 to 3 sprays or drops of 0.025% solution per nostril 2 times per day.

Do not administer to children under 2 unless under direction of physician. Dosage may vary based on infant or child's age.

OVERDOSE SYMPTOMS:
Headache, nausea, and vomiting, heart palpitations, raised blood pressure, muscle tremors and spasms. If you suspect an overdose, immediately seek medical attention.

SIDE EFFECTS:
Most common include: nasal dryness and stinging, headache, burning sensation. In rare cases, more severe side effects may result, including: heavy sweats, nervous agitation, hypertension, and irregular heartbeat. In these cases, discontinue medication and call your doctor immediately.

CHECK WITH YOUR DOCTOR OR PHARMACIST BEFORE COMBINING OXYMETAZOLINE WITH:
Cold, cough, allergy, or asthma medication, stimulants, sedatives, sleep aids, antidepressants, antihypertensives, digitalis or other heart medication, diuretics, or MAO (monoamine oxidase inhibitors) drugs. Ingestion of caffeinated beverages (coffee, tea, caffeine-containing soft drinks) while taking oxymetazoline-containing medication can result in agitation and insomnia.

PREGNANCY OR BREASTFEEDING:
Oxymetazoline use by a nursing mother should be considered a potential risk for a nursing child as the drug will be passed on to the infant in the mother's milk. In all cases, a physician should be consulted.

PRECAUTIONS FOR CHILDREN:
In general, oxymetazoline is not advised for children under 6. Administer oxymetazoline to infants or children only when consulting a

QUICK FACTS

physician and follow instructions on medication (see above).

PRECAUTIONS FOR SENIORS:
Seniors generally don't eliminate drugs as efficiently as younger persons, and should avoid high dosages. Seniors are more likely to experience stimulant effects of the drug.

SPECIAL WARNINGS:
Do not combine with any medication which contains caffeine. Prolonged, continuous use may lead to dependence.

INFORM YOUR DOCTOR BEFORE TAKING OXYMETAZOLINE IF YOU HAVE:
Diabetes, high blood pressure, heart disease, or thyroid condition. If you anticipate any surgery requiring general or spinal anesthesia within 2 months of taking oxymetazoline medication, inform your doctor.

ACTIVE INGREDIENT:

PHENYLEPHRINE HYDROCHLORIDE

BRAND NAMES:

- ALCONEFRIN/ ALCONEFRIN 25
- NEO-SYNEPHRINE
- NOSTRIL/CHILDREN'S NOSTRIL
- RHINALL
- SINEX

SYMPTOMS RELIEVED:

Nasal congestion due to common cold, sinusitis, hay fever, and other upper respiratory allergies.

HOW TO TAKE:

Comes in nasal spray or drop forms. Use dropper and spray pump per instructions on medication label. Always wash hands before applying product directly.

USUAL ADULT DOSE:

0.25% and 0.5% solutions: 2 to 3 sprays or drops per nostril every 3 to 4 hours.

1% solution: 2 to 3 sprays or drops per nostril no more than every 4 hours

USUAL CHILD DOSE:

For children 6 to 12:
0.25% and 0.5% solutions: 2 to 3 sprays or drops per nostril every 3 to 4 hours.

Do not administer to children under 6 unless under direction of physician. Dosage may vary based on infant or child's age.

OVERDOSE SYMPTOMS:

Headache, nausea and vomiting, heart palpitations, raised blood pressure, muscle tremors

and spasms. If you suspect an overdose, immediately seek medical attention.

SIDE EFFECTS:
Most common include: nasal dryness and stinging, headache, burning sensation. In rare cases, more severe side effects may result, including: heavy sweats, nervous agitation, hypertension, and irregular heartbeat. In these cases, discontinue medication and call your doctor immediately.

CHECK WITH YOUR DOCTOR OR PHARMACIST BEFORE COMBINING PHENYLEPHRINE WITH:
Cold, cough, allergy, or asthma medication, stimulants, sedatives, sleep aids, antidepressants, antihypertensives, digitalis or other heart medication, diuretics, or MAO (monoamine oxidase inhibitors) drugs. Ingestion of caffeinated beverages (coffee, tea, caffeine-containing soft drinks) while taking phenylephrine-containing medication can result in agitation and insomnia.

PREGNANCY OR BREASTFEEDING:
Phenylephrine use by a nursing mother should be considered a potential risk for a nursing child as the drug will be passed on to the infant in the mother's milk. In all cases, a physician should be consulted.

PRECAUTIONS FOR CHILDREN:
In general, phenylephrine is not advised for children under 6. Administer phenylephrine to infants or children only when consulting a physician and follow instructions on medication (see above).

55+ **PRECAUTIONS FOR SENIORS:**
Seniors generally don't eliminate drugs as efficiently as younger persons, and should avoid high dosages. Seniors are more likely to experience stimulant effects of the drug.

SPECIAL WARNINGS:
Do not combine with any medication which contains caffeine. Prolonged, continuous use may lead to dependence.

INFORM YOUR DOCTOR BEFORE TAKING PHENYLEPHRINE IF YOU HAVE:
Diabetes, high blood pressure, heart disease, or thyroid condition. If you anticipate any surgery requiring general or spinal anesthesia within 2 months of taking phenylephrine medication, inform your doctor.

Q U I C K F A C T S

ACTIVE INGREDIENTS:

PHENYLEPHRINE HYDROCHLORIDE, NAPHAZOLINE HYDROCHLORIDE, AND PYRLAMINE MALEATE

BRAND NAMES:

- 4-Way Fast Acting Original (regular and menthol)

SYMPTOMS RELIEVED:

Nasal congestion, runny nose, itchy and watery eyes, sneezing, scratchy throat, and irritated sinuses due to common cold, sinusitis, hay fever, and other upper respiratory allergies.

HOW TO TAKE:

Comes in nasal spray or drops forms. Use dropper and spray pump per instructions on medication label. Always wash hands before applying product directly.

USUAL ADULT DOSE:

1 to 2 sprays or drops per nostril as needed, not to exceed 1 dose every 6 hours

USUAL CHILD DOSE:

Do not administer to children under 12 unless under direction of physician. Dosage may vary based on infant or child's age.

OVERDOSE SYMPTOMS:

Headache, nausea and vomiting, heart palpitations, raised blood pressure, muscle tremors and spasms. If you suspect an overdose, immediately seek medical attention.

SIDE EFFECTS:

The most frequent side effect of antihistamine

use is drowsiness. Other common side effects include: nasal dryness and stinging, headache, burning sensation. In rare cases, more severe side effects may result, including: heavy sweats, nervous agitation, hypertension, and irregular heartbeat. In these cases, discontinue medication and call your doctor immediately.

CHECK WITH YOUR DOCTOR OR PHARMACIST BEFORE COMBINING THIS COMBINATION PRODUCT WITH:

Cold, cough, allergy, or asthma medication, stimulants, sedatives, sleep aids, antidepressants, antihypertensives, digitalis or other heart medication, diuretics, or MAO (monoamine oxidase inhibitors) drugs. Ingestion of caffeinated beverages (coffee, tea, caffeine-containing soft drinks) while taking naphazoline-containing medication can result in agitation and insomnia.

PREGNANCY OR BREASTFEEDING:

Use of this combination product by a nursing mother should be considered a potential risk for a nursing child as the drugs will be passed on to the infant in the mother's milk. In all cases, a physician should be consulted.

PRECAUTIONS FOR CHILDREN:

In general, this combination product is not advised for children under 6. Administer this combination product to infants or children only when consulting a physician and follow instructions on medication (see above).

55+ **PRECAUTIONS FOR SENIORS:**

Seniors generally don't eliminate drugs as efficiently as younger persons, and should avoid high dosages. Seniors are more likely to experience stimulant effects of the drugs in this product.

SPECIAL WARNINGS:

Because antihistamines often cause drowsiness, you should avoid activities or tasks such as driving, or other operations which require alertness, coordination, dexterity or quick reflexes. Do not use continuously for longer than 3 months.

INFORM YOUR DOCTOR BEFORE TAKING THIS COMBINATION PRODUCT IF YOU HAVE:

Diabetes, high blood pressure, heart disease, or thyroid condition. If you anticipate any surgery requiring general or spinal anesthesia within 2 months of taking this medication, inform your doctor.

ACTIVE INGREDIENTS:
PHENYLEPHRINE HYDROCHLORIDE AND PHENIRAMINE MALEATE

BRAND NAMES:
- DRISTAN NASAL (regular and menthol)

SYMPTOMS RELIEVED:
Nasal congestion, runny nose, itchy and watery eyes, sneezing, scratchy throat, and irritated sinuses due to common cold, sinusitis, hay fever, and other upper respiratory allergies.

HOW TO TAKE:
Comes in nasal spray form. Use spray pump per instructions on medication label. Always wash hands before applying product directly.

USUAL ADULT DOSE:
0.25% and 0.5% solutions: 2 to 3 sprays or drops per nostril every 3 to 4 hours.

1% solution: 2 to 3 sprays or drops per nostril no more than every 4 hours

USUAL CHILD DOSE:
For children 6 to 12:
0.25% and 0.5% solutions: 2 to 3 sprays or drops per nostril every 3 to 4 hours.

Do not administer to children under 6 unless under direction of physician. Dosage may vary based on infant or child's age.

OVERDOSE SYMPTOMS:
Headache, nausea, and vomiting, heart palpitations, raised blood pressure, muscle tremors and spasms. If you suspect an overdose, immediately seek medical attention.

SIDE EFFECTS:
The most frequent side effect of antihistamine use is drowsiness. Other common side effects include: nasal dryness and stinging, headache, burning sensation. In rare cases, more severe side effects may result, including: heavy sweats, nervous agitation, hypertension, and irregular heartbeat. In these cases, discontinue medication and call your doctor immediately.

CHECK WITH YOUR DOCTOR OR PHARMACIST BEFORE COMBINING PHENYLEPHRINE AND PHENIRAMINE MALEATE WITH:
Cold, cough, allergy, or asthma medication, stimulants, sedatives, sleep aids, antidepressants, antihypertensives, digitalis or other heart medication, diuretics, or MAO (monoamine oxidase inhibitors) drugs. Ingestion of caffeinated beverages (coffee, tea, caffeine-containing soft drinks) while taking phenylephrine and pheniramine maleate-containing medication can result in agitation and insomnia. Avoid ingestion of alcohol or use of sedatives or tranquilizers while taking chlorpheniramine maleate-containing medication or most other antihistamine-containing medication as the combination can produce severe drowsiness or sedation.

PREGNANCY OR BREASTFEEDING:
Phenylephrine and pheniramine maleate use by a nursing mother should be considered a potential risk for a nursing child as the drug will be passed on to the infant in the mother's milk. In all cases, a physician should be consulted.

PRECAUTIONS FOR CHILDREN:
In general, phenylephrine and pheniramine

maleate use is not advised for children under 6. Administer phenylephrine and pheniramine maleate to infants or children only when consulting a physician and follow instructions on medication (see above).

55+ **PRECAUTIONS FOR SENIORS:**
Seniors generally don't eliminate drugs as efficiently as younger persons, and should avoid high dosages. Seniors are more likely to experience stimulant effects of the drug.

SPECIAL WARNINGS:
Because antihistamines often cause drowsiness, you should avoid activities or tasks such as driving, or other operations which require alertness, coordination, dexterity or quick reflexes. Do not use continuously for longer than 3 months.

INFORM YOUR DOCTOR BEFORE TAKING PHENYLEPHRINE AND PHENIRAMINE MALEATE IF YOU HAVE:
Diabetes, high blood pressure, heart disease, or thyroid condition.

Q U I C K F A C T S

ACTIVE INGREDIENTS:

PHENYLEPHRINE HYDROCHLORIDE AND PYRLAMINE MALEATE

BRAND NAMES:

- MYCI-SPRAY

SYMPTOMS RELIEVED:
Nasal congestion, runny nose, itchy and watery eyes, sneezing, scratchy throat, and irritated sinuses due to common cold, sinusitis, hay fever, and other upper respiratory allergies.

HOW TO USE:
Comes in nasal spray form. Use spray pump per instructions on medication label. Always wash hands before applying product directly.

USUAL ADULT DOSE:
0.25% and 0.5% solutions: 2 to 3 sprays or drops per nostril every 3 to 4 hours.

1% solution: 2 to 3 sprays or drops per nostril no more than every 4 hours

USUAL CHILD DOSE:
For children 6 to 12:
0.25% and 0.5% solutions: 2 to 3 sprays or drops per nostril every 3 to 4 hours.

Do not administer to children under 6 unless under direction of physician. Dosage may vary based on infant or child's age.

OVERDOSE SYMPTOMS:
Headache, nausea and vomiting, heart palpitations, raised blood pressure, muscle tremors and spasms. If you suspect an overdose, immediately seek medical attention.

SIDE EFFECTS:
The most frequent side effect of antihistamine use is drowsiness. Other common side effects include: nasal dryness and stinging, headache, burning sensation. In rare cases, more severe side effects may result, including: heavy sweats, nervous agitation, hypertension, and irregular heartbeat. In these cases, discontinue medication and call your doctor immediately.

CHECK WITH YOUR DOCTOR OR PHARMACIST BEFORE COMBINING PHENYLEPHRINE AND PYRILAMINE MALEATE WITH:
Cold, cough, allergy, or asthma medication, stimulants, sedatives, sleep aids, antidepressants, antihypertensives, digitalis or other heart medication, diuretics, or MAO (monoamine oxidase inhibitors) drugs. Ingestion of caffeinated beverages (coffee, tea, caffeine-containing soft drinks) while taking phenylephrine and pyrilamine maleate-containing medication can result in agitation and insomnia. Avoid ingestion of alcohol or use of sedatives or tranquilizers while taking chlorpheniramine maleate-containing medication or most other antihistamine-containing medication as the combination can produce severe drowsiness or sedation.

PREGNANCY OR BREASTFEEDING:
Phenylephrine and pyrilamine maleate use by a nursing mother should be considered a potential risk for a nursing child as the drug will be passed on to the infant in the mother's milk. In all cases, a physician should be consulted.

PRECAUTIONS FOR CHILDREN:
In general, phenylephrine and pyrilamine

Q U I C K F A C T S

maleate use is not advised for children under 6. Administer phenylephrine and pyrilamine maleate to infants or children only when consulting a physician and follow instructions on medication (see above).

55+ **PRECAUTIONS FOR SENIORS:**
Seniors generally don't eliminate drugs as efficiently as younger persons, and should avoid high dosages. Seniors are more likely to experience stimulant effects of the drug.

SPECIAL WARNINGS:
Because antihistamines often cause drowsiness, you should avoid activities or tasks such as driving, or other operations which require alertness, coordination, dexterity or quick reflexes. Do not use continuously for longer than 3 months.

INFORM YOUR DOCTOR BEFORE TAKING PHENYLEPHRINE AND PYRILAMINE MALEATE IF YOU HAVE:
diabetes, high blood pressure, heart disease, or thyroid condition.

ACTIVE INGREDIENT:
SODIUM CHLORIDE

QUICK FACTS

BRAND NAMES:
- Afrin Saline Mist
- Ayr Saline
- Breathe Free
- Dristan Saline Spray
- HuMist Nasal Mist
- Nasal
- Nasal Moist
- Ocean
- Pretz/Pretz Irrigating/Pretz Moisturizing
- SalineX
- SeaMist

SYMPTOMS RELIEVED:
Nasal congestion, runny nose, itchy and watery eyes, sneezing, scratchy throat, and irritated sinuses due to common cold, sinusitis, hay fever, and other upper respiratory allergies.

HOW TO TAKE:
Comes in nasal spray, mist, or drop forms. Use dropper and spray pump per instructions on medication label. Always wash hands before applying product directly.

USUAL ADULT DOSE:
2 to 6 sprays or drops per nostril as needed or as directed by your doctor.

USUAL CHILD DOSE:
2 to 6 sprays or drops per nostril as needed or as directed by your doctor.

OVERDOSE SYMPTOMS:
Headache, nausea and vomiting, heart palpitations, raised blood pressure, muscle tremors

QUICK FACTS

and spasms. If you suspect an overdose, immediately seek medical attention.

SIDE EFFECTS:
Most common include: nasal burning and itching of membrane on application, and dryness and stinging during use. In rare cases, more severe side effects may result, including: heavy sweats, nervous agitation, hypertension, and irregular heartbeat. In these cases, discontinue medication and call your doctor immediately.

CHECK WITH YOUR DOCTOR OR PHARMACIST BEFORE COMBINING SODIUM CHLORIDE WITH:
Safe to use with other medications.

PREGNANCY OR BREASTFEEDING:
Adequate studies in pregnant women have failed to show a risk to the fetus in the first trimester of pregnancy, and no evidence of risk has been shown in later trimesters.

PRECAUTIONS FOR CHILDREN:
Carefully administer or supervise the use of these products with children and infants. To avoid contamination, always wipe nozzle clean after each use. Always follow instructions on medication (see above).

55+ **PRECAUTIONS FOR SENIORS:**
No known precautions.

SPECIAL WARNINGS:
Prolonged, continuous use may lead to dependence.

INFORM YOUR DOCTOR BEFORE TAKING SODIUM CHLORIDE IF YOU HAVE:
No known contraindications.

ACTIVE INGREDIENT:
XYLOMETAZOLINE HYDROCHLORIDE

QUICK FACTS

BRAND NAMES:
- OTRIVIN/OTRIVIN PEDIATRIC NASAL DROPS

SYMPTOMS RELIEVED:
Nasal congestion, runny nose, itchy and watery eyes, sneezing, scratchy throat, and irritated sinuses due to common cold, sinusitis, hay fever, and other upper respiratory allergies.

HOW TO TAKE:
Comes in nasal spray or drop forms. Use dropper and spray pump per instructions on medication label. Always wash hands before applying product directly.

USUAL ADULT DOSE:
2 to 3 sprays or drops of 0.1% solution per nostril 2 to 3 times per day.

USUAL CHILD DOSE:
For children 2 to 12: 2 to 3 sprays or drops of 0.05% solution per nostril 2 to 3 times per day.

Do not administer to children under 2 unless under direction of physician. Dosage may vary based on infant or child's age.

OVERDOSE SYMPTOMS:
Headache, nausea and vomiting, heart palpitations, raised blood pressure, muscle tremors and spasms. If you suspect an overdose, immediately seek medical attention.

SIDE EFFECTS:
Most common include: nasal dryness and stinging, headache, burning sensation. In rare cases,

QUICK FACTS

more severe side effects may result, including: heavy sweats, nervous agitation, hypertension, and irregular heartbeat. In these cases, discontinue medication and call your doctor immediately.

CHECK WITH YOUR DOCTOR OR PHARMACIST BEFORE COMBINING XYLOMETAZOLINE WITH:
Cold, cough, allergy, or asthma medication, stimulants, sedatives, sleep aids, antidepressants, antihypertensives, digitalis or other heart medication, diuretics, or MAO (monoamine oxidase inhibitors) drugs. Ingestion of caffeinated beverages (coffee, tea, caffeine-containing soft drinks) while taking xylometazoline-containing medication can result in agitation and insomnia.

PREGNANCY OR BREASTFEEDING:
Xylometazoline use by a nursing mother should be considered a potential risk for a nursing child as the drug will be passed on to the infant in the mother's milk. In all cases, a physician should be consulted.

PRECAUTIONS FOR CHILDREN:
In general, xylometazoline is not advised for children under 6. Administer xylometazoline to infants or children only when consulting a physician and follow instructions on medication (see above).

55+

PRECAUTIONS FOR SENIORS:
Seniors generally don't eliminate drugs as efficiently as younger persons, and should avoid high dosages. Seniors are more likely to experience stimulant effects of the drug.

SPECIAL WARNINGS:
Do not combine with any medication which contains caffeine. Prolonged, continuous use may lead to dependence.

INFORM YOUR DOCTOR BEFORE TAKING XYLOMETAZOLINE IF YOU HAVE:
Diabetes, high blood pressure, heart disease, or thyroid condition. If you anticipate any surgery requiring general or spinal anesthesia within 2 months of taking xylometazoline medication, inform your doctor.

QUICK REVIEW

• EXPECTORANT •

The most important considerations in choosing an expectorant are: its action in increasing productivity of coughs and potential side effects associated with the drug.

EXPECTORANTS ARE A CLASS OF DRUGS WHICH:

- help to relieve the typical coughing symptoms of various allergies, colds, bronchitis, flu and other nonchronic respiratory ailments, by reducing adhesiveness of respiratory tract and increasing the productivity of coughs, thereby lessening their occurrence,
- are commonly used to give an allergy, cold, bronchitis, flu, and other nonchronic respiratory ailment-sufferer sufficient relief from coughing spasms,
- may produce side effects such as drowsiness, nasal stuffiness, dryness of mouth and sinus passages, dizziness, and common gastrointestinal (GI) irritation or distress,
- are not recommended in treating chronic and lower respiratory symptoms including asthma, and emphysema,
- are often combined with other cough-related active ingredients such as antitussives, as well as analgesics, antihistamines, and decongestants—as well as other ingredients such as alcohol, sweeteners (natural and artificial) and flavorings (natural and artificial),
- do not affect the underlying cause of the symptoms which they are designed to relieve or suppress.

ACTIVE INGREDIENT:
GUAIFENESIN

℞ **BRAND NAMES:**

Capsules:
- AMONIDRIN
- BREONESIN
- GG-CEN
- GEE-GEE
- GLYCOTUSS
- GLYTUSS
- HYTUSS/HYTUSS 2X

Liquid:
- NALDECON SENIOR EX (also contains saccharin, sorbitol)

Syrup:
- ANTI-TUSS (also contains alcohol)
- GENATUSS (also contains alcohol)
- GLYATE (also contains alcohol)
- GUIATUSS
- HALOTUSSIN (also contains alcohol)
- MALOTUSS (also contains alcohol)
- MYTUSSIN (also contains alcohol, sugar, menthol, raspberry flavor)
- RESCON–GGLIQUID (combination with phenylephrine hydrochloride—a decongestant)
- ROBITUSSIN (also contains alcohol, glucose, corn syrup, saccharin)
- SCOT-TUSSIN EXPECTORANT (also contains alcohol, saccharin, menthol, sorbitol)
- UNI-TUSSIN (also contains alcohol)

Note: *Guaifenesin* is an active ingredient in many multi-symptom antitussive/expectorant medications which are formulated with other active ingredients.

Q U I C K F A C T S

SYMPTOMS RELIEVED:
Coughs associated with common cold, flu, hay fever, and other respiratory allergies by loosening bronchial congestion and phlegm, resulting in more productive coughs.

HOW TO TAKE:
Comes in capsule, liquid, or syrup forms. Swallow capsule with liquid. Do not crush or chew timed-release capsules.

USUAL ADULT DOSE:
100 to 400 milligrams 6 times per day, not to exceed 2.4 grams in a 24 hour period.

USUAL CHILD DOSE:
For children 6 to 12: 100 to 200 milligrams 6 times per day, not to exceed 1.2 grams in a 24 hour period.

For children 2 to 6 (syrup): 50 to 100 milligrams 6 times per day, not to exceed 600 milligrams in a 24 hour period.

Do not administer to children under 2 unless under direction of physician. Dosage may vary based on infant or child's age.

OVERDOSE SYMPTOMS:
Nausea and vomiting, drowsiness, dizziness, fatigue, rash. If you suspect an overdose, immediately seek medical attention.

SIDE EFFECTS:
No serious effects in most cases of common use. Less common side effects include dizziness, gastrointestinal (GI) upset including stomach cramps and diarrhea, drowsiness, fatigue.

CHECK WITH YOUR DOCTOR OR PHARMACIST BEFORE COMBINING GUAIFENESIN WITH:
Any anticoagulant medication.

PREGNANCY OR BREASTFEEDING:
Guaifenesin use by a nursing mother should be considered a potential risk for a nursing child as the drug will be passed on to the infant in the mother's milk. In all cases, a physician should be consulted.

PRECAUTIONS FOR CHILDREN:
In general, guaifenesin is not advised for children under 2. Administer guaifenesin to infants or children only when consulting a physician and follow instructions on medication (see above).

55+ **PRECAUTIONS FOR SENIORS:**
Seniors generally don't eliminate drugs as efficiently as younger persons, and should avoid high dosages.

SPECIAL WARNINGS:
Do not use for control of chronic cough related to conditions such as emphysema, asthma, or smoking, or if coughs are producing excessive secretions. If cough is accompanied by high fever, rash, nausea or vomiting, or persistent headache, use only if directed by your doctor.

ADDITIONAL WARNING:
Alcohol: Some guaifenesin-containing medications contain various amounts of alcohol. Check label of any cough medication if concerned about ingestion of alcohol.

Sugar/Sweeteners: Some dextromethorphan-containing medications contain various amounts of

Q U I C K F A C T S

sugar, sucrose, glucose, and/or artificial sweeteners such as aspartame, saccharin, sorbitol. Check label of cough medication before selecting, if concerned about diabetes and ingestion of sugar or artificial sweeteners.

INFORM YOUR DOCTOR BEFORE TAKING GUAIFENESIN IF YOU HAVE:

Asthma, emphysema, or other respiratory condition.

ACTIVE INGREDIENTS:

GUAIFENESIN AND DEXTROMETHORPHAN HYDROBROMIDE

℞ **BRAND NAMES:**

Liquid:

- Benylin Expectorant Liquid (also contains alcohol, saccharin, menthol, sucrose)
- Cheracol D Cough Liquid (also contains alcohol, fructose, sucrose)
- Diabetic Tussin DM (also contains saccharin, methylparaben, menthol)
- Guiatussin with Dextromethorphan Liquid (also contains alcohol)
- Halotussin-DM Liquid (also contains corn syrup, menthol, saccharin, sucrose, parabens)
- Halotussin-DM Sugar-Free Liquid (also contains saccharin, sorbitol, parabens)
- Kolephrin GG/DM Liquid (also contains glucose, saccharin, sucrose)
- Mytussin DM Liquid (also contains alcohol)
- Naldecon Senior DX Liquid (also contains saccharin, sorbitol)
- Robitussin–DM Liquid (also contains saccharin, glucose, high fructose corn syrup)
- Safe Tussin 30 Liquid
- Vicks Pediatric Formula 44E Liquid (also contains sorbitol, sucrose)

Syrup:

- Extra Action Cough Syrup (also contains alcohol, corn syrup, saccharin, sucrose)
- Genatuss DM Syrup (also contains sucrose)
- Rhinosyn–DMX Syrup
- Robafen DM Syrup (also contains alcohol, sugar, menthol, sorbitol, parabens)

QUICK FACTS

- TOLU-SED DM SYRUP (also contains alcohol)
- UNI-TUSSIN DM SYRUP (also contains saccharin, sucrose, methylparaben)

Tablets:

- GLYCOTUSS-DM TABLETS
- TUSS–DM TABLETS

Note: *Guaifenesin* and *dextromethorphan hydrobromide* are also active ingredient in other multi-symptom antitussive/expectorant medications which are formulated with other active ingredients.

SYMPTOMS RELIEVED:
Coughs associated with common cold, flu, hayfever, and other respiratory allergies by suppressing or moderating extreme cough activity, and by loosening bronchial congestion and phlegm, resulting in more productive coughs.

HOW TO TAKE:
Comes in tablet, liquid, or syrup forms. Swallow tablet with liquid. Do not crush or chew timed-release capsules.

USUAL ADULT DOSE:
Dosage varies per product and active ingredient formulation. Follow product dosage instructions.

USUAL CHILD DOSE:
Do not administer to children under 6 unless under direction of physician. Dosage may vary based on infant or child's age.

OVERDOSE SYMPTOMS:
Nervous agitation, severe anxiety, insomnia (sleeplessness), hallucinations, tremors,

convulsions, nausea, vomiting, cardiac arrhythmia (irregular pulse and heartbeat), drowsiness, dizziness, fatigue, rash. If you suspect an overdose, immediately seek medical attention.

SIDE EFFECTS:
No serious effects in most cases of common use. Less common side effects include nasal dryness, dizziness, nausea, and mild insomnia palpitations, insomnia, gastrointestinal (GI) upset including stomach cramps and diarrhea, drowsiness and fatigue. In rare cases, more severe side effects may result, including: painful and frequent urination, hypertension, and heart palpitations. In these cases, discontinue medication and call your doctor immediately.

CHECK WITH YOUR DOCTOR OR PHARMACIST BEFORE COMBINING GUAIFENESIN AND DEXTROMETHORPHAN WITH:
Anticoagulant medications and MAO (monoamine oxidase inhibitors) drugs.

PREGNANCY OR BREASTFEEDING:
Guaifenesin and dextromethorphan use by a nursing mother should be considered a potential risk for a nursing child as the drug will be passed on to the infant in the mother's milk. In all cases, a physician should be consulted.

PRECAUTIONS FOR CHILDREN:
In general, guaifenesin and dextromethorphan are not advised for children under 2. Administer guaifenesin and dextromethorphan to infants or children only when consulting a physician and follow instructions on medication (see above).

Q U I C K F A C T S

PRECAUTIONS FOR SENIORS:
Seniors generally don't eliminate drugs as efficiently as younger persons, and should avoid high dosages.

SPECIAL WARNINGS:
Do not use for control of chronic cough related to conditions such as emphysema, asthma, or smoking, or if coughs are producing excessive secretions. If cough is accompanied by high fever, rash, nausea or vomiting, or persistent headache, use only if directed by your doctor.

ADDITIONAL WARNING:
Alcohol: Some cough/cold medications contain various amounts of alcohol. Check label of any cough medication if concerned about ingestion of alcohol.

Sugar/Sweeteners: Some cough/cold medications contain various amounts of sugar, sucrose, glucose, and/or artificial sweeteners such as aspartame, saccharin, sorbitol. Check label of cough medication before selecting, if concerned about diabetes and ingestion of sugar or artificial sweeteners.

Abuse/Dependency: Reports indicate a rising rate of abuse of dextromethorphan-containing medications, particularly among teens. Sufficient data has not yet been collected, however, to determine the abuse and dependency potential of dextromethorphan-containing medications.

INFORM YOUR DOCTOR BEFORE TAKING GUAIFENESIN AND DEXTROMETHORPHAN IF YOU HAVE:
Asthma, emphysema, or other respiratory condition, or liver impairment or liver disease.

CONSTIPATION

QUICK REVIEW

• LAXATIVE •

The most important considerations in choosing a laxative are: its effectiveness in short-term treatment of constipation, and potential side effects associated with the drug.

LAXATIVES ARE A CLASS OF DRUGS WHICH:

- promote, facilitate or stimulate bowel movement and the passage of stools, through the following means:

  bulk-forming laxatives (psyllium, methylcellulose, polycarbophil) dissolve or swell in the intestinal fluid in order to stimulate bowel movement, and are considered the safest and most similar in action to the body's own function,

  stimulant laxatives (cascara sagrada, phenolphthalein, senna, castor oil, bisacodyl) act directly on intestines by irritation of mucous membrane and are also often used to evacuate bowels prior to surgery or X-ray examinations,

  saline laxatives (magnesium hydroxide, sodium phosphate), which promote retention of fluid in bowel, act similarly to bulk-forming laxatives, and are also used as purgatives in cases of food or drug poisoning,

  lubricant laxatives (mineral oil, docusate sodium), promote fecal softening, and are often used as stool softeners,

- should only be used for short-term symptomatic relief (unless your doctor directs otherwise), and with adequate fluid intake to prevent dehydration,

- should not be used as substitutes for sensible intake of fiber and fluid in daily diet, and regular exercise,
- should never be used when attempting to lose weight. (See Special Warnings sections on bulimia nervosa and anorexia nervosa in individual Quick Facts).

See also: Stool Softener

QUICK FACTS

ACTIVE INGREDIENT:

BISACODYL

BRAND NAMES:

- Bisco-Lax
- Dulcagen
- Dulcolax
  (also contains lactose, sucrose, parabens)
- Fleet Laxative

SYMPTOMS RELIEVED:

Irregular bowel movements (constipation).

HOW TO TAKE:

Comes in suppository and tablet forms. Swallow tablet and follow with full glass (8 oz.) of water. Remove wrapper of suppository and moisten carefully with water. If you have hemorrhoids or anal fissures, suppository tip may be lightly coated with petroleum jelly prior to insertion. Insertion may be easier if you lie on your side while pushing suppository (tapered or pointed end first) with finger high into rectum so it will not slip out. Do not retain longer than 20 to 30 minutes in rectum. Always wash hands before and after insertion of suppository. Unless directed otherwise, it is generally preferable to take these products at bedtime on an empty stomach. These products generally produce bowel movement within 6 to 10 hours.

USUAL ADULT DOSE:

Dosages vary with product. In all cases follow specific product instructions.

USUAL CHILD DOSE:

Ages 6 to 12: Dosages vary with product. In all cases follow specific product instructions.

Ages 3 to 6: Only administer to children between 3 to 6 under doctor's supervision or direction. These products are generally not advised for children younger than 3, and never for infants. In all cases follow specific product instructions.

QUICK FACTS

OVERDOSE SYMPTOMS:
Diarrhea, abdominal and muscular cramps, irregular heartbeat, fatigue.

SIDE EFFECTS:
No serious effects in most cases of common use. Occasional side effects may include: nausea, belching, dehydration, and loose stools or diarrhea. In rare cases skin hypersensitivity, skin rash, rectal bleeding or rectal pain have resulted. In these cases, discontinue use of the product and call your doctor immediately.

CHECK WITH YOUR DOCTOR OR PHARMACIST BEFORE COMBINING BISACODYL WITH:
Anticoagulants, antacids, or other drugs and preparations. Take any other medication 2 hours apart, as laxatives interfere with body's absorption of medicine.

PREGNANCY OR BREASTFEEDING:
Safety of this drug for use during pregnancy or while nursing has not been established. In all cases you should consult your doctor before using any drug during pregnancy or while nursing.

PRECAUTIONS FOR CHILDREN:
These products should only be used with doctor's supervision or direction for children under 6. These products are not recommended

Q U I C K F A C T S

for use with children under 3 and should never be used with infants. Consult your doctor and follow instructions on medication (see above).

55+ **PRECAUTIONS FOR SENIORS:**
Seniors generally may be more prone to side effects and possible adverse effects of these products than younger individuals. Avoid high dosages as laxative dependence may result.

SPECIAL WARNINGS:
Do not use any of these products if you are allergic to bisacodyl or any of the inactive ingredients contained in these products, if you are experiencing abdominal pain, cramps, nausea or vomiting, or if you have kidney disease. Do not use these products if you have experienced irregular bowel movements for less than 2 days. Do not use these products longer than one week as laxative dependence can result. If regular bowel movements have not returned within one week, consult your doctor.

ADDITIONAL WARNINGS:
Use of these products should be supplemented with liquids (preferably water) to prevent electrolyte/fluid depletion or dehydration.

Eating disorders: Chronic or excessive use of laxatives, particularly by young women, may be a sign of anorexia nervosa or bulimia nervosa.

INFORM YOUR DOCTOR BEFORE TAKING BISACODYL IF YOU HAVE:
Allergies—particularly to food types, high blood pressure, rectal bleeding, colostomy or ileostomy, or any form of kidney disease.

ACTIVE INGREDIENT:

CASCARA SAGRADA

Q U I C K F A C T S

BRAND NAMES:

- Caroid Laxative Tablets (combination with phenolphthalein)
- Herbal Laxative Tablets (combination with senna—also contains buckthorn bark)
- Nature's Remedy (combination with aloe—also contains lactose)

SYMPTOMS RELIEVED:

Irregular bowel movements (constipation).

HOW TO TAKE:

Comes in capsule and tablet forms. Swallow capsule or tablet with full glass (8 oz.) of water. Unless directed otherwise, it is generally preferable to take these products at bedtime. These products generally produce bowel movement within 6 to 12 hours.

USUAL ADULT DOSE:

Dosages vary with product. In all cases follow specific product instructions.

USUAL CHILD DOSE:

Ages 8 to 15: Dosages vary with product. In all cases follow specific product instructions.

Ages 3 to 8: Only administer to children between 3 to 8 under doctor's supervision or direction. These products are generally not advised for children younger than 3, and never for infants. In all cases follow specific product instructions.

QUICK FACTS

OVERDOSE SYMPTOMS:
Diarrhea, abdominal and muscular cramps, irregular heartbeat, fatigue.

SIDE EFFECTS:
No serious effects in most cases of common use, although use of products which contain cascara sagrada may result in discoloration of urine, usually to yellow-brown. If urine is alkaline, discoloration may be pink-red, red-violet or red-brown. Other occasional side effects may include: nausea, belching, dehydration, and loose stools or diarrhea. In rare cases, skin hypersensitivity, skin rash, rectal bleeding or rectal pain have resulted. In these cases, discontinue use of the product and call your doctor immediately.

CHECK WITH YOUR DOCTOR OR PHARMACIST BEFORE COMBINING CASCARA SAGRADA WITH:
Anticoagulants, antacids, or other drugs and preparations. Take any other medication 2 hours apart, as laxatives interfere with body's absorption of medicine.

PREGNANCY OR BREASTFEEDING:
Safety of this drug for use during pregnancy or while nursing has not been established. In all cases you should consult your doctor before using any drug during pregnancy or while nursing.

PRECAUTIONS FOR CHILDREN:
These products should only be used with doctor's supervision or direction for children under 8. These products are not recommended for use with children under 3 and should never be

used with infants. Consult your doctor and follow instructions on medication (see above).

55+

PRECAUTIONS FOR SENIORS:
Seniors generally may be more prone to side effects and possible adverse effects of these products than younger individuals. Avoid high dosages as laxative dependence may result.

SPECIAL WARNINGS:
Do not use any of these products if you are allergic to cascara sagrada or any of the inactive ingredients contained in these products, if you are experiencing abdominal pain, cramps, nausea or vomiting, or if you have kidney disease. Do not use these products if you have experienced irregular bowel movements for less than 2 days. Do not use these products longer than one week as laxative dependence can result. If regular bowel movements have not returned within one week, consult your doctor.

ADDITIONAL WARNINGS:
Use of these products should be supplemented with liquids (preferably water) to prevent electrolyte/fluid depletion or dehydration.

Eating disorders: Chronic or excessive use of laxatives, particularly by young women, may be a sign of anorexia nervosa or bulimia nervosa.

INFORM YOUR DOCTOR BEFORE TAKING CASCARA SAGRADA IF YOU HAVE:
Allergies—particularly to food types, high blood pressure, rectal bleeding, colostomy or ileostomy, or any form of kidney disease.

Q U I C K F A C T S

ACTIVE INGREDIENT:

CASTOR OIL

BRAND NAMES:
- EMULSOIL
- FLEET FLAVORED CASTOR OIL (also contains flavoring)
- PURGE (also contains lemon flavoring)

SYMPTOMS RELIEVED:
Irregular bowel movements (constipation)—also used in preparation of bowel for X-ray, surgery, proctological procedures, and related procedures.

HOW TO TAKE:
Comes in emulsion (mixture of two liquids) and liquid forms. Follow with full glass (8 oz.) of water. Unless directed otherwise, it is generally preferable to take these products in late afternoon or early evening. These products generally produce bowel movement within 2 to 6 hours, so plan accordingly.

USUAL ADULT DOSE:
Dosages vary with product. In all cases follow specific product instructions.

USUAL CHILD DOSE:
Ages 6 to 12: Dosages vary with product. In all cases follow specific product instructions.

Ages 3 to 6: Only administer to children between 3 to 6 under doctor's supervision or direction. These products are generally not advised for children younger than 3, and never for infants. In all cases follow specific product instructions.

OVERDOSE SYMPTOMS:
Diarrhea, abdominal and muscular cramps, irregular heartbeat, fatigue.

SIDE EFFECTS:
No serious effects in most cases of common use. Occasional side effects may include: nausea, belching, dehydration, and loose stools or diarrhea. In rare cases skin hypersensitivity, skin rash, rectal bleeding, or rectal pain have resulted. In these cases, discontinue use of the product and call your doctor immediately.

CHECK WITH YOUR DOCTOR OR PHARMACIST BEFORE COMBINING CASTOR OIL WITH:
Blood thinners, antacids, or other drugs and preparations. Take any other medication 2 hours apart, as laxatives interfere with body's absorption of medicine.

PREGNANCY OR BREASTFEEDING:
Safety of this drug for use during pregnancy or while nursing has not been established. In all cases you should consult your doctor before using any drug during pregnancy or while nursing.

PRECAUTIONS FOR CHILDREN:
These products should only be used with doctor's supervision or direction for children under 6. These products are not recommended for use with children under 3 and should never be used with infants. Consult your doctor and follow instructions on medication (see above).

Q U I C K F A C T S

55+ **PRECAUTIONS FOR SENIORS:**
Seniors generally may be more prone to side effects and possible adverse effects of these products than younger individuals. Avoid high dosages as laxative dependence may result.

SPECIAL WARNINGS:
Do not use any of these products if you are allergic to castor oil or any of the inactive ingredients contained in these products, if you are experiencing abdominal pain, cramps, nausea or vomiting, or if you have kidney disease. Do not use these products if you have experienced irregular bowel movements for less than 2 days. Do not use these products longer than one week as laxative dependence can result. If regular bowel movements have not returned within one week, consult your doctor.

ADDITIONAL WARNINGS:
Use of these products should be supplemented with liquids (preferably water) to prevent electrolyte/fluid depletion or dehydration.

Eating disorders: Chronic or excessive use of laxatives, particularly by young women, may be a sign of anorexia nervosa or bulimia nervosa.

INFORM YOUR DOCTOR BEFORE TAKING CASTOR OIL IF YOU HAVE:
Allergies—particularly to food types, high blood pressure, rectal bleeding, colostomy or ileostomy, or any form of kidney disease.

ACTIVE INGREDIENT:

DOCUSATE CALCIUM (DIOCTYL CALCIUM SULFOSUCCINATE)

Q U I C K F A C T S

BRAND NAMES:

- DC Softgels
- Pro-Cal-Sof
- Surfak Liquigels
  (also contains alcohol, sorbitol)

SYMPTOMS RELIEVED:
Irregular bowel movements (constipation).

HOW TO TAKE:
Comes in capsule forms. Take capsules with least one full glass (8 oz.) of water. These products generally produce more regular bowel movements within 12 to 72 hours.

USUAL ADULT DOSE:
240 milligrams per day, depending on symptoms and product, until normal bowel movements resume. In all cases follow specific product instructions.

USUAL CHILD DOSE:
Ages 12 and over and adults with less severe symptoms: 50 to 150 milligrams per day, depending on symptoms and product, until normal bowel movements resume. In all cases follow specific product instructions.

Ages 12 and younger: Only administer to children younger than 12 under doctor's supervision or direction. In all cases follow specific product instructions.

QUICK FACTS

OVERDOSE SYMPTOMS:
Muscular cramps, irregular heartbeat, fatigue, disorientation, and confusion.

SIDE EFFECTS:
No serious effects in most cases of common use. Occasional side effects may include nausea. In rare cases rectal bleeding, pain, itching, or burning sensation may occur. In these cases, discontinue use of the product and call your doctor immediately.

CHECK WITH YOUR DOCTOR OR PHARMACIST BEFORE COMBINING DOCUSATE CALCIUM WITH:
Anticoagulants, antacids, oral contraceptives, or other drugs and preparations. Take any other medication 2 hours apart, as laxatives interfere with body's absorption of medicine.

PREGNANCY OR BREASTFEEDING:
Safety of this drug for use during pregnancy or while nursing has not been established. In all cases you should consult your doctor before using any drug during pregnancy or while nursing.

PRECAUTIONS FOR CHILDREN:
These products should only be used with doctor's supervision or direction for children under 12. Consult your doctor and follow instructions on medication (see above).

PRECAUTIONS FOR SENIORS:
Seniors generally may be more prone to side effects and possible adverse effects of these products than younger individuals.

SPECIAL WARNINGS:
Do not use any of these if you are allergic to docusate calcium or any inactive ingredients contained in these products, if you are experiencing abdominal pain, cramps, nausea, or vomiting, or if you have intestinal obstruction or fecal impaction. Do not use these products if you have experienced irregular bowel movements for less than 2 days. If regular bowel movements have not returned within one week, consult your doctor.

ADDITIONAL WARNINGS:
Do not use any of these products in combination with a mineral oil laxative product. Use of these products should be supplemented with liquids (preferably water) to prevent electrolyte/fluid depletion or dehydration.

Eating disorders: Chronic or excessive use of laxatives, particularly by young women, may be a sign of anorexia nervosa or bulimia nervosa.

INFORM YOUR DOCTOR BEFORE TAKING DOCUSATE CALCIUM IF YOU HAVE:
Allergies—particularly to food types, high blood pressure, abdominal pain, cramps, nausea, vomiting, intestinal obstruction or fecal impaction, rectal bleeding, diabetes, heart trouble, colostomy, or ileostomy.

Q U I C K F A C T S

ACTIVE INGREDIENT:

DOCUSATE POTASSIUM (DIOCTYL POTASSIUM SULFOSUCCINATE)

BRAND NAMES:

- DIOCTO-K
- KASOF (also contains sorbitol)

SYMPTOMS RELIEVED:

Irregular bowel movements (constipation).

HOW TO TAKE:

Comes in capsule forms. Take capsules with least one full glass (8 oz.) of water. These products generally produce more regular bowel movements within 12 to 72 hours.

USUAL ADULT DOSE:

100 to 300 milligrams per day, depending on symptoms and product, until normal bowel movements resume. In all cases follow specific product instructions.

USUAL CHILD DOSE:

Ages 6 to 12: 100 milligrams per day at bedtime, depending on symptoms and product, until normal bowel movements resume. In all cases follow specific product instructions.

Only administer to children younger than 6 under doctor's supervision or direction. In all cases follow specific product instructions.

OVERDOSE SYMPTOMS:

Muscular cramps, irregular heartbeat, fatigue, disorientation, and confusion.

SIDE EFFECTS:

No serious effects in most cases of common

use. Occasional side effects may include nausea. In rare cases rectal bleeding, pain, itching, or burning sensation may occur. In these cases, discontinue use of the product and call your doctor immediately.

CHECK WITH YOUR DOCTOR OR PHARMACIST BEFORE COMBINING DOCUSATE POTASSIUM WITH:

Anticoagulants, antacids, oral contraceptives, or other drugs and preparations. Take any other medication 2 hours apart, as laxatives interfere with body's absorption of medicine.

PREGNANCY OR BREASTFEEDING:

Safety of this drug for use during pregnancy or while nursing has not been established. In all cases you should consult your doctor before using any drug during pregnancy or while nursing.

PRECAUTIONS FOR CHILDREN:

These products should only be used with doctor's supervision or direction for children under 6. Consult your doctor and follow instructions on medication (see above).

55+ **PRECAUTIONS FOR SENIORS:**

Seniors generally may be more prone to side effects and possible adverse effects of these products than younger individuals.

SPECIAL WARNINGS:

Do not use any of these if you are allergic to docusate potassium or any inactive ingredients contained in these products, if you are experiencing abdominal pain, cramps, nausea, or vomiting, or if you have intestinal obstruction

QUICK FACTS

or fecal impaction. Do not use these products if you have experienced irregular bowel movements for less than 2 days. If regular bowel movements have not returned within one week, consult your doctor.

ADDITIONAL WARNINGS:
Do not use any of these products in combination with a mineral oil laxative product. Use of these products should be supplemented with liquids (preferably water) to prevent electrolyte/fluid depletion or dehydration.

Eating disorders: Chronic or excessive use of laxatives, particularly by young women, may be a sign of anorexia nervosa or bulimia nervosa.

INFORM YOUR DOCTOR BEFORE TAKING DOCUSATE POTASSIUM IF YOU HAVE:
Allergies—particularly to food types, high blood pressure, abdominal pain, cramps, nausea, vomiting, intestinal obstruction or fecal impaction, rectal bleeding, diabetes, heart trouble, colostomy or ileostomy.

ACTIVE INGREDIENTS:

DOCUSATE POTASSIUM (DIOCTYL POTASSIUM SULFOSUCCINATE) IN COMBINATION WITH CASANTHRANOL

QUICK FACTS

BRAND NAMES:

- Dialose Tablets (also contains lactose)
- Diocto-K Plus Capsules
- Dioctolose Plus Capsules
- DSMC Plus Capsules

SYMPTOMS RELIEVED:

Irregular bowel movements (constipation) due to hard stools, anorectal pain, conditions such as cardiac cases in which straining or difficulty in defecation is undesirable.

HOW TO TAKE:

Comes in capsule and tablet forms. Take with one full glass (8 oz.) of water at bedtime. Follow with least one full glass (8 oz.) of water. These products generally produce softer stools (which usually means easier bowel movement) within 6 to 12 hours following initial dose.

USUAL ADULT DOSE:

1 to 2 tablets per day, at bedtime, depending on symptoms and product. In all cases follow specific product instructions.

USUAL CHILD DOSE:

Ages 6 to 12: Half the adult dose per day, at bedtime, depending on symptoms and product. In all cases follow specific product instructions. Only administer to children younger than 6 under doctor's supervision or direction. In all cases follow specific product instructions.

Q U I C K F A C T S

OVERDOSE SYMPTOMS:
Muscular cramps, irregular heartbeat, fatigue, disorientation, and confusion.

SIDE EFFECTS:
No serious effects in most cases of common use, although use of products which contain casanthranol may result in discoloration of alkaline urine, usually to pink-red, red-violet or red-brown. Other occasional side effects may include: bitter taste in mouth, nausea, belching, dehydration, and loose stools or diarrhea.
In rare cases rectal bleeding, pain, itching, burning sensation, skin irritation, or rash may occur. In these cases, discontinue use of the product and call your doctor immediately.

CHECK WITH YOUR DOCTOR OR PHARMACIST BEFORE COMBINING DOCUSATE SODIUM AND CASANTHRANOL WITH:
Blood thinners, antacids, oral contraceptives, or other drugs and preparations. Take any other medication 2 hours apart, as laxatives interfere with body's absorption of medicine.

PREGNANCY OR BREASTFEEDING:
Safety of this drug for use during pregnancy or while nursing has not been established. In all cases you should consult your doctor before using any drug during pregnancy or while nursing.

PRECAUTIONS FOR CHILDREN:
These products should only be used with doctor's supervision or direction for children under 6. Consult your doctor and follow instructions on medication (see above).

55+ **PRECAUTIONS FOR SENIORS:**
Seniors generally may be more prone to side effects and possible adverse effects of these products than younger individuals.

SPECIAL WARNINGS:
Do not use any of these if you are allergic to docusate sodium, casanthranol, or any inactive ingredients contained in these products, if you are experiencing abdominal pain, cramps, nausea or vomiting, or if you have intestinal obstruction or fecal impaction, or any form of kidney or liver disease. Do not use these products if you have experienced irregular bowel movements for less than 2 days. If regular bowel movements have not returned within one week, consult your doctor.

QUICK FACTS

ADDITIONAL WARNINGS:
Do not use any of these products in combination with a mineral oil laxative product. Use of these products should be supplemented with liquids (preferably water) to prevent electrolyte/fluid depletion or dehydration.

Eating disorders: Chronic or excessive use of laxatives, particularly by young women, may be a sign of anorexia nervosa or bulimia nervosa.

INFORM YOUR DOCTOR BEFORE TAKING DOCUSATE SODIUM AND CASANTHRANOL IF YOU HAVE:
Allergies—particularly to food types, high blood pressure, abdominal pain, cramps, nausea, vomiting, intestinal obstruction or fecal impaction, rectal bleeding, diabetes, heart trouble, kidney or liver disease, colostomy or ileostomy.

Q U I C K F A C T S

ACTIVE INGREDIENT:

DOCUSATE SODIUM (DIOCTYL SODIUM SULFOSUCCINATE; DSS)

BRAND NAMES:

- COLACE–CAPSULES
- COLACE–SYRUP (also contains alcohol, menthol, sucrose)
- DIALOSE
- DIALOSE PLUS (combination with phenolphthalein—also contains methylcellulose, magnesium stearate)
- DIOEZE
- DIOCTO
- DISONATE
- DOK
- DOS SOFTGELS
- DOXINATE–CAPSULES (also contains sorbitol)
- DOXINATE–SOLUTION (also contains alcohol)
- MODANE SOFT (also contains sorbitol)
- PRO-SOF
- REGULAX SS

SYMPTOMS RELIEVED:
Irregular bowel movements (constipation) due to hard stools, anorectal pain, conditions such as cardiac cases in which straining or difficulty in defecation is undesirable.

HOW TO TAKE:
Comes in capsule, liquid, syrup, and solution forms. Take liquid or syrup forms with one full glass (8 oz.) of nonalcoholic, noncarbonated liquid, such as water, fruit juice, or milk to prevent possible throat irritation. Follow with least one full glass (8 oz.) of water. These products

generally produce softer stools (which usually means easier bowel movement) within 1 to 3 days following first dose.

USUAL ADULT DOSE:
50 to 200 milligrams per day, depending on symptoms and product. In all cases follow specific product instructions.

USUAL CHILD DOSE:
Ages 6 to 12: 40 to 120 milligrams per day, depending on symptoms and product. In all cases follow specific product instructions.

Ages 3 to 6: 20 to 60 milligrams per day, depending on symptoms and product. In all cases follow specific product instructions. Only administer to children younger than 3 under doctor's supervision or direction. In all cases follow specific product instructions.

OVERDOSE SYMPTOMS:
Muscular cramps, irregular heartbeat, fatigue, disorientation, and confusion.

SIDE EFFECTS:
No serious effects in most cases of common use. Occasional side effects may include: sore or scratchy throat, bitter taste in mouth, or nausea. In rare cases rectal bleeding, pain, itching, or burning sensation may occur. In these cases, discontinue use of the product and call your doctor immediately.

CHECK WITH YOUR DOCTOR OR PHARMACIST BEFORE COMBINING DOCUSATE SODIUM WITH:
Anticoagulants, antacids, oral contraceptives, or other drugs and preparations. Take any other

Q U I C K F A C T S

medication 2 hours apart, as laxatives interfere with body's absorption of medicine.

PREGNANCY OR BREASTFEEDING:
Safety of this drug for use during pregnancy or while nursing has not been established. In all cases you should consult your doctor before using any drug during pregnancy or while nursing.

PRECAUTIONS FOR CHILDREN:
These products should only be used with doctor's supervision or direction for children under 3. Consult your doctor and follow instructions on medication (see above).

55+

PRECAUTIONS FOR SENIORS:
Seniors generally may be more prone to side effects and possible adverse effects of these products than younger individuals.

SPECIAL WARNINGS:
Do not use any of these if you are allergic to docusate sodium or any inactive ingredients contained in these products, if you are experiencing abdominal pain, cramps, nausea, or vomiting, or if you have intestinal obstruction or fecal impaction. Do not use these products if you have experienced irregular bowel movements for less than 2 days. If regular bowel movements have not returned within one week, consult your doctor.

ADDITIONAL WARNINGS:
Do not use any of these products in combination with a mineral oil laxative product. Use of these products should be supplemented with

liquids (preferably water) to prevent electrolyte/fluid depletion or dehydration.

Eating disorders: Chronic or excessive use of laxatives, particularly by young women, may be a sign of anorexia nervosa or bulimia nervosa.

INFORM YOUR DOCTOR BEFORE TAKING DOCUSATE SODIUM IF YOU HAVE:
Allergies—particularly to food types, high blood pressure, abdominal pain, cramps, nausea, vomiting, intestinal obstruction or fecal impaction, rectal bleeding, diabetes, heart trouble, colostomy, or ileostomy.

QUICK FACTS

ACTIVE INGREDIENTS:

DOCUSATE SODIUM (DIOCTYL SODIUM SULFOSUCCINATE; DSS) IN COMBINATION WITH CASANTHRANOL

℞ **BRAND NAMES:**

- Disanthrol Capsules,
- D-S-S Plus Capsules
- Disolan Forte Capsules
- Genasoft Plus Softgels
- Peri-Colace Capsules
- Peri-Dos Softgels
- Pro-Sof Plus Capsules
- Regulace Capsules

SYMPTOMS RELIEVED:
Irregular bowel movements (constipation) due to hard stools, anorectal pain, conditions such as cardiac cases in which straining or difficulty in defecation is undesirable.

HOW TO TAKE:
Comes in capsule and tablet forms. Take with one full glass (8 oz.) of water at bedtime. Follow with least one full glass (8 oz.) of water. These products generally produce softer stools (which usually means easier bowel movement) within 6 to 12 hours following initial dose.

USUAL ADULT DOSE:
1 to 2 tablets per day, at bedtime, depending on symptoms and product. In all cases follow specific product instructions.

USUAL CHILD DOSE:
Ages 6 to 12: Half the adult dose per day, at bedtime, depending on symptoms and product. In all cases follow specific product instructions.

Only administer to children younger than 6 under doctor's supervision or direction. In all cases follow specific product instructions.

OVERDOSE SYMPTOMS:
Muscular cramps, irregular heartbeat, fatigue, disorientation, and confusion.

SIDE EFFECTS:
No serious effects in most cases of common use, although use of products which contain casanthranol may result in discoloration of alkaline urine, usually to pink-red, red-violet or red-brown. Other occasional side effects may include: bitter taste in mouth, nausea, belching, dehydration, and loose stools or diarrhea. In these cases, discontinue use of the product and call your doctor immediately.

CHECK WITH YOUR DOCTOR OR PHARMACIST BEFORE COMBINING DOCUSATE SODIUM AND CASANTHRANOL WITH:
Anticoagulants, antacids, oral contraceptives, or other drugs and preparations. Take any other medication 2 hours apart, as laxatives interfere with body's absorption of medicine.

PREGNANCY OR BREASTFEEDING:
Safety of this drug for use during pregnancy or while nursing has not been established. In all cases you should consult your doctor before using any drug during pregnancy or while nursing.

PRECAUTIONS FOR CHILDREN:
These products should only be used with doctor's supervision or direction for children under 6. Consult your doctor and follow instructions on medication (see above).

PRECAUTIONS FOR SENIORS:
Seniors generally may be more prone to side effects and possible adverse effects of these products than younger individuals.

SPECIAL WARNINGS:
Do not use any of these if you are allergic to docusate sodium, casanthranol, or any inactive ingredients contained in these products, if you are experiencing abdominal pain, cramps, nausea or vomiting, or if you have intestinal obstruction or fecal impaction, or any form of kidney or liver disease. Do not use these products if you have experienced irregular bowel movements for less than 2 days. If regular bowel movements have not returned within one week, consult your doctor.

ADDITIONAL WARNINGS:
Do not use any of these products in combination with a mineral oil laxative product. Use of these products should be supplemented with liquids (preferably water) to prevent electrolyte/fluid depletion or dehydration.

Eating disorders: Chronic or excessive use of laxatives, particularly by young women, may be a sign of anorexia nervosa or bulimia nervosa.

INFORM YOUR DOCTOR BEFORE TAKING DOCUSATE SODIUM AND CASANTHRANOL IF YOU HAVE:
Allergies—particularly to food types, high blood pressure, abdominal pain, cramps, nausea, vomiting, intestinal obstruction or fecal impaction, rectal bleeding, diabetes, heart trouble, kidney or liver disease, colostomy, or ileostomy.

ACTIVE INGREDIENTS:

DOCUSATE SODIUM (DIOCTYL SODIUM SULFOSUCCINATE; DSS) IN COMBINATION WITH PHENOLPHTHALEIN

QUICK FACTS

℞ **BRAND NAMES:**

- Colax Tablets
- Correctol Tablets (also contains sugar)
- Disolan Capsules
- Docusal-P Softgels
- Doxidan (also contains sorbitol)
- Feen-a-Mint Pills (also contains sugar)
- Femilax Tablets
- Modane Plus Tablets (also contains sorbitol)
- Phillips' LaxCaps (also contains sorbitol)
- Unilax Capsules (also contains sorbitol)

SYMPTOMS RELIEVED:
Irregular bowel movements (constipation) due to hard stools, anorectal pain, conditions such as cardiac cases in which straining or difficulty in defecation is undesirable.

HOW TO TAKE:
Comes in capsule and tablet forms. Take with one full glass (8 oz.) of water at bedtime. Follow with least one full glass (8 oz.) of water. These products generally produce softer stools (which usually means easier bowel movement) within 6 to 12 hours following initial dose.

USUAL ADULT DOSE:
1 to 2 tablets per day, at bedtime, depending on symptoms and product. In all cases follow specific product instructions.

Q U I C K F A C T S

USUAL CHILD DOSE:
Ages 6 to 12: Half the adult dose per day, at bedtime, depending on symptoms and product. In all cases follow specific product instructions. Only administer to children younger than 6 under doctor's supervision or direction. In all cases follow specific product instructions.

OVERDOSE SYMPTOMS:
Muscular cramps, irregular heartbeat, fatigue, disorientation, and confusion.

SIDE EFFECTS:
No serious effects in most cases of common use, although use of products which contain phenolphthalein may result in discoloration of alkaline urine, usually to pink-red, red-violet or red-brown. Other occasional side effects may include: bitter taste in mouth, nausea, belching, dehydration, and loose stools or diarrhea.
In rare cases rectal bleeding, pain, itching, burning sensation, skin irritation or rash may occur. In these cases, discontinue use of the product and call your doctor immediately.

CHECK WITH YOUR DOCTOR OR PHARMACIST BEFORE COMBINING DOCUSATE SODIUM AND PHENOLPHTHALEIN WITH:
Anticoagulants, antacids, oral contraceptives, or other drugs and preparations. Take any other medication 2 hours apart, as laxatives interfere with body's absorption of medicine.

PREGNANCY OR BREASTFEEDING:
Safety of this drug for use during pregnancy or while nursing has not been established. In all cases you should consult your doctor before using any drug during pregnancy or while nursing.

PRECAUTIONS FOR CHILDREN:
These products should only be used with doctor's supervision or direction for children under 6. Consult your doctor and follow instructions on medication (see above).

PRECAUTIONS FOR SENIORS:
Seniors generally may be more prone to side effects and possible adverse effects of these products than younger individuals.

SPECIAL WARNINGS:
Do not use any of these if you are allergic to docusate sodium, phenolphthalein or any inactive ingredients contained in these products, if you are experiencing abdominal pain, cramps, nausea or vomiting, or if you have intestinal obstruction or fecal impaction, or any form of kidney or liver disease.

ADDITIONAL WARNINGS:
Do not use any of these products in combination with a mineral oil laxative product.
Use of these products should be supplemented with liquids (preferably water) to prevent electrolyte/fluid depletion or dehydration.

Eating disorders: Chronic or excessive use of laxatives, particularly by young women, may be a sign of anorexia nervosa or bulimia nervosa.

INFORM YOUR DOCTOR BEFORE TAKING DOCUSATE SODIUM AND PHENOLPHTHALEIN IF YOU HAVE:
Allergies—particularly to food types, high blood pressure, abdominal pain, cramps, nausea, vomiting, intestinal obstruction or fecal impaction, rectal bleeding, diabetes, heart trouble, kidney or liver disease, colostomy, or ileostomy.

QUICK FACTS

ACTIVE INGREDIENTS:

DOCUSATE SODIUM (DIOCTYL SODIUM SULFOSUCCINATE; DSS) IN COMBINATION WITH SENNA CONCENTRATE

BRAND NAMES:

- Ex-Lax Extra Gentle Pills (also contains sucrose)
- Gentlax Tablets (also contains lactose)
- Senokot-S Tablets (also contains lactose)

SYMPTOMS RELIEVED:
Irregular bowel movements (constipation) due to hard stools, anorectal pain, conditions such as cardiac cases in which straining or difficulty in defecation is undesirable.

HOW TO TAKE:
Comes in tablet forms. Take with one full glass (8 oz.) of water at bedtime. Follow with least one full glass (8 oz.) of water. These products generally produce softer stools (which usually means easier bowel movement) within 6 to 12 hours following initial dose.

USUAL ADULT DOSE:
1 to 2 tablets per day, at bedtime, depending on symptoms and product. In all cases follow specific product instructions.

USUAL CHILD DOSE:
Ages 6 to 12: Half the adult dose per day, at bedtime, depending on symptoms and product. In all cases follow specific product instructions. Only administer to children younger than 6 under doctor's supervision or direction. In all cases follow specific product instructions.

OVERDOSE SYMPTOMS:
Muscular cramps, irregular heartbeat, fatigue, disorientation, and confusion.

SIDE EFFECTS:
No serious effects in most cases of common use, although use of products which contain senna may result in discoloration of urine, usually to yellow-brown. If urine is alkaline, discoloration may be pink-red, red-violet or red-brown. Other occasional side effects may include: bitter taste in mouth, nausea, belching, dehydration, and loose stools or diarrhea. In rare cases rectal bleeding, pain, itching, burning sensation, skin irritation or rash may occur. In these cases, discontinue use of the product and call your doctor immediately.

CHECK WITH YOUR DOCTOR OR PHARMACIST BEFORE COMBINING DOCUSATE SODIUM AND SENNA WITH:
Anticoagulants, antacids, oral contraceptives, or other drugs and preparations. Take any other medication 2 hours apart, as laxatives interfere with body's absorption of medicine.

PREGNANCY OR BREASTFEEDING:
Safety of this drug for use during pregnancy or while nursing has not been established. In all cases you should consult your doctor before using any drug during pregnancy or while nursing.

PRECAUTIONS FOR CHILDREN:
These products should only be used with doctor's supervision or direction for children under 6. Consult your doctor and follow instructions on medication (see above).

Q U I C K F A C T S

PRECAUTIONS FOR SENIORS:
Seniors generally may be more prone to side effects and possible adverse effects of these products than younger individuals.

SPECIAL WARNINGS:
Do not use any of these if you are allergic to docusate sodium, senna, or any inactive ingredients contained in these products, if you are experiencing abdominal pain, cramps, nausea or vomiting, or if you have intestinal obstruction or fecal impaction, or any form of kidney or liver disease. Do not use these products if you have experienced irregular bowel movements for less than 2 days. If regular bowel movements have not returned within one week, consult your doctor.

ADDITIONAL WARNINGS:
Do not use any of these products in combination with a mineral oil laxative product. Use of these products should be supplemented with liquids (preferably water) to prevent electrolyte/fluid depletion or dehydration.

Eating disorders: Chronic or excessive use of laxatives, particularly by young women, may be a sign of anorexia nervosa or bulimia nervosa.

INFORM YOUR DOCTOR BEFORE TAKING DOCUSATE SODIUM AND SENNA IF YOU HAVE:
Allergies—particularly to food types, high blood pressure, abdominal pain, cramps, nausea, vomiting, intestinal obstruction or fecal impaction, rectal bleeding, diabetes, heart trouble, kidney or liver disease, colostomy or ileostomy.

ACTIVE INGREDIENT:
GLYCERIN

BRAND NAMES:
- Fleet Babylax
- Sani-Supp

SYMPTOMS RELIEVED:
Irregular bowel movements (constipation).

HOW TO TAKE:
Comes in rectal solution and suppository forms.

Suppository: Remove wrapper of suppository and moisten carefully with water. If you have hemorrhoids or anal fissures, suppository tip may be lightly coated with petroleum jelly prior to insertion. Insertion may be easier if you lie on your side while pushing suppository (tapered or pointed end first) with finger high into rectum so it will not slip out. Do not retain longer than 15 minutes in rectum. Always wash hands before and after insertion of suppository.

Rectal solution: Gently insert stem of applicator into rectum (with tip pointing towards navel). Squeeze applicator until nearly all liquid is expelled, then remove. Always wash hands before and after insertion of applicator. In all cases carefully read and follow specific product instructions on product packaging.

Do not use these products at bedtime on an empty stomach. These products generally produce bowel movement within 2 to 15 minutes.

USUAL ADULT DOSE:
Dosages vary with product. In all cases follow specific product instructions.

QUICK FACTS

USUAL CHILD DOSE:
Ages 6 to 12: Dosages vary with product. In all cases follow specific product instructions. Only administer to children younger than 6 under doctor's supervision or direction. In all cases follow specific product instructions.

OVERDOSE SYMPTOMS:
Abdominal and muscular cramps, irregular heartbeat, fatigue, profuse sweating, disorientation, and confusion.

SIDE EFFECTS:
No serious effects in most cases of common use. Occasional side effects may include: nausea, belching, dehydration, and loose stools or diarrhea. In these cases, discontinue use of the product and call your doctor immediately.

CHECK WITH YOUR DOCTOR OR PHARMACIST BEFORE COMBINING GLYCERIN WITH:
Anticoagulants, antacids, or other drugs and preparations. Take any other medication 2 hours apart, as laxatives interfere with body's absorption of medicine.

PREGNANCY OR BREASTFEEDING:
Safety of this drug for use during pregnancy or while nursing has not been established. In all cases you should consult your doctor before using any drug during pregnancy or while nursing.

PRECAUTIONS FOR CHILDREN:
These products should only be used with doctor's supervision or direction for children under 6. Consult your doctor and follow instructions on medication (see above).

PRECAUTIONS FOR SENIORS:
Seniors generally may be more prone to side effects and possible adverse effects of these products than younger individuals. Use of rectal solutions can result in excess fluid in the body. Avoid high dosages as laxative dependence may result.

SPECIAL WARNINGS:
Do not use any of these products if you are allergic to glycerin or any of the inactive ingredients contained in these products, if you are experiencing abdominal pain, cramps, nausea or vomiting, or if you have kidney disease. Do not use these products if you have experienced irregular bowel movements for less than 2 days. Do not use these products longer than one week as laxative dependence can result. If regular bowel movements have not returned within one week, consult your doctor.

ADDITIONAL WARNINGS:
Use of these products should be supplemented with liquids (preferably water) to prevent electrolyte/fluid depletion or dehydration.

Eating disorders: Chronic or excessive use of laxatives, particularly by young women, may be a sign of anorexia nervosa or bulimia nervosa.

INFORM YOUR DOCTOR BEFORE TAKING GLYCERIN IF YOU HAVE:
Allergies—particularly to food types, high blood pressure, rectal bleeding, colostomy, or ileostomy, or any form of kidney disease.

QUICK FACTS

ACTIVE INGREDIENT:
MAGNESIUM HYDROXIDE

BRAND NAMES:
- PHILLIPS' MILK OF MAGNESIA
- PHILLIPS' MILK OF MAGNESIA CONCENTRATED (also contains sorbitol, sugar; and strawberry, orange, or vanilla creme flavors)

SYMPTOMS RELIEVED:
Irregular bowel movements (constipation), acid indigestion, sour stomach, heartburn.

Note: For antacid action, see Quick Facts under Heartburn section.

HOW TO TAKE:
Comes in liquid forms. For laxative action: following dose, drink a full glass of water (preferable) or other nonalcoholic, noncarbonated liquid. Avoid taking late in day or on empty stomach. Since the laxative dosage will generally produce bowel movement 1/2 to 3 hours following dose, plan accordingly.

USUAL ADULT DOSE:
(For laxative action)
15 to 30 milliliters (2 to 4 tablespoonsful), followed by a 8 oz. (full glass) of liquid. In all cases follow specific product instructions.

USUAL CHILD DOSE:
(For laxative action)
Ages 6 to 12: 10 to 15 milliliters (1 to 2 tablespoonsful), followed by a full glass (8 oz.) of liquid.

Ages 3 to 6: Only administer to children

between 3 to 6 under doctor's supervision or direction. These products are generally not advised for children younger than 3, and never for infants. In all cases follow specific product instructions.

OVERDOSE SYMPTOMS:
Diarrhea, abdominal and muscular cramps, irregular heartbeat, fatigue.

SIDE EFFECTS:
No serious effects in most cases of common use. Occasionally nausea, belching, dehydration, and loose stools or diarrhea may occur. In rare cases rectal bleeding or rectal pain have resulted. In these cases, discontinue use of the product and call your doctor immediately.

CHECK WITH YOUR DOCTOR OR PHARMACIST BEFORE COMBINING MAGNESIUM HYDROXIDE WITH:
Anticoagulants, any other antacids, or other drugs and preparations. Take any other medication 2 hours apart, as laxatives interfere with body's absorption of medicine.

PREGNANCY OR BREASTFEEDING:
Safety of this drug for use during pregnancy or while nursing has not been established. In all cases you should consult your doctor before using any drug during pregnancy or while nursing.

PRECAUTIONS FOR CHILDREN:
These products should only be used with doctor's supervision or direction for children under 6. These products are not recommended for

Q U I C K F A C T S

use with children under 3 and should never be used with infants. Consult your doctor and follow instructions on medication (see above).

55+

PRECAUTIONS FOR SENIORS:
Seniors generally may be more prone to side effects and possible adverse effects of these products than younger individuals. Avoid high dosages as laxative dependence may result.

SPECIAL WARNINGS:
Do not use any of these products if you are allergic to magnesium hydroxide or any of the inactive ingredients contained in these products, if you are experiencing abdominal pain, cramps, nausea, or vomiting, or if you have kidney disease. Do not use these products if you have experienced irregular bowel movements for less than 2 days. Do not use these products longer than one week as laxative dependence can result. If regular bowel movements have not returned within one week, consult your doctor.

ADDITIONAL WARNINGS:
Use of these products should be supplemented with liquids (preferably water) to prevent electrolyte/fluid depletion or dehydration.

Eating disorders: Chronic or excessive use of laxatives, particularly by young women, may be a sign of anorexia nervosa or bulimia nervosa.

INFORM YOUR DOCTOR BEFORE TAKING MAGNESIUM HYDROXIDE IF YOU HAVE:
Allergies—particularly to food types, high blood pressure, rectal bleeding, colostomy, or ileostomy, or any form of kidney disease.

ACTIVE INGREDIENT:
MINERAL OIL

BRAND NAMES:
- Agoral Plain
- Kondremul
- Kondremul with Phenolphthalein
- Milkinol
- Neo-Cultol

(also contains sugar, chocolate flavoring)

SYMPTOMS RELIEVED:
Irregular bowel movements (constipation).

HOW TO TAKE:
Comes in emulsion (combination of two or more liquids) and jelly forms. Shake emulsion product well before taking. Unless directed otherwise, it is generally preferable to take these products at bedtime on an empty stomach. Follow with least one full glass (8 oz.) of water. These products generally produce bowel movement within 6 to 8 hours.

USUAL ADULT DOSE:
Emulsion: 2 to 5 tablespoonsful (30 to 75 milliliters), depending on symptoms and product. In all cases follow specific product instructions.

Jelly: See instructions of product packaging

USUAL CHILD DOSE:
Ages 6 to 12:
Emulsion: 2 to 5 teaspoonsful (10 to 25 milliliters), depending on symptoms and product. In all cases follow specific product instructions.

Jelly: See instructions of product packaging.

QUICK FACTS

Ages 3 to 6:
Only administer to children between 3 to 6 under doctor's supervision or direction. These products are generally not advised for children younger than 3, and never for infants. In all cases follow specific product instructions.

OVERDOSE SYMPTOMS:
Muscular cramps, irregular heartbeat, fatigue, disorientation, and confusion.

SIDE EFFECTS:
No serious effects in most cases of common use. Occasional side effects may include: stomach cramps, sore or scratchy throat, loose stools or diarrhea. In rare cases rectal bleeding, pain, itching, or burning sensation may occur. In these cases, discontinue use of the product and call your doctor immediately.

CHECK WITH YOUR DOCTOR OR PHARMACIST BEFORE COMBINING MINERAL OIL WITH:
Anticoagulants, antacids, oral contraceptives, or other drugs and preparations. Take any other medication 2 hours apart, as laxatives interfere with body's absorption of medicine.

PREGNANCY OR BREASTFEEDING:
Safety of this drug for use during pregnancy or while nursing has not been established. In all cases you should consult your doctor before using any drug during pregnancy or while nursing.

PRECAUTIONS FOR CHILDREN:
These products should only be used with doctor's supervision or direction for children under 6. These products are not recommended for use with children under 3 and should never be used with infants. Consult your doctor and

follow instructions on medication (see above).

55+ **PRECAUTIONS FOR SENIORS:**

Seniors generally may be more prone to side effects and possible adverse effects of these products than younger individuals. Avoid high dosages as laxative dependence may result.

SPECIAL WARNINGS:

Do not use any of these if you are allergic to mineral oil or any inactive ingredients contained in these products, if you are experiencing abdominal pain, cramps, nausea or vomiting, or if you have intestinal obstruction or fecal impaction. Do not use these products if you have experienced irregular bowel movements for less than 2 days. Do not use these products longer than one week as laxative dependence can result. If regular bowel movements have not returned within one week, consult your doctor.

ADDITIONAL WARNINGS:

Do not use any of these products in combination with a stool softener product. Use of these products should be supplemented with liquids (preferably water) to prevent electrolyte/fluid depletion or dehydration.

Eating disorders: Chronic or excessive use of laxatives, particularly by young women, may be a sign of anorexia nervosa or bulimia nervosa.

INFORM YOUR DOCTOR BEFORE TAKING MINERAL OIL IF YOU HAVE:

Allergies—particularly to food types, high blood pressure, difficulty swallowing (dysphagia), abdominal pain, cramps, nausea, vomiting, intestinal obstruction or fecal impaction, rectal bleeding, diabetes, heart trouble, colostomy, or ileostomy.

Q U I C K F A C T S

ACTIVE INGREDIENTS:

MISCELLANEOUS BULK-PRODUCING PRODUCTS

BRAND NAMES:

- MALTSUPEX (malt soup extract)
- UNIFIBER (powdered cellulose)

SYMPTOMS RELIEVED:

Irregular bowel movements (constipation), may also be used to relieve symptoms of irritable bowel syndrome

HOW TO TAKE:

Comes in liquid, powder, and tablet forms. Take with least one full glass (8 oz.) of water or other nonalcoholic or noncarbonated liquid. Mixing of products is easier in warm water or warm milk. Unifiber can also be mixed with soft foods, such as apple sauce, mashed potatoes, or pudding. Unless directed otherwise, it is generally preferable to take these products at meals or bedtime. These products generally produce bowel movement within 12 to 72 hours.

USUAL ADULT DOSE:

MALTSUPEX POWDER—up to 4 scoops (a scoop is provided with product) twice per day.

MALTSUPEX LIQUID—2 tablespoonsful twice per day with full glass (8 oz.) of liquid with each dose.

UNIFIBER—see instructions on product packaging.

In all cases follow specific product instructions.

USUAL CHILD DOSE:

Ages 6 to 12:

MALTSUPEX POWDER—up to 2 scoops twice per day.

MALTSUPEX LIQUID—1 tablespoonful twice per day with full glass (8 oz.) of liquid with each dose.

UNIFIBER—see instructions on product packaging.

In all cases follow specific product instructions.

Ages 3 to 6: Only administer to children between 3 to 6 under doctor's supervision or direction. These products are generally not advised for children younger than 3, and never for infants. In all cases follow specific product instructions.

OVERDOSE SYMPTOMS:

Diarrhea, abdominal and muscular cramps, irregular heartbeat, fatigue.

SIDE EFFECTS:

No serious effects in most cases of common use. Occasional side effects may include: nausea, belching, dehydration, and loose stools or diarrhea. In rare cases skin hypersensitivity, skin rash, rectal bleeding or rectal pain have resulted. In these cases, discontinue use of the product and call your doctor immediately.

CHECK WITH YOUR DOCTOR OR PHARMACIST BEFORE COMBINING THESE PRODUCTS WITH:

Anticoagulants, antacids, or other drugs and preparations. Take any other medication 2 hours apart, as laxatives interfere with body's absorption of medicine.

PREGNANCY OR BREASTFEEDING:
Safety of these products for use during pregnancy or while nursing has not been established. In all cases you should consult your doctor before using any drug during pregnancy or while nursing.

PRECAUTIONS FOR CHILDREN:
These products should only be used with doctor's supervision or direction for children under 6. These products are not recommended for use with children under 3 and should never be used with infants. Consult your doctor and follow instructions on medication (see above).

PRECAUTIONS FOR SENIORS:
Seniors generally may be more prone to side effects and possible adverse effects of these products than younger individuals. Avoid high dosages as laxative dependence may result.

SPECIAL WARNINGS:
Do not use any of these products if you are allergic to cellulose or malt soup extract or any inactive ingredients contained in these products; or if you are experiencing abdominal pain, cramps, nausea or vomiting, or if you have intestinal obstruction or fecal impaction.
Do not use these products if you have experienced irregular bowel movements for less than 2 days. Do not use these products longer than one week as laxative dependence can result.
If regular bowel movements have not returned within one week, consult your doctor.

ADDITIONAL WARNINGS:
Use of these products should be supplemented with liquids (preferably water) to prevent electrolyte/fluid depletion or dehydration.

Eating disorders: Chronic or excessive use of laxatives, particularly by young women, may be a sign of anorexia nervosa or bulimia nervosa.

INFORM YOUR DOCTOR BEFORE TAKING METHYLCELLULOSE IF YOU HAVE:
Allergies—particularly to food types, high blood pressure, abdominal pain, cramps, nausea, vomiting, intestinal obstruction or fecal impaction, rectal bleeding, colostomy, or ileostomy.

Q U I C K F A C T S

ACTIVE INGREDIENT:

METHYLCELLULOSE

BRAND NAMES:

- CITRUCEL (also contains sucrose, orange flavor)
- CITRUCEL SUGAR-FREE (combination with phenylalanine—also contains aspartame)

SYMPTOMS RELIEVED:

Irregular bowel movements (constipation), may also be used to relieve symptoms of irritable bowel syndrome, diverticular disease, and hemorrhoids.

HOW TO TAKE:

Comes in powder form. Take powder with least one full glass (8 oz.) of water. Taking product without sufficient liquid may cause choking. Unless directed otherwise, it is generally preferable to take these products with meals. These products generally produce bowel movement within 12 to 72 hours.

USUAL ADULT DOSE:

1 heaping tablespoonful (19 grams) in 8 oz. of cold water, 1 to 3 times per day. In all cases follow specific product instructions.

USUAL CHILD DOSE:

Ages 6 to 12: 1/2 half of adult dose in 4 oz. of cold water. In all cases follow specific product instructions.

Ages 3 to 6: Only administer to children between 3 to 6 under doctor's supervision or direction. These products are generally not advised for children younger than 3, and never for infants. In all cases follow specific product instructions.

OVERDOSE SYMPTOMS:
Diarrhea, abdominal and muscular cramps, irregular heartbeat, fatigue.

SIDE EFFECTS:
No serious effects in most cases of common use. Occasional side effects may include: nausea, belching, dehydration, and loose stools or diarrhea. In rare cases skin hypersensitivity, skin rash, rectal bleeding or rectal pain have resulted. In these cases, discontinue use of the product and call your doctor immediately.

CHECK WITH YOUR DOCTOR OR PHARMACIST BEFORE COMBINING METHYLCELLULOSE WITH:
Anticoagulants, antacids, or other drugs and preparations. Take any other medication 2 hours apart, as laxatives interfere with body's absorption of medicine.

PREGNANCY OR BREASTFEEDING:
Safety of this drug for use during pregnancy or while nursing has not been established. In all cases you should consult your doctor before using any drug during pregnancy or while nursing.

PRECAUTIONS FOR CHILDREN:
These products should only be used with doctor's supervision or direction for children under 6. These products are not recommended for use with children under 3 and should never be used with infants. Consult your doctor and follow instructions on medication (see above).

55+ PRECAUTIONS FOR SENIORS:
Seniors generally may be more prone to side effects and possible adverse effects of these

QUICK FACTS

products than younger individuals. Avoid high dosages as laxative dependence may result.

SPECIAL WARNINGS:
Do not use any of these products if you are allergic to methylcellulose or any inactive ingredients contained in these products, if you are experiencing abdominal pain, cramps, nausea or vomiting, or if you have intestinal obstruction or fecal impaction. Do not use these products if you have experienced irregular bowel movements for less than 2 days. Do not use these products longer than one week as laxative dependence can result. If regular bowel movements have not returned within one week, consult your doctor.

ADDITIONAL WARNINGS:
Do not take this product without adequate liquid, as it may swell and block throat or esophagus, resulting in choking. Use of these products should be supplemented with liquids (preferably water) to prevent electrolyte/fluid depletion or dehydration.

Eating disorders: Chronic or excessive use of laxatives, particularly by young women, may be a sign of anorexia nervosa or bulimia nervosa.

INFORM YOUR DOCTOR BEFORE TAKING METHYLCELLULOSE IF YOU HAVE:
Allergies—particularly to food types, high blood pressure, abdominal pain, cramps, nausea, vomiting, intestinal obstruction or fecal impaction, rectal bleeding, colostomy, or ileostomy.

ACTIVE INGREDIENT:

POLYCARBOPHIL

BRAND NAMES:

- Equalactin
- Fiberall
- FiberCon
- Fiber-Lax
- Mitrolan

SYMPTOMS RELIEVED:

Irregular bowel movements (constipation) or diarrhea associated with irritable bowel syndrome.

Note: *Polycarbophil* is also used as anti-diarrheal. In diarrhea conditions, it absorbs free fecal water, resulting in a gel which produces firmer stools.

HOW TO TAKE:

Comes in tablet and chewable tablet forms. Take tablets with least one full glass (8 oz.) of water. Unless directed otherwise, it is generally preferable to take these products with meals. These products generally produce bowel movement within 12 to 72 hours.

USUAL ADULT DOSE:

Dosages vary according to product. In all cases follow specific product instructions.

USUAL CHILD DOSE:

Ages 6 to 12: Dosages vary according to product. In all cases follow specific product instructions.

Ages 3 to 6: Only administer to children between 3 to 6 under doctor's supervision or

QUICK FACTS

direction. These products are generally not advised for children younger than 3, and never for infants. In all cases follow specific product instructions.

OVERDOSE SYMPTOMS:
Diarrhea, abdominal and muscular cramps, irregular heartbeat, fatigue.

SIDE EFFECTS:
No serious effects in most cases of common use. Occasional side effects may include: nausea, belching, dehydration, and loose stools or diarrhea. In rare cases skin hypersensitivity, skin rash, rectal bleeding or rectal pain have resulted. In these cases, discontinue use of the product and call your doctor immediately.

CHECK WITH YOUR DOCTOR OR PHARMACIST BEFORE COMBINING POLYCARBOPHIL WITH:
Anticoagulants, antacids, or other drugs and preparations. Take any other medication 2 hours apart, as laxatives interfere with body's absorption of medicine.

PREGNANCY OR BREASTFEEDING:
Safety of this drug for use during pregnancy or while nursing has not been established. In all cases you should consult your doctor before using any drug during pregnancy or while nursing.

PRECAUTIONS FOR CHILDREN:
These products should only be used with doctor's supervision or direction for children under 6. These products are not recommended for use with children under 3 and should never be used with infants. Consult your doctor and follow instructions on medication (see above).

55+

PRECAUTIONS FOR SENIORS:
Seniors generally may be more prone to side effects and possible adverse effects of these products than younger individuals. Avoid high dosages as laxative dependence may result.

SPECIAL WARNINGS:
Do not use any of these products if you are allergic to polycarbophil or any inactive ingredients contained in these products, if you are experiencing abdominal pain, cramps, nausea or vomiting, or if you have intestinal obstruction or fecal impaction. Do not use these products if you have experienced irregular bowel movements for less than 2 days. Do not use these products longer than one week as laxative dependence can result. If regular bowel movements have not returned within one week, consult your doctor.

ADDITIONAL WARNINGS:
Do not take this product without adequate liquid, as it may swell and block throat or esophagus, resulting in choking. Use of these products should be supplemented with liquids (preferably water) to prevent electrolyte/fluid depletion or dehydration.

Eating disorders: Chronic or excessive use of laxatives, particularly by young women, may be a sign of anorexia nervosa or bulimia nervosa.

INFORM YOUR DOCTOR BEFORE TAKING POLYCARBOPHIL IF YOU HAVE:
Allergies—particularly to food types, high blood pressure, abdominal pain, cramps, nausea, vomiting, intestinal obstruction or fecal impaction, rectal bleeding, colostomy, or ileostomy.

QUICK FACTS

ACTIVE INGREDIENT:
PSYLLIUM

℞ **BRAND NAMES:**

- EFFER-SYLLIUM (also contains saccharin, sucrose, lemon-lime flavoring)
- FIBERALL–WAFERS (also contains corn syrup, molasses, sugar, oatmeal raisin, fruit, nut flavorings)
- FIBERALL NATURAL FLAVOR
- FIBERALL ORANGE FLAVOR (also contains saccharin)
- HYDROCIL INSTANT
- KONSYL
- KONSYL-D (also contains dextrose)
- METAMUCIL–POWDER (also contains dextrose)
- METAMUCIL APPLE CRISP, CINNAMON SPICE–WAFERS (also contains sugar, fructose, molasses, sucrose, various flavorings)
- METAMUCIL LEMON-LIME FLAVOR–EFFERVESCENT POWDER (combination with phenylalanine—also contains aspartame)
- METAMUCIL ORANGE FLAVOR–POWDER (also contains sucrose, orange flavor)
- METAMUCIL ORANGE FLAVOR–EFFERVESCENT POWDER (combination with phenylalanine—also contains aspartame)
- METAMUCIL SUGAR-FREE (combination with phenylalanine—also contains aspartame)
- METAMUCIL SUGAR-FREE, ORANGE FLAVOR (combination with phenylalanine—also contains aspartame)
- MODANE BULK
- PERDIEM FIBER (also contains sucrose)
- REGULOID NATURAL
- REGULOID ORANGE

- REGULOID SUGAR-FREE ORANGE (combination with phenylalanine—also contains aspartame)
- REGULOID SUGAR-FREE REGULAR (combination with phenylalanine—also contains aspartame)
- SERUTAN–GRANULES (also contains saccharin, sugar)
- SERUTAN–POWDER (also contains dextrose)
- SIBLIN (also contains sugar)
- SYLLACT (also contains dextrose, saccharin)
- V-LAX

SYMPTOMS RELIEVED:
Chronic constipation, irregular bowel movements (nonspecific constipation), irritable bowel syndrome; as well as relief of symptoms of diverticular disease, hemorrhoid management, occasional pregnancy-related constipation (only under supervision of doctor).

HOW TO TAKE:
Comes in effervescent powder, granule, powder, and wafer forms. Take with at least one full glass (8 oz.) of water. Taking product without sufficient liquid may cause choking. Unless directed otherwise, it is generally preferable to take these products with meals. These products generally produce bowel movement within 12 to 72 hours.

USUAL ADULT DOSE:
Dosages vary according to product. In all cases follow specific product instructions.

USUAL CHILD DOSE:
Ages 6 to 12: Dosages vary according to product. In all cases follow specific product instructions.

Ages 3 to 6: Only administer to children between 3 to 6 under doctor's supervision or direction. These products are generally not advised for children younger than 3, and never for infants.

OVERDOSE SYMPTOMS:
Diarrhea, abdominal and muscular cramps, irregular heartbeat, fatigue.

SIDE EFFECTS:
No serious effects in most cases of common use. Occasional side effects may include: nausea, belching, dehydration, and loose stools or diarrhea. In rare cases skin hypersensitivity, skin rash, rectal bleeding or rectal pain have resulted. In these cases, discontinue use of the product and call your doctor immediately.

CHECK WITH YOUR DOCTOR OR PHARMACIST BEFORE COMBINING PSYLLIUM WITH:
Anticoagulants, antacids, or other drugs and preparations. Take any other medication 2 hours apart, as laxatives interfere with body's absorption of medicine.

PREGNANCY OR BREASTFEEDING:
Safety of this drug for use during pregnancy or while nursing has not been established. In all cases you should consult your doctor before using any drug during pregnancy or while nursing.

PRECAUTIONS FOR CHILDREN:
These products should only be used with doctor's supervision or direction for children under 6. These products are not recommended for use with children under 3 and should never

be used with infants. Consult your doctor and follow instructions on medication (see above).

55+ **PRECAUTIONS FOR SENIORS:**
Seniors generally may be more prone to side effects and possible adverse effects of these products than younger individuals. Avoid high dosages as laxative dependence may result.

SPECIAL WARNINGS:
Do not use any of these products if you are allergic to psyllium or any inactive ingredients contained in these products, if you are experiencing abdominal pain, cramps, nausea or vomiting, or if you have intestinal obstruction or fecal impaction. Do not use these products if you have experienced irregular bowel movements for less than 2 days. If regular bowel movements have not returned within one week, consult your doctor.

ADDITIONAL WARNINGS:
Do not take this product without adequate liquid, as it may swell and block throat or esophagus, resulting in choking. Use of these products should be supplemented with liquids (preferably water) to prevent electrolyte/fluid depletion or dehydration.

Eating disorders: Chronic or excessive use of laxatives, particularly by young women, may be a sign of anorexia nervosa or bulimia nervosa.

INFORM YOUR DOCTOR BEFORE TAKING PSYLLIUM IF YOU HAVE:
Allergies—particularly to food types, high blood pressure, abdominal pain, cramps, nausea, vomiting, intestinal obstruction or fecal impaction, rectal bleeding, colostomy, or ileostomy.

QUICK FACTS

ACTIVE INGREDIENT:
SENNA

BRAND NAMES:
- BLACK DRAUGHT–GRANULES (also contains sucrose, tartrazine)
- BLACK DRAUGHT–TABLETS (also contains sucrose)
- DR. CALDWELL SENNA LAXATIVE (also contains alcohol, salicylic acid, sucrose)
- EX-LAX UNFLAVORED (also contains sucrose)
- EX-LAX CHOCOLATED (also contains sucrose)
- EX-LAX MAXIMUM RELIEF FORMULA (also contains sucrose)
- FLETCHER'S CASTORIA (also contains alcohol, sucrose)
- GENTLAX (also contains malt extract, sucrose)
- SENEXON (also contains sucrose)
- SENOKOT–GRANULES (also contains sucrose)
- SENOKOT–SUPPOSITORIES
- SENOKOT–TABLETS (also contains lactose)
- SENOKOT-S (combination with docusate sodium)
- SENOKOT SYRUP (also contains alcohol)
- SENOKOT CHILDREN'S SYRUP
- SENOLAX

SYMPTOMS RELIEVED:
Irregular bowel movements (constipation).

HOW TO TAKE:
Comes in granule, liquid, suppository, syrup, and tablet forms. Swallow tablet, or follow chewable tablet, wafer, or gum with full glass (8 oz.) of water. Remove wrapper of suppository and moisten carefully with water. If you have hemorrhoids or anal fissures, suppository tip may be lightly coated with petroleum jelly prior to

insertion. Insertion may be easier if you lie on your side while pushing suppository (tapered or pointed end first) with finger high into rectum so it will not slip out. Do not retain longer than 20 to 30 minutes in rectum. Always wash hands before and after insertion of suppository. Unless directed otherwise, it is generally preferable to take these products at bedtime on an empty stomach. These products generally produce bowel movement within 6 to 10 hours.

USUAL ADULT DOSE:
Dosages vary with product. In all cases follow specific product instructions.

USUAL CHILD DOSE:
Ages 6 to 12: Dosages vary with product. In all cases follow specific product instructions.

Ages 3 to 6: Only administer to children between 3 to 6 under doctor's supervision or direction. These products are generally not advised for children younger than 3, and never for infants. In all cases follow specific product instructions.

OVERDOSE SYMPTOMS:
Diarrhea, abdominal and muscular cramps, irregular heartbeat, fatigue.

SIDE EFFECTS:
No serious effects in most cases of common use, although use of products which contain senna may result in discoloration of urine, usually to yellow-brown. If urine is alkaline, discoloration may be pink-red, red-violet or red-brown. Other occasional side effects may include: nausea, belching, dehydration, and loose

stools or diarrhea. In rare cases skin hypersensitivity, skin rash, rectal bleeding or rectal pain have resulted. In these cases, discontinue use of the product and call your doctor immediately.

CHECK WITH YOUR DOCTOR OR PHARMACIST BEFORE COMBINING SENNA WITH:

Anticoagulants, antacids, or other drugs and preparations. Take any other medication 2 hours apart, as laxatives interfere with body's absorption of medicine.

PREGNANCY OR BREASTFEEDING:

Safety of this drug for use during pregnancy or while nursing has not been established. In all cases you should consult your doctor before using any drug during pregnancy or while nursing.

PRECAUTIONS FOR CHILDREN:

These products should only be used with doctor's supervision or direction for children under 6. These products are not recommended for use with children under 3 and should never be used with infants. Consult your doctor and follow instructions on medication (see above).

55+ **PRECAUTIONS FOR SENIORS:**

Seniors generally may be more prone to side effects and possible adverse effects of these products than younger individuals. Avoid high dosages as laxative dependence may result.

SPECIAL WARNINGS:

Do not use any of these products if you are allergic to senna or any of the inactive ingredients contained in these products, if you are

experiencing abdominal pain, cramps, nausea or vomiting, or if you have kidney disease.
Do not use any of these products which contain tartrazine (a dye used in some food and medicines) if you are sensitive or allergic to aspirin.
Do not use these products if you have experienced irregular bowel movements for less than 2 days. Do not use these products longer than one week as laxative dependence can result.
If regular bowel movements have not returned within one week, consult your doctor.

ADDITIONAL WARNINGS:
Use of these products should be supplemented with liquids (preferably water) to prevent electrolyte/fluid depletion or dehydration.

Eating disorders: Chronic or excessive use of laxatives, particularly by young women, may be a sign of anorexia nervosa or bulimia nervosa.

INFORM YOUR DOCTOR BEFORE TAKING SENNA IF YOU HAVE:
Allergies—particularly to food types, high blood pressure, rectal bleeding, colostomy, or ileostomy, or any form of kidney disease.

QUICK REVIEW

• STOOL SOFTENER •

The most important considerations in choosing a stool softener are: its effectiveness in short-term treatment of difficult or painful bowel movement, and potential side effects associated with the drug.

STOOL SOFTENERS ARE A CLASS OF DRUGS WHICH:

- lubricate and soften feces in order to facilitate easier bowel movement when passage of firm stools or straining may cause adverse effects, such as post-surgery recovery or severe hemorrhoids conditions,
- usually contain mineral oil or docusate sodium,
- should only be used for short-term symptomatic relief (unless your doctor directs otherwise), and with adequate fluid intake to prevent dehydration,
- should not be used as substitutes for sensible intake of fiber and fluid in daily diet, and regular exercise,
- should never be used when attempting to lose weight. (See Special Warnings sections on bulimia nervosa and anorexia nervosa in individual Quick Facts.)

See also: Laxative

ACTIVE INGREDIENTS:

DOCUSATE POTASSIUM (DIOCTYL POTASSIUM SULFOSUCCINATE) IN COMBINATION WITH CASANTHRANOL

BRAND NAMES:

- Dialose Tablets (also contains lactose)
- Diocto-K Plus Capsules
- Dioctolose Plus Capsules
- DSMC Plus Capsules

SYMPTOMS RELIEVED:

Irregular bowel movements (constipation) due to hard stools, anorectal pain, conditions such as cardiac cases in which straining or difficulty in defecation is undesirable.

HOW TO TAKE:

Comes in capsule and tablet forms. Take with one full glass (8 oz.) of water at bedtime. Follow with least one full glass (8 oz.) of water. These products generally produce softer stools (which usually means easier bowel movement) within 6 to 12 hours following initial dose.

USUAL ADULT DOSE:

1 to 2 tablets per day, at bedtime, depending on symptoms and product. In all cases follow specific product instructions.

USUAL CHILD DOSE:

Ages 6 to 12: Half the adult dose per day, at bedtime, depending on symptoms and product. In all cases follow specific product instructions.

Only administer to children younger than 6 under doctor's supervision or direction. In all cases follow specific product instructions.

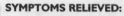

QUICK FACTS

OVERDOSE SYMPTOMS:
Muscular cramps, irregular heartbeat, fatigue, disorientation, and confusion.

SIDE EFFECTS:
No serious effects in most cases of common use, although use of products which contain casanthranol may result in discoloration of alkaline urine, usually to pink-red, red-violet or red-brown. Other occasional side effects may include: bitter taste in mouth, nausea, belching, dehydration, and loose stools or diarrhea. In rare cases rectal bleeding, pain, itching, burning sensation, skin irritation, or rash may occur. In these cases, discontinue use of the product and call your doctor immediately.

CHECK WITH YOUR DOCTOR OR PHARMACIST BEFORE COMBINING DOCUSATE SODIUM AND CASANTHRANOL WITH:
Anticoagulants, antacids, oral contraceptives, or other drugs and preparations. Take any other medication 2 hours apart, as laxatives interfere with body's absorption of medicine.

PREGNANCY OR BREASTFEEDING:
Safety of this drug for use during pregnancy or while nursing has not been established. In all cases you should consult your doctor before using any drug during pregnancy or while nursing.

55+ **PRECAUTIONS FOR CHILDREN:**
These products should only be used with doctor's supervision or direction for children under 6. Consult your doctor and follow instructions on medication (see above).

PRECAUTIONS FOR SENIORS:
Seniors generally may be more prone to side effects and possible adverse effects of these products than younger individuals.

Q U I C K F A C T S

SPECIAL WARNINGS:
Do not use any of these if you are allergic to docusate sodium, casanthranol, or any inactive ingredients contained in these products, if you are experiencing abdominal pain, cramps, nausea or vomiting, or if you have intestinal obstruction or fecal impaction, or any form of kidney or liver disease. Do not use these products if you have experienced irregular bowel movements for less than 2 days. If regular bowel movements have not returned within one week, consult your doctor.

ADDITIONAL WARNINGS:
Do not use any of these products in combination with a mineral oil laxative product. Use of these products should be supplemented with liquids (preferably water) to prevent electrolyte/ fluid depletion or dehydration.

Eating disorders: Chronic or excessive use of laxatives, particularly by young women, may be a sign of anorexia nervosa or bulimia nervosa.

INFORM YOUR DOCTOR BEFORE TAKING DOCUSATE SODIUM AND CASANTHRANOL IF YOU HAVE:
Allergies—particularly to food types, high blood pressure, abdominal pain, cramps, nausea, vomiting, intestinal obstruction or fecal impaction, rectal bleeding, diabetes, heart trouble, kidney or liver disease, colostomy or ileostomy.

QUICK FACTS

ACTIVE INGREDIENT:

DOCUSATE SODIUM (DIOCTYL SODIUM SULFOSUCCINATE; DSS)

BRAND NAMES:

- COLACE–CAPSULES
- COLACE–SYRUP (also contains alcohol, menthol, sucrose)
- DIALOSE
- DIALOSE PLUS (combination with phenolphthalein—also contains methylcellulose, magnesium stearate)
- DIOEZE
- DIOCTO
- DISONATE
- DOK
- DOS SOFTGELS
- DOXINATE–CAPSULES (also contains sorbitol)
- DOXINATE–SOLUTION (also contains alcohol)
- MODANE SOFT (also contains sorbitol)
- PRO-SOF
- REGULAX SS

SYMPTOMS RELIEVED:

Irregular bowel movements (constipation) due to hard stools, anorectal pain, conditions such as cardiac cases in which straining or difficulty in defecation is undesirable.

HOW TO TAKE:

Comes in capsule, liquid, syrup, and solution forms. Take liquid or syrup forms with one full glass (8 oz.) of nonalcoholic, noncarbonated liquid, such as water, fruit juice, or milk to prevent possible throat irritation. Follow with least one full glass (8 oz.) of water. These products generally produce softer stools (which usually means easier bowel movement) within 1 to 3 days following first dose.

USUAL ADULT DOSE:
50 to 200 milligrams per day, depending on symptoms and product. In all cases follow specific product instructions.

USUAL CHILD DOSE:
Ages 6 to 12: 40 to 120 milligrams per day, depending on symptoms and product. In all cases follow specific product instructions.

Ages 3 to 6: 20 to 60 milligrams per day, depending on symptoms and product. In all cases follow specific product instructions.

Only administer to children younger than 3 under doctor's supervision or direction. In all cases follow specific product instructions.

OVERDOSE SYMPTOMS:
Muscular cramps, irregular heartbeat, fatigue, disorientation, and confusion.

SIDE EFFECTS:
No serious effects in most cases of common use. Occasional side effects may include: sore or scratchy throat, bitter taste in mouth, or nausea. In rare cases rectal bleeding, pain, itching, or burning sensation may occur. In these cases, discontinue use of the product and call your doctor immediately.

CHECK WITH YOUR DOCTOR OR PHARMACIST BEFORE COMBINING DOCUSATE SODIUM WITH:
Anticoagulants, antacids, oral contraceptives, or

Q U I C K F A C T S

other drugs and preparations. Take any other medication 2 hours apart, as laxatives interfere with body's absorption of medicine.

PREGNANCY OR BREASTFEEDING:
Safety of this drug for use during pregnancy or while nursing has not been established. In all cases you should consult your doctor before using any drug during pregnancy or while nursing.

PRECAUTIONS FOR CHILDREN:
These products should only be used with doctor's supervision or direction for children under 3. Consult your doctor and follow instructions on medication (see above).

55+ **PRECAUTIONS FOR SENIORS:**
Seniors generally may be more prone to side effects and possible adverse effects of these products than younger individuals.

SPECIAL WARNINGS:
Do not use any of these if you are allergic to docusate sodium or any inactive ingredients contained in these products, if you are experiencing abdominal pain, cramps, nausea, or vomiting, or if you have intestinal obstruction or fecal impaction. Do not use these products if you have experienced irregular bowel movements for less than 2 days. If regular bowel movements have not returned within one week, consult your doctor.

ADDITIONAL WARNINGS:
Do not use any of these products in combination with a mineral oil laxative product. Use of

these products should be supplemented with liquids (preferably water) to prevent electrolyte/fluid depletion or dehydration.

Eating disorders: Chronic or excessive use of laxatives, particularly by young women, may be a sign of anorexia nervosa or bulimia nervosa.

INFORM YOUR DOCTOR BEFORE TAKING DOCUSATE SODIUM IF YOU HAVE:
Allergies—particularly to food types, high blood pressure, abdominal pain, cramps, nausea, vomiting, intestinal obstruction or fecal impaction, rectal bleeding, diabetes, heart trouble, colostomy, or ileostomy.

QUICK FACTS

ACTIVE INGREDIENTS:

DOCUSATE SODIUM (DIOCTYL SODIUM SULFOSUCCINATE; DSS) IN COMBINATION WITH CASANTHRANOL

BRAND NAMES:

- Disanthrol Capsules
- D-S-S Plus Capsules
- Disolan Forte Capsules
- Genasoft Plus Softgels
- Peri-Colace Capsules
- Peri-Dos Softgels
- Pro-Sof Plus Capsules
- Regulace Capsules

SYMPTOMS RELIEVED:

Irregular bowel movements (constipation) due to hard stools, anorectal pain, conditions such as cardiac cases in which straining or difficulty in defecation is undesirable.

HOW TO TAKE:

Comes in capsule and tablet forms. Take with one full glass (8 oz.) of water at bedtime. Follow with least one full glass (8 oz.) of water. These products generally produce softer stools (which usually means easier bowel movement) within 6 to 12 hours following initial dose.

USUAL ADULT DOSE:

1 to 2 tablets per day, at bedtime, depending on symptoms and product. In all cases follow specific product instructions.

USUAL CHILD DOSE:

Ages 6 to 12: Half the adult dose per day, at bedtime, depending on symptoms and product. In all cases follow specific product instructions.

Only administer to children younger than 6 under doctor's supervision or direction. In all cases follow specific product instructions.

OVERDOSE SYMPTOMS:
Muscular cramps, irregular heartbeat, fatigue, disorientation, and confusion.

SIDE EFFECTS:
No serious effects in most cases of common use, although use of products which contain casanthranol may result in discoloration of alkaline urine, usually to pink-red, red-violet or red-brown. Other occasional side effects may include: bitter taste in mouth, nausea, belching, dehydration, and loose stools or diarrhea. In rare cases rectal bleeding, pain, itching, burning sensation, skin irritation, or rash may occur. In these cases, discontinue use of the product and call your doctor immediately.

CHECK WITH YOUR DOCTOR OR PHARMACIST BEFORE COMBINING DOCUSATE SODIUM AND CASANTHRANOL WITH:
Anticoagulants, antacids, oral contraceptives, or other drugs and preparations. Take any other medication 2 hours apart, as laxatives interfere with body's absorption of medicine.

PREGNANCY OR BREASTFEEDING:
Safety of this drug for use during pregnancy or while nursing has not been established. In all cases you should consult your doctor before using any drug during pregnancy or while nursing.

QUICK FACTS

PRECAUTIONS FOR CHILDREN:
These products should only be used with doctor's supervision or direction for children under 6. Consult your doctor and follow instructions on medication (see above).

PRECAUTIONS FOR SENIORS:
Seniors generally may be more prone to side effects and possible adverse effects of these products than younger individuals.

SPECIAL WARNINGS:
Do not use any of these if you are allergic to docusate sodium, casanthranol, or any inactive ingredients contained in these products, if you are experiencing abdominal pain, cramps, nausea or vomiting, or if you have intestinal obstruction or fecal impaction, or any form of kidney or liver disease.

ADDITIONAL WARNINGS:
Do not use any of these products in combination with a mineral oil laxative product. Use of these products should be supplemented with liquids (preferably water) to prevent electrolyte/fluid depletion or dehydration.

Eating disorders: Chronic or excessive use of laxatives, particularly by young women, may be a sign of anorexia nervosa or bulimia nervosa.

INFORM YOUR DOCTOR BEFORE TAKING DOCUSATE SODIUM AND CASANTHRANOL IF YOU HAVE:
Allergies—particularly to food types, high blood pressure, abdominal pain, cramps, nausea, vomiting, intestinal obstruction or fecal impaction, rectal bleeding, diabetes, heart trouble, kidney or liver disease, colostomy, or ileostomy.

ACTIVE INGREDIENTS:

DOCUSATE SODIUM (DIOCTYL SODIUM SULFOSUCCINATE; DSS) IN COMBINATION WITH PHENOLPHTHALEIN

QUICK FACTS

BRAND NAMES:

- Colax Tablets
- Correctol Tablets (also contains sugar)
- Disolan Capsules
- Docusal-P Softgels
- Doxidan (also contains sorbitol)
- Feen-A-Mint Pills (also contains sugar)
- Femilax Tablets
- Modane Plus Tablets (also contains sorbitol)
- Phillips' LaxCaps (also contains sorbitol)
- Unilax Capsules (also contains sorbitol)

SYMPTOMS RELIEVED:
Irregular bowel movements (constipation) due to hard stools, anorectal pain, conditions such as cardiac cases in which straining or difficulty in defecation is undesirable.

HOW TO TAKE:
Comes in capsule and tablet forms. Take with one full glass (8 oz.) of water at bedtime. Follow with least one full glass (8 oz.) of water. These products generally produce softer stools (which usually means easier bowel movement) within 6 to 12 hours following initial dose.

USUAL ADULT DOSE:
1 to 2 tablets per day, at bedtime, depending on symptoms and product. In all cases follow specific product instructions.

QUICK FACTS

USUAL CHILD DOSE:
Ages 6 to 12: Half the adult dose per day, at bedtime, depending on symptoms and product. In all cases follow specific product instructions.

Only administer to children younger than 6 under doctor's supervision or direction. In all cases follow specific product instructions.

OVERDOSE SYMPTOMS:
Muscular cramps, irregular heartbeat, fatigue, disorientation, and confusion.

SIDE EFFECTS:
No serious effects in most cases of common use, although use of products which contain phenolphthalein may result in discoloration of alkaline urine, usually to pink-red, red-violet or red-brown. Other occasional side effects may include: bitter taste in mouth, nausea, belching, dehydration, and loose stools or diarrhea. In rare cases rectal bleeding, pain, itching, burning sensation, skin irritation or rash may occur. In these cases, discontinue use of the product and call your doctor immediately.

CHECK WITH YOUR DOCTOR OR PHARMACIST BEFORE COMBINING DOCUSATE SODIUM AND PHENOLPHTHALEIN WITH:
Anticoagulants, antacids, oral contraceptives, or other drugs and preparations. Take any other medication 2 hours apart, as laxatives interfere with body's absorption of medicine.

PREGNANCY OR BREASTFEEDING:
Safety of this drug for use during pregnancy or while nursing has not been established. In all

cases you should consult your doctor before using any drug during pregnancy or while nursing.

PRECAUTIONS FOR CHILDREN:
These products should only be used with doctor's supervision or direction for children under 6. Consult your doctor and follow instructions on medication (see above).

PRECAUTIONS FOR SENIORS:
Seniors generally may be more prone to side effects and possible adverse effects of these products than younger individuals.

SPECIAL WARNINGS:
Do not use any of these if you are allergic to docusate sodium, phenolphthalein or any inactive ingredients contained in these products, if you are experiencing abdominal pain, cramps, nausea or vomiting, or if you have intestinal obstruction or fecal impaction, or any form of kidney or liver disease. Do not use these products if you have experienced irregular bowel movements for less than 2 days. If regular bowel movements have not returned within one week, consult your doctor.

ADDITIONAL WARNINGS:
Do not use any of these products in combination with a mineral oil laxative product. Use of these products should be supplemented with liquids (preferably water) to prevent electrolyte/fluid depletion or dehydration.

Eating disorders: Chronic or excessive use of laxatives, particularly by young women, may be a sign of anorexia nervosa or bulimia nervosa.

QUICK FACTS

INFORM YOUR DOCTOR BEFORE TAKING DOCUSATE SODIUM AND PHENOLPHTHALEIN IF YOU HAVE:

Allergies—particularly to food types, high blood pressure, abdominal pain, cramps, nausea, vomiting, intestinal obstruction or fecal impaction, rectal bleeding, diabetes, heart trouble, kidney or liver disease, colostomy, or ileostomy.

ACTIVE INGREDIENTS:

DOCUSATE SODIUM (DIOCTYL SODIUM SULFOSUCCINATE; DSS) IN COMBINATION WITH SENNA CONCENTRATE

QUICK FACTS

BRAND NAMES:

- Ex-Lax Extra Gentle Pills (also contains sucrose)
- Gentlax Tablets (also contains lactose)
- Senokot-S Tablets (also contains lactose)

SYMPTOMS RELIEVED:

Irregular bowel movements (constipation) due to hard stools, anorectal pain, conditions such as cardiac cases in which straining or difficulty in defecation is undesirable.

HOW TO TAKE:

Comes in tablet forms. Take with one full glass (8 oz.) of water at bedtime. Follow with least one full glass (8 oz.) of water. These products generally produce softer stools (which usually means easier bowel movement) within 6 to 12 hours following initial dose.

USUAL ADULT DOSE:

1 to 2 tablets per day, at bedtime, depending on symptoms and product. In all cases follow specific product instructions.

USUAL CHILD DOSE:

Ages 6 to 12: Half the adult dose per day, at bedtime, depending on symptoms and product. In all cases follow specific product instructions.

Only administer to children younger than 6 under doctor's supervision or direction. In all cases follow specific product instructions.

OVERDOSE SYMPTOMS:
Muscular cramps, irregular heartbeat, fatigue, disorientation, and confusion.

SIDE EFFECTS:
No serious effects in most cases of common use, although use of products which contain senna may result in discoloration of urine, usually to yellow-brown. If urine is alkaline, discoloration may be pink-red, red-violet or red-brown. Other occasional side effects may include: bitter taste in mouth, nausea, belching, dehydration, and loose stools or diarrhea. In rare cases rectal bleeding, pain, itching, burning sensation, skin irritation or rash may occur. In these cases, discontinue use of the product and call your doctor immediately.

CHECK WITH YOUR DOCTOR OR PHARMACIST BEFORE COMBINING DOCUSATE SODIUM AND SENNA WITH:
Anticoagulants, antacids, oral contraceptives, or other drugs and preparations. Take any other medication 2 hours apart, as laxatives interfere with body's absorption of medicine.

PREGNANCY OR BREASTFEEDING:
Safety of this drug for use during pregnancy or while nursing has not been established. In all cases you should consult your doctor before using any drug during pregnancy or while nursing.

PRECAUTIONS FOR CHILDREN:
These products should only be used with doctor's supervision or direction for children under 6. Consult your doctor and follow instructions on medication (see above).

55+ **PRECAUTIONS FOR SENIORS:**
Seniors generally may be more prone to side effects and possible adverse effects of these products than younger individuals.

SPECIAL WARNINGS:
Do not use any of these if you are allergic to docusate sodium, senna, or any inactive ingredients contained in these products, if you are experiencing abdominal pain, cramps, nausea or vomiting, or if you have intestinal obstruction or fecal impaction, or any form of kidney or liver disease. Do not use these products if you have experienced irregular bowel movements for less than 2 days. If regular bowel movements have not returned within one week, consult your doctor.

ADDITIONAL WARNINGS:
Do not use any of these products in combination with a mineral oil laxative product. Use of these products should be supplemented with liquids (preferably water) to prevent electrolyte/fluid depletion or dehydration.

Eating disorders: Chronic or excessive use of laxatives, particularly by young women, may be a sign of anorexia nervosa or bulimia nervosa.

INFORM YOUR DOCTOR BEFORE TAKING DOCUSATE SODIUM AND SENNA IF YOU HAVE:
Allergies—particularly to food types, high blood pressure, abdominal pain, cramps, nausea, vomiting, intestinal obstruction or fecal impaction, rectal bleeding, diabetes, heart trouble, kidney or liver disease, colostomy or ileostomy.

CONTRACEPTIVE

•CONTRACEPTIVE• •SPERMICIDE•

The most important considerations in choosing a spermicide contraceptive are: its effectiveness in protecting against pregnancy, and potential side effects associated with the drug.

TOPICAL SPERMICIDES ARE A CLASS OF DRUGS WHICH:

- are intended only for topical use,
- act by releasing a chemical barrier between sperm and vaginal mucous membranes, and between sperm and cervix, and by killing sperm,
- may provide a degree of protection against sexually transmitted diseases (STDs),
- are usually more effective as protection against pregnancy and sexually transmitted diseases when combined with other contraceptive methods (see Quick Facts).

ACTIVE INGREDIENT:

NONOXYNOL 9

SPERMICIDE

BRAND NAMES:

- ENCARE

(also contains polyethylene glycols, sodium bicarbonate, sodium citrate, tartaric acid)

SYMPTOMS RELIEVED:

Protects against pregnancy.

HOW TO USE:

Comes in suppository form. This product is intended solely for vaginal use. Do not swallow.

USUAL ADULT DOSE:

Familiarize yourself with and follow all product instructions thoroughly before using this product. Product may be inserted up to one hour prior, but no later than 10 minutes before sexual intercourse. Further suppositories can be inserted as needed prior to each act of intercourse, or in the event that intercourse has not occurred within an hour of insertion. Use your fingertip to insert suppository gently as far as possible into the vagina, towards the small of your back. As the suppository distributes the spermicide, you may experience a warm sensation within the vagina. This is normal. In all cases follow specific product instructions.

USUAL CHILD DOSE:

This product is not recommended for children.

OVERDOSE SYMPTOMS:

None known.

Q U I C K F A C T S

SIDE EFFECTS:
No serious effects in most cases of common use. In rare cases, vaginal discharge, irritation, rash, or painful urination or discolored or bloody urine have resulted. In any of these cases, immediately discontinue use of product and call your doctor. If your partner experiences skin irritation following sexual intercourse, immediately discontinue use of product.

TS **TOXIC SHOCK SYNDROME:**
In very rare cases, toxic shock syndrome may be triggered by the use of intra-vaginal products. This extremely rare but life-threatening condition can produce the following symptoms: fever, chills, rash, muscle pains and aches, disorientation, severe fatigue and weakness, redness of vagina, nose, throat, eyes and inside of mouth. In any of these cases, also immediately discontinue use of product and call your doctor.

CHECK WITH YOUR DOCTOR OR PHARMACIST BEFORE COMBINING THIS PRODUCT WITH:
Any other drugs and preparations, including other forms of contraception.

PREGNANCY OR BREASTFEEDING:
Safety of this drug for use during pregnancy or while nursing has not been established. In all cases you should consult your doctor before using any drug during pregnancy or while nursing.

PRECAUTIONS FOR CHILDREN:
This product is not recommended for children.

55+ **PRECAUTIONS FOR SENIORS:**
None known.

SPECIAL WARNINGS:

Do not use this product if you are allergic to any forms of nonoxynol (including nonoxynol 9), or other spermicides, including octoxynol, benzalkonium chloride, or any of the inactive ingredients contained in this product. Do not use this product with other topical vaginal preparations which will adversely affect the effectiveness of the spermicidal agent. If using this product during your menstrual cycle, don't use cervical cap, vaginal sponge or diaphragm at the same time. Your partner should use a condom instead. When using this product, you should avoid douching until at least 6 hours following sexual intercourse.

ADDITIONAL WARNING:

This product's effectiveness may be enhanced by combining with barrier contraceptives, such as condom, and/or (except as during menstrual cycle as noted above) cervical cap, or vaginal diaphragm.

INFORM YOUR DOCTOR BEFORE TAKING THIS PRODUCT IF YOU HAVE:

Any allergies, vaginal infection, gynecological conditions, venereal disease, or if you are or plan to become pregnant during time that you will be taking this product.

COUGH PREPARATIONS

QUICK REVIEW

• ANALGESIC •

The most important considerations in choosing an analgesic are: pain relief; anti-inflammatory activity, and allergic reaction or sensitivity to certain active ingredients.

ANALGESICS (NONNARCOTIC) ARE A CLASS OF DRUGS WHICH:

- inhibit the action of prostaglandins (hormonelike substances) in the central nervous system, thereby temporarily reducing the perception of physical pain with little loss of sensibility to other physical sensation,
- are used to temporarily alleviate symptoms such as: headache, fever, backache, sinus pain, muscle strain, menstrual pain, and similar ailments. Some analgesics, such as aspirin (acetylsalicylic acid) and ibuprofen, also provide temporary anti-inflammatory relief for ailments such as arthritis. Aspirin has also been shown to be effective as a blood thinning antiplatelet agent in reducing heart attack and stroke risk,
- can have adverse effects in some instances. Aspirin intolerance can produce allergic and anaphylactic reactions in hypersensitive and asthmatic individuals. Aspirin can also aggravate aggravate gastrointestinal conditions such as heartburn and ulcer. Long-term acetaminophen use can damage liver (hepatic) and kidney (renal) functions.

ACTIVE INGREDIENTS:

ACETAMINOPHEN, CHLORPHENIRAMINE MALEATE, DEXTROMETHORPHAN HYDROBROMIDE, AND PSEUDOEPHREDINE HYDROCHLORIDE

℞ **BRAND NAMES:**

- ALKA-SELTZER PLUS COLD & COUGH LIQUI-GELS (also contains sorbitol)
- BAYER SELECT FLU RELIEF CAPLETS
- CO-APAP TABLETS
- COMTREX LIQUID (also contains alcohol, sucrose)
- COMTREX LIQUI-GELS (contains sorbitol)
- COMTREX MAXIMUM LIQUI-GELS (contains sorbitol)
- COMTREX MAX STRENGTH MULTI-SYMPTOM COLD & FLU RELIEF LIQUI-GELS
- COMTREX MAXIMUM STRENGTH MULTI-SYMPTOM COLD & FLU RELIEF CAPLETS & TABLETS (contains parabens)
- CONTAC SEVERE COLD & FLU NIGHTTIME LIQUID (also contains alcohol, saccharin, sorbitol, glucose)
- GENACOL TABLETS
- KOLEPHRIN/DM CAPLETS
- MAPAP COLD FORMULA TABLETS
- MEDI-FLU LIQUID (also contains alcohol, saccharin, sorbitol, sugar)
- THERAFLU FLU COLD & COUGH POWDER (contains sucrose)
- THERAFLU NIGHTTIME FLU POWDER (contains sucrose)
- TYLENOL CHILDREN'S COLD MULTI-SYMPTOM PLUS COUGH LIQUID (also contains sorbitol, corn syrup)

QUICK FACTS

- TYLENOL MULTI-SYMPTOM COLD CAPLETS & TABLETS
- TYLENOL MULTI-SYMPTOM HOT MEDICATION POWDER (combination with phenylalanine, also contains aspartame, sucrose)
- VICKS CHILDREN'S NYQUIL NIGHTTIME COLD/COUGH LIQUID (also contains sucrose)
- VICKS 44M COLD, FLU & COUGH LIQUICAPS
- VICKS PEDIATRIC FORMULA 44M MULTI-SYMPTOM COUGH & COLD LIQUID (also contains sorbitol, sucrose)

Note: *Dextromethorphan hydrobromide* is also an active ingredient in other multi-symptom antitussive/expectorant medications which are formulated with other active ingredients.

Pseudoephredine hydrochloride is a used as an active ingredient in decongestant and stimulant products.

Acetaminophen is a non-aspirin analgesic which is used primarily in pain-relief products.

Chlorpheniramine maleate is an antihistamine which is mostly used in combination with analgesic, antitussive, decongestant and expectorant active ingredients in OTC medications to provide relief of allergy, common cold, cough or flu symptoms.

SYMPTOMS RELIEVED:
Minor aches and pains such as those associated with the common cold, flu, headache, toothache, sinusitis, hay fever, and other respiratory allergies, muscular aches, backache, minor arthritis pain, menstrual discomfort, and reduction of fever.

HOW TO TAKE:
Comes in tablet, caplet, capsule, and liquid forms. Swallow tablet, caplet, or capsule with liquid. Sprinkle powder over liquid, then swallow. Do not crush or chew timed-release tablet.

USUAL ADULT DOSE:
Dosage varies per product and active ingredient formulation. Follow product dosage instructions.

USUAL CHILD DOSE:
Do not administer to children under 6 unless under direction of physician. Dosage may vary based on infant or child's age.

OVERDOSE SYMPTOMS:
Nervous agitation, severe anxiety, insomnia (sleeplessness), hallucinations, tremors, convulsions, nausea, vomiting, cardiac arrhythmia (irregular pulse and heartbeat), drowsiness, dizziness, fatigue, rash. If you suspect an overdose, immediately seek medical attention.

SIDE EFFECTS:
No serious effects in most cases of common use, although antihistamines can cause drowsiness. Less common side effects include nasal dryness, dizziness, nausea, and mild insomnia palpitations, insomnia, gastrointestinal (GI) upset including stomach cramps and diarrhea, drowsiness, and fatigue. In rare cases, more severe side effects may result, including: painful and frequent urination, hypertension, and heart palpitations. In these cases, discontinue medication and call your doctor immediately. Long-term ingestion of high dosages of acetaminophen-containing products may increase risk of liver and kidney damage.

QUICK FACTS

QUICK FACTS

CHECK WITH YOUR DOCTOR OR PHARMACIST BEFORE COMBINING THESE COMBINATION PRODUCTS WITH:
Anticoagulant medications, other cold, cough, or allergy medication, stimulants, antidepressants, antihypertensives, digitalis or other heart medication, diuretics, or MAO (monoamine oxidase inhibitors) drugs. Ingestion of caffeinated beverages (coffee, tea, caffeine-containing soft drinks) while taking pseudoephredine-containing medication can result in agitation and insomnia.
If taking combination products which contain acetaminophen, you should avoid Isoniazid (anti-tuberculosis) medication. Excessive ingestion of alcohol while taking acetaminophen-containing medication can increase the risk of liver damage or disease (hepatic toxicity). Alcohol use may also increase possible drowsiness effect of the antihistamine in these combination products.

PREGNANCY OR BREASTFEEDING:
Use of medications containing any of the active ingredients in these products by a nursing mother should be considered a potential risk for a nursing child as the drug(s) will be passed on to the infant in the mother's milk. In all cases, a physician should be consulted.

PRECAUTIONS FOR CHILDREN:
In general, these active ingredients are not advised for children under 2.

PRECAUTIONS FOR SENIORS:
Seniors generally don't eliminate drugs as efficiently as younger persons, and should avoid high dosages. Use of antihistamine-containing

medications by seniors can lead to urinary difficulties. In addition, seniors are more likely to experience potential drowsiness effects of the antihistamine in this combination.

SPECIAL WARNINGS:
Do not use for control of chronic cough related to conditions such as emphysema, asthma, or smoking, or if coughs are producing excessive secretions. If cough is accompanied by high fever, rash, nausea or vomiting, or persistent headache, use only if directed by your doctor. Because antihistamines may cause drowsiness, you should avoid activities or tasks such as driving, or other operations which require alertness, coordination, dexterity, or quick reflexes. Chronic alcoholics are at risk for hepatic (liver) function impairment if taking high dosages of acetaminophen-containing medication. Do not use medications which combine doxylamine succinate with tartrazine if you are intolerant or hypersensitive to aspirin.

ADDITIONAL WARNING:
Alcohol: Some cough/cold medications contain various amounts of alcohol. Check label of any cough medication if concerned about ingestion of alcohol.

Sugar/Sweeteners: Some cough/cold medications contain various amounts of sugar, sucrose, glucose, and/or artificial sweeteners such as aspartame, saccharin, sorbitol. Check label of cough medication before selecting, if concerned about diabetes and ingestion of sugar or artificial sweeteners.

Abuse/Dependency: Reports indicate a rising rate of abuse of dextromethorphan-containing medications, particularly among teens. Sufficient data has not yet been collected, however, to determine the abuse and dependency potential of dextromethorphan-containing medications.

INFORM YOUR DOCTOR BEFORE TAKING PRODUCTS CONTAINING THIS COMBINATION OF ACTIVE INGREDIENTS IF YOU HAVE:

Asthma, emphysema or other respiratory condition, liver impairment or liver disease, allergies to any sympathomimetic drug, aspirin or other salicylates, or if you have diabetes, thyroid condition, or urinary difficulty. If you anticipate any surgery requiring general or spinal anesthesia within 2 months of taking medication which contains pseudoephredine, inform your doctor.

ACTIVE INGREDIENTS:

ACETAMINOPHEN, DEXTROMETHORPHAN HYDROBROMIDE, GUAIFENESIN, AND PSEUDOEPHREDINE HYDROCHLORIDE

℞ **BRAND NAMES:**

- Comtrex Cough Formula Liquid (also contains alcohol, menthol, saccharin, sucrose)
- Contac Cough & Chest Cold Liquid (also contains alcohol, saccharin, sorbitol)
- Dimacol Caplets (also contains saccharin, parabens)
- Sudafed Cold & Cough Liquid Caps (also contains alcohol, menthol, methylparaben, saccharin, sorbitol, sucrose)
- Vicks DayQuil LiquiCaps

Note: *Guaifenesin* and *dextromethorphan hydrobromide* are also active ingredient in other multi-symptom antitussive/expectorant medications which are formulated with other active ingredients.

Pseudoephredine hydrochloride is a used as an active ingredient in decongestant and stimulant products.

Acetaminophen is a non-aspirin analgesic which is used primarily in pain-relief products.

HOW TO TAKE:
Comes in liquid forms.

USUAL ADULT DOSE:
Dosage varies per product and active ingredient formulation. Follow product dosage instructions.

QUICK FACTS

USUAL CHILD DOSE:
Do not administer to children under 6 unless under direction of physician. Dosage may vary based on infant or child's age.

OVERDOSE SYMPTOMS:
Nervous agitation, severe anxiety, insomnia (sleeplessness), hallucinations, tremors, convulsions, nausea, vomiting, cardiac arrhythmia (irregular pulse and heartbeat), drowsiness, dizziness, fatigue, rash. If you suspect an overdose, immediately seek medical attention.

SIDE EFFECTS:
No serious effects in most cases of common use, although antihistamines often cause drowsiness. Less common side effects include nasal dryness, dizziness, nausea, and mild insomnia palpitations, insomnia, GI upset including stomach cramps and diarrhea, drowsiness and fatigue. In rare cases, more severe side effects may result, including: painful and frequent urination, hypertension, and heart palpitations. In these cases, discontinue medication and call your doctor immediately. Long-term ingestion of high dosages of acetaminophen-containing products may increase risk of liver and kidney damage.

CHECK WITH YOUR DOCTOR OR PHARMACIST BEFORE COMBINING THESE COMBINATION PRODUCTS WITH:
Anticoagulant medications, other cold, cough,or allergy medication, stimulants, antidepressants, antihypertensives, digitalis or other heart medication, diuretics, or MAO (monoamine oxidase inhibitors) drugs. Ingestion of caffeinated beverages (coffee, tea, caffeine-containing soft drinks)

while taking pseudoephredine-containing medication can result in agitation and insomnia. If taking combination products which contain acetaminophen, you should avoid Isoniazid (anti-tuberculosis) medication. Excessive ingestion of alcohol while taking acetaminophen-containing medication can increase the risk of liver damage or disease (hepatic toxicity).

PREGNANCY OR BREASTFEEDING:
Use of medications containing any of the active ingredients in these products by a nursing mother should be considered a potential risk for a nursing child as the drug(s) will be passed on to the infant in the mother's milk. In all cases, a physician should be consulted.

PRECAUTIONS FOR CHILDREN:
In general, these active ingredients are not advised for children under 2. Administer to infants or children only when consulting a physician and follow instructions on medication (see above).

55+ **PRECAUTIONS FOR SENIORS:**
Seniors generally don't eliminate drugs as efficiently as younger persons, and should avoid high dosages.

SPECIAL WARNINGS:
Do not use for control of chronic cough related to conditions such as emphysema, asthma, or smoking, or if coughs are producing excessive secretions. If cough is accompanied by high fever, rash, nausea or vomiting, or persistent headache, use only if directed by your doctor. Because antihistamines often cause drowsiness, you should avoid activities or tasks such as

driving, or other operations which require alertness, coordination, dexterity or quick reflexes. Chronic alcoholics are at risk for hepatic (liver) function impairment if taking high dosages of acetaminophen-containing medication.

ADDITIONAL WARNING:
Alcohol: Some cough/cold medications contain various amounts of alcohol. Check label of any cough medication if concerned about ingestion of alcohol.

Sugar/Sweeteners: Some cough/cold medications contain various amounts of sugar, sucrose, glucose, and/or artificial sweeteners such as aspertame, saccharin, sorbitol. Check label of cough medication before selecting, if concerned about diabetes and ingestion of sugar or artificial sweeteners.

Abuse/Dependency: Reports indicate a rising rate of abuse of dextromethorphan-containing medications, particularly among teens. Sufficient data has not yet been collected, however, to determine the abuse and dependency potential of dextromethorphan-containing medications.

INFORM YOUR DOCTOR BEFORE TAKING PRODUCTS CONTAINING THIS COMBINATION OF ACTIVE INGREDIENTS IF YOU HAVE:
Asthma, emphysema or other respiratory condition, liver impairment or liver disease, allergies to any sympathomimetic drug, aspirin or other salicylates, or if you have diabetes, thyroid condition, or urinary difficulty. If you anticipate any surgery requiring general or spinal anesthesia within 2 months of taking medication which contains pseudoephredine, inform your doctor.

ACTIVE INGREDIENTS:
ACETAMINOPHEN, DEXTROMETHORPHAN HYDROBROMIDE, AND PSEUDOEPHREDINE HYDROCHLORIDE

℞ **BRAND NAMES:**

- Alka-Seltzer Plus Flu & Body Aches Non-Drowsy Liqui-Gels
- Bayer Select Nighttime Cold Caplets (combination with tripolidine hydrochloride)
- Comtrex Maximum Strength Non-Drowsy Caplets
- Contac Day & Night Cold & Flu Caplets (combination with diphenhydramine hydrochloride)
- Robitussin Night Relief Liquid (also contains saccharin, sorbitol)
- Saleto CF Tablets
- Sudafed Severe Cold Caplets & Tablets
- TheraFlu Non-Drowsy Formula Maximum Strength Caplets (also contains lactose, methylparaben)
- TheraFlu Non-Drowsy Flu, Cold & Cough Maximum Strength Powder (also contains sucrose)
- Triaminic Sore Throat Formula Liquid (also contains EDTA, sucrose)
- Tylenol Cold No Drowsiness Caplets & Gelcaps/Maximum Strength Gelcaps
- Tylenol Maximum Strength Cough with Decongestant Liquid (also contains alcohol, saccharin, sorbitol, sucrose)

Note: *Dextromethorphan hydrobromide* is also an active ingredient in other multi-symptom

Q U I C K F A C T S

antitussive/expectorant medications which are formulated with other active ingredients.

Pseudoephredine hydrochloride is a used as an active ingredient in decongestant and stimulant products.

Acetaminophen is a non-aspirin analgesic which is used primarily in pain-relief products.

SYMPTOMS RELIEVED:
Minor aches and pains such as those associated with the common cold, flu, headache, toothache, sinusitis, hay fever, and other respiratory allergies, muscular aches, backache, minor arthritis pain, menstrual discomfort, and reduction of fever.

HOW TO TAKE:
Comes in caplet, capsule, and liquid forms. Swallow caplet or capsule with liquid. Sprinkle powder over liquid, then swallow. Do not crush or chew timed-release tablet.

USUAL ADULT DOSE:
Dosage varies per product and active ingredient formulation. Follow product dosage instructions.

USUAL CHILD DOSE:
Do not administer to children under 6 unless under direction of physician. Dosage may vary based on infant or child's age.

OVERDOSE SYMPTOMS:
Nervous agitation, severe anxiety, insomnia (sleeplessness), hallucinations, tremors, convulsions, nausea, vomiting, cardiac arrhythmia (irregular pulse and heartbeat), drowsiness,

dizziness, fatigue, rash. If you suspect an overdose, immediately seek medical attention.

SIDE EFFECTS:
No serious effects in most cases of common use. Less common side effects include nasal dryness, dizziness, nausea, and mild insomnia palpitations, insomnia, gastrointestinal (GI) upset including stomach cramps and diarrhea, drowsiness and fatigue. In rare cases, more severe side effects may result, including: painful and frequent urination, hypertension, and heart palpitations. In these cases, discontinue medication and call your doctor immediately. Long-term ingestion of high dosages of acetaminophen-containing products may increase risk of liver and kidney damage.

CHECK WITH YOUR DOCTOR OR PHARMACIST BEFORE COMBINING THESE COMBINATION PRODUCTS WITH:
Anticoagulant medications, other cold, cough, or allergy medication, stimulants, antidepressants, antihypertensives, digitalis or other heart medication, diuretics, or MAO (monoamine oxidase inhibitors) drugs. Ingestion of caffeinated beverages (coffee, tea, caffeine-containing soft drinks) while taking pseudoephredine-containing medication can result in agitation and insomnia.
If taking combination products which contain acetaminophen, you should avoid Isoniazid (anti-tuberculosis) medication. Excessive ingestion of alcohol while taking acetaminophen-containing medication can increase the risk of liver damage or disease (hepatic toxicity).

QUICK FACTS

PREGNANCY OR BREASTFEEDING:
Use of medications containing any of the active ingredients in these products by a nursing mother should be considered a potential risk for a nursing child as the drug(s) will be passed on to the infant in the mother's milk. In all cases, a physician should be consulted.

PRECAUTIONS FOR CHILDREN:
In general, these active ingredients are not advised for children under 2.

PRECAUTIONS FOR SENIORS:
Seniors generally don't eliminate drugs as efficiently as younger persons, and should avoid high dosages. Use of pseudoephedrine-containing medications by seniors can lead to urinary difficulties. In addition, seniors are more likely to experience stimulant effects of pseudoephedrine.

SPECIAL WARNINGS:
Do not use for control of chronic cough related to conditions such as emphysema, asthma, or smoking, or if coughs are producing excessive secretions. If cough is accompanied by high fever, rash, nausea or vomiting, or persistent headache, use only if directed by your doctor. Chronic alcoholics are at risk for hepatic (liver) function impairment if taking high dosages of acetaminophen-containing medication.

ADDITIONAL WARNING:
Alcohol: Some cough/cold medications contain various amounts of alcohol. Check label of any cough medication if concerned about ingestion of alcohol.

Sugar/Sweeteners: Some cough/cold medications contain various amounts of sugar, sucrose, glucose, and/or artificial sweeteners such as aspartame, saccharin, sorbitol. Check label of cough medication before selecting, if concerned about diabetes and ingestion of sugar or artificial sweeteners.

Abuse/Dependency: Reports indicate a rising rate of abuse of dextromethorphan-containing medications, particularly among teens. Sufficient data has not yet been collected, however, to determine the abuse and dependency potential of dextromethorphan-containing medications.

INFORM YOUR DOCTOR BEFORE TAKING PRODUCTS CONTAINING THIS COMBINATION OF ACTIVE INGREDIENTS IF YOU HAVE:
Asthma, emphysema or other respiratory condition, liver impairment or liver disease, allergies to any sympathomimetic drug, aspirin or other salicylates, or if you have diabetes, thyroid condition, or urinary difficulty. If you anticipate any surgery requiring general or spinal anesthesia within 2 months of taking medication which contains pseudoephredine, inform your doctor.

QUICK REVIEW

• ANTIHISTAMINES •

The most important considerations in choosing an antihistamine are: its effectiveness in blocking or alleviating effects of histamine on the respiratory system, and the nature and extent of side effects which the drug may produce.

ANTIHISTAMINES ARE A CLASS OF DRUGS WHICH:

- are used in treating allergies and motion sickness,
- block the effects of histamine, a chemical substance released by the body as the result of injury or in reaction to an allergen. Histamine increases capillary permeability, which allows fluids to escape and cause swelling. It also constricts small air passages in the lungs. These properties result in symptoms such as sinus headache, congestion, sneezing, runny nose, wheezing, puffiness, and lowered blood pressure,
- act by blocking or displacing histamine, particularly in the blood vessels, skin, uterus, and bronchioles,
- as a result of the drugs' drying effects, thereby impede drainage and expectoration,
- may produce side effects such as drowsiness, nasal stuffiness, dryness of mouth and sinus passages, dizziness, and common gastrointestinal (GI) irritation or distress,
- are not recommended in treating lower respiratory symptoms including asthma, as the drug's effects may impede expectoration.

QUICK FACTS

ACTIVE INGREDIENT:
DIPHENHYDRAMINE HYDROCHLORIDE

BRAND NAMES:

- BENYLIN COUGH (also contains ammonium chloride, sodium citrate, alcohol, menthol, glucose, sucrose, saccharin)
- DIPHEN COUGH (also contains ammonium chloride, sodium citrate, alcohol, sugar, menthol, sorbitol, sucrose, raspberry flavor)
- HYDRAMINE COUGH (also contains alcohol)
- NORDRYL COUGH (also contains alcohol)
- UNI-BENT COUGH (also contains alcohol)

Note: As an antitussive *diphenhydramine* is also used in combinations with analgesics, antitussives, decongestants and expectorants including some or all of the following active ingredients: acetaminophen, dextromethorphan hydrobromide, guaifenesin, phenylpropanolamine hydrochloride, pseudoephedrine hydrochloride. Diphenhydramine is also used in allergy medications and sleep aids.

HOW TO TAKE:

Comes in syrup form. Diphenhydramine and other antihistamines can cause gastrointestinal (GI) irritation and should be taken with food or following meal.

USUAL ADULT DOSE:

25 milligrams 6 times per day, not to exceed 150 milligrams in a 24 hour period.

USUAL CHILD DOSE:

For children 6 to 12: 12.5 milligrams 6 times per day, not to exceed 75 milligrams in a 24 hour period.

Q U I C K F A C T S

For children 2 to 6: 6.25 milligrams 6 times per day, not to exceed 25 milligrams in a 24 hour period.

Do not administer to children under 2 unless under direction of physician. Dosage may vary based on infant or child's age.

OVERDOSE SYMPTOMS:
Nervous agitation, severe anxiety, insomnia (sleeplessness), hallucinations, tremors, convulsions, nausea, vomiting, cardiac arrhythmia (irregular pulse and heartbeat). If you suspect an overdose, immediately seek medical attention.

SIDE EFFECTS:
No serious effects in most cases of common use. Less common side effects include nasal dryness, dizziness, nausea, and mild insomnia palpitations, insomnia. In rare cases, more severe side effects may result, including: painful and frequent urination, hypertension, and heart palpitations. In these cases, discontinue medication and call your doctor immediately.

CHECK WITH YOUR DOCTOR OR PHARMACIST BEFORE COMBINING DIPHENHYDRAMINE WITH:
Cold, cough,or allergy medication, stimulants, antidepressants, antihypertensives, digitalis or other heart medication, diuretics, or MAO (monoamine oxidase inhibitors) drugs. Ingestion of caffeinated beverages (coffee, tea, caffeine-containing soft drinks) while taking diphenhydramine-containing medication can result in agitation and insomnia.

PREGNANCY OR BREASTFEEDING:
Diphenhydramine use by a nursing mother

should be considered a potential risk for a nursing child as the drug will be passed on to the infant in the mother's milk. In all cases, a physician should be consulted.

PRECAUTIONS FOR CHILDREN:
In general, diphenhydramine is not advised for children under 6. Administer diphenhydramine to infants or children only when consulting a physician and follow instructions on medication (see above).

55+ **PRECAUTIONS FOR SENIORS:**
Seniors generally don't eliminate drugs as efficiently as younger persons, and should avoid high dosages. Use of diphenhydramine medications by seniors can lead to urinary difficulties. In addition, seniors are more likely to experience drowsiness effects of the drug.

SPECIAL WARNINGS:
Because antihistamines often cause drowsiness, you should avoid activities or tasks such as driving, or other operations which require alertness, coordination, dexterity or quick reflexes.

INFORM YOUR DOCTOR BEFORE TAKING DIPHENHYDRAMINE IF YOU HAVE:
Allergies to: any sympathomimetic drug, aspirin or other salicylates, or if you have diabetes, thyroid condition, or urinary difficulty. If you anticipate any surgery requiring general or spinal anesthesia within 2 months of taking diphenhydramine medication, inform your doctor.

QUICK REVIEW

• ANTITUSSIVE •

The most important considerations in choosing an antitussive are: cough suppressant and relief action; and potential side effects associated with the drug.

ANTITUSSIVES ARE A CLASS OF DRUGS WHICH:

- help to suppress and relieve the spasmodic cough reflex typical of symptoms of various allergies, colds, bronchitis, flu, and other nonchronic respiratory ailments,
- are commonly used to give an allergy, cold, bronchitis, flu, and other nonchronic respiratory ailment-sufferer sufficient relief from coughing spasms, so that the person can rest,
- may produce side effects such as drowsiness, nasal stuffiness, dryness of mouth and sinus passages, dizziness, and common gastrointestinal (GI) irritation or distress,
- are not recommended in treating chronic and lower respiratory symptoms including asthma, and emphysema, as the drug's effects may impede expectoration,
- are often combined with other cough-related active ingredients such as expectorants, as well as analgesics, antihistamines, and decongestants—as well as other ingredients such as alcohol, sweeteners (natural and artificial) and flavorings (natural and artificial),
- do not affect the underlying cause of the symptoms which they are designed to relieve or suppress.

ACTIVE INGREDIENTS:

ACETAMINOPHEN, CHLORPHENIRAMINE MALEATE, DEXTROMETHORPHAN HYDROBROMIDE, AND PSEUDOEPHREDINE HYDROCHLORIDE

Q U I C K F A C T S

℞ **BRAND NAMES:**

- ALKA-SELTZER PLUS COLD & COUGH LIQUI-GELS (also contains sorbitol)
- BAYER SELECT FLU RELIEF CAPLETS
- CO-APAP TABLETS
- COMTREX LIQUID (also contains alcohol, sucrose)
- COMTREX LIQUI-GELS (contains sorbitol)
- COMTREX MAXIMUM LIQUI-GELS (contains sorbitol)
- COMTREX MAX STRENGTH MULTI-SYMPTOM COLD & FLU RELIEF LIQUI-GELS
- COMTREX MAXIMUM STRENGTH MULTI-SYMPTOM COLD & FLU RELIEF CAPLETS & TABLETS (contains parabens)
- CONTAC SEVERE COLD & FLU NIGHTTIME LIQUID (also contains alcohol, saccharin, sorbitol, glucose)
- GENACOL TABLETS
- KOLEPHRIN/DM CAPLETS
- MAPAP COLD FORMULA TABLETS
- MEDI-FLU LIQUID (also contains alcohol, saccharin, sorbitol, sugar)
- THERAFLU FLU, COLD & COUGH POWDER (contains sucrose)
- THERAFLU NIGHTTIME FLU POWDER (contains sucrose)
- TYLENOL CHILDREN'S COLD MULTI-SYMPTOM PLUS COUGH LIQUID (also contains sorbitol, corn syrup)

- TYLENOL MULTI-SYMPTOM COLD CAPLETS & TABLETS
- TYLENOL MULTI-SYMPTOM HOT MEDICATION POWDER (combination with phenylalanine, also contains aspartame, sucrose)
- VICKS CHILDREN'S NYQUIL NIGHTTIME COLD/ COUGH LIQUID (also contains sucrose)
- VICKS 44M COLD, FLU & COUGH LIQUICAPS
- VICKS PEDIATRIC FORMULA 44M MULTI-SYMPTOM COUGH & COLD LIQUID (also contains sorbitol, sucrose)

Note: *Dextromethorphan hydrobromide* is also an active ingredient in other multi-symptom antitussive/expectorant medications which are formulated with other active ingredients.

Pseudoephredine hydrochloride is a used as an active ingredient in decongestant and stimulant products.

Acetaminophen is a non-aspirin analgesic which is used primarily in pain-relief products.

Chlorpheniramine maleate is an antihistamine which is mostly used in combination with analgesic, antitussive, decongestant and expectorant active ingredients in OTC medications to provide relief of allergy, common cold, cough or flu symptoms.

SYMPTOMS RELIEVED:

Minor aches and pains, nasal congestion, and coughing such as those associated with the common cold, flu, sore throat, sinusitis, hay fever and other respiratory allergies, and reduction of fever.

HOW TO TAKE:
Comes in tablet, caplet, capsule, and liquid forms. Swallow tablet, caplet, or capsule with liquid. Sprinkle powder over liquid, then swallow. Do not crush or chew timed-release tablet.

USUAL ADULT DOSE:
Dosage varies per product and active ingredient formulation. Follow product dosage instructions.

USUAL CHILD DOSE:
Do not administer to children under 6 unless under direction of physician. Dosage may vary based on infant or child's age.

OVERDOSE SYMPTOMS:
Nervous agitation, severe anxiety, insomnia (sleeplessness), hallucinations, tremors, convulsions, nausea, vomiting, cardiac arrhythmia (irregular pulse and heartbeat), drowsiness, dizziness, fatigue, rash. If you suspect an overdose, immediately seek medical attention.

SIDE EFFECTS:
No serious effects in most cases of common use, although antihistamines can cause drowsiness. Less common side effects include nasal dryness, dizziness, nausea, and mild insomnia palpitations, insomnia, gastrointestinal (GI) upset including stomach cramps and diarrhea, drowsiness, and fatigue. In rare cases, more severe side effects may result, including: painful and frequent urination, hypertension, and heart palpitations. In these cases, discontinue medication and call your doctor immediately. Long-term ingestion of high dosages of acetaminophen-containing products may increase risk of liver and kidney damage.

QUICK FACTS

CHECK WITH YOUR DOCTOR OR PHARMACIST BEFORE COMBINING THESE COMBINATION PRODUCTS WITH:
Anticoagulant medications, other cold, cough, or allergy medication, stimulants, antidepressants, antihypertensives, digitalis or other heart medication, diuretics, or MAO (monoamine oxidase inhibitors) drugs. Ingestion of caffeinated beverages (coffee, tea, caffeine-containing soft drinks) while taking pseudoephredine-containing medication can result in agitation and insomnia.
If taking combination products which contain acetaminophen, you should avoid Isoniazid (antituberculosis) medication. Excessive ingestion of alcohol while taking acetaminophen-containing medication can increase the risk of liver damage or disease (hepatic toxicity). Alcohol use may also increase possible drowsiness effect of the antihistamine in these combination products.

PREGNANCY OR BREASTFEEDING:
Use of medications containing any of the active ingredients in these products by a nursing mother should be considered a potential risk for a nursing child as the drug(s) will be passed on to the infant in the mother's milk. In all cases, a physician should be consulted.

PRECAUTIONS FOR CHILDREN:
In general, these active ingredients are not advised for children under 2. Administer to infants or children only when consulting a physician and follow instructions on medication (see above).

55+ **PRECAUTIONS FOR SENIORS:**
Seniors generally don't eliminate drugs as efficiently as younger persons, and should avoid high dosages. Use of antihistamine-containing medications by seniors can lead to urinary difficulties. In addition, seniors are more likely to experience potential drowsiness effects of the antihistamine in this combination.

SPECIAL WARNINGS:
Do not use for control of chronic cough related to conditions such as emphysema, asthma, or smoking, or if coughs are producing excessive secretions. If cough is accompanied by high fever, rash, nausea or vomiting, or persistent headache, use only if directed by your doctor. Because antihistamines may cause drowsiness, you should avoid activities or tasks such as driving, or other operations which require alertness, coordination, dexterity, or quick reflexes. Chronic alcoholics are at risk for hepatic (liver) function impairment if taking high dosages of acetaminophen-containing medication. Do not use medications which combine doxylamine succinate with tartrazine if you are intolerant or hypersensitive to aspirin. Allergic reactions, including bronchial asthma, have occurred in susceptible individuals.

ADDITIONAL WARNING:
Alcohol: Some cough/cold medications contain various amounts of alcohol. Check label of any cough medication if concerned about ingestion of alcohol.

Sugar/Sweeteners: Some cough/cold medications contain various amounts of sugar, sucrose, glucose, and/or artificial sweeteners such as aspartame, saccharin, sorbitol. Check label of cough medication before selecting, if concerned about diabetes and ingestion of sugar or artificial sweeteners.

Abuse/Dependency: Reports indicate a rising rate of abuse of dextromethorphan-containing medications, particularly among teens. Sufficient data has not yet been collected, however, to determine the abuse and dependency potential of dextromethorphan-containing medications.

INFORM YOUR DOCTOR BEFORE TAKING PRODUCTS CONTAINING THIS COMBINATION OF ACTIVE INGREDIENTS IF YOU HAVE:

Asthma, emphysema or other respiratory condition, liver impairment or liver disease, allergies to any sympathomimetic drug, aspirin or other salicylates, or if you have diabetes, thyroid condition, or urinary difficulty. If you anticipate any surgery requiring general or spinal anesthesia within 2 months of taking medication which contains pseudoephredine, inform your doctor.

ACTIVE INGREDIENTS:

ACETAMINOPHEN AND DEXTROMETHORPHAN HYDROBROMIDE

QUICK FACTS

℞ **BRAND NAMES:**

- BAYER SELECT CHEST COLD CAPLETS
- CONTAC COUGH & SORE THROAT LIQUID (also contains alcohol, saccharin, sorbitol)
- DRIXORAL COUGH & SORE THROAT LIQUID CAPS (contains sorbitol)
- TYLENOL MAXIMUM STRENGTH COUGH LIQUID (also contains alcohol, saccharin, sorbitol, sucrose)

Note: *Dextromethorphan hydrobromide* is also an active ingredient in other multi-symptom antitussive/expectorant medications which are formulated with other active ingredients.

Acetaminophen is a non-aspirin analgesic which is used primarily in pain-relief products.

SYMPTOMS RELIEVED:

Minor aches and pains, nasal congestion and coughing such as those associated with the common cold, flu, sinusitis, hay fever and other respiratory allergies, as well as relief of headache, toothache, muscular aches, backache, minor arthritis pain, menstrual discomfort, and reduction of fever.

HOW TO TAKE:

Comes in caplet, capsule, and liquid forms. Swallow caplet or capsule with liquid. Do not crush or chew timed-release tablet.

Q U I C K F A C T S

USUAL ADULT DOSE:
Dosage varies per product and active ingredient formulation. Follow product dosage instructions.

USUAL CHILD DOSE:
Do not administer to children under 6 unless under direction of physician. Dosage may vary based on infant or child's age.

OVERDOSE SYMPTOMS:
Nervous agitation, severe anxiety, insomnia (sleeplessness), hallucinations, tremors, convulsions, nausea, vomiting, cardiac arrhythmia (irregular pulse and heartbeat), drowsiness, dizziness, fatigue, rash. If you suspect an overdose, immediately seek medical attention.

SIDE EFFECTS:
No serious effects in most cases of common use. Less common side effects include nasal dryness, dizziness, nausea, and mild insomnia palpitations, insomnia, gastrointestinal (GI) upset including stomach cramps and diarrhea, drowsiness and fatigue. In rare cases, more severe side effects may result, including: painful and frequent urination, hypertension, and heart palpitations. In these cases, discontinue medication and call your doctor immediately. Long-term ingestion of high dosages of acetaminophen-containing products may increase risk of liver and kidney damage.

CHECK WITH YOUR DOCTOR OR PHARMACIST BEFORE COMBINING THESE COMBINATION PRODUCTS WITH:
Anticoagulant medications, other cold, cough, or allergy medication, stimulants, antidepressants,

antihypertensives, digitalis or other heart medication, diuretics, or MAO (monoamine oxidase inhibitors) drugs. If taking combination products which contain acetaminophen, you should avoid Isoniazid (anti-tuberculosis) medication.
Excessive ingestion of alcohol while taking acetaminophen-containing medication can increase the risk of liver damage or disease (hepatic toxicity).

PREGNANCY OR BREASTFEEDING:
Use of medications containing any of the active ingredients in these products by a nursing mother should be considered a potential risk for a nursing child as the drug(s) will be passed on to the infant in the mother's milk. In all cases, a physician should be consulted.

PRECAUTIONS FOR CHILDREN:
In general, these active ingredients are not advised for children under 2. Administer to infants or children only when consulting a physician and follow instructions on medication (see above).

55+ **PRECAUTIONS FOR SENIORS:**
Seniors generally don't eliminate drugs as efficiently as younger persons, and should avoid high dosages.

SPECIAL WARNINGS:
Do not use for control of chronic cough related to conditions such as emphysema, asthma, or smoking, or if coughs are producing excessive secretions. If cough is accompanied by high fever, rash, nausea or vomiting, or persistent headache, use only if directed by your doctor.

Q U I C K F A C T S

Chronic alcoholics are at risk for hepatic (liver) function impairment if taking high dosages of acetaminophen-containing medication.

ADDITIONAL WARNING:
Alcohol: Some cough/cold medications contain various amounts of alcohol. Check label of any cough medication if concerned about ingestion of alcohol.

Sugar/Sweeteners: Some cough/cold medications contain various amounts of sugar, sucrose, glucose, and/or artificial sweeteners such as aspertame, saccharin, sorbitol. Check label of cough medication before selecting, if concerned about diabetes and ingestion of sugar or artificial sweeteners.

Abuse/Dependency: Reports indicate a rising rate of abuse of dextromethorphan-containing medications, particularly among teens. Sufficient data has not yet been collected, however, to determine the abuse and dependency potential of dextromethorphan-containing medications.

INFORM YOUR DOCTOR BEFORE TAKING PRODUCTS CONTAINING THIS COMBINATION OF ACTIVE INGREDIENTS IF YOU HAVE:
Asthma, emphysema, or other respiratory condition, liver impairment or liver disease, allergies to any sympathomimetic drug, aspirin or other salicylates, or if you have diabetes, thyroid condition, or urinary difficulty. If you anticipate any surgery requiring general or spinal anesthesia within 2 months of taking medication which contains pseudoephredine, inform your doctor.

ACTIVE INGREDIENTS:

ACETAMINOPHEN, DEXTROMETHORPHAN HYDROBROMIDE, DOXYLAMINE SUCCINATE, AND PSEUDOEPHREDINE HYDROCHLORIDE

QUICK FACTS

℞ **BRAND NAMES:**

- ALKA-SELTZER PLUS NIGHTTIME COLD LIQUI-GELS (also contains sorbitol)
- GENITE LIQUID (also contains alcohol, tartrazine)
- NYQUIL HOT THERAPY POWDER (also contains sucrose)
- NYQUIL NIGHTTIME COLD/FLU MEDICINE LIQUID (also contains alcohol, sucrose, saccharin [cherry flavor], tartrazine [original flavor])
- VICKS NYQUIL LIQUICAPS

Note: *Dextromethorphan hydrobromide* is also an active ingredient in other multi-symptom antitussive/expectorant medications which are formulated with other active ingredients.

Pseudoephredine hydrochloride is a used as an active ingredient in decongestant and stimulant products.

Acetaminophen is a non-aspirin analgesic which is used primarily in pain-relief products.

Doxylamine succinate is a drowsiness-producing antihistamine which is mostly used in combination with analgesic, antitussive, decongestant, and expectorant active ingredients in OTC medications to provide nighttime relief of allergy, common cold, cough or flu symptoms. It is also used as a sleep aid.

QUICK FACTS

SYMPTOMS RELIEVED:
Minor aches and pains, nasal congestion and coughing such as those associated with the common cold, flu, sore throat, sinusitis, hay fever and other respiratory allergies, and reduction of fever.

HOW TO TAKE:
Comes in capsule, liquid, and powder forms. Swallow capsule with liquid. Sprinkle powder over liquid, then swallow. Do not crush or chew timed-release capsule.

USUAL ADULT DOSE:
Dosage varies per product and active ingredient formulation. Follow product dosage instructions.

USUAL CHILD DOSE:
Do not administer to children under 6 unless under direction of physician. Dosage may vary based on infant or child's age.

OVERDOSE SYMPTOMS:
Nervous agitation, severe anxiety, insomnia (sleeplessness), hallucinations, tremors, convulsions, nausea, vomiting, cardiac arrhythmia (irregular pulse and heartbeat), drowsiness, dizziness, fatigue, rash. If you suspect an overdose, immediately seek medical attention.

SIDE EFFECTS:
No serious effects in most cases of common use, although antihistamines often cause drowsiness. Less common side effects include nasal dryness, dizziness, nausea, and mild insomnia palpitations, insomnia, gastrointestinal (GI) upset including stomach cramps and diarrhea, drowsiness, and fatigue. In rare cases, more severe

side effects may result, including: painful and frequent urination, hypertension, and heart palpitations. In these cases, discontinue medication and call your doctor immediately. Long-term ingestion of high dosages of acetaminophen-containing products may increase risk of liver and kidney damage.

CHECK WITH YOUR DOCTOR OR PHARMACIST BEFORE COMBINING THESE COMBINATION PRODUCTS WITH:

Anticoagulant medications, other cold, cough, or allergy medication, stimulants, antidepressants, antihypertensives, digitalis or other heart medication, diuretics, or MAO (monoamine oxidase inhibitors) drugs. Ingestion of caffeinated beverages (coffee, tea, caffeine-containing soft drinks) while taking pseudoephredine-containing medication can result in agitation and insomnia.

If taking combination products which contain acetaminophen, you should avoid Isoniazid (anti-tuberculosis) medication. Excessive ingestion of alcohol while taking acetaminophen-containing medication can increase the risk of liver damage or disease (hepatic toxicity). Alcohol use may also increase drowsiness effect of the antihistamine doxylamine succinate in these combination products.

PREGNANCY OR BREASTFEEDING:

Use of medications containing any of the active ingredients in these products by a nursing mother should be considered a potential risk for a nursing child as the drug(s) will be passed on to the infant in the mother's milk. In all cases, a physician should be consulted.

QUICK FACTS

PRECAUTIONS FOR CHILDREN:
In general, these active ingredients are not advised for children under 2. Administer to infants or children only when consulting a physician and follow instructions on medication (see above).

PRECAUTIONS FOR SENIORS:
Seniors generally don't eliminate drugs as efficiently as younger persons, and should avoid high dosages. Use of doxylamine succinate-containing medications by seniors can lead to urinary difficulties. In addition, seniors are more likely to experience drowsiness effects of doxylamine succinate.

SPECIAL WARNINGS:
Do not use for control of chronic cough related to conditions such as emphysema, asthma, or smoking, or if coughs are producing excessive secretions. If cough is accompanied by high fever, rash, nausea or vomiting, or persistent headache, use only if directed by your doctor. Because antihistamines such as doxylamine succinate often cause drowsiness, you should avoid activities or tasks such as driving, or other operations which require alertness, coordination, dexterity, or quick reflexes. Chronic alcoholics are at risk for hepatic (liver) function impairment if taking high dosages of acetaminophen-containing medication. Do not use medications which combine doxylamine succinate with tartrazine if you are intolerant or hypersensitive to aspirin. Allergic reactions, including bronchial asthma, have occurred in susceptible individuals.

ADDITIONAL WARNING:

Alcohol: Some cough/cold medications contain various amounts of alcohol. Check label of any cough medication if concerned about ingestion of alcohol.

Sugar/Sweeteners: Some cough/cold medications contain various amounts of sugar, sucrose, glucose, and/or artificial sweeteners such as aspartame, saccharin, sorbitol. Check label of cough medication before selecting, if concerned about diabetes and ingestion of sugar or artificial sweeteners.

Abuse/Dependency: Reports indicate a rising rate of abuse of dextromethorphan-containing medications, particularly among teens. Sufficient data has not yet been collected, however, to determine the abuse and dependency potential of dextromethorphan-containing medications.

INFORM YOUR DOCTOR BEFORE TAKING PRODUCTS CONTAINING THIS COMBINATION OF ACTIVE INGREDIENTS IF YOU HAVE:

Asthma, emphysema or other respiratory condition, liver impairment or liver disease, allergies to any sympathomimetic drug, aspirin or other salicylates, or if you have diabetes, thyroid condition, or urinary difficulty. If you anticipate any surgery requiring general or spinal anesthesia within 2 months of taking medication which contains pseudoephredine, inform your doctor.

QUICK FACTS

ACTIVE INGREDIENTS:

ACETAMINOPHEN, DEXTROMETHORPHAN HYDROBROMIDE, DOXYLAMINE SUCCINATE, AND PSEUDOEPHREDINE HYDROCHLORIDE

℞ **BRAND NAMES:**

- Alka-Seltzer Plus Nighttime Cold Liqui-Gels
  (also contains sorbitol)
- Genite Liquid
  (also contains alcohol, tartrazine)
- NyQuil Hot Therapy Powder
  (also contains sucrose)
- NyQuil Nighttime Cold/Flu Medicine Liquid
  (also contains alcohol, sucrose, saccharin [cherry flavor], tartrazine [original flavor])
- Vicks NyQuil LiquiCaps

Note: *Dextromethorphan hydrobromide* is also an active ingredient in other multi-symptom antitussive/expectorant medications which are formulated with other active ingredients.

Pseudoephredine hydrochloride is a used as an active ingredient in decongestant and stimulant products.

Acetaminophen is a non-aspirin analgesic which is used primarily in pain-relief products.

Doxylamine succinate is a drowsiness-producing antihistamine which is mostly used in combination with analgesic, antitussive, decongestant, and expectorant active ingredients in OTC medications to provide nighttime relief of allergy, common cold, cough or flu symptoms. It is also used as a sleep aid.

SYMPTOMS RELIEVED:
Minor aches and pains, nasal congestion and coughing such as those associated with the common cold, flu, sore throat, sinusitis, hay fever and other respiratory allergies, and reduction of fever.

HOW TO TAKE:
Comes in capsule, liquid, and powder forms. Swallow capsule with liquid. Sprinkle powder over liquid, then swallow. Do not crush or chew timed-release capsule.

USUAL ADULT DOSE:
Dosage varies per product and active ingredient formulation. Follow product dosage instructions.

USUAL CHILD DOSE:
Do not administer to children under 6 unless under direction of physician. Dosage may vary based on infant or child's age.

OVERDOSE SYMPTOMS:
Nervous agitation, severe anxiety, insomnia (sleeplessness), hallucinations, tremors, convulsions, nausea, vomiting, cardiac arrhythmia (irregular pulse and heartbeat), drowsiness, dizziness, fatigue, rash. If you suspect an overdose, immediately seek medical attention.

SIDE EFFECTS:
No serious effects in most cases of common use, although antihistamines often cause drowsiness. Less common side effects include nasal dryness, dizziness, nausea, and mild insomnia palpitations, insomnia, gastrointestinal (GI) upset including stomach cramps and diarrhea,

Q U I C K F A C T S

drowsiness, and fatigue. In rare cases, more severe side effects may result, including: painful and frequent urination, hypertension, and heart palpitations. In these cases, discontinue medication and call your doctor immediately.
Long-term ingestion of high dosages of acetaminophen-containing products may increase risk of liver and kidney damage.

CHECK WITH YOUR DOCTOR OR PHARMACIST BEFORE COMBINING THESE COMBINATION PRODUCTS WITH:
Anticoagulant medications, other cold, cough, or allergy medication, stimulants, antidepressants, antihypertensives, digitalis or other heart medication, diuretics, or MAO (monoamine oxidase inhibitors) drugs. Ingestion of caffeinated beverages (coffee, tea, caffeine-containing soft drinks) while taking pseudoephredine-containing medication can result in agitation and insomnia.
If taking combination products which contain acetaminophen, you should avoid Isoniazid (antituberculosis) medication. Excessive ingestion of alcohol while taking acetaminophen-containing medication can increase the risk of liver damage or disease (hepatic toxicity). Alcohol use may also increase drowsiness effect of the antihistamine doxylamine succinate in these combination products.

PREGNANCY OR BREASTFEEDING:
Use of medications containing any of the active ingredients in these products by a nursing mother should be considered a potential risk for a nursing child as the drug(s) will be passed on to the infant in the mother's milk. In all cases, a physician should be consulted.

PRECAUTIONS FOR CHILDREN:

In general, these active ingredients are not advised for children under 2. Administer to infants or children only when consulting a physician and follow instructions on medication (see above).

55+ **PRECAUTIONS FOR SENIORS:**

Seniors generally don't eliminate drugs as efficiently as younger persons, and should avoid high dosages. Use of doxylamine succinate-containing medications by seniors can lead to urinary difficulties. In addition, seniors are more likely to experience drowsiness effects of doxylamine succinate.

SPECIAL WARNINGS:

Do not use for control of chronic cough related to conditions such as emphysema, asthma, or smoking, or if coughs are producing excessive secretions. If cough is accompanied by high fever, rash, nausea or vomiting, or persistent headache, use only if directed by your doctor. Because antihistamines such as doxylamine succinate often cause drowsiness, you should avoid activities or tasks such as driving, or other operations which require alertness, coordination, dexterity, or quick reflexes. Chronic alcoholics are at risk for hepatic (liver) function impairment if taking high dosages of acetaminophen-containing medication. Do not use medications which combine doxylamine succinate with tartrazine if you are intolerant or hypersensitive to aspirin. Allergic reactions, including bronchial asthma, have occurred in susceptible individuals.

QUICK FACTS

ADDITIONAL WARNING:

Alcohol: Some cough/cold medications contain various amounts of alcohol. Check label of any cough medication if concerned about ingestion of alcohol.

Sugar/Sweeteners: Some cough/cold medications contain various amounts of sugar, sucrose, glucose, and/or artificial sweeteners such as aspartame, saccharin, sorbitol. Check label of cough medication before selecting, if concerned about diabetes and ingestion of sugar or artificial sweeteners.

Abuse/Dependency: Reports indicate a rising rate of abuse of dextromethorphan-containing medications, particularly among teens. Sufficient data has not yet been collected, however, to determine the abuse and dependency potential of dextromethorphan-containing medications.

INFORM YOUR DOCTOR BEFORE TAKING PRODUCTS CONTAINING THIS COMBINATION OF ACTIVE INGREDIENTS IF YOU HAVE:

Asthma, emphysema or other respiratory condition, liver impairment or liver disease, allergies to any sympathomimetic drug, aspirin or other salicylates, or if you have diabetes, thyroid condition, or urinary difficulty. If you anticipate any surgery requiring general or spinal anesthesia within 2 months of taking medication which contains pseudoephredine, inform your doctor.

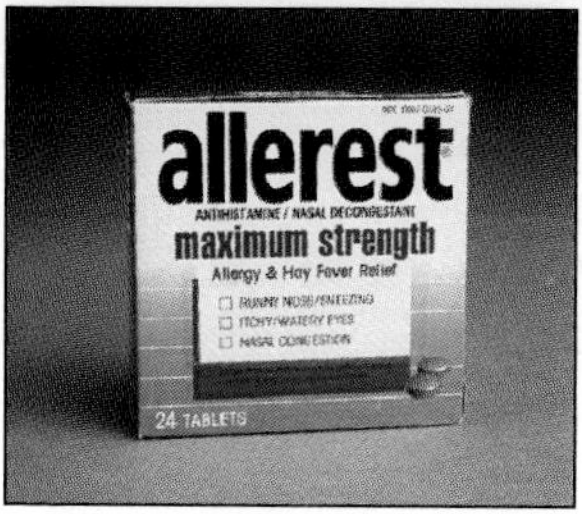

Allerest

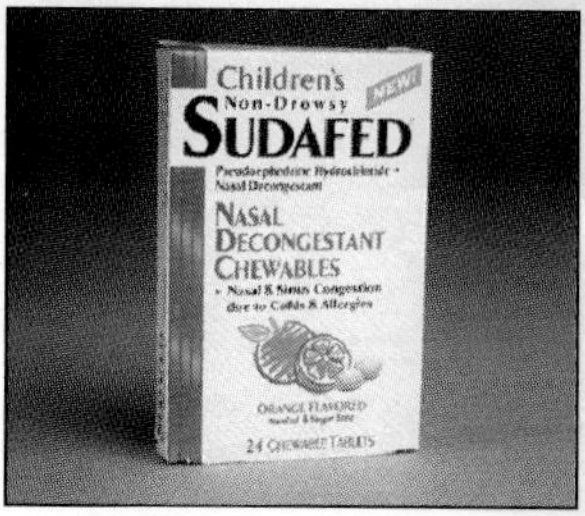

Children's Sudafed

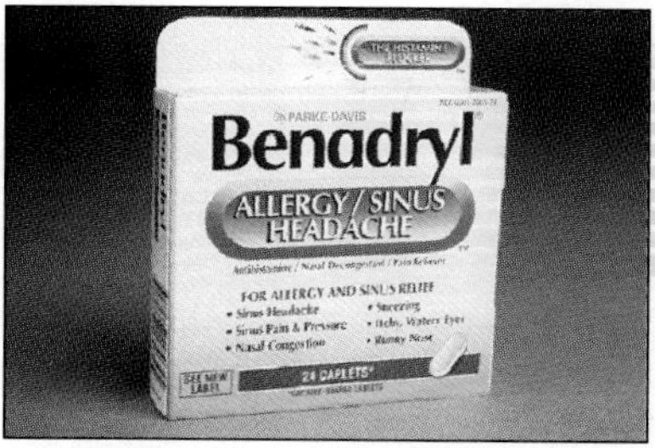

Benadryl Allergy/Sinus

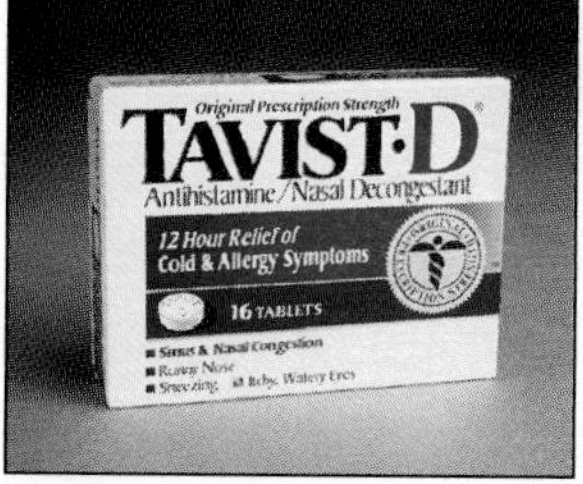

Tavist-D

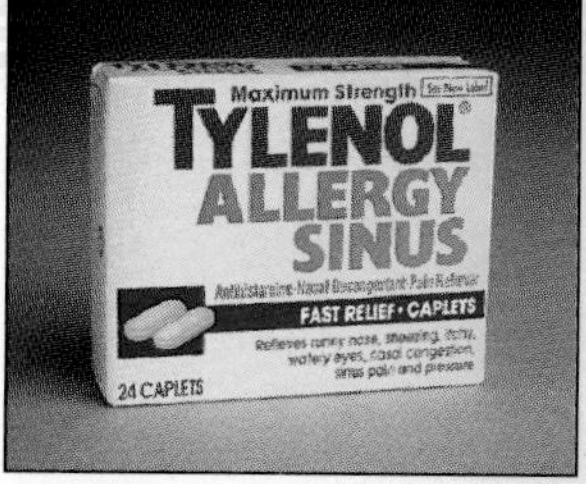

Tylenol Allergy Sinus

ARTHRITIS/BACKACHE AND PAIN

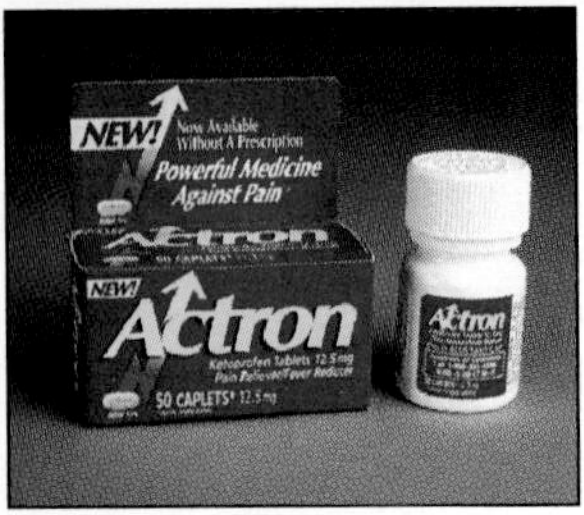

Actron

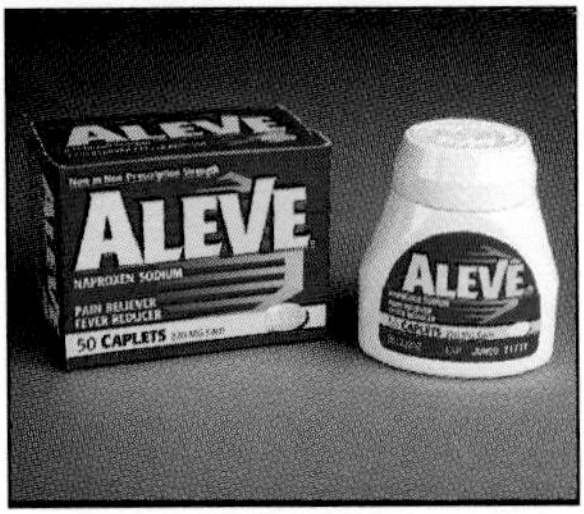

Aleve

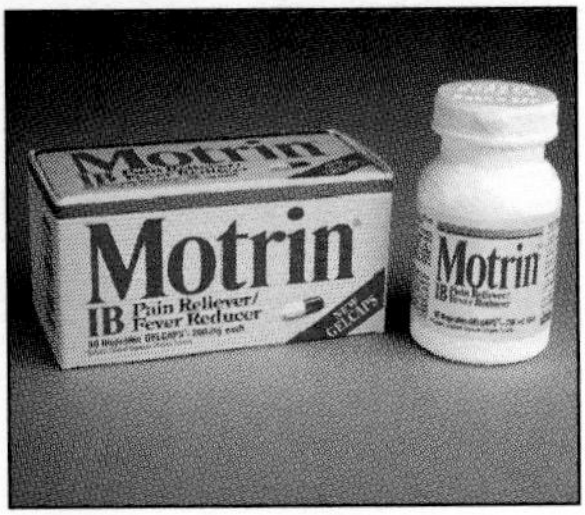

Motrin IB

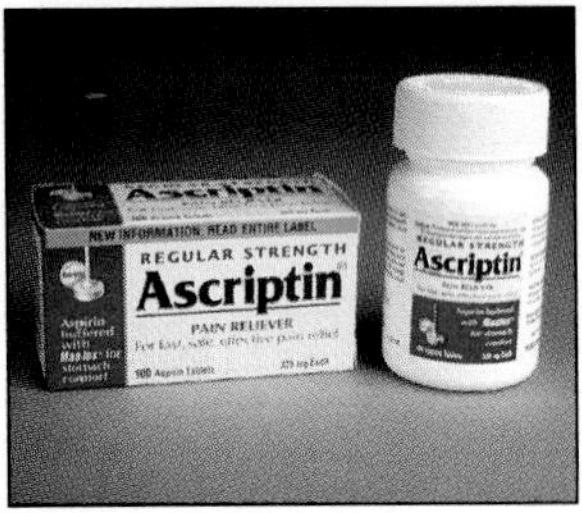

Ascriptin

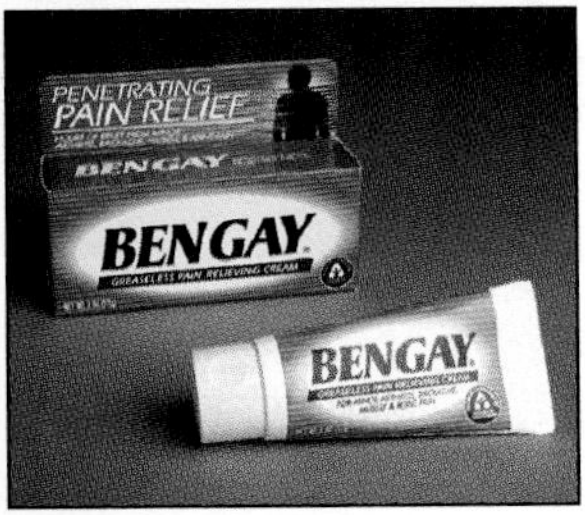

Bengay

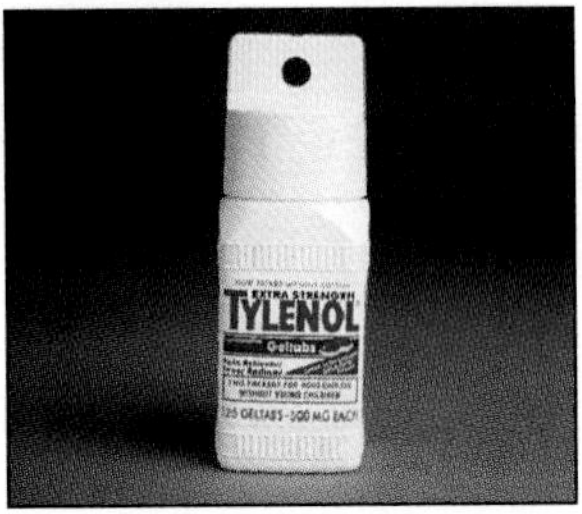

Tylenol

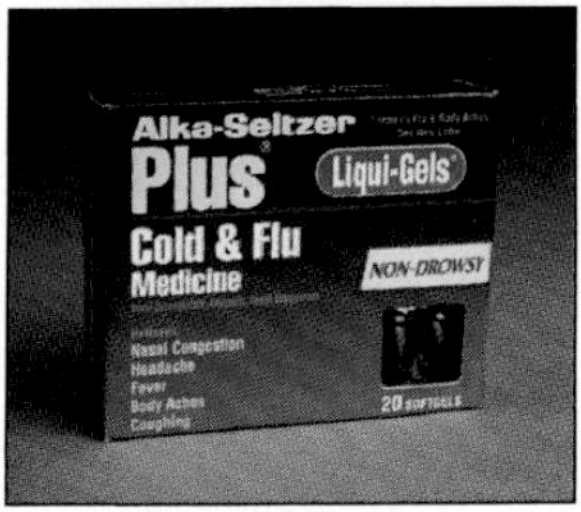

Alka-Seltzer Plus
Cold & Flu

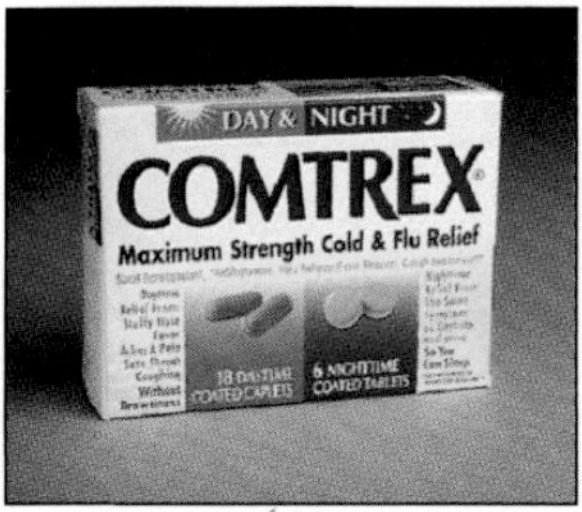

Comtrex Day & Night

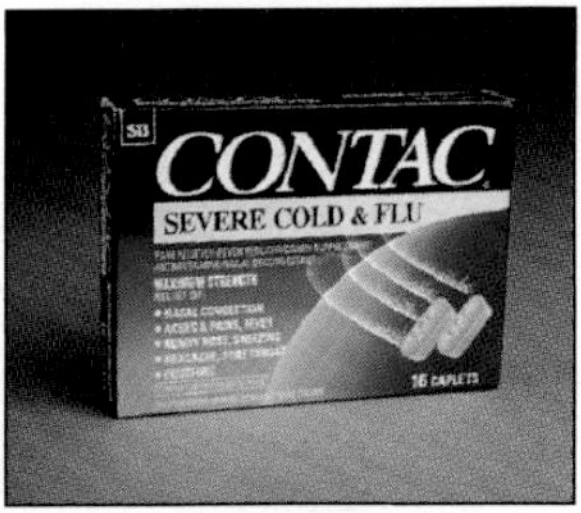

Contact
Severe Cold & Flu

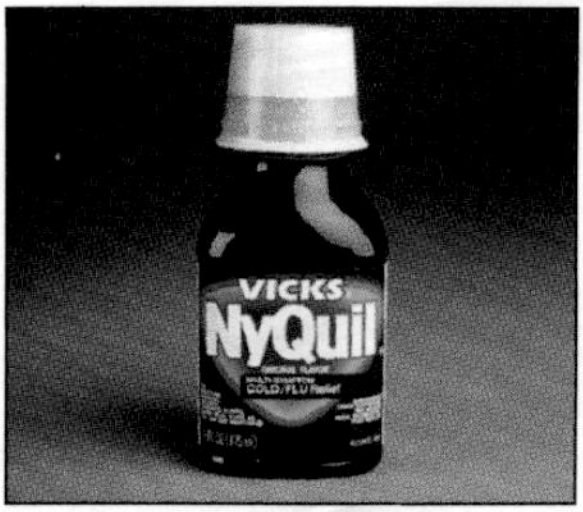

Nyquil

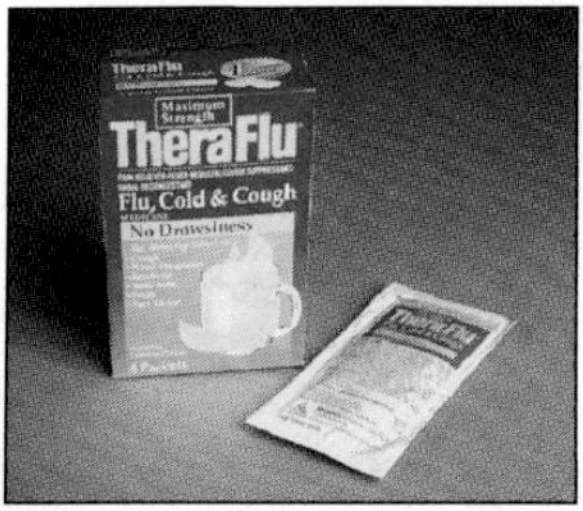

TheraFlu

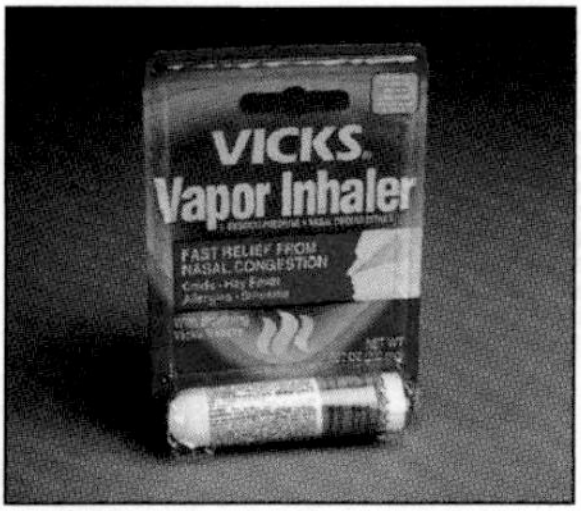

Vick's Inhaler

CONSTIPATION

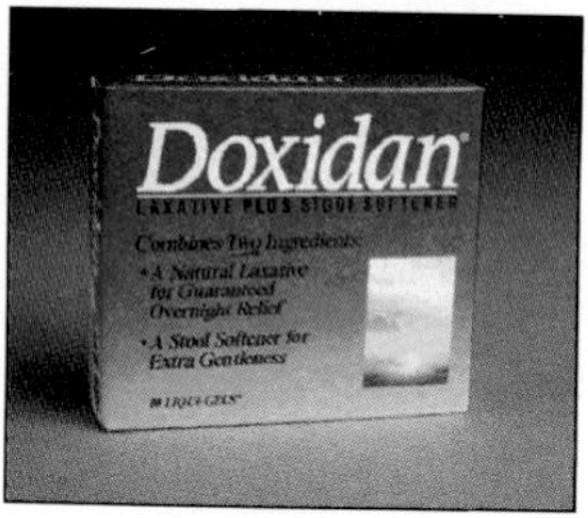

Doxidan

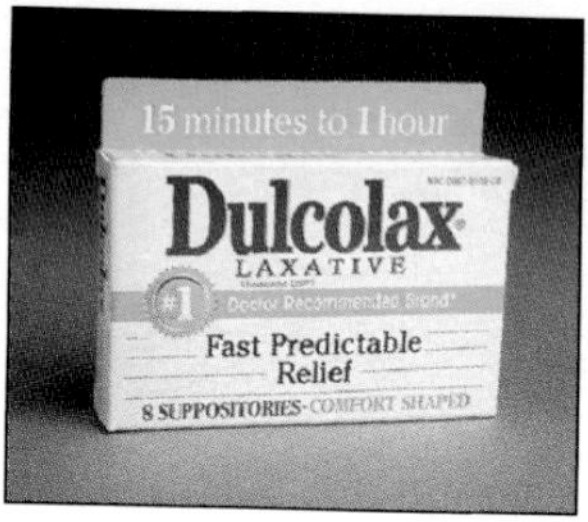

Dulcolax

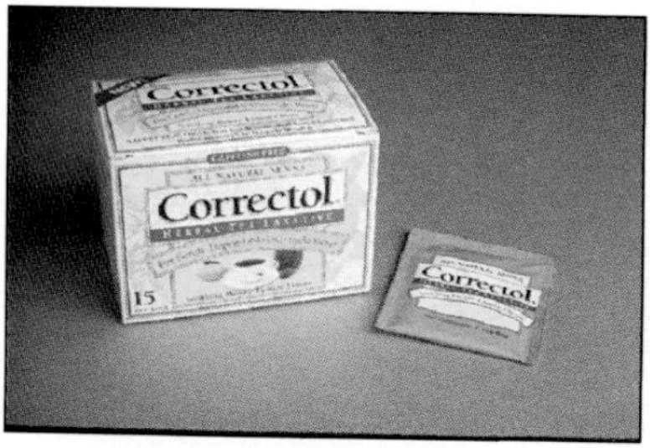

Correctol Tea

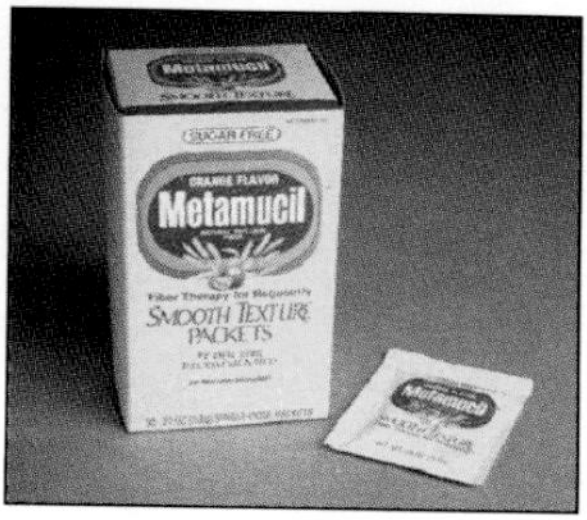

Metamucil

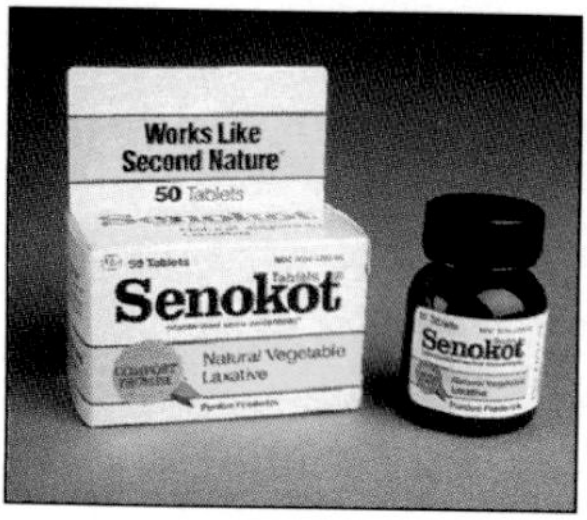

Senokot

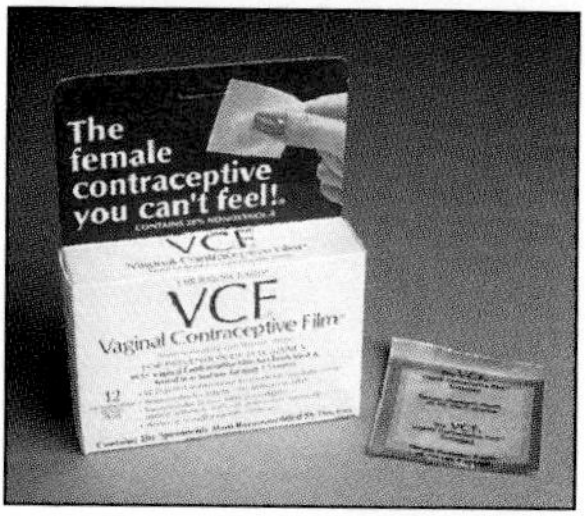

VCF—Vaginal Contraceptive Film

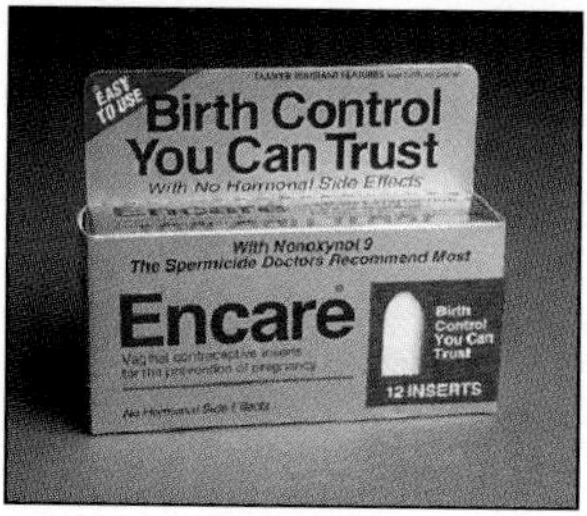

Encare

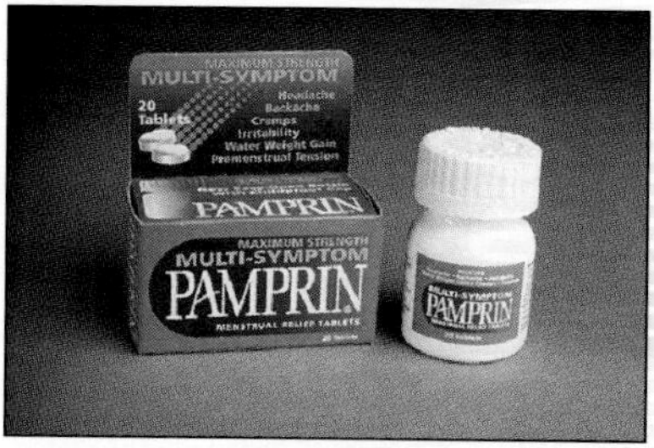

Pamprin

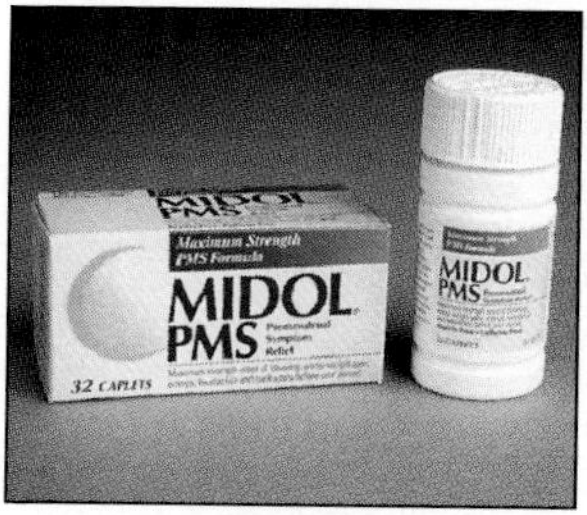

Midol PMS

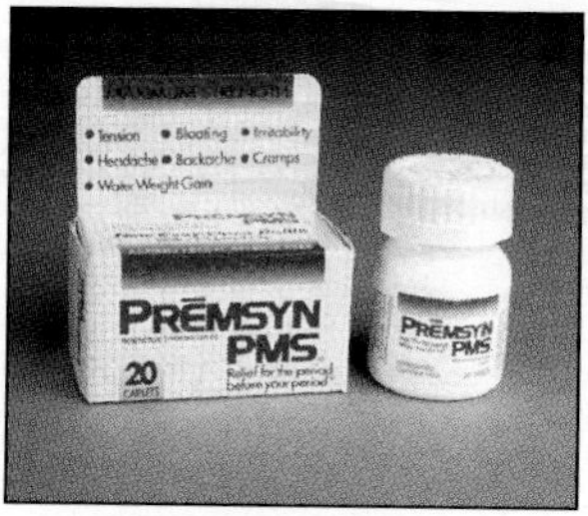

Premsyn PMS

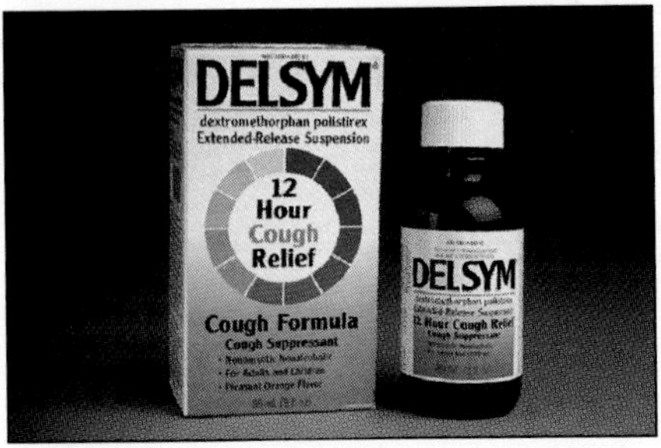

Delsym

Halls

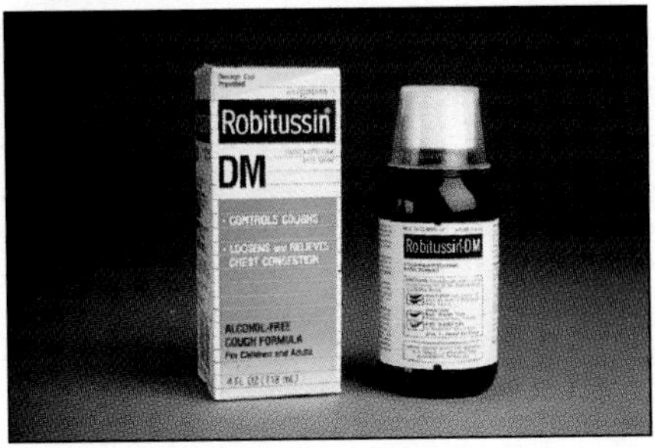

Robitussin DM

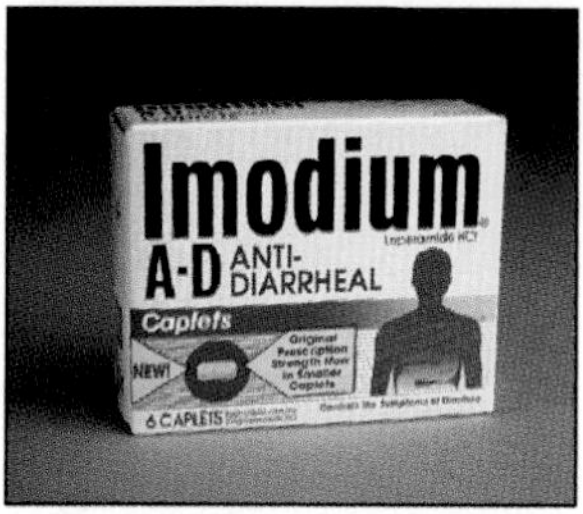

Imodium A-D

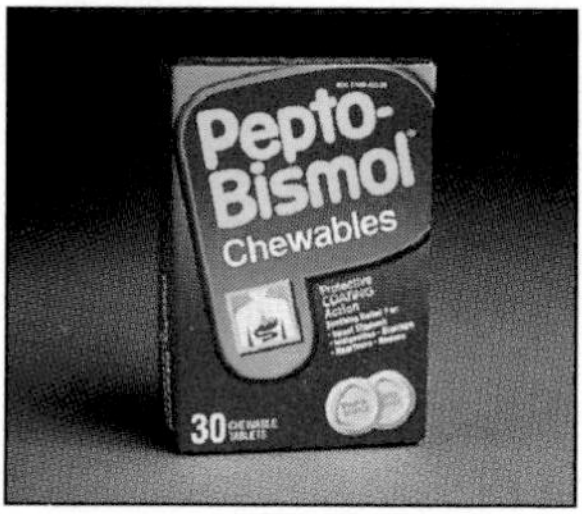

Pepto-Bismol

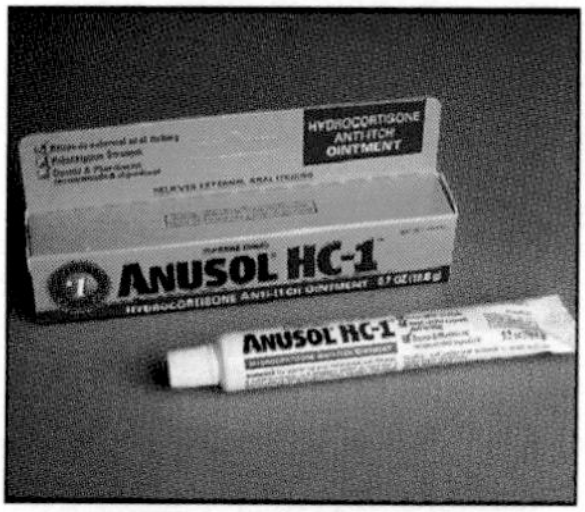

Anusol HC-1

Hemorid

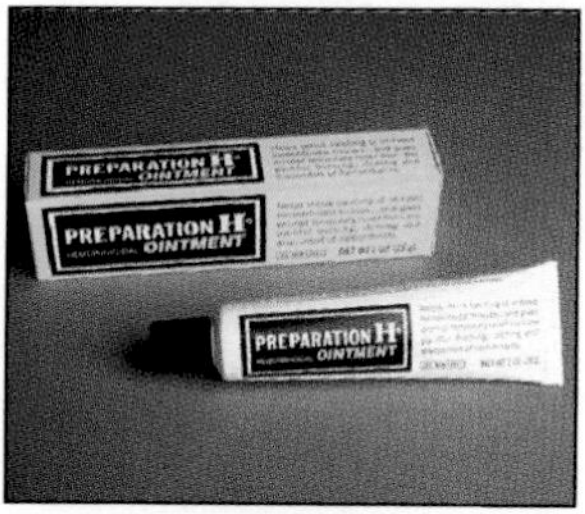

Preparation H

Tucks Medicated Pads

EYE PREPARATIONS

Clear Eyes

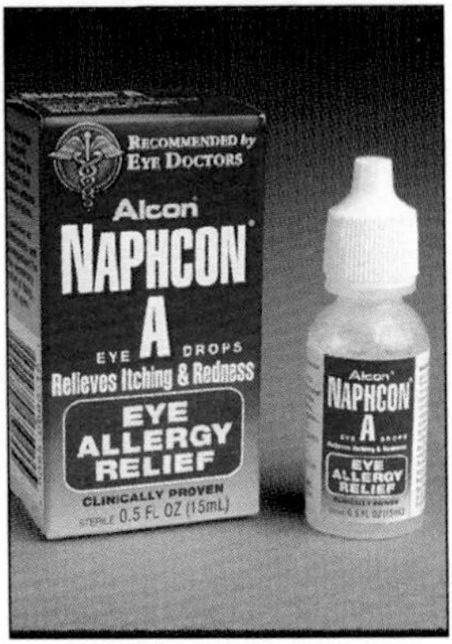

Naphcon A

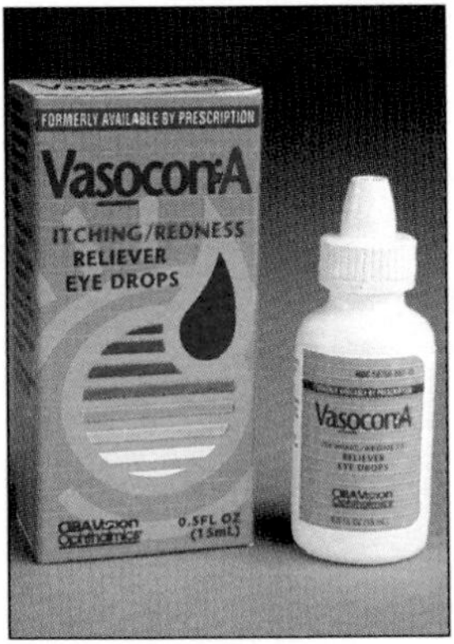

Vascon A

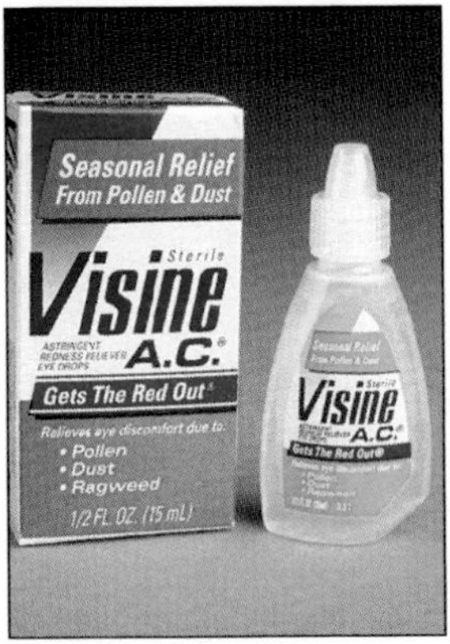

Visine A.C.

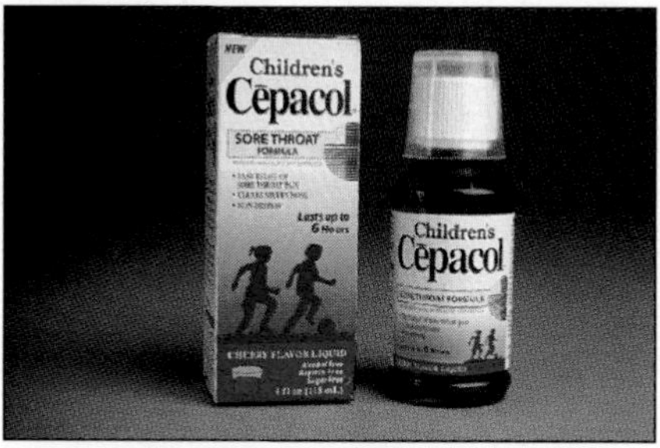

Children's Cepacol

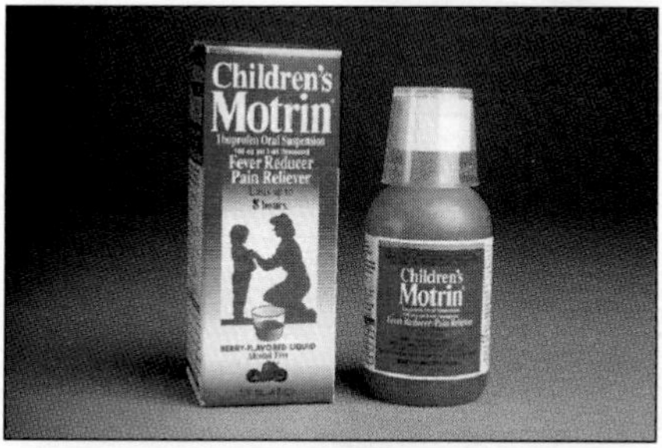

Children's Motrin

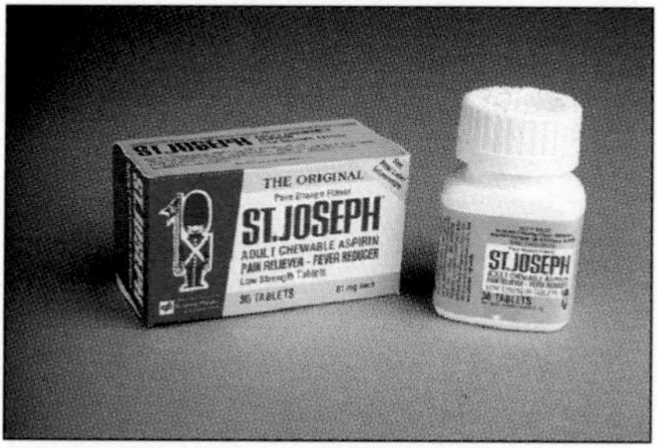

St. Joseph for Kids

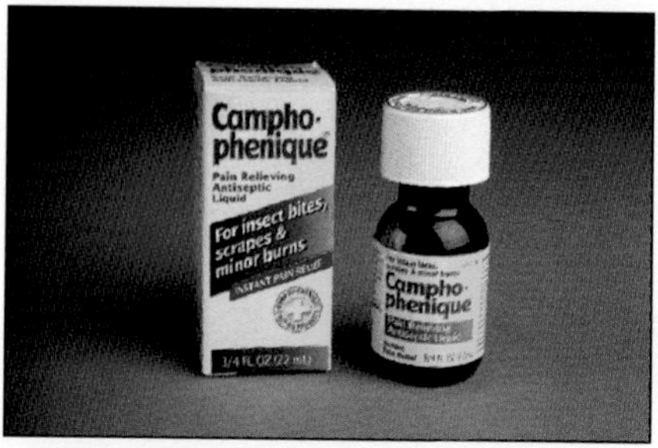

Campho-phenique

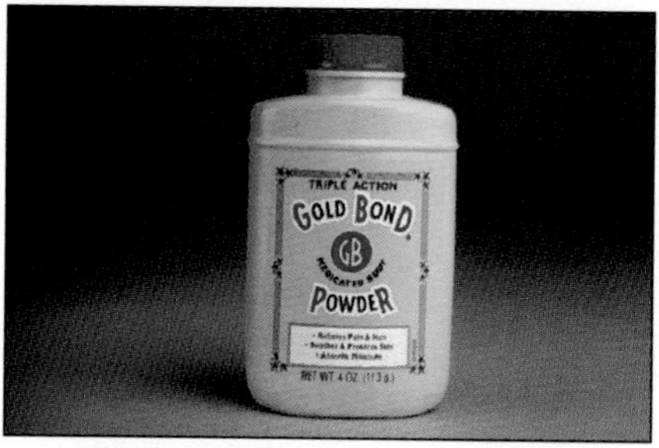

Gold Bond Medicated Powder

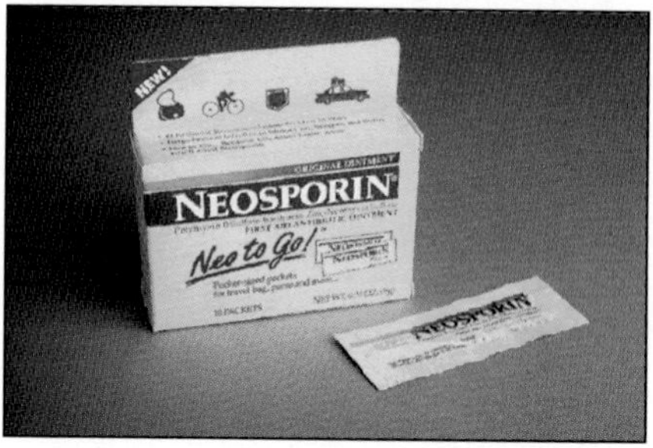

Neosporin

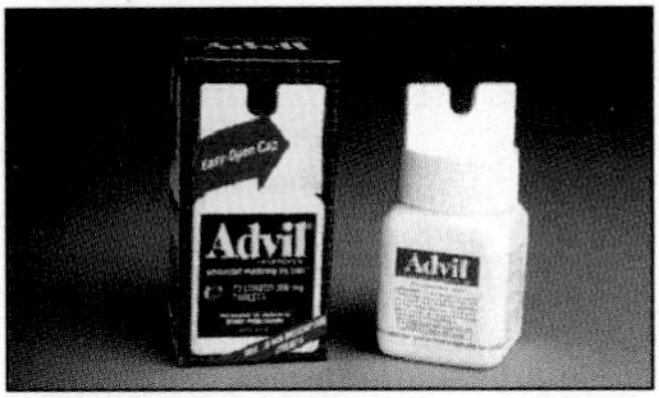

Advil

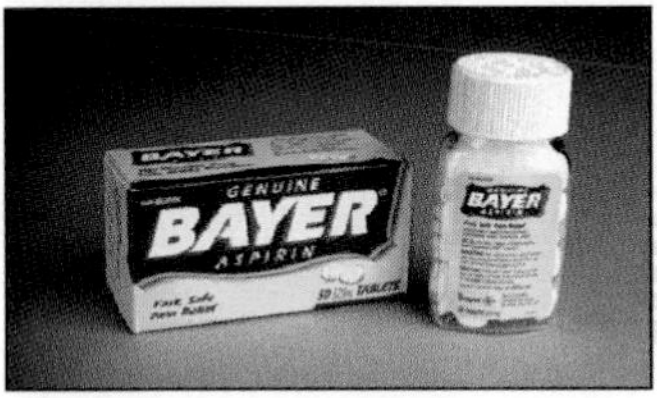

Bayer

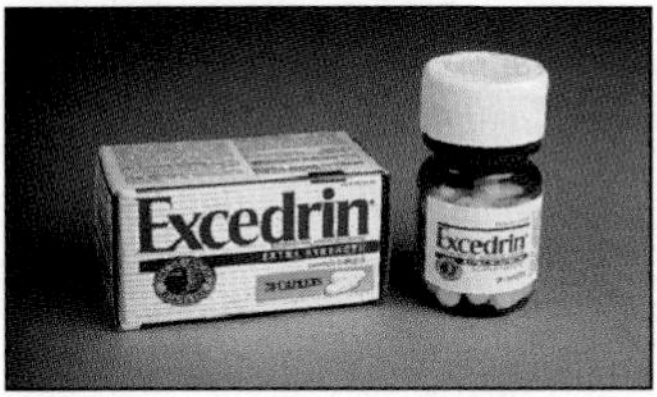

Excedrin

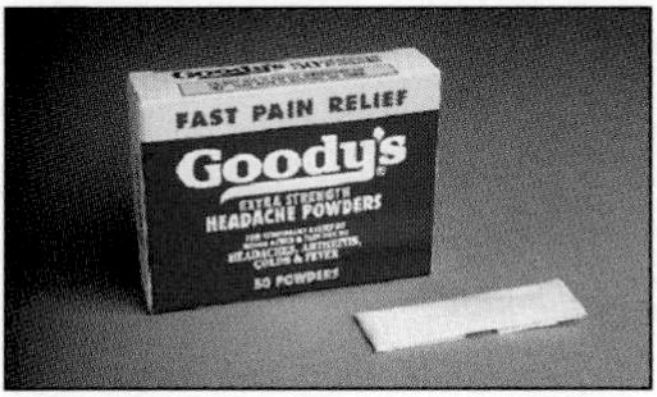

Goody's Headache Powders

HEARTBURN, STOMACH UPSET, AND GAS

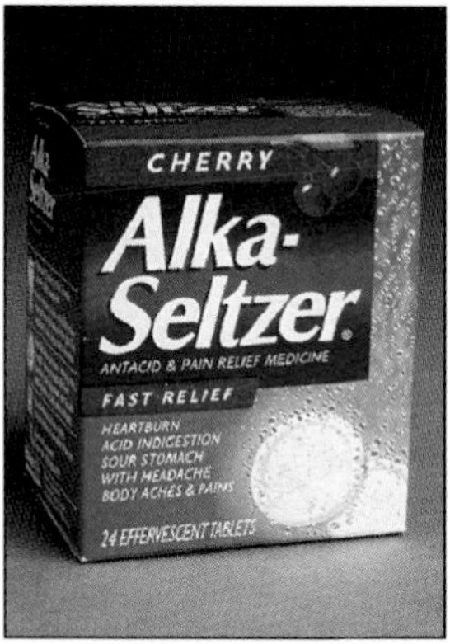

Alka-Seltzer

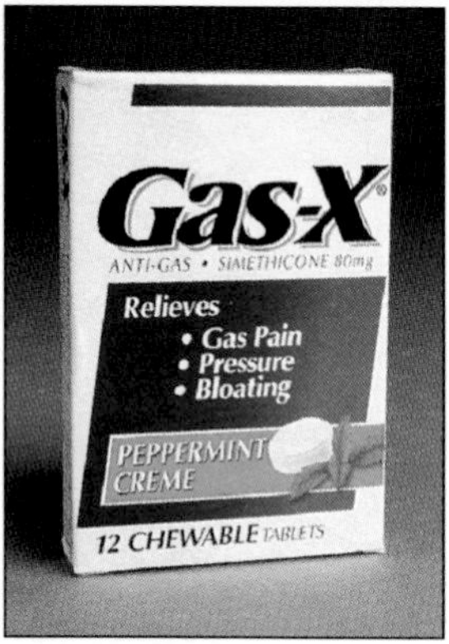

Gas-X

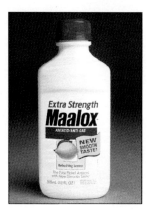

Extra Strength Maalox

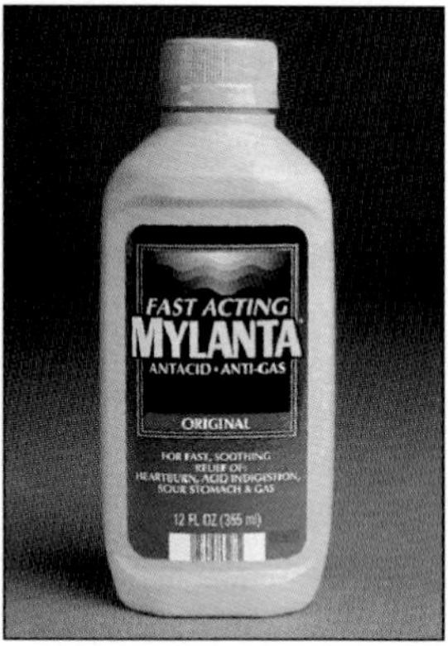

Mylanta

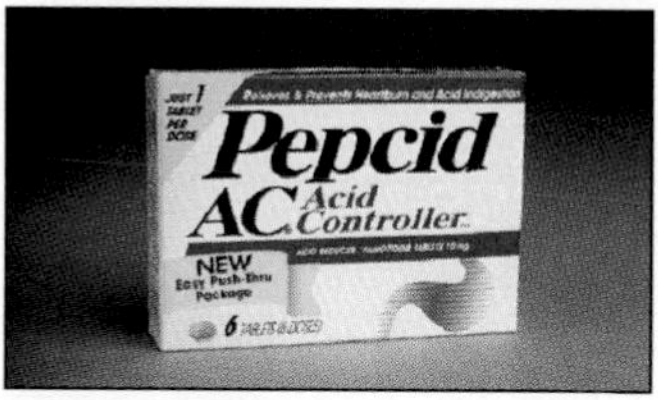

Pepcid AC

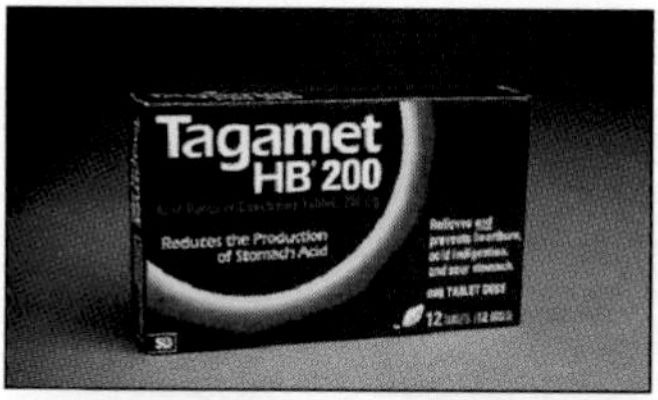

Tagamet HB 200

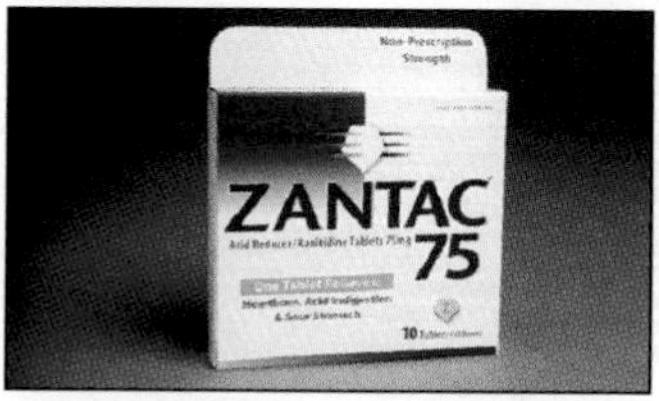

Zantac 75

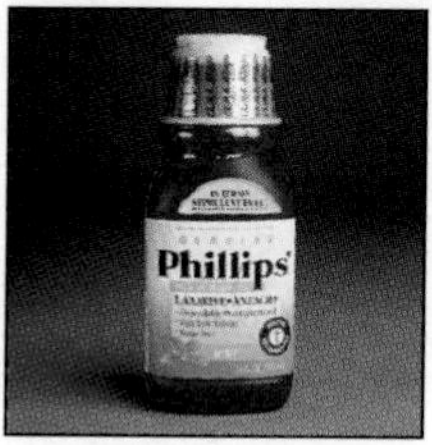

Phillips'
Milk of Magnesia

SKIN CONDITIONS

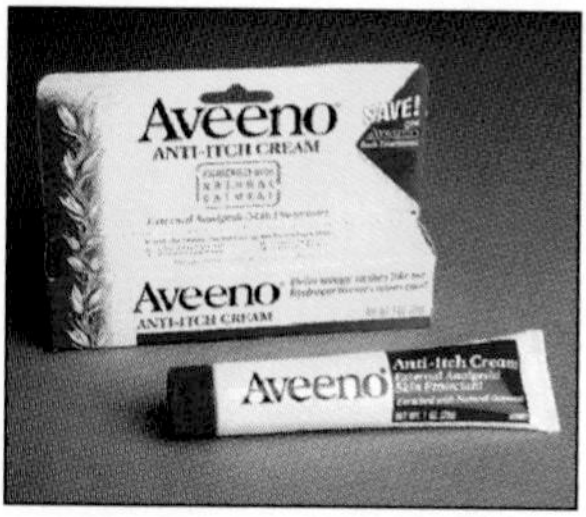

Aveeno

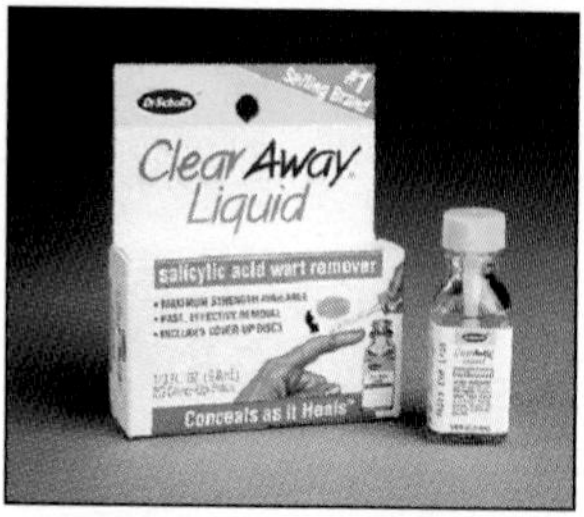

Clear Away Liquid

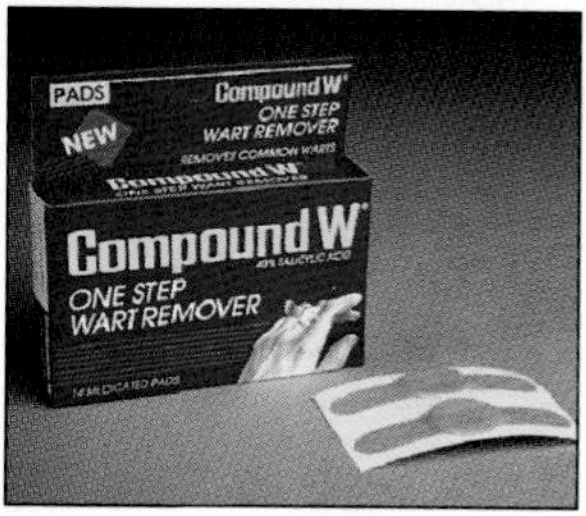

Compound W

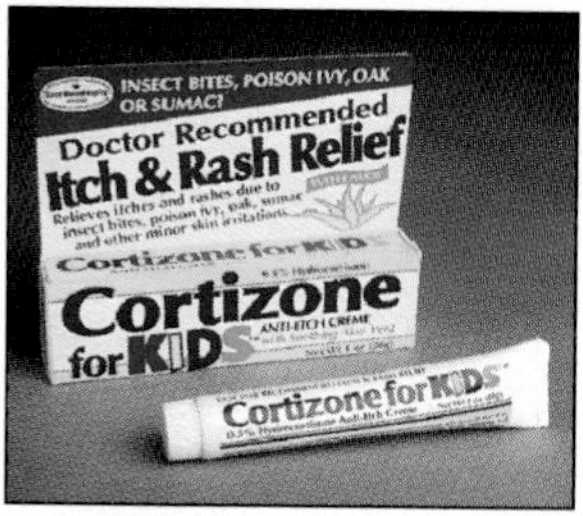

Cortizone for Kids

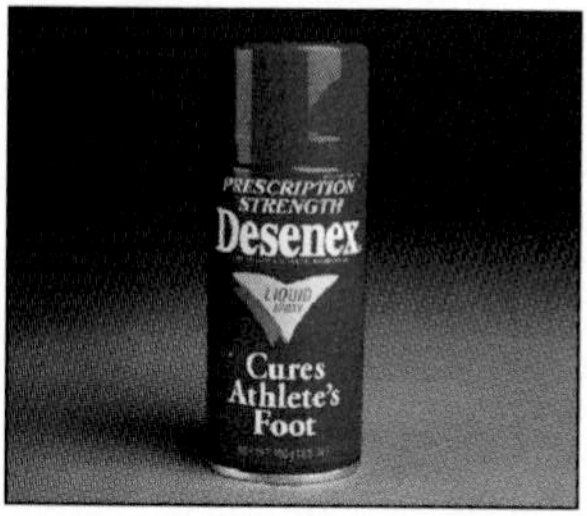

Desenex

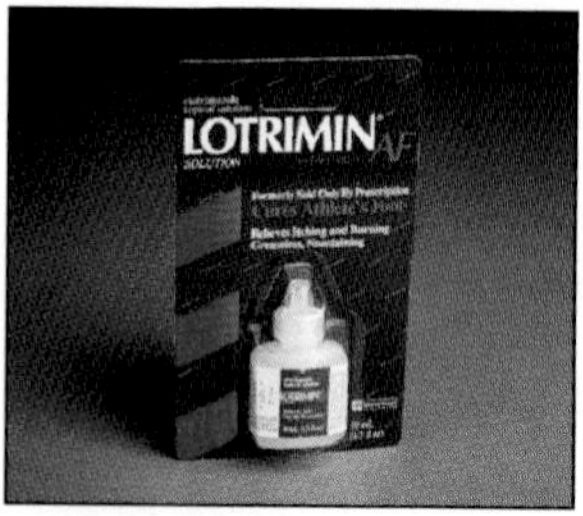

Lotrimin

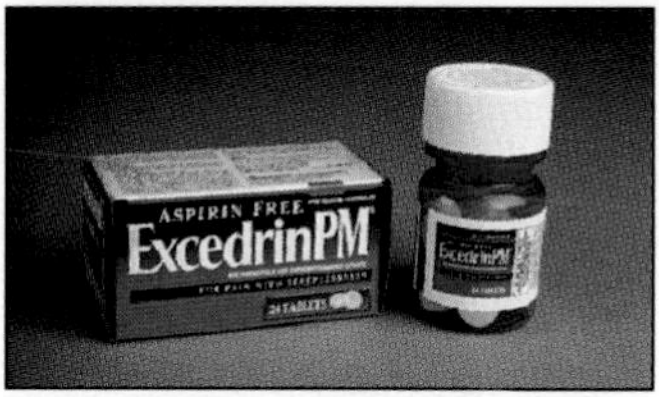

Excedrin PM

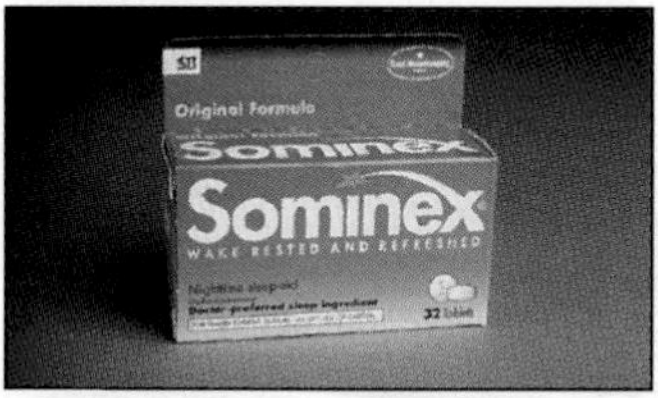

Sominex

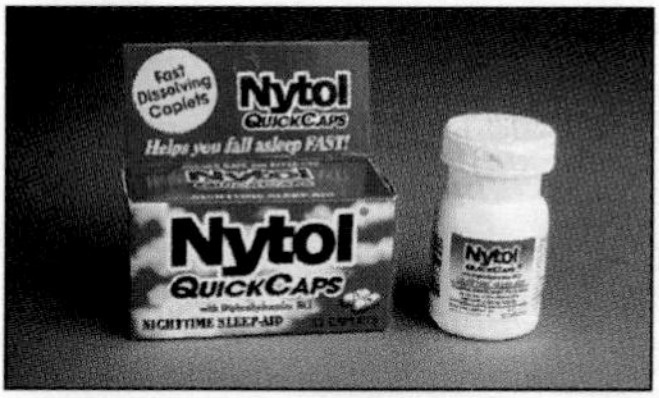

Nytol

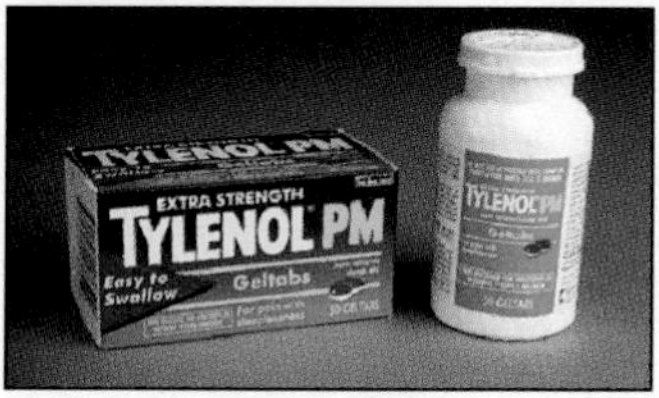

Tylenol PM

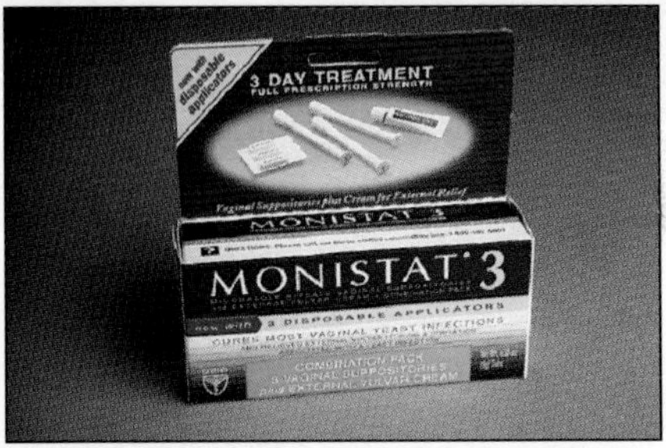

Monistat 3

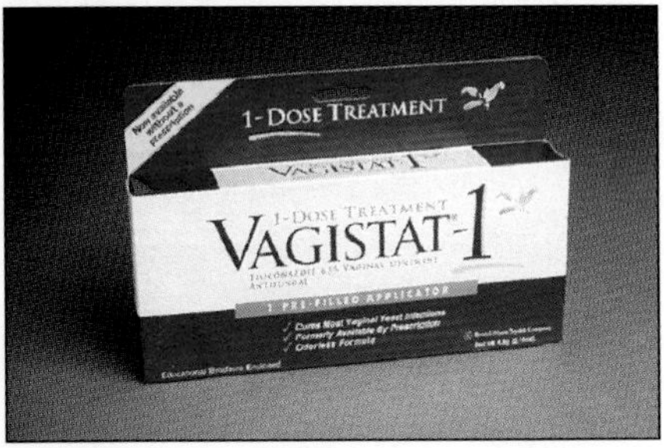

Vagistat 1

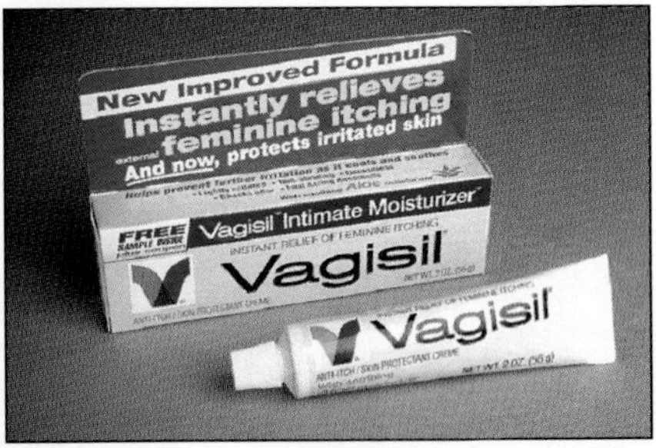

Vagisil

ACTIVE INGREDIENTS:
DEXTROMETHORPHAN HYDROBROMIDE AND BENZOCAINE

BRAND NAMES:
Lozenges:
- SPEC-T (combination with tartrazine, also contains sucrose, dextrose, glucose)
- VICKS FORMULA 44 COUGH CONTROL DISCS (also contains menthol, sucrose)
- VICKS COUGH SILENCERS (combination with tartrazine, menthol, anethole, also contains corn syrup, sucrose)

See also: Benzocaine, dextromethorphan hydrobromide

Note: *Dextromethorphan hydrobromide* is an active ingredient in many multi-symptom antitussive medications which are formulated with other active ingredients.

Benzocaine is also an active ingredient in oral anesthetics, topical analgesics and appetite suppressant products.

SYMPTOMS RELIEVED:
Cough associated with common cold, and minor throat and bronchial irritations.

HOW TO TAKE:
Comes in lozenge form.

USUAL ADULT DOSE:
Varies with product. Follow product information.

USUAL CHILD DOSE:
For children 3 to 12: Varies with product. Follow product information.

Q U I C K F A C T S

Do not administer to children under 3 unless under direction of physician. Dosage may vary based on infant or child's age.

OVERDOSE SYMPTOMS:
Intoxication, nervous agitation and overactivity, hallucinations, respiratory difficulty, severe anxiety, insomnia (sleeplessness), convulsions, cardiac arrhythmia (irregular pulse and heartbeat. If you suspect an overdose, immediately seek medical attention.

SIDE EFFECTS:
No serious effects in most cases of common use. Less common side effects include dizziness, stomach cramps, drowsiness, fatigue, nasal dryness, and mild insomnia. In rare cases, more severe side effects may result, including: painful and frequent urination, hypertension, and heart palpitations. In these cases, discontinue medication and call your doctor immediately.

CHECK WITH YOUR DOCTOR OR PHARMACIST BEFORE COMBINING DEXTROMETHORPHAN AND BENZOCAINE WITH:
Cold, cough, or allergy medication, stimulants, antidepressants, antihypertensives, digitalis or other heart medication, diuretics, or MAO (monoamine oxidase inhibitors) drugs. Ingestion of caffeinated beverages (coffee, tea, caffeine-containing soft drinks) while taking benzocaine-containing medication can result in agitation and insomnia.

PREGNANCY OR BREASTFEEDING:
Dextromethorphan and benzocaine use by a nursing mother should be considered a potential

risk for a nursing child as the drug will be passed on to the infant in the mother's milk. In all cases, a physician should be consulted.

QUICK FACTS

PRECAUTIONS FOR CHILDREN:
In general, dextromethorphan and benzocaine is not advised for children under 2. Administer dextromethorphan and benzocaine to infants or children only when consulting a physician and follow instructions on medication (see above).

55+ **PRECAUTIONS FOR SENIORS:**
Seniors generally don't eliminate drugs as efficiently as younger persons, and should avoid high dosages. Use of benzocaine medications by seniors can lead to cardiac arrhythmia (irregular pulse and heartbeat). In addition, seniors are more likely to experience stimulant effects of the drug.

SPECIAL WARNINGS:
Do not use for control of chronic cough related to conditions such as emphysema, asthma, or smoking, or if coughs are producing excessive secretions. If cough is accompanied by high fever, rash, nausea or vomiting, or persistent headache, use only if directed by your doctor. Do not use any benzocaine-containing medication continuously for longer than 3 months. Also do not use medications which combine benzocaine and tartrazine if you are intolerant or hypersensitive to aspirin. Allergic reactions, including bronchial asthma, have occurred in susceptible individuals.

ADDITIONAL WARNING:
Reports indicate a rising rate of abuse of

dextromethorphan-containing medications, particularly among teens. Sufficient data has not yet been collected, however, to determine the abuse and dependency potential of dextromethorphan-containing medications.

INFORM YOUR DOCTOR BEFORE TAKING DEXTROMETHORPHAN AND BENZOCAINE IF YOU HAVE:

Allergies to: any sympathomimetic drug, aspirin or other salicylates, or if you have asthma, impaired liver function or liver disease, diabetes, thyroid condition, or urinary difficulty. If you anticipate any surgery requiring general or spinal anesthesia within 2 months of taking a benzocaine-containing medication, inform your doctor.

QUICK FACTS

ACTIVE INGREDIENTS:

DEXTROMETHORPHAN HYDROBROMIDE AND PSEUDOEPHEDRINE HYDROCHLORIDE

BRAND NAMES:

- DRIXORAL COUGH & CONGESTION LIQUID CAPS
- PEDIA CARE NIGHTREST COUGH–COLD LIQUID (combination with chlorpheniramine maleate—also contains sorbitol, corn syrup)
- ROBITUSSIN MAXIMUM STRENGTH COUGH & COLD LIQUID (also contains alcohol, high fructose corn syrup, saccharin, glucose)
- TRIAMINIC NITE LIGHT LIQUID (combination with chlorpheniramine maleate—also contains sorbitol, sucrose)
- VICKS 44 NON-DROWSY COLD & COUGH LIQUICAPS (also contains sorbitol)
- VICKS PEDIATRIC FORMULA 44D COUGH & DECONGESTANT LIQUID (also contains sorbitol, sucrose)

See also: Pseudoephedrine hydrochloride

SYMPTOMS RELIEVED:
Cough and nasal congestion associated with common cold and minor throat and bronchial irritations.

HOW TO TAKE:
Comes in tablet, capsule, chewable forms. Swallow with liquid. Do not crush or chew timed-release tablets.

USUAL ADULT DOSE:
Dosage varies per product and active ingredient formulation. Follow product dosage instructions.

QUICK FACTS

USUAL CHILD DOSE:
Do not administer to children under 6 unless under direction of physician. Dosage may vary based on infant or child's age.

OVERDOSE SYMPTOMS:
Nervous agitation, severe anxiety, insomnia (sleeplessness), hallucinations, tremors, convulsions, nausea, vomiting, cardiac arrhythmia (irregular pulse and heartbeat). If you suspect an overdose, immediately seek medical attention.

SIDE EFFECTS:
No serious effects in most cases of common use. Less common side effects include nasal dryness, dizziness, nausea, and mild insomnia palpitations, insomnia. In rare cases, more severe side effects may result, including: painful and frequent urination, hypertension, and heart palpitations. In these cases, discontinue medication and call your doctor immediately.

CHECK WITH YOUR DOCTOR OR PHARMACIST BEFORE COMBINING DEXTROMETHORPHAN AND RELATED COMBINATION PRODUCTS WITH:
Cold, cough, or allergy medication, stimulants, antidepressants, antihypertensives, digitalis or other heart medication, diuretics, or MAO (monoamine oxidase inhibitors) drugs. Ingestion of caffeinated beverages (coffee, tea, caffeine-containing soft drinks) while taking dextromethorphan-containing medication can result in agitation and insomnia.

PREGNANCY OR BREASTFEEDING:
Dextromethorphan use by a nursing mother should be considered a potential risk for a nurs-

ing child as the drug will be passed on to the infant in the mother's milk. In all cases, a physician should be consulted.

PRECAUTIONS FOR CHILDREN:
In general, dextromethorphan is not advised for children under 6. Administer dextromethorphan to infants or children only when consulting a physician and follow instructions on medication (see above).

55+ **PRECAUTIONS FOR SENIORS:**
Seniors generally don't eliminate drugs as efficiently as younger persons, and should avoid high dosages. Use of dextromethorphan medications by seniors can lead to cardiac arrhythmia (irregular pulse and heartbeat). In addition, seniors are more likely to experience stimulant effects of the drug.

SPECIAL WARNINGS:
Do not use continuously for longer than 3 months. Do not use dextromethorphan medications containing tartrazine if you are intolerant or hypersensitive to aspirin. Allergic reactions, including bronchial asthma, have occurred in susceptible individuals.

ADDITIONAL WARNING:
Alcohol: Many dextromethorphan-containing medications contain various amounts of alcohol. Check label of any cough medication if concerned about ingestion of alcohol.

Abuse/Dependency: Reports indicate a rising rate of abuse of dextromethorphan-containing medications, particularly among teens. Sufficient

data has not yet been collected, however, to determine the abuse and dependency potential of dextromethorphan-containing medications.

INFORM YOUR DOCTOR BEFORE TAKING DEXTROMETHORPHAN IF YOU HAVE:
Allergies to: any sympathomimetic drug, aspirin or other salicylates, or if you have diabetes, thyroid condition, or urinary difficulty. If you anticipate any surgery requiring general or spinal anesthesia within 2 months of taking dextromethorphan medication, inform your doctor.

ACTIVE INGREDIENTS:

DEXTROMETHORPHAN HYDROBROMIDE, PHENYLPROPANOLAMINE, AND CHLORPHENIRAMINE MALEATE

℞ **BRAND NAMES:**

- Alka-Seltzer Plus Cold & Cough Tablets (combination with aspirin, phenylalanine, also contains aspartame)
- Alka-Seltzer Plus Nighttime Cold & Cough Tablets (combination with aspirin, phenylalanine, also contains aspartame, sucrose)
- Cerose DM Liquid
- Cheracol Plus Liquid
- Kophane Cough & Cold Formula Liquid
- Myminicol Liquid
- Rescon-DM Liquid
- Orthoxicol Cough Syrup
- Rhinosyn–DM Liquid
- Threamine DM Syrup
- Triaminic–DM Syrup
- Triaminicol Multi-Symptom Cough & Cold Tablets
- Triaminicol Multi-Symptom Relief Liquid
- Tricodene Forte Liquid/NN Liquid
- Triminol Cough Syrup
- Tussar DM Syrup
- Vicks 44M Cold, Flu & Cough LiquiCaps

SYMPTOMS RELIEVED:
Cough, nasal congestion and runny nose, itchy and watery eyes, sneezing, scratchy throat, and irritated sinuses associated with common cold, minor throat and bronchial irritations, sinusitis, hay fever, and other upper respiratory allergies.

QUICK FACTS

HOW TO TAKE:
Comes in tablet, capsule, liquid, and syrup forms. Swallow tablet or capsule with liquid. Do not crush or chew timed-release tablets.

USUAL ADULT DOSE:
Dosage varies per product and active ingredient formulation. Follow product dosage instructions.

USUAL CHILD DOSE:
Do not administer to children under 6 unless under direction of physician. Dosage may vary based on infant or child's age.

OVERDOSE SYMPTOMS:
Nervous agitation, severe anxiety, insomnia (sleeplessness), hallucinations, tremors, convulsions, nausea, vomiting, cardiac arrhythmia (irregular pulse and heartbeat). If you suspect an overdose, immediately seek medical attention.

SIDE EFFECTS:
No serious effects in most cases of common use, however, drowsiness is a common side effect produced by antihistamines. Less common side effects include nasal dryness, dizziness, nausea, and mild insomnia palpitations, insomnia. In rare cases, more severe side effects may result, including: painful and frequent urination, hypertension, and heart palpitations. In these cases, discontinue medication and call your doctor immediately.

CHECK WITH YOUR DOCTOR OR PHARMACIST BEFORE COMBINING DEXTROMETHORPHAN AND RELATED COMBINATION PRODUCTS WITH:
Cold, cough, or allergy medication, stimulants, antidepressants, antihypertensives, digitalis or

other heart medication, diuretics, or MAO (monoamine oxidase inhibitors) drugs. Ingestion of caffeinated beverages (coffee, tea, caffeine-containing soft drinks) while taking dextromethorphan-containing medication can result in agitation and insomnia.

PREGNANCY OR BREASTFEEDING:
Dextromethorphan use by a nursing mother should be considered a potential risk for a nursing child as the drug will be passed on to the infant in the mother's milk. In all cases, a physician should be consulted.

PRECAUTIONS FOR CHILDREN:
In general, dextromethorphan is not advised for children under 6. Administer dextromethorphan to infants or children only when consulting a physician and follow instructions on medication (see above).

55+ **PRECAUTIONS FOR SENIORS:**
Seniors generally don't eliminate drugs as efficiently as younger persons, and should avoid high dosages. Use of dextromethorphan medications by seniors can lead to cardiac arrhythmia (irregular pulse and heartbeat). In addition, seniors are more likely to experience stimulant effects of the drug.

SPECIAL WARNINGS:
Do not use for control of chronic cough related to conditions such as emphysema, asthma, or smoking, or if coughs are producing excessive secretions. If cough is accompanied by high fever, rash, nausea or vomiting, or persistent headache, use only if directed by your doctor.

Q U I C K F A C T S

Antihistamines: Because antihistamines often cause drowsiness, you should avoid activities or tasks such as driving, or other operations which require alertness, coordination, dexterity or quick reflexes while taking medications which include antihistamines—such as chlorpheniramine maleate as active ingredients.

Alcohol: Some dextromethorphan-containing medications contain various amounts of alcohol. Check label of any cough medication if concerned about ingestion of alcohol.

Sugar/Sweeteners: Some dextromethorphan-containing medications contain various amounts of sugar, sucrose, glucose, and/or artificial sweeteners such as aspartame, saccharin, sorbitol. Check label of cough medication before selecting, if concerned about diabetes and ingestion of sugar or artificial sweeteners.

ADDITIONAL WARNING:

Abuse/Dependency: Reports indicate a rising rate of abuse of dextromethorphan-containing medications, particularly among teens. Sufficient data has not yet been collected, however, to determine the abuse and dependency potential of dextromethorphan-containing medications.

INFORM YOUR DOCTOR BEFORE TAKING DEXTROMETHORPHAN AND RELATED COMBINATION PRODUCTS IF YOU HAVE:

Allergies to: any sympathomimetic drug, aspirin or other salicylates, or if you have diabetes, thyroid condition, or urinary difficulty. If you anticipate any surgery requiring general or spinal anesthesia within 2 months of taking dextromethorphan medication, inform your doctor.

ACTIVE INGREDIENTS:

DEXTROMETHORPHAN HYDROBROMIDE AND VARIOUS ANTIHISTAMINE COMBINATIONS

BRAND NAMES:

- DIMETAPP DM ELIXIR
  (combination with phenylpropanolamine hydrochloride and brompheniramine maleate—also contains saccharin, sorbitol)
- PRIMATUSS COUGH MIXTURE 4 LIQUID
  (combination with chlorpheniramine maleate—contains alcohol, sorbitol, sucrose)
- SCOT-TUSSIN DM LIQUID
  (combination with chlorpheniramine maleate)
- TRICODENE SUGAR-FREE
  (combination with chlorpheniramine maleate—also contains sorbitol)

See also: Brompheniramine maleate, chlorpheniramine maleate, phenylephrine hydrochloride

Q U I C K F A C T S

SYMPTOMS RELIEVED:
Cough and nasal congestion associated with common cold, and minor throat and bronchial irritations.

HOW TO TAKE:
Comes in tablet, capsule, and liquid forms.
Swallow tablet or capsule with liquid.
Do not crush or chew timed-release tablets.
Antihistamines can cause gastrointestinal (GI) irritation and should be taken with food or following meal.

USUAL ADULT DOSE:
Dosage varies per product and active ingredient formulation. Follow product dosage instructions.

QUICK FACTS

USUAL CHILD DOSE:
Do not administer to children under 6 unless under direction of physician. Dosage may vary based on infant or child's age.

OVERDOSE SYMPTOMS:
Nervous agitation, severe anxiety, insomnia (sleeplessness), hallucinations, tremors, convulsions, nausea, vomiting, cardiac arrhythmia (irregular pulse and heartbeat). If you suspect an overdose, immediately seek medical attention.

SIDE EFFECTS:
No serious effects in most cases of common use, however, drowsiness is a common side effect produced by antihistamines. Less common side effects include nasal dryness, dizziness, nausea, and mild insomnia palpitations, insomnia. In rare cases, more severe side effects may result, including: painful and frequent urination, hypertension, and heart palpitations. In these cases, discontinue medication and call your doctor immediately.

CHECK WITH YOUR DOCTOR OR PHARMACIST BEFORE COMBINING DEXTROMETHORPHAN AND RELATED COMBINATION PRODUCTS WITH:
Cold, cough, or allergy medication, stimulants, antidepressants, antihypertensives, digitalis or other heart medication, diuretics, or MAO (monoamine oxidase inhibitors) drugs. Ingestion of caffeinated beverages (coffee, tea, caffeine-containing soft drinks) while taking dextromethorphan-containing medication can result in agitation and insomnia.

PREGNANCY OR BREASTFEEDING:
Dextromethorphan use by a nursing mother should be considered a potential risk for a nursing child as the drug will be passed on to the infant in the mother's milk. In all cases, a physician should be consulted.

PRECAUTIONS FOR CHILDREN:
In general, dextromethorphan is not advised for children under 6. Administer dextromethorphan to infants or children only when consulting a physician and follow instructions on medication (see above).

PRECAUTIONS FOR SENIORS:
Seniors generally don't eliminate drugs as efficiently as younger persons, and should avoid high dosages. Use of dextromethorphan medications by seniors can lead to cardiac arrhythmia (irregular pulse and heartbeat). In addition, seniors are more likely to experience stimulant effects of the drug.

SPECIAL WARNINGS:
Do not use continuously for longer than 3 months. Do not use dextromethorphan medications containing tartrazine if you are intolerant or hypersensitive to aspirin. Allergic reactions, including bronchial asthma, have occurred in susceptible individuals.

Antihistamines: Because antihistamines often cause drowsiness, you should avoid activities or tasks such as driving, or other operations which require alertness, coordination, dexterity or quick reflexes while taking medications which include antihistamines as active ingredients.

QUICK FACTS

ADDITIONAL WARNING:
Abuse/Dependency: Reports indicate a rising rate of abuse of dextromethorphan-containing medications, particularly among teens. Sufficient data has not yet been collected, however, to determine the abuse and dependency potential of dextromethorphan-containing medications.

INFORM YOUR DOCTOR BEFORE TAKING DEXTROMETHORPHAN IF YOU HAVE:
Allergies to: any sympathomimetic drug, aspirin or other salicylates, or if you have diabetes, thyroid condition, or urinary difficulty. If you anticipate any surgery requiring general or spinal anesthesia within 2 months of taking dextromethorphan medication, inform your doctor.

ACTIVE INGREDIENTS:

DEXTROMETHORPHAN HYDROBROMIDE AND VARIOUS DECONGESTANT COMBINATIONS

BRAND NAMES:

- CODIMAL DM SYRUP (combination with phenylephrine hydrochloride, pyrilamine, also contains menthol, saccharin, sorbitol)
- DIMETAPP DM ELIXIR (combination with phenylpropanolamine hydrochloride and brompheniramine maleate—also contains saccharin, sorbitol)
- ROBITUSSIN PEDIATRIC COUGH & COLD LIQUID (combination with phenylephrine hydrochloride—also contains saccharin, sorbitol)
- SNAPLETS–DM GRANULES (combination with phenylephrine hydrochloride)
- TRICODENE PEDIATRIC COUGH & COLD LIQUID (combination with phenylephrine hydrochloride)

See also: Brompheniramine maleate, chlorpheniramine maleate, phenylephrine hydrochloride

SYMPTOMS RELIEVED:

Cough and nasal congestion associated with common cold, and minor throat and bronchial irritations.

HOW TO TAKE:

Comes in tablet, capsule, liquid, and chewable forms. Swallow with liquid. Do not crush or chew timed-release tablets.

QUICK FACTS

USUAL ADULT DOSE:
Dosage varies per product and active ingredient formulation. Follow product dosage instructions.

USUAL CHILD DOSE:
Do not administer to children under 6 unless under direction of physician. Dosage may vary based on infant or child's age.

OVERDOSE SYMPTOMS:
Nervous agitation, severe anxiety, insomnia (sleeplessness), hallucinations, tremors, convulsions, nausea, vomiting, cardiac arrhythmia (irregular pulse and heartbeat). If you suspect an overdose, immediately seek medical attention.

SIDE EFFECTS:
No serious effects in most cases of common use. Less common side effects include nasal dryness, dizziness, nausea, and mild insomnia palpitations, insomnia. In rare cases, more severe side effects may result, including: painful and frequent urination, hypertension, and heart palpitations. In these cases, discontinue medication and call your doctor immediately.

CHECK WITH YOUR DOCTOR OR PHARMACIST BEFORE COMBINING DEXTROMETHORPHAN AND RELATED COMBINATION PRODUCTS WITH:
Cold, cough, or allergy medication, stimulants, antidepressants, antihypertensives, digitalis or other heart medication, diuretics, or MAO (monoamine oxidase inhibitors) drugs. Ingestion of caffeinated beverages (coffee, tea, caffeine-containing soft drinks) while taking dextromethorphan-containing medication can result in agitation and insomnia.

PREGNANCY OR BREASTFEEDING:
Dextromethorphan use by a nursing mother should be considered a potential risk for a nursing child as the drug will be passed on to the infant in the mother's milk. In all cases, a physician should be consulted.

PRECAUTIONS FOR CHILDREN:
In general, dextromethorphan is not advised for children under 6. Administer dextromethorphan to infants or children only when consulting a physician and follow instructions on medication (see above).

55+

PRECAUTIONS FOR SENIORS:
Seniors generally don't eliminate drugs as efficiently as younger persons, and should avoid high dosages. Use of dextromethorphan medications by seniors can lead to cardiac arrhythmia (irregular pulse and heartbeat). In addition, seniors are more likely to experience stimulant effects of the drug.

SPECIAL WARNINGS:
Do not use continuously for longer than 3 months. Do not use dextromethorphan medications containing tartrazine if you are intolerant or hypersensitive to aspirin. Allergic reactions, including bronchial asthma, have occurred in susceptible individuals.

ADDITIONAL WARNING:
Abuse/Dependency: Reports indicate a rising rate of abuse of dextromethorphan-containing medications, particularly among teens. Sufficient data has not yet been collected, however, to

Q U I C K F A C T S

determine the abuse and dependency potential of dextromethorphan-containing medications.

INFORM YOUR DOCTOR BEFORE TAKING DEXTROMETHORPHAN IF YOU HAVE:
Allergies to: any sympathomimetic drug, aspirin or other salicylates, or if you have diabetes, thyroid condition, or urinary difficulty. If you anticipate any surgery requiring general or spinal anesthesia within 2 months of taking dextromethorphan medication, inform your doctor.

ACTIVE INGREDIENT:
DIPHENHYDRAMINE HYDROCHLORIDE

BRAND NAMES:
- BENYLIN COUGH (also contains ammonium chloride, sodium citrate, alcohol, menthol, glucose, sucrose, saccharin)
- BYDRAMINE (also contains alcohol)
- DIPHEN COUGH (also contains ammonium chloride, sodium citrate, alcohol, sugar, menthol, sorbitol, sucrose, raspberry flavor)
- UNI-BENT COUGH (also contains alcohol)

Note: *Diphenhydramine* is an antihistamine which is also used as a sleep aid. For information on these applications, see the Quick Facts sections under Antihistamines and Sleep Aids.

SYMPTOMS RELIEVED:
Nasal congestion, runny nose, itchy and watery eyes, sneezing, scratchy throat, and irritate sinuses due to common cold, sinusitis, hay fever and other upper respiratory allergies.

HOW TO TAKE:
Comes in syrup form. Diphenhydramine and other antihistamines can cause gastrointestinal (GI) irritation and should be taken with food or following meal.

USUAL ADULT DOSE:
25 milligrams 6 times per day, not to exceed 150 milligrams in a 24 hour period.

USUAL CHILD DOSE:
For children 6 to 12: 12.5 milligrams 6 times per day, not to exceed 75 milligrams in a 24 hour period.

For children 2 to 6: 6.25 milligrams 6 times per day, not to exceed 25 milligrams in a 24 hour period.

Do not administer to children under 2 unless under direction of physician. Dosage may vary based on infant or child's age.

OVERDOSE SYMPTOMS:
Nervous agitation, severe anxiety, insomnia (sleeplessness), hallucinations, tremors, convulsions, nausea, vomiting, cardiac arrhythmia (irregular pulse and heartbeat). If you suspect an overdose, immediately seek medical attention.

SIDE EFFECTS:
No serious effects in most cases of common use. Less common side effects include nasal dryness, dizziness, nausea, and mild insomnia palpitations, insomnia. In rare cases, more severe side effects may result, including: painful and frequent urination, hypertension, and heart palpitations. In these cases, discontinue medication and call your doctor immediately.

CHECK WITH YOUR DOCTOR OR PHARMACIST BEFORE COMBINING DIPHENHYDRAMINE WITH:
Cold, cough, or allergy medication, stimulants, antidepressants, antihypertensives, digitalis or other heart medication, diuretics, or MAO (monoamine oxidase inhibitors) drugs. Ingestion of caffeinated beverages (coffee, tea, caffeine-containing soft drinks) while taking diphenhydramine-containing medication can result in agitation and insomnia.

PREGNANCY OR BREASTFEEDING:
Diphenhydramine use by a nursing mother should be considered a potential risk for a nursing child as the drug will be passed on to the infant in the mother's milk. In all cases, a physician should be consulted.

PRECAUTIONS FOR CHILDREN:
In general, diphenhydramine is not advised for children under 6. Administer diphenhydramine to infants or children only when consulting a physician and follow instructions on medication (see above).

55+

PRECAUTIONS FOR SENIORS:
Seniors generally don't eliminate drugs as efficiently as younger persons, and should avoid high dosages. Use of diphenhydramine medications by seniors can lead to urinary difficulties. In addition, seniors are more likely to experience drowsiness effects of the drug.

SPECIAL WARNINGS:
Because antihistamines often cause drowsiness, you should avoid activities or tasks such as driving, or other operations which require alertness, coordination, dexterity or quick reflexes.

INFORM YOUR DOCTOR BEFORE TAKING DIPHENHYDRAMINE IF YOU HAVE:
Allergies to: any sympathomimetic drug, aspirin or other salicylates, or if you have diabetes, thyroid condition, or urinary difficulty. If you anticipate any surgery requiring general or spinal anesthesia within 2 months of taking diphenhydramine medication, inform your doctor.

QUICK FACTS

ACTIVE INGREDIENTS:

GUAIFENESIN AND DEXTROMETHORPHAN HYDROBROMIDE

℞ **BRAND NAMES:**

Liquid:

- BENYLIN EXPECTORANT LIQUID (also contains alcohol, saccharin, menthol, sucrose)
- CHERACOL D COUGH LIQUID (also contains alcohol, fructose, sucrose)
- DIABETIC TUSSIN DM (also contains saccharin, methylparaben, menthol)
- GUIATUSSIN WITH DEXTROMETHORPHAN LIQUID (also contains alcohol)
- HALOTUSSIN–DM LIQUID (also contains corn syrup, menthol, saccharin, sucrose, parabens)
- HALOTUSSIN–DM SUGAR FREE LIQUID (also contains saccharin, sorbitol, parabens)
- MYTUSSIN DM LIQUID (also contains alcohol)
- ROBITUSSIN–DM LIQUID (also contains saccharin, glucose, high fructose corn syrup)
- SAFE TUSSIN 30 LIQUID
- NALDECON SENIOR DX LIQUID (also contains saccharin, sorbitol)
- KOLEPHRIN GG/DM LIQUID (also contains glucose, saccharin, sucrose)
- VICKS PEDIATRIC FORMULA 44E LIQUID (also contains sorbitol, sucrose)

Syrup:

- EXTRA ACTION COUGH SYRUP (also contains alcohol, corn syrup, saccharin, sucrose)
- GENATUSS DM SYRUP (also contains sucrose)
- RHINOSYN-DMX SYRUP
- ROBAFEN DM SYRUP (also contains alcohol, sugar, menthol, sorbitol, parabens)

- TOLU-SED DM SYRUP (also contains alcohol)
- UNI-TUSSIN DM SYRUP (also contains saccharin, sucrose, methylparaben)

Tablets:

- GLYCOTUSS-DM TABLETS
- TUSS-DM TABLETS

Note: *Guaifenesin* and *dextromethorphan hydrobromide* are also active ingredient in other multisymptom antitussive/expectorant medications which are formulated with other active ingredients.

SYMPTOMS RELIEVED:
Coughs associated with common cold, flu, hay fever, and other respiratory allergies by suppressing or moderating extreme cough activity, and by loosening bronchial congestion and phlegm, resulting in more productive coughs.

HOW TO TAKE:
Comes in tablet, liquid, or syrup forms. Swallow tablet with liquid. Do not crush or chew timed-release capsules.

USUAL ADULT DOSE:
Dosage varies per product and active ingredient formulation. Follow product dosage instructions.

USUAL CHILD DOSE:
Do not administer to children under 6 unless under direction of physician. Dosage may vary based on infant or child's age.

OVERDOSE SYMPTOMS:
Nervous agitation, severe anxiety, insomnia (sleeplessness), hallucinations, tremors, convulsions, nausea, vomiting, cardiac arrhythmia

(irregular pulse and heartbeat), drowsiness, dizziness, fatigue, rash. If you suspect an overdose, immediately seek medical attention.

SIDE EFFECTS:
No serious effects in most cases of common use. Less common side effects include nasal dryness, dizziness, nausea, and mild insomnia palpitations, insomnia, gastrointestinal (GI) upset including stomach cramps and diarrhea, drowsiness and fatigue. In rare cases, more severe side effects may result, including: painful and frequent urination, hypertension, and heart palpitations. In these cases, discontinue medication and call your doctor immediately.

CHECK WITH YOUR DOCTOR OR PHARMACIST BEFORE COMBINING GUAIFENESIN AND DEXTROMETHORPHAN WITH:
Anticoagulant medications and MAO (monoamine oxidase inhibitors) drugs.

PREGNANCY OR BREASTFEEDING:
Guaifenesin and dextromethorphan use by a nursing mother should be considered a potential risk for a nursing child as the drug will be passed on to the infant in the mother's milk. In all cases, a physician should be consulted.

PRECAUTIONS FOR CHILDREN:
In general, guaifenesin and dextromethorphan are not advised for children under 2. Administer guaifenesin and dextromethorphan to infants or children only when consulting a physician and follow instructions on medication (see above).

55+ **PRECAUTIONS FOR SENIORS:**
Seniors generally don't eliminate drugs as effi-

ciently as younger persons, and should avoid high dosages.

SPECIAL WARNINGS:
Do not use for control of chronic cough related to conditions such as emphysema, asthma, or smoking, or if coughs are producing excessive secretions. If cough is accompanied by high fever, rash, nausea or vomiting, or persistent headache, use only if directed by your doctor.

ADDITIONAL WARNING:
Alcohol: Some cough/cold medications contain various amounts of alcohol. Check label of any cough medication if concerned about ingestion of alcohol.

Sugar/Sweeteners: Some cough/cold medications contain various amounts of sugar, sucrose, glucose, and/or artificial sweeteners such as aspartame, saccharin, sorbitol. Check label of cough medication before selecting, if concerned about diabetes and ingestion of sugar or artificial sweeteners.

Abuse/Dependency: Reports indicate a rising rate of abuse of dextromethorphan-containing medications, particularly among teens. Sufficient data has not yet been collected, however, to determine the abuse and dependency potential of dextromethorphan-containing medications.

INFORM YOUR DOCTOR BEFORE TAKING GUAIFENESIN AND DEXTROMETHORPHAN IF YOU HAVE:
Asthma, emphysema, or other respiratory condition, or liver impairment or liver disease.

Q U I C K F A C T S

ACTIVE INGREDIENTS:

GUAIFENESIN, DEXTROMETHORPHAN HYDROBROMIDE, AND PHENYLPROPANOLAMINE HYDROCHLORIDE

℞ **BRAND NAMES:**

- GUIACOUGH CF LIQUID (also contains alcohol, parabens, saccharin, sorbitol, sucrose)
- GUIATUSS CF LIQUID (also contains alcohol)
- NALDECON DX ADULT LIQUID (also contains saccharin, sorbitol)
- NALDELATE DX ADULT LIQUID (also contains saccharin, sorbitol)
- ROBAFEN CF LIQUID (also contains alcohol)
- ROBITUSSIN–CF LIQUID (also contains alcohol, saccharin, sorbitol)

Note: *Guaifenesin* and *dextromethorphan hydrobromide* are also active ingredient in other multi-symptom antitussive/expectorant medications which are formulated with other active ingredients.

Phenylpropanolamine hydrochloride is used as an active ingredient in decongestant and stimulant products.

SYMPTOMS RELIEVED:
Cough, nasal congestion and runny nose, itchy and watery eyes, sneezing, scratchy throat, and irritated sinuses associated with common cold, minor throat and bronchial irritations, sinusitis, hay fever and other upper respiratory allergies, by suppressing or moderating extreme cough activity, loosening bronchial congestion and phlegm—resulting in more productive coughs—and by clearing congested sinuses.

HOW TO TAKE:
Comes in liquid forms.

USUAL ADULT DOSE:
Dosage varies per product and active ingredient formulation. Follow product dosage instructions.

USUAL CHILD DOSE:
Do not administer to children under 6 unless under direction of physician. Dosage may vary based on infant or child's age.

OVERDOSE SYMPTOMS:
Nervous agitation, severe anxiety, insomnia (sleeplessness), hallucinations, tremors, convulsions, nausea, vomiting, cardiac arrhythmia (irregular pulse and heartbeat), drowsiness, dizziness, fatigue, rash. If you suspect an overdose, immediately seek medical attention.

SIDE EFFECTS:
No serious effects in most cases of common use. Less common side effects include nasal dryness, dizziness, nausea, and mild insomnia palpitations, insomnia, gastrointestinal (GI) upset including stomach cramps and diarrhea, drowsiness, and fatigue. In rare cases, more severe side effects may result, including: painful and frequent urination, hypertension, and heart palpitations. In these cases, discontinue medication and call your doctor immediately.

CHECK WITH YOUR DOCTOR OR PHARMACIST BEFORE COMBINING THESE COMBINATION PRODUCTS WITH:
Anticoagulant medications, other cold, cough, or allergy medication, stimulants, antidepressants,

antihypertensives, digitalis or other heart medication, diuretics, or MAO (monoamine oxidase inhibitors) drugs. Ingestion of caffeinated beverages (coffee, tea, caffeine-containing soft drinks) while taking phenylpropanolamine-containing medication can result in agitation and insomnia.

PREGNANCY OR BREASTFEEDING:
Use of medications containing any of the active ingredients in these products by a nursing mother should be considered a potential risk for a nursing child as the drug(s) will be passed on to the infant in the mother's milk. In all cases, a physician should be consulted.

PRECAUTIONS FOR CHILDREN:
In general, these active ingredients are not advised for children under 2. Administer to infants or children only when consulting a physician and follow instructions on medication (see above).

PRECAUTIONS FOR SENIORS:
Seniors generally don't eliminate drugs as efficiently as younger persons, and should avoid high dosages.

SPECIAL WARNINGS:
Do not use for control of chronic cough related to conditions such as emphysema, asthma, or smoking, or if coughs are producing excessive secretions. If cough is accompanied by high fever, rash, nausea or vomiting, or persistent headache, use only if directed by your doctor.

ADDITIONAL WARNING:
Alcohol: Some cough/cold medications contain

various amounts of alcohol. Check label of any cough medication if concerned about ingestion of alcohol.

Sugar/Sweeteners: Some cough/cold medications contain various amounts of sugar, sucrose, glucose, and/or artificial sweeteners such as aspartame, saccharin, sorbitol. Check label of cough medication before selecting, if concerned about diabetes and ingestion of sugar or artificial sweeteners.

Abuse/Dependency: Reports indicate a rising rate of abuse of dextromethorphan-containing medications, particularly among teens. Sufficient data has not yet been collected, however, to determine the abuse and dependency potential of dextromethorphan-containing medications.

INFORM YOUR DOCTOR BEFORE TAKING PRODUCTS CONTAINING THIS COMBINATION OF ACTIVE INGREDIENTS IF YOU HAVE:
Asthma, emphysema or other respiratory condition, liver impairment or liver disease, allergies to any sympathomimetic drug, aspirin or other salicylates, or if you have diabetes, thyroid condition, or urinary difficulty. If you anticipate any surgery requiring general or spinal anesthesia within 2 months of taking medication which contains phenylpropanolamine, inform your doctor.

QUICK FACTS

ACTIVE INGREDIENTS:

PHENYLPROPANOLAMINE AND BROMPHENIRAMINE MALEATE

BRAND NAMES:

- Bromaline Elixir (contains alcohol, saccharin, sorbitol)
- Bromanate Elixir (contains saccharin, sorbitol)
- Bromtapp Tablets
- Dimaphen Elixir (contains alcohol, saccharin, sorbitol)
- Dimetapp Elixir (contains alcohol, saccharin, sorbitol)
- Genatpp Elixir (contains saccharin, sorbitol)

SYMPTOMS RELIEVED:

Cough, nasal congestion and runny nose, itchy and watery eyes, sneezing, scratchy throat, and irritated sinuses associated with common cold, minor throat and bronchial irritations, sinusitis, hay fever and other upper respiratory allergies, by suppressing or moderating extreme cough activity, loosening bronchial congestion and phlegm—resulting in more productive coughs—and by clearing congested sinuses.

HOW TO TAKE:

Comes in tablet and liquid forms. Swallow tablets with liquid. Do not crush or chew timed-release tablets.

USUAL ADULT DOSE:

25 milligrams 3 times per day, (75 milligrams once daily for time release capsules) 1/2 hour before meals, not to exceed 75 milligrams in a 24 hour period, or as directed.

USUAL CHILD DOSE:
Do not administer to children under 6 unless under direction of physician. Dosage may vary based on infant or child's age.

OVERDOSE SYMPTOMS:
Nervous agitation, severe anxiety, insomnia (sleeplessness), hallucinations, tremors, convulsions, nausea, vomiting, cardiac arrhythmia (irregular pulse and heartbeat). If you suspect an overdose, immediately seek medical attention.

SIDE EFFECTS:
No serious effects in most cases of common use. Less common side effects include nasal dryness, dizziness, nausea, and mild insomnia palpitations, insomnia. In rare cases, more severe side effects may result, including: painful and frequent urination, hypertension, and heart palpitations. In these cases, discontinue medication and call your doctor immediately.

CHECK WITH YOUR DOCTOR OR PHARMACIST BEFORE COMBINING PHENYLPROPANOLAMINE WITH:
Cold, cough,or allergy medication, stimulants, antidepressants, antihypertensives, digitalis or other heart medication, diuretics, or MAO (monoamine oxidase inhibitors) drugs. Ingestion of caffeinated beverages (coffee, tea, caffeine-containing soft drinks) while taking phenylpropanolamine-containing medication can result in agitation and insomnia.

PREGNANCY OR BREASTFEEDING:
FDA category C. Animal studies have indicated an adverse effect on fetus, but no adequate studies have been performed on humans.

QUICK FACTS

Phenylpropanolamine use by a nursing mother should be considered a potential risk for a nursing child as the drug will be passed on to the infant in the mother's milk. In all cases, a physician should be consulted.

PRECAUTIONS FOR CHILDREN:
In general, phenylpropanolamine is not advised for children under 6. Administer phenylpropanolamine to infants or children only when consulting a physician and follow instructions on medication (see above).

55+ **PRECAUTIONS FOR SENIORS:**
Seniors generally don't eliminate drugs as efficiently as younger persons, and should avoid high dosages. Use of phenylpropanolamine medications by seniors can lead to cardiac arrhythmia (irregular pulse and heartbeat). In addition, seniors are more likely to experience stimulant effects of the drug.

SPECIAL WARNINGS:
Do not use continuously for longer than 3 months. Do not use phenylpropanolamine medications containing tartazine if you are intolerant or hypersensitive to aspirin. Allergic reactions, including bronchial asthma, have occurred in susceptible individuals.

INFORM YOUR DOCTOR BEFORE TAKING PHENYLPROPANOLAMINE IF YOU HAVE:
Allergies to: any sympathomimetic drug, aspirin or other salicylates, or if you have diabetes, thyroid condition, or urinary difficulty. If you anticipate any surgery requiring general or spinal anesthesia within 2 months of taking phenylpropanolamine medication, inform your doctor.

ACTIVE INGREDIENTS:

PHENYLPROPANOLAMINE AND CHLORPHENIRAMINE MALEATE COMBINATION WITH ACETAMINOPHEN

Q U I C K F A C T S

BRAND NAMES:

- TRIAMINICOL MULTI-SYMPTOM COUGH & COLD TABLETS (combination with caffeine)

SYMPTOMS RELIEVED:

Cough, nasal congestion and runny nose, itchy and watery eyes, sneezing, scratchy throat, and irritated sinuses associated with common cold, minor throat and bronchial irritations, sinusitis, hay fever and other upper respiratory allergies, by suppressing or moderating extreme cough activity, loosening bronchial congestion and phlegm—resulting in more productive coughs—and by clearing congested sinuses.

HOW TO TAKE:

Comes in tablet, capsule, chewable forms. Swallow with liquid. Do not crush or chew timed-release tablets.

USUAL ADULT DOSE:

25 milligrams 3 times per day, (75 milligrams once daily for timed-release capsules) 1/2 hour before meals, not to exceed 75 milligrams in a 24 hour period.

USUAL CHILD DOSE:

Do not administer to children under 6 unless under direction of physician. Dosage may vary based on infant or child's age.

OVERDOSE SYMPTOMS:

Nervous agitation, severe anxiety, insomnia

(sleeplessness), hallucinations, tremors, convulsions, nausea, vomiting, cardiac arrhythmia (irregular pulse and heartbeat). If you suspect an overdose, immediately seek medical attention.

SIDE EFFECTS:

No serious effects in most cases of common use. Less common side effects include nasal dryness, dizziness, nausea, and mild insomnia palpitations, insomnia. In rare cases, more severe side effects may result, including: painful and frequent urination, hypertension, and heart palpitations. In these cases, discontinue medication and call your doctor immediately.

CHECK WITH YOUR DOCTOR OR PHARMACIST BEFORE COMBINING PHENYLPROPANOLAMINE WITH:

Cold, cough,or allergy medication, stimulants, antidepressants, antihypertensives, digitalis or other heart medication, diuretics, or MAO (monoamine oxidase inhibitors) drugs. Ingestion of caffeinated beverages (coffee, tea, caffeine-containing soft drinks) while taking phenylpropanolamine-containing medication can result in agitation and insomnia.

PREGNANCY OR BREASTFEEDING:

Phenylpropanolamine use by a nursing mother should be considered a potential risk for a nursing child as the drug will be passed on to the infant in the mother's milk. In all cases, a physician should be consulted.

PRECAUTIONS FOR CHILDREN:

In general, phenylpropanolamine is not advised

for children under 6. Administer phenylpropanolamine to infants or children only when consulting a physician and follow instructions on medication (see above).

55+

PRECAUTIONS FOR SENIORS:
Seniors generally don't eliminate drugs as efficiently as younger persons, and should avoid high dosages. Use of phenylpropanolamine medications by seniors can lead to cardiac arrhythmia (irregular pulse and heartbeat). In addition, seniors are more likely to experience stimulant effects of the drug.

SPECIAL WARNINGS:
Do not use continuously for longer than 3 months. Do not use phenylpropanolamine medications containing tartrazine if you are intolerant or hypersensitive to aspirin. Allergic reactions, including bronchial asthma, have occurred in susceptible individuals.

INFORM YOUR DOCTOR BEFORE TAKING PHENYLPROPANOLAMINE IF YOU HAVE:
Allergies to: any sympathomimetic drug, aspirin or other salicylates, or if you have diabetes, thyroid condition, or urinary difficulty. If you anticipate any surgery requiring general or spinal anesthesia within 2 months of taking phenylpropanolamine medication, inform your doctor.

QUICK REVIEW

• DECONGESTANT •
(NASAL)

The most important considerations in choosing a decongestant are: relief of membrane congestion (usually in sinus areas) in cases of allergy, hay fever, and common cold; and potential side effects associated with these drugs.

DECONGESTANTS ARE A CLASS OF DRUGS WHICH:

- shrink swollen and irritated mucosal membranes. Decongestants function by acting on the sympathetic nervous system to constrict blood vessels. Many of these drugs can be effective in relieving nasal congestion, respiratory allergies, or sinusitis,
- often are often combined with other agents such as antihistamines, antipyretics, analgesics, antitussives, or expectorants to provide multisymptomatic relief for headaches, fever, cough, sleeplessness, and other symptoms of the common cold, flu, hay fever, and similar ailments. However, these drugs do not affect the underlying cause or course of such ailments,
- may produce side effects which can include dryness of mouth and sinuses, nervous agitation, sleeplessness, or drowsiness.

ACTIVE INGREDIENTS:

PHENYLPROPANOLAMINE AND CHLORPHENIRAMINE MALEATE

℞ **BRAND NAMES:**

- A.R.M. Caplets
- Allerest Sinus Pain Formula (combination with acetaminophen)
- Aspirin-Free Bayer Select Allergy Sinus Caplets (combination with acetaminophen)
- BC Cold-Sinus–Allergy Powder (combination with aspirin)
- Children's Allerest (also contains saccharin and sorbitol)
- Chlor-Trimeton Allergy Sinus Caplets (combination with acetaminophen)
- Chlor-Rest
- Cold-Gest Capsules
- Contac 12-Hour Capsules
- Coricidin D Tablets (combination with acetaminophen)
- Dapacin Cold Capsules (combination with acetaminophen)
- Demazin Syrup (also contains 7.5% alcohol, menthol, sugar, parabens)
- Duadacin Capsules (combination with acetaminophen)
- Gelpirin-CCF Tablets (combination with acetaminophen and guaifenesin)
- Gencold Capsules
- Histosal Tablets (combination with acetaminophen and caffeine)
- Maximum Strength Tylenol Allergy Sinus (combination with acetaminophen)
- Naldecon Pediatric Syrup/Drops (also contains sorbitol)

Q U I C K F A C T S

- Naldelate Pediatric Syrup (also contains sorbitol)
- Nalgest Pediatric Syrup/Drops (also contains sorbitol)
- Pyrroxate (combination with acetaminophen)
- Rescon Liquid (also contains 7.5% alcohol, menthol, sugar, parabens)
- Silaminic Cold Syrup (also contains 7.5% alcohol, menthol, sugar, parabens)
- Sinapils Tablets (combination with acetaminophen and caffeine)
- Sinarest Extra Strength Tablets (combination with acetaminophen)
- Sinulin (combination with acetaminophen)
- Teldrin 12-Hour Allergy Relief
- Temazin Cold Syrup (also contains 7.5% alcohol, menthol, sugar, parabens)
- Thera-Hist Syrup (also contains sorbitol and sucrose)
- Tri-Nefrin
- Tri-Phen-Chlor Pediatric Syrup/Drops (also contains sorbitol)
- Tri-Phen-Mine Pediatric Syrup/Drops (also contains sorbitol)
- Triaminic
- Triaminicin Cold, Allergy, Sinus Tablets (combination with acetaminophen)
- Triaminicol Multi-Symptom Cough & Cold Tablets (combination with acetaminophen and caffeine)

HOW TO TAKE:
Comes in tablet, capsule, chewable forms. Swallow with liquid. Do not crush or chew timed-release tablets. Phenylpropanolamine can cause GI irritation and should be taken with food or following meal.

USUAL ADULT DOSE:
25 milligrams 3 times per day, (75 milligrams once daily for time release capsules) 1/2 hour before meals, not to exceed 75 milligrams in a 24 hour period.

USUAL CHILD DOSE:
Do not administer to children under 6 unless under direction of physician. Dosage may vary based on infant or child's age.

OVERDOSE SYMPTOMS:
Nervous agitation, severe anxiety, insomnia (sleeplessness), hallucinations, tremors, convulsions, nausea, vomiting, cardiac arrhythmia (irregular pulse and heartbeat). If you suspect an overdose, immediately seek medical attention.

SIDE EFFECTS:
No serious effects in most cases of common use. Less common side effects include nasal dryness, dizziness, nausea, and mild insomnia palpitations, insomnia. In rare cases, more severe side effects may result, including: painful and frequent urination, hypertension, and heart palpitations. In these cases, discontinue medication and call your doctor immediately.

CHECK WITH YOUR DOCTOR OR PHARMACIST BEFORE COMBINING PHENYLPROPANOLAMINE WITH:
Stimulants, antidepressants, antihypertensives, digitalis or other heart medication, diuretics, or MAO (monoamine oxidase inhibitors) drugs. Ingestion of caffeinated beverages (coffee, tea, caffeine-containing soft drinks) while taking phenylpropanolamine-containing medication can result in agitation and insomnia.

QUICK FACTS

PREGNANCY OR BREASTFEEDING:
Phenylpropanolamine use by a nursing mother should be considered a potential risk for a nursing child as the drug will be passed on to the infant in the mother's milk. In all cases, a physician should be consulted.

PRECAUTIONS FOR CHILDREN:
In general, phenylpropanolamine is not advised for children under 6. Administer to infants or children only when consulting a physician.

55+

PRECAUTIONS FOR SENIORS:
Seniors generally don't eliminate drugs as efficiently as younger persons, and should avoid high dosages. Use of phenylpropanolamine medications by seniors can lead to cardiac arrhythmia (irregular pulse and heartbeat). In addition, seniors are more likely to experience stimulant effects of the drug.

SPECIAL WARNINGS:
Do not use continuously for longer the 3 months. Do not use phenylpropanolamine medications containing tartazine if you are intolerant or hypersensitive to aspirin. Allergic reactions, including bronchial asthma, have occurred in susceptible individuals.

INFORM YOUR DOCTOR BEFORE TAKING PHENYLPROPANOLAMINE IF YOU HAVE:
Allergies to: any sympathomimetic drug, aspirin or other salicylates, diabetes, thyroid condition, urinary difficulty. If you anticipate any surgery requiring general or spinal anesthesia within 2 months of taking phenylpropanolamine medication, inform your doctor.

ACTIVE INGREDIENT:

CAMPHOR

BRAND NAMES:

- MENTHOLATUM CHERRY CHEST RUB FOR KIDS (combination with menthol, eucalyptus oil—also contains fragrance, petrolatum, steareth-2, titanium dioxide)
- MENTHOLATUM OINTMENT (combination with menthol, eucalyptus oil—also contains fragrance, petrolatum, titanium dioxide)
- VICKS VAPORUB–CREAM (combination with menthol, eucalyptus oil—also contains cedarleaf oil, nutmeg oil, special petrolatum, spirits of turpentine, thymol)
- VICKS VAPORUB–OINTMENT (combination with menthol, eucalyptus oil—also contains carbomer 954, cedarleaf oil, cetyl alcohol, cetyl palminate, dimethicone, glycerin, imidazoliyl urea, isopropyl palminate, methylparaben, nutmeg oil, stearate, propylparaben, sodium hydroxide, spirits of turpentine, stearic acid, stearyl alcohol, thymol, titanium dioxide)

SYMPTOMS RELIEVED:
Nasal, sinus, and chest congestion, cough, and minor aches and pains of muscles associated with common cold, head cold, and flu.

HOW TO USE:
Comes in ointment and cream forms. Apply to affected areas. These products are for external use only. Do not swallow. Avoid contact with eyes while applying.

USUAL ADULT DOSE:
See specific product instructions. Generally,

Q U I C K F A C T S

apply externally to chest, throat, or below nostrils not more than 3 to 4 times per day, or as directed by your doctor. In all cases follow specific product instructions.

USUAL CHILD DOSE:
For ages 2 to 12: Apply same as adult, or as directed by your doctor. In all cases follow specific product instructions.

Only apply to children under 2 under doctor's supervision or direction. In all cases follow specific product instructions.

OVERDOSE SYMPTOMS:
None known.

SIDE EFFECTS:
No serious effects in most cases of common use.

CHECK WITH YOUR DOCTOR OR PHARMACIST BEFORE COMBINING THIS PRODUCT WITH:
Any other drugs and preparations.

PREGNANCY OR BREASTFEEDING:
Safety of this drug for use during pregnancy or while nursing has not been established. In all cases you should consult your doctor before using any drug during pregnancy or while nursing.

PRECAUTIONS FOR CHILDREN:
These products should only be used with doctor's supervision or direction for children under 2. Consult your doctor and follow instructions on medication (see above).

55+ **PRECAUTIONS FOR SENIORS:**
None known.

SPECIAL WARNINGS:
Do not use these products if you are allergic to camphor, menthol, or any of the inactive ingredients contained in these products. Do not apply these products to wounds, lesions, broken, damaged, or sensitive skin. Avoid contact with eyes and mucous membranes. Do not use in mouth or nose. Unless directed by your doctor, do not use these products to treat symptoms of persistent or chronic cough, such as those associated with smoking, asthma, emphysema, or coughs with excessive phlegm.

INFORM YOUR DOCTOR BEFORE USING THESE PRODUCTS IF YOU HAVE:
Any allergies, or if you are or plan to become pregnant during time that you will be taking this product.

QUICK REVIEW

• EXPECTORANT •

The most important considerations in choosing an expectorant are: its action in increasing productivity of coughs and potential side effects associated with the drug.

EXPECTORANTS ARE A CLASS OF DRUGS WHICH:

- help to relieve the typical coughing symptoms of various allergies, colds, bronchitis, flu and other nonchronic respiratory ailments, by reducing adhesiveness of respiratory tract and increasing the productivity of coughs, thereby lessening their occurrence,
- are commonly used to give an allergy, cold, bronchitis, flu, and other nonchronic respiratory ailment-sufferer sufficient relief from coughing spasms,
- may produce side effects such as drowsiness, nasal stuffiness, dryness of mouth and sinus passages, dizziness, and common gastrointestinal (GI) irritation or distress,
- are not recommended in treating chronic and lower respiratory symptoms including asthma, and emphysema,
- are often combined with other cough-related active ingredients such as antitussives, as well as analgesics, antihistamines, and decongestants—as well as other ingredients such as alcohol, sweeteners (natural and artificial) and flavorings (natural and artificial),
- do not affect the underlying cause of the symptoms which they are designed to relieve or suppress.

ACTIVE INGREDIENT:
GUAIFENESIN

℞ **BRAND NAMES:**

Capsules:
- AMONIDRIN
- BREONESIN
- GG-CEN
- GEE-GEE
- GLYCOTUSS
- GLYTUSS
- HYTUSS/HYTUSS 2X

Liquid:
- NALDECON SENIOR EX (also contains saccharin, sorbitol)

Syrup:
- ANTI-TUSS (also contains alcohol)
- GENATUSS (also contains alcohol)
- GLYATE (also contains alcohol)
- GUIATUSS
- HALOTUSSIN (also contains alcohol)
- MALOTUSS (also contains alcohol)
- MYTUSSIN (also contains alcohol, sugar, menthol, raspberry flavor)
- RESCON–GGLIQUID (combination with phenylephrine hydrochloride—a decongestant)
- ROBITUSSIN (also contains alcohol, glucose, corn syrup, saccharin)
- SCOT-TUSSIN EXPECTORANT (also contains alcohol, saccharin, menthol, sorbitol)
- UNI-TUSSIN (also contains alcohol)

Note: *Guaifenesin* is an active ingredient in many multi-symptom antitussive/expectorant medications which are formulated with other active ingredients.

QUICK FACTS

SYMPTOMS RELIEVED:
Coughs associated with common cold, flu, hay fever, and other respiratory allergies by loosening bronchial congestion and phlegm, resulting in more productive coughs.

HOW TO TAKE:
Comes in capsule, liquid, or syrup forms. Swallow capsule with liquid. Do not crush or chew timed-release capsules.

USUAL ADULT DOSE:
100 to 400 milligrams 6 times per day, not to exceed 2.4 grams in a 24 hour period.

USUAL CHILD DOSE:
For children 6 to 12: 100 to 200 milligrams 6 times per day, not to exceed 1.2 milligrams in a 24 hour period.

For children 2 to 6 (syrup): 50 to 100 milligrams 6 times per day, not to exceed 600 milligrams in a 24 hour period.

Do not administer to children under 2 unless under direction of physician. Dosage may vary based on infant or child's age.

OVERDOSE SYMPTOMS:
Nausea and vomiting, drowsiness, dizziness, fatigue, rash. If you suspect an overdose, immediately seek medical attention.

SIDE EFFECTS:
No serious effects in most cases of common use. Less common side effects include dizziness, gastrointestinal (GI) upset including stomach cramps and diarrhea, drowsiness, fatigue.

CHECK WITH YOUR DOCTOR OR PHARMACIST BEFORE COMBINING GUAIFENESIN WITH:
Any anticoagulant medication.

PREGNANCY OR BREASTFEEDING:
Guaifenesin use by a nursing mother should be considered a potential risk for a nursing child as the drug will be passed on to the infant in the mother's milk. In all cases, a physician should be consulted.

PRECAUTIONS FOR CHILDREN:
In general, guaifenesin is not advised for children under 2. Administer guaifenesin to infants or children only when consulting a physician and follow instructions on medication (see above).

55+

PRECAUTIONS FOR SENIORS:
Seniors generally don't eliminate drugs as efficiently as younger persons, and should avoid high dosages.

SPECIAL WARNINGS:
Do not use for control of chronic cough related to conditions such as emphysema, asthma, or smoking, or if coughs are producing excessive secretions. If cough is accompanied by high fever, rash, nausea or vomiting, or persistent headache, use only if directed by your doctor.

ADDITIONAL WARNING:
Alcohol: Some guaifenesin-containing medications contain various amounts of alcohol. Check label of any cough medication if concerned about ingestion of alcohol.

Sugar/Sweeteners: Some dextromethorphan-containing medications contain various amounts of

Q U I C K F A C T S

sugar, sucrose, glucose, and/or artificial sweeteners such as aspartame, saccharin, sorbitol. Check label of cough medication before selecting, if concerned about diabetes and ingestion of sugar or artificial sweeteners.

INFORM YOUR DOCTOR BEFORE TAKING GUAIFENESIN IF YOU HAVE:
Asthma, emphysema, or other respiratory condition.

ACTIVE INGREDIENTS:

GUAIFENESIN AND DEXTROMETHORPHAN HYDROBROMIDE

℞ **BRAND NAMES:**

Liquid:

- Benylin Expectorant Liquid (also contains alcohol, saccharin, menthol, sucrose)
- Cheracol D Cough Liquid (also contains alcohol, fructose, sucrose)
- Diabetic Tussin DM (also contains saccharin, methylparaben, menthol)
- Guiatussin with Dextromethorphan Liquid (also contains alcohol)
- Halotussin-DM Liquid (also contains corn syrup, menthol, saccharin, sucrose, parabens)
- Halotussin-DM Sugar Free Liquid (also contains saccharin, sorbitol, parabens)
- Kolephrin GG/DM Liquid (also contains glucose, saccharin, sucrose)
- Mytussin DM Liquid (also contains alcohol)
- Naldecon Senior DX Liquid (also contains saccharin, sorbitol)
- Robitussin–DM Liquid (also contains saccharin, glucose, high fructose corn syrup)
- Safe Tussin 30 Liquid
- Vicks Pediatric Formula 44E Liquid (also contains sorbitol, sucrose)

Syrup:

- Extra Action Cough Syrup (also contains alcohol, corn syrup, saccharin, sucrose)
- Genatuss DM Syrup (also contains sucrose)
- Rhinosyn–DMX Syrup
- Robafen DM Syrup (also contains alcohol, sugar, menthol, sorbitol, parabens)

- TOLU-SED DM SYRUP (also contains alcohol)
- UNI-TUSSIN DM SYRUP (also contains saccharin, sucrose, methylparaben)

Tablets:

- GLYCOTUSS-DM TABLETS
- TUSS–DM TABLETS

Note: *Guaifenesin* and *dextromethorphan hydrobromide* are also active ingredient in other multi-symptom antitussive/expectorant medications which are formulated with other active ingredients.

SYMPTOMS RELIEVED:
Coughs associated with common cold, flu, hay fever, and other respiratory allergies by suppressing or moderating extreme cough activity, and by loosening bronchial congestion and phlegm, resulting in more productive coughs.

HOW TO TAKE:
Comes in tablet, liquid, or syrup forms. Swallow tablet with liquid. Do not crush or chew timed-release capsules.

USUAL ADULT DOSE:
Dosage varies per product and active ingredient formulation. Follow product dosage instructions.

USUAL CHILD DOSE:
Do not administer to children under 6 unless under direction of physician. Dosage may vary based on infant or child's age.

OVERDOSE SYMPTOMS:
Nervous agitation, severe anxiety, insomnia (sleeplessness), hallucinations, tremors,

convulsions, nausea, vomiting, cardiac arrhythmia (irregular pulse and heartbeat), drowsiness, dizziness, fatigue, rash. If you suspect an overdose, immediately seek medical attention.

SIDE EFFECTS:
No serious effects in most cases of common use. Less common side effects include nasal dryness, dizziness, nausea, and mild insomnia palpitations, insomnia, gastrointestinal (GI) upset including stomach cramps and diarrhea, drowsiness and fatigue. In rare cases, more severe side effects may result, including: painful and frequent urination, hypertension, and heart palpitations. In these cases, discontinue medication and call your doctor immediately.

CHECK WITH YOUR DOCTOR OR PHARMACIST BEFORE COMBINING GUAIFENESIN AND DEXTROMETHORPHAN WITH:
Anticoagulant medications and MAO (monoamine oxidase inhibitors) drugs.

PREGNANCY OR BREASTFEEDING:
Guaifenesin and dextromethorphan use by a nursing mother should be considered a potential risk for a nursing child as the drug will be passed on to the infant in the mother's milk. In all cases, a physician should be consulted.

PRECAUTIONS FOR CHILDREN:
In general, guaifenesin and dextromethorphan are not advised for children under 2. Administer guaifenesin and dextromethorphan to infants or children only when consulting a physician and follow instructions on medication (see above).

Q U I C K F A C T S

55+ **PRECAUTIONS FOR SENIORS:**
Seniors generally don't eliminate drugs as efficiently as younger persons, and should avoid high dosages.

SPECIAL WARNINGS:
Do not use for control of chronic cough related to conditions such as emphysema, asthma, or smoking, or if coughs are producing excessive secretions. If cough is accompanied by high fever, rash, nausea or vomiting, or persistent headache, use only if directed by your doctor.

ADDITIONAL WARNING:
Alcohol: Some cough/cold medications contain various amounts of alcohol. Check label of any cough medication if concerned about ingestion of alcohol.

Sugar/Sweeteners: Some cough/cold medications contain various amounts of sugar, sucrose, glucose, and/or artificial sweeteners such as aspartame, saccharin, sorbitol. Check label of cough medication before selecting, if concerned about diabetes and ingestion of sugar or artificial sweeteners.

Abuse/Dependency: Reports indicate a rising rate of abuse of dextromethorphan-containing medications, particularly among teens. Sufficient data has not yet been collected, however, to determine the abuse and dependency potential of dextromethorphan-containing medications.

℞ **INFORM YOUR DOCTOR BEFORE TAKING GUAIFENESIN AND DEXTROMETHORPHAN IF YOU HAVE:**
Asthma, emphysema, or other respiratory condition, or liver impairment or liver disease.

DIARRHEA

QUICK REVIEW

• ANTIDIARRHEAL •

The most important considerations in choosing an antidiarrheal are: its effectiveness in short-term treatment of diarrhea, and potential side effects associated with the drug.

ANTIDIARRHEALS ARE A CLASS OF DRUGS WHICH:

- treat mild to moderate diarrhea symptoms, such as those associated with traveler or tourist diarrhea, and in the case of some products, also provides relief from chronic diarrhea caused by inflammatory bowel disease,
- act by limiting intestinal inflammation, contractions and motility, or by adsorbing (binding) certain intestinal toxins, or by absorbing fluids into fecal mass to produce firmer stools,
- should only be used for short-term symptomatic relief (unless your doctor directs otherwise), and with adequate fluid intake to prevent dehydration,
- should not be used for treatment of diarrhea resulting from more serious conditions such as toxigenic bacterial infections, or pseudomembranous enterocolitis.

ACTIVE INGREDIENT:
ATTAPULGITE

BRAND NAMES:
- DIASORB (also contains sorbitol)
- DONNAGEL (also contains saccharin, sorbitol)
- KAOPECTATE ADVANCED FORMULA (also contains sucrose—regular and peppermint flavors)
- KAOPECTATE CHILDREN'S–LIQUID (also contains sucrose, dextrose, cherry flavor)
- KAOPECTATE CHILDREN'S–CHEWABLE TABLETS (also contains sucrose, cherry flavor)
- KAOPECTATE MAXIMUM STRENGTH (also contains sucrose)
- RHEABAN MAXIMUM STRENGTH (also contains sucrose)

SYMPTOMS RELIEVED:
Mild to acute nonspecific diarrhea, including common symptoms of 'travelers' diarrhea.

Note: Not for relief of diarrhea resulting from colitis, or from severe food poisoning caused by toxigenic bacteria such as salmonella, e-coli, and shigella—see below.

HOW TO TAKE:
Comes in liquid and tablet forms. Swallow tablet(s) with liquid. Chewable tablet(s) should be chewed or allowed to dissolve in mouth.

USUAL ADULT DOSE:
2 tablets or 2 tablespoonsful (30 milliliters) as needed, not to exceed 6 doses in a 24 hour period. In all cases follow specific product instructions.

QUICK FACTS

USUAL CHILD DOSE:
Ages 6 to 12: 1 tablet or 1 tablespoonful (15 milliliters) as needed, not to exceed 6 doses in a 24 hour period.

Ages 3 to 6: 1/2 tablespoonful (7.5 milliliters) as needed, not to exceed 6 doses in a 24 hour period.

These products are generally not advised for children younger than 3, and never for infants. In all cases follow specific product instructions.

OVERDOSE SYMPTOMS:
None known.

SIDE EFFECTS:
No serious effects in most cases of common use. In some cases mild constipation may occur.

CHECK WITH YOUR DOCTOR OR PHARMACIST BEFORE COMBINING ATTAPULGITE WITH:
Any other drugs and preparations.

PREGNANCY OR BREASTFEEDING:
Safety of this drug for use during pregnancy or while nursing has not been established. In all cases you should consult your doctor before using any drug during pregnancy or while nursing.

PRECAUTIONS FOR CHILDREN:
These products are not recommended for use with children under 3 and should never be used with infants. Consult your doctor and follow instructions on medication (see above).

55+ **PRECAUTIONS FOR SENIORS:**
Seniors generally may be more prone to side effects and possible adverse effects of these products than younger individuals. Avoid high dosages as dehydration and constipation are more likely to result.

SPECIAL WARNINGS:
Do not use any of these products if you are allergic to attapulgite or any of the inactive ingredients contained in these products, or if you have an intestinal blockage. Do not use these products if you have colitis, or to treat symptoms associated with food poisoning caused by toxigenic bacteria such as salmonella, e-coli, and shigella.

ADDITIONAL WARNINGS:
Use of these products should be supplemented, in cases of acute diarrhea, with liquids to prevent electrolyte/fluid depletion or dehydration.

INFORM YOUR DOCTOR BEFORE TAKING ATTAPULGITE IF YOU HAVE:
Severe loss of fluids (dehydration).

QUICK FACTS

ACTIVE INGREDIENT:
BISMUTH SUBSALICYLATE

BRAND NAMES:
- BISMATROL (also contains saccharin)
- BISMATROL EXTRA STRENGTH
- PEPTO-BISMOL–TABLETS (also contains sodium, saccharin and cherry flavor)
- PEPTO-BISMOL/PEPTO–BISMOL MAXIMUM STRENGTH–LIQUID (also contains sodium, saccharin)

SYMPTOMS RELIEVED:
Heartburn, indigestion, mild to acute nonspecific diarrhea—including common symptoms of 'travelers' diarrhea, nausea, abdominal cramps.

HOW TO TAKE:
Comes in liquid and tablet forms. Chew tablet(s) or allow to dissolve in mouth.

USUAL ADULT DOSE:
2 tablets or 2 tablespoonsful (30 milliliters) as needed, not to exceed 8 doses in a 24 hour period. In all cases follow specific product instructions.

USUAL CHILD DOSE:
Ages 9 to 12: 1 tablet or 1 tablespoonful (15 milliliters) as needed, not to exceed 8 doses in a 24 hour period.

Ages 3 to 9: 1 teaspoonful (10 milliliters) as needed, not to exceed 8 doses in a 24 hour period.

These products are generally not advised for children younger than 3, and never for infants. In all cases follow specific product instructions.

OVERDOSE SYMPTOMS:
Severe nervous agitation, hearing loss, ringing or buzzing in ears, constipation, drowsiness, extreme fatigue, hyperventilation, rapid breathing.

SIDE EFFECTS:
No serious effects in most cases of common use, however, stools may temporarily appear gray or black during use of product. In rare cases, abdominal pain, nausea, vomiting, severe constipation, headache, sweats, confusion and disorientation may occur. In these cases, discontinue use of the product and call your doctor immediately.

CHECK WITH YOUR DOCTOR OR PHARMACIST BEFORE COMBINING BISMUTH SUBSALICYLATE WITH:
Anticoagulant medications, antidiabetic drugs such as insulin, or other salicylates—especially aspirin.

PREGNANCY OR BREASTFEEDING:
Safety of this drug for use during pregnancy or while nursing has not been established. In all cases you should consult your doctor before using any drug during pregnancy or while nursing.

PRECAUTIONS FOR CHILDREN:
These products are not recommended for use with children under 3 and should never be used with infants. Consult your doctor and follow instructions on medication (see above). See Special Warning (below) regarding Reye's syndrome.

QUICK FACTS

SPECIAL WARNING FOR CHILDREN:
Use of bismuth subsalicylate—as well as other salicylate and aspirin, in cases involving children and teenagers with influenza (flu), chicken pox, and other viral infections may be associated with development of Reye's syndrome. This rare but acute and often life-threatening condition has caused permanent brain damage in survivors.

PRECAUTIONS FOR SENIORS:
Seniors generally may be more prone to side effects and possible adverse effects of these products than younger individuals. Avoid high dosages, as severe constipation may result.

SPECIAL WARNINGS:
Do not use any of these products if you are allergic to bismuth subsalicylate, other salicylate and aspirin, or any of the inactive ingredients contained in these products.

ADDITIONAL WARNINGS:
Do not use these products if you have a sensitivity or allergy to aspirin, other salicylates, or nonsteroidal anti-inflammatory drugs (NSAIDs). Do not continue use for longer than 48 hours.

INFORM YOUR DOCTOR BEFORE TAKING BISMUTH SUBSALICYLATE IF YOU HAVE:
Severe loss of fluids (dehydration) due to diarrhea, kidney disease such as hepatitis, a history of bleeding ulcers; or if you are treating a child with a fever.

ACTIVE INGREDIENTS:
KAOLIN AND PECTIN

BRAND NAMES:
- K-C (combination with bismuth subcarbonate)
- KAODENE NON-NARCOTIC (combination with bismuth subsalicylate—also contains sucrose)
- KAOPECTOLIN
- KAO-SPEN

SYMPTOMS RELIEVED:
Mild to acute nonspecific diarrhea, including common symptoms of 'travelers' diarrhea.

Note: Not for relief of diarrhea resulting from colitis, or from severe food poisoning caused by toxigenic bacteria such as salmonella, e-coli, and shigella—see below.

HOW TO TAKE:
Comes in liquid forms.

USUAL ADULT DOSE:
2 tablespoonsful (30 milliliters) as needed, not to exceed 6 doses in a 24 hour period. In all cases follow specific product instructions.

USUAL CHILD DOSE:
Ages 6 to 12: 1 tablespoonful (15 milliliters) as needed, not to exceed 6 doses in a 24 hour period.

Ages *3 to 6:* ½ tablespoonful (7.5 milliliters) as needed, not to exceed 6 doses in a 24 hour period.

These products are generally not advised for children younger than 3, and never for infants. In all cases follow specific product instructions.

QUICK FACTS

OVERDOSE SYMPTOMS:
Fever, hallucinations, fecal impaction, dizziness, convulsions, nervous agitation, rapid pulse, coma.

SIDE EFFECTS:
Fatigue or drowsiness, increased frequency of urination, increased sweating, headache, dehydration, dizziness, constipation. In rare cases, blurry vision, nervous agitation, abdominal cramps, skin rash, hallucinations, and unusual heartbeat (rapid or slow) have been reported. In these cases, discontinue r use of the product and call your doctor immediately.

CHECK WITH YOUR DOCTOR OR PHARMACIST BEFORE COMBINING KAOLIN AND PECTIN WITH:
Antihistamines, antidepressants, analgesics, or any other drugs and preparations.

PREGNANCY OR BREASTFEEDING:
Safety of this drug for use during pregnancy or while nursing has not been established. In all cases you should consult your doctor before using any drug during pregnancy or while nursing.

PRECAUTIONS FOR CHILDREN:
These products are not recommended for use with children under 3 and should never be used with infants. Consult your doctor and follow instructions on medication (see above).

PRECAUTIONS FOR SENIORS:
Seniors generally may be more prone to side effects and possible adverse effects of these products than younger individuals. Avoid high

dosages as dizziness, drowsiness, dehydration, and constipation are more likely to result.

SPECIAL WARNINGS:
Do not use any of these products if you are allergic to kaolin and pectin or any of the inactive ingredients contained in these products, or if you have an intestinal blockage, colitis, bladder difficulties, or glaucoma.

ADDITIONAL WARNINGS:
Use of these products should be supplemented, in cases of acute diarrhea, with liquids to prevent electrolyte/fluid depletion or dehydration. You should avoid alcohol while using any of these products, as it will impede the medication's desired action and increase diarrhea.

INFORM YOUR DOCTOR BEFORE TAKING KAOLIN AND PECTIN IF YOU HAVE:
Severe loss of fluids (dehydration), glaucoma, angina, bronchitis, any form of liver or kidney disease or impairment, ulcer, fever above 101°F, heart disease, asthma, or enlarged prostate. Also inform your doctor if you anticipate any surgery requiring general or spinal anesthesia within 2 months of taking any kaolin or pectin products.

QUICK FACTS

ACTIVE INGREDIENT:

LOPERAMIDE HYDROCHLORIDE

BRAND NAMES:

- IMODIUM A-D–CAPLETS (also contains lactose)
- IMODIUM A-D–LIQUID (also contains alcohol and cherry or licorice flavor)
- KAOPECTATE II (also contains lactose)
- MAALOX ANTI-DIARRHEAL (also contains lactose)
- PEPTO DIARRHEA CONTROL (also contains alcohol, parabens, and cherry flavor)

SYMPTOMS RELIEVED:

Mild to acute nonspecific diarrhea, including common symptoms of 'travelers' diarrhea.

Note: Not for relief of diarrhea resulting from colitis, or from severe food poisoning caused by toxigenic bacteria such as salmonella, e-coli, and shigella—see below.

HOW TO TAKE:

Comes in liquid and tablet forms. Swallow tablet(s) with liquid, preferably also with food or following meal to lessen possible stomach irritation.

USUAL ADULT DOSE:

For acute symptoms: 4 milligrams after first loose bowel movement, then if required, 2 milligrams after subsequent loose bowel movements, not to exceed 8 milligrams in a 24 hour period over a two-day period. In all cases follow specific product instructions.

USUAL CHILD DOSE:

Ages 9 to 11 (60 to 95 lbs.): For acute symptoms: 2 milligrams after first loose bowel movement, then if required, 1 milligram after subsequent loose bowel movements, not to exceed 6 milligrams in a 24 hour period over a 2-day period.

Ages 6 to 8 (48 to 59 lbs.): For acute symptoms: 1 milligram after first loose bowel movement, then if required, 1 milligram after subsequent loose bowel movements, not to exceed 4 milligrams in a 24 hour period over a 2-day period.

For cases involving children younger than 6, consult your doctor. These products are generally not advised for children younger than 6, and never for infants. In all cases follow specific product instructions.

OVERDOSE SYMPTOMS:
constipation, gastrointestinal irritation, drowsiness, extreme fatigue, or depression.

SIDE EFFECTS:
No serious effects in most cases of common use. In some cases, drowsiness, dizziness, and dry mouth occur. In rarer cases, abdominal discomfort, nausea, vomiting, skin rash, have been reported. In these cases, discontinue use of the product and call your doctor immediately.

CHECK WITH YOUR DOCTOR OR PHARMACIST BEFORE COMBINING LOPERAMIDE HYDROCHLORIDE WITH:
Antibiotics—especially for treatment of colitis, or any other drugs and preparations.

PREGNANCY OR BREASTFEEDING:
Safety of this drug for use during pregnancy or while nursing has not been established. In all

Q U I C K F A C T S

cases you should consult your doctor before using any drug during pregnancy or while nursing.

PRECAUTIONS FOR CHILDREN:
These products are not recommended for use with children under 6 and should never be used with infants. Consult your doctor and follow instructions on medication (see above).

55+

PRECAUTIONS FOR SENIORS:
Seniors generally may be more prone to side effects and possible adverse effects of these products than younger individuals. Avoid high dosages.

SPECIAL WARNINGS:
Do not use any of these products if you are allergic to loperamide hydrochloride or any of the inactive ingredients contained in these products. Do not use these products if you have colitis, or to treat symptoms associated with food poisoning caused by toxigenic bacteria such as salmonella, e-coli, and shigella.

ADDITIONAL WARNINGS:
Do not continue use for longer than 48 hours. Use of these products should be supplemented, in cases of acute diarrhea, with liquids to prevent electrolyte/fluid depletion or dehydration.

INFORM YOUR DOCTOR BEFORE TAKING LOPERAMIDE HYDROCHLORIDE IF YOU HAVE:
Severe loss of fluids (dehydration) due to diarrhea, or have a liver condition or disease such as hepatitis.

EAR PREPARATIONS

QUICK REVIEW

• EAR PREPARATIONS •

The most important considerations in choosing an ear preparation are: its effectiveness in removing excessive ear wax, and method of application.

TOPICAL EAR PREPARATIONS ARE A CLASS OF PRODUCTS WHICH:

- are only intended for topical use in ear canal,
- act by loosening and emulsifying (liquefying) excessive ear wax,
- should only be used sparingly.

ACTIVE INGREDIENT:
CARBAMIDE PEROXIDE

BRAND NAMES:
- DEBROX DROPS (also contains citric acid, glycerin, propylene glycol, sodium stannate)

SYMPTOMS RELIEVED:
For occasional use in cleansing ears by softening, loosening, and removing excessive ear wax.

HOW TO TAKE:
Comes in liquid drop form with applicator. Use only with applicator. This product is intended solely for otic (ear) use. Do not swallow. Avoid contact with eyes while applying.

USUAL ADULT DOSE:
Apply to ear(s) 2 times per day, not to exceed four days of treatment, or as directed by your doctor. Do not allow applicator tip to enter or touch ear canal. Turn head sideways (so that ear is almost facing upward) and release 5 to 10 drops from applicator into ear. Drops should foam on contact with ear wax and a crackling sound may result due to release of oxygen. This is normal. Drops should remain in ear for several minutes: if uncomfortable or impractical to maintain tilted head position during that time, gently place cotton in ear. In all cases follow specific product instructions.

USUAL CHILD DOSE:
Only apply to children under 12 under doctor's supervision or direction. In all cases follow specific product instructions.

Q U I C K F A C T S

OVERDOSE SYMPTOMS:
None known.

SIDE EFFECTS:
No serious effects in most cases of common use. See Special Warnings section.

CHECK WITH YOUR DOCTOR OR PHARMACIST BEFORE COMBINING THIS PRODUCT WITH:
Any other drugs and preparations.

PREGNANCY OR BREASTFEEDING:
Safety of this drug for use during pregnancy or while nursing has not been established. In all cases you should consult your doctor before using any drug during pregnancy or while nursing.

PRECAUTIONS FOR CHILDREN:
This product should only be used with doctor's supervision or direction for children under 12. Consult your doctor and follow instructions on medication (see above).

PRECAUTIONS FOR SENIORS:
None known.

SPECIAL WARNINGS:
Do not use this product if you are allergic to carbamide peroxide or any of the inactive ingredients contained in this product, or if you are experiencing ear drainage or discharge, pain, irritation, or rash in ear(s), or feel dizzy. If your ear drum has been punctured or perforated, or if you have recently had ear surgery, only use this product under your doctor's direction. Do not use this product longer than four days

continuously. If excess ear wax remains after treatment with this product, consult your doctor.

INFORM YOUR DOCTOR BEFORE TAKING THIS PRODUCT IF YOU HAVE:

Any allergies, or if you are or plan to become pregnant during time that you will be taking this product.

EYE PREPARATIONS

QUICK REVIEW

•EYE PREPARATIONS•
•OPHTHALMIC PREPARATIONS•

The most important considerations in choosing an eye preparation are: its effectiveness in relieving eye irritation and discomfort, and method of application.

TOPICAL EYE PREPARATIONS ARE A CLASS OF PRODUCTS WHICH:

- are only intended for topical use in eyes,
- act as decongestant in eyes by constricting (shrinking) excessively dilated optic blood vessels to relieve redness and sensitivity,
- are often combined with an astringent component which helps to clear mucus from outer surface of eye,
- are usually applied as drops from eye dropper.

ACTIVE INGREDIENT:
HYDROXYPROPYL METHYLCELLULOSE
(EYES/CONTACT LENS RELIEF/TOPICAL)

BRAND NAMES:
- Clear Eyes CLR
  (combination with glycerin—also contains sorbic acid, sodium chloride)

SYMPTOMS RELIEVED:
Discomfort, irritation, blurring and dryness of eyes due to contact lense use.

HOW TO TAKE:
Comes in liquid drop form. These products are intended solely for ophthalmic (eye) use. Do not swallow. Do not allow tip of product to touch any surface.

USUAL ADULT DOSE:
This product is intended for the moistening of daily wear soft contact lenses and extended wear soft (hydrophilic) contact lenses, and may be used as needed during day, on awakening or before retiring in the evening. Squeeze 1 to 2 drops in affected eye(s) Blink 2 to 3 times to relieve eye irritation. Review product instructions thoroughly before using these products, wash hands before using product, and follow all product instructions carefully while applying.
A brief tingling sensation may be experienced on application of these products. This is normal.
In all cases follow specific product instructions.

USUAL CHILD DOSE:
Ages 12 and under: Only apply to children under

Q U I C K F A C T S

12 under doctor's supervision or direction. In all cases follow specific product instructions.

OVERDOSE SYMPTOMS:
None known.

SIDE EFFECTS:
No serious effects in most cases of common use. In some cases, increased eye irritation, blurred vision, dilation of pupils, drowsiness, lowered body temperature, nausea, dizziness, headache, nervous agitation, and slow heartbeat have been reported. In any of this cases, immediately discontinue use of product and call your doctor. See Special Warnings section.

CHECK WITH YOUR DOCTOR OR PHARMACIST BEFORE COMBINING THESE PRODUCTS WITH:
Any other drugs and preparations.

PREGNANCY OR BREASTFEEDING:
Safety of this drug for use during pregnancy or while nursing has not been established. In all cases you should consult your doctor before using any drug during pregnancy or while nursing.

PRECAUTIONS FOR CHILDREN:
These products should only be used with doctor's supervision or direction for children under 12. Consult your doctor and follow instructions on medication (see above).

PRECAUTIONS FOR SENIORS:
None known.

SPECIAL WARNINGS:
Do not use these products if you are allergic to

hydroxypropyl methylcellulose, glycerin, or any of the inactive ingredients contained in these products; if you have glaucoma or any eye disease, damage, or infection; or high blood pressure, heart disease, or any thyroid conditions. If discomfort, irritation, blurring or other symptom persists after application of this product, immediately remove contact lenses and consult your eye care professional.

INFORM YOUR DOCTOR BEFORE USING THESE PRODUCTS IF YOU HAVE:
Any allergies, or if you are or plan to become pregnant during time that you will be using these products.

QUICK FACTS

ACTIVE INGREDIENT:

NAPHAZOLINE HYDROCHLORIDE

(EYES/LUBRICANT/TOPICAL)

BRAND NAMES:

- CLEAR EYES (combination with glycerin—also contains boric acid, sodium borate)
- CLEAR EYES ACR (combination with glycerin—also contains boric acid, sodium chloride, sodium citrate)

SYMPTOMS RELIEVED:

Minor irritations, dryness and redness of eyes due to various environmental factors such as dust, smoke, pollen, ragweed, and airborne pollutants, as well as conditions associated with colds, allergies, excessive rubbing of eyes, swimming, contact lens irritation, eye strain due to close reading and writing, computer work or television viewing.

HOW TO TAKE:

Comes in liquid drop form. These products are intended solely for ophthalmic (eye) use. Do not swallow. Do not allow tip of product to touch any surface.

USUAL ADULT DOSE:

Squeeze 1 to 2 drops in affected eye(s) up to 4 times per day. Review product instructions thoroughly before using these products, wash hands before using product, and follow all product instructions carefully while applying. A brief tingling sensation may be experienced on application of these products. This is normal. In all cases follow specific product instructions.

USUAL CHILD DOSE:
Ages 12 and under: Only apply to children under 12 under doctor's supervision or direction. In all cases follow specific product instructions.

OVERDOSE SYMPTOMS:
None known.

SIDE EFFECTS:
No serious effects in most cases of common use. In some cases, increased eye irritation, blurred vision, dilation of pupils, drowsiness, lowered body temperature, nausea, dizziness, headache, nervous agitation, and slow heartbeat have been reported. In any of this cases, immediately discontinue use of product and call your doctor. See Special Warnings section.

CHECK WITH YOUR DOCTOR OR PHARMACIST BEFORE COMBINING THESE PRODUCTS WITH:
Any other drugs and preparations.

PREGNANCY OR BREASTFEEDING:
Safety of this drug for use during pregnancy or while nursing has not been established. In all cases you should consult your doctor before using any drug during pregnancy or while nursing.

PRECAUTIONS FOR CHILDREN:
These products should only be used with doctor's supervision or direction for children under 12. Consult your doctor and follow instructions on medication (see above).

PRECAUTIONS FOR SENIORS:
None known.

Q U I C K F A C T S

SPECIAL WARNINGS:
Do not use these products if you are allergic to naphazoline hydrochloride, glycerin, or any of the inactive ingredients contained in these products; if you have glaucoma or any eye disease, damage, or infection; or high blood pressure, heart disease, or any thyroid conditions. Do not use these products longer than 3 days continuously. Long-term use of these products can result in increased eye redness.

INFORM YOUR DOCTOR BEFORE USING THESE PRODUCTS IF YOU HAVE:
Any allergies, or if you are or plan to become pregnant during time that you will be using these products.

ACTIVE INGREDIENTS:

NAPHAZOLINE HYDROCHLORIDE WITH PHENIRAMINE MALEATE

(EYES/LUBRICANT/TOPICAL)

BRAND NAMES:
- NAPHCON-A
- VASOCLEAR
- VASOCON

SYMPTOMS RELIEVED:
Minor irritations, dryness and redness of eyes due to conditions associated with colds, allergies, excessive rubbing of eyes, swimming, contact lens irritation, eye strain due to close reading and writing, computer work or television viewing.

HOW TO TAKE:
Comes in liquid drop form. These products are intended solely for ophthalmic (eye) use. Do not swallow. Do not allow tip of product to touch any surface.

USUAL ADULT DOSE:
Squeeze 1 to 2 drops in affected eye(s) up to 4 times per day. Review product instructions thoroughly before using these products, wash hands before using product, and follow all product instructions carefully while applying. A brief tingling sensation may be experienced on application of these products. This is normal. In all cases follow specific product instructions.

USUAL CHILD DOSE:
Ages 12 and under: Only apply to children under 12 under doctor's supervision or direction. In all cases follow specific product instructions.

QUICK FACTS

OVERDOSE SYMPTOMS:
High blood pressure, irregular heartbeat

SIDE EFFECTS:
No serious effects in most cases of common use. In some cases, dilated pupils, drowsiness, high blood pressure, high blood sugar, increased pressure inside eyeball have been reported. In any of this cases, immediately discontinue use of product and call your doctor. See Special Warnings section.

CHECK WITH YOUR DOCTOR OR PHARMACIST BEFORE COMBINING THESE PRODUCTS WITH:
Any other drugs and preparations.

PREGNANCY OR BREASTFEEDING:
Safety of this drug for use during pregnancy or while nursing has not been established. In all cases you should consult your doctor before using any drug during pregnancy or while nursing.

PRECAUTIONS FOR CHILDREN:
These products should only be used with doctor's supervision or direction for children under 12. Consult your doctor and follow instructions on medication (see above).

PRECAUTIONS FOR SENIORS:
None known.

SPECIAL WARNINGS:
Do not use these products if you are using MAO inhibitors such as Nardil or Parnate, or if you have glaucoma or any eye disease, damage, or infection; or high blood pressure, heart disease,

or any thyroid conditions. Do not use these products longer than 3 days continuously. Long-term use of these products can result in increased eye redness.

INFORM YOUR DOCTOR BEFORE USING THESE PRODUCTS IF YOU HAVE:
Any allergies, or if you are or plan to become pregnant during time that you will be using these products.

QUICK FACTS

ACTIVE INGREDIENT:

OXYMETAZOLINE HYDROCHLORIDE

(EYES/DECONGESTANT/TOPICAL)

BRAND NAMES:

- VISINE L.R.
  (also contains boric acid, sodium borate, sodium chloride)

SYMPTOMS RELIEVED:

Minor irritations and redness of eyes due to various environmental factors such as dust, smoke, pollen, ragweed, and airborne pollutants, as well as conditions associated with colds, allergies, excessive rubbing of eyes, swimming, contact lens irritation, eye strain due to close reading and writing, computer work or television viewing.

HOW TO TAKE:

Comes in liquid drop form. These products are intended solely for ophthalmic (eye) use. Do not swallow. Do not allow tip of product to touch any surface.

USUAL ADULT DOSE:

Squeeze 1 to 2 drops in affected eye(s) up to 4 times per day. Review product instructions thoroughly before using these products, wash hands before using product, and follow all product instructions carefully while applying. A brief tingling sensation may be experienced on application of these products. This is normal. In all cases follow specific product instructions.

USUAL CHILD DOSE:

Ages 12 and under: Only apply to children under 6 under doctor's supervision or direction. In all cases follow specific product instructions.

OVERDOSE SYMPTOMS:
None known.

SIDE EFFECTS:
No serious effects in most cases of common use. In some cases, increased eye irritation, blurred vision, dilation of pupils, drowsiness, lowered body temperature, nausea, dizziness, headache, nervous agitation, and slow heartbeat have been reported. In any of this cases, immediately discontinue use of product and call your doctor. See Special Warnings section.

CHECK WITH YOUR DOCTOR OR PHARMACIST BEFORE COMBINING THESE PRODUCTS WITH:
Any other drugs and preparations.

PREGNANCY OR BREASTFEEDING:
Safety of this drug for use during pregnancy or while nursing has not been established. In all cases you should consult your doctor before using any drug during pregnancy or while nursing.

PRECAUTIONS FOR CHILDREN:
These products should only be used with doctor's supervision or direction for children under 6. Consult your doctor and follow instructions on medication (see above).

PRECAUTIONS FOR SENIORS:
None known.

SPECIAL WARNINGS:
Do not use these products if you are allergic to oxymetazoline hydrochloride or any of the inactive ingredients contained in these products; if you have glaucoma or any eye disease,

QUICK FACTS

damage, or infection; or high blood pressure, heart disease, or any thyroid conditions. Do not use these products longer than 3 days continuously. Long-term use of these products can result in increased eye redness.

INFORM YOUR DOCTOR BEFORE USING THESE PRODUCTS IF YOU HAVE:
Any allergies, or if you are or plan to become pregnant during time that you will be using these products.

ACTIVE INGREDIENTS:

PHENIRAMINE MALEATE AND NAPHAZOLINE HYDROCHLORIDE

(EYES/ANTIHISTAMINE & DECONGESTANT/ TOPICAL)

Q U I C K F A C T S

BRAND NAMES:

- OCUHIST (also contains boric acid)

SYMPTOMS RELIEVED:

Minor irritations, dryness and redness of eyes due to various environmental factors such as dust, smoke, pollen, ragweed, animal hair, dander, and airborne pollutants.

HOW TO TAKE:

Comes in liquid drop form. These products are intended solely for ophthalmic (eye) use. Do not swallow. Do not allow tip of product to touch any surface.

USUAL ADULT DOSE:

Squeeze 1 to 2 drops in affected eye(s) up to 4 times per day. Review product instructions thoroughly before using these products, wash hands before using product, and follow all product instructions carefully while applying. A brief tingling sensation may be experienced on application of these products. This is normal. In all cases follow specific product instructions.

USUAL CHILD DOSE:

Ages 12 and under: Only apply to children under 12 under doctor's supervision or direction. In all cases follow specific product instructions.

OVERDOSE SYMPTOMS:

None known.

QUICK FACTS

SIDE EFFECTS:
No serious effects in most cases of common use. In some cases, increased eye irritation, blurred vision, dilation of pupils, drowsiness, lowered body temperature, nausea, dizziness, headache, nervous agitation, and slow heartbeat have been reported. In any of this cases, immediately discontinue use of product and call your doctor. See Special Warnings section.

CHECK WITH YOUR DOCTOR OR PHARMACIST BEFORE COMBINING THESE PRODUCTS WITH:
Any other drugs and preparations.

PREGNANCY OR BREASTFEEDING:
Safety of this drug for use during pregnancy or while nursing has not been established. In all cases you should consult your doctor before using any drug during pregnancy or while nursing.

PRECAUTIONS FOR CHILDREN:
These products should only be used with doctor's supervision or direction for children under 12. Consult your doctor and follow instructions on medication (see above).

PRECAUTIONS FOR SENIORS:
None known.

SPECIAL WARNINGS:
Do not use these products if you are allergic to naphazoline hydrochloride, pheniramine maleate, or any of the inactive ingredients contained in these products; if you have glaucoma or any eye disease, damage, or infection; or high blood pressure, heart disease, or any thy-

roid conditions. Do not use these products longer than 3 days continuously. Long-term use of these products can result in increased eye redness.

INFORM YOUR DOCTOR BEFORE USING THESE PRODUCTS IF YOU HAVE:
Any allergies, or if you are or plan to become pregnant during time that you will be using these products.

Q U I C K F A C T S

ACTIVE INGREDIENTS:

POLYVINYL ALCOHOL AND POVIDONE

(EYES/LUBRICANT/TOPICAL)

BRAND NAMES:

- Murine Tears
  (also contains dextrose, potassium chloride, sodium bicarbonate, sodium chloride, sodium citrate, sodium phosphate)
- Murine Tears Plus
  (also contains dextrose, potassium chloride, sodium bicarbonate, sodium chloride, sodium citrate, sodium phosphate)

SYMPTOMS RELIEVED:

Minor irritations, dryness and redness of eyes due to various environmental factors such as dust,smoke, pollen, ragweed, animal hair, dander, and airborne pollutants.

HOW TO TAKE:

Comes in liquid drop form. These products are intended solely for ophthalmic (eye) use. Do not swallow. Do not allow tip of product to touch any surface.

USUAL ADULT DOSE:

Squeeze 1 to 2 drops in affected eye(s) up to 4 times per day. Review product instructions thoroughly before using these products, wash hands before using product, and follow all product instructions carefully while applying. A brief tingling sensation may be experienced on application of these products. This is normal. In all cases follow specific product instructions.

USUAL CHILD DOSE:
Ages 12 and under: Only apply to children under 12 under doctor's supervision or direction. In all cases follow specific product instructions.

OVERDOSE SYMPTOMS:
None known.

SIDE EFFECTS:
No serious effects in most cases of common use. In some cases, increased eye irritation, blurred vision, dilation of pupils, drowsiness, lowered body temperature, nausea, dizziness, headache, nervous agitation, and slow heartbeat have been reported. In any of this cases, immediately discontinue use of product and call your doctor. See Special Warnings section.

CHECK WITH YOUR DOCTOR OR PHARMACIST BEFORE COMBINING THESE PRODUCTS WITH:
Any other drugs and preparations.

PREGNANCY OR BREASTFEEDING:
Safety of this drug for use during pregnancy or while nursing has not been established. In all cases you should consult your doctor before using any drug during pregnancy or while nursing.

PRECAUTIONS FOR CHILDREN:
These products should only be used with doctor's supervision or direction for children under 12. Consult your doctor and follow instructions on medication (see above).

PRECAUTIONS FOR SENIORS:
None known.

Q U I C K F A C T S

SPECIAL WARNINGS:
Do not use these products if you are allergic to polyvinyl alcohol, povidone, or any of the inactive ingredients contained in these products; if you have glaucoma or any eye disease, damage, or infection; or high blood pressure, heart disease, or any thyroid conditions. Do not use these products longer than 3 days continuously. Long-term use of these products can result in increased eye redness.

INFORM YOUR DOCTOR BEFORE USING THESE PRODUCTS IF YOU HAVE:
Any allergies, or if you are or plan to become pregnant during time that you will be using these products.

ACTIVE INGREDIENT:
TETRAHYDROZOLINE HYDROCHLORIDE

BRAND NAMES:
- VISINE A.C.
  (combination with zinc sulfate—also contains boric acid, sodium chloride, sodium citrate)
- VISINE MOISTURIZING
  (combination with polyethelene glycol—also contains boric acid, sodium borate, sodium chloride)
- VISINE ORIGINAL
  (also contains boric acid, sodium chloride, sodium citrate)

SYMPTOMS RELIEVED:
Minor irritations and redness of eyes due to various environmental factors such as dust, smoke, pollen, ragweed, and airborne pollutants, as well as conditions associated with colds, allergies, excessive rubbing of eyes, swimming, contact lens irritation, eye strain due to close reading and writing, computer work or television viewing, and nonspecific conjunctivitis.

HOW TO TAKE:
Comes in liquid drop form. These products are intended solely for ophthalmic (eye) use. Do not swallow. Do not allow tip of product to touch any surface.

USUAL ADULT DOSE:
Squeeze 1 to 2 drops in affected eye(s) up to 4 times per day. Review product instructions thoroughly before using these products, wash hands before using product, and follow all product instructions carefully while applying. A brief

QUICK FACTS

tingling sensation may be experienced on application of these products. This is normal. In all cases follow specific product instructions.

USUAL CHILD DOSE:
Ages 12 and under: Only apply to children under 12 under doctor's supervision or direction. In all cases follow specific product instructions.

OVERDOSE SYMPTOMS:
None known.

SIDE EFFECTS:
No serious effects in most cases of common use. In some cases, increased eye irritation, blurred vision, dilation of pupils, drowsiness, lowered body temperature, nausea, dizziness, headache, nervous agitation, and slow heartbeat have been reported. In any of this cases, immediately discontinue use of product and call your doctor. See Special Warnings section.

CHECK WITH YOUR DOCTOR OR PHARMACIST BEFORE COMBINING THESE PRODUCTS WITH:
Any other drugs and preparations.

PREGNANCY OR BREASTFEEDING:
Safety of this drug for use during pregnancy or while nursing has not been established. In all cases you should consult your doctor before using any drug during pregnancy or while nursing.

PRECAUTIONS FOR CHILDREN:
These products should only be used with doctor's supervision or direction for children under 12. Consult your doctor and follow instructions on medication (see above).

55+ **PRECAUTIONS FOR SENIORS:**
None known.

SPECIAL WARNINGS:
Do not use these products if you are allergic to tetrahydrozoline hydrochloride, zinc sulfate, or any of the inactive ingredients contained in these products; if you have glaucoma or any eye disease, damage, or infection; or high blood pressure, heart disease, or any thyroid conditions. Do not use these products longer than 3 days continuously. Long-term use of these products can result in increased eye redness.

INFORM YOUR DOCTOR BEFORE USING THESE PRODUCTS IF YOU HAVE:
Any allergies, or if you are or plan to become pregnant during time that you will be taking these products.

FEVER REDUCER

QUICK REVIEW

• ANALGESIC •

The most important considerations in choosing an analgesic are: pain relief; anti-inflammatory activity, and allergic reaction or sensitivity to certain active ingredients.

ANALGESICS (NONNARCOTIC) ARE A CLASS OF DRUGS WHICH:

- inhibit the action of prostaglandins (hormonelike substances) in the central nervous system, thereby temporarily reducing the perception of physical pain with little loss of sensibility to other physical sensation,
- are used to temporarily alleviate symptoms such as: headache, fever, backache, sinus pain, muscle strain, menstrual pain, and similar ailments. Some analgesics, such as aspirin (acetylsalicylic acid) and ibuprofen, also provide temporary anti-inflammatory relief for ailments such as arthritis. Aspirin has also been shown to be effective as a blood thinning antiplatelet agent in reducing heart attack and stroke risk,
- can have adverse effects in some instances. Aspirin intolerance can produce allergic and anaphylactic reactions in hypersensitive and asthmatic individuals. Aspirin can also aggravate aggravate gastrointestinal conditions such as heartburn and ulcer. Long-term acetaminophen use can damage liver (hepatic) and kidney (renal) functions.

ACTIVE INGREDIENTS:
ASPIRIN AND CAFFEINE COMBINATION

BRAND NAMES:
- Anacin
- BC Powder
- Cope
- Dristan
- Excedrin
- Fendol
- Gensan

SYMPTOMS RELIEVED:
Reduction of fever; minor aches and pains such as those associated with the common cold, flu, headache, toothache, sinusitis, hay fever, and other respiratory allergies, muscular aches, backache, minor arthritis pain, menstrual discomfort.

HOW TO TAKE:
Comes in tablet, caplet, capsule, and powder forms. Swallow with liquid. Sprinkle powder over liquid, then swallow. Do not crush or chew timed-release tablets. Caffeine can cause gastrointestinal (GI) irritation and should be taken with food or following meal.

USUAL ADULT DOSE:
12.5 milligrams every 4 to 6 hours, not to exceed 25 milligrams in a 4 to 6 hour period or 75 milligrams in a 24 hour period.

USUAL CHILD DOSE:
Do not administer to children under 16 unless under direction of physician. Dosage may vary based on infant or child's age.

QUICK FACTS

OVERDOSE SYMPTOMS:
Nervous agitation, disorientation, confusion, severe headache, convulsions, GI bleeding or hemorrhage. If you suspect an overdose, immediately seek medical attention.

SIDE EFFECTS:
No serious effects in most cases of common use, however normal use of caffeine can result in common GI irritations such as heartburn and indigestion. Less common side effects include dizziness, nausea, stomach cramps, and headache.

CHECK WITH YOUR DOCTOR OR PHARMACIST BEFORE COMBINING CAFFEINE WITH:
Antacids, anticoagulants, aspirin, asthma medication, other nonsteroidal anti-inflammatory drugs (NSAIDs), tetracycline, and any other medication. Combination with acetaminophen increases risk of kidney damage. Ingestion of alcohol while taking salicylates can increase risk of GI ulceration. Avoid caffeine if you have a history of anemia. Also avoid use of caffeine, if possible, one week prior to surgery, as it may increase possibility of postoperative bleeding.

PREGNANCY OR BREASTFEEDING:
Animal studies have indicated an adverse effect on fetus, but no adequate studies have been performed on humans. No harmful effects have been reported regarding nursing infants, but caffeine use by a nursing mother should be considered a potential risk for a nursing child as the drug will be passed on to the infant in the mother's milk. In all cases, a physician should be consulted.

PRECAUTIONS FOR CHILDREN:
In general, caffeine and other NSAIDs are not advised for children under 15. Administer caffeine to infants or children only when consulting a physician and follow instructions on medication (see above).

PRECAUTIONS FOR SENIORS:
55+
Seniors generally don't eliminate drugs as efficiently as younger persons, and should avoid high dosages. Seniors (over 65) are at special risk for development of ulcers if taking caffeine in high doses. Prolonged use can also lead to kidney and liver damage.

SPECIAL WARNINGS:
Don't take caffeine medication if you are aspirin intolerant or allergic to other NSAIDs. If in doubt, always consult a pharmacist or physician. Also avoid if you have GI conditions such as gastritis, peptic ulcer, enteritis, ileitis, colitis; asthma, high blood pressure, or hematologic (bleeding) problems. Avoid alcohol while taking this or any other NSAID.

INFORM YOUR DOCTOR BEFORE TAKING CAFFEINE IF YOU HAVE:
An allergy or intolerance to aspirin or other NSAIDs, damaged or impaired renal (kidney) or hepatic (liver) functions, epilepsy, Parkinson's disease or mental illness.

QUICK REVIEW

• FEVER REDUCER •

The most important considerations in choosing a fever reducer are: its action in decreasing higher than normal body temperature and potential side effects associated with the drug.

FEVER REDUCERS ARE A CLASS OF DRUGS WHICH:

- decreases elevated body temperature by increasing the dissipation of body heat through perspiration and dilation of blood vessels, either by acting directly on the hypothalamus (the body's heat-regulating center located in the brain), or through other actions,
- include analgesics (aspirin, other salicylates, and acetaminophen) and nonsteroidal anti-inflammatory drugs (NSAIDs) such as ibuprofen, ketoprofen, and naproxen,
- do not affect the underlying cause of the symptoms which they are designed to relieve or suppress.

See also: Analgesics, Nonsteroidal Anti-Inflammatory Drugs (NSAIDs)

ACTIVE INGREDIENT:
ACETAMINOPHEN

BRAND NAMES:
Combination with pseudoephedrine hydrochloride:
- Allerest No-Drowsiness Tablets
- Allerest Sinus Pain Formula (combination with chlorpheniramine maleate)
- Bayer Select Aspirin-Free Allergy Sinus Caplets (combination with chlorpheniramine maleate)
- Bayer Select Head Cold Caplets/ Maximum Strength Sinus Pain Relief Caplets
- Coldrine Tablets
- Dristan AF (combination with caffeine)
- Dristan Cold Caplets
- Dynafed
- Excedrin Sinus Extra Strength Tablets & Caplets
- Ornex
- Sinarest
- Sine-Aid
- Sine-Off No Drowsiness Formula
- Sinutab Without Drowsiness
- Sudafed
- Tylenol (various formulations)
- Sinarest Extra Strength Tablets (combination with chlorpheniramine maleate)
- Vicks Dayquil Sinus Pressure & Pain Relief Caplets

SYMPTOMS RELIEVED:
Reduction of fever; minor aches and pains such as those associated with the common cold, flu, headache, toothache, sinusitis, hay fever, and

QUICK FACTS

other respiratory allergies, muscular aches, backache, minor arthritis pain, menstrual discomfort.

HOW TO TAKE:
Comes in tablet, chewable tablet, caplet, capsule, elixir, liquid, powder, solution, and suppository forms. Swallow tablet, capsule, or elixir with liquid. Sprinkle powder over liquid, then swallow. Follow medication instructions carefully for proper insertion of suppositories. Do not crush or chew timed-release tablet. In proper dosages in most cases, acetaminophen does not cause gastrointestinal (GI) irritation and can be taken with or without food.

USUAL ADULT DOSE:
325 to 650 milligrams every 4 to 6 hours, or 1 gram 3 to 4 times per day, not to exceed 4 grams a day.

USUAL CHILD DOSE:
4 to 5 doses per day, not to exceed 5 doses in 24 hours. Dosage varies based on infant or child's age.

OVERDOSE SYMPTOMS:
Nausea, vomiting, diaphoresis, discomfort, and malaise. In some cases, hepatic toxicity (liver poisoning) may result. If you suspect an overdose, immediately seek medical attention.

SIDE EFFECTS:
None in most cases of common use. Long-term ingestion of high dosages may increase risk of liver and kidney damage. In rare cases, extreme fatigue and drowsiness, allergic skin eruptions (rash, hives, itch), sore throat and fever,

bleeding or bruising, urinary discomfort or blood in urine, jaundiced skin or eyes may result.

CHECK WITH YOUR DOCTOR OR PHARMACIST BEFORE COMBINING ACETAMINOPHEN WITH:
Anticoagulants, aspirin, and other salicylates, Isoniazid (anti-tuberculosis) medication. Excessive ingestion of alcohol while taking acetaminophen can increase the risk of liver damage or disease (hepatic toxicity).

PREGNANCY OR BREASTFEEDING:
High dosage has in isolated cases caused anemia in mother and kidney failure in fetus. Nursing infants have shown no harmful effects.

PRECAUTIONS FOR CHILDREN:
In general, administer to infants or children only when consulting a physician and follow instructions on medication.

55+

PRECAUTIONS FOR SENIORS:
Seniors generally don't eliminate drugs as efficiently as younger persons, and should avoid high dosages.

SPECIAL WARNINGS:
Chronic alcoholics are at risk for hepatic (liver) function impairment if taking high dosages of acetaminophen.

INFORM YOUR DOCTOR BEFORE TAKING ACETAMINOPHEN IF YOU HAVE:
Liver or kidney disease or damage, an allergy to acetaminophen, or hypoglycemia.

QUICK FACTS

ACTIVE INGREDIENTS:
ACETAMINOPHEN AND ASPIRIN

BRAND NAMES:
- Extra Strength Excedrin
- Goody's Extra Strength Headache Powders

SYMPTOMS RELIEVED:
Reduction of fever; minor aches and pains such as those associated with the common cold, flu, headache, toothache, sinusitis, hay fever, and other respiratory allergies, muscular aches, backache, minor arthritis pain, menstrual discomfort.

HOW TO TAKE:
Comes in tablet, chewable tablet, caplet, capsule, and powder forms. Swallow tablet or capsule with liquid. Sprinkle powder over liquid, then swallow. Do not crush or chew timed-release tablet. Although acetaminophen does not normally cause GI irritation, aspirin can—as a result these medications should be taken with food.

USUAL ADULT DOSE:
Minor aches and pains: 325 to 650 milligrams every 4 hours or as needed, not to exceed 4 grams a day. For extra strength products, dosage may range to 500 milligrams every 3 hours to 1,000 milligrams every 6 hours.

USUAL CHILD DOSE:
4 to 5 doses per day, not to exceed 5 doses in 24 hours. Dosage varies based on infant or child's age.

OVERDOSE SYMPTOMS:
Nausea, vomiting, diaphoresis, diarrhea, discom-

fort, fever, impaired vision, sweats, bloody urine, abnormal thirst, nervous agitation, and malaise. In some cases, hepatic toxicity (liver poisoning), or capillary and other hematological abnormalities may result. If you suspect an overdose, immediately seek medical attention.

SIDE EFFECTS:

Aspirin: None in most cases of common use, however normal aspirin use can result in common gastrointestinal (GI) irritations such as heartburn and indigestion. Aspirin affects the hypothalamus, resulting in dilation of small blood vessels in skin. Low dosages may reduce risk of blood clotting as aspirin inhibits clotting of small blood cells. Aspirin use may however contribute to anemia in anemic individuals.

Acetaminophen: Long-term ingestion of high dosages of acetaminophen may increase risk of liver and kidney damage. In rare cases, extreme fatigue and drowsiness, allergic skin eruptions (rash, hives, itch), sore throat and fever, bleeding or bruising, urinary discomfort or blood in urine, jaundiced skin or eyes may result.

CHECK WITH YOUR DOCTOR OR PHARMACIST BEFORE COMBINING ACETAMINOPHEN/ASPIRIN COMBINATION WITH:

Anticoagulants, aspirin, and other salicylates, tetracycline, cellulose-based laxatives, Isoniazid (anti-tuberculosis) medication. Excessive ingestion of alcohol while taking acetaminophen can increase the risk of liver damage or disease (hepatic toxicity). Ingestion of alcohol while taking aspirin can increase risk of GI ulceration.

QUICK FACTS

Avoid use of medication containing aspirin if you have a history of anemia. Also avoid use of medication containing aspirin, if possible, one week prior to surgery, as aspirin may increase possibility of postoperative bleeding.

PREGNANCY OR BREASTFEEDING:
High dosage of acetaminophen has in isolated cases caused anemia in mother and kidney failure in fetus. In third trimester, use of medication containing aspirin should be discouraged. No harmful effects have been reported regarding nursing infants, but aspirin use by a nursing mother should be considered a potential risk for a nursing child as the drug will be passed on to the infant in milk. In all cases, a physician should be consulted.

PRECAUTIONS FOR CHILDREN:
In general, administer to infants or children only when consulting a physician and follow instructions on medication.

SPECIAL WARNING:
Aspirin use in children and teenagers with influenza (flu), chicken pox, and other viral infections may be associated with development of Reye's syndrome. This rare but acute and often life-threatening condition has caused permanent brain damage in survivors. Symptoms include: vomiting, lethargy, bellicosity, leading possibly to delirium and coma.

55+

PRECAUTIONS FOR SENIORS:
Seniors generally don't eliminate drugs as efficiently as younger persons, and should avoid high dosages. Aspirin use can cause GI irritation

and possibly stomach or intestinal bleeding in seniors, manifested usually by dark stools.

SPECIAL WARNINGS:

Chronic alcoholics are at risk for hepatic (liver) function impairment if taking high dosages of acetaminophen. Always check expiration date on label of medication. Do not take if medication has expired. Do not take medication containing aspirin which emits a vinegar-like odor. This indicates that it is decomposing and is unsafe for use.

INFORM YOUR DOCTOR BEFORE TAKING ACETAMINOPHEN/ASPIRIN COMBINATION IF YOU HAVE:

Liver or kidney disease or damage, an allergy to acetaminophen or aspirin, asthma, anemia, or other hematological condition, GI sensitivity, viral infection, hypoglycemia.

Q U I C K F A C T S

ACTIVE INGREDIENTS:

ACETAMINOPHEN AND CAFFEINE COMBINATION

BRAND NAMES:

- Bayer Select Maximum Strength
- Excedrin Aspirin-Free
- Fendol

SYMPTOMS RELIEVED:
Reduction of fever; minor aches and pains such as those associated with the common cold, flu, headache, toothache, sinusitis, hay fever, and other respiratory allergies, muscular aches, backache, minor arthritis pain, menstrual discomfort.

HOW TO TAKE:
Comes in tablet, caplet, capsule, and powder forms. Swallow with liquid. Sprinkle powder over liquid, then swallow. Do not crush or chew timed-release tablets. Caffeine can cause gastrointestinal (GI) irritation and should be taken with food or following a meal.

USUAL ADULT DOSE:
12.5 milligrams every 4 to 6 hours, not to exceed 25 milligrams in a 4 to 6 hour period or 75 milligrams in a 24 hour period.

USUAL CHILD DOSE:
Do not administer to children under 16 unless under direction of physician. Dosage may vary based on infant or child's age.

OVERDOSE SYMPTOMS:
Nervous agitation, disorientation, confusion, severe headache, convulsions, GI bleeding, or hemorrhage. If you suspect an overdose, seek medical attention immediately.

SIDE EFFECTS:
No serious effects in most cases of common use, however normal use of caffeine can result in common GI irritations such as heartburn and indigestion. Less common side effects include dizziness, nausea, stomach cramps, and headache.

CHECK WITH YOUR DOCTOR OR PHARMACIST BEFORE COMBINING ACETAMINOPHEN OR CAFFEINE WITH:
Antacids, anticoagulants, aspirin, asthma medication, other NSAIDs (anti-inflammatory nonsteroidal drugs), tetracycline, and any other medication.

PREGNANCY OR BREASTFEEDING:
Animal studies have indicated an adverse effect on fetus, but no adequate studies have been performed on humans. No harmful effects have been reported regarding nursing infants, but caffeine use by a nursing mother should be considered a potential risk for a nursing child as the drug will be passed on to the infant in the mother's milk. In all cases, a physician should be consulted.

PRECAUTIONS FOR CHILDREN:
In general, caffeine and other NSAIDs are not advised for children under 15. Administer caffeine to infants or children only when consulting a physician and follow instructions on medication (see above).

PRECAUTIONS FOR SENIORS:
Seniors generally don't eliminate drugs as efficiently as younger persons, and should avoid

Q U I C K F A C T S

high dosages. Seniors (over 65) are at special risk for development of ulcers if taking caffeine in high doses. Prolonged use can also lead to kidney and liver damage.

SPECIAL WARNINGS:
Don't take caffeine medication if you are aspirin intolerant or allergic to other NSAIDs. If in doubt, always consult a pharmacist or physician. Also avoid if you have GI conditions such as gastritis, peptic ulcer, enteritis, ileitis, colitis; asthma, high blood pressure, or hematologic (bleeding) problems. Avoid alcohol while taking this or any other NSAID.

INFORM YOUR DOCTOR BEFORE TAKING CAFFEINE IF YOU HAVE:
An allergy or intolerance to aspirin or other NSAIDs, damaged or impaired renal (kidney) or hepatic (liver) functions, epilepsy, Parkinson's disease or mental illness.

QUICK FACTS

ACTIVE INGREDIENTS:

ACETAMINOPHEN, CHLORPHENIRAMINE MALEATE, DEXTROMETHORPHAN HYDROBROMIDE, AND PSEUDOEPHREDINE HYDROCHLORIDE

℞ **BRAND NAMES:**

- Alka-Seltzer Plus Cold & Cough Liqui-Gels (also contains sorbitol)
- Bayer Select Flu Relief Caplets
- Co-Apap Tablets
- Comtrex Liquid (also contains alcohol, sucrose)
- Comtrex Liqui-Gels (contains sorbitol)
- Comtrex Maximum Liqui-Gels (contains sorbitol)
- Comtrex Max Strength Multi-Symptom Cold & Flu Relief Liqui-Gels
- Comtrex Maximum Strength Multi-Symptom Cold & Flu Relief Caplets and Tablets (contains parabens)
- Contac Severe Cold & Flu NightTime Liquid (also contains alcohol, saccharin, sorbitol, glucose)
- Genacol Tablets
- Kolephrin/DM Caplets
- Mapap Cold Formula Tablets
- Medi-Flu Liquid (also contains alcohol, saccharin, sorbitol, sugar)
- TheraFlu Flu Cold & Cough Powder (contains sucrose)
- TheraFlu NightTime Flu Powder (contains sucrose)
- Tylenol Children's Cold Multi-Symptom Plus Cough Liquid (also contains sorbitol, corn syrup)

QUICK FACTS

- Tylenol Multi-Symptom Cold Caplets & Tablets
- Tylenol Multi-Symptom Hot Medication Powder (combination with phenylalanine, also contains aspartame, sucrose)
- Vicks Children's NyQuil NightTime Cold/Cough Liquid (also contains sucrose)
- Vicks 44M Cold
- Flu & Cough LiquiCaps
- Vicks Pediatric Formula 44M Multi-Symptom Cough & Cold Liquid (also contains sorbitol, sucrose)

Note: *Dextromethorphan hydrobromide* is also an active ingredient in other multi-symptom antitussive/expectorant medications which are formulated with other active ingredients.

Pseudoephredine hydrochloride is a used as an active ingredient in decongestant and stimulant products.

Acetaminophen is a non-aspirin analgesic which is used primarily in pain-relief products.

Chlorpheniramine maleate is an antihistamine which is mostly used in combination with analgesic, antitussive, decongestant and expectorant active ingredients in OTC medications to provide relief of allergy, common cold, cough or flu symptoms.

SYMPTOMS RELIEVED:
Reduction of fever; minor aches and pains such as those associated with the common cold, flu, headache, toothache, sinusitis, hay fever, and other respiratory allergies, muscular aches, backache, minor arthritis pain, menstrual discomfort.

HOW TO TAKE:
Comes in tablet, caplet, capsule, and liquid forms. Swallow tablet, caplet, or capsule with liquid. Sprinkle powder over liquid, then swallow. Do not crush or chew timed-release tablet.

USUAL ADULT DOSE:
Dosage varies per product and active ingredient formulation. Follow product dosage instructions.

USUAL CHILD DOSE:
Do not administer to children under 6 unless under direction of physician. Dosage may vary based on infant or child's age.

OVERDOSE SYMPTOMS:
Nervous agitation, severe anxiety, insomnia (sleeplessness), hallucinations, tremors, convulsions, nausea, vomiting, cardiac arrhythmia (irregular pulse and heartbeat), drowsiness, dizziness, fatigue, rash. If you suspect an overdose, immediately seek medical attention.

SIDE EFFECTS:
No serious effects in most cases of common use, although antihistamines can cause drowsiness. Less common side effects include nasal dryness, dizziness, nausea, and mild insomnia palpitations, insomnia, gastrointestinal (GI) upset including stomach cramps and diarrhea, drowsiness, and fatigue. In rare cases, more severe side effects may result, including: painful and frequent urination, hypertension, and heart palpitations. In these cases, discontinue medication and call your doctor immediately. Long-term ingestion of high dosages of acetaminophen-containing products may increase risk of liver and kidney damage.

Q U I C K F A C T S

CHECK WITH YOUR DOCTOR OR PHARMACIST BEFORE COMBINING THESE COMBINATION PRODUCTS WITH:
Anticoagulant medications, other cold, cough, or allergy medication, stimulants, antidepressants, antihypertensives, digitalis or other heart medication, diuretics, or MAO (monoamine oxidase inhibitors) drugs. Ingestion of caffeinated beverages (coffee, tea, caffeine-containing soft drinks) while taking pseudoephredine-containing medication can result in agitation and insomnia.
If taking combination products which contain acetaminophen, you should avoid Isoniazid (anti-tuberculosis) medication. Excessive ingestion of alcohol while taking acetaminophen-containing medication can increase the risk of liver damage or disease (hepatic toxicity). Alcohol use may also increase possible drowsiness effect of the antihistamine in these combination products.

PREGNANCY OR BREASTFEEDING:
Use of medications containing any of the active ingredients in these products by a nursing mother should be considered a potential risk for a nursing child as the drug(s) will be passed on to the infant in the mother's milk. In all cases, a physician should be consulted.

PRECAUTIONS FOR CHILDREN:
In general, these active ingredients are not advised for children under 2.

55+ **PRECAUTIONS FOR SENIORS:**
Seniors generally don't eliminate drugs as efficiently as younger persons, and should avoid high dosages. Use of antihistamine-containing medications by seniors can lead to urinary diffi-

culties. In addition, seniors are more likely to experience potential drowsiness effects of the antihistamine in this combination.

SPECIAL WARNINGS:
Do not use for control of chronic cough related to conditions such as emphysema, asthma, or smoking, or if coughs are producing excessive secretions. If cough is accompanied by high fever, rash, nausea or vomiting, or persistent headache, use only if directed by your doctor. Because antihistamines may cause drowsiness, you should avoid activities or tasks such as driving, or other operations which require alertness, coordination, dexterity, or quick reflexes. Chronic alcoholics are at risk for hepatic (liver) function impairment if taking high dosages of acetaminophen-containing medication. Do not use medications which combine doxylamine succinate with tartrazine if you are intolerant or hypersensitive to aspirin.

ADDITIONAL WARNING:
Alcohol: Some cough/cold medications contain various amounts of alcohol. Check label of any cough medication if concerned about ingestion of alcohol.

Sugar/Sweeteners: Some cough/cold medications contain various amounts of sugar, sucrose, glucose, and/or artificial sweeteners such as aspartame, saccharin, sorbitol. Check label of cough medication before selecting, if concerned about diabetes and ingestion of sugar or artificial sweeteners.

Abuse/Dependency: Reports indicate a rising rate of abuse of dextromethorphan-containing medications, particularly among teens. Sufficient data has not yet been collected, however, to determine the abuse and dependency potential of dextromethorphan-containing medications.

INFORM YOUR DOCTOR BEFORE TAKING PRODUCTS CONTAINING THIS COMBINATION OF ACTIVE INGREDIENTS IF YOU HAVE:
Asthma, emphysema or other respiratory condition, liver impairment or liver disease, allergies to any sympathomimetic drug, aspirin or other salicylates, or if you have diabetes, thyroid condition, or urinary difficulty. If you anticipate any surgery requiring general or spinal anesthesia within 2 months of taking medication which contains pseudoephredine, inform your doctor.

ACTIVE INGREDIENTS:

ACETAMINOPHEN, DEXTROMETHORPHAN HYDROBROMIDE, DOXYLAMINE SUCCINATE, AND PSEUDOEPHREDINE HYDROCHLORIDE

℞ **BRAND NAMES:**

- Alka-Seltzer Plus NightTime Cold Liqui-Gels (also contains sorbitol)
- Genite Liquid (also contains alcohol, tartrazine)
- NyQuil Hot Therapy Powder (also contains sucrose)
- NyQuil NightTime Cold/Flu Medicine Liquid (also contains alcohol, sucrose, saccharin [cherry flavor], tartrazine [original flavor])
- Vicks NyQuil LiquiCaps

Note: *Dextromethorphan hydrobromide* is also an active ingredient in other multi-symptom antitussive/expectorant medications which are formulated with other active ingredients.

Pseudoephredine hydrochloride is a used as an active ingredient in decongestant and stimulant products.

Acetaminophen is a non-aspirin analgesic which is used primarily in pain-relief products.

Doxylamine succinate is a drowsiness-producing antihistamine which is mostly used in combination with analgesic, antitussive, decongestant, and expectorant active ingredients in OTC medications to provide nighttime relief of allergy, common cold, cough or flu symptoms. It is also used as a sleep aid.

QUICK FACTS

SYMPTOMS RELIEVED:
Reduction of fever; minor aches and pains such as those associated with the common cold, flu, headache, toothache, sinusitis, hay fever, and other respiratory allergies, muscular aches, backache, minor arthritis pain, menstrual discomfort.

HOW TO TAKE:
Comes in capsule, liquid, and powder forms. Swallow capsule with liquid. Sprinkle powder over liquid, then swallow. Do not crush or chew timed-release capsule.

USUAL ADULT DOSE:
Dosage varies per product and active ingredient formulation. Follow product dosage instructions.

USUAL CHILD DOSE:
Do not administer to children under 6 unless under direction of physician. Dosage may vary based on infant or child's age.

OVERDOSE SYMPTOMS:
Nervous agitation, severe anxiety, insomnia (sleeplessness), hallucinations, tremors, convulsions, nausea, vomiting, cardiac arrhythmia (irregular pulse and heartbeat), drowsiness, dizziness, fatigue, rash. If you suspect an overdose, immediately seek medical attention.

SIDE EFFECTS:
No serious effects in most cases of common use, although antihistamines often cause drowsiness. Less common side effects include nasal dryness, dizziness, nausea, and mild insomnia palpitations, insomnia, gastrointestinal (GI) upset including stomach cramps and diarrhea, drowsiness, and fatigue. In rare cases, more severe

side effects may result, including: painful and frequent urination, hypertension, and heart palpitations. In these cases, discontinue medication and call your doctor immediately. Long-term ingestion of high dosages of acetaminophen-containing products may increase risk of liver and kidney damage.

CHECK WITH YOUR DOCTOR OR PHARMACIST BEFORE COMBINING THESE COMBINATION PRODUCTS WITH:
Anticoagulant medications, other cold, cough, or allergy medication, stimulants, antidepressants, antihypertensives, digitalis or other heart medication, diuretics, or MAO (monoamine oxidase inhibitors) drugs. Ingestion of caffeinated beverages (coffee, tea, caffeine-containing soft drinks) while taking pseudoephredine-containing medication can result in agitation and insomnia.
If taking combination products which contain acetaminophen, you should avoid Isoniazid (anti-tuberculosis) medication. Excessive ingestion of alcohol while taking acetaminophen-containing medication can increase the risk of liver damage or disease (hepatic toxicity). Alcohol use may also increase drowsiness effect of the antihistamine doxylamine succinate in these combination products.

PREGNANCY OR BREASTFEEDING:
Use of medications containing any of the active ingredients in these products by a nursing mother should be considered a potential risk for a nursing child as the drug(s) will be passed on to the infant in the mother's milk. In all cases, a physician should be consulted.

Q U I C K F A C T S

PRECAUTIONS FOR CHILDREN:
In general, these active ingredients are not advised for children under 2. Administer to infants or children only when consulting a physician and follow instructions on medication (see above).

PRECAUTIONS FOR SENIORS:
Seniors generally don't eliminate drugs as efficiently as younger persons, and should avoid high dosages. Use of doxylamine succinate-containing medications by seniors can lead to urinary difficulties. In addition, seniors are more likely to experience drowsiness effects of doxylamine succinate.

SPECIAL WARNINGS:
Do not use for control of chronic cough related to conditions such as emphysema, asthma, or smoking, or if coughs are producing excessive secretions. If cough is accompanied by high fever, rash, nausea or vomiting, or persistent headache, use only if directed by your doctor. Because antihistamines such as doxylamine succinate often cause drowsiness, you should avoid activities or tasks such as driving, or other operations which require alertness, coordination, dexterity, or quick reflexes. Chronic alcoholics are at risk for hepatic (liver) function impairment if taking high dosages of acetaminophen-containing medication. Do not use medications which combine doxylamine succinate with tartrazine if you are intolerant or hypersensitive to aspirin. Allergic reactions, including bronchial asthma, have occurred in susceptible individuals.

ADDITIONAL WARNING:

Alcohol: Some cough/cold medications contain various amounts of alcohol. Check label of any cough medication if concerned about ingestion of alcohol.

Sugar/Sweeteners: Some cough/cold medications contain various amounts of sugar, sucrose, glucose, and/or artificial sweeteners such as aspartame, saccharin, sorbitol. Check label of cough medication before selecting, if concerned about diabetes and ingestion of sugar or artificial sweeteners.

Abuse/Dependency: Reports indicate a rising rate of abuse of dextromethorphan-containing medications, particularly among teens. Sufficient data has not yet been collected, however, to determine the abuse and dependency potential of dextromethorphan-containing medications.

INFORM YOUR DOCTOR BEFORE TAKING PRODUCTS CONTAINING THIS COMBINATION OF ACTIVE INGREDIENTS IF YOU HAVE:

Asthma, emphysema or other respiratory condition, liver impairment or liver disease, allergies to any sympathomimetic drug, aspirin or other salicylates, or if you have diabetes, thyroid condition, or urinary difficulty. If you anticipate any surgery requiring general or spinal anesthesia within 2 months of taking medication which contains pseudoephredine, inform your doctor.

QUICK FACTS

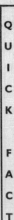

ACTIVE INGREDIENT:
IBUPROFEN

BRAND NAMES:
- Advil
- Advil Cold & Sinus Caplets
- Arthritis Foundation
- Bayer Select Pain Relief
- Dimetapp
- Dristan Sinus Caplets
- Genpril
- Ibuprohm
- Motrin
- Motrin IB Sinus Caplets
- Nupron
- Obuprin
- Sine-Aid IB Caplets (combination with pseudoephedrine hydrochloride)

SYMPTOMS RELIEVED:
Reduction of fever; minor aches and pains such as those associated with the common cold, flu, headache, toothache, sinusitis, hay fever, and other respiratory allergies, muscular aches, backache, minor arthritis pain, menstrual discomfort.

HOW TO TAKE:
Comes in tablet, caplet, and gelcap forms. Swallow with liquid. Do not crush or chew timed-release tablet. Ibuprofen can cause gastrointestinal (GI) irritation and should be taken with food or following meal.

USUAL ADULT DOSE:
Minor aches and pains: 200 milligrams every 4 to 6 hours as needed, not to exceed 1.2 grams per day.

Arthritis and related conditions: 1.2 grams to 3.2 grams per day divided into equal doses over 24 hours.

USUAL CHILD DOSE:
Always consult with a pharmacist or physician. Dosage may vary based on infant or child's age. Juvenile arthritis: 30 to 70 milligrams per day in 3 or 4 equal doses or as indicated.

Fever reduction: Maximum daily dose not to exceed 40 milligrams. Dosage should be adjusted based on initial temperature level. If less or equal to 102.5°F, 5 milligrams per dose is recommended. If temperature is greater than 102.5°F, 10 milligrams per dose is recommended.

OVERDOSE SYMPTOMS:
Nervous agitation, disorientation, confusion, severe headache, convulsions, GI bleeding or hemorrhage. If you suspect an overdose, immediately seek medical attention.

SIDE EFFECTS:
No serious effects in most cases of common use, however normal use of ibuprofen can result in common GI irritations such as heartburn and indigestion. Less common side effects include dizziness, nausea, stomach cramps, and headache.

CHECK WITH YOUR DOCTOR OR PHARMACIST BEFORE COMBINING IBUPROFEN WITH:
Antacids, anticoagulants, aspirin, asthma medication, other nonsteroidal anti-inflammatory drugs (NSAIDs), tetracycline, and any other medication. Combination with acetaminophen increases risk of kidney damage. Ingestion of alcohol while

taking ibuprofen can increase risk of GI ulceration. Avoid ibuprofen if you have a history of anemia. Also avoid use of ibuprofen, if possible, one week prior to surgery, as it may increase possibility of postoperative bleeding.

PREGNANCY OR BREASTFEEDING:
Animal studies have indicated an adverse effect on fetus, but no adequate studies have been performed on humans. No harmful effects have been reported regarding nursing infants, but ibuprofen use by a nursing mother should be considered a potential risk for a nursing child as the drug will be passed on to the infant in the mother's milk. In all cases, a physician should be consulted.

PRECAUTIONS FOR CHILDREN:
In general, ibuprofen and other NSAIDs are not advised for children under 15. Administer ibuprofen to infants or children only when consulting a physician and follow instructions on medication.

PRECAUTIONS FOR SENIORS:
Seniors generally don't eliminate drugs as efficiently as younger persons, and should avoid high dosages. Seniors (over 65) are at special risk for development of ulcers if taking ibuprofen in high doses. Prolonged use can also lead to kidney and liver damage.

SPECIAL WARNINGS:
Don't take ibuprofen medication if you are aspirin intolerant or allergic to other NSAIDs. If in doubt, always consult a pharmacist or physician. Also avoid if you have GI conditions such as

gastritis, peptic ulcer, enteritis, ileitis, colitis; asthma, high blood pressure, or hematologic (bleeding) problems. Avoid alcohol while taking this or any other NSAID.

INFORM YOUR DOCTOR BEFORE TAKING IBUPROFEN IF YOU HAVE:

An allergy or intolerance to aspirin or other NSAIDs, damaged or impaired renal (kidney) or hepatic (liver) functions, epilepsy, Parkinson's disease, or mental illness.

QUICK FACTS

ACTIVE INGREDIENT:
KETOPROFEN

BRAND NAMES:
- ACTRON
- ORUDIS

SYMPTOMS RELIEVED:
Reduction of fever; minor aches and pains such as those associated with the common cold, flu, headache, toothache, sinusitis, hay fever, and other respiratory allergies, muscular aches, backache, minor arthritis pain, menstrual discomfort.

HOW TO TAKE:
Comes in tablet forms. Swallow with liquid. Do not crush or chew timed-release tablets. Ketoprofen can cause gastrointestinal (GI) irritation and should be taken with food or following meal.

USUAL ADULT DOSE:
12.5 milligrams every 4 to 6 hours, not to exceed 25 milligrams in a 4 to 6 hour period or 75 milligrams in a 24 hour period.

USUAL CHILD DOSE:
Do not administer to children under 16 unless under direction of physician. Dosage may vary based on infant or child's age.

OVERDOSE SYMPTOMS:
Nervous agitation, disorientation, confusion, severe headache, convulsions, GI bleeding or hemorrhage. If you suspect an overdose, immediately seek medical attention.

SIDE EFFECTS:
No serious effects in most cases of common use, however normal use of ketoprofen can result in common GI irritations such as heartburn and indigestion. Less common side effects include dizziness, nausea, stomach cramps, and headache.

CHECK WITH YOUR DOCTOR OR PHARMACIST BEFORE COMBINING KETOPROFEN WITH:
Antacids, anticoagulants, aspirin, asthma medication, other nonsteroidal anti-inflammatory drugs (NSAIDs), tetracycline, and any other medication. Combination with acetaminophen increases risk of kidney damage. Ingestion of alcohol while taking ketoprofen can increase risk of GI ulceration. Avoid ketoprofen if you have a history of anemia. Also avoid use of ketoprofen, if possible, one week prior to surgery, as it may increase possibility of postoperative bleeding.

PREGNANCY OR BREASTFEEDING:
Animal studies have indicated an adverse effect on fetus, but no adequate studies have been performed on humans. No harmful effects have been reported regarding nursing infants, but ketoprofen use by a nursing mother should be considered a potential risk for a nursing child as the drug will be passed on to the infant in the mother's milk. In all cases, a physician should be consulted.

PRECAUTIONS FOR CHILDREN:
In general, ketoprofen and other NSAIDs are not advised for children under 15. Administer

Q U I C K F A C T S

ketoprofen to infants or children only when consulting a physician and follow instructions on medication (see above).

55+ **PRECAUTIONS FOR SENIORS:**
Seniors generally don't eliminate drugs as efficiently as younger persons, and should avoid high dosages. Seniors (over 65) are at special risk for development of ulcers if taking ketoprofen in high doses. Prolonged use can also lead to kidney and liver damage.

SPECIAL WARNINGS:
Don't take ketoprofen medication if you are aspirin intolerant or allergic to other NSAIDs. If in doubt, always consult a pharmacist or physician. Also avoid if you have GI conditions such as gastritis, peptic ulcer, enteritis, ileitis, colitis; asthma, high blood pressure, or hematologic (bleeding) problems. Avoid alcohol while taking this or any other NSAID.

INFORM YOUR DOCTOR BEFORE TAKING KETOPROFEN IF YOU HAVE:
An allergy or intolerance to aspirin or other NSAIDs, damaged or impaired renal (kidney) or hepatic (liver) functions, epilepsy, Parkinson's disease, or mental illness.

FIRST AID

QUICK REVIEW

• ANESTHETIC •
(TOPICAL)

The most important considerations in choosing a topical or local anesthetic are: its action in partially or completely eliminating the sensation of physical pain in one part of the body, and potential side effects associated with the drug.

TOPICAL ANESTHETICS ARE A CLASS OF DRUGS WHICH:

- act in some combination of the following ways: by limiting the production of energy in nerve cells—thereby reducing nerve impulses and related sensation of pain, by increasing the body's production of organic compounds which limit the transmission of pain messages through synapses, or by reducing nerve cell energy production, thereby limiting the cell's production of nerve impulses. These actions are not completely understood due to varying effects of topical anesthetics and the complex nature of the body's central nervous system (CNS),
- especially when used in high dosages or for long treatment periods, may be absorbed into the blood stream through the skin or mucous membranes, increasing the anesthetic's effectiveness but also the incidence and probability of adverse side effects,
- do not affect the underlying cause of the symptoms which they are designed to relieve or suppress.

ACTIVE INGREDIENT:
BENZOCAINE

BRAND NAMES:
- AMERICAINE FIRST AID (also contains benzethonium chloride)
- CHIGGEREX (also contains aloe vera, olive oil, camphor, menthol, methylparaben)
- CHIGGER-TOX (also contains benzyl benzoate)
- DERMOPLAST (also contains menthol, methylparaben, aloe, lanolin)
- FOILLE MEDICATED FIRST AID (also contains chloroxylenol, benzyl alcohol, EDTA)
- STING-KILL (also contains menthol, tartrazine, isopropyl alcohol)

SYMPTOMS RELIEVED:
Irritation, itching, and rashes due to minor skin conditions, discomfort of plant poisonings such as poison ivy, sumac, and oak, sunburn, common nonpoisonous insect bites and insect stings, and minor burns.

HOW TO USE:
Comes in aerosol, cream, liquid, lotion, and spray forms. Apply to affected area as needed, or in the case of creams and ointments, to a bandage or gauze pad before applying to skin. In all cases follow specific product instructions. These products are intended solely for external, topical use. Do not under any conditions ingest internally or use in eyes. Always wash hands before and after use.

USUAL ADULT DOSE:
Dosage varies according to product and condition. Use the minimum recommended dose in

QUICK FACTS

order to avoid side effects or complications. In all cases follow specific product instructions.

USUAL CHILD DOSE:
Do not use in children or infants under 1 year of age. Dosage varies according to product and condition. Use the minimum recommended dose in order to avoid side effects or complications. In all cases follow specific product instructions.

OVERDOSE SYMPTOMS:
Convulsions, agitation, euphoria, drowsiness, disorientation or dizziness, blurred vision, vomiting, numbness, hypotension—possibly leading to respiratory arrest; or cardiac arrhythmia (irregular pulse and heartbeat) leading to cardiac arrest or collapse. If you suspect an overdose, immediately seek medical attention.

SIDE EFFECTS:
No serious effects in most cases of common use. However, you may experience an increase in photosensitivity reaction resulting in higher risk of sunburn and other related skin damage. In this case, avoid unnecessary exposure to sun. In rare cases, some individuals have experienced swelling of skin or in mouth and throat, or rash, burning or stinging sensations, or pronounced skin sensitivity. In these cases, discontinue application or use of the product and call your doctor immediately.

CHECK WITH YOUR DOCTOR OR PHARMACIST BEFORE COMBINING BENZOCAINE WITH:
Sulfa drugs or Class I antiarrhythmia drugs (drugs used to treat irregular heartbeat, such as tocainide, mexiletine).

PREGNANCY OR BREASTFEEDING:
Safety of this drug for use during pregnancy or while nursing has not been established. In all cases you should consult your doctor before using any drug during pregnancy or while nursing.

PRECAUTIONS FOR CHILDREN:
In general, use caution when applying benzocaine products with children under 6, as the risk of product absorption through skin is greater. Do not use in children or infants under 1 year of age. Consult your doctor and follow instructions on medication (see above).

55+
PRECAUTIONS FOR SENIORS:
Seniors generally may be more prone to side effects and possible adverse effects of these products than younger individuals. Avoid high dosages.

SPECIAL WARNINGS:
Do not use any of these products if you are allergic to any topical anesthetic. Avoid applying more than three days continuously to same area, as this may lead to excess absorption. Do not continue overall use more than one week if condition hasn't improved.

INFORM YOUR DOCTOR BEFORE TAKING BENZOCAINE IF YOU HAVE:
Allergies to: any topical anesthetic, or if you have skin infection or skin conditions such as psoriasis or eczema.

QUICK FACTS

ACTIVE INGREDIENT:

BENZOCAINE (ETHYL AMINOBENZOATE)

℞ **BRAND NAMES:**

- AMERICAINE FIRST AID (also contains benzethonium chloride)
- AEROCAINE (also contains benzethonium chloride)
- AEROTHERM (also contains benzethonium chloride)
- ANBESOL (also contains phenol, povidone-iodine, alcohol, camphor, menthol, glycerin)
- BICOZENE–CREAM (also contains resorcinol, castor oil, glycerin)
- BOIL-EASE–OINTMENT (also contains camphor, lanolin, eucalyptus, menthol, petrolatum, phenol)
- CHIGGER-TOX–LIQUID (also contains benzyl benzoate)
- DERMOPLAST–LOTION (also contains menthol, methylparaben, aloe, lanolin)
- CHIGGEREX–LIQUID (also contains aloe vera, olive oil, camphor, menthol, methylparaben)
- DERMOPLAST–LOTION (also contains menthol, methylparaben, aloe, lanolin)
- DETANE (also contains carbomer 940)
- FOILLE–SPRAY (also contains chloroxylenol)
- FOILLE PLUS–AEROSOL (also contains chloroxylenol, alcohol)
- FOILLE MEDICATED FIRST AID–AEROSOL & OINTMENT (also contains chloroxylenol, benzyl alcohol, EDTA)
- LANACANE–CREAM (also contains benzethonium chloride, aloe, parabens, castor oil, glycerin, isopropyl alcohol)

- LANACANE–SPRAY (also contains benzethonium chloride, ethanol, aloe extract)
- SOLARCAINE–AEROSOL (also contains triclosan, SD alcohol, tocopheryl acetate)
- SOLARCAINE–LOTION (also contains triclosan, mineral oil, alcohol, aloe extract, tocopheryl acetate, menthol, camphor, parabens, EDTA)
- STING-KILL (also contains menthol, tartrazine, isopropyl alcohol)

SYMPTOMS RELIEVED:
Irritation, itching, and rashes due to minor skin conditions, discomfort of plant poisonings such as poison ivy, sumac, and oak, sunburn, common nonpoisonous insect bites and insect stings, and minor burns.

HOW TO USE:
Comes in aerosol, cream, liquid, lotion, and spray forms. Apply to affected area as needed, or in the case of creams and ointments, to a bandage or gauze pad before applying to skin. In all cases follow specific product instructions. These products are intended solely for external, topical use. Do not under any conditions ingest internally or use in eyes. Always wash hands before and after use.

USUAL ADULT DOSE:
Dosage varies according to product and condition. Use the minimum recommended dose in order to avoid side effects or complications. In all cases follow specific product instructions.

USUAL CHILD DOSE:
Do not use in children or infants under 1 year of age. Dosage varies according to product and

QUICK FACTS

condition. Use the minimum recommended dose in order to avoid side effects or complications. In all cases follow specific product instructions.

OVERDOSE SYMPTOMS:
Convulsions, agitation, euphoria, drowsiness, disorientation or dizziness, blurred vision, vomiting, numbness, hypotension—possibly leading to respiratory arrest; or cardiac arrhythmia (irregular pulse and heartbeat) leading to cardiac arrest or collapse. If you suspect an overdose, immediately seek medical attention.

SIDE EFFECTS:
No serious effects in most cases of common use. However, you may experience an increased in photosensitivity reaction resulting in higher risk of sunburn and other related skin damage. In this case, avoid unnecessary exposure to sun. In rare cases, some individuals have experienced swelling of skin or in mouth and throat, or rash, burning or stinging sensations, or pronounced skin sensitivity. In these cases, discontinue application or use of the product and call your doctor immediately.

CHECK WITH YOUR DOCTOR OR PHARMACIST BEFORE COMBINING BENZOCAINE WITH:
Sulfa drugs or Class I antiarrhythmia drugs (tocainide, mexiletine).

PREGNANCY OR BREASTFEEDING:
Benzocaine use by a nursing mother should be considered a potential risk for a nursing child as the drug will be passed on to the infant in the mother's milk. In all cases, a physician should be consulted.

PRECAUTIONS FOR CHILDREN:
In general, use caution when applying benzocaine products with children under 6, as the risk of product absorption through skin is greater. Do not use in children or infants under 1 year of age. Consulting your doctor and follow instructions on medication (see above).

55+ **PRECAUTIONS FOR SENIORS:**
Seniors generally may be more prone to side effects and possible adverse effects of these products than younger individuals. Avoid high dosages.

SPECIAL WARNINGS:
Do not use any of these products if you are allergic to any topical anesthetic. Avoid applying more than three days continuously to same area, as this may lead to excess absorption. Do not continue overall use more than one week if condition hasn't improved.

INFORM YOUR DOCTOR BEFORE TAKING BENZOCAINE IF YOU HAVE:
Allergies to: any topical anesthetic, or if you have skin infection or skin conditions such as psoriasis or eczema.

QUICK FACTS

ACTIVE INGREDIENT:

DIPHENHYDRAMINE HYDROCHLORIDE

℞ **BRAND NAMES:**

- BENADRYL–CREAM (also contains parabens)
- BENADRYL–NON-AEROSOL SPRAY (also contains alcohol)
- BENADRYL 2% MAXIMUM STRENGTH–CREAM (also contains parabens)
- BENADRYL 2% MAXIMUM STRENGTH–NON-AEROSOL SPRAY (also contains alcohol)
- CALADRYL–CREAM (also contains calamine, parabens, camphor)
- CALADRYL–LOTION (also contains calamine, camphor, alcohol)
- CALADRYL–SPRAY (also contains calamine, alcohol, camphor)
- CALADRYL CLEAR (also contains alcohol)
- CALA-GEN (also contains alcohol)
- DI-DELAMINE (also contains tripelennamine hydrochloride, benzalkonium chloride, menthol, EDTA)
- STING-EZE (also contains camphor, phenol, benzocaine, eucalyptol)
- ZIRADRYL (also contains zinc oxide, alcohol, camphor, parabens)

Note: *Diphenhydramine* is also used as: a sleep aid, as an antihistamine, and as an active ingredient in combination with other drugs in antitussive (anti-cough) products.

SYMPTOMS RELIEVED:

Irritation, itching and rashes due to minor skin conditions, discomfort of plant poisonings such as poison ivy, sumac, and oak, sunburn, common nonpoisonous insect bites and insect stings, and minor burns.

HOW TO USE:
Comes in concentrate, cream, gel, lotion, and spray forms. Wash and dry affected area before applying. Apply product as needed or as directed by your doctor.

In all cases follow specific product instructions. These products are intended solely for topical use. Do not under any conditions ingest internally or use in eyes. Always wash hands thoroughly before and after use.

USUAL ADULT DOSE:
See above. Use the minimum recommended dose in order to avoid side effects or complications. In all cases follow specific product instructions.

USUAL CHILD DOSE:
Do not use in cases involving children under 2 unless under medical supervision. For all others, use the minimum recommended dose in order to avoid side effects or complications. In all cases follow specific product instructions.

OVERDOSE SYMPTOMS:
No known overdose symptoms.

SIDE EFFECTS:
No serious effects in most cases of common use. However, in rare cases, individuals have experienced mild skin irritation. In these cases, discontinue application or use of the product and call your doctor immediately.

CHECK WITH YOUR DOCTOR OR PHARMACIST BEFORE COMBINING UNDECYLENIC ACID WITH:
Any other topical preparations, or any other antihistamine product.

QUICK FACTS

PREGNANCY OR BREASTFEEDING:
Safety of this drug for use during pregnancy or while nursing has not been established. In all cases you should consult your doctor before using any drug during pregnancy or while nursing.

PRECAUTIONS FOR CHILDREN:
These products should not be used to treat children under 2 unless under close medical supervision.

PRECAUTIONS FOR SENIORS:
No special precautions are known for seniors.

SPECIAL WARNINGS:
Do not use any other diphenhydramine products while using any of these topical products. Do not use any of these products if you are allergic to diphenhydramine hydrochloride or any topical antifungal medication, or any of the inactive ingredients listed, or if you have any form of liver disease or damage. Do not use longer than one week continuously.

ADDITIONAL WARNINGS:
Do not use these topical products to treat chicken pox, measles, blisters, or extensive skin areas, unless directed by your doctor.

INFORM YOUR DOCTOR BEFORE USING DIPHENHYDRAMINE IF YOU HAVE:
Urinary difficulty, glaucoma, ulcer, or if you are pregnant. If you anticipate any surgery requiring general or spinal anesthesia within 2 months of taking diphenhydramine-containing medication, inform your doctor.

QUICK FACTS

ACTIVE INGREDIENT:
LIDOCAINE

BRAND NAMES:
- BACTINE ANTISEPTIC ANESTHETIC (also contains benzalkonium chloride, EDTA)
- MEDI-QUIK (also contains benzalkonium chloride, benzyl alcohol)
- PRO-TECH (also contains povidone iodine)
- SOLARCAINE ALOE EXTRA BURN RELIEF–CREAM (also contains aloe, EDTA, lanolin, lanolin oil, camphor, propylparaben, eucalyptus oil, menthol, tartrazine)
- SOLARCAINE ALOE EXTRA BURN RELIEF–GEL (also contains aloe vera, glycerin, EDTA, isopropyl alcohol, menthol, diazolidinyl urea, tartrazine)
- SOLARCAINE ALOE EXTRA BURN RELIEF–SPRAY (also contains aloe vera gel, glycerin, EDTA, diazolidinyl urea, vitamin E, parabens)
- UNGUENTINE PLUS (also contains phenol, parabens, mineral oil, EDTA)
- ZILACTIN (also contains alcohol)

SYMPTOMS RELIEVED:
Irritation, itching, and rashes due to minor skin conditions, discomfort of plant poisonings such as poison ivy, sumac, and oak, sunburn, common nonpoisonous insect bites and insect stings, and minor burns.

HOW TO TAKE:
Comes in cream, gel, liquid, ointment, and spray forms. Apply to affected area as needed, or in the case of creams and ointments, to a bandage or gauze pad before applying to skin. In all cases follow specific product instructions. These

QUICK FACTS

products are intended solely for external use. Do not under any conditions ingest internally or use in eyes. Always wash hands before and after use.

USUAL ADULT DOSE:
Dosage varies according to product and condition. Use the minimum recommended dose in order to avoid side effects or complications. In all cases follow specific product instructions.

USUAL CHILD DOSE:
Do not use in children or infants under 1 year of age. Dosage varies according to product and condition. Use the minimum recommended dose in order to avoid side effects or complications.

OVERDOSE SYMPTOMS:
Convulsions, agitation, euphoria, drowsiness, disorientation or dizziness, blurred vision, vomiting, numbness, hypotension-possibly leading to respiratory arrest; or cardiac arrhythmia (irregular pulse and heartbeat) leading to cardiac arrest or collapse. If you suspect an overdose, immediately seek medical attention.

SIDE EFFECTS:
No serious effects in most cases of common use. However, you may experience an increased in photosensitivity reaction resulting in higher risk of sunburn and other related skin damage. In this case, avoid unnecessary exposure to sun. In rare cases, some individuals have experienced swelling of skin or in mouth and throat, or rash, burning or stinging sensations, or pronounced skin sensitivity. In these cases, discontinue application or use of the product and call your doctor immediately.

CHECK WITH YOUR DOCTOR OR PHARMACIST BEFORE COMBINING LIDOCAINE WITH:
Sulfa drugs or Class I antiarrhythmia drugs (drugs used to treat irregular heartbeat, such as tocainide, mexiletine).

PREGNANCY OR BREASTFEEDING:
Safety of this drug for use during pregnancy or while nursing has not been established. In all cases you should consult your doctor before using any drug during pregnancy or while nursing.

PRECAUTIONS FOR CHILDREN:
In general, use caution when applying lidocaine products with children under 6, as the risk of product absorption through skin is greater. Do not use in children or infants under 1 year of age.

PRECAUTIONS FOR SENIORS:
Seniors generally may be more prone to side effects and possible adverse effects of these products than younger individuals. Avoid high dosages.

SPECIAL WARNINGS:
Do not use any of these products if you are allergic to any topical anesthetic. Avoid applying more than three days continuously to same area, as this may lead to excess absorption. Do not continue overall use more than one week if condition hasn't improved.

INFORM YOUR DOCTOR BEFORE TAKING LIDOCAINE IF YOU HAVE:
Allergies to: any topical anesthetic, or if you have skin infection or skin conditions such as psoriasis or eczema.

QUICK REVIEW

• ANTI-ITCH •
(TOPICAL)

The most important considerations in choosing an anti-itch agent are: its effectiveness in treating and relieving skin itchiness, and potential side effects associated with the drug.

TOPICAL ANTI-ITCH AGENTS ARE A CLASS OF DRUGS WHICH:

- are only intended for topical use,
- are nonspecific in their action, and act against most causes of skin inflammation by depressing, neutralizing, or interfering with the activity of enzymes which produce skin inflammation and resultant itchiness,
- in over-the-counter (OTC) products, are primarily formulated with hydrocortisone (a topical adrenocorticoid) as the active ingredient,
- when used in high dosages or for long treatment periods, may be absorbed into the bloodstream through the skin or mucous membranes, increasing the incidence and probability of adverse side effects.

ACTIVE INGREDIENT:
BENZOCAINE

BRAND NAMES:
- AMERICAINE FIRST AID (also contains benzethonium chloride)
- CHIGGEREX (also contains aloe vera, olive oil, camphor, menthol, methylparaben)
- CHIGGER-TOX (also contains benzyl benzoate)
- DERMOPLAST (also contains menthol, methylparaben, aloe, lanolin)
- FOILLE MEDICATED FIRST AID (also contains chloroxylenol, benzyl alcohol, EDTA)
- STING-KILL (also contains menthol, tartrazine, isopropyl alcohol)

SYMPTOMS RELIEVED:
Irritation, itching, and rashes due to minor skin conditions, discomfort of plant poisonings such as poison ivy, sumac, and oak, sunburn, common nonpoisonous insect bites and insect stings, and minor burns.

HOW TO USE:
Comes in aerosol, cream, liquid, lotion, and spray forms. Apply to affected area as needed, or in the case of creams and ointments, to a bandage or gauze pad before applying to skin. In all cases follow specific product instructions. These products are intended solely for external, topical use. Do not under any conditions ingest internally or use in eyes. Always wash hands before and after use.

USUAL ADULT DOSE:
Dosage varies according to product and condition. Use the minimum recommended dose in

QUICK FACTS

order to avoid side effects or complications. In all cases follow specific product instructions.

USUAL CHILD DOSE:
Do not use in children or infants under 1 year of age. Dosage varies according to product and condition. Use the minimum recommended dose in order to avoid side effects or complications. In all cases follow specific product instructions.

OVERDOSE SYMPTOMS:
Convulsions, agitation, euphoria, drowsiness, disorientation or dizziness, blurred vision, vomiting, numbness, hypotension—possibly leading to respiratory arrest; or cardiac arrhythmia (irregular pulse and heartbeat) leading to cardiac arrest or collapse. If you suspect an overdose, immediately seek medical attention.

SIDE EFFECTS:
No serious effects in most cases of common use. However, you may experience an increase in photosensitivity reaction resulting in higher risk of sunburn and other related skin damage. In this case, avoid unnecessary exposure to sun. In rare cases, some individuals have experienced swelling of skin or in mouth and throat, or rash, burning or stinging sensations, or pronounced skin sensitivity. In these cases, discontinue application or use of the product and call your doctor immediately.

CHECK WITH YOUR DOCTOR OR PHARMACIST BEFORE COMBINING BENZOCAINE WITH:
Sulfa drugs or Class I antiarrhythmia drugs (drugs used to treat irregular heartbeat, such as tocainide, mexiletine).

PREGNANCY OR BREASTFEEDING:
Safety of this drug for use during pregnancy or while nursing has not been established. In all cases you should consult your doctor before using any drug during pregnancy or while nursing.

PRECAUTIONS FOR CHILDREN:
In general, use caution when applying benzocaine products with children under 6, as the risk of product absorption through skin is greater. Do not use in children or infants under 1 year of age. Consult your doctor and follow instructions on medication (see above).

PRECAUTIONS FOR SENIORS:
Seniors generally may be more prone to side effects and possible adverse effects of these products than younger individuals. Avoid high dosages.

SPECIAL WARNINGS:
Do not use any of these products if you are allergic to any topical anesthetic. Avoid applying more than three days continuously to same area, as this may lead to excess absorption. Do not continue overall use more than one week if condition hasn't improved.

INFORM YOUR DOCTOR BEFORE TAKING BENZOCAINE IF YOU HAVE:
Allergies to: any topical anesthetic, or if you have skin infection or skin conditions such as psoriasis or eczema.

QUICK FACTS

ACTIVE INGREDIENT:

BENZOCAINE (ETHYL AMINOBENZOATE)

℞ **BRAND NAMES:**

- AMERICAINE FIRST AID (also contains benzethonium chloride)
- AEROCAINE (also contains benzethonium chloride)
- AEROTHERM (also contains benzethonium chloride)
- ANBESOL (also contains phenol, povidone-iodine, alcohol, camphor, menthol, glycerin)
- BICOZENE–CREAM (also contains resorcinol, castor oil, glycerin)
- BOIL-EASE–OINTMENT (also contains camphor, lanolin, eucalyptus, menthol, petrolatum, phenol)
- CHIGGER-TOX–LIQUID (also contains benzyl benzoate)
- DERMOPLAST–LOTION (also contains menthol, methylparaben, aloe, lanolin)
- CHIGGEREX–LIQUID (also contains aloe vera, olive oil, camphor, menthol, methylparaben)
- DERMOPLAST–LOTION (also contains menthol, methylparaben, aloe, lanolin)
- DETANE (also contains carbomer 940)
- FOILLE–SPRAY (also contains chloroxylenol)
- FOILLE PLUS–AEROSOL (also contains chloroxylenol, alcohol)
- FOILLE MEDICATED FIRST AID–AEROSOL & OINTMENT (also contains chloroxylenol, benzyl alcohol, EDTA)
- LANACANE–CREAM (also contains benzethonium chloride, aloe, parabens, castor oil, glycerin, isopropyl alcohol)

- LANACANE–SPRAY (also contains benzethonium chloride, ethanol, aloe extract)
- SOLARCAINE–AEROSOL (also contains triclosan, SD alcohol, tocopheryl acetate)
- SOLARCAINE–LOTION (also contains triclosan, mineral oil, alcohol, aloe extract, tocopheryl acetate, menthol, camphor, parabens, EDTA)
- STING-KILL (also contains menthol, tartrazine, isopropyl alcohol)

SYMPTOMS RELIEVED:
Irritation, itching, and rashes due to minor skin conditions, discomfort of plant poisonings such as poison ivy, sumac, and oak, sunburn, common nonpoisonous insect bites and insect stings, and minor burns.

HOW TO USE:
Comes in aerosol, cream, liquid, lotion, and spray forms. Apply to affected area as needed, or in the case of creams and ointments, to a bandage or gauze pad before applying to skin. In all cases follow specific product instructions. These products are intended solely for external, topical use. Do not under any conditions ingest internally or use in eyes. Always wash hands before and after use.

USUAL ADULT DOSE:
Dosage varies according to product and condition. Use the minimum recommended dose in order to avoid side effects or complications. In all cases follow specific product instructions.

USUAL CHILD DOSE:
Do not use in children or infants under 1 year of age. Dosage varies according to product and

QUICK FACTS

Q U I C K F A C T S

condition. Use the minimum recommended dose in order to avoid side effects or complications. In all cases follow specific product instructions.

OVERDOSE SYMPTOMS:
Convulsions, agitation, euphoria, drowsiness, disorientation or dizziness, blurred vision, vomiting, numbness, hypotension-possibly leading to respiratory arrest; or cardiac arrhythmia (irregular pulse and heartbeat) leading to cardiac arrest or collapse. If you suspect an overdose, immediately seek medical attention.

SIDE EFFECTS:
No serious effects in most cases of common use. However, you may experience an increased in photosensitivity reaction resulting in higher risk of sunburn and other related skin damage. In this case, avoid unnecessary exposure to sun. In rare cases, some individuals have experienced swelling of skin or in mouth and throat, or rash, burning or stinging sensations, or pronounced skin sensitivity. In these cases, discontinue application or use of the product and call your doctor immediately.

CHECK WITH YOUR DOCTOR OR PHARMACIST BEFORE COMBINING BENZOCAINE WITH:
Sulfa drugs or Class I antiarrhythmia drugs (tocainide, mexiletine).

PREGNANCY OR BREASTFEEDING:
Benzocaine use by a nursing mother should be considered a potential risk for a nursing child as the drug will be passed on to the infant in the mother's milk. In all cases, a physician should be consulted.

PRECAUTIONS FOR CHILDREN:
In general, use caution when applying benzocaine products with children under 6, as the risk of product absorption through skin is greater. Do not use in children or infants under 1 year of age. Consulting your doctor and follow instructions on medication (see above).

PRECAUTIONS FOR SENIORS:
Seniors generally may be more prone to side effects and possible adverse effects of these products than younger individuals. Avoid high dosages.

SPECIAL WARNINGS:
Do not use any of these products if you are allergic to any topical anesthetic. Avoid applying more than three days continuously to same area, as this may lead to excess absorption. Do not continue overall use more than one week if condition hasn't improved.

INFORM YOUR DOCTOR BEFORE TAKING BENZOCAINE IF YOU HAVE:
Allergies to: any topical anesthetic, or if you have skin infection or skin conditions such as psoriasis or eczema.

QUICK FACTS

ACTIVE INGREDIENT:
DIPHENHYDRAMINE HYDROCHLORIDE

BRAND NAMES:
- BENADRYL–CREAM (also contains parabens)
- BENADRYL–NON-AEROSOL SPRAY (also contains alcohol)
- BENADRYL 2% MAXIMUM STRENGTH–CREAM (also contains parabens)
- BENADRYL 2% MAXIMUM STRENGTH–NON-AEROSOL SPRAY (also contains alcohol)
- CALADRYL–CREAM (also contains calamine, parabens, camphor)
- CALADRYL–LOTION (also contains calamine, camphor, alcohol)
- CALADRYL–SPRAY (also contains calamine, alcohol, camphor)
- CALADRYL CLEAR (also contains alcohol)
- CALA-GEN (also contains alcohol)
- DI-DELAMINE (also contains tripelennamine hydrochloride, benzalkonium chloride, menthol, EDTA)
- STING-EZE (also contains camphor, phenol, benzocaine, eucalyptol)
- ZIRADRYL (also contains zinc oxide, alcohol, camphor, parabens)

Note: *Diphenhydramine* is also used as: a sleep aid, as an antihistamine, and as an active ingredient in combination with other drugs in antitussive (anti-cough) products.

SYMPTOMS RELIEVED:
Irritation, itching, and rashes due to minor skin conditions, discomfort of plant poisonings such as poison ivy, sumac, and oak, sunburn, common nonpoisonous insect bites and insect stings, and minor burns.

HOW TO USE:

Comes in concentrate, cream, gel, lotion, and spray forms. Wash and dry affected area before applying. Apply product as needed or as directed by your doctor.

In all cases follow specific product instructions. These products are intended solely for topical use. Do not under any conditions ingest internally or use in eyes. Always wash hands thoroughly before and after use.

USUAL ADULT DOSE:

See above. Use the minimum recommended dose in order to avoid side effects or complications. In all cases follow specific product instructions.

USUAL CHILD DOSE:

Do not use in cases involving children under 2 unless under medical supervision. For all others, use the minimum recommended dose in order to avoid side effects or complications. In all cases follow specific product instructions.

OVERDOSE SYMPTOMS:

No known overdose symptoms.

SIDE EFFECTS:

No serious effects in most cases of common use. However, in rare cases, individuals have experienced mild skin irritation. In these cases, discontinue application or use of the product and call your doctor immediately.

CHECK WITH YOUR DOCTOR OR PHARMACIST BEFORE COMBINING UNDECYLENIC ACID WITH:

Any other topical preparations, or any other antihistamine product.

QUICK FACTS

PREGNANCY OR BREASTFEEDING:
Safety of this drug for use during pregnancy or while nursing has not been established. In all cases you should consult your doctor before using any drug during pregnancy or while nursing.

PRECAUTIONS FOR CHILDREN:
These products should not be used to treat children under 2 unless under close medical supervision.

PRECAUTIONS FOR SENIORS:
No special precautions are known for seniors.

SPECIAL WARNINGS:
Do not use any other diphenhydramine products while using any of these topical products. Do not use any of these products if you are allergic to diphenhydramine hydrochloride or any topical antifungal medication, or any of the inactive ingredients listed, or if you have any form of liver disease or damage. Do not use longer than one week continuously.

ADDITIONAL WARNINGS:
Do not use these topical products to treat chicken pox, measles, blisters, or extensive skin areas, unless directed by your doctor.

INFORM YOUR DOCTOR BEFORE USING DIPHENHYDRAMINE IF YOU HAVE:
Urinary difficulty, glaucoma, ulcer, or if you are pregnant. If you anticipate any surgery requiring general or spinal anesthesia within 2 months of taking diphenhydramine-containing medication, inform your doctor.

ACTIVE INGREDIENT:
LIDOCAINE

Q U I C K F A C T S

BRAND NAMES:
- BACTINE ANTISEPTIC ANESTHETIC (also contains benzalkonium chloride, EDTA)
- MEDI-QUIK (also contains benzalkonium chloride, benzyl alcohol)
- PRO-TECH (also contains povidone iodine)
- SOLARCAINE ALOE EXTRA BURN RELIEF–CREAM
- SOLARCAINE ALOE EXTRA BURN RELIEF–GEL
- SOLARCAINE ALOE EXTRA BURN RELIEF–SPRAY
- UNGUENTINE PLUS (also contains phenol, parabens, mineral oil, EDTA)
- ZILACTIN (also contains alcohol)

SYMPTOMS RELIEVED:
Irritation, itching, and rashes due to minor skin conditions, discomfort of plant poisonings such as poison ivy, sumac, and oak, sunburn, common nonpoisonous insect bites and insect stings, and minor burns.

HOW TO TAKE:
Comes in cream, gel, liquid, ointment, and spray forms. Apply to affected area as needed, or in the case of creams and ointments, to a bandage or gauze pad before applying to skin.

In all cases follow specific product instructions. These products are intended solely for external use. Do not under any conditions ingest internally or use in eyes. Always wash hands before and after use.

USUAL ADULT DOSE:
Dosage varies according to product and condition. Use the minimum recommended dose in

order to avoid side effects or complications. In all cases follow specific product instructions.

USUAL CHILD DOSE:
Do not use in children or infants under 1 year of age. Dosage varies according to product and condition. Use the minimum recommended dose in order to avoid side effects or complications. In all cases follow specific product instructions.

OVERDOSE SYMPTOMS:
Convulsions, agitation, euphoria, drowsiness, disorientation or dizziness, blurred vision, vomiting, numbness, hypotension—possibly leading to respiratory arrest; or cardiac arrhythmia (irregular pulse and heartbeat) leading to cardiac arrest or collapse. If you suspect an overdose, immediately seek medical attention.

SIDE EFFECTS:
No serious effects in most cases of common use. However, you may experience an increased in photosensitivity reaction resulting in higher risk of sunburn and other related skin damage. In this case, avoid unnecessary exposure to sun. In rare cases, some individuals have experienced swelling of skin or in mouth and throat, or rash, burning or stinging sensations, or pronounced skin sensitivity. In these cases, discontinue application or use of the product and call your doctor immediately.

CHECK WITH YOUR DOCTOR OR PHARMACIST BEFORE COMBINING LIDOCAINE WITH:
Sulfa drugs or Class I antiarrhythmia drugs (drugs used to treat irregular heartbeat, such as tocainide, mexiletine).

PREGNANCY OR BREASTFEEDING:
Safety of this drug for use during pregnancy or while nursing has not been established. In all cases you should consult your doctor before using any drug during pregnancy or while nursing.

PRECAUTIONS FOR CHILDREN:
In general, use caution when applying lidocaine products with children under 6, as the risk of product absorption through skin is greater. Do not use in children or infants under 1 year of age. Consulting your doctor and follow instructions on medication (see above).

PRECAUTIONS FOR SENIORS:
Seniors generally may be more prone to side effects and possible adverse effects of these products than younger individuals. Avoid high dosages.

SPECIAL WARNINGS:
Do not use any of these products if you are allergic to any topical anesthetic. Avoid applying more than three days continuously to same area, as this may lead to excess absorption. Do not continue overall use more than one week if condition hasn't improved.

INFORM YOUR DOCTOR BEFORE TAKING LIDOCAINE IF YOU HAVE:
Allergies to: any topical anesthetic, or if you have skin infection or skin conditions such as psoriasis or eczema.

Q U I C K F A C T S

ACTIVE INGREDIENT:

PRAMOXINE HYDROCHLORIDE

BRAND NAMES:

- ITCH-X–GEL (also contains benzyl alcohol, aloe vera, diazolidinyl urea, SD alcohol 40, parabens)
- ITCH-X–SPRAY (also contains benzyl alcohol, aloe vera gel, SD alcohol 40)
- PRAMAGEL (also contains menthol, benzyl alcohol, SD alcohol 40)
- PRAX–CREAM (also contains glycerin, cetyl alcohol, white petrolatum)
- PRAX–LOTION (also contains mineral oil, cetyl alcohol, glycerin, lanolin, potassium sorbate, sorbic acid)

SYMPTOMS RELIEVED:
Irritation, itching, and rashes due to minor skin conditions, discomfort of plant poisonings such as poison ivy, sumac, and oak, sunburn, common nonpoisonous insect bites and insect stings, and minor burns.

HOW TO TAKE:
Comes in cream, gel, lotion, and spray forms. Apply to affected area as needed, or in the case of creams, to a bandage or gauze pad before applying to skin. In all cases follow specific product instructions. These products are intended solely for external use. Do not under any conditions ingest internally or use in eyes. Always wash hands before and after use.

USUAL ADULT DOSE:
Dosage varies according to product and condition. Use the minimum recommended dose in

order to avoid side effects or complications. In all cases follow specific product instructions.

USUAL CHILD DOSE:
Do not use in children or infants under 1 year of age. Dosage varies according to product and condition. Use the minimum recommended dose in order to avoid side effects or complications. In all cases follow specific product instructions.

OVERDOSE SYMPTOMS:
Convulsions, agitation, euphoria, drowsiness, disorientation or dizziness, blurred vision, vomiting, numbness, hypotension-possibly leading to respiratory arrest; or cardiac arrhythmia (irregular pulse and heartbeat) leading to cardiac arrest or collapse. If you suspect an overdose, immediately seek medical attention.

SIDE EFFECTS:
No serious effects in most cases of common use. However, you may experience an increased in photosensitivity reaction resulting in higher risk of sunburn and other related skin damage. In this case, avoid unnecessary exposure to sun. In rare cases, some individuals have experienced swelling of skin or in mouth and throat, or rash, burning or stinging sensations, or pronounced skin sensitivity. In these cases, discontinue application or use of the product and call your doctor immediately.

CHECK WITH YOUR DOCTOR OR PHARMACIST BEFORE COMBINING PRAMOXINE WITH:
Sulfa drugs or Class I antiarrhythmia drugs (tocainide, mexiletine).

QUICK FACTS

PREGNANCY OR BREASTFEEDING:
Pramoxine use by a nursing mother should be considered a potential risk for a nursing child as the drug will be passed on to the infant in the mother's milk. In all cases, a physician should be consulted.

PRECAUTIONS FOR CHILDREN:
In general, use caution when applying pramoxine products with children under 6, as the risk of product absorption through skin is greater. Do not use in children or infants under 1 year of age. Consulting your doctor and follow instructions on medication (see above).

PRECAUTIONS FOR SENIORS:
Seniors generally may be more prone to side effects and possible adverse effects of these products than younger individuals. Avoid high dosages.

SPECIAL WARNINGS:
Do not use any of these products if you are allergic to any topical anesthetic. Avoid applying more than three days continuously to same area, as this may lead to excess absorption. Do not continue overall use more than one week if condition hasn't improved.

INFORM YOUR DOCTOR BEFORE TAKING PRAMOXINE IF YOU HAVE:
Allergies to: any topical anesthetic, or if you have skin infection or skin conditions such as psoriasis or eczema.

• ANTIBACTERIAL •
(TOPICAL)

The most important considerations in choosing an antibacterial are: its effectiveness in treating, healing, or preventing infections of minor cuts, wounds, burns, and skin abrasions, and potential side effects associated with the drug.

QUICK REVIEW

TOPICAL ANTIBACTERIALS ARE A CLASS OF DRUGS WHICH:

- are intended only for topical use,
- act by either neutralizing or destroying bacteria in affected area,
- when used in high dosages or for long treatment periods, may be absorbed into the blood stream through the skin or mucous membranes, increasing the incidence and probability of adverse side effects.

QUICK FACTS

ACTIVE INGREDIENTS:
POVIDONE-IODINE

BRAND NAMES:
- Betadine First Aid Cream (also contains glycerin, mineral oil, polyoxyethylene stearate, polysorbate, sorbitan monostearate, white petrolatum)
- Betadine Skin Cleanser (also contains ammonium nonoxynol-4-sulfate, lauramide DEA)
- Biodine Topical 1%
- Iodex
- Pro-Tech First Aid Stik (combination with lidocaine hydrochloride)

SYMPTOMS RELIEVED:
Minor burns, common nonpoisonous insect bites and insect stings, superficial boils, skin ulcers, minor surgical wounds.

HOW TO USE:
Comes in aerosol, cream, liquid, ointment, and solution forms. Application varies based on severity and extent of condition. In all cases follow specific product instructions. These products are intended solely for external, topical use. Do not under any conditions ingest internally or use in eyes. Always wash hands before and after use.

USUAL ADULT DOSE:
Dosage varies according to product and condition. Use the minimum recommended dose in order to avoid side effects or complications. In all cases follow specific product instructions.

USUAL CHILD DOSE:
Dosage varies according to product and condi-

tion. Use the minimum recommended dose in order to avoid side effects or complications. In all cases follow specific product instructions.

OVERDOSE SYMPTOMS:
None known.

SIDE EFFECTS:
No serious effects in most cases of common use. In rare cases, some individuals have experienced swelling of skin or rash, burning or stinging sensations, or pronounced skin sensitivity. In these cases, discontinue application or use of the product and call your doctor immediately.

CHECK WITH YOUR DOCTOR OR PHARMACIST BEFORE COMBINING POVIDONE-IODINE WITH:
None known.

PREGNANCY OR BREASTFEEDING:
Safety of this drug for use during pregnancy or while nursing has not been established. In all cases you should consult your doctor before using any drug during pregnancy or while nursing.

PRECAUTIONS FOR CHILDREN:
In general, use caution when applying povidone-iodine products with children under 2, as the risk of product absorption through skin is greater. Consult your doctor and follow instructions on medication (see above).

55+ **PRECAUTIONS FOR SENIORS:**
Seniors generally may be more prone to side effects and possible adverse effects of these products than younger individuals. Avoid high dosages.

QUICK FACTS

SPECIAL WARNINGS:
Do not use any of these products if you are allergic to any topical anesthetic. Do not use on open wounds without consulting your doctor. Do not continue overall use more than one week if condition hasn't improved.

INFORM YOUR DOCTOR BEFORE USING POVIDONE-IODINE IF YOU HAVE:
Allergies to: any topical anesthetic, or if you have skin infection or skin conditions such as psoriasis or eczema.

• ANTIHISTAMINES •

The most important considerations in choosing an antihistamine are: its effectiveness in blocking or alleviating effects of histamine on the respiratory system, and the nature and extent of side effects which the drug may produce.

QUICK REVIEW

ANTIHISTAMINES ARE A CLASS OF DRUGS WHICH:

- are used in treating allergies and motion sickness,
- block the effects of histamine, a chemical substance released by the body as the result of injury or in reaction to an allergen. Histamine increases capillary permeability, which allows fluids to escape and cause swelling. It also constricts small air passages in the lungs. These properties result in symptoms such as sinus headache, congestion, sneezing, runny nose, wheezing, puffiness, and lowered blood pressure,
- act by blocking or displacing histamine, particularly in the blood vessels, skin, uterus, and bronchioles,
- as a result of the drugs' drying effects, thereby impede drainage and expectoration,
- may produce side effects such as drowsiness, nasal stuffiness, dryness of mouth and sinus passages, dizziness, and common gastrointestinal (GI) irritation or distress,
- are not recommended in treating lower respiratory symptoms including asthma, as the drug's effects may impede expectoration.

QUICK FACTS

ACTIVE INGREDIENT:

DIPHENHYDRAMINE HYDROCHLORIDE

℞ **BRAND NAMES:**

- BENADRYL–CREAM (also contains parabens)
- BENADRYL–NON-AEROSOL SPRAY (also contains alcohol)
- BENADRYL 2% MAXIMUM STRENGTH–CREAM (also contains parabens)
- BENADRYL 2% MAXIMUM STRENGTH–NON-AEROSOL SPRAY (also contains alcohol)
- CALADRYL–CREAM (also contains calamine, parabens, camphor)
- CALADRYL–LOTION (also contains calamine, camphor, alcohol)
- CALADRYL–SPRAY (also contains calamine, alcohol, camphor)
- CALADRYL CLEAR (also contains alcohol)
- CALA-GEN (also contains alcohol)
- DI-DELAMINE (also contains tripelennamine hydrochloride, benzalkonium chloride, menthol, EDTA)
- STING-EZE (also contains camphor, phenol, benzocaine, eucalyptol)
- ZIRADRYL (also contains zinc oxide, alcohol, camphor, parabens)

Note: *Diphenhydramine* is also used as: a sleep aid, as an antihistamine, and as an active ingredient in combination with other drugs in antitussive (anti-cough) products.

SYMPTOMS RELIEVED:

Irritation, itching, and rashes due to minor skin conditions, discomfort of plant poisonings such as poison ivy, sumac, and oak, sunburn, common nonpoisonous insect bites and insect stings, and minor burns.

HOW TO USE:
Comes in concentrate, cream, gel, lotion, and spray forms. Wash and dry affected area before applying. Apply product as needed or as directed by your doctor.

In all cases follow specific product instructions. These products are intended solely for topical use. Do not under any conditions ingest internally or use in eyes. Always wash hands thoroughly before and after use.

Q U I C K F A C T S

USUAL ADULT DOSE:
See above. Use the minimum recommended dose in order to avoid side effects or complications. In all cases follow specific product instructions.

USUAL CHILD DOSE:
Do not use in cases involving children under 2 unless under medical supervision. For all others, use the minimum recommended dose in order to avoid side effects or complications. In all cases follow specific product instructions.

OVERDOSE SYMPTOMS:
No known overdose symptoms.

SIDE EFFECTS:
No serious effects in most cases of common use. However, in rare cases, individuals have experienced mild skin irritation. In these cases, discontinue application or use of the product and call your doctor immediately.

CHECK WITH YOUR DOCTOR OR PHARMACIST BEFORE COMBINING UNDECYLENIC ACID WITH:
Any other topical preparations, or any other antihistamine product.

Q U I C K F A C T S

PREGNANCY OR BREASTFEEDING:
Safety of this drug for use during pregnancy or while nursing has not been established. In all cases you should consult your doctor before using any drug during pregnancy or while nursing.

PRECAUTIONS FOR CHILDREN:
These products should not be used to treat children under 2 unless under close medical supervision.

55+ **PRECAUTIONS FOR SENIORS:**
No special precautions are known for seniors.

SPECIAL WARNINGS:
Do not use any other diphenhydramine products while using any of these topical products. Do not use any of these products if you are allergic to diphenhydramine hydrochloride or any topical antifungal medication, or any of the inactive ingredients listed, or if you have any form of liver disease or damage. Do not use longer than one week continuously.

ADDITIONAL WARNINGS:
Do not use these topical products to treat chicken pox, measles, blisters, or extensive skin areas, unless directed by your doctor.

INFORM YOUR DOCTOR BEFORE USING DIPHENHYDRAMINE IF YOU HAVE:
Urinary difficulty, glaucoma, ulcer, or if you are pregnant. If you anticipate any surgery requiring general or spinal anesthesia within 2 months of taking diphenhydramine-containing medication, inform your doctor.

• ANTISEPTIC •
(TOPICAL)

The most important considerations in choosing an antiseptic are: its effectiveness in treating, healing, or preventing infections of minor cuts, wounds, burns, and skin abrasions, and potential side effects associated with the drug.

TOPICAL ANTISEPTICS ARE A CLASS OF DRUGS WHICH:

- are intended only for topical use,
- act by killing bacteria, fungi, viruses, spores, protozoa, and yeasts in affected area,
- when used in high dosages or for long treatment periods, may be absorbed into the bloodstream through the skin or mucous membranes, increasing the incidence and probability of adverse side effects.

Q U I C K F A C T S

ACTIVE INGREDIENTS:
BACITRACIN AND NEOMYCIN COMBINATION

℞ **BRAND NAMES:**
- Bactine First Aid Antibiotic Plus Anesthetic Ointment (combination with polymixin B sulfate and diperodon hydrochloride—also contains mineral oil, white petrolatum)
- Campho-Phenique Antibiotic Plus Pain Reliever Ointment (combination with polymixin B sulfate and lidocaine—also contains white petrolatum)
- Medi-Quick Ointment (combination with polymixin B sulfate—also contains lanolin, mineral oil, petrolatum)
- Mycitracin Maximum Strength Triple Antibiotic Ointment (combination with polymixin B sulfate—also contains parabens, mineral oil, white petrolatum)
- Neosporin Maximum Strength Ointment (combination with polymixin B sulfate—also contains white petrolatum)
- Septa Ointment (combination with polymixin B sulfate)
- Spectrocin Plus Ointment (combination with polymixin B sulfate and lidocaine—also contains mineral oil, white petrolatum)

SYMPTOMS RELIEVED:
Pain or discomfort of minor cuts, scrapes, burns, or to prevent infection of same.

HOW TO USE:
Comes in ointment forms. Clean affected areas before application unless your doctor advises otherwise. Apply small amount (usually no more

than the surface of a fingertip) to affected area 1 to 3 times per day. In all cases follow specific product instructions. These products are intended solely for topical use. Do not under any conditions ingest internally or use in eyes, mouth, nose, ears or any mucous membrane. Always wash hands thoroughly before and after application.

USUAL ADULT DOSE:
See above. Use the minimum recommended dose in order to avoid side effects or complications. In all cases follow specific product instructions.

USUAL CHILD DOSE:
Consult your doctor before using in cases involving children or infants.

OVERDOSE SYMPTOMS:
None known overdose symptoms. However, if accidentally swallowed, immediately call for emergency medical aid.

SIDE EFFECTS:
No known adverse reactions or side effects in most cases of common use. However, in rare cases, individuals have experienced allergic dermatitis reactions, hearing loss, sore throat, fever, and bleeding or bruising. In these cases, discontinue application or use of the product and call your doctor immediately.

CHECK WITH YOUR DOCTOR OR PHARMACIST BEFORE COMBINING ANY OF THESE COMBINATION PRODUCTS WITH:
Any other topical product.

QUICK FACTS

PREGNANCY OR BREASTFEEDING:
Safety of this drug for use during pregnancy or while nursing has not been established. In all cases you should consult your doctor before using any drug during pregnancy or while nursing.

PRECAUTIONS FOR CHILDREN:
See Usual Child Dose above.

55+ **PRECAUTIONS FOR SENIORS:**
No special precautions are known for seniors.

SPECIAL WARNINGS:
Do not use these products if you are allergic to related "mycin" or "micin" antibiotics (e.g. mupirocin, polymixin, etc.) or chloramphenicol. Do not continue application longer than one week unless directed by your doctor.

INFORM YOUR DOCTOR BEFORE USING THESE COMBINATION PRODUCTS IF:
You have any open sores in the areas which you intend to treat, or if you have allergic contact dermatitis.

ACTIVE INGREDIENT:

NEOMYCIN SULFATE

BRAND NAMES:

- MYCIGUENT (also contains methylparaben)
- NEOSPORIN CREAM (combination with polymixin B sulfate—also contains white petrolatum)

SYMPTOMS RELIEVED:

Pain or discomfort of minor cuts, scrapes, burns, or to prevent infection of same.

HOW TO USE:

Comes in cream forms. Clean affected areas before application unless your doctor advises otherwise. Apply small amount (usually no more than the surface of a fingertip) to affected area 1 to 3 times per day. In all cases follow specific product instructions. These products are intended solely for topical use. Do not under any conditions ingest internally or use in eyes, mouth, nose, ears or any mucous membrane. Always wash hands thoroughly before and after application.

USUAL ADULT DOSE:

See above. Use the minimum recommended dose in order to avoid side effects or complications. In all cases follow specific product instructions.

USUAL CHILD DOSE:

Consult your doctor before using in cases involving children or infants.

OVERDOSE SYMPTOMS:

None known overdose symptoms. However, if accidentally swallowed, immediately call for emergency medical aid.

SIDE EFFECTS:
No known adverse reactions or side effects in most cases of common use. However, in rare cases, individuals have experienced allergic dermatitis reactions, hearing loss, sore throat, fever, and bleeding or bruising. In these cases, discontinue application or use of the product and call your doctor immediately.

CHECK WITH YOUR DOCTOR OR PHARMACIST BEFORE COMBINING NEOMYCIN SULFATE WITH:
Any other topical product.

PREGNANCY OR BREASTFEEDING:
Safety of this drug for use during pregnancy or while nursing has not been established. In all cases you should consult your doctor before using any drug during pregnancy or while nursing.

PRECAUTIONS FOR CHILDREN:
See Usual Child Dose above.

PRECAUTIONS FOR SENIORS:
No special precautions are known for seniors.

SPECIAL WARNINGS:
Do not use these products t if you are allergic to related "mycin" or "micin" antibiotics (e.g. mupirocin, polymixin, etc.) or chloramphenicol. Do not continue application longer than one week unless directed by your doctor.

INFORM YOUR DOCTOR BEFORE USING NEOMYCIN SULFATE IF:
You have any open sores in the areas which you intend to treat, or if you have allergic contact dermatitis.

HEADACHES

QUICK REVIEW

• ANALGESIC •

The most important considerations in choosing an analgesic are: pain relief; anti-inflammatory activity, and allergic reaction or sensitivity to certain active ingredients.

ANALGESICS (NONNARCOTIC) ARE A CLASS OF DRUGS WHICH:

- inhibit the action of prostaglandins (hormonelike substances) in the central nervous system, thereby temporarily reducing the perception of physical pain with little loss of sensibility to other physical sensation,
- are used to temporarily alleviate symptoms such as: headache, fever, backache, sinus pain, muscle strain, menstrual pain, and similar ailments. Some analgesics, such as aspirin (acetylsalicylic acid) and ibuprofen, also provide temporary anti-inflammatory relief for ailments such as arthritis. Aspirin has also been shown to be effective as a blood thinning antiplatelet agent in reducing heart attack and stroke risk,
- can have adverse effects in some instances. Aspirin intolerance can produce allergic and anaphylactic reactions in hypersensitive and asthmatic individuals. Aspirin can also aggravate aggravate gastrointestinal conditions such as heartburn and ulcer. Long-term acetaminophen use can damage liver (hepatic) and kidney (renal) functions.

QUICK FACTS

ACTIVE INGREDIENT:
ACETAMINOPHEN

BRAND NAMES:
- ACEPHEN
- ALKA-SELTZER FAST RELIEF (combination with calcium carbonate)
- ANACIN-3
- APACET
- BANESIN
- BAYER SELECT ASPIRIN-FREE
- EXCEDRIN ASPIRIN-FREE
- GENAPAP
- GENEBS
- GOODY'S
- PANADOL
- PERCOGESIC ANALGESIC TABLETS (combination with phenyltoloxamine citrate, also contains sucrose)
- PHENAPHEN
- ST. JOSEPH ASPIRIN-FREE
- TAPANOL
- TYLENOL (various formulations)
- VALADOL
- VANQUISH (combination with aspirin and caffeine)

SYMPTOMS RELIEVED:
Minor aches and pains such as those associated with headache(s).

HOW TO TAKE:
Comes in tablet, chewable tablet, caplet, capsule, elixir, liquid, powder, solution, and suppository forms. Swallow tablet, capsule, or elixir with liquid. Sprinkle powder over liquid, then swallow. Follow medication instructions

QUICK FACTS

carefully for proper insertion of suppositories. Do not crush or chew timed-release tablet. In proper dosages in most cases, acetaminophen does not cause gastrointestinal (GI) irritation and can be taken with or without food.

USUAL ADULT DOSE:
325 to 650 milligrams every 4 to 6 hours, or 1 gram 3 to 4 times per day, not to exceed 4 grams a day.

USUAL CHILD DOSE:
4 to 5 doses per day, not to exceed 5 doses in 24 hours. Dosage varies based on infant or child's age.

OVERDOSE SYMPTOMS:
Nausea, vomiting, diaphoresis, discomfort, and malaise. In some cases, hepatic toxicity (liver poisoning) may result. If you suspect an overdose, immediately seek medical attention.

SIDE EFFECTS:
None in most cases of common use. Long-term ingestion of high dosages may increase risk of liver and kidney damage. In rare cases, extreme fatigue and drowsiness, allergic skin eruptions (rash, hives, itch), sore throat and fever, bleeding or bruising, urinary discomfort or blood in urine, jaundiced skin or eyes may result.

CHECK WITH YOUR DOCTOR OR PHARMACIST BEFORE COMBINING ACETAMINOPHEN WITH:
Anticoagulants, aspirin and other salicylates, Isoniazid (anti-tuberculosis) medication. Excessive ingestion of alcohol while taking acetaminophen can increase the risk of liver damage or disease (hepatic toxicity).

PREGNANCY OR BREASTFEEDING:
No conclusive evidence of effects on fetus—benign or adverse—has been established. High dosage has in isolated cases caused anemia in mother and kidney failure in fetus. Nursing infants have shown no harmful effects.

PRECAUTIONS FOR CHILDREN:
In general, administer to infants or children only when consulting a physician and follow instructions on medication.

55+ **PRECAUTIONS FOR SENIORS:**
Seniors generally don't eliminate drugs as efficiently as younger persons, and should avoid high dosages.

SPECIAL WARNINGS:
Chronic alcoholics are at risk for hepatic (liver) function impairment if taking high dosages of acetaminophen.

INFORM YOUR DOCTOR BEFORE TAKING ACETAMINOPHEN IF YOU HAVE:
Liver or kidney disease or damage, an allergy to acetaminophen, or hypoglycemia.

QUICK FACTS

ACTIVE INGREDIENTS:
ACETAMINOPHEN AND ASPIRIN

BRAND NAMES:
- Extra Strength Excedrin
- Goody's Extra Strength Headache Powders

SYMPTOMS RELIEVED:
Minor aches and pains such as those associated with headache(s).

HOW TO TAKE:
Comes in tablet, chewable tablet, caplet, capsule, and powder forms. Swallow tablet or capsule with liquid. Sprinkle powder over liquid, then swallow. Do not crush or chew timed-release tablet. Although acetaminophen does not normally cause GI irritation, aspirin can—as a result these medications should be taken with food.

USUAL ADULT DOSE:
Minor aches and pains: 325 to 650 milligrams every 4 hours or as needed, not to exceed 4 grams a day. For extra strength products, dosage may range to 500 milligrams every 3 hours to 1,000 milligrams every 6 hours.

USUAL CHILD DOSE:
4 to 5 doses per day, not to exceed 5 doses in 24 hours. Dosage varies based on infant or child's age.

OVERDOSE SYMPTOMS:
Nausea, vomiting, diaphoresis, diarrhea, discomfort, fever, impaired vision, sweats, bloody urine, abnormal thirst, nervous agitation, and malaise.

In some cases, hepatic toxicity (liver poisoning), or capillary and other hematological abnormalities may result. If you suspect an overdose, immediately seek medical attention.

SIDE EFFECTS:
Aspirin: None in most cases of common use, however normal aspirin use can result in common gastrointestinal (GI) irritations such as heartburn and indigestion. Aspirin affects the hypothalamus, resulting in dilation of small blood vessels in skin. Low dosages may reduce risk of blood clotting as aspirin inhibits clotting of small blood cells. Aspirin use may however contribute to anemia in anemic individuals.

Acetaminophen: Long-term ingestion of high dosages of acetaminophen may increase risk of liver and kidney damage. In rare cases, extreme fatigue and drowsiness, allergic skin eruptions (rash, hives, itch), sore throat and fever, bleeding or bruising, urinary discomfort or blood in urine, jaundiced skin or eyes may result.

CHECK WITH YOUR DOCTOR OR PHARMACIST BEFORE COMBINING ACETAMINOPHEN/ASPIRIN COMBINATION WITH:
Anticoagulants, aspirin, and other salicylates, tetracycline, cellulose-based laxatives, Isoniazid (anti-tuberculosis) medication. Excessive ingestion of alcohol while taking acetaminophen can increase the risk of liver damage or disease (hepatic toxicity). Ingestion of alcohol while taking aspirin can increase risk of GI ulceration. Avoid use of medication containing aspirin if you have a history of anemia. Also avoid use of

medication containing aspirin, if possible, one week prior to surgery, as aspirin may increase possibility of postoperative bleeding.

PREGNANCY OR BREASTFEEDING:
High dosage of acetaminophen has in isolated cases caused anemia in mother and kidney failure in fetus. In third trimester, use of medication containing aspirin should be discouraged. No harmful effects have been reported regarding nursing infants, but aspirin use by a nursing mother should be considered a potential risk for a nursing child as the drug will be passed on to the infant in milk. In all cases, a physician should be consulted.

PRECAUTIONS FOR CHILDREN:
In general, administer to infants or children only when consulting a physician and follow instructions on medication.

SPECIAL WARNING:
Aspirin use in children and teenagers with influenza (flu), chicken pox, and other viral infections may be associated with development of Reye's syndrome. This rare but acute and often life-threatening condition has caused permanent brain damage in survivors. Symptoms include: vomiting, lethargy, bellicosity, leading possibly to delirium and coma.

55+ **PRECAUTIONS FOR SENIORS:**
Seniors generally don't eliminate drugs as efficiently as younger persons, and should avoid high dosages. Aspirin use can cause GI irritation and possibly stomach or intestinal bleeding in seniors, manifested usually by dark stools.

SPECIAL WARNINGS:
Chronic alcoholics are at risk for hepatic (liver) function impairment if taking high dosages of acetaminophen. Always check expiration date on label of medication. Do not take if medication has expired. Do not take medication containing aspirin which emits a vinegar-like odor. This indicates that it is decomposing and is unsafe for use.

INFORM YOUR DOCTOR BEFORE TAKING ACETAMINOPHEN/ASPIRIN COMBINATION IF YOU HAVE:
Liver or kidney disease or damage, an allergy to acetaminophen or aspirin, asthma, anemia, or other hematological condition, GI sensitivity, viral infection, hypoglycemia.

QUICK FACTS

ACTIVE INGREDIENTS:

ACETAMINOPHEN, ASPIRIN, AND CAFFEINE COMBINATION

BRAND NAMES:
- BUFFETS II TABLETS
- EXCEDRIN EXTRA-STRENGTH
- GELPIRIN
- GOODY'S EXTRA STRENGTH HEADACHE POWDERS
- PAIN RELIEVER TABS
- SUPAC
- VANQUISH

SYMPTOMS RELIEVED:
Minor aches and pains such as those associated with the common cold, flu, headache, toothache, sinusitis, hay fever, and other respiratory allergies, muscular aches, backache, minor arthritis pain, menstrual discomfort, and reduction of fever.

HOW TO TAKE:
Comes in tablet, caplet, capsule, and powder forms. Swallow with liquid. Sprinkle powder over liquid, then swallow. Do not crush or chew timed-release tablets. Aspirin and caffeine both can cause gastrointestinal (GI) irritation and should be taken with food or following meal.

USUAL ADULT DOSE:
1 or 2 capsules, tablets, caplets or 1 powder packet every 2 to 6 hours.

ACTIVE INGREDIENTS:

ACETAMINOPHEN AND CAFFEINE COMBINATION

QUICK FACTS

BRAND NAMES:

- Bayer: Select Maximum Strength
- Excedrin: Aspirin-Free
- Fendol

SYMPTOMS RELIEVED:

Minor aches and pains such as those associated with headache(s).

HOW TO TAKE:

Comes in tablet, caplet, capsule, and powder forms. Swallow with liquid. Sprinkle powder over liquid, then swallow. Do not crush or chew timed-release tablets. Caffeine can cause gastrointestinal (GI) irritation and should be taken with food or following a meal.

USUAL ADULT DOSE:

12.5 milligrams every 4 to 6 hours, not to exceed 25 milligrams in a 4 to 6 hour period or 75 milligrams in a 24 hour period.

USUAL CHILD DOSE:

Do not administer to children under 16 unless under direction of physician. Dosage may vary based on infant or child's age.

OVERDOSE SYMPTOMS:

Nervous agitation, disorientation, confusion, severe headache, convulsions, GI bleeding, or hemorrhage. If you suspect an overdose, seek medical attention immediately.

SIDE EFFECTS:

No serious effects in most cases of common

Q U I C K F A C T S

use, however normal use of caffeine can result in common GI irritations such as heartburn and indigestion. Less common side effects include dizziness, nausea, stomach cramps, and headache.

CHECK WITH YOUR DOCTOR OR PHARMACIST BEFORE COMBINING ACETAMINOPHEN OR CAFFEINE WITH:
Antacids, anticoagulants, aspirin, asthma medication, other (nonsteroidal anti-inflammatory drug) NSAIDs, tetracycline, and any other medication.

PREGNANCY OR BREASTFEEDING:
Animal studies have indicated an adverse effect on fetus, but no adequate studies have been performed on humans. No harmful effects have been reported regarding nursing infants, but caffeine use by a nursing mother should be considered a potential risk for a nursing child as the drug will be passed on to the infant in the mother's milk. In all cases, a physician should be consulted.

PRECAUTIONS FOR CHILDREN:
In general, caffeine and other NSAIDs are not advised for children under 15. Administer caffeine to infants or children only when consulting a physician and follow instructions on medication (see above).

55+ **PRECAUTIONS FOR SENIORS:**
Seniors generally don't eliminate drugs as efficiently as younger persons, and should avoid high dosages. Seniors (over 65) are at special risk for development of ulcers if taking caffeine in high doses. Prolonged use can also lead to kidney and liver damage.

SPECIAL WARNINGS:
Don't take caffeine medication if you are aspirin intolerant or allergic to other NSAIDs. If in doubt, always consult a pharmacist or physician. Also avoid if you have GI conditions such as gastritis, peptic ulcer, enteritis, ileitis, colitis; asthma, high blood pressure, or hematologic (bleeding) problems. Avoid alcohol while taking this or any other NSAID.

INFORM YOUR DOCTOR BEFORE TAKING CAFFEINE IF YOU HAVE:
An allergy or intolerance to aspirin or other NSAIDs, damaged or impaired renal (kidney) or hepatic (liver) functions, epilepsy, Parkinson's disease or mental illness.

QUICK FACTS

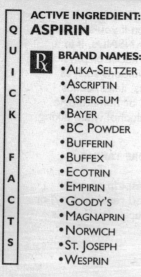

ACTIVE INGREDIENT:
ASPIRIN

BRAND NAMES:
- ALKA-SELTZER
- ASCRIPTIN
- ASPERGUM
- BAYER
- BC POWDER
- BUFFERIN
- BUFFEX
- ECOTRIN
- EMPIRIN
- GOODY'S
- MAGNAPRIN
- NORWICH
- ST. JOSEPH
- WESPRIN

SYMPTOMS RELIEVED:
Minor aches and pains such as those associated with headache(s).

HOW TO TAKE:
Comes in tablet, chewable tablet, caplet, capsule, powder, and solution forms. Swallow tablet, capsule, or caplet with liquid. Sprinkle powder over liquid, then swallow. Do not crush or chew timed-release tablet. Aspirin can cause gastrointestinal (GI) irritation and should be taken with food or following meal.

USUAL ADULT DOSE:
Minor aches and pains: 325 to 650 milligrams every 4 hours or as needed, not to exceed 4 grams a day. For extra strength products, dosage may range to 500 milligrams every 3 hours to 1,000 milligrams every 6 hours.

USUAL CHILD DOSE:
4 to 5 doses per day, not to exceed 5 doses in 24 hours. Dosage varies based on infant or child's age.

OVERDOSE SYMPTOMS:
Respiratory difficulty, hyperventilation, hyperthermia, nausea and vomiting, severe diarrhea, impaired vision, bloody urine, abnormal thirst, nervous agitation, disorientation and dizziness. In some cases, capillary and other hematological abnormalities may result. If you suspect an overdose, immediately seek medical attention.

SIDE EFFECTS:
No serious effects in most cases of common use, however normal aspirin use can result in common GI irritations such as heartburn and indigestion. Aspirin affects hypothalamus, resulting in dilation of small blood vessels in skin. Low dosages may reduce risk of blood clotting as aspirin inhibits blood clotting. Aspirin use may however contribute to anemia in anemic individuals.

CHECK WITH YOUR DOCTOR OR PHARMACIST BEFORE COMBINING ASPIRIN WITH:
Anticoagulants, asthma medication, other salicylates, tetracycline, and any other medication. Ingestion of alcohol while taking aspirin can increase risk of GI ulceration. Avoid aspirin use if you have aspirin intolerance, asthma, rhinitis, or a history of anemia (iron poor blood). Also avoid use of aspirin, if possible, one week prior to surgery, as it may increase possibility of postoperative bleeding.

QUICK FACTS

PREGNANCY OR BREASTFEEDING:
Animal studies have indicated an adverse effect on fetus, but no adequate studies have been performed on humans. In third trimester, aspirin use should be discouraged. No harmful effects have been reported regarding nursing infants, but aspirin use by a nursing mother should be considered a potential risk for a nursing child as the drug will be passed on to the infant in milk. In all cases, a physician should be consulted.

PRECAUTIONS FOR CHILDREN:
In general, administer to infants or children only when consulting a physician and follow instructions on medication.

SPECIAL WARNING:
Aspirin use in children and teenagers with influenza (flu), chicken pox and other viral infections may be associated with development of Reye's syndrome. This rare but acute and often life-threatening condition has caused permanent brain damage in survivors. Symptoms include: vomiting, lethargy, bellicosity, leading possibly to delirium and coma.

55+

PRECAUTIONS FOR SENIORS:
Seniors generally don't eliminate drugs as efficiently as younger persons, and should avoid high dosages. Buffered effervescent aspirin products contain high sodium content and should be avoided if on a restricted sodium diet. Aspirin use can cause GI irritation and possibly stomach or intestinal bleeding in seniors, manifested usually by dark stools.

SPECIAL WARNINGS:

Always check expiration date on label of medication. Do not take if medication has expired. Do not take aspirin which emits a vinegar-like odor. This indicates that it is decomposing and is unsafe for use.

INFORM YOUR DOCTOR BEFORE TAKING ASPIRIN IF YOU HAVE:

An allergy to aspirin, are asthmatic, anemic, or have other hematological conditions, or have GI sensitivity.

QUICK FACTS

ACTIVE INGREDIENTS:
ASPIRIN AND CAFFEINE COMBINATION

BRAND NAMES:
- ANACIN
- BC POWDER
- COPE
- DRISTAN
- EXCEDRIN
- FENDOL
- GENSAN

SYMPTOMS RELIEVED:
Minor aches and pains such as those associated with headache(s).

HOW TO TAKE:
Comes in tablet, caplet, capsule, and powder forms. Swallow with liquid. Sprinkle powder over liquid, then swallow. Do not crush or chew timed-release tablets. Caffeine can cause gastrointestinal (GI) irritation and should be taken with food or following meal.

USUAL ADULT DOSE:
12.5 milligrams every 4 to 6 hours, not to exceed 25 milligrams in a 4 to 6 hour period or 75 milligrams in a 24 hour period.

USUAL CHILD DOSE:
Do not administer to children under 16 unless under direction of physician. Dosage may vary based on infant or child's age.

OVERDOSE SYMPTOMS:
Nervous agitation, disorientation, confusion, severe headache, convulsions, GI bleeding or hemorrhage. If you suspect an overdose, immediately seek medical attention.

SIDE EFFECTS:
No serious effects in most cases of common use, however normal use of caffeine can result in common GI irritations such as heartburn and indigestion. Less common side effects include dizziness, nausea, stomach cramps, and headache.

CHECK WITH YOUR DOCTOR OR PHARMACIST BEFORE COMBINING CAFFEINE WITH:
Antacids, anticoagulants, aspirin, asthma medication, other nonsteroidal anti-inflammatory drugs (NSAIDs), tetracycline, and any other medication. Combination with acetaminophen increases risk of kidney damage. Ingestion of alcohol while taking salicylates can increase risk of GI ulceration. Avoid caffeine if you have a history of anemia. Also avoid use of caffeine, if possible, one week prior to surgery, as it may increase possibility of postoperative bleeding.

PREGNANCY OR BREASTFEEDING:
Animal studies have indicated an adverse effect on fetus, but no adequate studies have been performed on humans. No harmful effects have been reported regarding nursing infants, but caffeine use by a nursing mother should be considered a potential risk for a nursing child as the drug will be passed on to the infant in the mother's milk. In all cases, a physician should be consulted.

PRECAUTIONS FOR CHILDREN:
In general, caffeine and other NSAIDs are not advised for children under 15. Administer caffeine to infants or children only when consulting a physician and follow instructions on medication (see above).

Q U I C K F A C T S

55+ **PRECAUTIONS FOR SENIORS:**
Seniors generally don't eliminate drugs as efficiently as younger persons, and should avoid high dosages. Seniors (over 65) are at special risk for development of ulcers if taking caffeine in high doses. Prolonged use can also lead to kidney and liver damage.

SPECIAL WARNINGS:
Don't take caffeine medication if you are aspirin intolerant or allergic to other NSAIDs. If in doubt, always consult a pharmacist or physician. Also avoid if you have GI conditions such as gastritis, peptic ulcer, enteritis, ileitis, colitis; asthma, high blood pressure, or hematologic (bleeding) problems. Avoid alcohol while taking this or any other NSAID.

INFORM YOUR DOCTOR BEFORE TAKING CAFFEINE IF YOU HAVE:
An allergy or intolerance to aspirin or other NSAIDs, damaged or impaired renal (kidney) or hepatic (liver) functions, epilepsy, Parkinson's disease or mental illness.

ACTIVE INGREDIENT:

IBUPROFEN

BRAND NAMES:
- ADVIL
- ARTHRITIS FOUNDATION (backache and muscle pain)
- BAYER SELECT PAIN RELIEF
- GENPRIL
- OBUPRIN
- IBUPROHM
- MOTRIN
- NUPRON

SYMPTOMS RELIEVED:
Minor aches and pains such as those associated with headache(s).

HOW TO TAKE:
Comes in tablet, caplet, and gelcap forms. Swallow with liquid. Do not crush or chew timed-release tablet. Ibuprofen can cause gastrointestinal (GI) irritation and should be taken with food or following meal.

USUAL ADULT DOSE:
Minor aches and pains: 200 milligrams every 4 to 6 hours as needed, not to exceed 1.2 grams per day.

Arthritis and related conditions: 1.2 grams to 3.2 grams per day divided into equal doses over 24 hours.

USUAL CHILD DOSE:
Always consult with a pharmacist or physician. Dosage may vary based on infant or child's age.

Q U I C K F A C T S

OVERDOSE SYMPTOMS:
Nervous agitation, disorientation, confusion, severe headache, convulsions, GI bleeding or hemorrhage. If you suspect an overdose, immediately seek medical attention.

SIDE EFFECTS:
No serious effects in most cases of common use, however normal use of ibuprofen can result in common GI irritations such as heartburn and indigestion. Less common side effects include dizziness, nausea, stomach cramps, and headache.

CHECK WITH YOUR DOCTOR OR PHARMACIST BEFORE COMBINING IBUPROFEN WITH:
Antacids, anticoagulants, aspirin, asthma medication, other nonsteroidal anti-inflammatory drugs (NSAIDs), tetracycline, and any other medication. Combination with acetaminophen increases risk of kidney damage. Ingestion of alcohol while taking ibuprofen can increase risk of GI ulceration. Avoid ibuprofen if you have a history of anemia. Also avoid use of ibuprofen, if possible, one week prior to surgery, as it may increase possibility of postoperative bleeding.

PREGNANCY OR BREASTFEEDING:
No harmful effects have been reported regarding nursing infants, but ibuprofen use by a nursing mother should be considered a potential risk for a nursing child as the drug will be passed on to the infant in the mother's milk. In all cases, a physician should be consulted.

PRECAUTIONS FOR CHILDREN:
In general, ibuprofen and other NSAIDs are not advised for children under 15. Administer

ibuprofen to infants or children only when consulting a physician and follow instructions on medication.

55+

PRECAUTIONS FOR SENIORS:
Seniors generally don't eliminate drugs as efficiently as younger persons, and should avoid high dosages. Seniors (over 65) are at special risk for development of ulcers if taking ibuprofen in high doses. Prolonged use can also lead to kidney and liver damage.

SPECIAL WARNINGS:
Don't take ibuprofen medication if you are aspirin intolerant or allergic to other NSAIDs. If in doubt, always consult a pharmacist or physician. Avoid alcohol while taking this or any other NSAID.

INFORM YOUR DOCTOR BEFORE TAKING IBUPROFEN IF YOU HAVE:
An allergy or intolerance to aspirin or other NSAIDs, damaged or impaired renal (kidney) or hepatic (liver) functions, epilepsy, Parkinson's disease, or mental illness.

Q U I C K F A C T S

ACTIVE INGREDIENT:

KETOPROFEN

BRAND NAMES:

- ACTRON
- ORUDIS

SYMPTOMS RELIEVED:
Minor aches and pains such as those associated with headache(s).

HOW TO TAKE:
Comes in tablet forms. Swallow with liquid. Do not crush or chew timed-release tablets. Ketoprofen can cause gastrointestinal (GI) irritation and should be taken with food or following meal.

USUAL ADULT DOSE:
12.5 milligrams every 4 to 6 hours, not to exceed 25 milligrams in a 4 to 6 hour period or 75 milligrams in a 24 hour period.

USUAL CHILD DOSE:
Do not administer to children under 16 unless under direction of physician. Dosage may vary based on infant or child's age.

OVERDOSE SYMPTOMS:
Nervous agitation, disorientation, confusion, severe headache, convulsions, GI bleeding or hemorrhage. If you suspect an overdose, immediately seek medical attention.

SIDE EFFECTS:
No serious effects in most cases of common use, however normal use of ketoprofen can

result in common GI irritations such as heartburn and indigestion. Less common side effects include dizziness, nausea, stomach cramps, and headache.

CHECK WITH YOUR DOCTOR OR PHARMACIST BEFORE COMBINING KETOPROFEN WITH:
Antacids, anticoagulants, aspirin, asthma medication, other nonsteroidal anti-inflammatory drugs (NSAIDs), tetracycline, and any other medication. Combination with acetaminophen increases risk of kidney damage. Ingestion of alcohol while taking ketoprofen can increase risk of GI ulceration. Avoid ketoprofen if you have a history of anemia. Also avoid use of ketoprofen, if possible, one week prior to surgery, as it may increase possibility of postoperative bleeding.

PREGNANCY OR BREASTFEEDING:
Animal studies have indicated an adverse effect on fetus, but no adequate studies have been performed on humans. No harmful effects have been reported regarding nursing infants, but ketoprofen use by a nursing mother should be considered a potential risk for a nursing child as the drug will be passed on to the infant in the mother's milk. In all cases, a physician should be consulted.

PRECAUTIONS FOR CHILDREN:
In general, ketoprofen and other NSAIDs are not advised for children under 15. Administer ketoprofen to infants or children only when consulting a physician and follow instructions on medication (see above).

Q U I C K F A C T S

PRECAUTIONS FOR SENIORS:

Seniors generally don't eliminate drugs as efficiently as younger persons, and should avoid high dosages. Seniors (over 65) are at special risk for development of ulcers if taking ketoprofen in high doses. Prolonged use can also lead to kidney and liver damage.

SPECIAL WARNINGS:

Don't take ketoprofen medication if you are aspirin intolerant or allergic to other NSAIDs. If in doubt, always consult a pharmacist or physician. Also avoid if you have GI conditions such as gastritis, peptic ulcer, enteritis, ileitis, colitis; asthma, high blood pressure, or hematologic (bleeding) problems. Avoid alcohol while taking this or any other NSAID.

INFORM YOUR DOCTOR BEFORE TAKING KETOPROFEN IF YOU HAVE:

An allergy or intolerance to aspirin or other NSAIDs, damaged or impaired renal (kidney) or hepatic (liver) functions, epilepsy, Parkinson's disease, or mental illness.

ACTIVE INGREDIENT:
NAPROXEN

Q U I C K F A C T S

BRAND NAMES:
- ALEVE

SYMPTOMS RELIEVED:
Minor aches and pains such as those associated with headache(s).

HOW TO TAKE:
Comes in tablet forms. Swallow with liquid. Do not crush or chew timed-release tablets. Naproxen can cause gastrointestinal (GI) irritation and should be taken with food or following meal.

USUAL ADULT DOSE:
200 milligrams every 8 to 12 hours with full glass of liquid, not to exceed 600 milligrams in a 24 hour period. Seniors (over 65) should not exceed 200 milligrams in a 12 hour period.

USUAL CHILD DOSE:
Do not administer to children under 12 unless under direction of physician. Dosage may vary based on infant or child's age.

OVERDOSE SYMPTOMS:
Nervous agitation, disorientation, confusion, severe headache, convulsions, GI bleeding, or hemorrhage. If you suspect an overdose, immediately seek medical attention.

SIDE EFFECTS:
No serious effects in most cases of common use, however normal use of naproxen can result in common GI irritations such as heartburn and

indigestion. Less common side effects include dizziness, nausea, stomach cramps, and headache.

CHECK WITH YOUR DOCTOR OR PHARMACIST BEFORE COMBINING NAPROXEN WITH:
Antacids, anticoagulants, aspirin, asthma medication, other nonsteroidal anti-inflammatory drugs (NSAIDs), tetracycline, and any other medication. Combination with acetaminophen increases risk of kidney damage. Ingestion of alcohol while taking naproxen can increase risk of GI ulceration. Avoid naproxen if you have a history of anemia. Also avoid use of naproxen, if possible, one week prior to surgery, as it may increase possibility of postoperative bleeding.

PREGNANCY OR BREASTFEEDING:
Animal studies have indicated an adverse effect on fetus, but no adequate studies have been performed on humans. No harmful effects have been reported regarding nursing infants, but naproxen use by a nursing mother should be considered a potential risk for a nursing child as the drug will be passed on to the infant in the mother's milk. In all cases, a physician should be consulted.

PRECAUTIONS FOR CHILDREN:
In general, naproxen and other NSAIDs are not advised for children under 15. Administer naproxen to infants or children only when consulting a physician and follow instructions on medication (see above).

55+

PRECAUTIONS FOR SENIORS:
Seniors generally don't eliminate drugs as effi-

ciently as younger persons, and should avoid high dosages. Seniors (over 65) are at special risk for development of ulcers if taking naproxen in high doses. Prolonged use can also lead to kidney and liver damage.

SPECIAL WARNINGS:
Don't take naproxen medication if you are aspirin intolerant or allergic to other NSAIDs. If in doubt, always consult a pharmacist or physician. Also avoid if you have GI conditions such as gastritis, peptic ulcer, enteritis, ileitis, colitis; asthma, high blood pressure, or hematologic (bleeding) problems. Avoid alcohol while taking this or any other NSAID.

INFORM YOUR DOCTOR BEFORE TAKING NAPROXEN IF YOU HAVE:
An allergy or intolerance to aspirin or other NSAIDs, damaged or impaired renal (kidney) or hepatic (liver) functions, epilepsy, Parkinson's disease, or mental illness.

QUICK REVIEW

• ANTI-INFLAMMATORY •

The most important considerations in choosing an anti-inflammatory agent (nonsteroidal anti-inflammatory drug or "NSAID") are: pain relief; anti-inflammatory activity, and the potential for allergic reaction or sensitivity to certain active ingredients.

ANTI-INFLAMMATORY AGENTS (NSAIDS) ARE A CLASS OF DRUGS WHICH:

- inhibit the action of prostaglandins (hormonelike substances) in the central nervous system, thereby temporarily reducing the perception of physical pain with little loss of sensibility to other physical sensation,
- are used both for their anti-inflammatory and analgesic properties, to temporarily alleviate symptoms such as: headache, fever, backache, sinus pain, muscle strain, menstrual pain, and similar ailments. Some NSAIDs also provide temporary anti-inflammatory relief for ailments such as rheumatoid arthritis and osteoarthritis,
- can have adverse effects in some instances such as aggravation of gastrointestinal (GI) conditions such as heartburn and ulcer, and can produce allergic reactions in persons who are aspirin-intolerant or hypersensitive.

See also: Analgesics

ACTIVE INGREDIENTS:
ACETAMINOPHEN AND ASPIRIN

QUICK FACTS

BRAND NAMES:
- Extra Strength Excedrin
- Goody's Extra Strength Headache Powders

SYMPTOMS RELIEVED:
Minor aches and pains such as those associated with headache(s).

HOW TO TAKE:
Comes in tablet, chewable tablet, caplet, capsule, and powder forms. Swallow tablet or capsule with liquid. Sprinkle powder over liquid, then swallow. Do not crush or chew timed-release tablet. Although acetaminophen does not normally cause GI irritation, aspirin can—as a result these medications should be taken with food.

USUAL ADULT DOSE:
Minor aches and pains: 325 to 650 milligrams every 4 hours or as needed, not to exceed 4 grams a day. For extra strength products, dosage may range to 500 milligrams every 3 hours to 1,000 milligrams every 6 hours.

USUAL CHILD DOSE:
4 to 5 doses per day, not to exceed 5 doses in 24 hours. Dosage varies based on infant or child's age.

OVERDOSE SYMPTOMS:
Nausea, vomiting, diaphoresis, diarrhea, discomfort, fever, impaired vision, sweats, bloody urine, abnormal thirst, nervous agitation, and malaise. In some cases, hepatic toxicity (liver poisoning),

or capillary and other hematological abnormalities may result. If you suspect an overdose, immediately seek medical attention.

SIDE EFFECTS:
Aspirin: None in most cases of common use, however normal aspirin use can result in common gastrointestinal (GI) irritations such as heartburn and indigestion. Aspirin affects the hypothalamus, resulting in dilation of small blood vessels in skin. Low dosages may reduce risk of blood clotting as aspirin inhibits clotting of small blood cells. Aspirin use may however contribute to anemia in anemic individuals.

Acetaminophen: Long-term ingestion of high dosages of acetaminophen may increase risk of liver and kidney damage. In rare cases, extreme fatigue and drowsiness, allergic skin eruptions (rash, hives, itch), sore throat and fever, bleeding or bruising, urinary discomfort or blood in urine, jaundiced skin or eyes may result.

CHECK WITH YOUR DOCTOR OR PHARMACIST BEFORE COMBINING ACETAMINOPHEN/ASPIRIN COMBINATION WITH:
Anticoagulants, aspirin, and other salicylates, tetracycline, cellulose-based laxatives, Isoniazid (anti-tuberculosis) medication. Excessive ingestion of alcohol while taking acetaminophen can increase the risk of liver damage or disease (hepatic toxicity). Ingestion of alcohol while taking aspirin can increase risk of GI ulceration. Avoid use of medication containing aspirin if you have a history of anemia. Also avoid use of medication containing aspirin, if possible, one week

prior to surgery, as aspirin may increase possibility of postoperative bleeding.

PREGNANCY OR BREASTFEEDING:
High dosage of acetaminophen has in isolated cases caused anemia in mother and kidney failure in fetus. In third trimester, use of medication containing aspirin should be discouraged. No harmful effects have been reported regarding nursing infants, but aspirin use by a nursing mother should be considered a potential risk for a nursing child as the drug will be passed on to the infant in milk. In all cases, a physician should be consulted.

PRECAUTIONS FOR CHILDREN:
In general, administer to infants or children only when consulting a physician and follow instructions on medication.

SPECIAL WARNING:
Aspirin use in children and teenagers with influenza (flu), chicken pox, and other viral infections may be associated with development of Reye's syndrome. This rare but acute and often life-threatening condition has caused permanent brain damage in survivors. Symptoms include: vomiting, lethargy, bellicosity, leading possibly to delirium and coma.

55+

PRECAUTIONS FOR SENIORS:
Seniors generally don't eliminate drugs as efficiently as younger persons, and should avoid high dosages. Aspirin use can cause GI irritation and possibly stomach or intestinal bleeding in seniors, manifested usually by dark stools.

QUICK FACTS

SPECIAL WARNINGS:
Chronic alcoholics are at risk for hepatic (liver) function impairment if taking high dosages of acetaminophen. Always check expiration date on label of medication. Do not take if medication has expired. Do not take medication containing aspirin which emits a vinegar-like odor. This indicates that it is decomposing and is unsafe for use.

INFORM YOUR DOCTOR BEFORE TAKING ACETAMINOPHEN/ASPIRIN COMBINATION IF YOU HAVE:
Liver or kidney disease or damage, an allergy to acetaminophen or aspirin, asthma, anemia, or other hematological condition, GI sensitivity, viral infection, hypoglycemia.

ACTIVE INGREDIENTS:

ACETAMINOPHEN AND CAFFEINE COMBINATION

BRAND NAMES:
- BAYER SELECT MAXIMUM STRENGTH
- EXCEDRIN ASPIRIN-FREE
- FENDOL

SYMPTOMS RELIEVED:
Minor aches and pains such as those associated with headache(s).

HOW TO TAKE:
Comes in tablet, caplet, capsule, and powder forms. Swallow with liquid. Sprinkle powder over liquid, then swallow. Do not crush or chew timed-release tablets. Caffeine can cause gastrointestinal (GI) irritation and should be taken with food or following a meal.

USUAL ADULT DOSE:
12.5 milligrams every 4 to 6 hours, not to exceed 25 milligrams in a 4 to 6 hour period or 75 milligrams in a 24 hour period.

USUAL CHILD DOSE:
Do not administer to children under 16 unless under direction of physician. Dosage may vary based on infant or child's age.

OVERDOSE SYMPTOMS:
Nervous agitation, disorientation, confusion, severe headache, convulsions, GI bleeding, or hemorrhage. If you suspect an overdose, seek medical attention immediately.

SIDE EFFECTS:
No serious effects in most cases of common

QUICK FACTS

use, however normal use of caffeine can result in common GI irritations such as heartburn and indigestion. Less common side effects include dizziness, nausea, stomach cramps, and headache.

CHECK WITH YOUR DOCTOR OR PHARMACIST BEFORE COMBINING ACETAMINOPHEN OR CAFFEINE WITH:

Antacids, anticoagulants, aspirin, asthma medication, other nonsteroidal anti-inflammatory drugs (NSAIDs), tetracycline, and any other medication.

PREGNANCY OR BREASTFEEDING:

Animal studies have indicated an adverse effect on fetus, but no adequate studies have been performed on humans. No harmful effects have been reported regarding nursing infants, but caffeine use by a nursing mother should be considered a potential risk for a nursing child as the drug will be passed on to the infant in the mother's milk. In all cases, a physician should be consulted.

PRECAUTIONS FOR CHILDREN:

In general, caffeine and other NSAIDs are not advised for children under 15. Administer caffeine to infants or children only when consulting a physician and follow instructions on medication (see above).

55+ **PRECAUTIONS FOR SENIORS:**

Seniors generally don't eliminate drugs as efficiently as younger persons, and should avoid high dosages. Seniors (over 65) are at special risk for development of ulcers if taking caffeine in high doses. Prolonged use can also lead to kidney and liver damage.

SPECIAL WARNINGS:

Don't take caffeine medication if you are aspirin intolerant or allergic to other NSAIDs. If in doubt, always consult a pharmacist or physician. Also avoid if you have GI conditions such as gastritis, peptic ulcer, enteritis, ileitis, colitis; asthma, high blood pressure, or hematologic (bleeding) problems. Avoid alcohol while taking this or any other NSAID.

INFORM YOUR DOCTOR BEFORE TAKING CAFFEINE IF YOU HAVE:

An allergy or intolerance to aspirin or other NSAIDs, damaged or impaired renal (kidney) or hepatic (liver) functions, epilepsy, Parkinson's disease or mental illness.

QUICK FACTS

ACTIVE INGREDIENT:
ASPIRIN

BRAND NAMES:
- ALKA-SELTZER
- ASCRIPTIN
- ASPERGUM
- BAYER
- BC POWDER
- BUFFERIN
- BUFFEX
- ECOTRIN
- EMPIRIN
- GOODY'S
- MAGNAPRIN
- NORWICH
- ST. JOSEPH
- WESPRIN

SYMPTOMS RELIEVED:
Minor aches and pains such as those associated with headache(s).

HOW TO TAKE:
Comes in tablet, chewable tablet, caplet, capsule, powder, and solution forms. Swallow tablet, capsule, or caplet with liquid. Sprinkle powder over liquid, then swallow. Do not crush or chew timed-release tablet. Aspirin can cause gastrointestinal (GI) irritation and should be taken with food or following meal.

USUAL ADULT DOSE:
Minor aches and pains: 325 to 650 milligrams every 4 hours or as needed, not to exceed 4 grams a day. For extra strength products, dosage may range to 500 milligrams every 3 hours to 1,000 milligrams every 6 hours.

USUAL CHILD DOSE:
4 to 5 doses per day, not to exceed 5 doses in 24 hours. Dosage varies based on infant or child's age.

OVERDOSE SYMPTOMS:
Respiratory difficulty, hyperventilation, hyperthermia, nausea and vomiting, severe diarrhea, impaired vision, bloody urine, abnormal thirst, nervous agitation, disorientation and dizziness. In some cases, capillary and other hematological abnormalities may result. If you suspect an overdose, immediately seek medical attention.

SIDE EFFECTS:
No serious effects in most cases of common use, however normal aspirin use can result in common gastrointestinal (GI) irritations such as heartburn and indigestion. Aspirin affects hypothalamus, resulting in dilation of small blood vessels in skin. Low dosages may reduce risk of blood clotting as aspirin inhibits blood clotting. Aspirin use may however contribute to anemia in anemic individuals.

CHECK WITH YOUR DOCTOR OR PHARMACIST BEFORE COMBINING ASPIRIN WITH:
Anticoagulants, asthma medication, other salicylates, tetracycline, and any other medication. Ingestion of alcohol while taking aspirin can increase risk of GI ulceration. Avoid aspirin use if you have aspirin intolerance, asthma, rhinitis, or a history of anemia (iron poor blood). Also avoid use of aspirin, if possible, one week prior to surgery, as it may increase possibility of postoperative bleeding.

QUICK FACTS

PREGNANCY OR BREASTFEEDING:
Animal studies have indicated an adverse effect on fetus, but no adequate studies have been performed on humans. In third trimester, aspirin use should be discouraged. No harmful effects have been reported regarding nursing infants, but aspirin use by a nursing mother should be considered a potential risk for a nursing child as the drug will be passed on to the infant in milk. In all cases, a physician should be consulted.

PRECAUTIONS FOR CHILDREN:
In general, administer to infants or children only when consulting a physician and follow instructions on medication.

SPECIAL WARNING:
Aspirin use in children and teenagers with influenza (flu), chicken pox and other viral infections may be associated with development of Reye's syndrome. This rare but acute and often life-threatening condition has caused permanent brain damage in survivors. Symptoms include: vomiting, lethargy, bellicosity, leading possibly to delirium and coma.

55+

PRECAUTIONS FOR SENIORS:
Seniors generally don't eliminate drugs as efficiently as younger persons, and should avoid high dosages. Buffered effervescent aspirin products contain high sodium content and should be avoided if on a restricted sodium diet. Aspirin use can cause GI irritation and possibly stomach or intestinal bleeding in seniors, manifested usually by dark stools.

SPECIAL WARNINGS:
Always check expiration date on label of medication. Do not take if medication has expired. Do not take aspirin which emits a vinegar-like odor. This indicates that it is decomposing and is unsafe for use.

INFORM YOUR DOCTOR BEFORE TAKING ASPIRIN IF YOU HAVE:
An allergy to aspirin, are asthmatic, anemic, or have other hematological conditions, or have GI sensitivity.

QUICK FACTS

ACTIVE INGREDIENTS:
ASPIRIN AND CAFFEINE COMBINATION

BRAND NAMES:
- Anacin
- BC Powder
- Cope
- Dristan
- Excedrin
- Fendol
- Gensan

SYMPTOMS RELIEVED:
Minor aches and pains such as those associated with headache(s).

HOW TO TAKE:
Comes in tablet, caplet, capsule, and powder forms. Swallow with liquid. Sprinkle powder over liquid, then swallow. Do not crush or chew timed-release tablets. Caffeine can cause gastro-intestinal (GI) irritation and should be taken with food or following meal.

USUAL ADULT DOSE:
12.5 milligrams every 4 to 6 hours, not to exceed 25 milligrams in a 4 to 6 hour period or 75 milligrams in a 24 hour period.

USUAL CHILD DOSE:
Do not administer to children under 16 unless under direction of physician. Dosage may vary based on infant or child's age.

OVERDOSE SYMPTOMS:
Nervous agitation, disorientation, confusion, severe headache, convulsions, GI bleeding or hemorrhage. If you suspect an overdose, immediately seek medical attention.

SIDE EFFECTS:
No serious effects in most cases of common use, however normal use of caffeine can result in common GI irritations such as heartburn and indigestion. Less common side effects include dizziness, nausea, stomach cramps, and headache.

CHECK WITH YOUR DOCTOR OR PHARMACIST BEFORE COMBINING CAFFEINE WITH:
Antacids, anticoagulants, aspirin, asthma medication, other nonsteroidal anti-inflammatory drugs (NSAIDs), tetracycline, and any other medication. Combination with acetaminophen increases risk of kidney damage. Ingestion of alcohol while taking salicylates can increase risk of GI ulceration. Avoid caffeine if you have a history of anemia. Also avoid use of caffeine, if possible, one week prior to surgery, as it may increase possibility of postoperative bleeding.

PREGNANCY OR BREASTFEEDING:
Animal studies have indicated an adverse effect on fetus, but no adequate studies have been performed on humans. No harmful effects have been reported regarding nursing infants, but caffeine use by a nursing mother should be considered a potential risk for a nursing child as the drug will be passed on to the infant in the mother's milk. In all cases, a physician should be consulted.

PRECAUTIONS FOR CHILDREN:
In general, caffeine and other NSAIDs are not advised for children under 15. Administer caffeine to infants or children only when consulting a physician and follow instructions on medication (see above).

Q U I C K F A C T S

55+ **PRECAUTIONS FOR SENIORS:**

Seniors generally don't eliminate drugs as efficiently as younger persons, and should avoid high dosages. Seniors (over 65) are at special risk for development of ulcers if taking caffeine in high doses. Prolonged use can also lead to kidney and liver damage.

SPECIAL WARNINGS:

Don't take caffeine medication if you are aspirin intolerant or allergic to other NSAIDs. If in doubt, always consult a pharmacist or physician. Also avoid if you have GI conditions such as gastritis, peptic ulcer, enteritis, ileitis, colitis; asthma, high blood pressure, or hematologic (bleeding) problems. Avoid alcohol while taking this or any other NSAID.

INFORM YOUR DOCTOR BEFORE TAKING CAFFEINE IF YOU HAVE:

An allergy or intolerance to aspirin or other NSAIDs, damaged or impaired renal (kidney) or hepatic (liver) functions, epilepsy, Parkinson's disease or mental illness.

ACTIVE INGREDIENT:
IBUPROFEN

BRAND NAMES:
- Advil
- Arthritis Foundation (backache and muscle pain)
- Bayer Select Pain Relief
- Genpril
- Ibuprohm
- Motrin
- Nupron
- Obuprin

SYMPTOMS RELIEVED:
Minor aches and pains such as those associated with headache(s).

HOW TO TAKE:
Comes in tablet, caplet, and gelcap forms. Swallow with liquid. Do not crush or chew timed-release tablet. Ibuprofen can cause gastrointestinal (GI) irritation and should be taken with food or following meal.

USUAL ADULT DOSE:
Minor aches and pains: 200 milligrams every 4 to 6 hours as needed, not to exceed 1.2 grams per day.

USUAL CHILD DOSE:
Always consult with a pharmacist or physician. Dosage may vary based on infant or child's age.

OVERDOSE SYMPTOMS:
Nervous agitation, disorientation, confusion, severe headache, convulsions, GI bleeding or hemorrhage. If you suspect an overdose, immediately seek medical attention.

QUICK FACTS

QUICK FACTS

SIDE EFFECTS:
No serious effects in most cases of common use, however normal use of ibuprofen can result in common GI irritations such as heartburn and indigestion. Less common side effects include dizziness, nausea, stomach cramps, and headache.

CHECK WITH YOUR DOCTOR OR PHARMACIST BEFORE COMBINING IBUPROFEN WITH:
Antacids, anticoagulants, aspirin, asthma medication, other nonsteroidal anti-inflammatory drugs (NSAIDs), tetracycline, and any other medication. Combination with acetaminophen increases risk of kidney damage. Ingestion of alcohol while taking ibuprofen can increase risk of GI ulceration. Avoid ibuprofen if you have a history of anemia. Also avoid use of ibuprofen, if possible, one week prior to surgery, as it may increase possibility of postoperative bleeding.

PREGNANCY OR BREASTFEEDING:
No harmful effects have been reported regarding nursing infants, but ibuprofen use by a nursing mother should be considered a potential risk for a nursing child as the drug will be passed on to the infant in the mother's milk. In all cases, a physician should be consulted.

PRECAUTIONS FOR CHILDREN:
In general, ibuprofen and other NSAIDs are not advised for children under 15. Administer ibuprofen to infants or children only when consulting a physician and follow instructions on medication.

55+ **PRECAUTIONS FOR SENIORS:**
Seniors generally don't eliminate drugs as efficiently as younger persons, and should avoid high dosages. Seniors (over 65) are at special risk for development of ulcers if taking ibuprofen in high doses. Prolonged use can also lead to kidney and liver damage.

SPECIAL WARNINGS:
Don't take ibuprofen medication if you are aspirin intolerant or allergic to other NSAIDs. If in doubt, always consult a pharmacist or physician. Also avoid if you have GI conditions such as gastritis, peptic ulcer, enteritis, ileitis, colitis; asthma, high blood pressure, or hematologic (bleeding) problems. Avoid alcohol while taking this or any other NSAID.

INFORM YOUR DOCTOR BEFORE TAKING IBUPROFEN IF YOU HAVE:
An allergy or intolerance to aspirin or other NSAIDs, damaged or impaired renal (kidney) or hepatic (liver) functions, epilepsy, Parkinson's disease, or mental illness.

QUICK FACTS

ACTIVE INGREDIENT:
KETOPROFEN

BRAND NAMES:
- ACTRON
- ORUDIS

SYMPTOMS RELIEVED:
Minor aches and pains such as those associated with headache(s).

HOW TO TAKE:
Comes in tablet forms. Swallow with liquid. Do not crush or chew timed-release tablets. Ketoprofen can cause gastrointestinal (GI) irritation and should be taken with food or following meal.

USUAL ADULT DOSE:
12.5 milligrams every 4 to 6 hours, not to exceed 25 milligrams in a 4 to 6 hour period or 75 milligrams in a 24 hour period.

USUAL CHILD DOSE:
Do not administer to children under 16 unless under direction of physician. Dosage may vary based on infant or child's age.

OVERDOSE SYMPTOMS:
Nervous agitation, disorientation, confusion, severe headache, convulsions, GI bleeding or hemorrhage. If you suspect an overdose, immediately seek medical attention.

SIDE EFFECTS:
No serious effects in most cases of common use, however normal use of ketoprofen can result in common GI irritations such as heart-

burn and indigestion. Less common side effects include dizziness, nausea, stomach cramps, and headache.

CHECK WITH YOUR DOCTOR OR PHARMACIST BEFORE COMBINING KETOPROFEN WITH:
Antacids, anticoagulants, aspirin, asthma medication, other nonsteroidal anti-inflammatory drugs (NSAIDs), tetracycline, and any other medication. Combination with acetaminophen increases risk of kidney damage. Ingestion of alcohol while taking ketoprofen can increase risk of GI ulceration. Avoid ketoprofen if you have a history of anemia. Also avoid use of ketoprofen, if possible, one week prior to surgery, as it may increase possibility of postoperative bleeding.

PREGNANCY OR BREASTFEEDING:
Animal studies have indicated an adverse effect on fetus, but no adequate studies have been performed on humans. No harmful effects have been reported regarding nursing infants, but ketoprofen use by a nursing mother should be considered a potential risk for a nursing child as the drug will be passed on to the infant in the mother's milk. In all cases, a physician should be consulted.

PRECAUTIONS FOR CHILDREN:
In general, ketoprofen and other NSAIDs are not advised for children under 15. Administer ketoprofen to infants or children only when consulting a physician and follow instructions on medication (see above).

55+

PRECAUTIONS FOR SENIORS:
Seniors generally don't eliminate drugs as effi-

ciently as younger persons, and should avoid high dosages. Seniors (over 65) are at special risk for development of ulcers if taking ketoprofen in high doses. Prolonged use can also lead to kidney and liver damage.

SPECIAL WARNINGS:
Don't take ketoprofen medication if you are aspirin intolerant or allergic to other NSAIDs. If in doubt, always consult a pharmacist or physician. Also avoid if you have GI conditions such as gastritis, peptic ulcer, enteritis, ileitis, colitis; asthma, high blood pressure, or hematologic (bleeding) problems. Avoid alcohol while taking this or any other NSAID.

INFORM YOUR DOCTOR BEFORE TAKING KETOPROFEN IF YOU HAVE:
An allergy or intolerance to aspirin or other NSAIDs, damaged or impaired renal (kidney) or hepatic (liver) functions, epilepsy, Parkinson's disease, or mental illness.

•MIGRAINE RELIEF AGENT•

The most important considerations in choosing a migraine relief (vascoconstrictor) agent are: its effectiveness in helping to relieve pain of migraine headache, and side effects associated with the drug.

QUICK REVIEW

MIGRAINE RELIEF AGENTS ARE A CLASS OF DRUGS WHICH:

- stimulate the central nervous system (CNS) and constrict dilated blood vessels in brain in order to relieve pain of migraine headache,
- do not prevent migraine headache,
- in over-the-counter (OTC) products, contain caffeine as an active ingredient, usually in combination with analgesic drugs such as aspirin and/or acetaminophen,
- may produce adverse side effects (especially in high dosages), such as over-stimulation of CNS and irritability—due to caffeine content; stomach upset—due to aspirin content; or, in case of long-term use, may damage liver—due to acetaminophen content.

QUICK FACTS

ACTIVE INGREDIENTS:

ACETAMINOPHEN, ASPIRIN, AND CAFFEINE COMBINATION

BRAND NAMES:

- BUFFETS II TABLETS
- EXCEDRIN EXTRA-STRENGTH
- GELPIRIN
- GOODY'S EXTRA STRENGTH HEADACHE POWDERS
- PAIN RELIEVER TABS
- SUPAC
- VANQUISH

SYMPTOMS RELIEVED:
Minor aches and pains such as those associated with migraine headache(s).

HOW TO TAKE:
Comes in tablet, caplet, capsule, and powder forms. Swallow with liquid. Sprinkle powder over liquid, then swallow. Do not crush or chew timed-release tablets. Aspirin and caffeine both can cause gastrointestinal (GI) irritation and should be taken with food or following meal.

USUAL ADULT DOSE:
1 or 2 capsules, tablets, caplets or 1 powder packet every 2 to 6 hours.

ACTIVE INGREDIENTS:

ASPIRIN AND CAFFEINE COMBINATION

QUICK FACTS

BRAND NAMES:

- ANACIN
- BC POWDER
- COPE
- DRISTAN
- EXCEDRIN
- FENDOL
- GENSAN

SYMPTOMS RELIEVED:

Minor aches and pains such as those associated with the common cold, flu, headache, toothache, sinusitis, hay fever and other respiratory allergies, muscular aches, backache, minor arthritis pain, menstrual discomfort, and reduction of fever.

HOW TO TAKE:

Comes in tablet, caplet, capsule, and powder forms. Swallow with liquid. Sprinkle powder over liquid, then swallow. Do not crush or chew timed-release tablets. Caffeine can cause gastrointestinal (GI) irritation and should be taken with food or following meal.

USUAL ADULT DOSE:

12.5 milligrams every 4 to 6 hours, not to exceed 25 milligrams in a 4 to 6 hour period or 75 milligrams in a 24 hour period.

USUAL CHILD DOSE:

Do not administer to children under 16 unless under direction of physician. Dosage may vary based on infant or child's age.

Q U I C K F A C T S

OVERDOSE SYMPTOMS:
Nervous agitation, disorientation, confusion, severe headache, convulsions, GI bleeding or hemorrhage. If you suspect an overdose, immediately seek medical attention.

SIDE EFFECTS:
No serious effects in most cases of common use, however normal use of caffeine can result in common GI irritations such as heartburn and indigestion. Less common side effects include dizziness, nausea, stomach cramps, and headache.

CHECK WITH YOUR DOCTOR OR PHARMACIST BEFORE COMBINING CAFFEINE WITH:
Antacids, anticoagulants, aspirin, asthma medication, other nonsteroidal anti-inflammatory drugs (NSAIDs), tetracycline, and any other medication. Combination with acetaminophen increases risk of kidney damage. Ingestion of alcohol while taking salicylates can increase risk of GI ulceration. Avoid caffeine if you have a history of anemia. Also avoid use of caffeine, if possible, one week prior to surgery, as it may increase possibility of postoperative bleeding.

PREGNANCY OR BREASTFEEDING:
Animal studies have indicated an adverse effect on fetus, but no adequate studies have been performed on humans. No harmful effects have been reported regarding nursing infants, but caffeine use by a nursing mother should be considered a potential risk for a nursing child as the drug will be passed on to the infant in the mother's milk. In all cases, a physician should be consulted.

PRECAUTIONS FOR CHILDREN:
In general, caffeine and other NSAIDs are not advised for children under 15. Administer caffeine to infants or children only when consulting a physician and follow instructions on medication (see above).

PRECAUTIONS FOR SENIORS:
Seniors generally don't eliminate drugs as efficiently as younger persons, and should avoid high dosages. Seniors (over 65) are at special risk for development of ulcers if taking caffeine in high doses. Prolonged use can also lead to kidney and liver damage.

SPECIAL WARNINGS:
Don't take caffeine medication if you are aspirin intolerant or allergic to other NSAIDs. If in doubt, always consult a pharmacist or physician. Also avoid if you have GI conditions such as gastritis, peptic ulcer, enteritis, ileitis, colitis; asthma, high blood pressure, or hematologic (bleeding) problems. Avoid alcohol while taking this or any other NSAID.

INFORM YOUR DOCTOR BEFORE TAKING CAFFEINE IF YOU HAVE:
An allergy or intolerance to aspirin or other NSAIDs, damaged or impaired renal (kidney) or hepatic (liver) functions, epilepsy, Parkinson's disease or mental illness.

HEARTBURN, STOMACH UPSET, AND GAS

QUICK REVIEW

• ANTACID •

The most important considerations in choosing an antacid are: its action in reducing or neutralizing the degree acidity in the stomach and upper digestive tract, and potential side effects associated with the drug.

ANTACIDS ARE A CLASS OF DRUGS WHICH:

- are often taken to relieve the symptoms of common gastrointestinal upsets and conditions such as acid indigestion, sour stomach, and heartburn,
- are also used by doctors in stronger dosages and prescription forms to treat more serious gastrointestinal conditions such as peptic ulcer,
- are often grouped according to their action: systemic (containing sodium bicarbonate), nonsystemic—the fastest acting (calcium carbonate, simethicone), cathartic (magnesium carbonate), histamine H_2 antagonist—which block the stimulation of gastric-acid secretions (cimetidine and ranitidine), and phosphate-binding (aluminum),
- should only be used for short-term symptomatic relief as harmful side effects, such as high blood pressure, kidney stones, or urinary-tract infections (due to sodium content of bicarbonate) can result when used chronically or in repeated high dosages,
- do not affect the underlying cause of the symptoms which they are designed to relieve or suppress.

ACTIVE INGREDIENTS:

ALUMINUM HYDROXIDE AND MAGNESIUM CARBONATE

BRAND NAMES:

- GAVISCON (also contains benzyl alcohol, tartrazine—a dye, glycerin, saccharin, sodium alginate, sorbitol, flavors)
- GAVISCON EXTRA STRENGTH–LIQUID (also contains benzyl alcohol, edetate sodium, glycerin, saccharin, simethicone, sodium alginate, sorbitol, flavors)
- GAVISCON EXTRA STRENGTH–CHEWABLE TABLETS (also contains alginic acid, alginate, sodium bicarbonate, sucrose, flavors)
- MAALOX HEARTBURN RELIEF (also contains calcium carbonate, tartrazine—a dye, magnesium alginate, methylparaben, propylparaben, potassium bicarbonate, sorbitol, and mint flavor)

SYMPTOMS RELIEVED:

Acid indigestion, heartburn, sour stomach, associated with common upset stomach.

HOW TO TAKE:

Comes in liquid and tablet forms. Chew tablets well before swallowing. Do not swallow whole.

GAVISCON products–liquid and chewable tablets—should be taken after meals and at bedtime. Follow each dose with a half glass (4 oz.) of water.

USUAL ADULT DOSE:

Dosages vary according to product and symptoms. In all cases follow specific product instructions.

QUICK FACTS

USUAL CHILD DOSE:
Only administer to children between under 12 under doctor's supervision or direction. These products are generally not advised for children younger than 3, and never for infants. In all cases follow specific product instructions.

OVERDOSE SYMPTOMS:
Constipation, diarrhea, nausea, abdominal and muscular cramps, dehydration, irregular heartbeat, fatigue, disorientation, bone pain.

SIDE EFFECTS:
No serious effects in most cases of common use. Side effects with these products rarely occur unless medication is taken over long period of time. Occasionally, mild constipation may occur. In rare cases nausea, vomiting, nervous agitation, dizziness, disorientation, frequent urination, severe constipation fatigue, and swelling of feet and ankles have been reported. In any of these cases, discontinue use of the product and call your doctor immediately.

CHECK WITH YOUR DOCTOR OR PHARMACIST BEFORE COMBINING THIS PRODUCT WITH:
Anticoagulants, any other antacids—especially any containing sodium bicarbonate, or other drugs and preparations.

PREGNANCY OR BREASTFEEDING:
Safety of this drug for use during pregnancy or while nursing has not been established. In all cases you should consult your doctor before using any drug during pregnancy or while nursing.

PRECAUTIONS FOR CHILDREN:
These products should only be used with doctor's supervision or direction for children under 12. These products are not recommended for use with children under 3 and should never be used with infants. Consult your doctor and follow instructions on medication (see above).

55+

PRECAUTIONS FOR SENIORS:
Seniors generally may be more prone to side effects and possible adverse effects of these products than younger individuals.

SPECIAL WARNINGS:
Do not use this product if you are allergic to aluminum hydroxide and magnesium carbonate, or any of the inactive ingredients contained in these products, or if you have kidney disease. Avoid high dosages for longer more than two weeks, as "acid rebound" (secretion of excess stomach acid) can occur.

INFORM YOUR DOCTOR BEFORE TAKING THIS PRODUCT IF YOU HAVE:
High calcium levels in your blood, or any form of kidney disease (including kidney stones).

QUICK FACTS

ACTIVE INGREDIENTS:

ALUMINUM HYDROXIDE AND MAGNESIUM HYDROXIDE

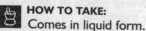

BRAND NAMES:

- MAALOX

SYMPTOMS RELIEVED:
Acid indigestion, heartburn, sour stomach, associated with common upset stomach.

HOW TO TAKE:
Comes in liquid form.

USUAL ADULT DOSE:
2 to 4 teaspoonsful 4 times per day, or as directed by your doctor, not to exceed 16 teaspoonsful in a 24 hour period.

USUAL CHILD DOSE:
Only administer to children under 12 under doctor's supervision or direction. These products are generally not advised for children younger than 3, and never for infants. In all cases follow specific product instructions.

OVERDOSE SYMPTOMS:
Constipation, diarrhea, nausea, abdominal and muscular cramps, dehydration, irregular heartbeat, fatigue, disorientation, bone pain.

SIDE EFFECTS:
No serious effects in most cases of common use. Side effects with these products rarely occur unless medication is taken over long period of time. Occasionally, mild constipation may occur. In any of these cases, discontinue use of the product and call your doctor immediately.

CHECK WITH YOUR DOCTOR OR PHARMACIST BEFORE COMBINING THIS PRODUCT WITH:
Anticoagulants, any other antacids—especially any containing sodium bicarbonate, or other drugs and preparations.

PREGNANCY OR BREASTFEEDING:
Safety of this drug for use during pregnancy or while nursing has not been established. In all cases you should consult your doctor before using any drug during pregnancy or while nursing.

PRECAUTIONS FOR CHILDREN:
These products should only be used with doctor's supervision or direction for children under 12. These products are not recommended for use with children under 3 and should never be used with infants. Consult your doctor and follow instructions on medication (see above).

55+

PRECAUTIONS FOR SENIORS:
Seniors generally may be more prone to side effects and possible adverse effects of these products than younger individuals.

SPECIAL WARNINGS:
Do not use this product if you are allergic to aluminum hydroxide and magnesium hydroxide, or any of the inactive ingredients contained in these products, or if you have kidney disease. Avoid high dosages for longer more than two weeks, as "acid rebound" (secretion of excess stomach acid) can occur.

INFORM YOUR DOCTOR BEFORE TAKING THIS PRODUCT IF YOU HAVE:
High calcium levels in your blood, or any form of kidney disease (including kidney stones).

QUICK FACTS

ACTIVE INGREDIENTS:

ALUMINUM HYDROXIDE AND MAGNESIUM TRISILICATE

BRAND NAMES:

- GAVISCON (also contains alginic acid, sodium bitrisilicate, sucrose, flavors)
- GAVISCON-2 (also contains alginic acid, sodium bitrisilicate, sucrose, flavors)

SYMPTOMS RELIEVED:

Acid indigestion, heartburn, sour stomach, associated with common upset stomach.

HOW TO TAKE:

Comes in chewable tablet forms. Chew tablets well before swallowing. Do not swallow whole. These products should be taken after meals and at bedtime. Follow each dose with a half glass (4 oz.) of water.

USUAL ADULT DOSE:

GAVISCON: Chew 2 to 4 tablets 4 times per day, or as directed by your doctor, not to exceed 16 tablets in a 24 hour period.

GAVISCON-2: Chew 1 to 2 tablets 4 times per day, or as directed by your doctor, not to exceed 8 tablets in a 24 hour period.

USUAL CHILD DOSE:

Only administer to children between under 12 under doctor's supervision or direction. These products are generally not advised for children younger than 3, and never for infants. In all cases follow specific product instructions.

OVERDOSE SYMPTOMS:
Constipation, diarrhea, nausea, abdominal and muscular cramps, dehydration, irregular heartbeat, fatigue, disorientation, bone pain.

SIDE EFFECTS:
No serious effects in most cases of common use. Side effects with these products rarely occur unless medication is taken over long period of time. Occasionally, mild constipation may occur. In rare cases nausea, vomiting, nervous agitation, dizziness, disorientation, frequent urination, severe constipation fatigue, and swelling of feet and ankles have been reported. In any of these cases, discontinue use of the product and call your doctor immediately.

CHECK WITH YOUR DOCTOR OR PHARMACIST BEFORE COMBINING THIS PRODUCT WITH:
Anticoagulants, any other antacids—especially any containing sodium bicarbonate, or other drugs and preparations.

PREGNANCY OR BREASTFEEDING:
Safety of this drug for use during pregnancy or while nursing has not been established. In all cases you should consult your doctor before using any drug during pregnancy or while nursing.

PRECAUTIONS FOR CHILDREN:
These products should only be used with doctor's supervision or direction for children under 12. These products are not recommended for use with children under 3 and should never be used with infants. Consult your doctor and follow instructions on medication (see above).

Q U I C K F A C T S

PRECAUTIONS FOR SENIORS:
Seniors generally may be more prone to side effects and possible adverse effects of these products than younger individuals.

SPECIAL WARNINGS:
Do not use this product if you are allergic to aluminum hydroxide and magnesium trisilicate, or any of the inactive ingredients contained in these products, or if you have kidney disease. Avoid high dosages for longer more than two weeks, as "acid rebound" (secretion of excess stomach acid) can occur.

INFORM YOUR DOCTOR BEFORE TAKING THIS PRODUCT IF YOU HAVE:
High calcium levels in your blood, or any form of kidney disease (including kidney stones).

ACTIVE INGREDIENTS:

ALUMINUM HYDROXIDE, MAGNESIUM HYDROXIDE, AND SIMETHICONE

Rx **BRAND NAMES:**

- Di-Gel–liquid
  (also contains methylcellulose, sodium, saccharin, sorbitol and assorted flavors)
- Maalox Extra Strength–liquid
  (also contains saccharin, sorbitol and assorted flavors)
- Maalox Extra Strength–tablet
  (also contains dextrose, saccharin, sorbitol, sugar, and assorted flavors)
- Mylanta Fast-Acting
  (also contains methylcellulose, sodium, saccharin, sorbitol and assorted flavors)
- Mylanta Maximum Strength Fast-Acting
  (also contains methylcellulose, sodium, saccharin, sorbitol, and assorted flavors)

SYMPTOMS RELIEVED:
Acid indigestion, heartburn, sour stomach, upset stomach as well as pain and discomfort associated with retention of excess gas in digestive tract and accompanying, bloating, pressure and fullness.

HOW TO TAKE:
Comes in liquid and tablet forms. Chew tablets well before swallowing. Take dose 1 to 3 hours after meal, or as directed by your doctor. Follow each dose with a full glass (8 oz.) of water.

USUAL ADULT DOSE:
Dosages vary according to product and symptoms. In all cases follow specific product instructions.

USUAL CHILD DOSE:
Only administer to children between under 12 under doctor's supervision or direction. These products are generally not advised for children younger than 3, and never for infants. In all cases follow specific product instructions.

OVERDOSE SYMPTOMS:
Constipation, diarrhea, nausea, abdominal and muscular cramps, dehydration, irregular heartbeat, fatigue, disorientation, bone pain.

SIDE EFFECTS:
No serious effects in most cases of common use. Side effects with these products rarely occur unless medication is taken over long period of time. Occasionally, mild constipation may occur. In rare cases nausea, vomiting, nervous agitation, dizziness, disorientation, frequent urination, severe constipation fatigue, and swelling of feet and ankles have been reported. In any of these cases, discontinue use of the product and call your doctor immediately.

CHECK WITH YOUR DOCTOR OR PHARMACIST BEFORE COMBINING THIS PRODUCT WITH:
Anticoagulants, any other antacids—especially any containing sodium bicarbonate, or other drugs and preparations.

PREGNANCY OR BREASTFEEDING:
Safety of this drug for use during pregnancy or while nursing has not been established. In all cases you should consult your doctor before using any drug during pregnancy or while nursing.

PRECAUTIONS FOR CHILDREN:

These products should only be used with doctor's supervision or direction for children under 12. These products are not recommended for use with children under 3 and should never be used with infants. Consult your doctor and follow instructions on medication (see above).

55+

PRECAUTIONS FOR SENIORS:

Seniors generally may be more prone to side effects and possible adverse effects of these products than younger individuals. Seniors should specifically avoid high dosages of these products as the calcium content of this combination may provoke constipation, or the magnesium content may provoke diarrhea.

SPECIAL WARNINGS:

Do not use this product if you are allergic to aluminum hydroxide, magnesium hydroxide, simethicone, or any of the inactive ingredients contained in these products, if you are experiencing abdominal pain, cramps, nausea or vomiting, or if you have kidney disease. Avoid high dosages for longer more than two weeks, as "acid rebound" (secretion of excess stomach acid) can occur.

INFORM YOUR DOCTOR BEFORE TAKING THIS PRODUCT IF YOU HAVE:

High calcium levels in your blood, or any form of kidney disease (including kidney stones).

QUICK FACTS

ACTIVE INGREDIENT:
BISMUTH SUBSALICYLATE

BRAND NAMES:
- Bismatrol (also contains saccharin)
- Bismatrol Extra Strength
- Pepto-Bismol–tablets (also contains sodium, saccharin and cherry flavor)
- Pepto-Bismol/Pepto-Bismol Maximum Strength–liquid (also contains sodium, saccharin)

SYMPTOMS RELIEVED:
Heartburn, indigestion, mild to acute nonspecific diarrhea—including common symptoms of 'travelers' diarrhea, nausea, abdominal cramps.

HOW TO TAKE:
Comes in liquid and tablet forms. Chew tablet(s) or allow to dissolve in mouth.

USUAL ADULT DOSE:
2 tablets or 2 tablespoonsful (30 milliliters) as needed, not to exceed 8 doses in a 24 hour period. In all cases follow specific product instructions.

USUAL CHILD DOSE:
For ages 9 to 12: 1 tablet or 1 tablespoonful (15 milliliters) as needed, not to exceed 8 doses in a 24 hour period.

For ages 3 to 9: 1 teaspoonful (10 milliliters) as needed, not to exceed 8 doses in a 24 hour period.

These products are generally not advised for children younger than 3, and never for infants. In all cases follow specific product instructions.

OVERDOSE SYMPTOMS:
Severe nervous agitation, hearing loss, ringing or buzzing in ears, constipation, drowsiness, extreme fatigue, hyperventilation, rapid breathing.

SIDE EFFECTS:
No serious effects in most cases of common use, however, stools may temporarily appear gray or black during use of product. In rare cases, abdominal pain, nausea, vomiting, severe constipation, headache, sweats, confusion and disorientation may occur. In these cases, discontinue use of the product and call your doctor immediately.

CHECK WITH YOUR DOCTOR OR PHARMACIST BEFORE COMBINING BISMUTH SUBSALICYLATE WITH:
Blood thinning medications, antidiabetic drugs or other salicylates—especially aspirin.

PREGNANCY OR BREASTFEEDING:
Safety of this drug for use during pregnancy or nursing has not been established. In all cases you should consult your doctor before using any drug during pregnancy or while nursing.

PRECAUTIONS FOR CHILDREN:
These products are not recommended for use with children under 3 and should never be used with infants. Consult your doctor and follow instructions on medication (see above). See Special Warning (below) regarding Reye's syndrome.

SPECIAL WARNING FOR CHILDREN:
Use of bismuth subsalicylate—as well as other

QUICK FACTS

Q U I C K F A C T S

salicylate and aspirin, in cases involving children and teenagers with influenza (flu), chicken pox and other viral infections may be associated with development of Reye's syndrome. This rare but acute and often life-threatening condition has caused permanent brain damage in survivors. Symptoms include: vomiting, lethargy, bellicosity, leading possibly to delirium and coma.

55+

PRECAUTIONS FOR SENIORS:
Seniors generally may be more prone to side effects and possible adverse effects of these products than younger individuals. Avoid high dosages, as severe constipation may result.

SPECIAL WARNINGS:
Do not use any of these products if you are allergic to bismuth subsalicylate, other salicylate and aspirin, or any of the inactive ingredients contained in these products.

ADDITIONAL WARNINGS:
Do not use these products if you have a sensitivity or allergy to aspirin, other salicylates, or nonsteroidal anti-inflammatory drugs (NSAIDs). Do not continue use for longer than 48 hours. Use of these products should be supplemented, in cases of acute diarrhea, with liquids to prevent electrolyte/fluid depletion or dehydration.

INFORM YOUR DOCTOR BEFORE TAKING BISMUTH SUBSALICYLATE IF YOU HAVE:
Severe loss of fluids (dehydration) due to diarrhea, kidney disease such as hepatitis, a history of bleeding ulcers; or if you are treating a child with a fever.

ACTIVE INGREDIENT:
CALCIUM CARBONATE

QUICK FACTS

BRAND NAMES:
- ALKA-MINTS (also contains sorbitol, sugar, polyethylene glycol, artificial flavors)
- MYLANTA CHILDREN'S UPSET STOMACH RELIEF (also contains sugar, sorbitol, assorted flavors)
- TUMS (also contains sucrose, peppermint, or other assorted flavors)
- TUMS E-X (also contains sucrose, wintergreen, or other assorted mint and fruit flavors)
- TUMS E-X SUGAR-FREE (also contains sorbitol, aspartame, wintergreen, or other assorted mint and fruit flavors)
- TUMS ULTRA (also contains sucrose, assorted fruit and mint flavors)

SYMPTOMS RELIEVED:
Acid indigestion, heartburn, sour stomach, upset stomach.

HOW TO TAKE:
Comes in chewable tablet and liquid forms. Chew tablets thoroughly before swallowing. Take dose 1 to 3 hours after meal, or as directed by your doctor. Follow each dose with a full glass (8 oz.) of water.

USUAL ADULT DOSE:
ALKA-MINTS: Chew 1 to 2 tablets every 2 hours, or as directed by your doctor, not to exceed 9 tablets in a 24 hour period. In all cases follow specific product instructions.

TUMS: Chew 2 to 4 tablets as symptoms occur, or as directed by your doctor, continuing with hourly doses if symptoms persist or return, not to exceed 16 tablets in a 24 hour period. In all cases follow specific product instructions.

TUMS E-X: Chew 2 to 4 tablets as symptoms occur, or as directed by your doctor, continuing with hourly doses if symptoms persist or return, not to exceed 10 tablets in a 24 hour period. In all cases follow specific product instructions.

TUMS ULTRA: Chew 2 to 3 tablets as symptoms occur, or as directed by your doctor, continuing with hourly doses if symptoms persist or return, not to exceed 8 tablets in a 24 hour period. In all cases follow specific product instructions.

USUAL CHILD DOSE:
MYLANTA CHILDREN'S UPSET STOMACH RELIEF: Use weight and age chart on product packaging to determine proper child dose, not to exceed 3 tablets or 3 teaspoonsful in a 24 hour period (ages 2 to 5) or 6 tablets or 6 teaspoonsful in a 24 hour period (ages 6 to 11).

Except for Mylanta Children's Upset Stomach Relief, these products are generally not advised for children younger than 3, and never for infants. In all cases follow specific product instructions. For other products, only administer to children between under 12 under doctor's supervision or direction.

OVERDOSE SYMPTOMS:
Constipation, diarrhea, nausea, abdominal and muscular cramps, dehydration, irregular heart-beat, fatigue, disorientation, bone pain.

SIDE EFFECTS:
No serious effects in most cases of common use. Side effects with these products rarely occur unless medication is taken over long period of time. Occasionally, mild constipation may occur. In rare cases nausea, vomiting, nervous agitation, dizziness, disorientation, frequent urination, severe constipation fatigue, and swelling of feet and ankles have been reported. In any of these cases, discontinue use of the product and call your doctor immediately.

CHECK WITH YOUR DOCTOR OR PHARMACIST BEFORE COMBINING CALCIUM CARBONATE WITH:
Anticoagulants, any other antacids—especially any containing sodium bicarbonate, or other drugs and preparations.

PREGNANCY OR BREASTFEEDING:
Safety of this drug for use during pregnancy or while nursing has not been established. In all cases you should consult your doctor before using any drug during pregnancy or while nursing.

PRECAUTIONS FOR CHILDREN:
These products, except for Mylanta Children's Upset Stomach Relief should only be used with doctor's supervision or direction for children under 12. These products are not recommended for use with children under 3 and should never be used with infants. Consult your doctor and follow instructions on medication (see above).

QUICK FACTS

55+ **PRECAUTIONS FOR SENIORS:**
Seniors generally may be more prone to side effects and possible adverse effects of these products than younger individuals. Avoid high dosages as constipation is more likely to result.

SPECIAL WARNINGS:
Do not use any of these products if you are allergic to calcium carbonate or any of the inactive ingredients contained in these products, if you are experiencing abdominal pain, cramps, nausea or vomiting, or if you have kidney disease. Avoid high dosages for longer more than two weeks, as "acid rebound" (secretion of excess stomach acid) can occur.

INFORM YOUR DOCTOR BEFORE TAKING CALCIUM CARBONATE IF YOU HAVE:
High calcium levels in your blood, or any form of kidney disease (including kidney stones).

ACTIVE INGREDIENTS:

CALCIUM CARBONATE AND MAGNESIUM HYDROXIDE

Q U I C K F A C T S

BRAND NAMES:

- MYLANTA FAST-ACTING (also contains sugar, sorbitol, and various flavors)
- MYLANTA GELCAPS (also contains alcohol—may contain propylene glycol)
- MYLANTA MAXIMUM STRENGTH FAST ACTING (also contains sugar, sorbitol, and various flavors)
- ROLAIDS ANTACID TABLETS (also contains sucrose and assorted mint and fruit flavors)

SYMPTOMS RELIEVED:

Acid indigestion, heartburn, sour stomach, upset stomach.

HOW TO TAKE:

Comes in capsule and chewable tablet forms. Chew tablets thoroughly before swallowing. Take dose 1 to 3 hours after meal, or as directed by your doctor. Follow each dose with a full glass (8 oz.) of water.

USUAL ADULT DOSE:

MYLANTA FAST-ACTING: 2 to 4 tablets as symptoms occur, or as directed by your doctor, continuing with hourly doses if symptoms persist or return, not to exceed 20 tablets in a 24 hour period. In all cases follow specific product instructions.

MYLANTA MAXIMUM STRENGTH FAST ACTING: 2 to 4 tablets as symptoms occur, or as directed by your doctor, continuing with hourly doses if symptoms persist or return, not to exceed

10 tablets in a 24 hour period. In all cases follow specific product instructions.

MYLANTA GELCAPS: 2 to 4 tablets as symptoms occur, or as directed by your doctor, continuing with hourly doses if symptoms persist or return, not to exceed 24 tablets in a 24 hour period. In all cases follow specific product instructions.

ROLAIDS ANTACID TABLETS: 1 to 4 tablets as symptoms occur, or as directed by your doctor, continuing with hourly doses if symptoms persist or return, not to exceed 12 tablets in a 24 hour period. In all cases follow specific product instructions.

USUAL CHILD DOSE:
Only administer to children between under 12 under doctor's supervision or direction. These products are generally not advised for children younger than 3, and never for infants. In all cases follow specific product instructions.

OVERDOSE SYMPTOMS:
Constipation, diarrhea, nausea, abdominal and muscular cramps, dehydration, irregular heartbeat, fatigue, disorientation, bone pain.

SIDE EFFECTS:
No serious effects in most cases of common use. Side effects with these products rarely occur unless medication is taken over long period of time. Occasionally, mild constipation may occur. In rare cases nausea, vomiting, nervous agitation, dizziness, disorientation, frequent urination, severe constipation fatigue, and swelling of feet and ankles have been reported. In any of

these cases, discontinue use of the product and call your doctor immediately.

CHECK WITH YOUR DOCTOR OR PHARMACIST BEFORE COMBINING CALCIUM CARBONATE AND MAGNESIUM HYDROXIDE WITH:
Anticoagulants, any other antacids—especially any containing sodium bicarbonate, or other drugs and preparations.

PREGNANCY OR BREASTFEEDING:
Safety of this drug for use during pregnancy or while nursing has not been established. In all cases you should consult your doctor before using any drug during pregnancy or while nursing.

PRECAUTIONS FOR CHILDREN:
These products should only be used with doctor's supervision or direction for children under 12. These products are not recommended for use with children under 3 and should never be used with infants. Consult your doctor and follow instructions on medication (see above).

55+

PRECAUTIONS FOR SENIORS:
Seniors generally may be more prone to side effects and possible adverse effects of these products than younger individuals. Seniors should specifically avoid high dosages of these products as the calcium content of this combination may provoke constipation, or the magnesium content may provoke diarrhea.

SPECIAL WARNINGS:
Do not use any of these products if you are allergic to calcium carbonate and magnesium

QUICK FACTS

hydroxide or any of the inactive ingredients contained in these products, if you are experiencing abdominal pain, cramps, nausea or vomiting, or if you have kidney disease. Avoid high dosages for longer more than two weeks, as "acid rebound" (secretion of excess stomach acid) can occur.

INFORM YOUR DOCTOR BEFORE TAKING CALCIUM CARBONATE AND MAGNESIUM HYDROXIDE IF YOU HAVE:

High calcium levels in your blood, or any form of kidney disease (including kidney stones).

ACTIVE INGREDIENTS:

CALCIUM CARBONATE, MAGNESIUM HYDROXIDE AND SIMETHICONE

BRAND NAMES:

- Di-Gel

(also contains sucrose and assorted flavors)

SYMPTOMS RELIEVED:

Acid indigestion, heartburn, sour stomach, upset stomach, and accompanying symptoms of gas.

HOW TO TAKE:

Comes in chewable tablet form. Chew tablets thoroughly before swallowing. Take dose 1 to 3 hours after meal, or as directed by your doctor. Follow each dose with a full glass (8 oz.) of water.

USUAL ADULT DOSE:

2 to 4 tablets every 2 hours, or as directed by your doctor, not to exceed 20 tablets in a 24 hour period. In all cases follow specific product instructions.

USUAL CHILD DOSE:

Only administer to children between under 12 under doctor's supervision or direction. These products are generally not advised for children younger than 3, and never for infants. In all cases follow specific product instructions.

OVERDOSE SYMPTOMS:

Constipation, diarrhea, nausea, abdominal and muscular cramps, dehydration, irregular heartbeat, fatigue, disorientation, bone pain.

QUICK FACTS

QUICK FACTS

SIDE EFFECTS:
No serious effects in most cases of common use. Side effects with these products rarely occur unless medication is taken over long period of time. Occasionally, mild constipation may occur. In rare cases nausea, vomiting, nervous agitation, dizziness, disorientation, frequent urination, severe constipation fatigue, and swelling of feet and ankles have been reported. In any of these cases, discontinue use of the product and call your doctor immediately.

CHECK WITH YOUR DOCTOR OR PHARMACIST BEFORE COMBINING THIS PRODUCT WITH:
Anticoagulants, any other antacids—especially any containing sodium bicarbonate, or other drugs and preparations.

PREGNANCY OR BREASTFEEDING:
Safety of this drug for use during pregnancy or while nursing has not been established. In all cases you should consult your doctor before using any drug during pregnancy or while nursing.

PRECAUTIONS FOR CHILDREN:
These products should only be used with doctor's supervision or direction for children under 12. These products are not recommended for use with children under 3 and should never be used with infants. Consult your doctor and follow instructions on medication (see above).

PRECAUTIONS FOR SENIORS:
Seniors generally may be more prone to side effects and possible adverse effects of these products than younger individuals. Seniors

should specifically avoid high dosages of these products as the calcium content of this combination may provoke constipation, or the magnesium content may provoke diarrhea.

SPECIAL WARNINGS:

Do not use this product if you are allergic to calcium carbonate, magnesium hydroxide, simethicone, or any of the inactive ingredients contained in these products, if you are experiencing abdominal pain, cramps, nausea or vomiting, or if you have kidney disease. Avoid high dosages for longer more than two weeks, as "acid rebound" (secretion of excess stomach acid) can occur.

INFORM YOUR DOCTOR BEFORE TAKING THIS PRODUCT IF YOU HAVE:

High calcium levels in your blood, or any form of kidney disease (including kidney stones).

Q U I C K F A C T S

ACTIVE INGREDIENTS:

CIMETIDINE

(HISTAMINE H_2 ANTAGONIST)

BRAND NAMES:

- TAGAMET HB 200
  (also contains cellulose, methylcellulose, polyethylene glycol)

SYMPTOMS RELIEVED:
Acid indigestion, heartburn, sour stomach, upset stomach. Also can be used prophylatically to prevent these symptoms (see below).

HOW TO TAKE:
Comes in tablet form. Swallow tablet with water.

USUAL ADULT DOSE:
For relief of symptoms: Take 1 tablet with water not to exceed 2 tablets in a 24 hour period. In all cases follow specific product instructions.

For prevention of symptoms: Take 1 tablet with water (not to exceed 2 tablets in a 24 hour period) 30 minutes prior to a meal which you believe may cause symptoms. In all cases follow specific product instructions.

USUAL CHILD DOSE:
This product is generally not advised for children under 12, and never for infants. Only administer to children under 12 under doctor's supervision or direction. In all cases follow specific product instructions.

OVERDOSE SYMPTOMS:
Disorientation, delirium, rapid pulse, slurred speech.

SIDE EFFECTS:
No serious effects in most cases of common use. Occasionally, dizziness, headache, fatigue, or diarrhea, impotence may result. In rare cases nervous agitation, disorientation, constipation, irregular heartbeat, muscular pain, bleeding, and bruising have been reported. In any of these cases, discontinue use of the product and call your doctor immediately.

CHECK WITH YOUR DOCTOR OR PHARMACIST BEFORE COMBINING CIMETIDINE WITH:
Anticoagulants, oral asthma medication, anti-seizure medication, antacids, aspirin, or other drugs and preparations.

PREGNANCY OR BREASTFEEDING:
Safety of this drug for use during pregnancy or while nursing has not been established. In all cases you should consult your doctor before using any drug during pregnancy or while nursing.

PRECAUTIONS FOR CHILDREN:
This product is not recommended for use with children under 12 and should never be used with infants. Consult your doctor and follow instructions on medication.

55+ **PRECAUTIONS FOR SENIORS:**
Seniors generally may be more prone to side effects and possible adverse effects of this product than younger individuals..

SPECIAL WARNINGS:
Do not use any of this product if you are allergic to cimetidine or any of the inactive ingredients

QUICK FACTS

contained in this product. Do not take this product for more than two weeks continuously as liver damage can result from prolonged use. Stagger any doses of other antacids while taking this medication.

INFORM YOUR DOCTOR BEFORE TAKING CIMETIDINE IF YOU HAVE:
Any form of liver or kidney disease (including kidney stones).

ACTIVE INGREDIENT:

MAGNESIUM HYDROXIDE

QUICK FACTS

BRAND NAMES:

- PHILLIPS' MILK OF MAGNESIA
- PHILLIPS' MILK OF MAGNESIA CONCENTRATED (also contains sorbitol, sugar; and strawberry, orange, or vanilla creme flavors)

SYMPTOMS RELIEVED:

Irregular bowel movements (constipation), acid indigestion, sour stomach, heartburn.

Note: For laxative action, see Quick Facts under Constipation section.

HOW TO TAKE:

Comes in liquid forms. For laxative action: following dose, drink a full glass of water (preferable) or other nonalcoholic, noncarbonated liquid. Avoid taking late in day or on empty stomach. Since the laxative dosage will generally produce bowel movement ½ to 3 hours following dose, plan accordingly.

USUAL ADULT (AND CHILDREN 12 AND OLDER) DOSE:

1 to 3 teaspoonsful, not to exceed 4 doses in a 24 hour period. In all cases follow specific product instructions.

USUAL CHILD DOSE:

Only administer to children between 3 to 12 under doctor's supervision or direction. These products are generally not advised for children younger than 3, and never for infants. In all cases follow specific product instructions.

QUICK FACTS

OVERDOSE SYMPTOMS:
Diarrhea, abdominal and muscular cramps, irregular heartbeat, fatigue.

SIDE EFFECTS:
No serious effects in most cases of common use. Occasionally nausea, belching, dehydration, and loose stools or diarrhea may occur. In rare cases rectal bleeding or rectal pain have resulted. In these cases, discontinue use of the product and call your doctor immediately.

CHECK WITH YOUR DOCTOR OR PHARMACIST BEFORE COMBINING MAGNESIUM HYDROXIDE WITH:
Anticoagulants, any other antacids, or other drugs and preparations. Take any other medication 2 hours apart, as laxatives interfere with body's absorption of medicine.

PREGNANCY OR BREASTFEEDING:
Safety of this drug for use during pregnancy or while nursing has not been established. In all cases you should consult your doctor before using any drug during pregnancy or while nursing.

PRECAUTIONS FOR CHILDREN:
These products should only be used with doctor's supervision or direction for children under 6. These products are not recommended for use with children under 3 and should never be used with infants. Consult your doctor and follow instructions on medication (see above).

PRECAUTIONS FOR SENIORS:
Seniors generally may be more prone to side

effects and possible adverse effects of these products than younger individuals. Avoid high dosages as laxative dependence may result.

SPECIAL WARNINGS:
Do not use any of these products if you are allergic to magnesium hydroxide or any of the inactive ingredients contained in these products, if you are experiencing abdominal pain, cramps, nausea, or vomiting, or if you have kidney disease. Do not use these products if you have experienced irregular bowel movements for less than 2 days. Do not use these products longer than one week as laxative dependence can result. If regular bowel movements have not returned within one week, consult your doctor.

ADDITIONAL WARNINGS:
Use of these products should be supplemented with liquids (preferably water) to prevent electrolyte/fluid depletion or dehydration.

Eating disorders: Chronic or excessive use of laxatives, particularly by young women, may be a sign of anorexia nervosa or bulimia nervosa.

INFORM YOUR DOCTOR BEFORE TAKING MAGNESIUM HYDROXIDE IF YOU HAVE:
Allergies—particularly to food types, high blood pressure, rectal bleeding, colostomy, or ileostomy, or any form of kidney disease.

QUICK FACTS

ACTIVE INGREDIENT:

RANITIDINE HYDROCHLORIDE

(HISTAMINE H_2 ANTAGONIST)

BRAND NAMES:

- ZANTAC 75

SYMPTOMS RELIEVED:
Acid indigestion, heartburn, sour stomach, upset stomach.

HOW TO TAKE:
Comes in tablet form. Swallow tablet with water.

USUAL ADULT DOSE:
Take 1 tablet with water not to exceed 2 tablets in a 24 hour period. In all cases follow specific product instructions.

USUAL CHILD DOSE:
This product is generally not advised for children under 12, and never for infants. Only administer to children under 12 under doctor's supervision. In all cases follow specific product instructions.

OVERDOSE SYMPTOMS:
Disorientation, delirium, rapid pulse, slurred speech.

SIDE EFFECTS:
No serious effects in most cases of common use. Occasionally, dizziness, headache, fatigue, or diarrhea, impotence may result. In rare cases nervous agitation, disorientation, constipation, irregular heartbeat, muscular pain, bleeding, and bruising have been reported. In any of these cases, discontinue use of the product and call your doctor immediately.

CHECK WITH YOUR DOCTOR OR PHARMACIST BEFORE COMBINING RANITIDINE HYDROCHLORIDE WITH:
Anticoagulants, oral asthma medication, anti-seizure medication, antacids, aspirin, or other drugs and preparations.

PREGNANCY OR BREASTFEEDING:
Safety of this drug for use during pregnancy or while nursing has not been established. In all cases you should consult your doctor before using any drug during pregnancy or while nursing.

PRECAUTIONS FOR CHILDREN:
This product is not recommended for use with children under 12 and should never be used with infants. Consult your doctor and follow instructions on medication.

PRECAUTIONS FOR SENIORS:
Seniors generally may be more prone to side effects and possible adverse effects of this product than younger individuals..

SPECIAL WARNINGS:
Do not use any of this product if you are allergic to ranitidine hydrochloride or any of the inactive ingredients contained in this product. Do not take this product for more than two weeks continuously as liver damage can result from prolonged use. Stagger any doses of other antacids while taking this medication.

INFORM YOUR DOCTOR BEFORE TAKING RANITIDINE HYDROCHLORIDE IF YOU HAVE:
Any form of liver or kidney disease (including kidney stones).

Q U I C K F A C T S

ACTIVE INGREDIENT:

SODIUM BICARBONATE

BRAND NAMES:

- ALKA-SELTZER GOLD

SYMPTOMS RELIEVED:
Acid indigestion, heartburn, sour stomach, associated with common upset stomach.

HOW TO TAKE:
Comes in effervescent tablet form. Fully dissolve tablets in 4 oz. of water before swallowing. Do not swallow whole.

USUAL ADULT DOSE:
Take 2 tablets every 4 hours, or as directed by your doctor, not to exceed 8 tablets in a 24 hour period.

USUAL CHILD DOSE:
Only administer to children under 12 under doctor's supervision or direction. These products are generally not advised for children younger than 3, and never for infants. In all cases follow specific product instructions.

OVERDOSE SYMPTOMS:
Excessive swelling of limbs—especially lower legs and feet.

SIDE EFFECTS:
No serious effects in most cases of common use. Side effects with these products rarely occur unless medication is taken over long period of time. Occasionally, stomach cramps may occur. In rare cases nervous agitation, muscular soreness or spasms, breathing difficulty, and

swelling of feet and ankles have been reported. In any of these cases, discontinue use of the product and call your doctor immediately.

CHECK WITH YOUR DOCTOR OR PHARMACIST BEFORE COMBINING THIS PRODUCT WITH:
Anticoagulants, any other antacids, or other drugs and preparations.

PREGNANCY OR BREASTFEEDING:
Safety of this drug for use during pregnancy or while nursing has not been established. In all cases you should consult your doctor.

PRECAUTIONS FOR CHILDREN:
These products should only be used with doctor's supervision or direction for children under 12. These products are not recommended for use with children under 3 and should never be used with infants.

55+

PRECAUTIONS FOR SENIORS:
Seniors generally may be more prone to side effects and possible adverse effects of these products than younger individuals.

SPECIAL WARNINGS:
Do not use this product if you are allergic to sodium bicarbonate, or any of the inactive ingredients contained in these products, or if you have kidney disease, or if you are on a restricted sodium diet. Avoid high dosages for longer more than two weeks, as "acid rebound" (secretion of excess stomach acid) can occur.

INFORM YOUR DOCTOR BEFORE TAKING THIS PRODUCT IF YOU HAVE:
high calcium levels in your blood, or any form of kidney disease (including kidney stones).

Q U I C K F A C T S

ACTIVE INGREDIENTS:

SODIUM BICARBONATE AND ASPIRIN

BRAND NAMES:

- ALKA-SELTZER EXTRA STRENGTH (also contains flavors)
- ALKA-SELTZER LEMON LIME/CHERRY (also contains aspartame, flavors)
- ALKA-SELTZER ORIGINAL

SYMPTOMS RELIEVED:
Acid indigestion, heartburn, sour stomach, associated with common upset stomach, with headache, or body aches and pains.

HOW TO TAKE:
Comes in effervescent tablet form. Fully dissolve tablets in 4 oz. of water before swallowing. Do not swallow whole.

USUAL ADULT DOSE:
ALKA-SELTZER EXTRA STRENGTH: Take 2 tablets every 6 hours, or as directed by your doctor, not to exceed 7 tablets in a 24 hour period.

Others: Take 2 tablets every 4 hours, or as directed by your doctor, not to exceed 8 tablets in a 24 hour period.

USUAL CHILD DOSE:
Only administer to children between under 12 under doctor's supervision or direction. These products are generally not advised for children younger than 3, and never for infants. In all cases follow specific product instructions.

OVERDOSE SYMPTOMS:
Respiratory difficulty, hyperventilation,

hyperthermia, nausea and vomiting, severe diarrhea, impaired vision, bloody urine, abnormal thirst, nervous agitation, disorientation and dizziness, and excessive swelling of limbs—especially lower legs and feet.

SIDE EFFECTS:
No serious effects in most cases of common use. Side effects with these products rarely occur unless medication is taken over long period of time. Occasionally, stomach cramps may occur. In rare cases nervous agitation, muscular soreness or spasms, breathing difficulty, and swelling of feet and ankles have been reported. In any of these cases, discontinue use of the product and call your doctor immediately.

Aspirin side effects: Normal aspirin use can result in common gastrointestinal (GI) irritations such as heartburn and indigestion. Aspirin affects hypothalamus, resulting in dilation of small blood vessels in skin. Low dosages may reduce risk of blood clotting as aspirin inhibits clustering of small blood cells. Aspirin use may contribute to anemia in anemic individuals.

CHECK WITH YOUR DOCTOR OR PHARMACIST BEFORE COMBINING THIS COMBINATION WITH:
Anticoagulants, asthma medication, other salicylates, tetracycline, any other antacids, or other drugs and preparations. Ingestion of alcohol while taking aspirin can increase risk of GI ulceration.

PREGNANCY OR BREASTFEEDING:
Safety of this drug for use during pregnancy or while nursing has not been established. In all

QUICK FACTS

cases you should consult your doctor before using any drug during pregnancy or while nursing.

PRECAUTIONS FOR CHILDREN:
These products should only be used with doctor's supervision or direction for children under 12. These products are not recommended for use with children under 3 and should never be used with infants. Consult your doctor and follow instructions on medication (see above).

SPECIAL WARNING:
Aspirin use in children and teenagers with influenza (flu), chicken pox, and other viral infections may be associated with development of Reye's syndrome. This rare but acute and often life-threatening condition has caused permanent brain damage in survivors. Symptoms include: vomiting, lethargy, bellicosity, leading possibly to delirium and coma.

55+ **PRECAUTIONS FOR SENIORS:**
Seniors generally don't eliminate drugs as efficiently as younger persons, and should avoid high dosages. Buffered effervescent aspirin products contain high sodium content and should be avoided if on a restricted sodium diet. Aspirin use can cause GI irritation and possibly stomach or intestinal bleeding in seniors, manifested usually by dark stools.

SPECIAL WARNINGS:
Do not use these products if you are allergic to sodium bicarbonate and aspirin, or any of the inactive ingredients contained in these products; or if you have asthma, rhinitis, a history of

anemia (iron poor blood), kidney disease, or if you are on a restricted sodium diet. Avoid high dosages for longer more than two weeks, as "acid rebound" (secretion of excess stomach acid) can occur. Do not take any product with aspirin which emits a vinegar-like odor. This indicates that it is decomposing and is unsafe for use. Also avoid use of aspirin, if possible, one week prior to surgery, as it may increase possibility of postoperative bleeding.

INFORM YOUR DOCTOR BEFORE TAKING THIS PRODUCT IF YOU HAVE:

An allergy to aspirin, asthma, anemia, a sensitive digestive system, high calcium levels in your blood, or any form of kidney disease (including kidney stones).

Q U I C K F A C T S

ACTIVE INGREDIENT:
SIMETHICONE

℞ **BRAND NAMES:**
- GAS-X
  (also contains dextrose and assorted flavors)
- GAS-X EXTRA STRENGTH—TABLETS
  (also contains dextrose and assorted flavors)
- GAS-X EXTRA STRENGTH SODIUM-FREE—SOFTGELS
  (also contains glycerin, sorbitol, and assorted flavors)
- MAALOX ANTI-GAS (also contains gelatin, sucrose, and assorted flavors)
- MAALOX ANTI-GAS EXTRA STRENGTH (also contains gelatin, sucrose, and assorted flavors)
- MYLANTA GAS RELIEF
  (also contains sorbitol and assorted flavors)
- MYLANTA GAS RELIEF MAXIMUM STRENGTH—GELCAPS (also contains benzyl alcohol, castor oil, methylcellulose, methylparaben, propylene glycol, sodium, saccharin, sorbitol, and assorted flavors)
- MYLANTA GAS RELIEF MAXIMUM STRENGTH—TABLETS
  (also contains sorbitol and assorted flavors)
- PHAZYME-95
  (also contains acacia, compressible sugar, methylcellulose, sodium benzoate, sucrose)
- PHAZYME INFANT DROPS
  (also contains citric acid, methylcellulose, sodium benzoate, sodium citrate)
- PHAZYME-125—CAPSULES
  (also contains gelatin, glycerin, hydrogenated soybean oil, lecithin, methylparaben, propylparaben, soybean oil, vegetable shortening)
- PHAZYME-125—LIQUID (also contains bentonite, glycerin, sodium benzoate, flavors)

- PHAZYME-125–TABLETS (also contains citric acid, sorbitol, sucrose, flavors)

SYMPTOMS RELIEVED:
Pain and discomfort associated with retention of excess gas in digestive tract and accompanying, bloating, pressure, and fullness.

HOW TO TAKE:
Comes in capsule, drops, liquid, and chewable tablet forms. Shake liquid well before taking. Use dropper (supplied with PHAZYME INFANT DROPS) to administer medication to children and infants. Chew tablets well before swallowing. Take dose 1 to 3 hours after meal, or as directed by your doctor. Follow each dose with a full glass (8 oz.) of water.

USUAL ADULT DOSE:
Dosages vary according to product and symptoms. In all cases follow specific product instructions.

USUAL CHILD DOSE:
Ages 2 to 12:
PHAZYME INFANT DROPS only: 0.6 milliliters 4 times per day following meals and at bedtime or as directed by your doctor.

Infants to 2 years and under:
PHAZYME INFANT DROPS only: 0.3 milliliters 4 times per day following meals and at bedtime or as directed by your doctor. Drops may be mixed with other liquids for easier administration to infants and young children.

Except for PHAZYME INFANT DROPS, these products are generally not advised for children younger than 3, and never for infants.

QUICK FACTS

OVERDOSE SYMPTOMS:
None known.

SIDE EFFECTS:
No known side effects in most cases of common use. Side effects with these products rarely occur unless medication is taken over long period of time.

CHECK WITH YOUR DOCTOR OR PHARMACIST BEFORE COMBINING THIS PRODUCT WITH:
Any other antacids, or other drugs and preparations.

PREGNANCY OR BREASTFEEDING:
Safety of this drug for use during pregnancy or while nursing has not been established. In all cases you should consult your doctor before using any drug during pregnancy or while nursing.

PRECAUTIONS FOR CHILDREN:
Except for the product noted above, these products should only be used with doctor's supervision or direction for children under 12. These products are not recommended for use with children under 3 and should never be used with infants, except as noted above. Consult your doctor and follow instructions on medication (see above).

PRECAUTIONS FOR SENIORS:
None known.

SPECIAL WARNINGS:
Do not use this product if you are allergic to simethicone, or any of the inactive ingredients contained in these products.

• ANTIDIARRHEAL •

The most important considerations in choosing an antidiarrheal are: its effectiveness in short-term treatment of diarrhea, and potential side effects associated with the drug.

QUICK REVIEW

ANTIDIARRHEALS ARE A CLASS OF DRUGS WHICH:

- treat mild to moderate diarrhea symptoms, such as those associated with traveler or tourist diarrhea, and in the case of some products, also provides relief from chronic diarrhea caused by inflammatory bowel disease,
- act by limiting intestinal inflammation, contractions and motility, or by adsorbing (binding) certain intestinal toxins, or by absorbing fluids into fecal mass to produce firmer stools,
- should only be used for short-term symptomatic relief (unless your doctor directs otherwise), and with adequate fluid intake to prevent dehydration,
- should not be used for treatment of diarrhea resulting from more serious conditions such as toxigenic bacterial infections, or pseudomembranous enterocolitis.

Q U I C K   F A C T S

ACTIVE INGREDIENT:

BISMUTH SUBSALICYLATE

BRAND NAMES:

- BISMATROL (also contains saccharin)
- BISMATROL EXTRA STRENGTH
- PEPTO-BISMOL–TABLETS (also contains sodium, saccharin and cherry flavor)
- PEPTO-BISMOL/PEPTO–BISMOL MAXIMUM STRENGTH–LIQUID (also contains sodium, saccharin)

SYMPTOMS RELIEVED:
Heartburn, indigestion, mild to acute nonspecific diarrhea—including common symptoms of 'travelers' diarrhea, nausea, abdominal cramps.

HOW TO TAKE:
Comes in liquid and tablet forms. Chew tablet(s) or allow to dissolve in mouth.

USUAL ADULT DOSE:
2 tablets or 2 tablespoonsful (30 milliliters) as needed, not to exceed 8 doses in a 24 hour period. In all cases follow specific product instructions.

USUAL CHILD DOSE:
Ages 9 to 12: 1 tablet or 1 tablespoonful (15 milliliters) as needed, not to exceed 8 doses in a 24 hour period.

Ages 3 to 9: 1 teaspoonful (10 milliliters) as needed, not to exceed 8 doses in a 24 hour period.

These products are generally not advised for children younger than 3, and never for infants. In all cases follow specific product instructions.

OVERDOSE SYMPTOMS:
Severe nervous agitation, hearing loss, ringing or buzzing in ears, constipation, drowsiness, extreme fatigue, hyperventilation, rapid breathing.

SIDE EFFECTS:
No serious effects in most cases of common use, however, stools may temporarily appear gray or black during use of product. In rare cases, abdominal pain , nausea, vomiting, severe constipation, headache, sweats, confusion and disorientation may occur. In these cases, discontinue r use of the product and call your doctor immediately.

CHECK WITH YOUR DOCTOR OR PHARMACIST BEFORE COMBINING BISMUTH SUBSALICYLATE WITH:
Anticoagulants, antidiabetic drugs such as insulin, or other salicylates—especially aspirin.

PREGNANCY OR BREASTFEEDING:
Safety of this drug for use during pregnancy or while nursing has not been established. In all cases you should consult your doctor before using any drug during pregnancy or while nursing.

PRECAUTIONS FOR CHILDREN:
These products are not recommended for use with children under 3 and should never be used with infants. Consult your doctor and follow instructions on medication (see above). See Special Warning (below) regarding Reye's syndrome.

QUICK FACTS

SPECIAL WARNING FOR CHILDREN:
Use of bismuth subsalicylate—as well as other salicylate and aspirin, in cases involving children and teenagers with influenza (flu), chicken pox, and other viral infections may be associated with development of Reye's syndrome. This rare but acute and often life-threatening condition has caused permanent brain damage in survivors.

55+

PRECAUTIONS FOR SENIORS:
Seniors generally may be more prone to side effects and possible adverse effects of these products than younger individuals. Avoid high dosages, as severe constipation may result.

SPECIAL WARNINGS:
Do not use any of these products if you are allergic to bismuth subsalicylate, other salicylate and aspirin, or any of the inactive ingredients contained in these products.

ADDITIONAL WARNINGS:
Do not use these products if you have a sensitivity or allergy to aspirin, other salicylates, or nonsteroidal anti-inflammatory drugs (NSAIDs). Do not continue use for longer than 48 hours.

INFORM YOUR DOCTOR BEFORE TAKING BISMUTH SUBSALICYLATE IF YOU HAVE:
Severe loss of fluids (dehydration) due to diarrhea, kidney disease such as hepatitis, a history of bleeding ulcers; or if you are treating a child with a fever.

HEMORRHOIDS AND RECTAL ITCHING

QUICK REVIEW

• ANESTHETIC •
(TOPICAL)

The most important considerations in choosing a topical or local anesthetic are: its action in partially or completely eliminating the sensation of physical pain in one part of the body, and potential side effects associated with the drug.

TOPICAL ANESTHETICS ARE A CLASS OF DRUGS WHICH:

- act in some combination of the following ways: by limiting the production of energy in nerve cells—thereby reducing nerve impulses and related sensation of pain, by increasing the body's production of organic compounds which limit the transmission of pain messages through synapses, or by reducing nerve cell energy production, thereby limiting the cell's production of nerve impulses. These actions are not completely understood due to varying effects of topical anesthetics and the complex nature of the body's central nervous system (CNS),
- especially when used in high dosages or for long treatment periods, may be absorbed into the blood stream through the skin or mucous membranes, increasing the anesthetic's effectiveness but also the incidence and probability of adverse side effects,
- do not affect the underlying cause of the symptoms which they are designed to relieve or suppress.

ACTIVE INGREDIENT:

BENZOCAINE (ETHYL AMINOBENZOATE)

BRAND NAMES:

- AMERICAINE
- MEDICONE
- PREPARATION-H

SYMPTOMS RELIEVED:

Irritation, itching, and rashes due to minor skin conditions, discomfort from hemorrhoids or other rectal conditions.

HOW TO TAKE:

Comes in ointment form. Apply to affected area as needed, with finger or applicator. Do not insert applicator further than halfway for internal application. Discard or thoroughly wash applicator with soap and water following use. Always wash hands before and after use. In all cases follow specific product instructions.

USUAL ADULT DOSE:

Dosage varies according to product and condition. Use the minimum recommended dose in order to avoid side effects or complications. In all cases follow specific product instructions.

USUAL CHILD DOSE:

Do not use in children or infants under 1 year of age. Dosage varies according to product and condition. Use the minimum recommended dose in order to avoid side effects or complications. In all cases follow specific product instructions.

QUICK FACTS

OVERDOSE SYMPTOMS:
Convulsions, agitation, euphoria, drowsiness, disorientation or dizziness, blurred vision, vomiting, numbness, hypotension-possibly leading to respiratory arrest; or cardiac arrhythmia (irregular pulse and heartbeat) leading to cardiac arrest or collapse. If you suspect an overdose, immediately seek medical attention.

SIDE EFFECTS:
No serious effects in most cases of common use. In rare cases, some individuals have experienced swelling of skin, mouth, throat or feet, rash, burning or stinging sensations, or bloody or painful urine. In these cases, discontinue application or use of the product and call your doctor immediately.

CHECK WITH YOUR DOCTOR OR PHARMACIST BEFORE COMBINING BENZOCAINE WITH:
Sulfa drugs or Class I antiarrhythmia drugs (tocainide, mexiletine).

PREGNANCY OR BREASTFEEDING:
Consult your doctor in all cases.

PRECAUTIONS FOR CHILDREN:
In general, use caution when applying benzocaine products with children under 6, as the risk of product absorption through skin is greater. Do not use in children or infants under 1 year of age. Consulting your doctor and follow instructions on medication (see above).

PRECAUTIONS FOR SENIORS:
Seniors generally may be more prone to side effects and possible adverse effects of these products than younger individuals. Avoid high dosages.

SPECIAL WARNINGS:

Do not use any of these products if you are allergic to any topical anesthetic. Avoid applying more than three days continuously to same area, as this may lead to excess absorption. Inform your doctor immediately if you experience any rectal bleeding.

INFORM YOUR DOCTOR BEFORE TAKING BENZOCAINE IF YOU HAVE:

Allergies to: any topical anesthetic, or if you have skin infection or skin conditions such as psoriasis or eczema, or bleeding hemorrhoids.

QUICK FACTS

QUICK REVIEW

• ANTI-ITCH •

(TOPICAL)

The most important considerations in choosing an anti-itch agent are: its effectiveness in treating and relieving skin itchiness, and potential side effects associated with the drug.

TOPICAL ANTI-ITCH AGENTS ARE A CLASS OF DRUGS WHICH:

- are only intended for topical use,
- are nonspecific in their action, and act against most causes of skin inflammation by depressing, neutralizing, or interfering with the activity of enzymes which produce skin inflammation and resultant itchiness,
- in over-the-counter (OTC) products, are primarily formulated with hydrocortisone (a topical adrenocorticoid) as the active ingredient,
- when used in high dosages or for long treatment periods, may be absorbed into the bloodstream through the skin or mucous membranes, increasing the incidence and probability of adverse side effects.

ACTIVE INGREDIENT:

BENZOCAINE (ETHYL AMINOBENZOATE)

Q U I C K F A C T S

BRAND NAMES:

- Americaine
- Medicone
- Preparation-H

SYMPTOMS RELIEVED:
Irritation, itching, and rashes due to minor skin conditions, discomfort from hemorrhoids or other rectal conditions.

HOW TO TAKE:
Comes in ointment form. Apply to affected area as needed, with finger or applicator. Do not insert applicator further than halfway for internal application. Discard or thoroughly wash applicator with soap and water following use. Always wash hands before and after use. In all cases follow specific product instructions.

USUAL ADULT DOSE:
Dosage varies according to product and condition. Use the minimum recommended dose in order to avoid side effects or complications. In all cases follow specific product instructions.

USUAL CHILD DOSE:
Do not use in children or infants under 1 year of age. Dosage varies according to product and condition. Use the minimum recommended dose in order to avoid side effects or complications. In all cases follow specific product instructions.

QUICK FACTS

OVERDOSE SYMPTOMS:
Convulsions, agitation, euphoria, drowsiness, disorientation or dizziness, blurred vision, vomiting, numbness, hypotension-possibly leading to respiratory arrest; or cardiac arrhythmia (irregular pulse and heartbeat) leading to cardiac arrest or collapse. If you suspect an overdose, immediately seek medical attention.

SIDE EFFECTS:
No serious effects in most cases of common use. In rare cases, some individuals have experienced swelling of skin, mouth, throat or feet, rash, burning or stinging sensations, or bloody or painful urine. In these cases, discontinue application or use of the product and call your doctor immediately.

CHECK WITH YOUR DOCTOR OR PHARMACIST BEFORE COMBINING BENZOCAINE WITH:
Sulfa drugs or Class I antiarrhythmia drugs (tocainide, mexiletine).

PREGNANCY OR BREASTFEEDING:
Consult your doctor in all cases.

PRECAUTIONS FOR CHILDREN:
In general, use caution when applying benzocaine products with children under 6, as the risk of product absorption through skin is greater. Do not use in children or infants under 1 year of age. Consulting your doctor and follow instructions on medication (see above).

PRECAUTIONS FOR SENIORS:
Seniors generally may be more prone to side effects and possible adverse effects of these

products than younger individuals. Avoid high dosages.

SPECIAL WARNINGS:

Do not use any of these products if you are allergic to any topical anesthetic. Avoid applying more than three days continuously to same area, as this may lead to excess absorption. Inform your doctor immediately if you experience any rectal bleeding.

INFORM YOUR DOCTOR BEFORE TAKING BENZOCAINE IF YOU HAVE:

Allergies to: any topical anesthetic, or if you have skin infection or skin conditions such as psoriasis or eczema, or bleeding hemorrhoids.

MENSTRUAL CONDITIONS

QUICK REVIEW

• ANALGESIC •

The most important considerations in choosing an analgesic are: pain relief; anti-inflammatory activity, and allergic reaction or sensitivity to certain active ingredients.

ANALGESICS (NONNARCOTIC) ARE A CLASS OF DRUGS WHICH:

- inhibit the action of prostaglandins (hormonelike substances) in the central nervous system, thereby temporarily reducing the perception of physical pain with little loss of sensibility to other physical sensation,
- are used to temporarily alleviate symptoms such as: headache, fever, backache, sinus pain, muscle strain, menstrual pain, and similar ailments. Some analgesics, such as aspirin (acetylsalicylic acid) and ibuprofen, also provide temporary anti-inflammatory relief for ailments such as arthritis. Aspirin has also been shown to be effective as a blood thinning antiplatelet agent in reducing heart attack and stroke risk,
- can have adverse effects in some instances. Aspirin intolerance can produce allergic and anaphylactic reactions in hypersensitive and asthmatic individuals. Aspirin can also aggravate aggravate gastrointestinal conditions such as heartburn and ulcer. Long-term acetaminophen use can damage liver (hepatic) and kidney (renal) functions.

ACTIVE INGREDIENT:

ACETAMINOPHEN

BRAND NAMES:

- MIDOL MAXIMUM STRENGTH TEEN MENSTRUAL FORMULA (also contains pamabrom)
- MIDOL PMS FORMULA (also contains pyrilamine maleate and pamabrom)
- PAMPRIN MULTI-SYMPTOM (also contains magnesium salicylate and pamabrom)

SYMPTOMS RELIEVED:
Minor aches, discomfort, and pains associated with menstruation.

HOW TO TAKE:
Comes in caplet or gelcap forms. Swallow with liquid. Do not crush or chew timed-release tablets. Although acetaminophen usually doesn't cause gastrointestinal (GI) upset, caffeine can cause GI irritation and medications formulated with this drug should be taken with food.

USUAL ADULT DOSE:
2 caplets or gelcaps every 4 to 6 hours, as needed not to exceed 8 doses in a 24 hour period.

USUAL CHILD DOSE:
Do not administer to children under 12 unless under direction of physician. Dosage may vary based on infant or child's age.

OVERDOSE SYMPTOMS:
Nervous agitation, disorientation, confusion, severe headache, convulsions, GI bleeding, or hemorrhage. If you suspect an overdose, immediately seek medical attention.

Q U I C K F A C T S

SIDE EFFECTS:
The antihistamine pyrilamine maleate may cause drowsiness. Magnesium salicylate can cause common GI irritations such as heartburn and indigestion. Less common side effects include dizziness, nausea, stomach cramps, and headache.

CHECK WITH YOUR DOCTOR OR PHARMACIST BEFORE COMBINING THESE MEDICATIONS WITH:
Sedatives, tranquilizers, antacids, anticoagulants, aspirin, asthma medication, nonsteroidal anti-inflammatory drugs (NSAIDs), tetracycline, and any other medication.

PREGNANCY OR BREASTFEEDING:
No harmful effects have been reported regarding nursing infants, but caffeine use by a nursing mother should be considered a potential risk for a nursing child as the drug will be passed on to the infant in the mother's milk. In all cases, a physician should be consulted.

PRECAUTIONS FOR CHILDREN:
In general, not advised for children under 12. Administer to infants or children only when consulting a physician (see above).

55+

SPECIAL WARNINGS:
Avoid alcohol while taking any drug containing antihistamines.

INFORM YOUR DOCTOR BEFORE TAKING THIS COMBINATION IF YOU HAVE:
Respiratory conditions such as bronchitis or emphysema, glaucoma, or urinary difficulties.

QUICK FACTS

ACTIVE INGREDIENTS:

ACETAMINOPHEN AND CAFFEINE COMBINATION

BRAND NAMES:

- MIDOL MAXIMUM STRENGTH MULTI-SYMPTOM FORMULA (combination with pyrilamine maleate)

SYMPTOMS RELIEVED:
Minor aches, discomfort, and pains associated with menstruation.

HOW TO TAKE:
Comes in caplet or gelcap forms. Swallow with liquid. Do not crush or chew timed-release tablets. Although acetaminophen usually doesn't cause gastrointestinal (GI) upset, caffeine can cause GI irritation and medications formulated with this drug should be taken with food or following meal.

USUAL ADULT DOSE:
2 caplets or gelcaps every 4 to 6 hours, as needed not to exceed 8 doses in a 24 hour period.

USUAL CHILD DOSE:
Do not administer to children under 12 unless under direction of physician.

OVERDOSE SYMPTOMS:
Nervous agitation, disorientation, confusion, severe headache, convulsions, GI bleeding, or hemorrhage. If you suspect an overdose, immediately seek medical attention.

SIDE EFFECTS:
The antihistamine in this combination may cause

Q U I C K F A C T S

drowsiness. Normal use of caffeine can result in common GI irritations such as heartburn and indigestion. Less common side effects include dizziness, nausea, stomach cramps, and headache.

CHECK WITH YOUR DOCTOR OR PHARMACIST BEFORE COMBINING ACETAMINOPHEN OR CAFFEINE WITH:
Sedatives, tranquilizers, antacids, anticoagulants, aspirin, asthma medication, nonsteroidal anti-inflammatory drugs (NSAIDs), tetracycline, and any other medication.

PREGNANCY OR BREASTFEEDING:
No harmful effects have been reported regarding nursing infants, but caffeine use by a nursing mother should be considered a potential risk for a nursing child as the drug will be passed on to the infant in the mother's milk. In all cases, a physician should be consulted.

PRECAUTIONS FOR CHILDREN:
Administer to infants or children only when consulting a physician (see above).

SPECIAL WARNINGS:
Avoid if you have GI conditions such as gastritis, peptic ulcer, enteritis, ileitis, colitis; asthma, high blood pressure, as the caffeine contained in each recommended dose is equivalent to approximately one cup of coffee. Avoid alcohol while taking this drug.

INFORM YOUR DOCTOR BEFORE TAKING THIS COMBINATION IF YOU HAVE:
Respiratory conditions such as bronchitis or emphysema, glaucoma, or urinary difficulties.

ACTIVE INGREDIENT:

IBUPROFEN

BRAND NAMES:
- GENPRIL
- OBUPRIN
- MENADOL
- MIDOL IB

SYMPTOMS RELIEVED:
Minor aches, discomfort, and pains associated with menstruation.

HOW TO TAKE:
Comes in tablet, caplet, and gelcap forms. Swallow with liquid. Do not crush or chew timed-release tablet. Ibuprofen can cause gastrointestinal (GI) irritation and should be taken with food or following meal.

USUAL ADULT DOSE:
Minor aches and pains: 200 milligrams every 4 to 6 hours as needed, not to exceed 1.2 grams per day.

USUAL CHILD DOSE:
Always consult with a pharmacist or physician. Dosage may vary based on infant or child's age.

OVERDOSE SYMPTOMS:
Nervous agitation, disorientation, confusion, severe headache, convulsions, GI bleeding or hemorrhage. If you suspect an overdose, immediately seek medical attention.

SIDE EFFECTS:
No serious effects in most cases of common use, however normal use of ibuprofen can result

QUICK FACTS

Q U I C K   F A C T S

in common GI irritations such as heartburn and indigestion. Less common side effects include dizziness, nausea, stomach cramps, and headache.

CHECK WITH YOUR DOCTOR OR PHARMACIST BEFORE COMBINING IBUPROFEN WITH:
Antacids, anticoagulants, aspirin, asthma medication, other nonsteroidal anti-inflammatory drugs (NSAIDs), tetracycline, and any other medication. Combination with acetaminophen increases risk of kidney damage. Ingestion of alcohol while taking ibuprofen can increase risk of GI ulceration. Avoid ibuprofen if you have a history of anemia. Also avoid use of ibuprofen, if possible, one week prior to surgery, as it may increase possibility of postoperative bleeding.

PREGNANCY OR BREASTFEEDING:
Animal studies have indicated an adverse effect on fetus, but no adequate studies have been performed on humans. No harmful effects have been reported regarding nursing infants, but ibuprofen use by a nursing mother should be considered a potential risk for a nursing child as the drug will be passed on to the infant in the mother's milk. In all cases, a physician should be consulted.

PRECAUTIONS FOR CHILDREN:
In general, ibuprofen and other NSAIDs are not advised for children under 15. Administer ibuprofen to infants or children only when consulting a physician and follow instructions on medication.

SPECIAL WARNINGS:

Don't take ibuprofen medication if you are aspirin intolerant or allergic to other NSAIDs (anti-inflammatory nonsteroidal drugs). If in doubt, always consult a pharmacist or physician. Also avoid if you have GI conditions such as gastritis, peptic ulcer, enteritis, ileitis, colitis; asthma, high blood pressure, or hematologic (bleeding) problems. Avoid alcohol while taking this or any other NSAID.

INFORM YOUR DOCTOR BEFORE TAKING IBUPROFEN IF YOU HAVE:

An allergy or intolerance to aspirin or other NSAIDs, damaged or impaired renal (kidney) or hepatic (liver) functions, epilepsy, Parkinson's disease, or mental illness.

QUICK REVIEW

• ANTI-INFLAMMATORY •

The most important considerations in choosing an anti-inflammatory agent (nonsteroidal anti-inflammatory drugs or "NSAID") are: pain relief; anti-inflammatory activity, and the potential for allergic reaction or sensitivity to certain active ingredients.

ANTI-INFLAMMATORY AGENTS (NSAIDS) ARE A CLASS OF DRUGS WHICH:

- inhibit the action of prostaglandins (hormonelike substances) in the central nervous system, thereby temporarily reducing the perception of physical pain with little loss of sensibility to other physical sensation,
- are used both for their anti-inflammatory and analgesic properties, to temporarily alleviate symptoms such as: headache, fever, backache, sinus pain, muscle strain, menstrual pain, and similar ailments. Some NSAIDs also provide temporary anti-inflammatory relief for ailments such as rheumatoid arthritis and osteoarthritis,
- can have adverse effects in some instances such as aggravation of gastrointestinal (GI) conditions such as heartburn and ulcer, and can produce allergic reactions in persons who are aspirin-intolerant or hypersensitive.

See *also:* Analgesics

ACTIVE INGREDIENTS:

ACETAMINOPHEN AND CAFFEINE COMBINATION

BRAND NAMES:
- Midol Maximum Strength Multi-Symptom Formula

SYMPTOMS RELIEVED:
Minor aches, discomfort, and pains associated with menstruation.

HOW TO TAKE:
Comes in caplet or gelcap forms. Swallow with liquid. Do not crush or chew timed-release tablets. Although acetaminophen usually doesn't cause gastrointestinal (GI) upset, caffeine can cause GI irritation and medications formulated with this drug should be taken with food.

USUAL ADULT DOSE:
2 caplets or gelcaps every 4 to 6 hours, as needed not to exceed 8 doses in a 24 hour period.

USUAL CHILD DOSE:
Do not administer to children under 12 unless under direction of physician. Dosage may vary based on infant or child's age.

OVERDOSE SYMPTOMS:
Nervous agitation, disorientation, confusion, severe headache, convulsions, GI bleeding, or hemorrhage. If you suspect an overdose, immediately seek medical attention.

SIDE EFFECTS:
The antihistamine in this combination may cause drowsiness. Normal use of caffeine can result in

QUICK FACTS

common GI irritations such as heartburn and indigestion. Less common side effects include dizziness, nausea, stomach cramps, and headache.

CHECK WITH YOUR DOCTOR OR PHARMACIST BEFORE COMBINING ACETAMINOPHEN OR CAFFEINE WITH:
Sedatives, tranquilizers, antacids, anticoagulants, aspirin, asthma medication, nonsteroidal anti-inflammatory drugs (NSAIDs), tetracycline, and any other medication.

PREGNANCY OR BREASTFEEDING:
No harmful effects have been reported regarding nursing infants, but caffeine use by a nursing mother should be considered a potential risk for a nursing child as the drug will be passed on to the infant in the mother's milk. In all cases, a physician should be consulted.

PRECAUTIONS FOR CHILDREN:
In general, not advised for children under 12. Administer to infants or children only when consulting a physician (see above).

SPECIAL WARNINGS:
Avoid if you have GI conditions such as gastritis, peptic ulcer, enteritis, ileitis, colitis; asthma, high blood pressure, as the caffeine contained in each recommended dose is equivalent to approximately one cup of coffee. Avoid alcohol while taking this or any other drug containing antihistamines.

INFORM YOUR DOCTOR BEFORE TAKING THIS COMBINATION IF YOU HAVE:
Respiratory conditions such as bronchitis or emphysema, glaucoma, or urinary difficulties.

QUICK FACTS

ACTIVE INGREDIENT:
IBUPROFEN

BRAND NAMES:
- GENPRIL
- OBUPRIN
- MENADOL
- MIDOL IB

SYMPTOMS RELIEVED:
Minor aches, discomfort, and pains associated with menstruation.

HOW TO TAKE:
Comes in tablet, caplet, and gelcap forms. Swallow with liquid. Do not crush or chew timed-release tablet. Ibuprofen can cause gastrointestinal (GI) irritation and should be taken with food or following meal.

USUAL ADULT DOSE:
Minor aches and pains: 200 milligrams every 4 to 6 hours as needed, not to exceed 1.2 grams per day.

USUAL CHILD DOSE:
Always consult with a pharmacist or physician. Dosage may vary based on infant or child's age.

OVERDOSE SYMPTOMS:
Nervous agitation, disorientation, confusion, severe headache, convulsions, GI bleeding or hemorrhage. If you suspect an overdose, immediately seek medical attention.

SIDE EFFECTS:
No serious effects in most cases of common use, however normal use of ibuprofen can result

QUICK FACTS

in common GI irritations such as heartburn and indigestion. Less common side effects include dizziness, nausea, stomach cramps, and headache.

CHECK WITH YOUR DOCTOR OR PHARMACIST BEFORE COMBINING IBUPROFEN WITH:
Antacids, anticoagulants, aspirin, asthma medication, other nonsteroidal anti-inflammatory drugs (NSAIDs), tetracycline, and any other medication. Combination with acetaminophen increases risk of kidney damage. Ingestion of alcohol while taking ibuprofen can increase risk of GI ulceration. Avoid ibuprofen if you have a history of anemia. Also avoid use of ibuprofen, if possible, one week prior to surgery, as it may increase possibility of postoperative bleeding.

PREGNANCY OR BREASTFEEDING:
Animal studies have indicated an adverse effect on fetus, but no adequate studies have been performed on humans. No harmful effects have been reported regarding nursing infants, but ibuprofen use by a nursing mother should be considered a potential risk for a nursing child as the drug will be passed on to the infant in the mother's milk. In all cases, a physician should be consulted.

PRECAUTIONS FOR CHILDREN:
In general, ibuprofen and other NSAIDs are not advised for children under 15. Administer ibuprofen to infants or children only when consulting a physician and follow instructions on medication.

SPECIAL WARNINGS:

Don't take ibuprofen medication if you are aspirin intolerant or allergic to other NSAIDs (anti-inflammatory nonsteroidal) drugs. If in doubt, always consult a pharmacist or physician. Also avoid if you have GI conditions such as gastritis, peptic ulcer, enteritis, ileitis, colitis; asthma, high blood pressure, or hematologic (bleeding) problems. Avoid alcohol while taking this or any other NSAID.

INFORM YOUR DOCTOR BEFORE TAKING IBUPROFEN IF YOU HAVE:

An allergy or intolerance to aspirin or other NSAIDs, damaged or impaired renal (kidney) or hepatic (liver) functions, epilepsy, Parkinson's disease, or mental illness.

MOTION SICKNESS

QUICK REVIEW

• ANTIEMETIC •

The most important considerations in choosing an antiemetic are: its action in preventing or relieving nausea and vomiting, and side effects associated with the drug.

ANTIEMETICS ARE A CLASS OF DRUGS WHICH:

- are used to treat nausea and vomiting associated with motion sickness and vertigo, as well as common gastrointestinal conditions such as upset stomach, overindulgence, or food poisoning,
- act by reducing or suppressing over-stimulus of the inner ear (meclizine, cyclizine and dimenhydrinate), or by coating and soothing gastrointestinal tract to reduce muscle contractions which produce vomiting (phosphoric acid-glucose combination),
- do not affect the underlying cause of the symptoms which they are designed to relieve or suppress.

See also: Antacid

ACTIVE INGREDIENT:

DIMENHYDRINATE

BRAND NAMES:

- CALM-X
- DRAMAMINE CHILDREN'S LIQUID (also contains flavors, glycerin, methylparaben, sucrose)
- DRAMAMINE–CHEWABLE TABLETS (also contains aspartame, magnesium stearate, methacrylic acid, tartrazine—a dye, sorbitol, flavors)
- DRAMAMINE–TABLETS (also contains acacia, carboxymehtylcellulose sodium, magnesium stearate, sodium sulfate)
- MARMINE

SYMPTOMS RELIEVED:
Nausea, vomiting, dizziness associated with motion sickness.

HOW TO TAKE:
Comes in chewable tablet, liquid, and tablet forms. Chewable tablets should be well chewed before swallowing. Do not swallow whole. Swallow regular tablets with liquid. For prevention of motion sickness, take first dose ½ hour to 1 hour before beginning an activity (such as sailing) which you believe will produce symptoms of motion sickness.

USUAL ADULT DOSE:
1 to 2 tablets every 4 to 6 hours, not to exceed 8 tablets in a 24 hour period, or as directed by your doctor. In all cases follow specific product instructions.

USUAL CHILD DOSE:
For children 6 to 12: ½ to 1 tablet every 6 to 8 hours, not to exceed 3 tablets in a 24 hour

period, or as directed by your doctor; or 2 to 4 teaspoonsful of DRAMAMINE CHILDREN'S LIQUID every 6 to 8 hours, not to exceed 12 teaspoonsful, or as directed by your doctor. In all cases follow specific product instructions.

For children 2 to 6: 1/4 to 1/2 tablet every 6 to 8 hours, not to exceed 1 1/2 tablets in a 24 hour period, or as directed by your doctor; or 1 to 2 teaspoonsful of DRAMAMINE CHILDREN'S LIQUID every 6 to 8 hours, not to exceed 6 teaspoonsful, or as directed by your doctor. In all cases follow specific product instructions.

Do not administer to children under 2 unless under direction of physician. Dosage may vary based on infant or child's age. In all cases follow specific product instructions.

OVERDOSE SYMPTOMS:

Severe drowsiness and fatigue, difficulty breathing, convulsions, coma.

SIDE EFFECTS:

The most frequent side effect of this type of antihistamines use is drowsiness. Other common side effects include: include dryness of mouth, throat, and nasal passages, dizziness, gastrointestinal (GI) distress (including vomiting, diarrhea, and constipation or change in bowel regularity), and diminished muscle coordination. In rare cases, more severe side effects may result, such as painful and frequent urination or urinary retention, blurred vision, loss of appetite, and respiratory difficulty, nervous agitation, severe anxiety, insomnia (sleeplessness), or severe drowsiness and fatigue, rapid heartbeat, hallucinations, and tremors. In these cases, discontinue medication and call your doctor immediately.

CHECK WITH YOUR DOCTOR OR PHARMACIST BEFORE COMBINING DIMENHYDRINATE WITH: Cold, cough, or allergy medication—including other antihistamines; aspirin, stimulants, antidepressants, antihypertensives, digitalis or other heart medication, diuretics, or MAO (monoamine oxidase inhibitors) drugs, or any other drugs or medications. Avoid ingestion of alcohol or use of sedatives or tranquilizers while taking these products or most other antihistamine medication as the combination can produce severe drowsiness or sedation.

PREGNANCY OR BREASTFEEDING: Safety of this drug for use during pregnancy or while nursing has not been established. In all cases you should consult your doctor before using any drug during pregnancy or while nursing.

PRECAUTIONS FOR CHILDREN: In general, dimenhydrinate is not advised for children under 2. Administer dimenhydrinate to infants or children only when consulting a physician and follow instructions on medication (see above).

55+ **PRECAUTIONS FOR SENIORS:** Seniors generally don't eliminate drugs as efficiently as younger persons, and should avoid high dosages. Use of dimenhydrinate medications by seniors can lead to urinary difficulties. In addition, seniors are more likely to experience drowsiness effects of the drug.

QUICK FACTS

SPECIAL WARNINGS:

Do not use these products if you are allergic to dimenhydrinate, or any of the inactive ingredients contained in these products. Because antihistamines often cause drowsiness, you should avoid activities or tasks such as driving, or other operations which require alertness, coordination, dexterity or quick reflexes. Do not use continuously for longer than 3 months. Do not use dimenhydrinate medications containing tartrazine if you are intolerant or hypersensitive to aspirin. Allergic reactions, including bronchial asthma, have occurred in susceptible individuals.

INFORM YOUR DOCTOR BEFORE TAKING DIMENHYDRINATE IF YOU HAVE:

Urinary difficulty, glaucoma, ulcer, or if you are pregnant. If you anticipate any surgery requiring general or spinal anesthesia within 2 months of taking any of these products, inform your doctor.

QUICK FACTS

ACTIVE INGREDIENT:

MECLIZINE HYDROCHLORIDE

BRAND NAMES:

- Bonine
- Dizmiss
- Dramamine II Less Drowsy (also contains colloidal silicon dioxide, croscarmellose sodium, dibasic calcium phosphate, microcrystalline cellulose, magnesium stearate)

SYMPTOMS RELIEVED:
Nausea, vomiting, dizziness associated with motion sickness.

HOW TO TAKE:
Comes in tablet forms. Swallow tablet s with liquid. For prevention of motion sickness, take first dose 1 hour before beginning an activity (such as sailing) which you believe will produce symptoms of motion sickness.

USUAL ADULT DOSE:
1 to 2 tablets every per day, not to exceed 2 tablets in a 24 hour period, or as directed by your doctor. In all cases follow specific product instructions.

USUAL CHILD DOSE:
Do not administer to children under 12 unless under direction of physician. Dosage may vary based on infant or child's age. In all cases follow specific product instructions.

OVERDOSE SYMPTOMS:
Severe drowsiness and fatigue, difficulty breathing, convulsions, coma.

Q U I C K F A C T S

SIDE EFFECTS:
The most frequent side effect of this type of antihistamines use is drowsiness. Other common side effects include: include dryness of mouth, throat, and nasal passages, dizziness, gastrointestinal (GI) distress (including vomiting, diarrhea and constipation, or change in bowel regularity), and diminished muscle coordination. In rare cases, more severe side effects may result, such as painful and frequent urination or urinary retention, blurred vision, loss of appetite, and respiratory difficulty, nervous agitation, severe anxiety, insomnia (sleeplessness) or severe drowsiness and fatigue, rapid heartbeat, hallucinations, and tremors. In these cases, discontinue medication and call your doctor immediately.

CHECK WITH YOUR DOCTOR OR PHARMACIST BEFORE COMBINING MECLIZINE HYDROCHLORIDE WITH:
Cold, cough, or allergy medication—including other antihistamines; aspirin, stimulants, antidepressants, antihypertensives, digitalis or other heart medication, diuretics, or MAO (monoamine oxidase inhibitors) drugs, or any other drugs or medications. Avoid ingestion of alcohol or use of sedatives or tranquilizers while taking these products or most other antihistamine medication as the combination can produce severe drowsiness or sedation.

PREGNANCY OR BREASTFEEDING:
Safety of this drug for use during pregnancy or while nursing has not been established. In all cases you should consult your doctor before using any drug during pregnancy or while nursing.

QUICK FACTS

PRECAUTIONS FOR CHILDREN:
In general, meclizine hydrochloride is not advised for children under 2. Administer meclizine hydrochloride to infants or children only when consulting a physician and follow instructions on medication (see above).

PRECAUTIONS FOR SENIORS:
Seniors generally don't eliminate drugs as efficiently as younger persons, and should avoid high dosages. Use of meclizine hydrochloride medications by seniors can lead to urinary difficulties. In addition, seniors are more likely to experience drowsiness effects of the drug.

SPECIAL WARNINGS:
Do not use these products if you are allergic to meclizine, or any of the inactive ingredients contained in these products. Because antihistamines often cause drowsiness, you should avoid activities or tasks such as driving, or other operations which require alertness, coordination, dexterity, or quick reflexes. Do not use continuously for longer than 3 months. Do not use meclizine hydrochloride medications containing tartrazine if you are intolerant or hypersensitive to aspirin. Allergic reactions, including bronchial asthma, have occurred in susceptible individuals.

INFORM YOUR DOCTOR BEFORE TAKING MECLIZINE HYDROCHLORIDE IF YOU HAVE:
Urinary difficulty, glaucoma, ulcer, or if you are pregnant. If you anticipate any surgery requiring general or spinal anesthesia within 2 months of taking any of these products, inform your doctor.

MOUTH AND DENTAL CARE

QUICK REVIEW

• ANESTHETIC •
(TOPICAL)

The most important considerations in choosing a topical or local anesthetic are: its action in partially or completely eliminating the sensation of physical pain in one part of the body, and potential side effects associated with the drug.

TOPICAL ANESTHETICS ARE A CLASS OF DRUGS WHICH:

- act in some combination of the following ways: by limiting the production of energy in nerve cells—thereby reducing nerve impulses and related sensation of pain, by increasing the body's production of organic compounds which limit the transmission of pain messages through synapses, or by reducing nerve cell energy production, thereby limiting the cell's production of nerve impulses. These actions are not completely understood due to varying effects of topical anesthetics and the complex nature of the body's central nervous system (CNS),
- especially when used in high dosages or for long treatment periods, may be absorbed into the blood stream through the skin or mucous membranes, increasing the anesthetic's effectiveness but also the incidence and probability of adverse side effects,
- do not affect the underlying cause of the symptoms which they are designed to relieve or suppress.

Q U I C K F A C T S

ACTIVE INGREDIENT:
BENZOCAINE

BRAND NAMES:
- ANBESOL MAXIMUM STRENGTH–LIQUID AND GEL (also contains alcohol, saccharin)
- HURRICANE–LIQUID, GEL, AND SPRAY (cherry, piña colada, watermelon flavors)
- ORABASES GEL (also contains ethyl alcohol, saccharin)
- ORAJEL MOUTH-AID–GEL (also contains benzalkonium chloride, zinc chloride, saccharin)
- ORAJEL MOUTH-AID–LIQUID (also contains cetylpyridinium chloride, ethyl alcohol, tartrazine, saccharin)

SYMPTOMS RELIEVED:
Minor sore throat and sore mouth pain, including pain associated with common canker sores, and minor oral irritation or pain caused by dental or orthodontic procedures.

HOW TO TAKE:
Comes in gel, liquid, and spray forms.

Liquid: Gargle and spit out. Do not swallow.

Gel: Apply to affected area as needed with applicator. Do not swallow.

Spray: Spray affected area. Do not inhale.
In all cases follow specific product instructions.

These products are intended solely for topical use. Do not under any conditions ingest internally or use in eyes. Always wash hands before and after use.

Q U I C K F A C T S

USUAL ADULT DOSE:
Dosage varies according to product and condition. Use the minimum recommended dose in order to avoid side effects or complications. In all cases follow specific product instructions.

USUAL CHILD DOSE:
Do not use in children or infants under 1 year of age. Dosage varies according to product and condition. Use the minimum recommended dose in order to avoid side effects or complications. In all cases follow specific product instructions.

OVERDOSE SYMPTOMS:
Convulsions, agitation, euphoria, drowsiness, disorientation or dizziness, blurred vision, vomiting, numbness, hypotension—possibly leading to respiratory arrest; or cardiac arrhythmia (irregular pulse and heartbeat) leading to cardiac arrest or collapse. If you suspect an overdose, immediately seek medical attention.

SIDE EFFECTS:
No serious effects in most cases of common use. In rare cases, some individuals have experienced swelling of skin or in mouth and throat, or rash, burning or stinging sensations, or pronounced skin sensitivity. In these cases, discontinue application or use of the product and call your doctor immediately.

CHECK WITH YOUR DOCTOR OR PHARMACIST BEFORE COMBINING BENZOCAINE WITH:
Sulfa drugs or any medication for treatment of glaucoma.

PREGNANCY OR BREASTFEEDING:
Consult your doctor.

PRECAUTIONS FOR CHILDREN:
In general, use caution when applying benzocaine products with children under 6, as the risk of product absorption through skin is greater. Do not use in children or infants under 1 year of age. Consulting your doctor and follow instructions on medication (see above).

PRECAUTIONS FOR SENIORS:
Seniors generally may be more prone to side effects and possible adverse effects of these products than younger individuals. Avoid high dosages.

SPECIAL WARNINGS:
Do not ingest food or liquids, or chew gum for one hour following use of these products (or any other oral anesthetic). Do not continue overall use more than one week if condition hasn't improved.

ADDITIONAL WARNINGS:
If you anticipate any dental procedure which will require anesthesia, inform your dentist about your use of any of these or any other oral anesthetic products.

INFORM YOUR DOCTOR BEFORE TAKING BENZOCAINE IF YOU HAVE:
Allergies to: any topical anesthetic, or if you have any infections such as canker sores or other types of oral sores.

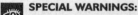

QUICK FACTS

ACTIVE INGREDIENTS:

DYCLONINE HYDROCHLORIDE AND ALLANTOIN

BRAND NAMES:

- ORAJEL COVERMED
- TANAC MEDICATED GEL

SYMPTOMS RELIEVED:

Minor sore throat and sore mouth pain, including pain associated with common canker sores, and minor oral irritation or pain caused by dental or orthodontic procedures.

HOW TO USE:

Comes in gel forms. Apply to affected areas. These products are for external use only. Do not swallow. Avoid contact with eyes while applying.

USUAL ADULT DOSE:

Apply to affected areas 3 to 4 times per day, or as directed by your doctor or dentist. In all cases follow specific product instructions.

USUAL CHILD DOSE:

For ages 2 to 12: Apply to affected areas 3 to 4 times per day, or as directed by your doctor or dentist. In all cases follow specific product instructions.

Only administer to children under 2 under doctor or dentist's supervision or direction. In all cases follow specific product instructions.

OVERDOSE SYMPTOMS:

None known.

SIDE EFFECTS:
No serious effects in most cases of common use.

CHECK WITH YOUR DOCTOR OR PHARMACIST BEFORE COMBINING THIS COMBINATION WITH:
Any other drugs and preparations.

PREGNANCY OR BREASTFEEDING:
Safety of this drug for use during pregnancy or while nursing has not been established. In all cases you should consult your doctor before using any drug during pregnancy or while nursing.

PRECAUTIONS FOR CHILDREN:
These products should only be used with doctor or dentist's supervision or direction for children under 2. Consult your doctor or dentist and follow instructions on medication (see above).

PRECAUTIONS FOR SENIORS:
Seniors generally don't eliminate drugs as efficiently as younger persons, and should avoid high dosages.

SPECIAL WARNINGS:
Do not use these products if you are allergic to dyclonine hydrochloride or allantoin, or any of the inactive ingredients contained in these products. Call your doctor if condition persists longer than one week or worsens.

INFORM YOUR DOCTOR BEFORE TAKING THIS PRODUCT IF YOU HAVE:
Any allergies, or if you are or plan to become pregnant during time that you will be taking this product.

QUICK FACTS

ACTIVE INGREDIENT:

DYCLONINE HYDROCHLORIDE

BRAND NAMES:

- Cepacol Maximum Strength Sore Throat Spray/Cherry and Cool Menthol

SYMPTOMS RELIEVED:

Minor sore throat and sore mouth pain, including pain associated with common canker sores, and minor oral irritation or pain caused by dental or orthodontic procedures.

HOW TO TAKE:

Comes in spray form. Spray into throat or affected area of mouth or gums, and swallow.

USUAL ADULT DOSE:

Spray 4 times, not to exceed 4 doses per day, or as directed by your doctor or dentist. In all cases follow specific product instructions.

USUAL CHILD DOSE:

For ages 2 to 12: Spray 2 to 3 times, not to exceed 4 doses per day, or as directed by your doctor or dentist. Children should be supervised when administering this product. In all cases follow specific product instructions.

Only administer to children under 2 under doctor or dentist's supervision or direction. In all cases follow specific product instructions.

OVERDOSE SYMPTOMS:

None known.

SIDE EFFECTS:

No serious effects in most cases of common use.

CHECK WITH YOUR DOCTOR OR PHARMACIST BEFORE COMBINING THIS COMBINATION WITH:
Any other drugs and preparations.

PREGNANCY OR BREASTFEEDING:
Safety of this drug for use during pregnancy or while nursing has not been established. In all cases you should consult your doctor before using any drug during pregnancy or while nursing.

PRECAUTIONS FOR CHILDREN:
This product should only be used with doctor or dentist's supervision or direction for children under 2. Consult your doctor or dentist and follow instructions on medication (see above).

PRECAUTIONS FOR SENIORS:
Seniors generally don't eliminate drugs as efficiently as younger persons, and should avoid high dosages.

SPECIAL WARNINGS:
Do not use this product if you are allergic to dyclonine hydrochloride or any of the inactive ingredients contained in this product. Call your doctor if sore throat persists longer than two days, or is severe, and is accompanied by other symptoms such as fever, headache, rash, nausea or vomiting, or other severe symptoms.

INFORM YOUR DOCTOR BEFORE TAKING THIS PRODUCT IF YOU HAVE:
Any allergies, any of the symptoms listed above, or if you are or plan to become pregnant during time that you will be taking this product.

QUICK FACTS

ACTIVE INGREDIENT:
PHENOL

BRAND NAMES:
- VICKS CHLORASEPTIC SORE THROAT SPRAY–CHERRY AND MENTHOL FLAVORS (also contains flavors, glycerin, saccharin, sodium)

SYMPTOMS RELIEVED:
Minor sore throat and sore mouth pain, including pain associated with common canker sores, and minor oral irritation or pain caused by dental or orthodontic procedures.

HOW TO TAKE:
Comes in spray form. Spray into throat or affected area of mouth or gums, and swallow.

USUAL ADULT DOSE:
Spray 5 times, not to exceed 4 doses per day, or as directed by your doctor or dentist. In all cases follow specific product instructions.

USUAL CHILD DOSE:
For ages 2 to 12: Spray 2 to 3 times, repeating dosage every 2 hours, not to exceed 4 doses per day, or as directed by your doctor or dentist. Children should be supervised when administering this product. In all cases follow specific product instructions.

OVERDOSE SYMPTOMS:
None known.

SIDE EFFECTS:
No serious effects in most cases of common use.

CHECK WITH YOUR DOCTOR OR PHARMACIST BEFORE COMBINING THIS COMBINATION WITH:
Any other drugs and preparations.

PREGNANCY OR BREASTFEEDING:
Safety of this drug for use during pregnancy or while nursing has not been established. In all cases you should consult your doctor before using any drug during pregnancy or while nursing.

PRECAUTIONS FOR CHILDREN:
This product should only be used with doctor or dentist's supervision or direction for children under 2. Consult your doctor or dentist and follow instructions on medication (see above).

PRECAUTIONS FOR SENIORS:
Seniors generally don't eliminate drugs as efficiently as younger persons, and should avoid high dosages.

SPECIAL WARNINGS:
Do not use this product if you are allergic to phenol or any of the inactive ingredients contained in this product. Call your doctor if sore throat persists longer than two days, or is severe, and is accompanied by other symptoms such as fever, headache, rash, nausea or vomiting, or other severe symptoms.

INFORM YOUR DOCTOR BEFORE USING THIS PRODUCT IF YOU HAVE:
Any allergies, any of the symptoms listed above, or if you are or plan to become pregnant during time that you will be using this product.

QUICK REVIEW

• ANTI-ITCH •
(TOPICAL)

The most important considerations in choosing an anti-itch agent are: its effectiveness in treating and relieving skin itchiness, and potential side effects associated with the drug.

TOPICAL ANTI-ITCH AGENTS ARE A CLASS OF DRUGS WHICH:

- are only intended for topical use,
- are nonspecific in their action, and act against most causes of skin inflammation by depressing, neutralizing, or interfering with the activity of enzymes which produce skin inflammation and resultant itchiness,
- in over-the-counter (OTC) products, are primarily formulated with hydrocortisone (a topical adrenocorticoid) as the active ingredient,
- when used in high dosages or for long treatment periods, may be absorbed into the bloodstream through the skin or mucous membranes, increasing the incidence and probability of adverse side effects.

ACTIVE INGREDIENT:

ALLANTOIN

BRAND NAMES:

- Herpecin-L Cold Sore Lip Balm (also contains padimate O—a sunscreen, titanium dioxide, petrolatum)

SYMPTOMS RELIEVED:

Dryness and chapping of lips and cold sores, sun and fever blisters associated with herpes simplex infections.

HOW TO USE:

Comes in gel form. Apply to affected areas. This product is for external use only. Do not swallow. Avoid contact with eyes while applying.

USUAL ADULT DOSE:

For recurrent cold sores, sun and fever blisters: Apply liberally and as often as convenient to affected areas, preferably as soon as you are aware of symptoms (tingling, burning, itching), or as directed by your doctor. In all cases follow specific product instructions.

For sun protection: Apply before and during outdoor activities which involve exposure to sun (such as swimming, hiking, or sunbathing), and at bedtime, or as directed by your doctor.

For dry, chapped lips: Apply to affected area as needed, or as directed by your doctor.

USUAL CHILD DOSE:

Ages 2 to 12: Same as adult, or as directed by your doctor. In all cases follow specific product instructions. Only apply to children under 2 under doctor's supervision or direction. In all cases follow specific product instructions.

QUICK FACTS

OVERDOSE SYMPTOMS:
None known.

SIDE EFFECTS:
No serious effects in most cases of common use.

CHECK WITH YOUR DOCTOR OR PHARMACIST BEFORE COMBINING THIS PRODUCT WITH:
Any other drugs and preparations.

PREGNANCY OR BREASTFEEDING:
Safety of this drug for use during pregnancy or while nursing has not been established. In all cases you should consult your doctor before using any drug during pregnancy or while nursing.

PRECAUTIONS FOR CHILDREN:
This product should only be used with doctor's supervision or direction for children under 2. Consult your doctor and follow instructions on medication (see above).

PRECAUTIONS FOR SENIORS:
Seniors generally don't eliminate drugs as efficiently as younger persons, and should avoid high dosages.

SPECIAL WARNINGS:
Do not use this product if you are allergic to allantoin, or any of the inactive ingredients contained in this product.

INFORM YOUR DOCTOR BEFORE TAKING THIS PRODUCT IF YOU HAVE:
Any allergies, or if you are or plan to become pregnant during time that you will be taking this product.

• ANTISEPTIC •
(TOPICAL)

The most important considerations in choosing an antiseptic are: its effectiveness in treating, healing, or preventing infections of minor cuts, wounds, burns, and skin abrasions, and potential side effects associated with the drug.

TOPICAL ANTISEPTICS ARE A CLASS OF DRUGS WHICH:

- are intended only for topical use,
- act by killing bacteria, fungi, viruses, spores, protozoa, and yeasts in affected area,
- when used in high dosages or for long treatment periods, may be absorbed into the bloodstream through the skin or mucous membranes, increasing the incidence and probability of adverse side effects.

QUICK FACTS

ACTIVE INGREDIENT:
ALLANTOIN

BRAND NAMES:
- HERPECIN-L COLD SORE LIP BALM

SYMPTOMS RELIEVED:
Dryness and chapping of lips and cold sores, sun and fever blisters associated with herpes simplex infections.

HOW TO USE:
Comes in gel form. Apply to affected areas. This product is for external use only. Do not swallow. Avoid contact with eyes while applying.

USUAL ADULT DOSE:
For recurrent cold sores, sun and fever blisters: Apply liberally and as often as convenient to affected areas, preferably as soon as you are aware of symptoms (tingling, burning, itching), or as directed by your doctor. In all cases follow specific product instructions.

For sun protection: Apply before and during outdoor activities which involve exposure to sun (such as swimming, hiking, or sunbathing), and at bedtime, or as directed by your doctor.

For dry, chapped lips: Apply to affected area as needed, or as directed by your doctor.

USUAL CHILD DOSE:
Ages 2 to 12: Same as adult, or as directed by your doctor. In all cases follow specific product instructions.

Only apply to children under 2 under doctor's supervision or direction. In all cases follow specific product instructions.

OVERDOSE SYMPTOMS:
None known.

SIDE EFFECTS:
No serious effects in most cases of common use. In rare cases, a skin sensitivity has been reported.

CHECK WITH YOUR DOCTOR OR PHARMACIST BEFORE COMBINING THIS PRODUCT WITH:
Any other drugs and preparations.

PREGNANCY OR BREASTFEEDING:
Safety of this drug for use during pregnancy or while nursing has not been established. In all cases you should consult your doctor before using any drug during pregnancy or while nursing.

PRECAUTIONS FOR CHILDREN:
This product should only be used with doctor's supervision or direction for children under 2. Consult your doctor and follow instructions on medication (see above).

PRECAUTIONS FOR SENIORS:
Seniors generally don't eliminate drugs as efficiently as younger persons, and should avoid high dosages.

SPECIAL WARNINGS:
Do not use this product if you are allergic to allantoin, or any of the inactive ingredients contained in this product.

INFORM YOUR DOCTOR BEFORE TAKING THIS PRODUCT IF YOU HAVE:
Any allergies, or if you are or plan to become pregnant during time that you will be taking this product.

NAUSEA AND VOMITING

QUICK REVIEW

• ANTACID •

The most important considerations in choosing an antacid are: its action in reducing or neutralizing the degree acidity in the stomach and upper digestive tract, and potential side effects associated with the drug.

ANTACIDS ARE A CLASS OF DRUGS WHICH:

- are often taken to relieve the symptoms of common gastrointestinal upsets and conditions such as acid indigestion, sour stomach, and heartburn,
- are also used by doctors in stronger dosages and prescription forms to treat more serious gastrointestinal conditions such as peptic ulcer,
- are often grouped according to their action: systemic (containing sodium bicarbonate), nonsytemic— the fastest acting (calcium carbonate, simethicone), cathartic (magnesium carbonate), histamine H_2 antagonist—which block the stimulation of gastric-acid secretions (cimetidine and ranitidine), and phosphate-binding (aluminum),
- should only be used for short-term symptomatic relief as harmful side effects, such as high blood pressure, kidney stones, or urinary-tract infections (due to sodium content of bicarbonate) can result when used chronically or in repeated high dosages,
- do not affect the underlying cause of the symptoms which they are designed to relieve or suppress.

ACTIVE INGREDIENT:

BISMUTH SUBSALICYLATE

BRAND NAMES:

- BISMATROL (also contains saccharin)
- BISMATROL EXTRA STRENGTH
- PEPTO-BISMOL–TABLETS (also contains sodium, saccharin and cherry flavor)
- PEPTO-BISMOL/PEPTO-BISMOL MAXIMUM STRENGTH–LIQUID (also contains sodium, saccharin)

SYMPTOMS RELIEVED:
Heartburn, indigestion, mild to acute nonspecific diarrhea—including common symptoms of 'travelers' diarrhea, nausea, abdominal cramps.

HOW TO TAKE:
Comes in liquid and tablet forms. Chew tablet(s) or allow to dissolve in mouth.

USUAL ADULT DOSE:
2 tablets or 2 tablespoonsful (30 milliliters) as needed, not to exceed 8 doses in a 24 hour period. In all cases follow specific product instructions.

USUAL CHILD DOSE:
For ages 9 to 12: 1 tablet or 1 tablespoonful (15 milliliters) as needed, not to exceed 8 doses in 24 hour period.

For ages 3 to 9: 1 teaspoonful (10 milliliters) as needed, not to exceed 8 doses in a 24 hour period.

These products are generally not advised for children younger than 3, and never for infants. In all cases follow specific product instructions.

QUICK FACTS

OVERDOSE SYMPTOMS:
Severe nervous agitation, hearing loss, ringing or buzzing in ears, constipation, drowsiness, extreme fatigue, hyperventilation, rapid breathing.

SIDE EFFECTS:
No serious effects in most cases of common use, however, stools may temporarily appear gray or black during use of product. In rare cases, abdominal pain, nausea, vomiting, severe constipation, headache, sweats, confusion and disorientation may occur. In these cases, discontinue use of the product and call your doctor immediately.

CHECK WITH YOUR DOCTOR OR PHARMACIST BEFORE COMBINING BISMUTH SUBSALICYLATE WITH:
Blood thinning medications, antidiabetic drugs or other salicylates—especially aspirin.

PREGNANCY OR BREASTFEEDING:
Safety of this drug for use during pregnancy or nursing has not been established. In all cases you should consult your doctor before using any drug during pregnancy or while nursing.

PRECAUTIONS FOR CHILDREN:
These products are not recommended for use with children under 3 and should never be used with infants. Consult your doctor and follow instructions on medication (see above). See Special Warning (below) regarding Reye's syndrome.

SPECIAL WARNING FOR CHILDREN:
Use of bismuth subsalicylate—as well as other

salicylate and aspirin, in cases involving children and teenagers with influenza (flu), chicken pox and other viral infections may be associated with development of Reye's syndrome. This rare but acute and often life-threatening condition has caused permanent brain damage in survivors. Symptoms include: vomiting, lethargy, bellicosity, leading possibly to delirium and coma.

55+ **PRECAUTIONS FOR SENIORS:**
Seniors generally may be more prone to side effects and possible adverse effects of these products than younger individuals. Avoid high dosages, as severe constipation may result.

SPECIAL WARNINGS:
Do not use any of these products if you are allergic to bismuth subsalicylate, other salicylate and aspirin, or any of the inactive ingredients contained in these products.

ADDITIONAL WARNINGS:
Do not use these products if you have a sensitivity or allergy to aspirin, other salicylates, or nonsteroidal anti-inflammatory drugs (NSAIDs). Do not continue use for longer than 48 hours. Use of these products should be supplemented, in cases of acute diarrhea, with liquids to prevent electrolyte/fluid depletion or dehydration.

INFORM YOUR DOCTOR BEFORE TAKING BISMUTH SUBSALICYLATE IF YOU HAVE:
Severe loss of fluids (dehydration) due to diarrhea, kidney disease such as hepatitis, a history of bleeding ulcers; or if you are treating a child with a fever.

QUICK REVIEW

• ANTIEMETIC •

The most important considerations in choosing an antiemetic are: its action in preventing or relieving nausea and vomiting, and side effects associated with the drug.

ANTIEMETICS ARE A CLASS OF DRUGS WHICH:

- are used to treat nausea and vomiting associated with motion sickness and vertigo, as well as common gastrointestinal conditions such as upset stomach, overindulgence, or food poisoning,
- act by reducing or suppressing over-stimulus of the inner ear (meclizine, cyclizine and dimenhydrinate), or by coating and soothing gastrointestinal tract to reduce muscle contractions which produce vomiting (phosphoric acid-glucose combination),
- do not affect the underlying cause of the symptoms which they are designed to relieve or suppress.

See also: Antacid

ACTIVE INGREDIENT:

DIMENHYDRINATE

BRAND NAMES:

- CALM-X
- DRAMAMINE CHILDREN'S LIQUID (also contains flavors, glycerin, methylparaben, sucrose)
- DRAMAMINE–CHEWABLE TABLETS (also contains aspartame, magnesium stearate, methacrylic acid, tartrazine—a dye, sorbitol, flavors)
- DRAMAMINE–TABLETS (also contains acacia, carboxymehtylcellulose sodium, magnesium stearate, sodium sulfate)
- MARMINE

SYMPTOMS RELIEVED:

Nausea, vomiting, dizziness associated with motion sickness.

HOW TO TAKE:

Comes in chewable tablet, liquid, and tablet forms. Chewable tablets should be well chewed before swallowing. Do not swallow whole. Swallow regular tablets with liquid. For prevention of motion sickness, take first dose ½ hour to 1 hour before beginning an activity (such as sailing) which you believe will produce symptoms of motion sickness.

USUAL ADULT DOSE:

1 to 2 tablets every 4 to 6 hours, not to exceed 8 tablets in a 24 hour period, or as directed by your doctor. In all cases follow specific product instructions.

USUAL CHILD DOSE:

For children 6 to 12: ½ to 1 tablet every 6 to 8 hours, not to exceed 3 tablets in a 24 hour period, or as directed by your doctor; or 2 to 4 teaspoonsful of DRAMAMINE CHILDREN'S LIQUID every 6 to 8 hours, not to exceed 12 teaspoonsful, or as directed by your doctor. In all cases follow specific product instructions.

For children 2 to 6: 1/4 to 1/2 tablet every 6 to 8 hours, not to exceed 1 1/2 tablets in a 24 hour period, or as directed by your doctor; or 1 to 2 teaspoonsful of DRAMAMINE CHILDREN'S LIQUID every 6 to 8 hours, not to exceed 6 teaspoonsful, or as directed by your doctor. In all cases follow specific product instructions.

Do not administer to children under 2 unless under direction of physician. Dosage may vary based on infant or child's age. In all cases follow specific product instructions.

OVERDOSE SYMPTOMS:
Severe drowsiness and fatigue, difficulty breathing, convulsions, coma.

SIDE EFFECTS:
The most frequent side effect of this type of antihistamines use is drowsiness. Other common side effects include: include dryness of mouth, throat, and nasal passages, dizziness, gastrointestinal (GI) distress (including vomiting, diarrhea, and constipation or change in bowel regularity), and diminished muscle coordination. In rare cases, more severe side effects may result, such as painful and frequent urination or urinary retention, blurred vision, loss of appetite, and respiratory difficulty, nervous agitation, severe anxiety, insomnia (sleeplessness), or severe drowsiness and fatigue, rapid heartbeat,

hallucinations, and tremors. In these cases, discontinue medication and call your doctor immediately.

CHECK WITH YOUR DOCTOR OR PHARMACIST BEFORE COMBINING DIMENHYDRINATE WITH:
Cold, cough, or allergy medication—including other antihistamines; aspirin, stimulants, antidepressants, antihypertensives, digitalis or other heart medication, diuretics, or MAO (monoamine oxidase inhibitors) drugs, or any other drugs or medications. Avoid ingestion of alcohol or use of sedatives or tranquilizers while taking these products or most other antihistamine medication as the combination can produce severe drowsiness or sedation.

PREGNANCY OR BREASTFEEDING:
Safety of this drug for use during pregnancy or while nursing has not been established. In all cases you should consult your doctor before using any drug during pregnancy or while nursing.

PRECAUTIONS FOR CHILDREN:
In general, dimenhydrinate is not advised for children under 2. Administer dimenhydrinate to infants or children only when consulting a physician and follow instructions on medication (see above).

55+

PRECAUTIONS FOR SENIORS:
Seniors generally don't eliminate drugs as efficiently as younger persons, and should avoid high dosages. Use of dimenhydrinate medications by seniors can lead to urinary difficulties. In addition, seniors are more likely to experience drowsiness effects of the drug.

QUICK FACTS

SPECIAL WARNINGS:

Do not use these products if you are allergic to dimenhydrinate, or any of the inactive ingredients contained in these products. Because antihistamines often cause drowsiness, you should avoid activities or tasks such as driving, or other operations which require alertness, coordination, dexterity or quick reflexes. Do not use continuously for longer than 3 months. Do not use dimenhydrinate medications containing tartrazine if you are intolerant or hypersensitive to aspirin. Allergic reactions, including bronchial asthma, have occurred in susceptible individuals.

INFORM YOUR DOCTOR BEFORE TAKING DIMENHYDRINATE IF YOU HAVE:

Urinary difficulty, glaucoma, ulcer, or if you are pregnant. If you anticipate any surgery requiring general or spinal anesthesia within 2 months of taking any of these products, inform your doctor.

ACTIVE INGREDIENT:

MECLIZINE HYDROCHLORIDE

BRAND NAMES:

- BONINE
- DIZMISS
- DRAMAMINE II LESS DROWSY (also contains colloidal silicon dioxide, croscarmellose sodium, dibasic calcium phosphate, microcrystalline cellulose, magnesium stearate)

SYMPTOMS RELIEVED:
Nausea, vomiting, dizziness associated with motion sickness.

HOW TO TAKE:
Comes in tablet forms. Swallow tablet s with liquid. For prevention of motion sickness, take first dose 1 hour before beginning an activity (such as sailing) which you believe will produce symptoms of motion sickness.

USUAL ADULT DOSE:
1 to 2 tablets every per day, not to exceed 2 tablets in a 24 hour period, or as directed by your doctor. In all cases follow specific product instructions.

USUAL CHILD DOSE:
Do not administer to children under 12 unless under direction of physician. Dosage may vary based on infant or child's age. In all cases follow specific product instructions.

OVERDOSE SYMPTOMS:
Severe drowsiness and fatigue, difficulty breathing, convulsions, coma.

Q U I C K F A C T S

QUICK FACTS

SIDE EFFECTS:
The most frequent side effect of this type of antihistamines use is drowsiness. Other common side effects include: include dryness of mouth, throat, and nasal passages, dizziness, gastrointestinal (GI) distress (including vomiting, diarrhea and constipation, or change in bowel regularity), and diminished muscle coordination. In rare cases, more severe side effects may result, such as painful and frequent urination or urinary retention, blurred vision, loss of appetite, and respiratory difficulty, nervous agitation, severe anxiety, insomnia (sleeplessness) or severe drowsiness and fatigue, rapid heartbeat, hallucinations, and tremors. In these cases, discontinue medication and call your doctor immediately.

CHECK WITH YOUR DOCTOR OR PHARMACIST BEFORE COMBINING MECLIZINE HYDROCHLORIDE WITH:
Cold, cough, or allergy medication—including other antihistamines; aspirin, stimulants, antidepressants, antihypertensives, digitalis or other heart medication, diuretics, or MAO (monoamine oxidase inhibitors) drugs, or any other drugs or medications. Avoid ingestion of alcohol or use of sedatives or tranquilizers while taking these products or most other antihistamine medication as the combination can produce severe drowsiness or sedation.

PREGNANCY OR BREASTFEEDING:
Safety of this drug for use during pregnancy or while nursing has not been established. In all cases you should consult your doctor before using any drug during pregnancy or while nursing.

PRECAUTIONS FOR CHILDREN:
In general, meclizine hydrochloride is not advised for children under 2. Administer meclizine hydrochloride to infants or children only when consulting a physician and follow instructions on medication (see above).

PRECAUTIONS FOR SENIORS:
Seniors generally don't eliminate drugs as efficiently as younger persons, and should avoid high dosages. Use of meclizine hydrochloride medications by seniors can lead to urinary difficulties. In addition, seniors are more likely to experience drowsiness effects of the drug.

SPECIAL WARNINGS:
Do not use these products if you are allergic to meclizine, or any of the inactive ingredients contained in these products. Because antihistamines often cause drowsiness, you should avoid activities or tasks such as driving, or other operations which require alertness, coordination, dexterity, or quick reflexes. Do not use continuously for longer than 3 months. Do not use meclizine hydrochloride medications containing tartrazine if you are intolerant or hypersensitive to aspirin. Allergic reactions, including bronchial asthma, have occurred in susceptible individuals.

INFORM YOUR DOCTOR BEFORE TAKING MECLIZINE HYDROCHLORIDE IF YOU HAVE:
Urinary difficulty, glaucoma, ulcer, or if you are pregnant. If you anticipate any surgery requiring general or spinal anesthesia within 2 months of taking any of these products, inform your doctor.

QUICK FACTS

ACTIVE INGREDIENT:

PHOSPHORIC ACID

BRAND NAMES:

- EMETROL

SYMPTOMS RELIEVED:

Nausea and vomiting associated with upset stomach, intestinal flu, food poisoning, or overindulgence.

HOW TO TAKE:

Comes in liquid form. Do not dilute or take with other liquid of any kind immediately before dose or until at least 15 minutes after dose.

USUAL ADULT DOSE:

1 to 2 tablepoonsful every 15 minutes, not to exceed 5 doses in a 1 hour period, or as directed by your doctor. In all cases follow specific product instructions.

Note: If symptoms persist or quickly recur, immediately consult your doctor.

USUAL CHILD DOSE:

1 to 2 teaspoonsful every 15 minutes, not to exceed 5 doses in a 1 hour period, or as directed by your doctor. In all cases follow specific product instructions.

Note: If symptoms persist or quickly recur, immediately consult your doctor.

OVERDOSE SYMPTOMS:

Severe abdominal pain and diarrhea.

SIDE EFFECTS:

None in most cases of common use. Occasionally, some abdominal pain or diarrhea may occur.

CHECK WITH YOUR DOCTOR OR PHARMACIST BEFORE COMBINING PHOSPHORIC ACID (GLUCOSE, FRUCTOSE, AND PHOSPHORIC ACID SOLUTION) WITH:
Any other drugs or medications.

PREGNANCY OR BREASTFEEDING:
Safety of this drug for use during pregnancy or while nursing has not been established. In all cases you should consult your doctor before using any drug during pregnancy or while nursing.

PRECAUTIONS FOR CHILDREN:
Administer this product to infants or children only when consulting a physician and follow instructions on medication (see above).

55+

PRECAUTIONS FOR SENIORS:
Seniors generally don't eliminate drugs as efficiently as younger persons, and should avoid high dosages.

SPECIAL WARNINGS:
Do not use these products if you are allergic to phosphoric acid, or any of the inactive ingredients contained in these products. Do not use continuously for longer than 1 hour (see above). Do not use this product if you are diabetic, or if you have HFI (hereditary fructose intolerance).

INFORM YOUR DOCTOR BEFORE TAKING PHOSPHORIC ACID (GLUCOSE, FRUCTOSE AND PHOSPHORIC ACID SOLUTION) IF YOU HAVE:
Any allergies or food intolerance, urinary difficulty, glaucoma, ulcer, intestinal obstruction, or if you are pregnant.

QUICK FACTS

SKIN CONDITIONS

QUICK REVIEW

• ANESTHETIC •
(TOPICAL)

The most important considerations in choosing a topical or local anesthetic are: its action in partially or completely eliminating the sensation of physical pain in one part of the body, and potential side effects associated with the drug.

TOPICAL ANESTHETICS ARE A CLASS OF DRUGS WHICH:

- act in some combination of the following ways: by limiting the production of energy in nerve cells—thereby reducing nerve impulses and related sensation of pain, by increasing the body's production of organic compounds which limit the transmission of pain messages through synapses, or by reducing nerve cell energy production, thereby limiting the cell's production of nerve impulses. These actions are not completely understood due to varying effects of topical anesthetics and the complex nature of the body's central nervous system (CNS),
- especially when used in high dosages or for long treatment periods, may be absorbed into the blood stream through the skin or mucous membranes, increasing the anesthetic's effectiveness but also the incidence and probability of adverse side effects,
- do not affect the underlying cause of the symptoms which they are designed to relieve or suppress.

ACTIVE INGREDIENT:

BENZOCAINE (ETHYL AMINOBENZOATE)

℞ **BRAND NAMES:**

- AMERICAINE FIRST AID (also contains benzethonium chloride)
- AEROCAINE (also contains benzethonium chloride)
- AEROTHERM (also contains benzethonium chloride)
- ANBESOL (also contains phenol, povidone-iodine, alcohol, camphor, menthol, glycerin)
- BICOZENE–CREAM (also contains resorcinol, castor oil, glycerin)
- BOIL-EASE–OINTMENT (also contains camphor, lanolin, eucalyptus, menthol, petrolatum, phenol)
- CHIGGER-TOX–LIQUID (also contains benzyl benzoate)
- DERMOPLAST–LOTION (also contains menthol, methylparaben, aloe, lanolin)
- CHIGGEREX–LIQUID (also contains aloe vera, olive oil, camphor, menthol, methylparaben)
- DERMOPLAST–LOTION (also contains menthol, methylparaben, aloe, lanolin)
- DETANE (also contains carbomer 940)
- FOILLE–SPRAY (also contains chloroxylenol)
- FOILLE PLUS–AEROSOL (also contains chloroxylenol, alcohol)
- FOILLE MEDICATED FIRST AID–AEROSOL & OINTMENT (also contains chloroxylenol, benzyl alcohol, EDTA)
- LANACANE–CREAM (also contains benzethonium chloride, aloe, parabens, castor oil, glycerin, isopropyl alcohol)

QUICK FACTS

- LANACANE–SPRAY (also contains benzethonium chloride, ethanol, aloe extract)
- SOLARCAINE–AEROSOL (also contains triclosan, SD alcohol, tocopheryl acetate)
- SOLARCAINE–LOTION (also contains triclosan, mineral oil, alcohol, aloe extract, tocopheryl acetate, menthol, camphor, parabens, EDTA)
- STING-KILL (also contains menthol, tartrazine, isopropyl alcohol)

SYMPTOMS RELIEVED:
Irritation, itching, and rashes due to minor skin conditions, discomfort of plant poisonings such as poison ivy, sumac, and oak, sunburn, common nonpoisonous insect bites and insect stings, and minor burns.

HOW TO USE:
Comes in aerosol, cream, liquid, lotion, and spray forms. Apply to affected area as needed, or in the case of creams and ointments, to a bandage or gauze pad before applying to skin. In all cases follow specific product instructions. These products are intended solely for external, topical use. Do not under any conditions ingest internally or use in eyes. Always wash hands before and after use.

USUAL ADULT DOSE:
Dosage varies according to product and condition. Use the minimum recommended dose in order to avoid side effects or complications. In all cases follow specific product instructions.

USUAL CHILD DOSE:
Do not use in children or infants under 1 year of age. Dosage varies according to product and

condition. Use the minimum recommended dose in order to avoid side effects or complications. In all cases follow specific product instructions.

OVERDOSE SYMPTOMS:

Convulsions, agitation, euphoria, drowsiness, disorientation or dizziness, blurred vision, vomiting, numbness, hypotension-possibly leading to respiratory arrest; or cardiac arrhythmia (irregular pulse and heartbeat) leading to cardiac arrest or collapse. If you suspect an overdose, immediately seek medical attention.

SIDE EFFECTS:

No serious effects in most cases of common use. However, you may experience an increased in photosensitivity reaction resulting in higher risk of sunburn and other related skin damage. In this case, avoid unnecessary exposure to sun. In rare cases, some individuals have experienced swelling of skin or in mouth and throat, or rash, burning or stinging sensations, or pronounced skin sensitivity. In these cases, discontinue application or use of the product and call your doctor immediately.

CHECK WITH YOUR DOCTOR OR PHARMACIST BEFORE COMBINING BENZOCAINE WITH:

Sulfa drugs or Class I antiarrhythmia drugs (tocainide, mexiletine).

PREGNANCY OR BREASTFEEDING:

Benzocaine use by a nursing mother should be considered a potential risk for a nursing child as the drug will be passed on to the infant in the mother's milk. In all cases, a physician should be consulted.

QUICK FACTS

PRECAUTIONS FOR CHILDREN:
In general, use caution when applying benzocaine products with children under 6, as the risk of product absorption through skin is greater. Do not use in children or infants under 1 year of age. Consulting your doctor and follow instructions on medication (see above).

PRECAUTIONS FOR SENIORS:
Seniors generally may be more prone to side effects and possible adverse effects of these products than younger individuals. Avoid high dosages.

SPECIAL WARNINGS:
Do not use any of these products if you are allergic to any topical anesthetic. Avoid applying more than three days continuously to same area, as this may lead to excess absorption. Do not continue overall use more than one week if condition hasn't improved.

INFORM YOUR DOCTOR BEFORE TAKING BENZOCAINE IF YOU HAVE:
Allergies to: any topical anesthetic, or if you have skin infection or skin conditions such as psoriasis or eczema.

ACTIVE INGREDIENTS:

BENZOCAINE IN COMBINATION WITH ICHTAMMOL

QUICK FACTS

BRAND NAMES:

- BOIL-EASE (also contains lanolin, camphor, eucalyptus oil, juniper tar, phenol, menthol, paraffin, petrolatum, rosin, sexadecyl alcohol, thymol, yellow wax, zinc oxide)
- BOYOL SALVE (also contains lanolin, petrolatum)

SYMPTOMS RELIEVED:
Boils and related topical conditions.

HOW TO USE:
Comes in salve forms. Application varies based on severity of condition. In all cases follow specific product instructions. These products are intended solely for external, topical use. Do not under any conditions ingest internally or use in eyes. Always wash hands before and after use.

USUAL ADULT DOSE:
Dosage varies according to product and condition. Use the minimum recommended dose in order to avoid side effects or complications. In all cases follow specific product instructions.

USUAL CHILD DOSE:
Do not use in children or infants under 1 year of age. Dosage varies according to product and condition. Use the minimum recommended dose in order to avoid side effects or complications. In all cases follow specific product instructions.

QUICK FACTS

OVERDOSE SYMPTOMS:
Convulsions, agitation, euphoria, drowsiness, disorientation or dizziness, blurred vision, vomiting, numbness, hypotension-possibly leading to respiratory arrest; or cardiac arrhythmia (irregular pulse and heartbeat) leading to cardiac arrest or collapse. If you suspect an overdose, immediately seek medical attention.

SIDE EFFECTS:
No serious effects in most cases of common use. However, you may experience an increased in photosensitivity reaction resulting in higher risk of sunburn and other related skin damage. In this case, avoid unnecessary exposure to sun. In rare cases, some individuals have experienced swelling of skin or in mouth and throat, or rash, burning or stinging sensations, or pronounced skin sensitivity. In these cases, discontinue application or use of the product and call your doctor immediately.

CHECK WITH YOUR DOCTOR OR PHARMACIST BEFORE COMBINING BENZOCAINE WITH:
Sulfa drugs or Class I antiarrhythmia drugs (drugs used to treat irregular heartbeat, such as tocainide, mexiletine).

PREGNANCY OR BREASTFEEDING:
Safety of this drug for use during pregnancy or while nursing has not been established. In all cases you should consult your doctor before using any drug during pregnancy or while nursing.

PRECAUTIONS FOR CHILDREN:
In general, use caution when applying benzocaine products with children under 6, as the risk of product absorption through skin is greater. Do not use in children or infants under 1 year of age. Consult your doctor and follow instructions on medication (see above).

55+

PRECAUTIONS FOR SENIORS:
Seniors generally may be more prone to side effects and possible adverse effects of these products than younger individuals. Avoid high dosages.

SPECIAL WARNINGS:
Do not use any of these products if you are allergic to any topical anesthetic. Avoid applying more than three days continuously to same area, as this may lead to excess absorption. Do not continue overall use more than one week if condition hasn't improved.

INFORM YOUR DOCTOR BEFORE USING BENZOCAINE IF YOU HAVE:
Allergies to: any topical anesthetic, or if you have skin infection or skin conditions such as psoriasis or eczema.

QUICK FACTS

ACTIVE INGREDIENT:
DIBUCAINE

BRAND NAMES:
- NUPERCAINAL

SYMPTOMS RELIEVED:
Irritation, itching, and rashes due to minor skin conditions, discomfort of plant poisonings such as poison ivy, sumac, and oak, sunburn, common nonpoisonous insect bites and insect stings, and minor burns.

HOW TO TAKE:
Comes in cream and ointment forms. Apply to affected area as needed, or to a bandage or gauze pad before applying to skin. In all cases follow specific product instructions. This product is intended solely for external use. Do not under any conditions ingest internally or use in eyes. Always wash hands before and after use.

USUAL ADULT DOSE:
Dosage varies according to product and condition. Use the minimum recommended dose in order to avoid side effects or complications. In all cases follow specific product instructions.

USUAL CHILD DOSE:
Do not use in children or infants under 1 year of age. Dosage varies according to product and condition. Use the minimum recommended dose in order to avoid side effects or complications. In all cases follow specific product instructions.

OVERDOSE SYMPTOMS:
Convulsions, agitation, euphoria, drowsiness,

disorientation or dizziness, blurred vision, vomiting, numbness, hypotension-possibly leading to respiratory arrest; or cardiac arrhythmia (irregular pulse and heartbeat) leading to cardiac arrest or collapse. If you suspect an overdose, immediately seek medical attention.

SIDE EFFECTS:

No serious effects in most cases of common use. However, you may experience an increased in photosensitivity reaction resulting in higher risk of sunburn and other related skin damage. In this case, avoid unnecessary exposure to sun. In rare cases, some individuals have experienced swelling of skin or in mouth and throat, or rash, burning or stinging sensations, or pronounced skin sensitivity. In these cases, discontinue application or use of the product and call your doctor immediately.

CHECK WITH YOUR DOCTOR OR PHARMACIST BEFORE COMBINING DIBUCAINE WITH:

Sulfa drugs or Class I antiarrhythmia drugs (tocainide, mexiletine).

PREGNANCY OR BREASTFEEDING:

Dibucaine use by a nursing mother should be considered a potential risk for a nursing child as the drug will be passed on to the infant in the mother's milk. In all cases, a physician should be consulted.

PRECAUTIONS FOR CHILDREN:

In general, use caution when applying dibucaine products with children under 6, as the risk of product absorption through skin is greater. Do not use in children or infants under 1 year

QUICK FACTS

of age. Consulting your doctor and follow instructions on medication (see above).

55+ **PRECAUTIONS FOR SENIORS:**

Seniors generally may be more prone to side effects and possible adverse effects of these products than younger individuals. Avoid high dosages.

SPECIAL WARNINGS:

Do not use any of these products if you are allergic to any topical anesthetic. Avoid applying more than three days continuously to same area, as this may lead to excess absorption. Do not continue overall use more than one week if condition hasn't improved.

INFORM YOUR DOCTOR BEFORE TAKING DIBUCAINE IF YOU HAVE:

Allergies to: any topical anesthetic, or if you have skin infection or skin conditions such as psoriasis or eczema.

ACTIVE INGREDIENT:

LIDOCAINE

QUICK FACTS

BRAND NAMES:

- BACTINE ANTISEPTIC ANESTHETIC (also contains benzalkonium chloride, EDTA)
- DERMAFLEX (also contains alcohol)
- DR. SCHOLL'S CRACKED HEEL RELIEF (also contains benzalkonium chloride)
- MEDI-QUIK (also contains benzalkonium chloride, benzyl alcohol)
- PRO-TECH (also contains povidone iodine)
- SOLARCAINE ALOE EXTRA BURN RELIEF–CREAM (also contains aloe, EDTA, lanolin, lanolin oil, camphor, propylparaben,eucalyptus oil, menthol, tartrazine)
- SOLARCAINE ALOE EXTRA BURN RELIEF–GEL (also contains aloe vera, glycerin, EDTA, isopropyl alcohol, menthol, diazolidinyl urea, tartrazine)
- SOLARCAINE ALOE EXTRA BURN RELIEF–SPRAY (also contains aloe vera gel, glycerin, EDTA, diazolidinyl urea, vitamin E, parabens)
- UNGUENTINE PLUS (also contains phenol, parabens, mineral oil, EDTA)
- ZILACTIN (also contains alcohol)

SYMPTOMS RELIEVED:

Irritation, itching, and rashes due to minor skin conditions, discomfort from poison ivy, sumac, and oak, sunburn, common nonpoisonous insect bites and stings, and minor burns.

HOW TO TAKE:

Comes in cream, gel, liquid, ointment, and spray forms. Apply to affected area as needed, or in the case of creams and ointments, to a bandage

QUICK FACTS

or gauze pad before applying to skin. In all cases follow specific product instructions. These products are intended solely for external use. Do not under any conditions ingest internally or use in eyes. Always wash hands before and after use.

USUAL ADULT DOSE:
Dosage varies according to product and condition. Use the minimum recommended dose in order to avoid side effects or complications. In all cases follow specific product instructions.

USUAL CHILD DOSE:
Do not use in children or infants under 1 year of age. Dosage varies according to product and condition. Use the minimum recommended dose in order to avoid side effects or complications. In all cases follow specific product instructions.

OVERDOSE SYMPTOMS:
Convulsions, agitation, euphoria, drowsiness, disorientation or dizziness, blurred vision, vomiting, numbness, hypotension-possibly leading to respiratory arrest; or cardiac arrhythmia (irregular pulse and heartbeat) leading to cardiac arrest or collapse. If you suspect an overdose, immediately seek medical attention.

SIDE EFFECTS:
No serious effects in most cases of common use. However, you may experience an increased in photosensitivity reaction resulting in higher risk of sunburn and other related skin damage. In this case, avoid unnecessary exposure to sun. In rare cases, some individuals have experienced swelling of skin or in mouth and throat, or rash, burning or stinging sensations, or pronounced

skin sensitivity. In these cases, discontinue application or use of the product and call your doctor immediately.

CHECK WITH YOUR DOCTOR OR PHARMACIST BEFORE COMBINING LIDOCAINE WITH:
Sulfa drugs or Class I antiarrhythmia drugs.

PREGNANCY OR BREASTFEEDING:
Lidocaine use by a nursing mother should be considered a potential risk for a nursing child as the drug will be passed on to the infant in the mother's milk. In all cases consult a physician.

PRECAUTIONS FOR CHILDREN:
In general, use caution when applying lidocaine products with children under 6, as the risk of product absorption through skin is greater. Do not use in children or infants under 1 year of age.

55+

PRECAUTIONS FOR SENIORS:
Seniors generally may be more prone to side effects and possible adverse effects of these products than younger individuals. Avoid high dosages.

SPECIAL WARNINGS:
Do not use any of these products if you are allergic to any topical anesthetic. Avoid applying more than three days continuously to same area, as this may lead to excess absorption. Do not continue overall use more than one week if condition hasn't improved.

INFORM YOUR DOCTOR BEFORE TAKING LIDOCAINE IF YOU HAVE:
Allergies to: any topical anesthetic, or if you have skin infection or skin conditions such as psoriasis or eczema.

QUICK FACTS

ACTIVE INGREDIENT:
PRAMOXINE HYDROCHLORIDE

BRAND NAMES:
- ITCH-X–GEL (also contains benzyl alcohol, aloe vera, diazolidinyl urea, SD alcohol 40, parabens)
- ITCH-X–SPRAY (also contains benzyl alcohol, aloe vera gel, SD alcohol 40)
- PRAMAGEL (also contains menthol, benzyl alcohol, SD alcohol 40)
- PRAX–CREAM (also contains glycerin, cetyl alcohol, white petrolatum)
- PRAX–LOTION (also contains mineral oil, cetyl alcohol, glycerin, lanolin, potassium sorbate, sorbic acid)

SYMPTOMS RELIEVED:
Irritation, itching, and rashes due to minor skin conditions, discomfort of plant poisonings such as poison ivy, sumac, and oak, sunburn, common nonpoisonous insect bites and insect stings, and minor burns.

HOW TO TAKE:
Comes in cream, gel, lotion, and spray forms. Apply to affected area as needed, or in the case of creams, to a bandage or gauze pad before applying to skin. In all cases follow specific product instructions. These products are intended solely for external use. Do not under any conditions ingest internally or use in eyes. Always wash hands before and after use.

USUAL ADULT DOSE:
Dosage varies according to product and condition. Use the minimum recommended dose in

order to avoid side effects or complications. In all cases follow specific product instructions.

USUAL CHILD DOSE:
Do not use in children or infants under 1 year of age. Dosage varies according to product and condition. Use the minimum recommended dose in order to avoid side effects or complications. In all cases follow specific product instructions.

OVERDOSE SYMPTOMS:
Convulsions, agitation, euphoria, drowsiness, disorientation or dizziness, blurred vision, vomiting, numbness, hypotension-possibly leading to respiratory arrest; or cardiac arrhythmia (irregular pulse and heartbeat) leading to cardiac arrest or collapse. If you suspect an overdose, immediately seek medical attention.

SIDE EFFECTS:
No serious effects in most cases of common use. However, you may experience an increased in photosensitivity reaction resulting in higher risk of sunburn and other related skin damage. In this case, avoid unnecessary exposure to sun. In rare cases, some individuals have experienced swelling of skin or in mouth and throat, or rash, burning or stinging sensations, or pronounced skin sensitivity. In these cases, discontinue application or use of the product and call your doctor immediately.

CHECK WITH YOUR DOCTOR OR PHARMACIST BEFORE COMBINING PRAMOXINE WITH:
Sulfa drugs or Class I antiarrhythmia drugs (tocainide, mexiletine).

QUICK FACTS

PREGNANCY OR BREASTFEEDING:
Pramoxine use by a nursing mother should be considered a potential risk for a nursing child as the drug will be passed on to the infant in the mother's milk. In all cases, a physician should be consulted.

PRECAUTIONS FOR CHILDREN:
In general, use caution when applying pramoxine products with children under 6, as the risk of product absorption through skin is greater. Do not use in children or infants under 1 year of age. Consulting your doctor and follow instructions on medication (see above).

55+

PRECAUTIONS FOR SENIORS:
Seniors generally may be more prone to side effects and possible adverse effects of these products than younger individuals. Avoid high dosages.

SPECIAL WARNINGS:
Do not use any of these products if you are allergic to any topical anesthetic. Avoid applying more than three days continuously to same area, as this may lead to excess absorption. Do not continue overall use more than one week if condition hasn't improved.

INFORM YOUR DOCTOR BEFORE TAKING PRAMOXINE IF YOU HAVE:
Allergies to: any topical anesthetic, or if you have skin infection or skin conditions such as psoriasis or eczema.

ACTIVE INGREDIENT:
TETRACAINE

BRAND NAMES:
- PONTOCAINE
  (also contains menthol, white petrolatum)

SYMPTOMS RELIEVED:
Irritation, itching, and rashes due to minor skin conditions, discomfort of plant poisonings such as poison ivy, sumac, and oak, sunburn, common nonpoisonous insect bites and insect stings, and minor burns.

HOW TO TAKE:
Comes in cream and ointment forms. Apply to affected area as needed, or to a bandage or gauze pad before applying to skin. In all cases follow specific product instructions. This product is intended solely for external use. Do not under any conditions ingest internally or use in eyes. Always wash hands before and after use.

USUAL ADULT DOSE:
Dosage varies according to product and condition. Use the minimum recommended dose in order to avoid side effects or complications. In all cases follow specific product instructions.

USUAL CHILD DOSE:
Do not use in children or infants under 1 year of age. Dosage varies according to product and condition. Use the minimum recommended dose in order to avoid side effects or complications. In all cases follow specific product instructions.

QUICK FACTS

OVERDOSE SYMPTOMS:
Convulsions, agitation, euphoria, drowsiness, disorientation or dizziness, blurred vision, vomiting, numbness, hypotension-possibly leading to respiratory arrest; or cardiac arrhythmia (irregular pulse and heartbeat) leading to cardiac arrest or collapse. If you suspect an overdose, immediately seek medical attention.

SIDE EFFECTS:
No serious effects in most cases of common use. However, you may experience an increased in photosensitivity reaction resulting in higher risk of sunburn and other related skin damage. In this case, avoid unnecessary exposure to sun. In rare cases, some individuals have experienced swelling of skin or in mouth and throat, or rash, burning or stinging sensations, or pronounced skin sensitivity. In these cases, discontinue application or use of the product and call your doctor immediately.

CHECK WITH YOUR DOCTOR OR PHARMACIST BEFORE COMBINING TETRACAINE WITH:
Sulfa drugs or Class I antiarrhythmia drugs (tocainide, mexiletine).

PREGNANCY OR BREASTFEEDING:
Tetracaine use by a nursing mother should be considered a potential risk for a nursing child as the drug will be passed on to the infant in the mother's milk. In all cases, a physician should be consulted.

PRECAUTIONS FOR CHILDREN:
In general, use caution when applying tetracaine products with children under 6, as the risk of

product absorption through skin is greater. Do not use in children or infants under 1 year of age. Consulting your doctor and follow instructions on medication (see above).

55+ **PRECAUTIONS FOR SENIORS:**

Seniors generally may be more prone to side effects and possible adverse effects of these products than younger individuals. Avoid high dosages.

SPECIAL WARNINGS:

Do not use any of these products if you are allergic to any topical anesthetic. Avoid applying more than three days continuously to same area, as this may lead to excess absorption. Do not continue overall use more than one week if condition hasn't improved.

INFORM YOUR DOCTOR BEFORE TAKING TETRACAINE IF YOU HAVE:

Allergies to: any topical anesthetic, or if you have skin infection or skin conditions such as psoriasis or eczema.

QUICK REVIEW

• ANTI-ITCH •
(TOPICAL)

The most important considerations in choosing an anti-itch agent are: its effectiveness in treating and relieving skin itchiness, and potential side effects associated with the drug.

TOPICAL ANTI-ITCH AGENTS ARE A CLASS OF DRUGS WHICH:

- are only intended for topical use,
- are nonspecific in their action, and act against most causes of skin inflammation by depressing, neutralizing, or interfering with the activity of enzymes which produce skin inflammation and resultant itchiness,
- in over-the-counter (OTC) products, are primarily formulated with hydrocortisone (a topical adrenocorticoid) as the active ingredient,
- when used in high dosages or for long treatment periods, may be absorbed into the bloodstream through the skin or mucous membranes, increasing the incidence and probability of adverse side effects.

ACTIVE INGREDIENT:

BENZOCAINE (ETHYL AMINOBENZOATE)

Q U I C K F A C T S

℞ **BRAND NAMES:**

- AMERICAINE FIRST AID (also contains benzethonium chloride)
- AEROCAINE (also contains benzethonium chloride)
- AEROTHERM (also contains benzethonium chloride)
- ANBESOL (also contains phenol, povidone-iodine, alcohol, camphor, menthol, glycerin)
- BICOZENE–CREAM (also contains resorcinol, castor oil, glycerin)
- BOIL-EASE–OINTMENT (also contains camphor, lanolin, eucalyptus, menthol, petrolatum, phenol)
- CHIGGER-TOX–LIQUID (also contains benzyl benzoate)
- DERMOPLAST–LOTION (also contains menthol, methylparaben, aloe, lanolin)
- CHIGGEREX–LIQUID (also contains aloe vera, olive oil, camphor, menthol, methylparaben)
- DERMOPLAST–LOTION (also contains menthol, methylparaben, aloe, lanolin)
- DETANE (also contains carbomer 940)
- FOILLE–SPRAY (also contains chloroxylenol)
- FOILLE PLUS–AEROSOL (also contains chloroxylenol, alcohol)
- FOILLE MEDICATED FIRST AID–AEROSOL & OINTMENT (also contains chloroxylenol, benzyl alcohol, EDTA)
- LANACANE–CREAM (also contains benzethonium chloride, aloe, parabens, castor oil, glycerin, isopropyl alcohol)

QUICK FACTS

- LANACANE–SPRAY (also contains benzethonium chloride, ethanol, aloe extract)
- SOLARCAINE–AEROSOL (also contains triclosan, SD alcohol, tocopheryl acetate)
- SOLARCAINE–LOTION (also contains triclosan, mineral oil, alcohol, aloe extract, tocopheryl acetate, menthol, camphor, parabens, EDTA)
- STING-KILL (also contains menthol, tartrazine, isopropyl alcohol)

SYMPTOMS RELIEVED:
Irritation, itching, and rashes due to minor skin conditions, discomfort of plant poisonings such as poison ivy, sumac, and oak, sunburn, common nonpoisonous insect bites and insect stings, and minor burns.

HOW TO USE:
Comes in aerosol, cream, liquid, lotion, and spray forms. Apply to affected area as needed, or in the case of creams and ointments, to a bandage or gauze pad before applying to skin. In all cases follow specific product instructions. These products are intended solely for external, topical use. Do not under any conditions ingest internally or use in eyes. Always wash hands before and after use.

USUAL ADULT DOSE:
Dosage varies according to product and condition. Use the minimum recommended dose in order to avoid side effects or complications. In all cases follow specific product instructions.

USUAL CHILD DOSE:
Do not use in children or infants under 1 year of age. Dosage varies according to product and

condition. Use the minimum recommended dose in order to avoid side effects or complications. In all cases follow specific product instructions.

OVERDOSE SYMPTOMS:
Convulsions, agitation, euphoria, drowsiness, disorientation or dizziness, blurred vision, vomiting, numbness, hypotension-possibly leading to respiratory arrest; or cardiac arrhythmia (irregular pulse and heartbeat) leading to cardiac arrest or collapse. If you suspect an overdose, immediately seek medical attention.

SIDE EFFECTS:
No serious effects in most cases of common use. However, you may experience an increased in photosensitivity reaction resulting in higher risk of sunburn and other related skin damage. In this case, avoid unnecessary exposure to sun. In rare cases, some individuals have experienced swelling of skin or in mouth and throat, or rash, burning or stinging sensations, or pronounced skin sensitivity. In these cases, discontinue application or use of the product and call your doctor immediately.

CHECK WITH YOUR DOCTOR OR PHARMACIST BEFORE COMBINING BENZOCAINE WITH:
Sulfa drugs or Class I antiarrhythmia drugs (tocainide, mexiletine).

PREGNANCY OR BREASTFEEDING:
Benzocaine use by a nursing mother should be considered a potential risk for a nursing child as the drug will be passed on to the infant in the mother's milk. In all cases, a physician should be consulted.

Q U I C K F A C T S

PRECAUTIONS FOR CHILDREN:
In general, use caution when applying benzocaine products with children under 6, as the risk of product absorption through skin is greater. Do not use in children or infants under 1 year of age. Consulting your doctor and follow instructions on medication (see above).

55+ **PRECAUTIONS FOR SENIORS:**
Seniors generally may be more prone to side effects and possible adverse effects of these products than younger individuals. Avoid high dosages.

SPECIAL WARNINGS:
Do not use any of these products if you are allergic to any topical anesthetic. Avoid applying more than three days continuously to same area, as this may lead to excess absorption. Do not continue overall use more than one week if condition hasn't improved.

INFORM YOUR DOCTOR BEFORE TAKING BENZOCAINE IF YOU HAVE:
Allergies to: any topical anesthetic, or if you have skin infection or skin conditions such as psoriasis or eczema.

ACTIVE INGREDIENT:
DIBUCAINE

BRAND NAMES:
- NUPERCAINAL

SYMPTOMS RELIEVED:
Irritation, itching, and rashes due to minor skin conditions, discomfort of plant poisonings such as poison ivy, sumac, and oak, sunburn, common nonpoisonous insect bites and insect stings, and minor burns.

HOW TO TAKE:
Comes in cream and ointment forms. Apply to affected area as needed, or to a bandage or gauze pad before applying to skin. In all cases follow specific product instructions. This product is intended solely for external use. Do not under any conditions ingest internally or use in eyes. Always wash hands before and after use.

USUAL ADULT DOSE:
Dosage varies according to product and condition. Use the minimum recommended dose in order to avoid side effects or complications. In all cases follow specific product instructions.

USUAL CHILD DOSE:
Do not use in children or infants under 1 year of age. Dosage varies according to product and condition. Use the minimum recommended dose in order to avoid side effects or complications. In all cases follow specific product instructions.

OVERDOSE SYMPTOMS:
Convulsions, agitation, euphoria, drowsiness,

Q U I C K F A C T S

disorientation or dizziness, blurred vision, vomiting, numbness, hypotension-possibly leading to respiratory arrest; or cardiac arrhythmia (irregular pulse and heartbeat) leading to cardiac arrest or collapse. If you suspect an overdose, immediately seek medical attention.

SIDE EFFECTS:
No serious effects in most cases of common use. However, you may experience an increased in photosensitivity reaction resulting in higher risk of sunburn and other related skin damage. In this case, avoid unnecessary exposure to sun. In rare cases, some individuals have experienced swelling of skin or in mouth and throat, or rash, burning or stinging sensations, or pronounced skin sensitivity. In these cases, discontinue application or use of the product and call your doctor immediately.

CHECK WITH YOUR DOCTOR OR PHARMACIST BEFORE COMBINING DIBUCAINE WITH:
Sulfa drugs or Class I antiarrhythmia drugs (tocainide, mexiletine).

PREGNANCY OR BREASTFEEDING:
Dibucaine use by a nursing mother should be considered a potential risk for a nursing child as the drug will be passed on to the infant in the mother's milk. In all cases, a physician should be consulted.

PRECAUTIONS FOR CHILDREN:
In general, use caution when applying dibucaine products with children under 6, as the risk of product absorption through skin is greater. Do not use in children or infants under 1 year

of age. Consulting your doctor and follow instructions on medication (see above).

55+ **PRECAUTIONS FOR SENIORS:**

Seniors generally may be more prone to side effects and possible adverse effects of these products than younger individuals. Avoid high dosages.

SPECIAL WARNINGS:

Do not use any of these products if you are allergic to any topical anesthetic. Avoid applying more than three days continuously to same area, as this may lead to excess absorption. Do not continue overall use more than one week if condition hasn't improved.

INFORM YOUR DOCTOR BEFORE TAKING DIBUCAINE IF YOU HAVE:

Allergies to: any topical anesthetic, or if you have skin infection or skin conditions such as psoriasis or eczema.

Q U I C K F A C T S

ACTIVE INGREDIENT:

DIPHENHYDRAMINE HYDROCHLORIDE

℞ **BRAND NAMES:**

- BENADRYL–CREAM (also contains parabens)
- BENADRYL–NON-AEROSOL SPRAY (also contains alcohol)
- BENADRYL 2% MAXIMUM STRENGTH–CREAM (also contains parabens)
- BENADRYL 2% MAXIMUM STRENGTH–NON-AEROSOL SPRAY (also contains alcohol)
- CALADRYL–CREAM (also contains calamine, parabens, camphor)
- CALADRYL–LOTION (also contains calamine, camphor, alcohol)
- CALADRYL–SPRAY (also contains calamine, alcohol, camphor)
- CALADRYL CLEAR (also contains alcohol)
- CALA-GEN (also contains alcohol)
- DI-DELAMINE (also contains tripelennamine hydrochloride, benzalkonium chloride, menthol, EDTA)
- STING-EZE (also contains camphor, phenol, benzocaine, eucalyptol)
- ZIRADRYL (also contains zinc oxide, alcohol, camphor, parabens)

Note: *Diphenhydramine* is also used as: a sleep aid, as an antihistamine, and as an active ingre-dient in combination with other drugs in antitussive (anti-cough) products.

SYMPTOMS RELIEVED:

Irritation, itching, and rashes due to minor skin conditions, discomfort of plant poisonings such as poison ivy, sumac, and oak, sunburn, common nonpoisonous insect bites and insect stings, and minor burns.

HOW TO USE:
Comes in concentrate, cream, gel, lotion, and spray forms. Wash and dry affected area before applying. Apply product as needed or as directed by your doctor.

In all cases follow specific product instructions. These products are intended solely for topical use. Do not under any conditions ingest internally or use in eyes. Always wash hands thoroughly before and after use.

USUAL ADULT DOSE:
See above. Use the minimum recommended dose in order to avoid side effects or complications. In all cases follow specific product instructions.

USUAL CHILD DOSE:
Do not use in cases involving children under 2 unless under medical supervision. For all others, use the minimum recommended dose in order to avoid side effects or complications. In all cases follow specific product instructions.

OVERDOSE SYMPTOMS:
No known overdose symptoms.

SIDE EFFECTS:
No serious effects in most cases of common use. However, in rare cases, individuals have experienced mild skin irritation. In these cases, discontinue application or use of the product and call your doctor immediately.

CHECK WITH YOUR DOCTOR OR PHARMACIST BEFORE COMBINING UNDECYLENIC ACID WITH:
Any other topical preparations, or any other antihistamine product.

Q U I C K F A C T S

PREGNANCY OR BREASTFEEDING:
Safety of this drug for use during pregnancy or while nursing has not been established. In all cases you should consult your doctor before using any drug during pregnancy or while nursing.

PRECAUTIONS FOR CHILDREN:
These products should not be used to treat children under 2 unless under close medical supervision.

55+ **PRECAUTIONS FOR SENIORS:**
No special precautions are known for seniors.

SPECIAL WARNINGS:
Do not use any other diphenhydramine products while using any of these topical products. Do not use any of these products if you are allergic to diphenhydramine hydrochloride or any topical antifungal medication, or any of the inactive ingredients listed, or if you have any form of liver disease or damage. Do not use longer than one week continuously.

ADDITIONAL WARNINGS:
Do not use these topical products to treat chicken pox, measles, blisters, or extensive skin areas, unless directed by your doctor.

INFORM YOUR DOCTOR BEFORE USING DIPHENHYDRAMINE IF YOU HAVE:
Urinary difficulty, glaucoma, ulcer, or if you are pregnant. If you anticipate any surgery requiring general or spinal anesthesia within 2 months of taking diphenhydramine-containing medication, inform your doctor.

ACTIVE INGREDIENT:
HYDROCORTISONE

℞ **BRAND NAMES:**

- CALDECORT ANTI-ITCH CREAM (also contains cetostearyl alcohol, sodium lauryl sulfate, white petrolatum, propylene glycol)
- CORTAID INTENSIVE THERAPY (also contains cetyl alcohol, citric acid, glyceryl stearate, isopropyl myristate, methylparaben, poloxyl 40 stearate, polysorbate 60, propylene glycol, propylparaben, sodium citrate, sorbic acid, sorbitan monostearate, stearyl alcohol, white wax)
- CORTAID MAXIMUM STRENGTH CREAM (also contains aloe vera gel, ceteareth alcohol, cetyl palminate, glycerin, isoproply myristate, isostearyl neopentanoate, methylparaben)
- CORTAID MAXIMUM STRENGTH OINTMENT (also contains butylparaben, cholesterol, methylparaben, microcrystalline wax, mineral oil, white petrolatum)
- CORTAID MAXIMUM STRENGTH SPRAY & FAST-STICK (also contains alcohol, glycerin, methylparaben)
- CORTAID MAXIMUM SENSITIVE SKIN FORMULA CREAM (also contains aloe vera gel, butylparaben, cetyl palminate, glyceryl stearate, methylparaben, polyethelene glycol, stearamidoethyl diethylamine)
- CORTAID MAXIMUM SENSITIVE SKIN FORMULA OINTMENT (also contains butylparaben, cholesterol, methylparaben, microcrystalline wax, mineral oil, white petrolatum)

QUICK FACTS

QUICK FACTS

SYMPTOMS RELIEVED:
Itching associated with minor skin irritations, inflammations, and rashes, such as those associated with eczema, common nonpoisonous insect bites and stings, poison ivy, oak and sumac, products such as soaps, detergents, cosmetics, and jewelry, and external anal and feminine itching.

HOW TO USE:
Comes in ointment, nonaerosol spray, roll-on stick and cream forms. Apply to affected areas. These products are for external use only. Do not swallow. Avoid contact with eyes while applying.

USUAL ADULT DOSE:
See specific product instructions. Generally, apply externally to affected areas not more than 3 to 4 times per day, or as directed by your doctor. In all cases follow specific product instructions.

USUAL CHILD DOSE:
For ages 2 to 12: Apply same as adult, or as directed by your doctor. In all cases follow specific product instructions.

Only apply to children under 2 under doctor's supervision or direction. In all cases follow specific product instructions.

OVERDOSE SYMPTOMS:
None known.

SIDE EFFECTS:
No serious effects in most cases of common use. In rare cases, blisters, skin infection, acne-

like eruptions have been reported. These adverse effects are extremely unlikely to occur when these products are used in reasonable dosages for brief periods.

CHECK WITH YOUR DOCTOR OR PHARMACIST BEFORE COMBINING THIS PRODUCT WITH:
Any topical antibacterials or antifungals, or any other drugs and preparations.

PREGNANCY OR BREASTFEEDING:
Safety of this drug for use during pregnancy or while nursing has not been established. In all cases you should consult your doctor before using any drug during pregnancy or while nursing.

PRECAUTIONS FOR CHILDREN:
Use caution when applying these or any other cortisone products with children, as the risk of product absorption through skin is greater. These products should only be used with doctor's supervision or direction for children under 2. Consult your doctor and follow instructions on medication (see above).

55+

PRECAUTIONS FOR SENIORS:
Seniors generally may be more prone to side effects and possible adverse effects of these products than younger individuals. Avoid high dosages.

SPECIAL WARNINGS:
Do not use these products if you are allergic to hydrocortisone, any other topical cortisone medication, or any of the inactive ingredients contained in these products. Do not apply these

Q U I C K F A C T S

products to wounds, lesions, broken, damaged, or sensitive skin. Avoid contact with eyes and mucous membranes. Do not use in mouth or nose.

INFORM YOUR DOCTOR BEFORE USING THESE PRODUCTS IF YOU HAVE:
Diabetes, any skin infection—especially in area which requires treatment, any allergies, stomach ulcers, tuberculosis, or if you are or plan to become pregnant during time that you will be taking this product.

ACTIVE INGREDIENT:

LIDOCAINE

QUICK FACTS

BRAND NAMES:

- BACTINE ANTISEPTIC ANESTHETIC (also contains benzalkonium chloride, EDTA)
- DERMAFLEX (also contains, alcohol)
- DR. SCHOLL'S CRACKED HEEL RELIEF (also contains benzalkonium chloride)
- MEDI-QUIK (also contains benzalkonium chloride, benzyl alcohol)
- PRO-TECH (also contains povidone iodine)
- SOLARCAINE ALOE EXTRA BURN RELIEF–CREAM
- SOLARCAINE ALOE EXTRA BURN RELIEF–GEL
- SOLARCAINE ALOE EXTRA BURN RELIEF–SPRAY
- UNGUENTINE PLUS (also contains phenol, parabens, mineral oil, EDTA)
- ZILACTIN (also contains alcohol)

SYMPTOMS RELIEVED:

Irritation, itching, and rashes due to minor skin conditions, discomfort of plant poisonings such as poison ivy, sumac, and oak, sunburn, common nonpoisonous insect bites and insect stings, and minor burns.

HOW TO TAKE:

Comes in cream, gel, liquid, ointment, and spray forms. Apply to affected area as needed, or in the case of creams and ointments, to a bandage or gauze pad before applying to skin.

In all cases follow specific product instructions. These products are intended solely for external use. Do not under any conditions ingest internally or use in eyes. Always wash hands before and after use.

QUICK FACTS

USUAL ADULT DOSE:
Dosage varies according to product and condition. Use the minimum recommended dose in order to avoid side effects or complications. In all cases follow specific product instructions.

USUAL CHILD DOSE:
Do not use in children or infants under 1 year of age. Dosage varies according to product and condition. Use the minimum recommended dose in order to avoid side effects or complications. In all cases follow specific product instructions.

OVERDOSE SYMPTOMS:
Convulsions, agitation, euphoria, drowsiness, disorientation or dizziness, blurred vision, vomiting, numbness, hypotension—possibly leading to respiratory arrest; or cardiac arrhythmia (irregular pulse and heartbeat) leading to cardiac arrest or collapse. If you suspect an overdose, immediately seek medical attention.

SIDE EFFECTS:
No serious effects in most cases of common use. However, you may experience an increased in photosensitivity reaction resulting in higher risk of sunburn and other related skin damage. In this case, avoid unnecessary exposure to sun. In rare cases, some individuals have experienced swelling of skin or in mouth and throat, or rash, burning or stinging sensations, or pronounced skin sensitivity. In these cases, discontinue application or use of the product and call your doctor immediately.

CHECK WITH YOUR DOCTOR OR PHARMACIST BEFORE COMBINING LIDOCAINE WITH:
Sulfa drugs or Class I antiarrhythmia drugs (tocainide, mexiletine).

PREGNANCY OR BREASTFEEDING:
Lidocaine use by a nursing mother should be considered a potential risk for a nursing child as the drug will be passed on to the infant in the mother's milk. In all cases, a physician should be consulted.

PRECAUTIONS FOR CHILDREN:
In general, use caution when applying lidocaine products with children under 6, as the risk of product absorption through skin is greater. Do not use in children or infants under 1 year of age. Consulting your doctor and follow instructions on medication (see above).

PRECAUTIONS FOR SENIORS:
Seniors generally may be more prone to side effects and possible adverse effects of these products than younger individuals. Avoid high dosages.

SPECIAL WARNINGS:
Do not use any of these products if you are allergic to any topical anesthetic. Avoid applying more than three days continuously to same area, as this may lead to excess absorption. Do not continue overall use more than one week if condition hasn't improved.

INFORM YOUR DOCTOR BEFORE TAKING LIDOCAINE IF YOU HAVE:
Allergies to: any topical anesthetic, or if you have skin infection or skin conditions such as psoriasis or eczema.

QUICK FACTS

ACTIVE INGREDIENT:

TETRACAINE

BRAND NAMES:

- PONTOCAINE
  (also contains menthol, white petrolatum)

SYMPTOMS RELIEVED:

Irritation, itching, and rashes due to minor skin conditions, discomfort of plant poisonings such as poison ivy, sumac, and oak, sunburn, common nonpoisonous insect bites and insect stings, and minor burns.

HOW TO TAKE:

Comes in cream and ointment forms. Apply to affected area as needed, or to a bandage or gauze pad before applying to skin. In all cases follow specific product instructions. This product is intended solely for external use. Do not under any conditions ingest internally or use in eyes. Always wash hands before and after use.

USUAL ADULT DOSE:

Dosage varies according to product and condition. Use the minimum recommended dose in order to avoid side effects or complications. In all cases follow specific product instructions.

USUAL CHILD DOSE:

Do not use in children or infants under 1 year of age. Dosage varies according to product and condition. Use the minimum recommended dose in order to avoid side effects or complications. In all cases follow specific product instructions.

QUICK FACTS

OVERDOSE SYMPTOMS:
Convulsions, agitation, euphoria, drowsiness, disorientation or dizziness, blurred vision, vomiting, numbness, hypotension-possibly leading to respiratory arrest; or cardiac arrhythmia (irregular pulse and heartbeat) leading to cardiac arrest or collapse. If you suspect an overdose, immediately seek medical attention.

SIDE EFFECTS:
No serious effects in most cases of common use. However, you may experience an increased in photosensitivity reaction resulting in higher risk of sunburn and other related skin damage. In this case, avoid unnecessary exposure to sun. In rare cases, some individuals have experienced swelling of skin or in mouth and throat, or rash, burning or stinging sensations, or pronounced skin sensitivity. In these cases, discontinue application or use of the product and call your doctor immediately.

CHECK WITH YOUR DOCTOR OR PHARMACIST BEFORE COMBINING TETRACAINE WITH:
Sulfa drugs or Class I antiarrhythmia drugs (tocainide, mexiletine).

PREGNANCY OR BREASTFEEDING:
Tetracaine use by a nursing mother should be considered a potential risk for a nursing child as the drug will be passed on to the infant in the mother's milk. In all cases, a physician should be consulted.

PRECAUTIONS FOR CHILDREN:
In general, use caution when applying tetracaine products with children under 6, as the risk of

Q U I C K F A C T S

product absorption through skin is greater. Do not use in children or infants under 1 year of age. Consulting your doctor and follow instructions on medication (see above).

55+

PRECAUTIONS FOR SENIORS:
Seniors generally may be more prone to side effects and possible adverse effects of these products than younger individuals. Avoid high dosages.

SPECIAL WARNINGS:
Do not use any of these products if you are allergic to any topical anesthetic. Avoid applying more than three days continuously to same area, as this may lead to excess absorption. Do not continue overall use more than one week if condition hasn't improved.

INFORM YOUR DOCTOR BEFORE TAKING TETRACAINE IF YOU HAVE:
Allergies to: any topical anesthetic, or if you have skin infection or skin conditions such as psoriasis or eczema.

• ANTIBACTERIAL •
(TOPICAL)

The most important considerations in choosing an antibacterial are: its effectiveness in treating, healing, or preventing infections of minor cuts, wounds, burns, and skin abrasions, and potential side effects associated with the drug.

TOPICAL ANTIBACTERIALS ARE A CLASS OF DRUGS WHICH:

- are intended only for topical use,
- act by either neutralizing or destroying bacteria in affected area,
- when used in high dosages or for long treatment periods, may be absorbed into the blood stream through the skin or mucous membranes, increasing the incidence and probability of adverse side effects.

QUICK REVIEW

QUICK FACTS

ACTIVE INGREDIENTS:
POVIDONE-IODINE

BRAND NAMES:
- Aerodine
- Betadine First Aid Cream (also contains glycerin, mineral oil, polyoxyethylene stearate, polysorbate, sorbitan monostearate, white petrolatum)
- Betadine Ointment (also contains polyethylene glycols)
- Betadine Skin Cleanser (also contains ammonium nonoxynol-4-sulfate, lauramide DEA)
- Betagen
- Biodine Topical 1%
- Efodine
- Iodex
- Mallisol
- Minidyne (also contains citric acid, sodium phosphate dibasic)
- Polydine
- Pro-Tech First Aid Stik (combination with lidocaine hydrochloride)

SYMPTOMS RELIEVED:
Minor burns, common nonpoisonous insect bites and insect stings, superficial boils, skin ulcers, minor surgical wounds.

HOW TO USE:
Comes in aerosol, cream, liquid, ointment, and solution forms. Application varies based on severity and extent of condition. In all cases follow specific product instructions. These products are intended solely for external, topical use. Do not under any conditions ingest internally or use in eyes. Always wash hands before and after use.

USUAL ADULT DOSE:
Dosage varies according to product and condition. Use the minimum recommended dose in order to avoid side effects or complications. In all cases follow specific product instructions.

USUAL CHILD DOSE:
Dosage varies according to product and condition. Use the minimum recommended dose in order to avoid side effects or complications. In all cases follow specific product instructions.

OVERDOSE SYMPTOMS:
None known.

SIDE EFFECTS:
No serious effects in most cases of common use. In rare cases, some individuals have experienced swelling of skin or rash, burning or stinging sensations, or pronounced skin sensitivity. In these cases, discontinue application or use of the product and call your doctor immediately.

CHECK WITH YOUR DOCTOR OR PHARMACIST BEFORE COMBINING POVIDONE-IODINE WITH:
None known.

PREGNANCY OR BREASTFEEDING:
Safety of this drug for use during pregnancy or while nursing has not been established. In all cases you should consult your doctor before using any drug during pregnancy or while nursing.

PRECAUTIONS FOR CHILDREN:
In general, use caution when applying povidone-iodine products with children under 2, as the risk of product absorption through skin is

Q U I C K F A C T S

greater. Consult your doctor and follow instructions on medication (see above).

55+ **PRECAUTIONS FOR SENIORS:**
Seniors generally may be more prone to side effects and possible adverse effects of these products than younger individuals. Avoid high dosages.

SPECIAL WARNINGS:
Do not use any of these products if you are allergic to any topical anesthetic. Do not use on open wounds without consulting your doctor. Do not continue overall use more than one week if condition hasn't improved.

INFORM YOUR DOCTOR BEFORE USING POVIDONE-IODINE IF YOU HAVE:
Allergies to: any topical anesthetic, or if you have skin infection or skin conditions such as psoriasis or eczema.

• ANTIFUNGAL •

The most important considerations in choosing a topical antifungal are: its effectiveness in fighting fungus infections, and potential side effects associated with the drug.

QUICK REVIEW

TOPICAL ANTIFUNGALS ARE A CLASS OF DRUGS WHICH:

- act by interfering with or inhibiting growth of common fungal parasites (dermatophytes) and yeasts,
- are often combined with astringent, antibacterial, antiseptic, anesthetic, and anti-itch components to promote drying, cleansing, disinfecting, and relief of pain and itching in affected areas,
- should only be applied topically,
- especially when used in high dosages or for long treatment periods, may be absorbed into the blood stream through the skin or mucous membranes, increasing the antifungal's effectiveness but also the incidence and probability of adverse side effects.

QUICK FACTS

ACTIVE INGREDIENT:

CLIOQUINOL (LOCHOCHLORHYDROXYQUIN)

BRAND NAMES:

- VIOFORM

SYMPTOMS RELIEVED:

Eczema, athlete's foot, and other fungal infections.

HOW TO USE:

Comes in cream or ointment forms.

Wash and dry affected area before applying. Apply product to affected area 2 to 3 times per day as needed or as directed by your doctor.

In all cases follow specific product instructions. These products are intended solely for topical use. Do not under any conditions ingest internally or use in eyes. Always wash hands thoroughly before and after use.

USUAL ADULT DOSE:

See above. Use the minimum recommended dose in order to avoid side effects or complications. In all cases follow specific product instructions.

USUAL CHILD DOSE:

Do not use in cases involving children under 2 unless under medical supervision. For all others, use the minimum recommended dose in order to avoid side effects or complications. In all cases follow specific product instructions.

OVERDOSE SYMPTOMS:

No known overdose symptoms.

SIDE EFFECTS:
No serious effects in most cases of common use. However, in rare cases, individuals have experienced mild skin irritation. In these cases, discontinue application or use of the product and call your doctor immediately.

CHECK WITH YOUR DOCTOR OR PHARMACIST BEFORE COMBINING CLIOQUINOL WITH:
Any other topical preparations.

PREGNANCY OR BREASTFEEDING:
Safety of clioquinol use by a nursing mother has not been established. In all cases, a physician should be consulted.

PRECAUTIONS FOR CHILDREN:
These products should not be used to treat children under 2 unless under close medical supervision.

PRECAUTIONS FOR SENIORS:
No special precautions are known for seniors.

SPECIAL WARNINGS:
Do not use any of these products if you are allergic to clioquinol or any topical antifungal medication or if you have any form of liver disease or damage. Do not use longer than one week.

INFORM YOUR DOCTOR BEFORE TAKING CLIOQUINOL IF:
You are pregnant.

Q U I C K F A C T S

ACTIVE INGREDIENT:

UNDECYLENIC ACID (AND DERIVATIVES)

BRAND NAMES:

- BREEZE MIST AEROSOL (also contains talc)
- CALDESENE (also contains talc)
- CRUEX–AEROSOL (also contains menthol and talc)
- CRUEX–CREAM (also contains lanolin, parabens, white petrolatum)
- CRUEX–POWDER (also contains talc)
- DECLYENES
- DESENEX–AEROSOL »(also contains menthol and talc)
- DESENEX–CREAM (also contains lanolin, parabens, white petrolatum)
- DESENEX–POWDER (also contains talc)
- DESENEX–FOAM
- DESENEX–SOAP
- PEDI-PRO (also contains starch)
- PHICON F
- PROTECTROL MEDICATED (also contains starch)

SYMPTOMS RELIEVED:
Athlete's foot, diaper rash, jock itch, skin conditions including itching, burning, and chafing discomfort.

HOW TO USE:
Comes in aerosol powder, cream, foam, ointment, powder, and soap forms.

Wash and dry affected area before applying. Apply product as needed or as directed by your doctor.

In all cases follow specific product instructions. These products are intended solely for topical use. Do not under any conditions ingest internally or use in eyes. Always wash hands thoroughly before and after use.

Q U I C K F A C T S

USUAL ADULT DOSE:
See above. Use the minimum recommended dose in order to avoid side effects or complications. In all cases follow specific product instructions.

USUAL CHILD DOSE:
Do not use in cases involving children under 2 unless under medical supervision. For all others, use the minimum recommended dose in order to avoid side effects or complications. In all cases follow specific product instructions.

OVERDOSE SYMPTOMS:
No known overdose symptoms.

SIDE EFFECTS:
No serious effects in most cases of common use. However, in rare cases, individuals have experienced mild skin irritation. In these cases, discontinue application or use of the product and call your doctor immediately.

CHECK WITH YOUR DOCTOR OR PHARMACIST BEFORE COMBINING UNDECYLENIC ACID WITH:
Any other topical preparations.

PREGNANCY OR BREASTFEEDING:
Safety of undecylenic acid use by a nursing mother has not been established. In all cases, a physician should be consulted.

Q U I C K F A C T S

PRECAUTIONS FOR CHILDREN:
These products should not be used to treat children under 2 unless under close medical supervision.

PRECAUTIONS FOR SENIORS:
No special precautions are known for seniors.

SPECIAL WARNINGS:
Do not use any of these products if you are allergic to undecylenic acid or any topical antifungal medication, or any of the inactive ingredients listed, or if you have any form of liver disease or damage. Do not discontinue use before suggested course of medication is complete, as recurrence of infection is likely to result.

INFORM YOUR DOCTOR BEFORE TAKING UNDECYLENIC ACID IF:
You are pregnant, diabetic, or have impaired or poor blood circulation.

QUICK FACTS

ACTIVE INGREDIENTS:

UNDECYLENIC ACID (AND DERIVATIVES) IN COMBINATION WITH SODIUM PROPIONATE, BENZOIC ACID AND SODIUM THIOSULFATE

BRAND NAMES:

- ANTINEA (also contains salicylic acid)
- BLIS-TO-SOL (also contains salicylic acid)
- CASTADERM (also contains, resorcinol, boric acid, acetone, basic fuschin, phenol, alcohol)
- CASTEL MINUS (also contains basic fuschin, phenol, resorcinol, acetone)
- CASTEL PLUS (also contains resorcinol, acetone, basic fuschin, hydroxyethylcellulose, alcohol)
- DERMASEPT ANTIFUNGAL (also contains tannic acid, zinc chloride, benzocaine, methylbenzethonium, tolnaftate, ethanol, phenol, benzyl alcohol, coal tar, camphor, menthol)
- FUNGI-NAIL (also contains resorcinol, salicylic acid, chloroxylenol, benzocaine, isopropyl alcohol)
- NEO-CASTADERM (also contains, resorcinol, boric acid, acetone, sodium bisulfite, phenol, alcohol)
- PROPHYLLIN
- WHITFIELD'S (also contains salicylic acid)

SYMPTOMS RELIEVED:
Athlete's foot, diaper rash, jock itch, skin conditions including itching, burning, and chafing discomfort of sensitive areas.

HOW TO USE:
Comes in cream, liquid, ointment, powder, soap, and solution forms.

QUICK FACTS

Wash and dry affected area before applying. Apply product as needed or as directed by your doctor.

In all cases follow specific product instructions. These products are intended solely for topical use. Do not under any conditions ingest internally or use in eyes. Always wash hands thoroughly before and after use.

USUAL ADULT DOSE:
See above. Use the minimum recommended dose in order to avoid side effects or complications. In all cases follow specific product instructions.

USUAL CHILD DOSE:
Do not use in cases involving children under 2 unless under medical supervision. For all others, use the minimum recommended dose in order to avoid side effects or complications. In all cases follow specific product instructions.

OVERDOSE SYMPTOMS:
No known overdose symptoms.

SIDE EFFECTS:
No serious effects in most cases of common use. However, in rare cases, individuals have experienced mild skin irritation. In these cases, discontinue application or use of the product and call your doctor immediately.

CHECK WITH YOUR DOCTOR OR PHARMACIST BEFORE COMBINING UNDECYLENIC ACID WITH:
Any other topical preparations.

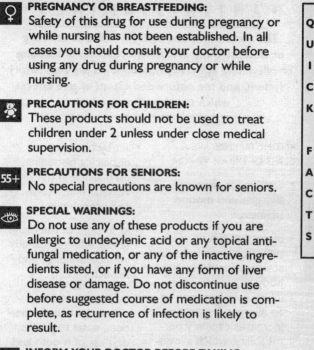

PREGNANCY OR BREASTFEEDING:
Safety of this drug for use during pregnancy or while nursing has not been established. In all cases you should consult your doctor before using any drug during pregnancy or while nursing.

PRECAUTIONS FOR CHILDREN:
These products should not be used to treat children under 2 unless under close medical supervision.

PRECAUTIONS FOR SENIORS:
No special precautions are known for seniors.

SPECIAL WARNINGS:
Do not use any of these products if you are allergic to undecylenic acid or any topical antifungal medication, or any of the inactive ingredients listed, or if you have any form of liver disease or damage. Do not discontinue use before suggested course of medication is complete, as recurrence of infection is likely to result.

INFORM YOUR DOCTOR BEFORE TAKING UNDECYLENIC ACID IF:
You are pregnant, diabetic or have impaired or poor blood circulation.

QUICK REVIEW

• ANTIHISTAMINES •

The most important considerations in choosing an antihistamine are: its effectiveness in blocking or alleviating effects of histamine on the respiratory system, and the nature and extent of side effects which the drug may produce.

ANTIHISTAMINES ARE A CLASS OF DRUGS WHICH:

- are used in treating allergies and motion sickness,
- block the effects of histamine, a chemical substance released by the body as the result of injury or in reaction to an allergen. Histamine increases capillary permeability, which allows fluids to escape and cause swelling. It also constricts small air passages in the lungs. These properties result in symptoms such as sinus headache, congestion, sneezing, runny nose,wheezing, puffiness, and lowered blood pressure,
- act by blocking or displacing histamine, particularly in the blood vessels, skin, uterus, and bronchioles,
- as a result of the drugs' drying effects, thereby impede drainage and expectoration,
- may produce side effects such as drowsiness, nasal stuffiness, dryness of mouth and sinus passages, dizziness, and common gastrointestinal (GI) irritation or distress,
- are not recommended in treating lower respiratory symptoms including asthma, as the drug's effects may impede expectoration.

ACTIVE INGREDIENT:

DIPHENHYDRAMINE HYDROCHLORIDE

Q U I C K F A C T S

BRAND NAMES:

- BENADRYL–CREAM (also contains parabens)
- BENADRYL–NON-AEROSOL SPRAY (also contains alcohol)
- BENADRYL 2% MAXIMUM STRENGTH–CREAM (also contains parabens)
- BENADRYL 2% MAXIMUM STRENGTH–NON-AEROSOL SPRAY (also contains alcohol)
- CALADRYL–CREAM (also contains calamine, parabens, camphor)
- CALADRYL–LOTION (also contains calamine, camphor, alcohol)
- CALADRYL–SPRAY (also contains calamine, alcohol, camphor)
- CALADRYL CLEAR (also contains alcohol)
- CALA-GEN (also contains alcohol)
- DI-DELAMINE (also contains tripelennamine hydrochloride, benzalkonium chloride, menthol, EDTA)
- STING-EZE (also contains camphor, phenol, benzocaine, eucalyptol)
- ZIRADRYL (also contains zinc oxide, alcohol, camphor, parabens)

Note: *Diphenhydramine* is also used as: a sleep aid, as an antihistamine, and as an active ingredient in combination with other drugs in antitussive (anti-cough) products.

SYMPTOMS RELIEVED:

Irritation, itching, and rashes due to minor skin conditions, discomfort of plant poisonings such as poison ivy, sumac, and oak, sunburn, common nonpoisonous insect bites and insect stings, and minor burns.

QUICK FACTS

HOW TO USE:
Comes in concentrate, cream, gel, lotion, and spray forms. Wash and dry affected area before applying. Apply product as needed or as directed by your doctor.

In all cases follow specific product instructions. These products are intended solely for topical use. Do not under any conditions ingest internally or use in eyes. Always wash hands thoroughly before and after use.

USUAL ADULT DOSE:
See above. Use the minimum recommended dose in order to avoid side effects or complications. In all cases follow specific product instructions.

USUAL CHILD DOSE:
Do not use in cases involving children under 2 unless under medical supervision. For all others, use the minimum recommended dose in order to avoid side effects or complications. In all cases follow specific product instructions.

OVERDOSE SYMPTOMS:
No known overdose symptoms.

SIDE EFFECTS:
No serious effects in most cases of common use. However, in rare cases, individuals have experienced mild skin irritation. In these cases, discontinue application or use of the product and call your doctor immediately.

CHECK WITH YOUR DOCTOR OR PHARMACIST BEFORE COMBINING UNDECYLENIC ACID WITH:
Any other topical preparations, or any other antihistamine product.

PREGNANCY OR BREASTFEEDING:
Safety of this drug for use during pregnancy or while nursing has not been established. In all cases you should consult your doctor before using any drug during pregnancy or while nursing.

PRECAUTIONS FOR CHILDREN:
These products should not be used to treat children under 2 unless under close medical supervision.

PRECAUTIONS FOR SENIORS:
No special precautions are known for seniors.

SPECIAL WARNINGS:
Do not use any other diphenhydramine products while using any of these topical products. Do not use any of these products if you are allergic to diphenhydramine hydrochloride or any topical antifungal medication, or any of the inactive ingredients listed, or if you have any form of liver disease or damage. Do not use longer than one week continuously.

ADDITIONAL WARNINGS:
Do not use these topical products to treat chicken pox, measles, blisters, or extensive skin areas, unless directed by your doctor.

INFORM YOUR DOCTOR BEFORE USING DIPHENHYDRAMINE IF YOU HAVE:
Urinary difficulty, glaucoma, ulcer, or if you are pregnant. If you anticipate any surgery requiring general or spinal anesthesia within 2 months of taking diphenhydramine-containing medication, inform your doctor.

QUICK REVIEW

• ANTISEPTIC •
(TOPICAL)

The most important considerations in choosing an antiseptic are: its effectiveness in treating, healing, or preventing infections of minor cuts, wounds, burns, and skin abrasions, and potential side effects associated with the drug.

TOPICAL ANTISEPTICS ARE A CLASS OF DRUGS WHICH:

- are intended only for topical use,
- act by killing bacteria, fungi, viruses, spores, protozoa, and yeasts in affected area,
- when used in high dosages or for long treatment periods, may be absorbed into the bloodstream through the skin or mucous membranes, increasing the incidence and probability of adverse side effects.

ACTIVE INGREDIENT:
NEOMYCIN SULFATE

BRAND NAMES:
- MYCIGUENT (also contains methylparaben)
- NEOSPORIN CREAM (combination with polymixin B sulfate—also contains white petrolatum)

SYMPTOMS RELIEVED:
Pain or discomfort of minor cuts, scrapes, burns, or to prevent infection of same.

HOW TO USE:
Comes in cream forms. Clean affected areas before application unless your doctor advises otherwise. Apply small amount (usually no more than the surface of a fingertip) to affected area 1 to 3 times per day. In all cases follow specific product instructions. These products are intended solely for topical use. Do not under any conditions ingest internally or use in eyes, mouth, nose, ears or any mucous membrane. Always wash hands thoroughly before and after application.

USUAL ADULT DOSE:
See above. Use the minimum recommended dose in order to avoid side effects or complications. In all cases follow specific product instructions.

USUAL CHILD DOSE:
Consult your doctor before using in cases involving children or infants.

OVERDOSE SYMPTOMS:
None known overdose symptoms. However, if accidentally swallowed, immediately call for emergency medical aid.

QUICK FACTS

SIDE EFFECTS:
No known adverse reactions or side effects in most cases of common use. However, in rare cases, individuals have experienced allergic dermatitis reactions, hearing loss, sore throat, fever, and bleeding or bruising. In these cases, discontinue application or use of the product and call your doctor immediately.

CHECK WITH YOUR DOCTOR OR PHARMACIST BEFORE COMBINING NEOMYCIN SULFATE WITH:
Any other topical product.

PREGNANCY OR BREASTFEEDING:
Safety of this drug for use during pregnancy or while nursing has not been established. In all cases you should consult your doctor before using any drug during pregnancy or while nursing.

PRECAUTIONS FOR CHILDREN:
See Usual Child Dose above.

55+ **PRECAUTIONS FOR SENIORS:**
No special precautions are known for seniors.

SPECIAL WARNINGS:
Do not use these products t if you are allergic to related "mycin" or "micin" antibiotics (e.g. mupirocin, polymixin, etc.) or chloramphenicol. Do not continue application longer than one week unless directed by your doctor.

INFORM YOUR DOCTOR BEFORE USING NEOMYCIN SULFATE IF:
You have any open sores in the areas which you intend to treat, or if you have allergic contact dermatitis.

• KERATOLYTIC •
(TOPICAL)

The most important considerations in choosing an antiwart product are: its effectiveness in treating and removing common, plantar, and flat warts, as well as calluses and corns, and potential side effects associated with the drug.

TOPICAL ANTIWART PRODUCTS ARE A CLASS OF DRUGS WHICH:

- are intended only for topical use,
- for over-the-counter use, contain salicylic acid as the active ingredient,
- act by promoting the shedding or scaling off (desquamation) of cornified skin in affected area,
- when used in high dosages or for long treatment periods, may be absorbed into the blood stream through the skin or mucous membranes, increasing the incidence and probability of adverse side effects.

QUICK FACTS

ACTIVE INGREDIENT:
SALICYLIC ACID

℞ **BRAND NAMES:**

- Compound W–liquid
- Compound W–gel (also contains alcohol, camphor, castor oil, collodion, colloidal silicon dioxide, hydroxypropyl cellulose, hypophosphorous acid, polysorbate 80)
- Dr Scholl's Advanced Pain Relief Corn Removers
- Dr Scholl's Callus Removers
- Dr Scholl's Clear Away Plantar
- Dr Scholl's Corn Removers
- Dr Scholl's Moisturizing Corn Remover Kit
- Dr Scholl's Clear Away OneStep
- Dr Scholl's OneStep Corn Removers
- Dr Scholl's Corn/Callus Remover (also contains alcohol, ether, acetone, hydrogenated vegetable oil)
- DuoFilm–liquid (also contains alcohol, castor oil, ether)
- DuoFilm–transdermal patch
- DuoPlant (also contains alcohol, ether, ethyl lactate, hydroxypropyl cellulose, polybutene)
- Fostex
- Gets-It (combination with zinc chloride)
- Gordofilm
- Mediaplast
- Mosco
- Occlusal-HP (also contains isopropyl alcohol)
- Panscol
- PediaPatch
- Sal-Plant
- Trans-Plantar
- Trans-Ver-Sal

- WART-OFF (also contains alcohol, propylene glycol, dipelargonate)

SYMPTOMS RELIEVED:
Used for removal of common, plantar, and flat warts, calluses, and corns.

HOW TO USE:
Comes in cream, disk, gel, liquid, plaster, ointment, solution, and transdermal patch forms. Application varies based on severity and extent of condition. In all cases follow specific product instructions. These products are intended solely for external, topical use. Do not, under any conditions, ingest internally, or apply to genitals, mucous membranes, or eyes. Avoid contact with unaffected skin near affected area. Always wash hands before and after use.

USUAL ADULT DOSE:
Dosage varies according to product and condition. Use the minimum recommended dose in order to avoid side effects or complications. In all cases follow specific product instructions.

USUAL CHILD DOSE:
Dosage varies according to product and condition. Use the minimum recommended dose in order to avoid side effects or complications. In all cases follow specific product instructions.

OVERDOSE SYMPTOMS:
None known.

SIDE EFFECTS:
No serious effects in most cases of common use. However, you may experience a change in pigment in the treated area, as well as stinging

QUICK FACTS

sensations or peeling. In some cases, individuals have experienced swelling of skin or rash, burning sensations, blistering or crusting, and other forms of skin irritation. If any of these effects occur, discontinue application or use of the product and call your doctor immediately. In rare cases, when these products are applied to extensive skin areas, poisoning can occur, especially in young children or individuals with impaired kidney or livers. Warning signs include: diarrhea, nausea, dizziness, severe headache, fatigue, shortness of breath, and other respiratory difficulty. In these cases, discontinue application or use of the product and call your doctor immediately.

CHECK WITH YOUR DOCTOR OR PHARMACIST BEFORE COMBINING SALICYLIC ACID WITH:
Topical anti-acne products, other topical skin products—especially those containing alcohol, medicated cosmetics, or any other drugs and preparations.

PREGNANCY OR BREASTFEEDING:
Safety of this drug for use during pregnancy or while nursing has not been established. In all cases you should consult your doctor before using any drug during pregnancy or while nursing.

PRECAUTIONS FOR CHILDREN:
In general, these products are not recommended for use with children, as the risk of product absorption through skin is greater. Consult your doctor and follow instructions on medication (see above).

PRECAUTIONS FOR SENIORS:
Seniors generally may be more prone to side effects and possible adverse effects of these products than younger individuals. Avoid high dosages.

SPECIAL WARNINGS:
Do not use any of these products if you are allergic to aspirin or other salicylic acid derivatives, resorcinol, or any of the inactive ingredients contained in these products. Do not use on open wounds without consulting your doctor.

ADDITIONAL WARNINGS:
Use caution when applying any of these products as they can damage or stain clothing, fabric, or other materials, including common household items made of plastic, wood, and metal.

INFORM YOUR DOCTOR BEFORE USING SALICYLIC ACID IF YOU HAVE:
Skin infection or condition such as psoriasis or eczema, diabetes, or poor blood circulation.

SLEEP AIDS

QUICK REVIEW

• ANALGESIC •

The most important considerations in choosing an analgesic are: pain relief; anti-inflammatory activity, and allergic reaction or sensitivity to certain active ingredients.

ANALGESICS (NONNARCOTIC) ARE A CLASS OF DRUGS WHICH:

- inhibit the action of prostaglandins (hormonelike substances) in the central nervous system, thereby temporarily reducing the perception of physical pain with little loss of sensibility to other physical sensation,
- are used to temporarily alleviate symptoms such as: headache, fever, backache, sinus pain, muscle strain, menstrual pain, and similar ailments. Some analgesics, such as aspirin (acetylsalicylic acid) and ibuprofen, also provide temporary anti-inflammatory relief for ailments such as arthritis. Aspirin has also been shown to be effective as a blood thinning antiplatelet agent in reducing heart attack and stroke risk,
- can have adverse effects in some instances. Aspirin intolerance can produce allergic and anaphylactic reactions in hypersensitive and asthmatic individuals. Aspirin can also aggravate aggravate gastrointestinal conditions such as heartburn and ulcer. Long-term acetaminophen use can damage liver (hepatic) and kidney (renal) functions.

ACTIVE INGREDIENT:
ACETAMINOPHEN

BRAND NAMES:
- UNISOM WITH PAIN RELIEF

SYMPTOMS RELIEVED:
Sleeplessness as a result of minor aches and pains such as those associated with the common cold, flu, headache, toothache, sinusitis, hay fever, and other respiratory allergies, muscular aches, minor arthritis pain, and reduction of fever.

HOW TO TAKE:
Comes in tablet forms. Swallow tablet with liquid. Do not crush or chew timed-release tablet. In proper dosages in most cases, acetaminophen does not cause gastrointestinal (GI) irritation and can be taken with or without food.

USUAL ADULT DOSE:
650 milligrams at bedtime or as directed by your doctor.

USUAL CHILD DOSE:
Unisom is intended for adults only and should not be given to children under 12. Consult your doctor.

OVERDOSE SYMPTOMS:
Nausea, vomiting, diaphoresis, discomfort, and malaise. In some cases, hepatic toxicity (liver poisoning) may result. If you suspect an overdose, immediately seek medical attention.

SIDE EFFECTS:
Drowsiness. In rare cases: allergic skin eruptions (rash, hives, itch), sore throat and fever, bleeding or bruising, urinary discomfort or blood in urine, jaundiced skin or eyes may result.

Q U I C K F A C T S

CHECK WITH YOUR DOCTOR OR PHARMACIST BEFORE COMBINING ACETAMINOPHEN AND ANTIHISTAMINE WITH:
Sedatives, tranquilizers, anticoagulants, aspirin and other salicylates, Isoniazid (anti-tuberculosis) medication. Ingestion of alcohol while taking acetaminophen can increase the risk of liver damage or disease (hepatic toxicity).

PREGNANCY OR BREASTFEEDING:
Animal studies have indicated an adverse effect on fetus, but no adequate studies have been performed on humans. No harmful effects have been reported regarding nursing infants, but ibuprofen use by a nursing mother should be considered a potential risk for a nursing child as the drug will be passed on to the infant in the mother's milk. In all cases, a physician should be consulted.

PRECAUTIONS FOR CHILDREN:
See above.

PRECAUTIONS FOR SENIORS:
Seniors generally don't eliminate drugs as efficiently as younger persons, and should avoid high dosages or chronic use as hepatic (liver) function impairment may result.

SPECIAL WARNINGS:
Avoid alcohol when taking this combination. Chronic alcoholics are also at risk for liver function impairment if taking high dosages.

INFORM YOUR DOCTOR BEFORE TAKING ACETAMINOPHEN IF YOU HAVE:
Liver or kidney disease or damage, an allergy to acetaminophen, or hypoglycemia.

• ANTIHISTAMINES •

The most important considerations in choosing an antihistamine are: its effectiveness in blocking or alleviating effects of histamine on the respiratory system, and the nature and extent of side effects which the drug may produce.

ANTIHISTAMINES ARE A CLASS OF DRUGS WHICH:

- are used in treating allergies and motion sickness,
- block the effects of histamine, a chemical substance released by the body as the result of injury or in reaction to an allergen. Histamine increases capillary permeability, which allows fluids to escape and cause swelling. It also constricts small air passages in the lungs. These properties result in symptoms such as sinus headache, congestion, sneezing, runny nose,wheezing, puffiness, and lowered blood pressure,
- act by blocking or displacing histamine, particularly in the blood vessels, skin, uterus, and bronchioles,
- as a result of the drugs' drying effects, thicken bronchial and sinus secretions, thereby impeding drainage and expectoration,
- may produce side effects such as drowsiness, nasal stuffiness, dryness of mouth and sinus passages, dizziness, and common gastrointestinal (GI) irritation or distress,
- are not recommended in treating lower respiratory symptoms including asthma, as the drug's effects may impede expectoration.

QUICK FACTS

ACTIVE INGREDIENT:
ACETAMINOPHEN

BRAND NAMES:
- UNISOM WITH PAIN RELIEF (combination with diphenhydramine hydrochloride)

SYMPTOMS RELIEVED:
Sleeplessness as a result of minor aches and pains such as those associated with the common cold, flu, headache, toothache, sinusitis, hay fever and other respiratory allergies, muscular aches, back ache, minor arthritis pain, menstrual discomfort, and reduction of fever.

HOW TO TAKE:
Comes in tablet forms. Swallow tablet with liquid. Do not crush or chew timed-release tablet. In proper dosages in most cases, acetaminophen does not cause gastrointestinal (GI) irritation and can be taken with or without food.

USUAL ADULT DOSE:
650 milligrams at bedtime or as directed by your doctor.

USUAL CHILD DOSE:
UNISOM is intended for adults only and should not be given to children under 12.

OVERDOSE SYMPTOMS:
Nausea, vomiting, diaphoresis, discomfort, and malaise. In some cases, hepatic toxicity (liver poisoning) may result. If you suspect an overdose, immediately seek medical attention.

SIDE EFFECTS:
Drowsiness. In rare cases: allergic skin eruptions (rash, hives, itch), sore throat and fever, bleed-

ing or bruising, urinary discomfort or blood in urine, jaundiced skin or eyes may result.

CHECK WITH YOUR DOCTOR OR PHARMACIST BEFORE COMBINING ACETAMINOPHEN AND ANTIHISTAMINE WITH:

Sedatives, tranquilizers, anticoagulants, aspirin and other salicylates, Isoniazid (anti-tuberculosis) medication. Ingestion of alcohol while taking acetaminophen can increase the risk of liver damage or disease (hepatic toxicity).

PREGNANCY OR BREASTFEEDING:

No harmful effects have been reported regarding nursing infants, but ibuprofen use by a nursing mother should be considered a potential risk for a nursing child as the drug will be passed on to the infant in the mother's milk. In all cases, a physician should be consulted.

PRECAUTIONS FOR CHILDREN:

See above.

55+

PRECAUTIONS FOR SENIORS:

Seniors generally don't eliminate drugs as efficiently as younger persons, and should avoid high dosages or chronic use as hepatic (liver) function impairment may result.

SPECIAL WARNINGS:

Avoid alcohol when taking this combination. Chronic alcoholics are also at risk for hepatic (liver) function impairment if taking high dosages of acetaminophen.

INFORM YOUR DOCTOR BEFORE TAKING ACETAMINOPHEN IF YOU HAVE:

Liver or kidney disease or damage, an allergy to acetaminophen, or hypoglycemia.

QUICK FACTS

ACTIVE INGREDIENTS:

ACETAMINOPHEN, DEXTROMETHORPHAN HYDROBROMIDE, DOXYLAMINE SUCCINATE, AND PSEUDOEPHREDINE HYDROCHLORIDE

℞ **BRAND NAMES:**

- ALKA-SELTZER PLUS NIGHTTIME COLD LIQUI-GELS (also contains sorbitol)
- GENITE LIQUID (also contains alcohol, tartrazine)
- NYQUIL HOT THERAPY POWDER (also contains sucrose)
- NYQUIL NIGHTTIME COLD/FLU MEDICINE LIQUID (also contains alcohol, sucrose, saccharin [cherry flavor], tartrazine [original flavor])
- VICKS NYQUIL LIQUICAPS

Note: *Dextromethorphan hydrobromide* is also an active ingredient in other multi-symptom anti-tussive/expectorant medications which are formulated with other active ingredients.

Pseudoephredine hydrochloride is a used as an active ingredient in decongestant and stimulant products.

Acetaminophen is a non-aspirin analgesic which is used primarily in pain-relief products.

Doxylamine succinate is a drowsiness-producing antihistamine which is mostly used in combination with analgesic, antitussive, decongestant, and expectorant active ingredients in OTC medications to provide nighttime relief of allergy, common cold, cough or flu symptoms. It is also used as a sleep aid.

SYMPTOMS RELIEVED:
Sleeplessness as a result of minor aches and pains, nasal congestion and coughing such as those associated with the common cold, flu, sore throat, sinusitis, hay fever and other respiratory allergies, and reduction of fever.

HOW TO TAKE:
Comes in capsule, liquid, and powder forms. Swallow capsule with liquid. Sprinkle powder over liquid, then swallow. Do not crush or chew timed-release capsule.

USUAL ADULT DOSE:
Dosage varies per product and active ingredient formulation. Follow product dosage instructions.

USUAL CHILD DOSE:
Do not administer to children under 6 unless under direction of physician. Dosage may vary based on infant or child's age.

OVERDOSE SYMPTOMS:
Nervous agitation, severe anxiety, insomnia (sleeplessness), hallucinations, tremors, convulsions, nausea, vomiting, cardiac arrhythmia (irregular pulse and heartbeat), drowsiness, dizziness, fatigue, rash. If you suspect an overdose, immediately seek medical attention.

SIDE EFFECTS:
No serious effects in most cases of common use, although antihistamines often cause drowsiness. Less common side effects include nasal dryness, dizziness, nausea, and mild insomnia palpitations, insomnia, gastrointestinal (GI) upset including stomach cramps and diarrhea,

drowsiness, and fatigue. In rare cases, more severe side effects may result, including: painful and frequent urination, hypertension, and heart palpitations. In these cases, discontinue medication and call your doctor immediately. Long-term ingestion of high dosages of acetaminophen-containing products may increase risk of liver and kidney damage.

CHECK WITH YOUR DOCTOR OR PHARMACIST BEFORE COMBINING THESE COMBINATION PRODUCTS WITH:
Anticoagulant medications, other cold, cough, or allergy medication, stimulants, antidepressants, antihypertensives, digitalis or other heart medication, diuretics, or MAO (monoamine oxidase inhibitors) drugs. Ingestion of caffeinated beverages (coffee, tea, caffeine-containing soft drinks) while taking pseudoephredine-containing medication can result in agitation and insomnia.
If taking combination products which contain acetaminophen, you should avoid Isoniazid (anti-tuberculosis) medication. Excessive ingestion of alcohol while taking acetaminophen-containing medication can increase the risk of liver damage or disease (hepatic toxicity). Alcohol use may also increase drowsiness effect of the antihistamine doxylamine succinate in these combination products.

PREGNANCY OR BREASTFEEDING:
Use of medications containing any of the active ingredients in these products by a nursing mother should be considered a potential risk for a nursing child as the drug(s) will be passed on to the infant in the mother's milk. In all cases, a physician should be consulted.

PRECAUTIONS FOR CHILDREN:
In general, these active ingredients are not advised for children under 2. Administer to infants or children only when consulting a physician and follow instructions on medication (see above).

PRECAUTIONS FOR SENIORS:
Seniors generally don't eliminate drugs as efficiently as younger persons, and should avoid high dosages. Use of doxylamine succinate-containing medications by seniors can lead to urinary difficulties. In addition, seniors are more likely to experience drowsiness effects of doxylamine succinate.

SPECIAL WARNINGS:
Do not use for control of chronic cough related to conditions such as emphysema, asthma, or smoking, or if coughs are producing excessive secretions. If cough is accompanied by high fever, rash, nausea or vomiting, or persistent headache, use only if directed by your doctor. Because antihistamines such as doxylamine succinate often cause drowsiness, you should avoid activities or tasks such as driving, or other operations which require alertness, coordination, dexterity, or quick reflexes. Chronic alcoholics are at risk for hepatic (liver) function impairment if taking high dosages of acetaminophen-containing medication. Do not use medications which combine doxylamine succinate with tartrazine if you are intolerant or hypersensitive to aspirin. Allergic reactions, including bronchial asthma, have occurred in susceptible individuals.

ADDITIONAL WARNING:
Alcohol: Some cough/cold medications contain various amounts of alcohol. Check label of any cough medication if concerned about ingestion of alcohol.

Sugar/Sweeteners: Some cough/cold medications contain various amounts of sugar, sucrose, glucose, and/or artificial sweeteners such as aspartame, saccharin, sorbitol. Check label of cough medication before selecting, if concerned about diabetes and ingestion of sugar or artificial sweeteners.

Abuse/Dependency: Reports indicate a rising rate of abuse of dextromethorphan-containing medications, particularly among teens. Sufficient data has not yet been collected, however, to determine the abuse and dependency potential of dextromethorphan-containing medications.

INFORM YOUR DOCTOR BEFORE TAKING PRODUCTS CONTAINING THIS COMBINATION OF ACTIVE INGREDIENTS IF YOU HAVE:
Asthma, emphysema or other respiratory condition, liver impairment or liver disease, allergies to any sympathomimetic drug, aspirin or other salicylates, or if you have diabetes, thyroid condition, or urinary difficulty. If you anticipate any surgery requiring general or spinal anesthesia within 2 months of taking medication which contains pseudoephredine, inform your doctor.

ACTIVE INGREDIENT:

DOXYLAMINE SUCCINATE

BRAND NAMES:

- UNISOM NIGHTTIME SLEEP AID

SYMPTOMS RELIEVED:

Insomnia and difficulty of falling asleep.

HOW TO TAKE:

Doxylamine succinate is a drowsiness-producing antihistamine which is mostly used in combination with analgesic, antitussive, decongestant, and expectorant active ingredients in over-the-counter medications to provide nighttime relief of allergy, common cold, cough, or flu symptoms. It is also used as a sleep aid. For information on this application, see the Quick Facts section under Sleep Aids.

USUAL ADULT DOSE:

See dosage information for active ingredients in combination with doxylamine succinate

USUAL CHILD DOSE:

Do not administer to children under 6 unless under direction of physician. Dosage may vary based on infant or child's age.

OVERDOSE SYMPTOMS:

See overdose information for active ingredients in combination with doxylamine succinate.

SIDE EFFECTS:

The most frequent side effect of antihistamines use is drowsiness. Other common side effects include: include dryness of mouth, throat, and nasal passages, dizziness, GI distress (including

QUICK FACTS

vomiting, diarrhea and constipation or change in bowel regularity), and diminished muscle coordination. In rare cases, more severe side effects may result, such as painful and frequent urination or urinary retention, vision problems, loss of appetite, and respiratory difficulty. In these cases, discontinue medication and call your doctor immediately.

CHECK WITH YOUR DOCTOR OR PHARMACIST BEFORE COMBINING DOXYLAMINE SUCCINATE WITH:
Cold, cough, or allergy medication—including other antihistamines; aspirin, stimulants, antidepressants, antihypertensives, digitalis or other heart medication, diuretics, or MAO (monoamine oxidase inhibitors) drugs. Avoid ingestion of alcohol or use of sedatives or tranquilizers while taking doxylamine succinate-containing medication or most other antihistamine-containing medication as the combination can produce severe drowsiness or sedation.

PREGNANCY OR BREASTFEEDING:
Doxylamine succinate should not be used by a pregnant or nursing woman.

PRECAUTIONS FOR CHILDREN:
Doxylamine succinate is not advised for children under 6. Administer only to infants or children only when consulting a physician and follow instructions on medication (see above).

55+

PRECAUTIONS FOR SENIORS:
Seniors generally don't eliminate drugs as efficiently as younger persons, and should avoid high dosages. Use of doxylamine succinate

medications by seniors can lead to urinary difficulties. In addition, seniors are more likely to experience sedative effects of the drug.

SPECIAL WARNINGS:
Because antihistamines often cause drowsiness, you should avoid activities or tasks such as driving, or other operations which require alertness, coordination, dexterity or quick reflexes. Do not use continuously for longer than 3 months. Do not use doxylamine succinate medications containing tartrazine if you are intolerant or hypersensitive to aspirin. Allergic reactions, including bronchial asthma, have occurred in susceptible individuals.

INFORM YOUR DOCTOR BEFORE TAKING DOXYLAMINE SUCCINATE IF YOU HAVE:
Urinary difficulty (such as enlarged prostate), glaucoma, ulcer, or if you are pregnant. If you anticipate any surgery requiring general or spinal anesthesia within 2 months of taking doxylamine succinate-containing medication, inform your doctor.

SMOKING CESSATION

QUICK REVIEW

• ANTISMOKING AGENT •

The most important considerations in choosing an antismoking agent are: its effectiveness in helping the user to quit smoking, and potential side effects associated with the drug.

ANTISMOKING AGENTS ARE A CLASS OF DRUGS WHICH:

- are only intended to help a person quit smoking,
- are used to alleviate smoking withdrawal symptoms,
- contain nicotine as the active ingredient,
- are available mostly in transdermal (through the skin) patch or chewing gum forms,
- in the case of transdermal patches, deliver decreasing amounts of nicotine to the user during a regulated treatment period,
- in order for treatment to be effective, require the smoker to completely stop using any type of tobacco product.

QUICK FACTS

ACTIVE INGREDIENT:
NICOTINE

BRAND NAMES:
- NicoDerm CQ
- Nicorette
- Nicotrol

SYMPTOMS RELIEVED:
Aids in quitting smoking, and alleviates smoking withdrawal symptoms.

HOW TO USE:
Comes in chewing gum and transdermal (through the skin) patch forms. These products are intended solely as stop smoking aids. Do not smoke, chew tobacco, or use snuff while using these products. In order to use these products effectively, you must be motivated to quit smoking. In the case of transdermal patch products, you will also need to complete the full treatment program. Because nicotine is both physically and mentally addictive, quitting smoking may be one of the hardest things you do.
In order to effectively quit, support programs are recommended. Ask your doctor, and read the product guides and instructions for more information. You may also want to contact the following groups:
American Lung Association (800/586-4872)
American Cancer Association (800/227-2345)
American Heart Association (800/242-8721)

USUAL ADULT DOSE:
Amount and dosage varies based on product and on the amount of nicotine you are presently consuming. Review product instructions thoroughly before using these products, and

Q U I C K F A C T S

follow all product instructions carefully while applying or using. This is especially important in the case of transdermal patch products, which require a multiweek commitment in order for treatment to have the desired effect. Always wash hands before and after applying skin patch. In all cases follow specific product instructions.

USUAL CHILD DOSE:
Persons under 18 years of age should not use these products.

OVERDOSE SYMPTOMS:
None known.

SIDE EFFECTS:
Common side effects include: itching, skin rash, burning, redness around skin patch. If any of these symptoms persist more than four days, immediately discontinue use of product and call your doctor. In some cases, nicotine withdrawal symptoms may include: digestive and stomach upset such as diarrhea, indigestion, constipation, and nausea, as well as nervous agitation, dizziness, muscle aches and pains, cough, fatigue, variation in menstrual cycle, headache, change in sleep habits, insomnia, unusual dreams, and unusual or changed taste of flavors. In rare cases, chest pains, vomiting, dehydration, sinus pains, and numb or tingling extremities have been reported. These may be symptoms of nicotine overdose. In these cases, immediately discontinue use of product and call your doctor.

CHECK WITH YOUR DOCTOR OR PHARMACIST BEFORE COMBINING THESE PRODUCTS WITH:
Any other drugs and preparations, including

other transdermal (skin patch) products or insulin.

PREGNANCY OR BREASTFEEDING:
Safety of this drug for use during pregnancy or while nursing has not been established. In all cases you should consult your doctor before using any drug during pregnancy or while nursing.

PRECAUTIONS FOR CHILDREN:
Persons under 18 years of age should not use these products.

55+

PRECAUTIONS FOR SENIORS:
Seniors generally don't eliminate drugs as efficiently as younger persons, and may be more susceptible to possible side effects of these products.

SPECIAL WARNINGS:
Do not use these products if you are allergic to nicotine, or any of the inactive ingredients contained in these products. Do not continue to smoke, chew tobacco or use snuff while using these products, or at any time during treatment period, even when not wearing patch, nicotine will still be entering your bloodstream.

INFORM YOUR DOCTOR BEFORE USING THESE PRODUCTS IF YOU HAVE:
Any allergies to adhesive tape, skin conditions, asthma, heart disease, liver disease, kidney disease, diabetes, peptic ulcer, high blood pressure, or if you are or plan to become pregnant during time that you will be using these products

other nonsteroidal [illegible] products or them.

STIMULANTS

QUICK REVIEW

• STIMULANTS •

The most important considerations in choosing a stimulant are: its effectiveness in treating drowsiness and fatigue, and potential side effects associated with the drug.

STIMULANTS ARE A CLASS OF DRUGS WHICH:

- are only intended to help a person restore mental alertness in temporary cases of fatigue or drowsiness,
- should not be used as a substitute for sensible sleep and rest patterns,
- act by stimulating the central nervous system (CNS),
- in over-the-counter (OTC) products, mostly contain caffeine as the active ingredient,
- may also act to suppress appetite,
- if taken for long periods or in high dosages, can produce serious adverse side effects, such as irritability, nervousness, restlessness, sleeplessness, and rapid heart beat, as well as symptoms of withdrawal when use ceases.

ACTIVE INGREDIENT:
CAFFEINE

Q U I C K F A C T S

BRAND NAMES:
- CAFFEDRINE
- COFFEE BREAK
- NODOZ
- QUICK PEP
- TIREND (combination with aspirin)
- VIVARIN (combination with aspirin)

SYMPTOMS RELIEVED:
Drowsiness and mental fatigue.

HOW TO TAKE:
Comes in tablet forms. Swallow with liquid. Do not crush or chew timed-release tablets. Caffeine can cause gastrointestinal (GI) irritation and should be taken with food or following meal.

USUAL ADULT DOSE:
100 to 200 milligrams (200 milligrams for timed release capsules) every 3 to 4 hours, as needed, not to exceed 2 grams in a 24 hour period.

USUAL CHILD DOSE:
Do not administer to children under 16 unless under direction of physician. Dosage may vary based on infant or child's age.

OVERDOSE SYMPTOMS:
Nervous agitation, insomnia (sleeplessness), disorientation, fast or irregular heartbeat, (slow heartbeat in cases involving infants), confusion, convulsions, diarrhea and general GI upset, coma. If you suspect an overdose, immediately seek medical attention.

QUICK FACTS

SIDE EFFECTS:
No serious effects in most cases of common use, however normal use of caffeine can result in faster heartbeat, lower blood sugar, irritability, minor GI upsets such as loose stools or diarrhea, insomnia, frequent urination. Less common side effects include severe irritability, dizziness, nausea, stomach cramps, indigestion, heartburn, and confusion.

CHECK WITH YOUR DOCTOR OR PHARMACIST BEFORE COMBINING CAFFEINE WITH:
Other stimulants—including other caffeine-containing drugs, oral contraceptives, Isoniazid, sedatives, sleep aids, thyroid hormones, tranquilizers, asthma medication, nonsteroidal anti-inflammatory drugs (NSAIDs), tetracycline, and any other medication. Ingestion of caffeinated beverages (coffee, tea, caffeine-containing soft drinks) will increase medication's effect. Smoking while using caffeine medication should be avoided as it can lead to increased heartbeat.

PREGNANCY OR BREASTFEEDING:
Caffeine use by a nursing mother should be considered a potential risk for a nursing child as the drug will be passed on to the infant in the mother's milk. In all cases, a physician should be consulted.

PRECAUTIONS FOR CHILDREN:
In general, caffeine is not advised for children under 16. Administer caffeine to infants or children only when consulting a physician and follow instructions on medication (see above).

55+

PRECAUTIONS FOR SENIORS:
Seniors generally don't eliminate drugs as efficiently as younger persons, and should avoid high dosages. Chronic or prolonged use of caffeine medications can lead to stomach ulcers.

SPECIAL WARNINGS:
It is advisable to discontinue use gradually of caffeine-containing medication after continuous, prolonged usage period (over a month), as you may otherwise experience withdrawal symptoms. Special Warning for Women: Use of caffeine-containing medication may aggravate or lead to development of fibrocystic breast disease.

INFORM YOUR DOCTOR BEFORE TAKING CAFFEINE IF YOU HAVE:
Hypoglycemia, ulcer, epilepsy, irregular heartbeat, high blood pressure, insomnia, or other sleep disorder.

VAGINAL IRRITATION AND INFECTIONS

QUICK REVIEW

• ANESTHETIC •
(TOPICAL)

The most important considerations in choosing a topical or local anesthetic are: its action in partially or completely eliminating the sensation of physical pain in one part of the body, and potential side effects associated with the drug.

TOPICAL ANESTHETICS ARE A CLASS OF DRUGS WHICH:

- act in some combination of the following ways: by limiting the production of energy in nerve cells—thereby reducing nerve impulses and related sensation of pain, by increasing the body's production of organic compounds which limit the transmission of pain messages through synapses, or by reducing nerve cell energy production, thereby limiting the cell's production of nerve impulses. These actions are not completely understood due to varying effects of topical anesthetics and the complex nature of the body's central nervous system (CNS),
- especially when used in high dosages or for long treatment periods, may be absorbed into the blood stream through the skin or mucous membranes, increasing the anesthetic's effectiveness but also the incidence and probability of adverse side effects,
- do not affect the underlying cause of the symptoms which they are designed to relieve or suppress.

ACTIVE INGREDIENT:

BENZOCAINE

BRAND NAMES:

- VAGISIL

(also contains resorcinol, aloe, cetyl and lanolin alcohols, methylparaben, trisodium HEDTA, mineral oil, sodium sulfite)

SYMPTOMS RELIEVED:

Vaginal irritation, itching, and discomfort.

HOW TO USE:

Comes in cream forms. Apply to affected area as needed. In all cases follow specific product instructions. These products are intended solely for external, topical use. Do not under any conditions ingest internally or use in eyes. Always wash hands before and after use.

USUAL ADULT DOSE:

Dosage varies according to product and condition. Use the minimum recommended dose in order to avoid side effects or complications. In all cases follow specific product instructions.

USUAL CHILD DOSE:

Do not use in children or infants under 1 year of age. Dosage varies according to product and condition. Use the minimum recommended dose in order to avoid side effects or complications. In all cases follow specific product instructions.

OVERDOSE SYMPTOMS:

Convulsions, agitation, euphoria, drowsiness, disorientation or dizziness, blurred vision, vomiting, numbness, hypotension-possibly

QUICK FACTS

leading to respiratory arrest; or cardiac arrhythmia (irregular pulse and heartbeat) leading to cardiac arrest or collapse. If you suspect an overdose, immediately seek medical attention.

SIDE EFFECTS:
No serious effects in most cases of common use. However, you may experience an increased in photosensitivity reaction resulting in higher risk of sunburn and other related skin damage. In this case, avoid unnecessary exposure to sun. In rare cases, some individuals have experienced swelling of skin or in mouth and throat, or rash, burning or stinging sensations, or pronounced skin sensitivity. In these cases, discontinue application or use of the product and call your doctor immediately.

CHECK WITH YOUR DOCTOR OR PHARMACIST BEFORE COMBINING BENZOCAINE WITH:
Sulfa drugs or Class I antiarrhythmia drugs (tocainide, mexiletine).

PREGNANCY OR BREASTFEEDING:
Benzocaine use by a nursing mother should be considered a potential risk for a nursing child as the drug will be passed on to the infant in the mother's milk. In all cases, a physician should be consulted.

PRECAUTIONS FOR CHILDREN:
Consult your doctor before using this medication on children under 12.

55+

PRECAUTIONS FOR SENIORS:
Seniors generally may be more prone to side effects and possible adverse effects of these

products than younger individuals. Avoid high dosages.

SPECIAL WARNINGS:

Do not use any of these products if you are allergic to any topical anesthetic. Avoid applying more than three days continuously to same area, as this may lead to excess absorption. Do not continue overall use more than one week if condition hasn't improved.

INFORM YOUR DOCTOR BEFORE TAKING BENZOCAINE IF YOU HAVE:

Allergies to: any topical anesthetic, or if you have skin infection or skin conditions such as psoriasis or eczema.

QUICK REVIEW

• ANTI-ITCH •
(TOPICAL)

The most important considerations in choosing an anti-itch agent are: its effectiveness in treating and relieving skin itchiness, and potential side effects associated with the drug.

TOPICAL ANTI-ITCH AGENTS ARE A CLASS OF DRUGS WHICH:

- are only intended for topical use,
- are nonspecific in their action, and act against most causes of skin inflammation by depressing, neutralizing, or interfering with the activity of enzymes which produce skin inflammation and resultant itchiness,
- in over-the-counter (OTC) products, are primarily formulated with hydrocortisone (a topical adrenocorticoid) as the active ingredient,
- when used in high dosages or for long treatment periods, may be absorbed into the bloodstream through the skin or mucous membranes, increasing the incidence and probability of adverse side effects.

ACTIVE INGREDIENT:

BENZOCAINE

BRAND NAMES:

- VAGISIL (also contains resorcinol, aloe, cetyl and lanolin alcohols, methylparaben, trisodium HEDTA, mineral oil, sodium sulfite)

SYMPTOMS RELIEVED:

Vaginal irritation, itching, and discomfort.

HOW TO USE:

Comes in cream forms. Apply to affected area as needed. In all cases follow specific product instructions. These products are intended solely for external, topical use. Do not under any conditions ingest internally or use in eyes. Always wash hands before and after use.

USUAL ADULT DOSE:

Dosage varies according to product and condition. Use the minimum recommended dose in order to avoid side effects or complications. In all cases follow specific product instructions.

USUAL CHILD DOSE:

Do not use in cases involving children or infants unless under medical supervision.

OVERDOSE SYMPTOMS:

Convulsions, agitation, euphoria, drowsiness, disorientation or dizziness, blurred vision, vomiting, numbness, hypotension—possibly leading to respiratory arrest; or cardiac arrhythmia (irregular pulse and heartbeat) leading to cardiac arrest or collapse. If you suspect an overdose, immediately seek medical attention.

Q U I C K F A C T S

SIDE EFFECTS:
No serious effects in most cases of common use. However, you may experience an increased in photosensitivity reaction resulting in higher risk of sunburn and other related skin damage. In this case, avoid unnecessary exposure to sun. In rare cases, some individuals have experienced swelling of skin or in mouth and throat, or rash, burning or stinging sensations, or pronounced skin sensitivity. In these cases, discontinue application or use of the product and call your doctor immediately.

CHECK WITH YOUR DOCTOR OR PHARMACIST BEFORE COMBINING BENZOCAINE WITH:
Sulfa drugs or Class I antiarrhythmia drugs (tocainide, mexiletine).

PREGNANCY OR BREASTFEEDING:
Benzocaine use by a nursing mother should be considered a potential risk for a nursing child as the drug will be passed on to the infant in the mother's milk. In all cases, a physician should be consulted.

PRECAUTIONS FOR CHILDREN:
Consult your doctor before using this medication on children under 12.

PRECAUTIONS FOR SENIORS:
Seniors generally may be more prone to side effects and possible adverse effects of these products than younger individuals. Avoid high dosages.

SPECIAL WARNINGS:
Do not use any of these products if you are

allergic to any topical anesthetic. Avoid applying more than three days continuously to same area, as this may lead to excess absorption. Do not continue overall use more than one week if condition hasn't improved.

INFORM YOUR DOCTOR BEFORE TAKING BENZOCAINE IF YOU HAVE:

Allergies to: any topical anesthetic, or if you have skin infection or skin conditions such as psoriasis or eczema.

QUICK REVIEW

• ANTIFUNGAL •

The most important considerations in choosing a topical antifungal are: its effectiveness in fighting fungus infections, and potential side effects associated with the drug.

TOPICAL ANTIFUNGALS ARE A CLASS OF DRUGS WHICH:

- act by interfering with or inhibiting growth of common fungal parasites (dermatophytes) and yeasts,
- are often combined with astringent, antibacterial, antiseptic, anesthetic, and anti-itch components to promote drying, cleansing, disinfecting, and relief of pain and itching in affected areas,
- should only be applied topically,
- especially when used in high dosages or for long treatment periods, may be absorbed into the blood stream through the skin or mucous membranes, increasing the antifungal's effectiveness but also the incidence and probability of adverse side effects.

ACTIVE INGREDIENT:
CLOTRIMAZOLE

BRAND NAMES:

- FEMCARE–VAGINAL TABLETS
- FEMCARE–VAGINAL CREAM
  (also contains benzyl and cetostearyl alcohols)
- GYNE-LOTRIMIN
- GYNE-LOTRIMIN COMBINATION PACK–VAGINAL TABLETS & TOPICAL CREAM
  (also contains benzyl and cetostearyl alcohols)
- MYCELEX-7–VAGINAL TABLETS
  (also contains lactose)
- MYCELEX-7–VAGINAL CREAM
  (also contains benzyl and cetostearyl alcohols)
- MYCELEX TWIN PACK–VAGINAL TABLETS & TOPICAL CREAM
  (also contains benzyl and cetostearyl alcohols)

SYMPTOMS RELIEVED:
Vaginal irritation, itching, and discomfort from yeast and other fungal conditions.

HOW TO USE:
Comes in topical cream, and vaginal cream and tablet forms.

Tablets/100 milligrams: Insert one tablet vaginally as directed before retiring for 7 consecutive days.

Tablets/500 milligrams: Insert one tablet vaginally as directed.

Topical cream: Apply to affected area in morning and evening for 7 consecutive days.

Vaginal cream: Apply with applicator (per product instructions) before retiring for 7 consecutive days.

In all cases follow specific product instructions. These products are intended solely for vaginal and topical use. Do not under any conditions ingest internally or use in eyes. Wash applicator thoroughly after use with soap and water. Always wash hands before and after use.

USUAL ADULT DOSE:
See above. Use the minimum recommended dose in order to avoid side effects or complications. In all cases follow specific product instructions.

USUAL CHILD DOSE:
Do not use in cases involving children or infants unless under medical supervision.

OVERDOSE SYMPTOMS:
None known overdose symptoms.

SIDE EFFECTS:
No serious effects in most cases of common use. However, in some cases, individuals have experienced vaginal burning or other irritations, labial swelling, gastrointestinal upset or abdominal cramps, or increased discharge not previously present, rash, hives or other skin condition. In these cases, discontinue application or use of the product and call your doctor immediately.

CHECK WITH YOUR DOCTOR OR PHARMACIST BEFORE COMBINING CLOTRIMAZOLE WITH:
Any other vaginal preparations or douches.

PREGNANCY OR BREASTFEEDING:
Safety of clotrimazole use by a nursing mother has not been established. In all cases, a physician should be consulted.

PRECAUTIONS FOR CHILDREN:
These products should not be used to treat children unless under close medical supervision.

PRECAUTIONS FOR SENIORS:
No special precautions are known for seniors.

SPECIAL WARNINGS:
Do not use any of these products if you are allergic to miconazole nitrate or any of the inactive ingredients listed, or if you have any form of liver (hepatic) disease or damage. Do not discontinue use before suggested course of medication is complete, as recurrence of infection is likely to result. Do not use with other vaginal preparations or douches unless advised by your doctor. Do not use tampons while using these products. Use sanitary napkin or minipad to prevent staining.

ADDITIONAL WARNINGS:
You should refrain from sexual intercourse while using these products. You should also be aware that some inactive ingredients in these medications may weaken products used in condoms and diaphragms. Wait at least 72 hours after completing course of medication before resuming sexual intercourse with theses types of contraceptive devices.

INFORM YOUR DOCTOR BEFORE TAKING CLOTRIMAZOLE IF:
You are pregnant.

Q U I C K F A C T S

ACTIVE INGREDIENT:

MICONAZOLE NITRATE

BRAND NAMES:

- MONISTAT 7–VAGINAL SUPPOSITORIES (also contains hydrogenated vegetable oil)
- MONISTAT 7–VAGINAL CREAM (also contains mineral oil)
- MONISTAT 7 COMBINATION PACK–VAGINAL SUPPOSITORIES & TOPICAL CREAM (also contains hydrogenated vegetable oil)

SYMPTOMS RELIEVED:

Vaginal irritation, itching, and discomfort from yeast and other fungal conditions.

HOW TO TAKE:

Comes in topical cream, and vaginal cream and tablet forms.

Suppository tablets/100 milligrams: Insert one tablet as directed before retiring for 7 consecutive days.

Suppository tablets/200 milligrams: Insert one tablet as directed for 3 consecutive days.

Topical cream: Apply to affected area in morning and evening for 7 consecutive days.

In all cases follow specific product instructions. These products are intended solely for vaginal and topical use. Do not under any conditions ingest internally or use in eyes. Wash applicator thoroughly after use with soap and water. Always wash hands before and after use.

USUAL ADULT DOSE:

See above. Use the minimum recommended dose in order to avoid side effects or complications. In all cases follow specific product instructions.

USUAL CHILD DOSE:
Do not use in cases involving children or infants unless under medical supervision.

OVERDOSE SYMPTOMS:
None known overdose symptoms.

SIDE EFFECTS:
No serious effects in most cases of common use. However, in some cases, individuals have experienced vaginal burning or other irritations, labial swelling, gastrointestinal upset or abdominal cramps, or increased discharge not previously present, rash, hives or other skin condition. In these cases, discontinue application or use of the product and call your doctor immediately.

CHECK WITH YOUR DOCTOR OR PHARMACIST BEFORE COMBINING MICONAZOLE NITRATE WITH:
Any other vaginal preparations or douches.

PREGNANCY OR BREASTFEEDING:
Safety of miconazole nitrate use by a nursing mother has not been established. In all cases, a physician should be consulted.

PRECAUTIONS FOR CHILDREN:
These products should not be used to treat children unless under close medical supervision.

55+

PRECAUTIONS FOR SENIORS:
No special precautions are known for seniors.

SPECIAL WARNINGS:
Do not use any of these products if you are

allergic to miconazole nitrate or any of the inactive ingredients listed, or if you have any form of liver (hepatic) disease or damage. Do not discontinue use before suggested course of medication is complete, as recurrence of infection is likely to result. Do not use with other vaginal preparations or douches unless advised by your doctor. Do not use tampons while using these products. Use sanitary napkin or minipad to prevent staining.

ADDITIONAL WARNINGS:
You should refrain from sexual intercourse while using these products. You should also be aware that some inactive ingredients in these medications may weaken products used in condoms and diaphragms. Wait at least 72 hours after completing course of medication before resuming sexual intercourse with theses types of contraceptive devices.

INFORM YOUR DOCTOR BEFORE TAKING MICONAZOLE NITRATE IF:
You are pregnant.

Complimentary Medicine Appendix

If you're reading this book, you're already one of the millions of Americans who have chosen self-care options for your health. Another mode of thinking, alternative—or complementary—therapies, is rapidly being mainstreamed into our health care system and these therapies focus on the preventative and self care aspects of healing. Below are brief descriptions of some of the more popular therapies:

Acupuncture uses very thin, disposable needles to increase the body's energy or to block out the transmission of pain. Needles are inserted along acupuncture meridians, which are paths through which the body's electrical energy has been proven to move.

Acupressure uses the pressure of the fingers and hands—in place of acupuncture needles—to stimulate certain points in the body. This is thought to not only alleviate pain, but to stimulate better operation of the body's internal systems. *Shiatsu* massage is a prime example of acupressure (the word *shiatsu* literally means "finger pressure" in Japanese).

Applied Kinesiology identifies and attempts to correct the weaknesses in certain muscles. By stimulating or relaxing these muscles, an applied kinesiolgist can diagnose and resolve a variety of mobility-related health concerns.

Aromatherapy uses essential oils extracted from

herbs and plants to treat a wide ranging group of health concerns including stress, infections, and skin disorders. The oils have distinct properties and specific uses and are available in a variety of forms including candles, bath oils, and pure essential oils.

Ayurvedic Medicine is centered around three body types, or *doshas.* Like the Chinese and Greeks, the traditional healers of India developed a healing system based on an underlying life energy. The body is considered to maintain harmony and health by balancing the three forces within it—*vata, pitta,* or *kapha.* Ayurvedic medicine believes that when the three doshas are balanced, the body functions harmoniously. When there is an imbalance, Ayurvedic practitioners will often treat the imbalance dietarily, with movement therapies, or with Ayurvedic herbal medicine.

Biological Dentistry explores the health of the mouth and teeth as part of overall health. The most commonly form of biological dentistry is the replacement of silver amalgam fillings, which contain mercury that is believed to be toxic, with white, composite fillings.

Bodywork commonly refers to such therapies as massage and deep tissue manipulation which are used to reduce pain, soothe injured muscles, stimulate circulation, and promote relaxation.

Chelation Therapy is a method of purging the bloodstream of toxins and metabolic wastes by the use of intravenous or oral chelating agents. These agents vary based on the type of chelation recommended, but can include such common substances as garlic and cayenne (for oral use) or may be prescription-only substances (for intravenous use) that your doctor or practitioner suggests.

Chiropractic is the adjustment of the spine and joints, which is thought to influence the body's central nervous system to reduce pain and improve overall health. As one of the most commonly used complimentary therapies, chiropractic is already used by many for the relief of symptoms from back and neck injury, and an increasing number of people consider chiropractic care a beneficial form of preventative medicine.

Colon Therapy is a method of healing that purports the manual cleaning of the colon, by a practitioner, to encourage the natural elimination of body waste and toxins.

Craniosacral Therapy manipulates the bones of the skull to treat a range of conditions. It is thought to increase energy, reduce tension, improve vision, or relieve headaches.

Detoxification Therapy stems from the belief that the human body absorbs many toxins that are unfamiliar to it and must be purged in order to maintain and/or restore good health. Forms of detoxification therapies range from chelation and colon therapy to fasting and allergy testing. Detoxification therapy is also a commonly used adjunct to environmental medicine (see below).

Diet and Nutrition has long been considered to have a central role in good health. However, achieving a balanced diet can be a challenge for many people due to varying nutritional needs. Supporters of alternative therapies believe that certain foods can help or hinder the treatment of specific health conditions.

Environmental Medicine is the study of the role of dietary and environmental factors to our overall health. Factors such as dusts, molds, pesticides, and certain food allergens can cause allergic reactions that can dramatically influence health, particularly headaches and so-called "airborne" allergies such as hay fever.

Fasting is considered a method or relieving the body of toxins by eliminating solid food for a period of time. The body is then fed high-nutrient, clean (read: organic) foods such as vegetable and fruit juices and water to flush the body's waste toxins out. Common cleansing fasts range in time from 3 days to 7 days.

Guided Imagery uses the power of the mind to create positive physical responses. This form of mind/body healing that encourages the person to visualize their health situation in a controlled setting.

Herbal Medicine has been used in all cultures throughout history and has been enjoying a renaissance in American as studies continue to prove its efficacy for a wide range of illnesses.

Homeopathy is a nontoxic form of healing used virtually worldwide. By diluting an organic substance—such as a flower essence or natural mineral—to hundreds or even thousands of an original "curative" dose, homeopaths believe that the trace elements in these remedies stimulate the body's own system of healing.

Magnetic Field Therapy is the theory of creating an external magnetic force to diagnose and treat physical and emotional disorders either through pulsing or static magnets. Magnetic therapy is commonly used to treat pain, aid in the healing of broken bones, and to help reduce stress.

Meditation is any activity that stimulates the relaxation response—physiological response produced by quieting the mind. Meditation is often used to reduce stress, and promote healing. Meditation has been proven so thoroughly effective in reducing stress and tension that, in 1984, the National Institutes of Health recommended meditation over prescription drugs as the first treatment for mild hypertension.

Naturopathic Medicine is perhaps the most commonly practiced form of alternative medicine in the United States. With over 1,100 credentialed universities in the U.S., alone, naturopaths use a myriad of healing modalities to assist their patients. These remedies may include acupuncture, dietary modifications, herbal medicine, homeopathy, magnetic field therapy, and nutritional supplementation.

Nutritional Supplementation is the application of outside nutrients or "supplements" to amend our dietary needs. Nutritional supplements are used for a variety of conditions, injuries, and age-related problems and are also considered to aid in chronic disease prevention.

Orthomolecular Medicine is rapidly emerging as a significant force in the field of alternative medicine. The basic tenet of orthomolecular thinking is to find the perfect nutritional balance for each individual's biochemical needs through diet and nutritional supplementation. Because people's needs may vary greatly—even if they eat the same foods and exist in the same environment—orthomolecular practitioners use very precise nutritional testing to make a diagnosis, and then work closely with their patients to develop individualized nutritional remedies.

Oxygen Therapy refers to a wide range of therapies which use oxygen in various forms to promote healing and destroy toxins in the body. Currently, oxygen therapy is most commonly used in the treatment of burns and stroke patients.

Traditional Chinese Medicine roots its healing in the balance of *yin* and *yang*. Certain organs are considered *yin*, while others are considered *yang*. The attraction of *yin* and *yang* creates movement and energy, an energy known as *qi*, or the vital life force. Traditional Chinese Medicine believes that a stagnation or imbalance of *qi* leads to health dysfunction or illness. Often, these imbalances are treated with healing modalities such as acupuncture, Chinese herbal medicine, diet, movement therapies such as yoga, or reflexology.

Yoga is perhaps the most common form of movement therapy in America, as well as one of the oldest known practiced. Yoga has been found to reduce stress, lower blood pressure, and regulate heart rate.

For more information on Brenda Adderly's medical discoveries, visit her Web site at www.BrendaAdderly.com

Vitamins & Minerals

Nutritional supplementation is one of today's most commonly used health buzzwords, given the prevalent belief that it is difficult to obtain all your nutrients through diet alone. The following is a list of the most commonly needed and used nutritional supplements.

Acidophilus and **Bifidobacteria** are two "healthy" bacteria that grow within the body and are partly responsible for keeping the body's natural flora in balance.

Beta-carotene is a primary antioxidant that helps to protect body tissues. It is converted by the body to vitamin A as needed. Beta-carotene is considered to help the body battle cancer and has also been suggested to protect the lungs against secondhand smoke.

Biotin is essential for food metabolism and release of energy. It assists in the biosynthesis of amino acids, nucleic acid, and fatty acids, and aids in the utilization of other B vitamins by the body.

Calcium essential for strong bones and teeth. It serves as a vital cofactor in cellular energy production, and nerve and heart function. The best form of natural calcium is found in green, leafy vegetables.

Chromium regulates the body's flow of insulin and has been found to be helpful in enhancing food metabolism, enzyme activation, and the regulation of cholesterol. It is also packaged as chromium picolinate.

Coenzyme Q10 (CoQ10) has been found to help improve heart function and circulation. Some claim that CoQ10 also enhances the functioning of the immune system.

Chondroitan and **Glucosamine sulfate** have been found to be instrumental in reducing the symptoms of osteoarthritis and aid in the rebuilding of healthy cartilage.

Folate (or folic acid) is essential for healthy blood formation and is essential for the proper synthesis of RNA and DNA.

Iodine is known to stimulate the thyroid gland, which regulates the body's rate of metabolism. Iodine is also considered to protect against breast cancer.

Iron works in combination with other nutrients to maintain healthy blood. It is also involved in the vital metabolism process.

Magnesium: Is necessary to maintain the pH balance of blood and tissue, as well as the synthesis of RNA and DNA. Is considered to help fight cancer.

Melatonin is a supplement that is commonly used to aid in the regulation of restful sleep.

Omega-3 Fatty Acids: These substances, found naturally in oilier fish such as salmon and in substances such as flaxseed oil and evening primrose oil, are essential for the proper functioning of cells and has also been found to improve the texture of the skin.

Phosphorus plays a big role in energy production and assists the action of the B vitamins. It is also an active component of healthy bones and teeth.

Potassium helps to regulate the body's water and acid (pH) base. Potassium is the mineral that chronic dieters often are depleted of.

Sodium is a primary electrolyte and is important in regulating pH balance and water balance in the body's systems.

Vitamin A is essential for healthy growth and development and the maintenance of healthy skin, hair, and eyes.

B vitamins should also be taken in a B-complex form because of their close interrelationship in the metabolic process.

Vitamin B_1 is essential for food metabolism and the release of energy for cellular function.

Vitamin B_2 is essential for food metabolism and the release of energy for cellular function. It is also important in the formation of red blood cells and also facilitates the body's usage of the other B vitamins.

Vitamin B_3 is essential for food metabolism and the release of energy for cellular function.

Vitamin B_5 is involved in food metabolism and release of energy for cellular function. It is vital for biosynthesis of hormones and support of the adrenal glands.

Vitamin B_6 is involved in food metabolism and release of energy for cellular function. It is essential for amino acid metabolism, and formation of blood proteins and antibodies, and helps to regulate electrolytic balance. Vitamin B6 is considered to help strengthen the immune system by helping to maintain healthy mucous membranes in the respiratory tract, providing a natural barrier to pollution and infection.

Vitamin B_{12} is essential for normal formation of red blood cells. It is involved in food metabolism, release of energy and maintenance of epithelial cells and the central nervous system.

Vitamin C is a primary antioxidant, essential for tissue growth, wound healing, absorption of calcium and iron and utilization of the B vitamin folic acid. It is involved in neurotransmitter biosynthesis, cholesterol regulation and formation of collagen. Vitamin C is considered to be integrally involved in boosting and maintaining the immune system, as well as protecting against a variety of cancers.

Vitamin D is considered essential for the metabolism of calcium and phosphorus—required for healthy teeth and bones.

Vitamin E is an antioxidant which keeps the red blood cells healthy and enhances cellular respiration.

Some claims have been made that suggest vitamin E can reduce the damage done by ozone and other substances found in smog. Topically, vitamin E is known for helping to improve the surface appearance of healing skin.

Vitamin K is important for blood clotting and is considered good for skin's regeneration.

Zinc is a cofactor in numerous enzymatic processes and reactions. It is involved in taste, wound healing, and digestion.

INDEX

The following triple index is a unique feature to *The Doctors' Guide to Over-the-Counter Drugs.* Designed to give you all the information you need—right at your fingertips—our three indexes give you an added boost in locating the correct medication for your symptoms or condition.

The first index is categorized by the **Brand Name** of the drug and was created to give you easy access to drug(s) you may already use or identify by name.

The second index, our **Symptom Guide,** directs you toward the many remedies available for your condition.

The **Active Ingredient** index rounds out the trio, offering you a broad look at the drugs and drug combinations that are used everyday.

Brand Name Index

A

B

C

D

U

V

Symptom Guide Index

Colds and Flu

Constipation

Contraceptives

Cough Preparations

Fever Reducers

First Aid

Headaches

Skin Conditions

Active Ingredients Index

ABOUT THE AUTHOR

BRENDA ADDERLY, M.H.A., is a health care researcher and strategic management consultant. She holds a masters degree in health services administration from the George Washington University, Washington, D.C. Her health care career includes cofounding a managed care consulting practice, strategic planning and business development for a major national HMO, benefits consulting to corporations, and the U.S. Public Health Service as a staff assistant under Dr. C. Everett Koop. She is currently Senior Manager, Business Development and Client Services at the RAND Corporation. Ms. Adderly is the editor of *The Complete Guide to Pills* (Ballantine Books), a consumer guide which profiles the most common prescription drugs; and co-author of *The Arthritis Cure* (St. Martin's Press), and *The Fat Blocker Diet* (St. Martin's Press). She lives in Los Angeles.

Visit Brenda Adderly's Web site address at
www.BrendaAdderly.com